DATE DUE

OCT 1 4 1998	
DEC 0 4 1998	
OCT 3 1 1999	
NOV - 9 1999	
APR	
OCT 2 5 2000	
NOV 1 2000	
NOV 2 1 2000	
JUL - 6 2001	
JUL 2 4 2001	
NOV - 5 2001	
APR 1 0	

BRODART   Cat. No. 23-221

THE MILLON INVENTORIES

THE MILLON INVENTORIES

Clinical and Personality Assessment

Edited by

THEODORE MILLON

THE GUILFORD PRESS
New York   London

© 1997 The Guilford Press
A Division of Guilford Publications, Inc.
72 Spring Street, New York, NY 10012

Printed in the United States of America

This book is printed on acid-free paper.

Last digit is print number: 9   8   7   6   5   4   3   2   1

Library of Congress Cataloging-in-Publication Data
The Millon inventories : clinical and personality assessment / edited
  by Theodore Millon.
       p.   cm.
    Includes bibliographical references and index.
    ISBN 1-57230-184-8
    1. Personality assessment.   2. Personality tests.   I. Millon,
Theodore.
    [DNLM: 1. Personality Assessment.   2. Mental Disorders—
diagnosis.
    WM 145 M656 1997]
    RC554.M55 1997
    155.2'8—dc21
    DNLM/DLC
    for Library of Congress   97-7702
                                                                  CIP

Contributors

Michael H. Antoni, PhD, Institute for Advanced Studies in Personology and Psychopathology, Coral Gables, Florida

Stephanie Boyd, PhD, Medical College of Georgia and VA Medical Center, Augusta, Georgia

Jeffrey Brandsma, PhD, Medical College of Georgia and VA Medical Center, Augusta, Georgia

James P. Choca, PhD, Lakeside VA Medical Center, Chicago, Illinois

Robert J. Craig, PhD, ABPP, Illinois School of Professional Psychology, Chicago, and Director, Drug Abuse Program, West Side VA Medical Center, Chicago

Roger D. Davis, PhD, Institute for Advanced Studies in Personology and Psychopathology, Coral Gables, Florida

Jan J. L. Derksen, PhD, Catholic University Nijmegen, The Netherlands

Darwin Dorr, PhD, Wichita State University, Wichita, Kansas

Frank J. Dyer, PhD, ABPP, Private Practice, Montclair, New Jersey

Luis A. Escovar, PhD, Department of Psychology, Florida International University, Miami, Florida, and Director, Study Groups Institute for Advanced Studies in Personology and Psychopathology, Coral Gables, Florida

George S. Everly, Jr., PhD, Chief Executive Officer, International Critical Incident Stress Foundation, and Department of Psychology, Loyola College, Severna Park, Maryland

Patrick M. Flynn, PhD, National Development and Research Institute, Inc., Raleigh, North Carolina

Alexandra Guzman, BS, Institute for Advanced Studies in Personology and Psychopathology, Coral Gables, Florida

Lee Hyer, PhD, Medical College of Georgia and VA Medical Center, Augusta, Georgia

Joseph T. McCann, PsyD, JD, Private Practice, Binghamton, New York

Robert C. McMahon, PhD, Director of Training and Counseling Psychology, University of Miami, Coral Gables, Florida

Carrie M. Millon, PhD, Institute for Advanced Studies in Personology and Psychopathology, Coral Gables, Florida

Theodore Millon, PhD, DSc, Dean and Scientific Director, Institute for Advanced Studies in Personology and Psychopathology, Coral Gables, Florida

Eileen C. Newman, PhD, Sheppard and Enoch Pratt Hospital, Towson, Maryland

A. Rodney Nurse, PhD, ABPP, Co-director, Family Psychological Services and Collaborative Divorce, Orinda, California

Paul Retzlaff, PhD, Department of Psychology, University of Northern Colorado, Greeley, Colorado

Elbert W. Russell, PhD, Director Emeritus, Neuropsychology Laboratory, VA Medical Center, Miami, Florida

Sally L. Kolitz Russell, PhD, Private Practice, Miami, Florida

Hedwig V. Sloore, PhD, Free University of Brussels, Brussels, Belgium

Stephen Strack, PhD, U.S. Department of Veterans Affairs Outpatient Clinic, Los Angeles, California

Robert F. Tringone, PhD, Division of Child and Adolescent Psychiatry, Schneider Children's Hospital, Long Island Jewish Medical Center, New Hyde Park, New York

Eric J. Van Denburg, PhD, Lakeside VA Medical Center, Chicago, Illinois

Lawrence G. Weiss, PhD, Senior Project Director, The Psychological Corporation, San Antonio, Texas

Andrew Wenger, PhD Candidate, Institute for Advanced Studies in Personology and Psychopathology, Coral Gables, Florida

Preface

The MCMI and its sister inventories originated as a defensive act, a shield against the proliferation of potentially misconceived or poorly designed efforts on the part of well-meaning others to "operationalize" concepts I had proposed in an earlier publication. Rather than sit back and enjoy the dissemination of my ideas, I began to see this burgeoning of divergent instrument development, not only as uncontrolled, and possibly misguided, but as a process ultimately endangering the very theoretical notions they were designed to strengthen.

To establish a measure of instrumental uniformity for future investigators, as well as to assure at least a modicum of psychometric quality among tools that ostensibly reflected the theory's constructs, I was prompted (perhaps "driven" is a more accurate word) to consider undertaking the test-construction task myself. At that time, in early 1971, I fortunately was directing a research supervision group composed of psychologists- and psychiatrists-in-training during their internship and residency periods. All of them had read my 1969 *Modern Psychopathology* text, and found my suggestion that we work together to develop instruments to identify and quantify the text's novel personality constructs to be both worthy and challenging.

Naively, we assumed that the construction task could be completed in about 18 months, a time period that would allow several members of the research group to participate on a continuing basis. Despite the fact that we "postponed" developing a structured interview schedule after an initial effort, the "more limited" task of constructing a self-report inventory took almost 7 years to complete. The framework and preliminary item selections of the inventory were well underway by the end of the first full year of our work; it was described briefly in a book I cowrote in 1972 entitled *Research Methods in Psychopathology*. The initial forms of the clinical instrument were entitled the *Millon–Illinois Self-Report Inventory*.

Psychodiagnostic procedures in the past contained more than their share of mystique. Not only were assessments often an exercise in oracular craft and intuitive artistry, but they typically were clothed in obscure and esoteric jargon. A change in the character of personality theory and assessment began to brew in the late 1960s. Slow though these advances progressed, there were clear signs that new ideas would soon emerge. Projective techniques such as the Rorschach began to be analyzed quantitatively and were increasingly anchored to the empirical domain. The so-called objective inventories, such as the MMPI, were being interpreted increasingly in terms of configural profiles. No longer approached as sets of separate scales, formerly segmented instruments were increasingly analyzed as holistic integrations that possessed clinical significance only as gestalt composites. In addition, the former insistence that diagnostic interpretation be "objective," that is, anchored solely to empirical correlates, gave way to clinical syntheses, including the "dynamics" of the previously maligned projectives. Although part-function instruments, oriented toward one expressive form of pathology or another (e.g., Beck Depression Inventory) are still popular, the newest tools moved increasingly toward composite structures, (i.e., "whole" personalities). These personality formulations were not conceived of as random sets or discrete attributes (i.e., factors) that must be individually deduced and then pieced together, but as integrated configurations from the start. Hence, we have seen the development of various tools explicitly designed to diagnose, for example, the "borderline" personality. The MCMI represents this trend in holistic personality measures, going one step beyond most techniques by including all of the *Diagnostic and Statistical Manual* (DSM) personality disorders in a single inventory. Holism is not limited to inventories alone. New structured interview schedules and clinical rating scales have been developed to provide another rich source of data. Not to be overlooked is the sound psychometric manner in which most of these newer tools have been constructed, thereby wedding the empirical and quantitative features that were the major strength of the structured objective inventories with the dynamic and integrative qualities that characterized the more intuitive projective techniques.

We should also not overlook the very special status assigned to the personality disorders in the DSM. With the third edition of this official classification in 1980, personality not only gained a place of consequence among syndromal categories but became central to its multiaxial schema. The logic for assigning personality its own special status was more than a matter of differentiating syndromes of a more acute and dramatic nature from those of a longstanding and prosaic character. More relevant to this partitioning decision was the assertion that personality (Axis II) serves usefully as a dynamic substrate from which clinicians can better grasp the significance and meaning of their patient's transient and florid disorders (Axis I). In the DSM, then, personality disorders not only attained a nosological status of prominence in their own right but were assigned a contextual role that made them fundamental to the understanding and interpretation of all other psychopathologies.

As is evident by the variety of "Millon" instruments reported in this book, I have judged it best to opt in favor of focusing an inventory on target rather than broad-based populations; hence, the MCMI is oriented toward matters of import among adult mental health patients, the MACI focuses on adolescent clinical populations, the MBHI and the forthcoming MBMC focus on those whose primary ailments are of a medical or physical nature, and the recently developed MIPS (Millon Index of Personality Styles) addresses traits among nonclinical or so-called normal adults (as can be seen, I have chosen the term "style" for persons who do not evince discernible psychic pathology).

I must admit, much to both my surprise and pleasure, that the defensively constructed MCMI, as well as its sister inventories, quickly matched in acceptance and clinical usage the theory upon which they were based. Only the MMPI and Rorschach continue to supersede the Millon Inventories as the most used and published of clinically oriented tests. In the past decade, numerous clinicians and researchers have begun to publish books (six at last count) and articles (approximately a thousand) evaluating the Millon instruments. The present volume is, however, the first book organized and edited by the inventories' primary author.

Perhaps the greatest value to this text's readers will be an implicit one, namely, the growing heuristic fertility of the Millon inventories. These inventories are more than another "objective" tool in the diagnostician's assessment kit. They provide clinicians with a theoretical foundation for mastering the realm of clinical and personality pathology, a means for understanding the principles that underlie their patient's functional and dysfunctional behaviors, thoughts, and feelings. Moreover, the openness of the theory not only illuminates the patient's personal life but encourages the clinician to deduce and uncover insights beyond those on which the inventories interpretive reports have been grounded.

Finally, we believe this book will provide professors of psychological assessment courses a comprehensive text for teaching the foundations, development, and applications of the several Millon inventories.

THEODORE MILLON

Contents

III   THE MACI, MBHI, MBMC, AND MPDC

IV   THE PACL AND MIPS

V EPILOGUE

THE MILLON INVENTORIES

I

INTRODUCTION

1

The Place of Assessment in Clinical Science

THEODORE MILLON
ROGER D. DAVIS

The study of personality may be approached from either of two great historical traditions, the nomothetic or the idiographic, both of which go back at least to the time of the ancient Greeks. The nomothetic approach is focused primarily on constructs and the theoretical propositions which relate them, and not on any one individual. In contrast, the idiographic approach is primarily clinical, and thus is focused on understanding the individual person. While their purposes are obviously different, these perspectives are not necessarily antagonistic. In fact, we shall argue that they are complementary, not by accident or intent, but by necessity: The success of theoretical propositions can be judged only in terms of the extent to which they facilitate idiographic or clinical goals; conversely, if idiographic propositions are to possess a validity which is distinctly psychological, as opposed to being merely descriptive (however elegantly done), this requires that case conceptualization proceed from some theoretical basis—an assessment should meet certain criteria of scientific respectability. This chapter is devoted to tracking out these conceptual reciprocities and their implications for theory building and clinical work.

THE NOMOTHETIC PERSPECTIVE: UNIVERSAL TRUTH IN PERSONALITY

The first of the two traditions to be discussed, the nomothetic or construct-centered (Allport, 1937) approach, is concerned with personality in an abstract sense and not with any one individual. The emphasis is on discovering how certain constructs tend to relate or cohere with others and why. Most often the focus is on constructs subsidiary to personality as an integrated phenomenon, such as needs, motives, mechanisms, traits, schemas, and defenses, that is, on part functions. Questions grounded in this approach include "What is the relationship of locus of control to depression?" and "How does the continuum of self-schema complexity relate to stress vulnerability?" Nowhere is mention made of the individual person.

The nomothetic approach is inherently taxonomy seeking. While strongly nomothetically oriented psychologists do not deny the existence of individuality, they do believe that once the fundamental units of personality are isolated it will be possible to express each particular personality in terms of these units, with little or no "residual variance," or relevant information, left over. Individuals are simply different combinations of different levels of the same variables. This attitude, inherited from the worldview of determinism or mechanism, holds that as science advances, the shrouds of mystery will recede indefinitely, and that every fact, no matter how small, trivial, or individual, will be accounted for in some scientific context. Experimental error or residual variance is seen as reflecting our ignorance of important independent variables that, when accounted for, render what is yet to be explained vanishingly small. In classical psychometric terms, personality is described along many dimensions in terms of the deviation of each individual score from the group mean. In modern psychometric terms, the individual's score may be described in terms of sample-free logits. Either way, the subject's profile or codetype is regarded as the complete representation of his or her personality.

An expression of these characteristics is seen in taxonomies constructed using factor-analytic methods. Here, numerous scales representing a broad selection of personality traits are factor analyzed for latent patterns of covariation, the dimensions that, according to its proponents, underlie the true or fundamental structure of personality. Variance not accounted for by the factor model is rejected as irrelevant, that is, as being due to measurement error. The derived factors are then accorded causal primacy in the specification of other more circumscribed traits or facets of personality, and ultimately these factors become the axes of a nomothetic hyperspace in which any particular personality may be plotted. Parsimony is paramount; thousands of traits may be telescoped into a handful of dimensions. Whether this approach can sustain important challenges to the auxiliary assumptions required to support it (for example, whether the linear nature of the methodology distorts the structure of the subject domain in its inexorable extraction of a purely dimensional model) is, of course, another matter completely. Nevertheless, it embodies important characteristics of the nomothetic ideal.

The advantage of the nomothetic perspective is that it serves the needs of science. Because science thrives on generalizability, a science of personality cannot afford to be limited to the discovery and explication of laws of behavior specific to one person, or at most to a very small group of persons. If science is the discovery and explanation of invariances across instances, the instances cannot be singular. Instead, science must show the applicability of its theories to realms of manifest phenomenon not heretofore seen, approached, or understood. To locate such universal propositions about behavior, personality psychologists look for regularities or covariations which hold across many different people, rather than merely within one person. Allport (1937, p. 4) compared the nomothetic approach to "finding a single thread running from individual nature to individual nature, visible only through the magical spectacles of a special, theoretic attitude."

THE IDIOGRAPHIC PERSPECTIVE: PARTICULAR TRUTHS ABOUT PARTICULAR PERSONS

While the nomothetically oriented perspective emphasizes commonalities between people, that is, regularities consistent across a class of objects, the idiographic perspective emphasizes the individuality, complexity, and uniqueness of each person or object. Obviously, people have different personalities; otherwise assessment would need not exist at all. Were everyone the same, were there no variation between persons, then personality as a construct would be entirely unnecessary. The idiographic perspective reminds us that just as personality is not only that which makes each individual what he or she is, it is also that which makes each person different from others, and potentially different from *all* others. At the extreme end, it may even be held that there is something ineffable about each of us which cannot be gotten wholly into any symbolic system of description. The psychodynamic idea that personality consists of a series of layers of defense and compromise, through which the impulses of sex and aggression may be transformed in circuitous and unexpected ways, begins to approximate this complexity.

Perhaps the most important point of this perspective is the idea that individuality is the result of a unique history of transactions between biological (e.g., temperament and genetic constitution) and contextual factors (e.g., the mother's womb, the family environment, social roles to which the child is exposed, culture, and socioeconomic status), a history which has never existed before and will never be repeated. Because each personality is such a singular product, it cannot be understood through either the application of universal laws or through dimensions of individual differences. Instead, understanding personality requires a developmental approach, one whose descriptive potential is as rich as the person's own history, so rich in fact that ultimately it might only be called biographical. Accordingly to Henry Murray (1938, p. 604), originator of the term "personology," "the history of personality *is* the personality." Whereas the nomothetic approach asks about the "what" of personality, the idiographic perspective asks about the "how" and the "why." The question is: How has the person become the unique creature he or she is? Accordingly, the focus in this perspective shifts from the description of each individual personality as a positive phenomenon, that is, from the classification of the person as an "antisocial" (or as the dimensionalization of the person as a codetype in some nomothetic space) to the view that personality is a richly contextualized and intrinsically transactional phenomenon which emerges with stochastic indeterminateness from a nearly infinite ground of possibilities. In this view, cross-sectional descriptions or personality diagnoses are only the beginning point. Scientific explanation requires discovering why each individual has evolved into just exactly who they have become, rather than into someone else. Personology, then, is an exercise in elucidating the developmentally necessary and sufficient conditions through which the particular individual as a distinct entity was "culled" from an infinite universe of possibilities. Given the antithesis of this perspective to universal laws, it is not impossible that these constraints might include such "softer" concepts as free will and chance.

LINKING THE NOMOTHETIC
AND IDIOGRAPHIC APPROACHES

The nomothetic–idiographic duality is a classic and inevitable problem, and one for which no easy solution is forthcoming. One way out is reductionism: to simply reduce one pole of the duality to the other, effectively ignoring the existence of contrary views. Thus, strongly nomothetically oriented psychologists typically maintain that variance unaccounted for by their pet dimensions consists wholly of error and nothing more. Any other admission impugns the completeness of the preferred model by acknowledging the omission of relevant and substantive content and thus begs for supplementary constructs or dimensions that may not easily fit with the author's theoretical preconceptions. Any theorist may argue that his or her set of dimensions is fundamental, of course, but such rationales are particularly apparent in factor-analytically derived schemes, which always extract a small number of dimensions, followed by so-called "error factors."

Where the idiographic pole is emphasized, each person may be regarded as an entity so ineffably complex that any form of description simplifies, and so trivializes, the totality of the individual's unique "existential situation." Psychodynamically "deep" case analyses, which emphasize the circuitous transformations of drives and impulses through multiple latent layers of character formation, begin to approximate the hermeneutic potential of the idiographic perspective. As this potential increases, that is, as the interpretive thread is spun more and more finely to reflect the mutually intercontextualized and developmentally transactional nature of the individual personality, the approach itself becomes less objective and therefore seemingly antiscientific, if only because the individual has been specified to the point of existing *sui generis*. Clearly, reductionism is not a solution. How then are we to reconcile these two approaches?

THE STRUCTURE OF CLINICAL SCIENCE

Clinical science may be said to consist of four intercontextualized domains: theory, taxonomy, assessment, and intervention. All of the activities of clinical scientists are oriented toward one or more of these clinical domains. Theory may be said to consist of a corpus of propositions that relate various constructs in personality and psychopathology to observed clinical realities; taxonomy refers to the categories into, or dimensions along which, pathologies and personalities may be classified or appraised. Assessment is concerned with the description and explanation of individual pathology, while intervention seeks to address and remedy this pathology. The first two domains are more construct centered, reflecting psychopathology and personality considered as a pure science that focuses on clinical "diseases" (Axis I), such as anxiety and depression, and their relationships to other traits (Axis II), physical characteristics (Axis III), and environmental factors (Axis IV). The second two domains are focused more on the individual, reflecting clinical science as it exists in its applied form, focused on the person who must be understood as the particular being who actually has the so-called disease, and for whom help must be found.

If the nomothetic–idiographic issue is linked to clinical science in this way (one which frames the duality as complementary, rather than antagonistic), then each domain places constraints upon the structure of the others and so acts as a check on the validity of the science as a whole (see Figure 1.1). The conceptual opposite is a disconnected science consisting of the same four domains, each independent of the others, built on its own specific principles and evolved exclusively out of itself, content in the cognizance of its own internal consistency. In such an unintegrated science, theory exists as a self-perpetuating, unverifiable mass; taxonomy consists of categories of convenience; instrumentation is informed only by history and tradition; and interventions rely mainly on placebo effects and nonspecific factors and tend to multiply without bound. Unfortunately, the state of clinical science today, fueled in part by the distinction between academician and clinician, largely favors the independence of domains rather than their integration.

While it is obvious that the clinical domains are, and should be, interrelated, the history of clinical science bears out what intuition knows to be true. As genuinely interdependent parts of a single science, developments in each domain influence the form of the others and of the science as a whole. Thus, with the publication of the third edition of the *Diagnostic and Statistical Manual* (DSM-III) in 1980, the psychodynamic foundation of much of psychopathology was officially overthrown, with the result that the value and relevance

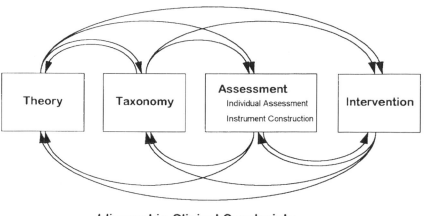

FIGURE 1.1. Domains of clinical science and their relationships.

of instruments oriented toward constructs no longer officially sanctioned, such as the Rorschach and the Thematic Apperception Test (TAT), became more limited. With the evolution of managed care, assessment has become more integral to intervention. Clients may now start down the so-called clinical pathways depending upon testing results, for which a particular intervention may be operationalized in great detail. These essentially historical facts illustrate the interdependence of taxonomy and assessment. Other examples could easily be given for any given pair of domains.

The fundamental thesis, however, is that the integration of clinical domains is not merely historical, in the way, for example, that the Eiffel Tower is integrated into the cultural history of Paris, but that it is also logically necessary. The ideal of an integrated science leads us to require that there be certain relationships between the various domains, which, if we were unaware of the ideal of integration, or if in fact we were to regard the domains as independent, we most definitely would not propose. In general, idiographic formulations must be held to scientific standards; conversely, nomothetic propositions must be tested against clinical realities. It may be said, for example, that while interventions guided by the intuition of a seasoned professional are often admirably effective, they are not truly scientific in a strict sense unless guided by clinical theory; that while taxonomy should ultimately be based in theory, clinical observation may suggest additional categories or subcategories of pathology for the investigation and elaboration of theory; that case conceptualization is dependent upon theory if it is to be genuinely explanatory, rather than merely descriptive; and so on. Many such propositions might be enumerated. Each domain is connected to, constrained according to, or informed by, the others. In Figure 1.1, these constraints or informational pathways are grouped into two kinds: those oriented toward theory and taxonomy, which tend to be nomothetic in nature, and those that are oriented toward assessment and intervention, which tend to be more idiographic. Grouping the constraints in this way not only brings the reciprocity between traditionally academic or theoretical work and traditionally clinical or applied work into the foreground, but also it allows them to be discussed in reciprocal pairs. For example, the question "How does psychological theory constrain psychological assessment?" can easily and legitimately be turned around to read "How do the results of psychological assessment constrain psychological theory?"

In this chapter, we are interested only in those constraints that impinge upon assessment and those that issue from it. These form a set of necessary (but probably not sufficient) criteria that must be met if assessment is to be fully integrated into clinical science, listed as propositions in Table 1.1. These form the outline headings for the remainder of this chapter.

THEORY AND THE ASSESSMENT OF THE INDIVIDUAL

As long as science remains incomplete, there will always be a certain reciprocity between scientific theory and observation, for observation, which in its more rigorous forms consists of empirical experimentation, is needed to test theory. This is also true for theories of the individual.

Nomothetic Proposition: Theory Provides the Only Point of Departure for a Genuinely Scientific Assessment of the Individual

What prescriptions does the nomothetic approach make for assessment? Recall that this perspective is concerned with personality in the abstract and with the theoretical linkages among its constructs. Any psychological assessment must then, in Allport's (1937, p. 4) words, pay homage to the "theoretic thread that runs from individual to individual." To possess a validity which is distinctly psychological, as opposed to what might be termed "Theophrastean" (after Theophrastus, the ancient Greek writer who provided vivid portrayals of certain commonly seen personality types), the constructs used to appraise personality should possess a genuine explanatory power.

TABLE 1.1. Relation of Assessment to Other Domains of Clinical Science

Theory–Individual assessment

Nomothetic proposition: A theoretical system provides the only point of departure for a genuinely scientific assessment of the individual.

Idiographic proposition: The purpose of psychological theory is to aid in understanding the individual as a whole person.

Theory–Instrument construction

Nomothetic proposition: Assessment instruments should be coordinated with theoretical propositions and derivations.

Idiographic proposition: Theory and taxonomy should be refined on the basis of accumulated clinical knowledge.

Intervention–Assessment

Nomothetic proposition: Therapy should be based on a plan developed for those theory-based clinical prototypes most relevant to the individual's personality style.

Idiographic proposition: The therapeutic plan must be elaborated to accommodate individual specificities not easily gotten into clinical prototypes.

To do so, they must somehow be more "fundamental" than terms taken from that store of descriptors usually referred to as the "common lexicon." Scientific languages differ from the natural language not only because they serve a different purpose, but also because they have been refined of theoretical ambiguities and surface similarities present in the terms of the natural language. In its beginning stages, science is mainly concerned with the questions "What is there?" and "What is it like?," a strategy of inventory and description. The philosopher of science, Carl Hempel (1965), noted:

> The development of a scientific discipline may often be said to proceed from an initial "natural history" stage ... to subsequent more and more theoretical stages. ... The vocabulary required in the early stages of this development will be largely observational. ... The shift toward theoretical systematization is marked by the introduction of new, "theoretical" terms ... more or less removed from the level of directly observable things and events. ... These terms have a distinct meaning and function only in the context of a corresponding theory. (pp. 139–140)

Even at this natural history stage, however, knowledge is never theory neutral or paradigm free. Surplus meanings are inevitable. Even what we term as "facts" are not objective statements about the natural world. They are, rather, statements whose assumptive context has become so consensual that it need not be explicitly stated in order to communicate. Such assumptions are neither conscious nor preconscious, but are unconscious, so much so in fact that their elucidation often becomes the stuff of philosophical and scientific revolutions. Consider gravity: In Newton's world, gravity was understood as a force. No less a genius than Einstein was required for gravity to be understood as a curvature of space. After relativity, our experience of gravity as a force could be seen as an artifact of our own perceptual mechanisms.

In the area of personality disorders, for example, the term "disorders" brings to the assessment enterprise a set of assumptions which are paradigmatically inappropriate. Personality disorders are not illnesses for which some discrete pathogen can be found, or for which there exists some underlying unitary cause, either past or present. The use of such language as "disorder" is indeed unfortunate, for personality pathologies are not disorders at all in the medical sense. Instead, personality disorders are best conceptualized as disorders of the entire matrix of the person. Hence, we prefer the terms "pattern" or "style" rather than the intrinsically reifying "disorder." This misconception is more paradigmatic than diagnostic, but it leads to subsequent distortions in multiaxial logic, encouraging the view that classical clinical syndromes and personality disorders exist alongside each other in a horizontal relationship, when in fact, clinical symptoms are best viewed as being embedded in the context of a personality pattern.

A second sense in which theory is relevant to assessment concerns not content, but process: How are we to get from clinical theory to case conceptualization? The fractionated person, the person who has been dispersed across scales, instruments, and interviews, must be put back together again as the organic whole he or she is. How is such a venture to be achieved? We would argue that assessment is an eminently theoretical process which requires a weighing of this and a disqualifying of that across the idiosyncrasies and commonalities of methods and data sources through multiple iterations of hypothesis generation and testing. The ideal result is *the* "theory of the client," a theory in which every loose end has been tied up in a logic so compelling that it seems to follow from the logic of the client's own psyche, so convincing that one gets the feeling that things could not be otherwise.

To achieve this ideal insofar as is possible, theories of the person should pay homage to the same virtues as do other scientific theories. For one thing, they should be made as internally consistent, that is, as free of internal contradictions, as possible. Individuals cannot possess both psychopathic indifference to suffering and altruistic sacrifice for others as cardinal traits, for example. Where contradictions are indicated by the data, they may often be resolved by invoking the dynamic idea of conflict, and by inspecting the data for objects around which the conflict is expressed. In addition, a good theory of the patient should be as complete as possible; that is, it is should avail itself of as much data, in as many domains, as can be expeditiously gathered, a fact that makes sense both psychometrically and personologically. Psychometrically, confidence is increased when aggregated data converge toward a single result. Personologically, information within a particular domain speaks more strongly about that domain than does other data. While we might expect, for example, someone who is interpersonally dramatic and gregarious to also be cognitively scattered, evidence directly relevant to the ideational process is preferred for such a conclusion. Directly relevant data not only allow us to have higher confidence in our conclusions, but also allow the theory to be as specific as possible.

Idiographic Proposition: The Ultimate Purpose of Assessment Must Be to Understand the Person

From an extreme idiographic perspective, taxonomy is only a point of departure used in understanding individuals. Individuality is ultimately too complex to be organized into classes or placed along dimensions of individual differences. If taxonomies are used at all, they must be used self-consciously as contrivances which facilitate the investigation of individuality, not as clinical endpoints. As clinical heuristics, they are guidelines to be replaced and reformulated as necessary; it is the unique instantiation of the construct or trait in the particular individual that is of immediate clinical interest. Any personality construct, any literary metaphor, is free game if it is relevant and effective in conceptualizing and communicating clinically relevant matters.

Even widely consensual and officially sanctioned taxonomies of personality and personality disorders are limited in their explanatory power and clinical utility. Not only is the DSM not an exhaustive listing of personality constructs that might be relevant to any particular individual, it does not even begin to scratch the surface. Nomothetic propositions and diagnostic labels are mere superficialities to be overcome and replaced by more complete hypotheses as test results and other data are gathered and understanding is gained. To clinicians, who might justifiably be called "scientists of the individual," it is the categories of DSM that represent a kind of natural history stage, a gross, cross-sectional description of pathology that must be augmented with biographical data before the individual can be understood and treated. Questions to be answered include: Why does the patient have this particular personality style rather than some other? What are the developmental antecedents of his or her defensive mechanisms? How is the patient's personality related to symptom production? What psychosocial forces undermine the adequacy of the patient's coping mechanisms?

While nomothetically it is constructs that are viewed as open concepts, from an idiographic perspective it is individuality that is to be pinned down and understood to the degree that it can be brought to closure through links with scientific constructs. Individuals may be viewed as open concepts, as well. In fact, we might identify a continuum of interpretive openness running from very incomplete to extremely idiographic. At the first level would be a score on a single dimension. Here, the individual is spoken of as being self-conscious, or extroverted, for example. To the extent that this dimension is indeed the organizing principle of the whole personality, what Allport (1937) referred to as an individual's cardinal trait, it describes how the person will behave in a given situation, and in fact functions as a rather good inductive summary for the entire matrix of the individual.

Unfortunately, very few subjects are pure prototypes of any particular construct; cardinal traits are rare. The second level of interpretation is configural and hierarchical, but remains cross-sectional. Here, "configural" simply means that the scores on particular traits or dimensions are not interpreted in and of themselves, but in relation to one another. At a bare minimum, two dimensions are involved in the clinician's configural efforts, as for example with the interpersonal circle, which features love–hate and dominance–submission. As the number of dimensions increases, profile interpretation becomes successively more nuanced as the meaning of each trait is transformed by virtue of its existence in the context of the others. Thus, for example, a high Narcissistic score may be considered in conjunction with a secondary Antisocial elevation. Such individuals are likely to be grandiose and entitled, and to act out when their self-esteem is deflated, or to become explosive if their entitlement is not honored by others. If yet a third elevation is added, say Masochistic, we would be required to integrate certain aspects of this prototype into our formulation. We might conclude that such individual is likely to realize their errors at a later date and attempt to undo their transgressions through some form of self-torment. Note that nowhere in these formulations is developmental information explicitly considered. Accordingly, interpretations produced at this level lie somewhere between description and explanation, being descriptive in the sense that they cannot explain the origins of the particular personality, and explanatory in that they are nevertheless formulated in terms that are theoretically anchored.

The deepest level of interpretation is distinctly biographical, asking "How is it that the person has come to be as he or she is?" Here, the substance of the individual's personality is subjected to developmental inquiry, in context of developmental theory and the individual's unique biography. If the clinical interview reveals, for example, rigid, compulsive parents, we might conclude that the Narcissistic elevation is in fact a defense against highly critical introjects and that his or her grandiosity allows him or her to transcend these disparaging internal voices and keeps him or her compensated.

THEORY AND INSTRUMENT CONSTRUCTION

Just as the understanding of any physical phenomenon is limited by the paradigms available, so also is the validity of the individual assessment. In fact, the availability of theory is a primary constraint on the validity of the assessment (just as the experience of the clinician is another constraint). No assessment can be stronger than its limiting conditions. Just as water cannot rise higher than its source, no case conceptualization can be more valid than the perspectives brought to bear in its formulation. While this principle holds for any diagnostic syndrome, it is even more relevant to the personality disorders, which are, as disorders of the entire matrix of the individual, anchored to multiple domains of structure and functioning—behavioral, phenomenological, intrapsychic, and biophysical. The clinician must draw from these perspectives to discover the relationship between the symptom and the larger matrix. It is the intent to draw upon deeper and more precise principles that distinguishes this activity as genuinely scientific and sets it apart from more commonsense ascriptions. Interpretive accuracy, however, requires valid instrumentation.

Nomothetic Proposition: Assessment Instruments
Should Be Constructed on the Basis of Theory

Assessment instruments in psychological science tend to endure. A comparison of the top 20 instruments of 20 years ago with those of today shows little change. The Rorschach has been with us for almost 75 years, the Minnesota Multiphasic Personality Inventory (MMPI) for over 50 years. These instruments are somewhat like the character armor of our field. Their existence ritualizes clinical assessment activities, assures us that the more difficult and essentially philosophical questions have already been answered, and so encourages us to put aside these truly troublesome quandaries and get on with our work. And like good defensive armor, their future use is set, even if their relevance and utility are questionable.

Whatever the current state of clinical knowledge, it is the generativity of theory that suggests not only the latent structure of a subject domain, but also those gauges that might be shown, upon further empirical research, to be optimally suited to the assessment of this structure. If a researcher wishes to construct a self-report scale to measure narcissistic personality disorder, the researcher's theory of the disorder becomes a major guiding force in shaping the character of the items written for the initial pool; they are not simply a random selection of stimulus materials. Unfortunately, a review of the most frequently used projective and objective tests, the Rorschach and the MMPI, shows their structure and content to be much less theoretically grounded that might at first be believed. As a field, we appear to be far more concerned with retrofitting modern psychological innovations, whether theoretical or taxonomic, to old instruments than with revising and optimizing the instruments themselves.

When Herman Rorschach began to explore the use of inkblots in his studies with schizophrenics in the 1920s, for example, he originally used about 40 cards (Exner, 1986). From these he selected 15 that, from his own empirical experience, were most clinically useful. Unfortunately, even 15 proved too expensive to reproduce given the technology of the times, so he rewrote his classic *Psychodiagnostik* to feature only the 10 blots he used most often. If the reader has ever watched the Mel Brooks film *History of the World, Part 1*, there is a point in the movie whereupon Moses, having descended from his mountaintop conference with God, stands dramatically on a rocky ledge before the Hebrew people, holding three stone tablets, on which are inscribed 15 commandments. Just as Moses is presenting the law of God, he loses his grasp on one of the tablets and it drops to the ground and shatters on the earth below. A long moment of anticlimactic silence follows, during which Moses quickly and cleverly conceives a means of concealing his awkwardness: "I give you these 15 . . . (*crash*) . . . no 10 . . . 10 commandments!" The effect upon the audience is a mix of humor, amazement, and curiosity. What did the five lost commandments say? Is this one clumsy error the reason the world has been screwed up ever since? How might things be different if the lost commandments had survived?

Given the rather desultory development of the final Rorschach plates, we are entitled to ask the same questions of Herman Rorschach, though in fairness, Rorschach expired before he could develop the inkblot technique more fully. The point is, however, while there was some selection of stimulus materials through Rorschach's own research and personal experience, it is by no means clear that this set of plates was optimized for the nosologic categories of the 1920s, much less for use with the DSM-IV today. Were modern clinicians to attempt the construction of a new set of plates, optimized to the structure and content of modern DSMs with the idea of providing meaningful information for Axes I, II, and IV, the resulting set of stimulus materials would probably bear little resemblance to the Rorschach. Yet, there is also little doubt that it is the same 10 plates that will be with us 75 years in the future, if only because it is these plates that set the whole enterprise in motion and on which thousands of research studies are based. For assessment instruments, the importance of continuity with the past cannot be underestimated.

A similar case may be made with regard to the clinical scales of the MMPI. At the time of its construction, an exclusively empirical approach to inventory construction seemed worthwhile. The philosophy of science known as logical positivism was in its ascendancy and psychological theory was considered as yet too weak to inform inventory construction. If items of ostensibly unrelated content were found to differentiate psychiatric groups, then this could simply be considered a point of departure for scientific interest that might be explored at some future date.

Unfortunately, the native MMPI scales proved unsatisfactory. First, the clinical scales proved difficult to interpret. Not only were the latent elements important to particular elevations and profile patterns difficult to resolve, but also the same elevation or profile pattern might mean different things for different patients. The Harris–Lingoes subscales (1955, 1968), which group items of each MMPI scale into rationally coherent subgroups, were constructed to address these considerations. Clusters of item endorsements could now be examined to explain profile patterns at a more molecular level. Later, Wiggins (1969) would construct his own content scales, grouping together items from the entire pool. And today we have the MMPI-2 Content scales, constructed as part of the restandardization project itself.

In the larger picture, however, the reason that the MMPI clinical scales proved disappointing was that clinical taxonomy evolved out from underneath them. Unlike the MMPI, the categories of mental illness on which the instrument was based did not endure. Had this psychiatric nosology in fact "carved nature at its joints," the criterion–groups method of instrument construction might still be with us today. The item-selection statistics would almost certainly be revved up, but the essential idea that items can be chosen and be diagnostically effective while being ostensibly unrelated to their diagnostic criterion would be sound, from a practical viewpoint. After all, if nature exists in categories, then predicting these categories is all that is important.

In turn, the categories of the 1940s evolved because they lacked the kind of generative power about which Hempel (1965) has written. Fortunately, the MMPI has survived by recombining its items in ways more fruitful than those of the clinical scales, namely the content scales of the MMPI-2. The lesson is that it is extremely difficult, if not impossible, to get more out of an assessment than what is afforded by the generativity of the underlying constructs on which an instrument is based. Earlier it was argued that theory forms the only scientific point of departure for an assessment. Scientific theories are always in a state of evolution. However, it is the generativity of theoretical propositions upon which the validity of the case conceptualization stands. The upper bound of precision and explanatory power for the assessment is the precision and explanatory power of the propositions of the underlying science.

Idiographic Proposition: The Results of Clinical Observation Must Inform the Content and Structure of Clinical Instrumentalities

For nosologists, the inexact fit between patient and diagnosis is a nagging and noisome reminder of individuality, one which has continued to fuel the development of modern psychiatric taxonomies. Ideally, a diagnosis alone should be both necessary and sufficient to begin treatment, and all the clinician needs to know. Were ideals realities, individuals would fit their diagnostic categories perfectly with pristinely prototypal presentations. Yet such a thing seldom occurs. A famous developmental theorist, Heinz Werner, argued that development always proceeds from the global to the more differentiated. The monotypic categories of earlier DSMs may be seen as the global beginnings of later specifications and accommodations. In the initial phases of its development, a diagnostic taxonomy consists generally of entities of broad bandwidth, but little specificity. Inevitably, some diagnostic categories begin to be viewed as invalid and are simply discarded. As theoretical knowledge and empirical studies accrue, however, broad diagnostic taxons begin to be broken down into multiple, narrow taxons of greater specificity and descriptive value. As the process continues, an interesting structural change occurs: The taxonomy begins to take on a hierarchical structure, one which allows it to accommodate to the contextualism which exists in the world at large. Coverage increases as big taxons are broken down into little taxons. The big taxons are now merely what the little taxons have in common, as anxiety is for panic disorder, agoraphobia, and posttraumatic stress disorder, among others.

The same kind of hierarchical evolution is now occurring on Axis II. Whenever kinds of schizoids or antisocials or borderlines are discussed, a hierarchical conception is implicit. Subvarieties of the Axis II constructs have been abstracted from historical works to provide further refinement, sharper distinctions, and greater descriptive power within these diagnostic entities (Millon & Davis, 1996). In addition, Millon (1986, 1990) has articulated each of the Axis II prototypes as integrative personality patterns which are expressed in a variety of functional and structural clinical domains. Among assessment instruments, which are much more easily constructed and altered than are official nosologies, the emergence of contextualism is even more clear. Despite its metatheoretical weaknesses, one strength of the lexical approach is its assertion that personality traits are hierarchically organized. Personality descriptors are broad but somewhat inaccurate near the top of the hierarchy, becoming increasingly narrow but more precise as one moves down into regions of lower traits and ultimately into behavioral acts. The NEO Personality Inventory—Revised (NEO-PI; Costa & McCrae, 1985), for example, includes facet scales of each of its five broad-band factors. The MMPI-2 Content scales have been broken up into experimental Content Component scales (Butcher, Graham, Williams, & Ben-Porath, 1990). Investigations are underway which look at content subscales for the Millon family of instruments, as well.

ASSESSMENT AND THERAPY

The form of therapy and its content are the two principle considerations in setting forth a logical model for the therapy of personality disorders. The ideal form of therapy can be derived without considerations of content, being implicit in the structural properties of the personality construct itself. Modern therapies are often practiced in a "linear" format, one which assumes that a simple additivity of therapeutic effects will be sufficient to deal with the problems at hand. Unfortunately, many mental health professionals continue to apply the same therapeutic modality, exclusively cognitive therapy, exclusively behavioral therapy, exclusively pharmacological therapy, exclusively family therapy, and so on, to every patient they encounter. If personality disorders were anchored exclusively to one of these domains (as phobias are thought of as being primarily behavioral in nature), such single-minded approaches would be both appropriate and desirable. Personality disorders, however, are not exclusively behavioral or cognitive or intrapsychic constructs. Instead, they are multioperational and systemic. No part of the system exists in complete isolation. Instead, every part is directly or indirectly tied to every other. An emergent synergism lends the whole a clinical tenacity which makes personality a "real" thing to be reckoned with in any therapeutic endeavor.

Two integrative procedures have been put forward for the personality disorders. In the first of these, which has been called "potentiated pairings," treatment methods are combined simultaneously to overcome problematic characteristics that might be refractory to each technique if they were administered separately. These composites pull and push for change on many different fronts, so that the therapy becomes as multioperational and as tenacious as the disorder itself. The term "catalytic sequences" has been proposed to represent procedures whose intent is to plan the order in which coordinated treatments are executed. They comprise therapeutic arrangements and timing series which should optimize the impact of changes that would be less effective if the sequential combination were otherwise arranged. In a catalytic sequence, for example, one might seek first to alter a patient's stuttering by direct modification procedures which, if achieved, may facilitate the use of cognitive methods in producing self-image changes in confidence which may, in its turn, foster the utility of interpersonal techniques in effecting improvements in social relationships.

Nomothetic Proposition: The Therapeutic Plan Should Be Developed from Those Prototypes Assessed as Being Most Relevant to the Individual's Personality Style

While we may know that personality disorders require a fundamentally different kind of therapy than do the Axis I disorders, this does not in itself tell us what to do when confronted with an actual patient. The integrative forms of personologic therapy are dictated by the nature of the construct. The content of personologic therapy, however, must be specified on some other basis. Personality is, by definition, the patterning of intraindividual variables, but the nature of these variables does not follow from the definition, and must be supplied by some principle or on some basis which is "outside" the personality construct itself. Personality is a structural–functional concept that refers to the intraorganismic patterning of variables; it does not in itself say what these variables are, nor can it be expected to, just as the generic idea of personality cannot be expected to tell us anything particular about the personality of a specific individual.

To ask the question "How do I address the personality pathologies of the patient that sits before me?" is once again to ask about the fundamental nature of the forces or elements that give rise to, or combine to form, the personality disorders. As a construct, personality seeks to capture the entire matrix of the person, to distill from the major currents and subtle eddies of the behavioral stream some set of underlying, logical, organizing principles which capture precisely individual functioning. Personality asks us to look at manifest behaviors not one at a time as if each were simply the next on the list or next in a sequence relevant to, yet isolated from the larger whole, but rather to examine behaviors in connection with one another as a means by which to infer some underlying theme or unity of purpose to which each aspect of the whole is somehow accountable. As a construct, personality begs us to dive beneath the surface, to make inferences, and to integrate manifest diversities according to latent logical principles. As scientists, we are called upon not merely to record behavior in this or that domain, but to explain it.

In Millon's model, for example, the content of personality is derived from evolutionary theory, a discipline which informs and serves as a basis for, but exists apart from, personology. By comparing and contrasting the specific person against the personality prototypes deduced from the theory, a therapeutic plan can be formed which provides a basis for approaching the individual's pathologies in terms of the fundamental "forces" of which personality is composed. Table 1.2 provides a synopsis of polarity-oriented goals for the Axis II disorders.

Idiographic Proposition: The Therapeutic Plan Must Be Elaborated to Accommodate Idiographic Specificities That Do Not Fit Readily into the Schema of Clinical Prototypes

In the DSM, the personality disorders are operationalized as prototypes. Each prototype consists of a variety of diagnostic attributes. Possessing a threshold number of these attributes qualifies one for a particular personality diagnosis. For example, if five of nine are required, then a patient positive for any five of the nine will be diagnosed with the disorder. While every pair of patients will inevitably have at least two attributes in common, no one particular criterion is either necessary or sufficient for the diagnosis. The resemblance of an individual to the prototype is necessarily a qualitative as well as a quantitative affair. That is, by its heuristic nature, the prototype asks both how and how much the individual resembles the ideal, implicitly looking beyond the one-disorder, one-cause, one-therapy perspective implicit in the current diagnostic system. Heterogeneity, then, is seen not as an epistemic problem reflecting our ignorance of an individual's true diagnostic disposition, but rather as a substantive part of the diagnostic landscape that must be considered *in addition* to whatever diagnoses are made.

Thus, diagnosing a patient into a particular set of prototypes does not represent a stopping point, but is instead a point of departure for creating that much longer a narrative which conceptualizes the individual's whole personality. On what basis will this nar-

TABLE 1.2. Goals of Polarity-Oriented Personologic Therapy

Modifying the pain–pleasure polarity

+ Pleasure (schizoid, avoidant, depressive)
– Pain (avoidant, depressive)
Pain ↔ Pleasure (masochistic, sadistic)

Balancing the passive–active polarity

+ Passive – Active (avoidant, histrionic, antisocial, sadistic, negativistic)
– Passive + Active (schizoid, depressive, dependent, narcissistic, masochistic, compulsive)

Altering the other–self polarity

– Other + Self (dependent, histrionic)
+ Other – Self (narcissistic, antisocial)
Other ↔ Self (compulsive, negativistic)

Rebuilding the personality structure

+ Cognitive, Interpersonal Cohesion   schizotypal
+ Affective, Self Cohesion   borderline
– Cognitive, Affective-Rigidity   paranoid

rative be generated? Currently, there are two directions within Millon's model in which the clinician can proceed. In the first, the clinical prototypes are operationalized in terms of their manifestations in eight functional–structural domains of personality. These domains suggest additional and more specific characteristics that may be inquired to derive rich and relatively complete conceptions of a patient's personality structure and functioning. Assume, for example, that an individual, upon completing an MCMI, obtains a narcissistic–dependent profile. Specific domain attributes can then be examined in conjunction with auxiliary evidence to generate more detailed, idiographically valid portrayals of personality. Domain attributes and associated descriptive paragraphs for the narcissistic and dependent personalities are given in Table 1.3.

As a second means of deriving more idiographic conceptions of individual personality, the clinician may wish to inspect what are being called the *adult subtypes* of the personality disorders (Millon & Davis, 1996). While the major prototypes represent "inevitable deductions" from the evolutionary theory, the subtypes represent instead what are believed, on the basis of clinical experience and a reading of the historical literature for personality, to be the more common manifestations of the major clinical variants in our particular times and culture. Often, they represent the convergence of the major types with organizing principles from particular domains of personality, for example, the idea of the "compensating narcissistic" type. And often, they represent commonly found fusions of the major types, for example, the histrionic and the borderline. Nevertheless, while the increased specificity of the subtypes relative to the major prototypes promises an increase in the fit of actual patients to the diagnostic system, the subtypes should be viewed, again, as protosubtypes, rather than taxonomic endpoints. They are simply another waystation or frame of reference that clinicians may avail themselves of on the way to a narrative formulation of high "fit" with the individual, that is, one that brings the person-as-open concept to closure in terms of constructs anchored within a schema that is genuinely explanatory, rather than descriptive.

One question we may want to ask concerns the limits to which the content of personologic therapy can be specified in advance at a tactical level, that is, the extent to which specific potentiating pairings and catalytic sequences can be identified for each of the personality disorders. Many of the clinical chapters in this text contain a chart which presents the salience of each of the clinical domains for that disorder. To the extent that each patient's presentations is prototypal, the potentiating pairings and catalytic sequences that are actually used should derive from modality tactics oriented to several of the more salient domains. That, however, probably represents the limits to which theory can guide practice in an abstract sense, that is, without knowing anything about the history and characteristics of the specific individual case to which the theory is to be applied. Just as individuality is ultimately so rich that it cannot be exhausted by any taxonomic schema, personologic therapy, ideally performed, is full of specificities which cannot readily be resolved into more general statements. Potentiating pairings, catalytic sequences, and whatever other higher-order composites that therapists may evolve are conducted at an idiographic rather than at a nomothetic (or disorder) level. Accordingly, their precise content is specified as much by the logic of the individual case as by the logic of the disorders themselves.

Perhaps we can best grasp the integrative process of personologic therapy if we think of personality domains as analogous to the sections of an orchestra, and the pathological characteristics of a patient as a clustering of discordant instruments. To extend the analogy, therapists may be seen as conductors whose task is to bring forth a harmonious balance among all the instruments, muting some here, accentuating others there, all to the

TABLE 1.3. Domain Tables for Narcissistic and Dependent Personality Disorders

Narcissistic personality	Dependent personality
Behavioral level	**Behavioral level**
(F) Expressively haughty (e.g., acts in an arrogant, supercilious, pompous, and disdainful manner, flouting conventional rules of shared social living, viewing them as naive or inapplicable to self; reveals a careless disregard for personal integrity and a self-important indifference to the rights of others)	*(F) Expressively incompetent* (e.g., withdraws from adult responsibilities by acting helpless and seeking nurturance from others; is docile and passive, lacks functional competencies, and avoids self-assertion)
(F) Interpersonally exploitive (e.g., feels entitled, is unempathic and expects special favors without assuming reciprocal responsibilities; shamelessly takes others for granted and uses them to enhance self and indulge desires)	*(F) Interpersonally submissive* (e.g., needs excessive advice and reassurance, as well as subordinates self to stronger, nurturing figure, without whom may feel anxiously alone and helpless; is compliant, conciliatory, and placating, fearing being left to care for oneself)
Phenomenological level	**Phenomenological level**
(F) Cognitively expansive (e.g., has an undisciplined imagination and exhibits a preoccupation with immature and self-glorifying fantasies of success, beauty, or love; is minimally constrained by objective reality, takes liberties with facts, and often lies to redeem self-illusions)	*(F) Cognitively naive* (e.g., rarely disagrees with others and is easily persuaded; is unsuspicious and gullible; reveals a Pollyanna attitude toward interpersonal difficulties, watering down objective problems and smoothing over troubling events)
(S) Admirable self-image (e.g., believes self to be meritorious, special, if not unique, deserving of great admiration, and acting in a grandiose or self-assured manner, often without commensurate achievements; has a sense of high self-worth, despite being seen by others as egotistic, inconsiderate, and arrogant)	*(S) Inept self-image* (e.g., views self as weak, fragile, and inadequate; exhibits lack of self-confidence by belittling own attitudes and competencies, and hence not capable of doing things on one's own)
(S) Contrived objects (e.g., internalized representations are composed far more than usual of illusory and changing memories of past relationships; unacceptable drives and conflicts are readily refashioned as the need arises, as are others often simulated and pretentious)	*(S) Immature objects* (e.g., internalized representations are composed of infantile impressions of others, unsophisticated ideas, incomplete recollections, rudimentary drives and childlike impulses, as well as minimal competencies to manage and resolve stressors)
Intrapsychic level	**Intrapsychic level**
(F) Rationalization mechanism (e.g., is self-deceptive and facile in devising plausible reasons to justify self-centered and socially inconsiderate behaviors; offers alibis to place oneself in the best possible light, despite evident shortcomings or failures)	*(F) Introjection mechanism* (e.g., is firmly devoted to another to strengthen the belief that an inseparable bond exists between them; jettisons independent views in favor of those of others to preclude conflicts and threats to relationship)
(S) Spurious organization (e.g., morphologic structures underlying coping and defensive strategies tend to be flimsy and transparent, appear more substantial and dynamically orchestrated than they are in fact, regulating impulses only marginally, channeling needs	*(S) Inchoate organization* (e.g., owing to entrusting others with the responsibility to fulfill needs and to cope with adult tasks, there is both a deficient morphologic structure and a lack of diversity in internal regulatory controls, leaving a miscellany of relatively

(continued)

TABLE 1.3. (*continued*)

with minimal restraint, and creating an inner world in which conflicts are dismissed, failures are quickly redeemed, and self-pride is effortlessly reasserted)	undeveloped and undifferentiated adaptive abilities, as well as an elementary system for functioning independently)

Biophysical level	Biophysical level
(S) Insouciant mood (e.g., manifests a general air of nonchalance, imperturbability, and feigned tranquility; appears coolly unimpressionable or buoyantly optimistic, except when narcissistic confidence is shaken, at which time either rage, shame, or emptiness is briefly displayed)	*(S) Pacific mood* (e.g., is characteristically warm, tender, and noncompetitive; timidly avoids social tension and interpersonal conflicts)

Note. F, functional domains; S, structural domains.

end of fulfilling their knowledge of how "the composition" can best be made consonant. The task is not that of altering just one instrument, but of altering all, in concert. Just as music requires a balanced score, one composed of harmonic counterpoints, rhythmic patterns, and melodic combinations, what is needed in personologic therapy is a likewise balanced and synergistic program, a coordinated strategy of counterpoised techniques designed to optimize treatment effects in an idiographically combinatorial and sequential manner.

Obviously, a tremendous amount of knowledge, both about the nature of the patient's disorders and about diverse modes of intervention, is required to perform personologic therapy. To maximize this synergism requires that the therapist be a little like a jazz soloist. Not only should the professional be fully versed in the various musical keys, that is, in techniques of psychotherapy which span all personologic domains, but also he or she should be prepared to respond to subtle fluctuations in the patient's thoughts, actions, and emotions, any of which could take the composition in a wide variety of directions, and integrate these with the overall plan of therapy as it evolves. After the instruments have been packed away and the band goes home, a retrospective account on the entire process should reveal a level of thematic continuity and logical order commensurate with that which would have existed, had all relevant constraints been known in advance.

REFERENCES

Allport, G. (1937). *Personality: A psychological interpretation.* New York: Holt.

American Psychiatric Association. (1980). *Diagnostic and statistical manual of mental disorders* (3rd ed.). Washington, DC: Author.

Butcher, J. N., Graham, J. R., Williams, C. L., & Ben-Porath, Y. S. (1990). *Development and use of the MMPI-2 content scales.* Minneapolis: University of Minnesota Press.

Costa, P. T., & McCrae, R. R. (1985). *The NEO Personality Inventory manual.* Odessa, FL: Psychological Assessment Resources.

Exner, J. E., Jr. (1986). *The Rorschach: A comprehensive system.* New York: Wiley-Interscience.

Hempel, C. G. (1965). *Aspects of scientific explanation.* New York: Free Press.

Harris, R. E., & Lingoes, J. C. (1955, 1968). *Subscales for the MMPI: An aid to profile interpretation.* Unpublished manuscript, Langley–Porter Neuropsychiatric Institute.

Millon, T. (1986). Personality prototypes and their diagnostic criteria. In T. Millon & G. L. Klerman (Eds.), *Contemporary directions in psychopathology: Toward the DSM-IV* (pp. 571–712). New York: Guilford Press

Millon, T. (1990). *Toward a new personology.* New York: Wiley.

Millon, T., & Davis, R. D. (1996). *Disorders of personality: DSM-IV and beyond.* New York: Wiley-Interscience.

Murray, H. A. (Ed.). (1938). *Explorations in personality.* New York: Oxford University Press.

Rorschach, H. (1921). *Psychodiagnostik* (Hans Huber Verlag, Trans.). Bern, Switzerland: Bircher.

Wiggins, J. S. (1969). Content dimensions in the MMPI. In J. N. Butcher (Ed.), *MMPI: Research developments and clinical applications* (pp. 129–180). New York: McGraw-Hill.

II
THE MILLON CLINICAL MULTIAXIAL INVENTORY (MCMI)

2

History, Theory, and Validation of the MCMI

THEODORE MILLON
CARRIE M. MILLON

This chapter is intended for readers who wish to explore the history, theoretical models, and validation steps undergirding the Millon Clinical Multiaxial Inventories (MCMI) (Millon, 1977, 1987a, 1994). While the logic and rationale presented here may be more abstract than in other sections of this text, the discussion will furnish a perspective regarding how the constructs were derived and why we believe them to be consonant with recent developments in the field of personology.

As we have noted elsewhere (Millon, 1990), this is a time of rapid scientific and clinical advances, a time that seems optimal for ventures designed to generate new ideas and syntheses. The territory where "personality" and "psychopathology" intersect is one of the areas of significant academic activity and clinical responsibility. Providing theoretical formulations that bridge these intersections would alone represent a major intellectual step, but we want to do more. To limit our focus to contemporary research models that address these junctions directly might lead us to overlook the solid footings provided by our field's historic thinkers (such as Freud and Jung), as well as our more mature sciences (such as physics and evolutionary biology). If we fail to coordinate propositions and constructs with principles and laws established by these intellectual giants and advanced disciplines, the different domains comprising our subject will continue to float on their own, so to speak, unconnected to other realms of nature, and, hence, will require that we return to the important task of synthesis another day. Therefore, in this chapter we go beyond current conceptual and research boundaries in personology and incorporate the contributions of past theorists as well as those of our more firmly grounded "adjacent" sciences. Not only may such steps bear new conceptual fruits, but they also may provide a foundation to guide our own discipline's explorations.

Much of psychology as a whole remains adrift, divorced from broader spheres of scientific knowledge, isolated from deeper and more fundamental, if not universal, principles. As the history of psychology amply illustrates, the propositions of our science are not in themselves sufficient to orient its development in a consistent and focused fashion. Consequently, psychology has built a patchwork quilt of dissonant concepts and diverse data domains. Preoccupied with but a small part of the larger pie, or fearing accusations of reductionism, we have failed to draw on the rich possibilities that may be found in both historical and adjacent realms of scholarly pursuit. With few exceptions, cohering concepts that would connect current topics to those of the past have not been developed. We seem repeatedly trapped in (obsessed with?) contemporary fads and horizontal refinements.

A search for integrative schemas and constructs that will link us to relevant observations and laws in other fields of contemporary "science" is also needed. The goal, admittedly a rather "grandiose" one, is to refashion our patchwork quilt into a well-tailored and cohesive tapestry that interweaves the diverse forms in which nature expresses itself. There is no better sphere within the psychological sciences to undertake such a synthesis than the subject matter of personology—the study of persons. The individual person is the only organically integrated system in the psychological domain, evolved through the millennia and basically created from birth as a natural entity. The individual person is not simply a culture-bound and experience-derived gestalt. The intrinsic cohesion of the person is not a rhetorical construction but an authentic substantive unity. Personologic features may be differentiated into normal or pathological, and may be partitioned conceptually for pragmatic or scientific purposes, but they are segments of an inseparable biopsychosocial entity.

HISTORY OF THE MCMI

It may be of interest to record a few words regarding the origin and sequential development of the various forms of the MCMI. As noted in the Preface, a year or two after the publication in 1969 of *Modern Psychopathology* (Millon, 1969), Theodore Millon, the senior author, began with some regularity to receive letters and phone calls from graduate students who had read the book and thought it provided ideas that could aid them in formulating their dissertations. Most inquired about the availability of an "operational" measure they could use to assess or diagnose the pathologies of personality that were generated by the text's theoretical model. Regretfully, no such tool was available. Nevertheless, they were encouraged to pursue whatever lines of interest they may have had in the subject. Some were sufficiently motivated to state that they would attempt to develop their own "Millon" instrument as part of the dissertation enterprise.

As the number of these potential "Millon" progenies grew into the teens, however, concern grew proportionately regarding both the diversity and the adequacy of these representations of the theory. To establish a measure of instrumental uniformity for future investigators, as well as to assure at least a modicum of psychometric quality among tools that ostensibly reflected the theory's constructs, Millon was prompted (perhaps "driven" is a more accurate word) to consider undertaking the test construction task himself. At that time, in early 1971, Millon was directing a research supervision group composed of psychologists and psychiatrists-in-training during their internship and residency periods. All of them had read *Modern Psychopathology* and found the proposal of working together to develop instruments to identify and quantify the text's personality constructs to be both worthy and challenging.

The initial task was that of exploring alternate methods for gathering relevant clinical data. About 11 or 12 persons were involved in that early phase. Some were asked to analyze the possibilities of identifying new indexes from well-established projective tests, such as the Rorschach and the Thematic Apperception Test; others were to investigate whether we could compose relevant scales from existing objective inventories, such as the

Sixteen Personality Factor Questionnaire (16PF) and the Minnesota Multiphasic Personality Inventory (MMPI). Another group examined the potential inherent in developing a new and original structured interview. After 4 or 5 months of weekly discussions, the group concluded that an entirely new instrument would be required if we were to represent the full scope of the theory, especially its diverse and then-novel "pathological" personality patterns (our work, it should be recalled, preceded by several years that undertaken by the DSM-III Task Force). It was judged further that we would attempt to construct both a self-report inventory and a semistructured interview schedule.

Naively, it was assumed that both construction tasks could be completed in about 18 months, a time period that would allow several members of the research group to participate on a continuing basis. Despite the fact that we "postponed" developing the interview schedule after a brief initial period, the "more limited" task of the inventory took almost 7 years to complete. The framework and preliminary item selections of the inventory were well underway, however, by the end of the first full year of our work and was described briefly in a book Millon coauthored in 1972: *Research Methods in Psychopathology* (Millon & Diesenhaus, 1972). The initial forms of the clinical instrument were entitled the Millon–Illinois Self-Report Inventory (MI-SRI).

Millon became involved thereafter in the development of the DSM-III (American Psychiatric Association, 1980), playing a major role in formulating both the constructs and the criteria that were to characterize its Axis II personality disorders. Although the MI-SRI was regularly refined and strengthened on the basis of theoretic logic and research data, an effort was made during this period to coordinate both its items and scales with the forthcoming syndromes of DSM-III. So modified, its name was changed to the Millon Clinical Multiaxial Inventory (MCMI), published in 1977 by National Computer Systems, Inc. (NCS).

In the ensuing 10-year period numerous refinements of the inventory were introduced (e.g., corrections for response-distorting tendencies such as current emotional state) and expansions were made to incorporate theoretical extensions and the newly published DSM-III-R (e.g., the addition of the Self-defeating and Sadistic Personality Disorder scales; American Psychiatric Association, 1987). The MCMI-II, reflecting the preceding changes and additions, was published in 1987 (Millon, 1987a). Ongoing investigations, further refinements in its undergirding theory, and modifications in the anticipated DSM-IV personality disorders criteria served as the primary impetus to refashion the inventory into its latest form, the MCMI-III, published in 1994, designed to reflect its theory optimally and to maximize its consonance with the most recent and empirically grounded official classification system.

THEORY

Philosophers of science agree that it is theory which provides the conceptual glue that binds a nosology together. Moreover, a good theory not only summarizes and incorporates extant knowledge, but it also possesses systematic import in that it originates and develops new observations and new methods. In setting out a theory of personality prototypes, what is desired is not merely a *descriptive* list of disorders and their correlated attributes, but also an *explanatory* derivation based on theoretical principles. Again, the question of interest is: Why these particular personality disorders rather than others?

To address this question, a taxonomy must seek a theoretical schema which "carves nature at its joints," so to speak. The philosopher of science Carl Hempel (1965) clearly distinguished between natural and artificial classification systems. The difference, according to Hempel, is that natural classifications possess "systematic import." Hempel writes:

> Distinctions between "natural" and "artificial" classifications may well be explicated as referring to the difference between classifications that are scientifically fruitful and those that are not: in a classification of the former kind, those characteristics of the elements which serve as criteria of membership in a given class are associated, universally or with high-probability, with more or less extensive clusters of other characteristics. . . . A classification of this sort should be viewed as somehow having objective existence in nature, as "carving nature at the joints." . . . (pp. 146–147)

The biological sexes (male and female) and the periodic table of elements are both examples of classifications schemes which can be viewed as possessing "objective" existence in nature. The items we seek to classify are not sexes or chemical elements, however, but persons. In so doing, we seek the ideal of a classification scheme or taxonomy which is "natural," one which "inheres" in the subject domain, and is not "imposed" on it.

Again, to achieve such an end, the system of kinds which undergirds any domain of inquiry must itself be answerable to the question that forms the very point of departure for the scientific enterprise: Why does nature take this particular form rather than some other? The goal of science is to explain the objects and events we find in the world, and among the objects we find in the world are classification systems for objects themselves. Applied to a taxonomy, the question is thus rephrased: Why this particular system of kinds rather than some other? Accordingly, a taxonomic scheme must be justified, and to be justified scientifically it must be justified theoretically. Consonant with integrative principles, then, theory and taxonomy are intimately intertwined. Rather than remaining an uncoordinated and free-floating fragment, each taxon finds its true nexus with others in transcending theoretical principles through which the entire taxonomy can be deduced as an organic whole: The validity of a taxonomy is linked to its theoretical construction. Quine (1977) makes a parallel case:

> One's sense of similarity or one's system of kinds develops and changes . . . as one matures. . . . And at length standards of similarity set in which are geared to theoretical science. The development is away from the immediate, subjective, animal sense of similarity to the remoter objectivity of a similarity determined by scientific hypotheses . . . and constructs. Things are similar in the later or theoretical sense to the degree that they are . . . revealed by science. (p. 171)

This "remoter sense of objectivity" is essentially what is sought in the assessment process, most obviously in terms of the referral question, but also in terms of the intermediate constructs required to address the referral question, such as personality style. The purpose of an integrative assessment is to develop a theory of the person. That anyone would want to develop an integrative theory of the person without a proportionally integrative theory of the constructs used to explain the person is somewhat puzzling, if not amazing. But when theory is ignored in favor of exclusively empirical inductions or factor-analytically derived orthogonal dimensions, that is essentially what is being done.

Does this mean that one has to buy into the theory which underlies the MCMI to buy into the test? Not at all. While no other instrument is as coordinated with the official DSM taxonomy of personality disorders as is the MCMI, the official position of the DSM with regard to all taxonomic categories, including personality prototypes, is atheoretical. Moreover, the MCMI was designed from the beginning to function as an explicitly clinical inventory. It is not set in stone. As substantive advances in knowledge take place, whether as the result of compelling empirical research or well-justified theoretical deduction, the MCMI will be upgraded and refined as well. Minor elaborations and modifications have been introduced since the original MCMI formal publication 20 years ago; these fine-tunings will continue regularly as our understanding of the MCMI's strengths, limits, and potentials develops further.

We must add, however, that to jettison the theory would be to sell the MCMI short. In the absence of a theoretical foundation, the outline of this chapter could be effectively abbreviated to read something like the following: "These are the disorders and this is the test and this is how to give the test and this is what to watch out for and this is what to expect when such and such shows up." No "why?," just "that." In contrast, a theoretical perspective embodies well-ordered and codified links between constructs, providing a *generative* basis for making clinical inferences founded on a small number of fundamental principles. We now turn to these principles.

One goal of this chapter is to connect the conceptual structure of personality to its foundations in the natural world, which also was an aim of both Freud and Jung. The formulation that will be presented here is akin to Freud's abandoned "Project for a Scientific Psychology" (1966). Freud was endeavoring to advance our understanding of human nature by exploring interconnections among disciplines that evolved from ostensibly unrelated bodies of research and that used manifestly dissimilar languages. The approach here is also akin to Jung's effort to explicate personality functions with reference to the balancing of deeply rooted bipolarities, a theory most clearly formulated in his book *Psychological Types* (1971).

Contemporary formulations by psychologists likewise have set forth the potential and analyzed the problems involved in combining evolutionary notions with theories of individual differences and personality traits (e.g., Buss, 1990). The common goal among these proposals is not only to apply analogous principles across diverse scientific realms but also to reduce the enormous range of psychological concepts that have proliferated throughout history; this might be achieved by exploring the power of evolutionary theory to simplify and order previously disparate personality features.

For example, all organisms seek to avoid injury, find nourishment, and reproduce their kind if they are to survive and maintain their populations. Each species is marked by commonalities in its adaptive or survival style among all members. Within each species, however, there are differences in style and in the success with which various members adapt to the diverse and changing environments they face. On this basic level, "personality" would be employed as a term to represent the more or less distinctive style of adaptive functioning that a particular member of a species exhibits as it relates to its typical range of habitats, or environments. "Normal personality," so conceived, would reflect a species member's specific modes of adaptation that are effective in "average" or "expectable" environments. "Disorders of personality," in this context, would represent different styles of maladaptive functioning that can be traced to deficiencies, imbalances, or conflicts in a member's capacity to relate to the environments it faces.

A few more words should be said concerning comparisons made between evolution and ecology, on the one hand, and normal and abnormal personality, on the other. During its life history, an organism develops an assemblage of traits that contributes to its individual survival and reproductive success—the two essential components of fitness formulated by Darwin. Such assemblages, termed "complex adaptations and strategies" in the literature of evolutionary ecology, may be conceptualized as the biological equivalents to personality styles in the mental health literature. Biological explanations of an organism's lifetime strategy of adaptations refer primarily to variations among constituent biogenetic traits, their overall covariance structure, and the nature and ratio of favorable to unfavorable ecological resources that have been available for purposes of extending longevity and optimizing reproduction. Such explanations are not appreciably different from those used to account for the development of normal and pathological personality styles.

A relevant and intriguing parallel may be drawn between the phylogenetic evolution of a species' genetic composition and the ontogenetic development of an individual organism's adaptive strategies (i.e., its "personality style"). At any point in time, a species will possess a limited set of genes that serve as trait potentials. Over succeeding generations, the frequency distribution of these genes will likely change in their relative proportions, depending on how well the traits they undergird contribute to the species' "fittedness" within its varying ecological habitats.

In a similar fashion, individual organisms begin life with a limited subset of their species' genes and the trait potentials they subserve. Over time, the salience of these trait potentials—not the proportion of the genes themselves—will become differentially prominent as the organism interacts with its environments. It "learns" from these experiences which of its traits "fit" best—that is, which are optimally suited to its ecosystem. In phylogenesis, then, actual gene frequencies change during the generation-to-generation adaptive process, whereas in ontogenesis, it is the salience or prominence of gene-based traits that change as adaptive learning takes place. Parallel evolutionary processes occur, both within the life of a species and within the life of a member organism, respectively.

What is seen in the individual organism is a shaping of latent potentialities into adaptive and manifest styles of perceiving, feeling, thinking, and acting. It is the authors' view that these distinctive modes of adaptation, engendered by the interaction of biological endowment and social experience, comprise the elements of what are termed personality styles, whether normal or abnormal. There is a formative process over the course of a single individual's lifetime that parallels gene redistributions within a whole species during its entire evolutionary history.

The Polarity Model of Personality Disorders

The theoretical model that follows is grounded in evolutionary theory (Millon, 1990; Millon & Davis, 1996). In essence, it seeks to explicate the structure and styles of personality with reference to deficient, imbalanced, or conflicted modes of ecological adaptation and reproductive strategy. The proposition that the development and functions of personologic traits may be usefully explored through the lens of evolutionary principles has a long, if yet unfulfilled tradition. Spencer (1870) and Huxley (1870) offered suggestions of this nature shortly after Darwin's seminal *Origins* was published. In more recent times, we have seen the emergence of sociobiology, an interdisciplinary science that explores the interface between human social functioning and evolutionary biology (Wilson, 1975, 1978).

Four periods or phases in which evolutionary principles are demonstrated are labeled as *existence, adaptation, replication,* and *abstraction.* The first, "existence," relates the serendipitous transformation of random or less organized states into those possessing distinct structures of greater organization; the second, "adaptation," refers to homeostatic processes employed to sustain survival in open ecosystems; the third, "replication," pertains to reproductive styles that maximize the diversification and selection of ecologically effective attributes; and the fourth, "abstraction," concerns the emergence of competencies that foster anticipatory planning and reasoned decision making. Polarities derived from the first three phases (pleasure–pain, passive–active, and other–self) are used to construct a theoretically embedded classification system of personality disorders.

These polarities have forerunners in psychological theory that may be traced as far back as the early 1900s. A number of pre-World War I theorists, including Freud, proposed a set of three polarities that were used time and again as the raw materials for constructing psychological processes. Aspects of these polarities were "discovered" and employed by theorists in France, Germany, Russia, and other European nations, as well as the United States (Millon, 1990). In addition, there is a growing group of contemporary scholars whose work has begun to illuminate aspects of these polar dimensions, including Eysenck (1957, 1967), Gray (1973), Buss and Plomin (1975, 1984), Russell (1980), Tellegen (1985), and Cloninger (1986, 1987).

Much as Godel (1931) argued that the consistency of a system cannot be proven at the same level as that system, disputations between "subdisciplines" cannot be resolved by means of imperial ambitions and internecine battles; they can only be transcended at a superordinate level of integration in metatheory. Interested readers should consult Millon (1990) for an explication of these relationships.

The first period, "existence," concerns the maintenance of integrative phenomena, whether nuclear particle, virus, or human being, against the background of entropic decompensation. Evolutionary mechanisms derived from this phase regard life enhancement and life preservation. The former are concerned with orienting individuals toward improvement in the quality of life, and the latter with orienting individuals away from actions or environments that decrease the quality of life or even jeopardize existence itself. These may be called *existential aims*. At the highest level of abstraction such mechanisms form, phenomenologically or metaphorically expressed, a pleasure–pain polarity. Some individuals are conflicted in regard to these existential aims (e.g., the sadistic), while others possess deficits in these crucial substrates (e.g., the schizoid). In terms of neuropsychological growth stages (Millon, 1969, 1981; Millon & Davis, 1996), the pleasure–pain polarity is recapitulated in a "sensory–attachment" phase, the purpose of which is the largely innate and rather mechanical discrimination of pain and pleasure signals.

Existence, however, is but an initial phase. Once an integrative structure exists, it must maintain its existence through exchanges of energy and information with its environment. The second evolutionary phase relates to what is termed the "modes of adaptation"; it is also framed as a two-part polarity: a passive orientation, a tendency to accommodate to one's ecological niche, versus an active orientation, a tendency to modify or intervene in one's surrounds. These "modes of adaptation" differ from the first phase of evolution in that they regard how that which exists, endures. In terms of neuropsychological growth stages, these modes are recapitulated in a "sensorimotor–autonomy" stage, during which the child either progresses to active disposition toward his or her physical and social context, or perpetuates the passive and dependent mode of prenatal and infantile existence.

Although organisms may be well-adapted to their environments, the existence of any life-form is time-limited. To circumvent this limitation, organisms have developed "replicatory strategies" by which to generate progeny. These strategies regard what biologists have referred to as an "r- (or self-propagating) strategy" at one polar extreme, and a "K- (or other-nurturing) strategy" at the second extreme. Psychologically, the former strategy is disposed toward actions which are egotistic, insensitive, inconsiderate, and uncaring, whereas the latter is disposed toward actions which are affiliative, intimate, protective, and solicitous (Gilligan, 1982; Rushton, 1985; Wilson, 1978). Like pleasure–pain, the self–other polarity is often deficient or conflicted. Some personality disorders are ambivalent on this polarity, such as the compulsive and passive–aggressive. In terms of a neuro-psychological growth stages, an individual's orientation toward self and/or others is reca-pitulated in the pubertal gender identity stage (Millon & Davis, 1996).

VALIDATION

According to Loevinger (1957) and Jackson (1970), validation should be an ongoing pro-cess involved in all phases of test construction, rather than a procedure for corroborating the instrument's effectiveness after its completion. With this principle in mind, validation of the MCMI, MCMI-II, and MCMI-III became an integral element at each step of devel-opment rather than an afterthought.

Once a commitment was made to this strategy, the question remained as to what validation procedures should be used to make the final product as efficient as possible in achieving the goals of differential diagnostic and clinical interpretive utility. In her highly illuminating monograph, Loevinger (1957) proposes that development validation pos-sesses three sequential components: substantive, structural, and external. Each of these is a necessary component in construction, but not a sufficient one. Where feasible, steps should be taken to progress from the first stage through the third. A validation sequence such as this departs from procedures employed in the construction of past clinical inven-tories. A brief introduction to the rationale and methods of each of these three compo-nents may be a useful précis of the procedures followed in developing the MCMI, MCMI-II, and MCMI-III.

The first validation step, relabeled "theoretical–substantive validation," and more recently termed the "deductive approach" by Burisch (1984), examines the extent to which the items comprising the instrument derive their content from an explicit theoretical frame-work. Such a theory has been developed (Millon, 1969, 1981, 1986, 1990). In the MCMIs, it provides a series of clinically relevant constructs for personality trait and syndrome defi-nition to be used as a guide in writing relevant scale items. Moreover, because both clear boundaries and anticipated relationships between syndromes can be established on ratio-nal grounds, the test can be constructed with either distinct or interrelated scales at the initial stage of development.

The second step, "internal–structural validation," refers to the model (that is, the purity of the separate scales or the character of their expected relationships) to which the instru-ments' items are expected to conform. For example, each scale may be constructed as a measure of an independent trait in accord with a factorial model. In another model, each scale may be designed to possess a high degree of internal consistency and also expected to display considerable overlap with other specific scales. In the internal–structural stage, items that have already been substantively validated are administered to appropriate popula-tions. For the MCMI, MCMI-II, and MCMI-III, the items that survived this second stage were those which maximized scale homogeneity, displayed a measure of overlap with other theoretically congruent scales, and demonstrated satisfactory levels of endorsement fre-quency and temporal stability.

The third step, noted here as "external–criterion validation," includes only those items and scales which have met the requirements of both the substantive and the structural steps of development. It pertains to the empirical correspondence between each test scale and a variety of nonscale measures of the trait or syndrome under study. This third step entails correlating results obtained on preliminary forms of the inventory with relevant clinical behaviors. When performed in conjunction with other assessment methods and employing diverse external criteria, this procedure may also establish each scale's convergent and discriminant validity (Campbell & Fiske, 1959).

In a classic article, Hase and Goldberg (1967) compared alternative construction strategies and found that each displayed equivalent levels of validity across a set of diverse criteria. After reviewing several subsequent parallel studies, Burisch (1984) concluded that these findings of method equivalence continued to be supported. It would seem, nevertheless, that a sequential validation strategy that employed all three of these approaches would at the very least prove equal to and perhaps enjoy a measure of superiority over any single method alone. With this untested assumption in mind, developmental validation studies were begun on the MCMI. It was hoped that each stage would produce increasingly more refined and accurate forms of the inventory.

Theoretical–Substantive Validation

Some of the major principles and aims that guided the development of the MCMI are presented in this section. The steps taken to generate the preliminary items of the MCMI are also presented.

Reflecting on her years of experience in test construction and evaluation, Loevinger (1972) concludes:

> If I were to draw a single conclusion from my own studies of personality measurement, it would be this: I consider it exceedingly unlikely that either by accident or by automation one will discover a measure of a major personality variable. There is no substitute for having a psychologist in charge who has at least a first-approximation conception of the trait he wishes to measure, always open to revision, of course, as data demand. Theory has always been the mark of a mature science. The time is overdue for psychology, in general, and personality measurement, in particular, to come of age. (p. 56)

Commenting on the development of the MMPI, Norman (1972) notes that criterion keying was the only recourse possible, as no adequate theory or body of established empirical data was available as an alternative. Meehl (1954), the most persuasive exponent of the criterion keying approach, has shifted from an earlier antitheoretical position to one in which a guiding theory is seen as a valuable test development tool (Meehl, 1972). In his usual insightful fashion, Meehl (1972) states:

> One reason for the difficulties of psychometric personology, a reason I did not appreciate in my "dustbowl empiricist" paper of 1945, is the sad state of psychological theory . . .
>
> I now think that at all stages in personality test development, from initial phase of item pool construction to a late-stage optimized clinical interpretive procedure for the fully developed and "validated" instrument, theory and by this I mean all sorts of theory, including trait theory, developmental theory, learning theory, psychodynamics, and behavior genetics-should play an important role. . . .
>
> I believe that psychology can no longer afford to adopt psychometric procedures whose methodology proceeds with almost zero reference to what bets it is reasonable to lay upon substantive personological horses. The "theory" . . . may be only weakly corroborated but I think we have to make do with it anyway. (pp. 149–151)
>
> . . . the preliminary item pool should be constructed in reliance upon all of the facts and theories bearing upon the test. Even one who advocates a relatively atheoretical "blind empirical criterion keying" . . . need not deprive himself of whatever theoretical insight is available at the item construction stage. . . . I now believe (as I did not formerly) that an item ought to make theoretical sense. . . . (p. 155)

Although Meehl maintains his strong commitment to the critical role played by external validation, his recognition of the guiding value of a theoretical model served significantly to reinforce the strategy undertaken in developing the MCMI, MCMI-II, and MCMI-III. Together with Loevinger, Meehl's growing appreciation of the use of theory, strengthened the belief that such a course would prove both wise and fruitful.

Internal–Structural Validation

As described and elaborated by Loevinger (1957), the structural component of validity refers to an instrument's fidelity to its underlying model. Thus, relationships found among the test's items and scales should correspond to the structural pattern of the instrument's theory. For example, assume that a theory posits the existence of personality characteristics formulated as independent or "pure" traits. In this case, the instrument should be designed with a factorial structure; that is, the items comprising each scale should intercorrelate positively with one another and correlate negatively with all other scales of the instrument. The test would then exhibit fidelity to its guiding theory. Despite its popularity with many distinguished psychometricians (e.g., the Eysenck Personality Inventory [1957], and Cattell's 16PF [1946]), a factorial model is not universally applicable, as many personality theories do not accept the notion of trait independence (Allport, 1937, 1950).

The MCMI was constructed in accord with a "polythetic" structural model that stresses internal scale consistency but does not require the scale independence that characterizes factorial approaches. To accord with the underlying "prototypal" model of its guiding theory and its polythetic syndromal structure (Cantor, Smith, French, & Mezzich, 1980; Horowitz, Wright, Lowenstein, & Parad, 1981; Millon, 1986, 1987b; Rosch, 1978), the scales of the MCMI should possess a high level of internal consistency, yet at the same time display selective overlap and a high degree of correlation with other theoretically related scales. For example, according to the theory, the basic personality scale, Avoidant, is viewed as a less severe precursor of the pathological personality disorder scale, Schizotypal. Because they represent relatively coherent clinical syndromes, each scale should exhibit reasonably strong evidence of internal consistency. At the same time, because of their polythetic structure and, hence, the inherent commonalities between these two syndromes, many items should overlap both scales, resulting in substantial interscale correlations. When high interscale correlations of this sort occur, it is often suggested that one scale could be readily substituted for the other. For a variety of reasons beyond their polythetic nature, not the least of which are the different prevalence base rates for these scale syndromes, this contention is neither logical nor pragmatic in terms of clinical theory.

In contrast to the MMPI, for which scale overlap through joint item keying evolved strictly as a result of empirically derived commonalities in diagnostic efficiency (Wakefield, Bradley, Doughtie, & Kraft, 1975), item overlap is both anticipated and guided by the polythetic structural model and the dynamic features of its underlying theory. In addition, as stated by Dahlstrom, Welsh, and Dahlstrom (1972, p. 23): "If the syndrome used in developing a given scale is relatively complex and is characterized by a wide variety of symptoms, then the scale, reflecting this behavioral heterogeneity, is likely to show important relationships with some other scales in the profile."

It is Dahlstrom (1969), a distinguished and active MMPI researcher, who has provided an articulate rationale for scale redundancy. Reflecting on whether two scales showing a high level of intercorrelation are really two measures or one, Dahlstrom recounts the experience of McKinley and Hathaway (1944), who found a substantial overlap between the Hysteria and the Hypochondriasis scales. Dahlstrom writes:

These investigators indicated that their initial temptation was to drop one or the other of these scales on general psychiatric cases because the two scales correlated .71. Yet careful examination of the clinical contributions of each of these scales led McKinley and Hathaway to retain both scales. . . . Several kinds of evidence were used (such as the fact that 32% of the cases of conversion hysteria had scores beyond the arbitrary cutting score on Hysteria, while being missed by the Hypochondriasis scale), but the most compelling reasons for retaining both scales lay in their configural relationships. The way these scales related to each other and the third scale in the neurotic triad, the Depression scale, provided useful data in psychodiagnostic evaluations of anxiety, depression, and somatic reactions. Information provided by such indices as hit rates or summarized in nonlinear combinations of test scales is not adequately represented in tables of intercorrelations nor accurately preserved in factor solutions . . . [which do] serious injustice to clinical assessment formulations that operate outside a narrow, geometrical view of human personality. (pp. 23–24)

Dahlstrom's suggestion for revising the MMPI consists largely of devising separate scales for personologic predispositions (personality pattern scales) and for psychopathological states (clinical syndrome scales), precisely the distinction developed in constructing the MCMIs. And, in accord with these instruments' underlying theory, Dahlstrom comments that a separation of scales along these lines would enable researchers to test the thesis that specific ties exist between particular personality types and the clinical disorders each will exhibit under stress, as well as the specific kinds of disorders to which each type is most susceptible. The underlying theory of the MCMI, MCMI-II, and MCMI-III can contribute most usefully in formulating these hypothesized relationships.

External–Criterion Validation

The central idea behind using external–criterion validation is quite straightforward. Items comprising a test scale should be selected on the basis of their empirically verified association with a significant and relevant criterion measure. The procedure by which this association is gauged is also direct. Preliminary items should be administered to two groups of subjects which differ on the criterion measure. The "criterion" group exhibits the trait with which the item is to be associated; the "comparison" group does not. After the test is administered, the True and False endorsement frequencies for both groups on every item are calculated. Items that statistically differentiate the criterion group from the comparison group are judged "externally valid." To ensure that these item discriminations are not spurious or do not occur merely by chance, they should be reassessed through additional studies with new, cross-validation samples.

The prime virtue of the external–criterion method is that it verifies, in fact, what is only intuitively, structurally, or theoretically assumed to be an item–criterion relationship. Moreover, the method may uncover associations which are neither obvious nor readily deduced on consistency or theoretical grounds. Among the incidental advantages that may accrue from the criterion method is the identification of subtle or indirect items which subjects would have difficulty falsifying or dissembling.

There are several disadvantages to test development procedures that depend exclusively on external validation methods. These are especially problematic when diverse cross-validation follow-up studies have not been done. The items this method produces may stem from chance relationships that characterize the particular population sample used for item selections. Significant item discriminations that emerge with the construction sample, particularly those that are surprising in terms of clinical "logic," often fail to hold up when reevaluated with an apparently similar, but new, cross-validation sample.

One of the merits of the MCMI construction procedure is that all items survived the criteria of theoretical–substantive and internal–structural validity before being subjected to external validation. Hence, those which survive this final stage are not likely to be judged either "surprising" or logically "inconsistent."

Accepting the rationale of external–criterion validation still leaves two additional problems. First, there is the question of the nature of the criteria to be chosen for external reference. Second, a decision must be made about which comparison groups would be most relevant for contrast with the criterion groups.

The use of practical or pragmatic criteria for external validation reference has been a subject of much debate for many years. (Cattell, 1946; Lord, 1955; Loevinger, 1957; Gough, 1965). The issue is whether the criteria chosen should be composed of real clinical functions and decisions for which the test will be a substitute gauge or whether the criteria should be less specific and reflect more generalized functions, traits, and purposes.

Lord (1955) writes that the goal of generalized, nonpragmatic validity is neither feasible nor relevant. Rather, the true measure of validation is the instrument's discriminating power for specific decision problems. Similarly, Gough (1965) argues that the ultimate standard for validation should be the setting within which the test will be used; that is, the instrument should be evaluated by its predictive or descriptive use in a real-world, functional setting. This pragmatic philosophy for external criteria, successfully applied in validating the Strong Vocational Blank, the MMPI, and the California Psychological Inventory (CPI), achieves its greatest value by ensuring that an instrument is directly relevant to the operational services it is intended to perform.

Applying the pragmatic model to the MCMIs (I, II, and III) suggests that its use would be best gauged by its ability to predict what clinicians are likely to say in describing their patient's personality characteristics and symptom disorders. Because the items of the MCMIs had already been screened in accord with theoretical–substantive and internal–structural validation procedures, the instrument fulfilled the goals of those who espouse less pragmatic and more generalizable criteria. Enhancing the practical use of the MCMIs seemed to be fully justified for the ensuing external state of validation. A careful selection of pragmatic criteria would not only refine the instrument by providing additional validation data, but would also help make the MCMIs maximally useful to clinicians who employ them primarily for differential diagnostic and interpretive purposes.

There are numerous methods by which useful data can be gathered about patients. The most direct and clinically relevant approach would be to obtain assessments by mental health professionals who are well acquainted with the specific psychological traits and disorders of particular patients. Diagnostic appraisals by experienced psychologists, psychiatrists, and psychiatric social workers, in contrast to those of nonprofessional relatives and acquaintances, would discriminate psychologically subtle, as well as gross, differences among patients. Thus, an operational criteria composed of professional clinical assessments would not only be pertinent and practical, but would also furnish those more precise discriminations necessary to make the instrument an efficient differential diagnostic tool.

The MCMI-III is not a general personality instrument to be used for "normal" populations or for purposes other than diagnostic screening or clinical assessment. Hence, it contrasts with other, more broadly applied, inventories whose presumed utility for diverse populations may not be as suitable as is often thought.

Normative data and transformation scores for the MCMI-III are based entirely on clinical samples and are applicable only to persons who evidence psychological symptoms or are engaged in a program of professional psychotherapy or psychodiagnostic evaluation. Although its use as an operational measure of relevant theoretical constructs is fully justified, the samples employed for such purposes are best drawn only from comparable clinical populations. To administer the MCMI-III to a wider range of problems or class of subjects such as those found in business and industry, or to identify neurologic lesions, or to use it for the assessment of general personality traits among college students, is to apply the instrument to settings and samples for which it is neither intended nor appropriate.

Clinicians working with physically ill, behavioral medicine, or rehabilitation patients are directed to one of the MCMI-III's associated inventories, the Millon Behavioral Health Inventory, also termed the MBHI (Millon, Green, & Meagher, 1982). Similarly, when the population to be assessed is composed of psychologically troubled teenagers at the junior or senior high school or beginning college levels, the clinician is advised to employ the Millon Adolescent Clinical Inventory, known also as the MACI (Millon, Millon, & Davis, 1993). Both of these instruments are available through NCS Assessment Services. Those who wish to appraise the psychological attributes and traits of nonclinical (i.e., normal) adults may wish to utilize the Millon Index of Personality Styles, also termed the MIPS (Millon, Millon, Weiss, & Davis, 1994). This latter inventory is especially suitable as a gauge of the broader theory's constructs; it may be obtained from the offices of The Psychological Corporation.

The MCMI, MCMI-II, and MCMI-III provide in-depth clinical reports that can be transmitted via U.S. mail, on-site software programs, or electronic teleprocessing methods with instant turnaround. Several principles should be followed to protect confidentiality and to assure appropriate professional standards among those who use the instrument or who avail themselves of its associated computer scoring and interpretive services (Zachary & Pope, 1984). To maintain anonymity, the use of code numbers rather than names is recommended in completing answer sheets; furthermore, only the mental health professional responsible for each case should possess the code for patient identification. This recommendation is warranted especially when the automated interpretive report is used.

In general, those who use the instrument and its associated reports or those who supervise its use should have a sufficient background in test logic, psychometric methods, and clinical practice theory to understand test manuals (Skinner & Pakula, 1986). Those who use the MCMI-III and its reports should have as a minimum a master's degree in clinical or counseling psychology or psychiatric social work, or should have internship or psychiatric residency status. With the exception of graduate school training or research situations in which supervision should be mandatory, the use of the automated scoring and interpretive services should be limited to clinicians who meet full membership qualifications for the American Psychological Association, the American Psychiatric Association, the American Medical Association, American Association for Marriage and Family Therapy, or the National Association of Social Workers. In short, the reading of a computerized report is no substitute for clinical judgment. Only those trained in the limits of psychological tests should make use of them.

Because the automated interpretive report service is considered a professional-to-professional consultation, it is the responsibility of the consultee to view the report as only one facet of a total patient evaluation and to recognize that the information it contains is a series of tentative judgments rather than a set of definitive statements. The integration of selected features of the report into ongoing management and treatment decisions with patients is fully appropriate, but the direct sharing of the report's explicit content with either patients or their relatives is strongly discouraged.

The paragraphs that precede all MCMI-III interpretive reports state that the narrative text "should be evaluated in conjunction with additional clinical data (e.g., current life circumstances, observed behavior, biographic history, interview responses, and information from other tests)." The accuracy and richness of any self-report measure is enhanced when its findings are appraised in the context of other clinical sources. Not only does the combination of various gauges from diverse settings provide the data aggregates (Epstein, 1979, 1983) that increase the likelihood of drawing correct inferences, but multimethod approaches (Campbell & Fiske, 1959) provide both the experienced and the novice clinician with an optimal base for deciphering those special, if not unique, features that characterize each patient.

No less important than the insights provided by non-self-report sources of clinical data is the interpretive guidance furnished by a variety of nonclinical demographic indices (e.g., age, sex, marital status, vocation, ethnicity, socioeconomic factors, educational level). Although higher or lower MCMI-III scale elevations associated with these population characteristics often reflect "real" differences in prevalence rates (e.g., male police officers score higher on certain scales than do male teachers, and do so in a manner consistent with nontest personality data), it is important for clinicians to have a reasonable notion of what is typical for patients of particular social backgrounds. Special scoring norms are being developed for ethnicity to accommodate this major demographic variable. Similarly, a number of scale "modifiers" are utilized in the MCMI-III to compensate for differences among patients in their distortion tendencies, notably candor and exaggeration. Whatever the efficacy of these corrections may be, it behooves the clinician to consider carefully the impact of important demographics, not only to compensate for their effects, but for the insights they may furnish and for their ability to individualize and enrich the meaning of the MCMI-III's clinical data.

Important implications for evaluating MCMI-III results stem from the fact that certain personality scales are sensitive to the current affective state of a patient. All self-report inventory scales, be they personality (Axis II) or syndrome-oriented (Axis I), reflect in varying degrees both "traits" and "states." Despite methodological and psychometric procedures to tease the enduring characteristics of personality apart from clinical features of a more transient quality, every scale reflects a mix of predisposing and generalizing attributes, as well as those of a more situational or acute nature. Noteworthy are the partial blurring effects of current depressive and anxiety states upon specific personality scales (Hirschfeld et al., 1983). These results stem in part from shared scale items (Wiggins, 1982), but the level of covariation is appreciably greater than can be accounted for by item overlap alone. Experience with earlier versions of the MCMI indicates that the presence of dysthymic and anxious states accentuate scores on certain MCMI personality scales while unduly diminishing those obtained on others, a view consistent with recent research by Shea, Glass, Pilkonis, Watkins, and Docherty (1987).

Compensatory efforts have been made to counter the effect of other potentially distorting effects by rephrasing MCMI-III items so as to more clearly separate clinical and state phenomena from those of a more longstanding or trait nature, as well as to build in scoring adjustments that automatically correct for the influences of marked or acute affective states. Nevertheless, clinicians should bear in mind the possibility of occasional personality disorder misrenderings when scores on the Anxiety and Dysthymia scales appear unusually or unexpectedly high or low, in light of other sources of clinical evidence.

Users of computer-based interpretive reports register high levels of satisfaction both in their overall quality and in their correspondence with independently derived clinical observations and judgments (Green, 1982; Craig, 1993). Encouraging as studies such as these may be in affirming "customer satisfaction," they may prove spurious in failing to recognize the so-called "Barnum effect," that is, the tendency of recipients of personality characterizations to conclude that such reports are accurate, not because they are, but because they present attributes of such high generality or commonality as to be applicable to almost all individuals. Moreover, the mysterious and seemingly mythic powers of computer technologies have no doubt imbued its reports, at least for some, with an undue measure of scientific merit and clinical acumen.

Users of diagnostic characterizations provided via computer systems should be wary lest they find themselves lulled over time into an uncritical acceptance of computer-based reports; they should routinely compare the interpretive statements contained in such reports against independently generated clinical evidence. However—and notwithstanding the preceding—the findings of recent investigations into the validity of MCMI interpretive reports provide strong evidence that ratings of that inventory's accuracy are higher than can be accounted for by either the Barnum effect or the computer-generated format (Moreland & Onstad, 1987; Sandberg, 1987; Craig, 1993).

As should be evident, there are distinct boundaries to the accuracy of the self-report method of clinical data collection; by no means is it a perfect data source. The inherent psychometric limits of the tool, the tendency of similar patients to interpret questions differently, the effect of current affective states on trait measures, and the efforts of patients to effect certain false appearances and impressions all narrow the upper boundaries of this method's potential accuracy. However, by constructing a self-report instrument in line with accepted techniques of validation (Loevinger, 1957), an inventory should begin to approach these upper boundaries. Given that it has progressed through such a developmental background, we find that MCMI reports prove to be on the mark in about 55% to 65% of patients to whom it is administered; it is appraised as both useful and generally valid, although with partial misjudgments in about another 25% to 30% of cases; and they appear off target, that is, appreciably in error, about 10% to 15% of the time. These positive figures, we should note, are in the quantitative range of five to six times greater than chance.

Although accuracy levels vary from setting to setting, these differences largely reflect difficulties in decoding the presence of a disorder at the time it is being appraised (e.g., identifying a histrionic personality disorder during a patient's depression). Also problematic is the disorder's prevalence or base rate; on purely mathematical grounds, diagnostic groups with notably low (e.g., suicide) or high (e.g., dysthymia) base rates prove statistically troublesome in that even the most optimal of selected cutoffs often produce hit rates that are only marginally superior to chance (Meehl & Rosen, 1955; Rorer & Dawes, 1982).

Not unrelated to the preceding, the MCMI-III's diagnostic scale cutoffs and profile interpretations are oriented to the majority of patients who take the inventory, that is, to those displaying psychic disturbances in the midranges of severity, rather than to those whose difficulties are either close to "normal" (e.g., worker's compensation litigants, spouses of patients in marital therapy) or of manifest clinical severity (e.g., acute psychotics, chronic schizophrenics). To optimize both diagnostic and interpretive validity, narratives have been written to focus on moderate levels of pathology; this results in a slightly diminished degree of diagnostic and interpretive accuracy among patients in both the lesser and the most severe ranges of psychological disturbance, a fact that users of the interpretive reports should bear in mind. Narrative analyses of patients experiencing ordinary life difficulties or minor adjustment disorders will tend to be construed as more troubled than they are; conversely, those with the most serious pathologies will often be considered as less severe than they are.

The preceding sections stress the importance of having the results of the MCMI-III evaluated concurrently with a variety of other clinical data, and that it be undertaken by properly trained clinicians who know the limitations both of the self-report modality in general and of the MCMI-III in particular.

REFERENCES

Allport, G. (1937). *Personality: A psychological interpretation.* New York: Holt.

Allport, G. W. (1950). *The nature of personality: Selected papers.* Cambridge, MA: Addison-Wesley.

American Psychiatric Association. (1980). *Diagnostic and statistical manual of mental disorders* (3rd ed.). Washington, DC: Author.

American Psychiatric Association. (1987). *Diagnostic and statistical manual of mental disorders* (3rd ed., rev.). Washington, DC: Author.

Burisch, M. (1984). Approaches to personality inventory construction: A comparison of merits. *American Psychologist, 39,* 214–227.

Buss, A., & Plomin, R. (1975). *A temperament theory of personality development.* New York: Wiley.

Buss, A., & Plomin, R. (1984). *Temperament: Early developing personality traits.* Hillsdale, NJ: Erlbaum.

Buss, D. (Ed.). (1990). Biological foundations of personality. *Journal of Personality, 58,* 1–34.

Campbell, D. T., & Fiske, D. W. (1959). Convergent and discriminant validation by the multitrait–multimethod matrix. *Psychological Bulletin, 56,* 81–105.

Cantor, N., Smith, E. E., French, R. D., & Mezzich, J. (1980). Psychiatric diagnosis as prototype categorization. *Journal of Abnormal Psychology, 89,* 181–193.

Cattell, R. B. (1946). *Description and measurement of personality.* Yonkers, NY: World Book.

Cloninger, C. R. (1986). A unified biosocial theory of personality and its role in the development of anxiety states. *Psychiatric Developments, 3,* 167–226.

Cloninger, C. R. (1987). A systematic method for clinical description and classification of personality variants. *Archives of General Psychiatry, 44,* 573–588.

Craig, R. J. (Ed.). (1993). *The Millon Clinical Multiaxial Inventory: A clinical research information synthesis.* Hillsdale, NJ: Erlbaum.

Dahlstrom, W. G. (1969). Recurrent issues in the development of the MMPI. In J. N. Butcher (Ed.), *MMPI: Research developments and clinical applications* (pp. 1–40). New York: McGraw-Hill.

Dahlstrom, W. G., Welsh, G. S., & Dahlstrom, L. E. (1972). *An MMPI handbook* (Vol. I). Minneapolis: University of Minnesota Press.

Epstein, S. (1979). The stability of behavior: 1. On predicting most of the people much of the time. *Journal of Personality and Social Psychology, 37,* 1097–1126.

Epstein, S. (1983). Aggregation and beyond: Some basic issues on the prediction of behavior. *Journal of Personality, 51,* 360–392.

Eysenck, H. J. (1957). *The dynamics of anxiety and hysteria.* London: Routledge & Paul.

Eysenck, H. J. (1967). *The biological basis of personality.* Springfield, IL: Thomas.

Freud, S. (1966). Project for a scientific psychology. In *Standard Edition* (Vol. 1, pp. 283–291). London: Hogarth Press. (Original work published 1895)

Gilligan, C. (1982). *In a different voice.* Cambridge, MA. Harvard University Press.

Godel, K. (1931). *On formally undecidable propositions of principia mathematica and related systems.* Unpublished doctoral dissertation, University of Vienna.

Gough, H. G. (1965). *Some thoughts on test usage and test development.* Paper presented at the annual meeting of the American Personnel and Guidance Association, Los Angeles, CA.

Gray, J. A. (1973). Causal theories of personality and how to test them. In J. R. Royce (Ed.), *Multivariate analysis and psychological theory.* New York: Academic Press.

Green, C. J. (1982). The diagnostic accuracy and utility of MMPI and MCMI computer interpretive reports. *Journal of Personality Assessment, 46,* 359–365.

Hase, H. E., & Goldberg, L. R. (1967). Comparative validity of different strategies of devising personality inventory scales. *Psychological Bulletin, 67,* 231–248.

Hempel, C. (1965). *Aspects of scientific explanation.* New York: Free Press.

Hirschfeld, R. M., Klerman, G. L., Clayton, P. J., Keller, M. P., McDonald-Scott, M. A., & Larkin, B. H. (1983). Assessing personality: Effects of the depressive state on trait measurement. *American Journal of Psychiatry, 140,* 695–699.

Horowitz, L. M., Wright, J. C., Lowenstein, E., & Parad, H. W. (1981). The prototype as a construct in abnormal psychology: 1. A method for deriving prototypes. *Journal of Abnormal Psychology, 90,* 568–574.

Huxley, T. H. (1870). Mr. Darwin's critics. *Contemporary Review, 18,* 443–476.

Jackson, D. N. (1970). A sequential system for personality scale development. In C. D. Spielberger (Ed.), *Current topics in clinical and community psychology* (Vol. 2, pp. 61–92). New York: Academic Press.

Jung, C. (1971). *Psychological types.* Zurich: Rasher Verlag. (Original work published 1921)

Loevinger, J. (1957). Objective tests as instruments of psychological theory. *Psychological Reports, 3,* 635–694.

Loevinger, J. (1972). Some limitations of objective personality tests. In J. N. Butcher (Ed.), *Objective personality assessment* (pp. 45–58). New York: Academic Press.

Lord, F. M. (1955). Some perspectives on "the alternation paradox in test theory." *Psychological Bulletin, 52,* 505–510.

McKinley, J. C., & Hathaway, S. R. (1944). The Minnesota Multiphasic Personality Inventory: V. Hysteria, hypomania, and psychopathic deviate. *Journal of Applied Psychology, 28,* 153–174.

Meehl, P. (1954). *Clinical versus statistical prediction.* Minneapolis: University of Minnesota Press.

Meehl, P. (1972). Specific genetic etiology, psychodynamics, and therapeutic nihilism. *International Journal of Mental Health, 1,* 10–27.

Meehl, P. E., & Rosen, A. (1955). Antecedent probability and the efficiency of psychometric signs, patterns, or cutting scores. *Psychological Bulletin, 52,* 194–216.

Millon, T. (1969). *Modern psychopathology: A biosocial approach to maladaptive learning and functioning.* Philadelphia: W. B. Saunders.

Millon, T. (1977). *Millon Clinical Multiaxial Inventory manual.* Minneapolis: National Computer Systems.

Millon, T. (1981). *Disorders of personality: DSM-III, Axis II.* New York: Wiley-Interscience.

Millon, T. (1986). A theoretical derivation of pathological personalities. In T. Millon & G. L. Klerman (Eds.), *Contemporary directions in psychopathology: Toward the DSM-IV.* New York: Guilford Press.

Millon, T. (1987a). *Manual for the MCMI-II* (2nd ed.). Minneapolis: National Computer Systems.

Millon, T. (1987b). On the nature of taxonomy in psychopathology. In C. Last & M. Hersen (Eds.), *Issues in diagnostic research.* New York: Plenum.

Millon, T. (1990). *Toward a new personology: An evolutionary model.* New York: Wiley-Interscience.

Millon, T., Millon, C., & Davis, R. (1994). *Millon Clinical Multiaxial Inventory—III manual.* Minneapolis: National Computer Systems.

Millon, T., & Davis, R. (1996). *Disorders of personality: DSM-IV and beyond.* New York: Wiley.

Millon, T., & Diesenhaus, H. (1972). *Research methods in psychopathology.* New York: Wiley.

Millon, T., Green, C. J., & Meagher, R. B., Jr. (1982). *Millon Behavioral Health Inventory manual* (3rd ed.). Minneapolis: National Computer Systems.

Millon, T., Millon, C., & Davis, R. (1993). *Millon Adolescent Clinical Inventory.* Minneapolis: National Computer Systems.

Millon, T., Millon, C., Weiss, L., & Davis, R. (1994). *Millon Index of Personality Styles.* San Antonio, TX: Psychological Corporation.

Moreland, K. L., & Onstad, J. A. (1987). Validity of Millon's computerized interpretation system for the MCMI: A controlled study. *Journal of Consulting and Clinical Psychology, 55,* 113–114.

Norman, W. T. (1972). Psychometric considerations for a revision of the MMPI. In J. N. Butcher (Ed.), *Objective personality assessment* (pp. 59–84). New York: Academic Press.

Quine, W.V.O. (1977). Natural kinds. In S. P. Schwartz (Ed.), *Naming, necessity, and natural groups.* Ithaca, NY: Cornell University Press.

Rorer, L. G., & Dawes, R. M. (1982). A base-rate bootstrap. *Journal of Consulting and Clinical Psychology, 50,* 419–425.

Rosch, E. (1978). Principles of categorization. In E. Rosch & D. B. Lloyds (Eds.), *Cognition and categorization.* Hillsdale, NJ: Erlbaum.

Rushton, J. P. (1985). Differential K theory: The sociobiology of individual and group differences. *Personality and Individual Differences*, 6, 441–452.

Russell, J. A. (1980). A circumplex model of affect. *Journal of Personality and Social Psychology*, 39(1), 1611–1678.

Sandberg, M. L. (1987). Is the ostensive accuracy of computer interpretive reports a result of the Barnum effect? A study of the MCMI. In C. Green (Ed.), *Conference on the Millon clinical inventories (MCMI, MBHI, MAPI)* (pp. 155–164). Minneapolis: National Computer Systems.

Shea, M. T., Glass, D. R., Pilkonis, P. A., Watkins, J., & Docherty, J. P. (1987). Frequency and complications of personality disorders in a sample of depressed outpatients. *Journal of Personality Disorders*, 1, 27–42.

Skinner, H. A., & Pakula, A. (1986). Challenge of computers in psychological assessment. *Professional Psychology: Research and Practice*, 17, 44–50.

Spencer, H. (1870). *The principles of psychology*. London: Williams and Norgate.

Tellegen, A. (1985). Structures of mood and personality and relevance to assessing anxiety with an emphasis on self-report. In A. H. Tuma & J. Maser (Eds.), *Anxiety and the anxiety disorders*. Hillsdale, NJ: Erlbaum.

Wakefield, J. A., Bradley, P. E., Doughtie, E. B., & Kraft, I. A. (1975). Influence of overlapping and nonoverlapping items on the theoretical interrelationships of MMPI scales. *Journal of Consulting and Clinical Psychology*, 43, 851–857.

Wiggins, J. (1982). Circumplex models of interpersonal behavior in clinical psychology. In P. Kendall & J. N. Butcher (Eds.), *Handbook of research methods in clinical psychology* (pp. 183–222). New York: Wiley.

Wilson, E. O. (1975). *Sociobiology: The new synthesis*. Cambridge: Harvard University Press.

Wilson, E. O. (1978). *On human nature*. Cambridge: Harvard University Press.

Zachary, R. A., & Pope, K. S. (1984). Legal and ethical issues in the clinical use of computerized testing. In M. D. Schwartz (Ed.), *Using computers in clinical practice* (pp. 212–238). New York: Haworth Press.

3

Interpretation of the MCMI-III

ERIC J. VAN DENBURG
JAMES P. CHOCA

This chapter will present our method of interpreting the Millon Clinical Multiaxial Inventory—III (MCMI-III; Millon, 1994). While other methods are possible, we have found the process we will describe in this chapter to be helpful. Of course, there is no substitute for experience. Careful, extensive use of the MCMI-III, ideally with patients with whom one is well acquainted, will help users to best understand and utilize the instrument.

We assume that the majority of our readers have some rudimentary knowledge of the current psychiatric diagnostic nosology, the fourth edition of the *Diagnostic and Statistical Manual of Mental Disorders* (DSM-IV; American Psychiatric Association, 1994). We also assume that most readers will be using the National Computer Systems (NCS) interpretive readout of their patient's MCMI-III results. This chapter will be geared, then, to extend the readers' knowledge so that they can assume a more informed, independent stance toward some of the interpretations put forward within the NCS computerized readout. To even better use this chapter and the NCS printout, it is also recommended that users make themselves familiar with other recent texts pertaining to the use and interpretation of the MCMI (Choca & Van Denburg, 1997; Craig, 1993a, 1993b; Retzlaff, 1995).

In this chapter we will first cover briefly the changes in the MCMI-III from the MCMI-II. Second, we will review the multiplicity of issues in assessing the validity of a profile. Next, the complex problems of interpreting the underlying personality patterns will be discussed, and the question of the functionality of a given personality profile pattern will be addressed. In the next section, we will review the matter of interpreting syndromal (Axis I) elevations, particularly within the context of the previously covered personality structure. Finally, we plan to discuss issues pertaining to integration of the profile, which will also serve as a summary of the above material.

CHANGES IN THE MCMI-III

The newest version of the MCMI, the third edition, comes after 8 years of experience with the second edition. As the new manual articulates in detail, a revised version of the test was deemed necessary for several reasons (Millon, 1994). First, with the publication of the DSM-IV, it was an appropriate time to make item content of the MCMI more clearly consistent with the new diagnostic system. Many of the new items were rewritten explicitly in line with DSM-IV criteria. Appendix A of the MCMI-III manual goes through items within each of the personality and syndromal scales that directly correlate with DSM-IV criteria. This change was a direct response to prior criticism of the Millon inventories for not being sufficiently consonant with the DSMs (Bonato, Cyr, Kalprin, Prendergast, & Sanhueza, 1988; Widiger, Williams, Spitzer, & Frances, 1986; Widiger & Sanderson, 1987).

Second, the issue of extensive item overlap and subsequent interscale correlation, often raised as a possible problem with the MCMI (Choca, Peterson, & Shanley, 1986; Wiggins, 1982), was addressed. The MCMI-III was designed to have fewer items per scale and reduced item overlap. Third, two new scales were added to the MCMI-III for a broader coverage of current Axis I and II issues. The Depressive scale (2B) is included to reflect this new prototype, contained in the DSM-IV Appendix B. The Post-Traumatic Stress Disorder (PTSD) scale (R) attempts to measure this Axis I diagnosis. Fourth, the item weighting system of the MCMI-III was simplified, again in response to empirical criticisms of the prior practice (Streiner, Goldberg, & Miller, 1993). Finally, the NCS interpretive algorithm of the MCMI-III was made more complex and differentiated to include the changes in theory. The new narratives also reflect the progress in short-term treatment modalities that had been accomplished since publication of the MCMI-II.

The structure of the MCMI-III is presented in Table 3.1.

VALIDITY OF THE PROFILE

To assure that a given MCMI-III profile is a valid indicator of the patient's true psychological state, one must first check several bits of data. At the most basic and rudimentary level, one needs to examine the responses to the Validity scale (V). This scale is composed of three items, each of which is very unusual, and grossly unlikely to be endorsed, if the person is reliably reading the test items. An example is an item that reads "I have not seen a car in the last ten years" (item 157). Barring the most unusual of cases, an examinee should not endorse this item as true. If any of the three Validity scale items is marked as true, the NCS program will note this and will urge the examiner to carefully assess whether the profile is valid. When two or more of the items are endorsed in the true direction, the profile is considered invalid.

The first of the modifier indices, the Disclosure scale (X), is not a scale in the true sense of the word, but is instead based on a formula that includes personality scale scores. This composite was originally intended as a measure of the examinee's tendency to respond in a frank and open manner, rather than in a closed and reticent fashion. Several authors (Retzlaff, Ofman, Hyer, & Matheson, 1994; Retzlaff, 1995) suggest that if the Disclosure scale is below a base rate (BR) score of 35 or above 85, the profile should be considered invalid. The Disclosure scale is the only MCMI-III scale that is interpreted in both directions; that is, both low and high scores are examined.

The Disclosure scale is used to apply a correction factor to other scales on the MCMI-III, to adjust for test-taking distortion in either an "underreporting" or "overreporting" direction. If the Disclosure scale falls above or below a certain value, adjustments to the BR scores of a number of other scales are made. It should be noted that these corrections evoked some criticism when they were instituted for the MCMI-II (Miller, Goldberg, & Streiner, 1993), although studies of their true usefulness have not yet been conducted.

TABLE 3.1. Structure of the MCMI-III

Clinical Personality Patterns

1	Schizoid
2A	Avoidant
2B	Depressive
3	Dependent
4	Histrionic
5	Narcissistic
6A	Antisocial
6B	Aggressive (Sadistic)
7	Compulsive
8A	Passive–Aggressive (Negativistic)
8B	Self-Defeating (Masochistic)

Severe Personality Pathology

S	Schizotypal
C	Borderline
P	Paranoid

Clinical Syndromes

A	Anxiety
H	Somatoform
N	Bipolar: Manic
D	Dysthymia
B	Alcohol Dependence
T	Drug Dependence
R	Post-Traumatic Stress Disorder

Severe Syndromes

SS	Thought Disorder
CC	Major Depression
PP	Delusional Disorder

Modifying Indices

X	Disclosure
Y	Desirability
Z	Debasement
V	Validity

Information pertaining to the nature and extent of these adjustments may be found in Appendix D of the MCMI-III manual (Millon, 1994). The psychometric properties of the Disclosure scale have been examined, albeit with the MCMI and MCMI-II. The evidence supports the validity of the scale in detecting "fake bad" profiles, but the scale has been found to have greater difficulty distinguishing the "fake good" profile (McNeil & Meyer, 1990; Retzlaff, Sheehan, & Fiel, 1991; Van Gorp & Meyer, 1986).

The Desirability scale (Y) attempts to assess the examinee's tendency to present a favorable image of him or herself. The scale is very roughly analogous to the K scale of the Minnesota Multiphasic Personality Inventory (MMPI-2) (Butcher, Dahlstrom, Graham, Tellegen, & Kaemmer, 1989). The Desirability scale items on the MCMI-III were taken from the MCMI-II Y scale items that were retained; any items from the MCMI-II Scale Y that were not retained were replaced with new items of similar content. BR scores over 75 on the Desirability scale suggest that the examinee was attempting to "look good" when the inventory was completed. Reasons for this test-taking style should be examined by the clinician. In our clinical work, we have found that patients seeking discharge from the hospital, or those in massive denial of their problems (e.g., untreated alcoholics, pedophiles, parents in custody evaluations) will often obtain an elevation on the Desirability scale. More rigorous experimental work (Retzlaff et al., 1991) urges caution with this scale, however, as it had some difficulty clearly distinguishing "fake good" profiles at better than chance levels.

The Debasement scale (Z) is used to assess whether a given patient has distorted their profile in the direction of presenting more pathology than may, in fact, be objectively present. A heightened score on the Debasement scale is roughly analogous to obtaining a high F score on the MMPI. As with Scale Y, the Debasement scale items on the MCMI-III were taken from MCMI-II Z scale items that were retained, and any items that were not retained were replaced with new items of similar content. Those examinees obtaining BR scores of 75 or higher may be exaggerating their degree of psychological distress. Our experience is that this scale tends to be elevated in cases of marked, acute decompensation, when a patient is attempting, for whatever reason, to appear psychologically disturbed (e.g., compensation and pension cases within the VA system), or with borderline patients who maintain fixed, unremitting negative views of themselves and others. Empirical studies are obviously needed to help correlate Debasement scale scores with clinical presentations.

As with the other moderator indices, the Debasement scale has generated some empirical study. The strength of the scale in detecting malingering was seen as modest in an analogue study assessing test-taking styles (Retzlaff et al., 1991), and as useful with post-traumatic stress disorder (PTSD) claimants (Lees-Haley, 1992).

PERSONALITY PATTERNS

To interpret well the personality scales of the MCMI-III, the clinician needs to (1) decide which of the obtained scores are elevated enough to be of clinical relevance, (2) integrate the different aspects of the elevated scales into a cohesive description of the individual's personality, and (3) reach an understanding about the level of severity or dysfunctionality of the individual's personality.

The issue of choosing which scales to interpret is not as straightforward as it would appear at first sight. One strategy, that of interpreting the single highest point, is appealing in its simplicity, but generally does not do justice to the intricacies of the person being examined, or to the discriminating power of the test. We often discuss the personality prototypes as if they were all-or-none categorical variables; we speak of one person being avoidant and another histrionic, without paying much attention to the fact that very few people are only avoidant or histrionic, or to the fact that a person who is extremely avoidant will have a different clinical presentation from that of a person who is only mildly avoidant. As is well recognized (Hirschfeld, 1993; Widiger, 1992), the personality of the typical individual has traits that cut across the established personality prototypes and demonstrate different levels of extremeness on any given trait. The reality is that we may all be, for example, compulsive to some degree, and may distribute ourselves in a continuum with regard to the prevalence of that trait. The use of the single high point distributes individuals into categorical personality classes at the expense of the accuracy gained by considering what other traits may be present. The single high point remains the best possible strategy when one of the personality scales in the profile is much more elevated than the rest, say, 15 or 20 points higher than the second highest score. In this case, the prototype measured by the highest elevation can be seen as being, indeed, so much more characteristic of the individual than any of the other prototypes that only that prototype needs to be considered.

Once the idea of considering more than one of the personality scales is accepted, the issue to be raised is how many of the personality prototypes may be clinically significant when there are several scales elevated. To answer that question the clinician needs to look at how elevated the scores are, and at how wide is the gap between the score of one scale and the next highest score. An interpretation that includes the highest two prototypes (a two-point interpretation) is most appropriate when only two scales are significantly elevated, when there is a gap between the score obtained on the second highest scale and the third, and when the score of the third highest scale is closer to the cluster of scores to follow than to the cluster made up by the two highest scales.

Clinicians using the MCMI typically take into consideration the highest three personality scores (a three-point interpretation) in their interpretation. Some elements of the fourth or the fifth elevations are occasionally added, in cases where those scores also cluster with the other high scores, and especially in cases where such additions offer some information that appears to be of particular clinical relevance for the examinee.

A BR score of 75 is typically used as the cutoff determining whether or not a scale is elevated. A knowledgeable clinician does not have to strictly adhere to that guideline. In cases where the entire score profile is elevated, the clinician may decide to disregard or deemphasize some of the scales that did not yield the predominant elevations, even if the BR score was actually above 75. Conversely, with a low score profile, a clinician may use data from scales with scores that did not quite reach the cutoff, especially in cases where such decision can be supported with other sources of information about the individual. In other words, the emphasis when the clinician is personally interpreting an MCMI protocol should be on the cluster of scores that has primacy, rather than on adopting a mechanistic rule about what scores are to be interpreted. Of course, the license to interpret scores below the cutoff has to be exercised with caution: we must remember that the BR score of 50 represents the average for the non-patient population so that, as the scores get into the 60s range, they become more indistinguishable from the mass of scores that, being in the average range, do not indicate a salient characteristic.

Even if only the original eight personality styles are used, and the profile code is determined by considering only the highest three elevations, there would be 336 possible permutations, or distinct profile codes. Our work is made somewhat easier by the fact that some of the possible profile codes are seldom, if ever, found. Retzlaff and his coworkers, for instance, found that only 20 single and two high-point codes occurred with a frequency of more than 2%, and that those 20 code types explained 82% of their variance (Retzlaff et al., 1994). We offer a table in our book that allows the user to map all the possible permutations of the eight basic scales into a more manageable number (67) of narratives (Choca & Van Denburg, 1997).

Once the clinician has decided which scales to consider in the interpretation of the test, the meaning of any particular scale elevation has to be conceptualized. To develop such a conceptualization, the clinician can use one of four approaches, or a combination of more than one of these approaches. Millon (see Chapter 1, this volume) offers a theoretical approach based on his Polarity Model. Millon attempts in his theoretical writings to understand the various attributes of personality disorders within varying domains or levels of clinical analysis: behavioral, phenomenological, intrapsychic, and biophysical. None of these levels is seen as more central or primary than the others; instead, they are seen as varying perspectives, or viewpoints, from which we might better understand a given personality.

We follow mostly a prototypical approach that relies on the original descriptions of the type of person that a particular scale was designed to characterize, and which Millon also endorses. Closely related to the prototypical approach is the item analysis approach, based on examining the statements that the person has endorsed to elevate a particular scale. Finally, there is the actuarial approach that attempts to use empirical findings to describe the elevations of individuals who typically have elevated scores on a particular scale. The latter approach is unfortunately hampered by a lack of literature characterizing individuals with a particular MCMI-III personality profile on other measures or sources of information.

The next step in interpreting the personality scales is to integrate the findings from the different scales into one cohesive view of the personality. We like to start with the original eight personality styles proposed by Millon (1969) and create a description on the basis of the profile the examinee obtained on those eight scales. As a general rule, we describe first the common elements of the different prototypes in the elevated cluster, later noting, with less emphasis, the more specific attributes of each of the elevated scales. Let us consider, for instance, a description for profile code 2A–3–1 (i.e., the Avoidant scale [2A] is the highest elevation, followed by the Dependent scale [3], followed by the Schizoid scale [1]). An ideal description of this profile would emphasize the fear of rejection and low self-esteem included in both the avoidant and the dependent prototypes, and the social withdrawal implied by both the avoidant and schizoid prototypes. After the common elements are developed, the narrative may then consider the unique elements of each of the elevations, such as the nervousness implied by the avoidant tendencies, or the emotional blandness of the schizoid. The descriptions we have developed (Choca & Van Denburg, 1997) were originally written for an actual individual being assessed and have, as a result, the advantage of some validation against the clinical realities of at least one person.

We have argued that the original eight personality scales (Schizoid, Avoidant, Dependent, Histrionic, Narcissistic, Antisocial, Compulsive, and Negativistic) measure personality *styles* and do not necessarily indicate the presence of a personality *disorder* (Choca & Van Denburg, 1997). In our view, each of these styles brings to the bearer some advantages and some disadvantages, and one style is not necessarily better than any other style across all situations. Some of the available data does suggest that some styles (e.g., histrionic, narcissistic, compulsive) may provide some insulation against life stressors or psychiatric problems, while others (e.g., schizoid, avoidant, or negativistic) may have the opposite effect (Leaf, Alington, Moss, DiGiuseppe, & Ellis, 1991; Leaf et al., 1990; Nakao et al., 1992; Strack, Lorr, & Campbell, 1989). However, we find individuals with any one of these styles who are able to function well and, as a result, we do not see any of these styles as inherently problematic.

The next task in the MCMI interpretation, however, is to decide how functional a particular style is for a particular individual. We feel that high elevations in one or more of the basic personality scales do not necessarily point to a problem area. The assessment of whether the individual's personality style is dysfunctional and actually represents a personality *disorder* is made in two ways. First, the clinician should look at the scores of the personality scales that do imply some inherent pathology (the Depressive, Aggressive, and Self-Defeating scales, as well as the severe personality scales). Second, the clinician needs to take into account the person's history from the point of view of whether it demonstrates the type of chronic difficulties that would be expected with a personality disorder.

The severe personality scales in the MCMI-III are the Schizotypal (S), Borderline (C), and Paranoid (P) scales. When there are elevations on these scales, a dysfunctional personality is almost always present, and the possibility of a diagnosable Axis II personality disorder should be seriously considered, especially if the BR score is greater than 85. In support of this rule of thumb, Divac-Jovanovic, Svrakic, and Lecic-Tosevski (1993) reported that those examinees with personality disorders were more likely to have elevations on the Borderline scale than were participants in a control group.

There is little way in which elevations on these scales can be seen as reflecting adaptive psychological functioning, in contrast to the basic personality style scales. These elevations often co-occur with the basic personality scales, lending a certain coloration to the basic pattern. For example, let us consider a person with elevations on Scales 1 and 2A (Schizoid and Avoidant), who also has an elevated score on the Schizotypal scale. Such a person is likely to be someone with a distant, detached manner, wary of rejection, much like a usual 1–2A high-point code, but having a more damaged underlying personality structure. This additional finding would lead us to expect a vulnerability to decompensate into the psychotic realm of functioning.

It might be useful to briefly examine a few items on each of the severe personality scales to capture the flavor of what is being assessed. In all examples, prototypical items (which receive 2 points in the computation of raw scores) will be mentioned. With the Schizotypal scale, such items include "People make fun of me behind my back, talking about the way I act or look" (item 8) and "I often get lost in my thoughts and forget what's going on around me" (item 162). The Borderline scale includes such items as "Lately, I have begun to feel like smashing things" (item 30) and "I'll do something desperate to prevent a person I love from abandoning me" (item 120). The Paranoid scale has items such as "Since I was a child, I have always had to watch out for people who were trying to cheat me" (item 49) and "I always wonder what the real reason is when someone is acting especially nice to me" (item 146).

Millon describes the Schizotypal individual as a person with a dysfunctional personality who is peculiar in their mannerisms and reticent with others (Millon, 1995). Subtle cognitive slippage is likely, and both self and object representations are confused and jumbled. Magical thinking may be present, as well as defenses that are chaotic and haphazard. The schizotypal person probably is ill at ease with others and demonstrates odd affective expression.

His view of the borderline personality is again that of a dysfunctional personality, with abrupt shifts in behavior and interpersonal relations. The borderline's world view is shifting constantly due to lack of identity consolidation and to a splitting of self and object representations. Regression to more primitive defenses is frequent, and the internal world is composed of contradictory and compartmentalized memories and feelings. The mood of the borderline is unstable and fluctuating, ranging from moments of euphoria and elation to profound despair and self-hatred.

The paranoid, again a dysfunctional personality variant, is seen by Millon as a hypervigilant, well-armored individual who can be testy and provocative with others. The paranoid is wary of the motives other people may have, tries to stand apart from others to maintain feelings of independence and self-control, and is quite fixed and rigid in views of others. The paranoid relies on projection to rid him or herself of uncomfortable feelings or memories, and does so in a consistently unremitting fashion. Unpleasant to be around, the paranoid is likely crusty, a bit of a curmudgeon, irritable, and hostile.

Research on these severe personality scales of various versions of the MCMI will now be discussed, where such research is available. Once again, we must keep in mind that these studies were carried out with prior versions of the MCMI and it is unclear to what extent the data can be generalized to the current version of the test.

Recent work by Retzlaff and his coworkers (1994) on the Severe Personality scales of the MCMI-II suggests that it is very unlikely for one of these scales to be the sole high-point code of a profile. In fact, in their sample of VA patients at four different sites, they found no individuals who had an elevation in one of the severe personality disorders and no other elevated personality scale scores. Further, their data point out that it is relatively uncommon for elevations of the severe personality scales to occur with any great frequency with common personality style high-point codes. At least with their data, the Schizotypal and Borderline scales are associated to a moderate degree with several personality elevations; when examined they seem relatively orthogonal. For example, the Schizotypal scale is most frequently associated with elevations on scales 1 and 2A, 1 and 8A, 2A and 8A, and 2A and 8B; the Borderline scale is most frequently associated with scales 2 and 6A, 6A, 8A, and 6B and 8A. The Paranoid scale is most frequently associated with scales 6B and 7, but failed to occur at any greater than 20% with any of the high-point configuration codes.

The Borderline scale has probably generated the largest number of empirical studies, perhaps because the borderline personality disorder is one of the most frequently made personality disorder diagnoses, when the clinical population contains personality disorders (American Psychiatric Association, 1994). The overall findings concerning the efficacy of the MCMI-II scale have been mixed. Jackson, Gazis, Rudd, and Edwards (1991) found that the Borderline scale showed good concordance with the Structured Interview for DSM-III Personality (SIDP; Pfohl, Stangl, & Zimmerman, 1983), unlike other scales. Lewis and Harder (1990) found the MCMI-II to be effective, but less so than other measures, in identifying borderlines and in differentiating a borderline personality disorder group from a control group of people with other diagnoses. McCann, Flynn, and Gersh (1992) looked at the ability of the MCMI-II scale to differentiate borderlines from patients without personality disorders, and demonstrated that the scale actually performed best when the number of prototypic items endorsed, rather than the BR score on the scale, was utilized to make the differential diagnostic decision. Using this method, they were able to correctly classify 80% of their borderline patients. Patrick (1993) demonstrated some problems with the operating characteristics of the MCMI Borderline scale. In his study, he compared how experienced clinicians' diagnoses of the borderline personality disorder matched with MCMI results, and concluded that the scale "has very limited utility as a screening instrument for individual diagnoses when a well-defined borderline sample is used as a criterion" (p. 28).

As far as the Schizotypal scale is concerned, there have been a few studies examining the relationship of MMPI with MCMI-II personality disorder scales for the entire test, with inconsistent findings concerning the concordance on the Schizotypal scales of each instrument (McCann, 1991; Schuler, Snibbe, & Buckwalter, 1994). A recent study conducted at our medical center (Rouff, Van Denburg, Newman, & Choca, 1995) highlighted the Schizotypal scale. We tried to predict premature termination from our outpatient clinic using a mixture of the MCMI-II results and demographic and diagnostic information obtained when patients first entered the clinic. A logistic regression model led to the finding that only the Schizotypal scale was a significant predictor of dropout; interestingly, those patients who continued in treatment scored *higher* on this scale than did those who precipitously dropped out of treatment.

A few specific findings with the Paranoid scale should be noted. First, at least with the MCMI, African Americans tend to score higher on this scale than do European Americans. Whether this is a function of racial bias of the test (Choca, Shanley, Peterson, & Van Denburg, 1990), a reflection of differing adaptive strategies within U.S. society, or a valid description of underlying personality differences is not clear (Hamberger & Hastings, 1992).

Further, the MCMI showed a tendency to overdiagnose the paranoid disorder with drug abusers (Craig & Weinberg, 1992).

INTERPRETING SYNDROMAL (AXIS I) ELEVATIONS
Clinical Syndrome Scales

This section will cover the clinical syndromes as assessed by the MCMIs. Once again, it should be understood that any published research utilized the first two versions of this test and the findings may not generalize to the current version. There are reliability and validity data available concerning how the MCMI-III compares with other commonly used psychological instruments in the test manual, and these findings will be discussed where appropriate.

There are seven clinical syndrome scales, almost all keyed in the "True" direction. As with the personality scales, there is much less item overlap than in prior versions of the test, hopefully leading to greater specificity of symptomatic constructs. Millon views the clinical syndromes as "extensions or distortions of the patient's basic personality pattern" (Millon, 1994, p. 14). These symptoms can theoretically occur within any of the personality types, are thought to be more transient over time, and are psychometrically less stable than are personality traits.

The Millon perspective, of course, runs counter to some current emphases in biological psychiatry and to some of the symptom-based treatment approaches. In our experience, however, if one does not take into account the personality structure of a given patient, brief, symptom-based treatments are less effective and even potentially destructive. For example, the meanings and impact of depression to a person with a histrionic style is vastly different than to a person with obsessional tendencies. With the former, the meanings often cohere around themes of loss and abandonment of interpersonal supplies (e.g., losing one's spouse during a divorce), while with the latter, the meanings often have to do with themes of loss of control, or self-recriminations (e.g., dejection over not living up to one's moral standards). Such a model is consistent with work that acknowledges the complex interactional effects of personality structure and symptoms (e.g., Blatt, 1974; Blatt & Shichman, 1983).

The first scale, the Anxiety scale (A) relates to the patient's experience of tension, restlessness, possible phobic responses, some physiological sequelae of anxiety (e.g., increased sweating), and worry. Prototypic items include "I've become very jumpy in the last few weeks" (item 58), and "There are certain thoughts that keep coming back again and again in my mind" (item 147). It has been noted that this scale is "the most sensitive of the MCMI scales as a measure of psychological stress and disturbance" (Smith, Carroll, & Fuller, 1988, p. 172).

The Somatoform scale (H) taps into complaints of fatigue, pains, aches, and strange sensory experiences. Sample prototypic items of this scale are "I feel weak and tired much of the time (item 4), and "I very often lose my ability to feel any sensations in parts of my body" (item 37). In a recent chapter, Retzlaff (1995) mentions several possible problems with this scale. First, he wonders whether the scale will turn out to be psychometrically sound, as the number of items (13) is fairly small. He also comments that the positive predictive power of the prior version of the scale in MCMI-II was low, possibly because of difficulty generating adequate items for this domain. In support of the current scale's validity, we find that the Somatoform scale correlates .63 with Scale 1 (Hypochondriasis) of the MMPI-2, greater than any other scale on the MCMI-III (Millon, 1994).

The Bipolar Manic scale (N) assesses the degree to which a patient reports times of elation, overactivity, impulsiveness, flight of ideas, and rapid shifts of mood. Prototypic items on this scale are "I enjoy doing so many different things that I can't make up my mind what to do first" (item 3), and "There are many times, when for no reason, I feel very cheerful and full of excitement" (item 54). Retzlaff (1995) had some concerns with the relative brevity of this scale (13 items) and a modest alpha coefficient (.71, the lowest of any of the MCMI-III scales). On the other hand, the scale was one of the most highly correlated of the MCMI-III scales with the MMPI-2 (.43; Millon, 1994). Results of empirical studies of the scale with prior versions of the test have been mixed (DeWolfe, Larson, & Ryan, 1985; Choca, Bresolin, Okonek, & Ostrow, 1988), although the MMPI Mania (Scale 9) fares no better in terms of sensitivity (Wetzler & Marlow, 1993).

The Dysthymia scale (D) has been one of the best of the syndrome scales in terms of its validity. This scale taps into a person's feelings of guilt, dejection, futility, pessimism, problems with concentration, and decreased interest in the interpersonal world. Prototypic items include "For some time now I've been feeling sad and blue and can't seem to snap out of it" (item 86), and "I seem to have lost interest in most things that I used to find pleasurable, such as sex" (item 111). In prior versions of the test, the positive predictive power was strong; the alpha coefficient of the scale on the MCMI-III is excellent (.89), while correlations with other measures of depression are solid (.71 with the Beck Depression Inventory (BDI) (Beck, 1967); .68 with Scale 2 of the MMPI-2; Millon, 1994). Most studies with the MCMI (e.g., Choca et al., 1988; Goldberg, Shaw, & Segal, 1987; Wetzler, Kahn, Strauman, & Dubro, 1989) have shown the scale to be useful diagnostically, while work with the scale on the MCMI-II (Piersma, 1991) suggests that the scale is a strong indicator of unipolar depressive disorders.

Scales B (Alcohol Dependence) and T (Drug Dependence) were designed to detect the presence of substance dependence. Although we clinically sometimes group these problems together, the scales, with 15 and 14 items respectively, share only 4 items, and no prototypic items. The scales correlate moderately with one another (.62), although this leaves 62% of the variance unaccounted for. With the Alcohol and Drug scales, all of the prototypic items are face valid, attempting to assess directly alcohol or drug use; the remainder of the scale items are subtle and do not directly reflect issues concerning alcohol or drug dependence. If all of the subtle items, and none of the prototypic items were endorsed by a patient, it would still be possible to obtain an uncorrected BR score higher than 75 on the Alcohol scale, but not on the Drug scale.

The substance abuse scales have generated a great deal of empirical work with both prior versions of the MCMIs. For example, Craig and Weinberg (1992) note that as of 1992, the tests had been used with more than 2,000 patients in the published literature. However, some studies with these scales have yielded disappointing results. For example, Calsyn, Saxon, and Daisy (1990) found that Scale T of the MCMI was only able to detect 59% of their drug-dependent sample with a BR score higher than 74. A few studies have moved beyond using simple scale elevations to using cluster analytic or discriminant function analyses, and have successfully predicted dropout and relapse from substance dependence programs (McMahon, Kelley, & Kouzekanani, 1993; Fals-Stewart, 1992). The overall findings with these scales seem to be that they may be useful for differentiating subtypes of alcoholics and drug addicts, but when used singly they tend to produce too many false negatives (substance dependence actually present but patient denies it on testing).

Scale R (Post-Traumatic Stress Disorder) is the only new clinical syndrome scale on the MCMI-III. It attempts to mirror the DSM-IV criteria, and it includes such prototypic items as "The memory of a very upsetting experience in my past keeps coming back to haunt my thoughts" (item 109) and "My current life is still upset by flashbacks of something terrible that happened to me" (item 160). This scale has strong internal consistency (alpha coefficient of .89), and seems to correlate fairly well with other instrument scales assessing anxiety and depression. However, as Retzlaff (1995) notes, in certain settings the scale may have too much face validity, so that those patients seeking to present a certain picture may have no difficulty in artificially boosting the score to meet their ends. Thus, it is recommended that psychologists doing assessments with such patients (e.g., within a VA system to determine disability) use collaborative data and other clinical information to reach a final diagnostic decision.

Severe Syndrome Scales

There are three severe syndrome scales on the MCMI-III designed to tap the more severe symptomatic psychopathology. The first, Scale SS, or Thought Disorder, is putatively elevated with patients presenting with symptoms of schizophrenia, schizophreniform disorder, or brief reactive psychosis. Items on this scale include more blatantly psychotic items such as "Even when I'm awake, I don't seem to notice people who are near me" (item 78), and items having more to do with thought control issues, such as "Ideas keep turning over and over in my mind and they won't go away" (item 61). The scale has a moderate correlation with other standardized measures used to assess psychotic processes, including the Psychoticism subscale of the Symptom Checklist 90—Revised (SCL-90-R) (.58) and Scale 8 of the MMPI-2 (.61; Millon, 1994). Unfortunately, prior versions of the test lead one to question the scale's validity. Greenblatt and Davis (1993), in a summary chapter on the use of the prior versions of the MCMI with schizophrenics, caution that schizophrenics are prone to underreport symptoms and that the MCMI yields far too many false negatives. In addition, false positives on the scale also occur, especially with nonpsychotic African American patients. Greenblatt and Davis wonder if part of the problem with the scale was that, in the MCMI construction, there were very few schizophrenics in the initial normative sample.

Scale PP, Delusional Disorder, was designed to pick up paranoid individuals with a psychotic level of symptomatic presentation. Such patients likely have systematized delusions, possibly ideas of reference, hypervigilance, and a hostile mood. Items on this severe symptomatic scale include "Many people have been spying into my private life for years" (item 63), and "People are trying to make me believe that I'm crazy" (item 119). The scale on the MCMI-III appears to have strong internal consistency (alpha coefficient of .79; Millon, 1994), although the positive predictive power was modest with the MCMI-II (.4; Millon, 1987). Retzlaff (1995) speculated that this may have to do with the low prevalence of the disorders and the difficulty in constructing items for such a narrowly defined construct. In our experience this scale can pick up frankly delusional thinking, if the patient does not have a motive for concealing the bizarre ideas. In a case with which one of us (E.V.) was familiar, a hostile and difficult patient with systematized delusions concerning the Veteran's Administration obtained a BR score higher than 100, despite the fact that he was quite guarded about such issues in an interview. Research on the scale demonstrates the same problems mentioned earlier with the Thought Disorder scale, however, including a tendency to misdiagnose paranoid schizophrenics who are not currently floridly psychotic (Greenblatt & Davis, 1993; Patrick, 1988).

The final severe clinical syndrome scale, Major Depression (CC), is designed to assess the presence of a profoundly debilitating depressive disorder. Those scoring high on the scale may not be able to function and are likely display psychomotor changes of either a retarded or an agitated type. Somatic problems and difficulties with concentration and attention are common. The future is viewed very pessimistically. A few sample items are "I feel terribly depressed and sad much of the time now" (item 44) and "I have completely lost my appetite and have trouble sleeping most nights" (item 107). The new scale seems to have strong internal consistency (.90 Cronbach alpha) and correlates well with other commonly utilized measures of depression (.74 with the BDI, .74 with the Depression subscale of the SCL-90-R, and .71 with Scale 2 of the MMPI-2; Millon, 1994).

Unfortunately, as with the other severe syndrome scales, research support has at times been mixed with the Major Depression scale of the previous versions of the test. According to Choca and Bresolin's (1993) summary the research data on affective disorders and the MCMI, "many authors have felt (the Major Depression scale) to be of little clinical utility" (p. 113). For example, Piersma (1991) found that using a BR of 75 cutoff, 39% of those participants in his sample with major depression were missed; he further noted that the overall diagnostic power of the CC scale was quite a bit less than it was for the Dysthymia scale (D) (73% with the D vs. 59% with the CC scale).

Prior criticisms of the validity problems with the Major Depression scale have pointed to the lack of items tapping somatic and vegetative symptoms, a hallmark of the disorder. Perhaps in response to these critiques, it appears as though Millon has increased the percentage of such items for this scale. In examining the current item content of scale CC on the MCMI-III, 59% of the 17 items have content directly relevant to issues of appetite problems, sleep disturbances, decreased energy, loss of libido, and anhedonia. It remains an open empirical question, however, whether these item changes will increase scale validity.

INTEGRATIVE INTERPRETATION

Now that we have covered the validity indices, personality disorder scales, and syndromal scales, we are at a point when we need to put all the pieces together into an integrated picture. Because many clinicians have the NCS automated report available, our goal for this section is to increase the practitioner's ability to integrate the findings at a higher and more individualized level than would be possible for a computer program.

The NCS report does a nice job of beginning with a capsule summary. After presenting the usual caveats, the summary (1) urges the clinician to look at the global response style, (2) mentions profile severity, (3) suggests Axes I and II diagnoses, and (4) gives treatment suggestions.

Utilizing this clear outline, we would add the following to the above four sections. Concerning response style, the score on the Disclosure scale is probably the best, most valid indicator of test-taking attitude. It can be interpreted in both directions, with the low scores indicating tendencies toward reticence and guardedness and the high scores suggesting possible exaggeration. While there is controversy, some researchers and clinicians (Retzlaff, 1995) suggest that the protocol be seen as technically invalid if the BR score of this scale is above 85. Millon does not follow this; in fact, the NCS extended case example in the manual exceeds this level. Lest the reader fret over this ambiguity, realize that there is also some controversy in the MMPI camp over F and F–K validity levels (Berry, Baer, & Harris, 1991). Clinicians can also glance at the Debasement (fake bad) and Desirability (fake good) scales, but it is probably best to take these findings with a grain of salt. These scales are less psychometrically sound than are the other MCMI scales (Retzlaff, 1995). Also, as mentioned above, the Desirability scale has been shown to have difficulty clearly distinguishing "fake good" profiles at better than chance levels, and the Debasement scale has had mixed reviews (Lees-Haley, 1992; Retzlaff et al., 1991).

Concerning response style, we find it helpful to always think of the motives and context of a person taking the Millon and then to use those hypotheses to frame and understand the validity indices. For example, the first author was asked to examine the MCMIs of an adult woman in psychotherapy and her two elderly parents. The young woman was accusing the parents of having engaged in satanic ritual abuse of her when she was a child, which they adamantly denied. Regardless of the veracity of her claims, the response style indices were as one might imagine, given the test-taking situation. The adult child was highly disclosing of pathology and problems, whereas her parents were extremely closed and definitely appearing to be socially appropriate and above board.

The next step, checking profile severity, is aided by the visual representation of the NCS profile. Simply glancing at the number and elevation of the varying scales gives one a sense of the intensity of the patient's problems. As the NCS report suggests, with extreme elevations one needs to deliberately upwardly adjust subsequent interpretive statements of the readout to take this into account.

Like the NCS manual and consistent with Millon's model, we next look at Axis II pathology, rather than seeing Axis I problems as prominent in understanding a person. We often invoke the structural metaphor of viewing the personality as an actual physical container buffeted by stressors from the outside (Axis IV of the DSM-IV—Psychosocial and Environmental Problems) and struggling at times to accommodate the Axis I contents of the vessel (e.g., bubbling acute anxiety, fragmenting psychotic ideation, or the near-viscous slowing of a major depression).

Although, as mentioned above, there are some empirical problems with the severe personality scales, we first try to give serious attention to these scales next (Borderline, Paranoid, and Schizotypal). Elevations on these scales can provide cues that a person is either decompensating from a higher level of psychic development or has a vulnerable, and maladaptive characterological structure. Millon (1994) is cognizant of the fact that these scales may artificially elevate during acute psychic disruptions; thus, he has included in the MCMI-III (Appendix D) adjustment factors applied to the Borderline and Schizotypal scales, if the Axis I duration is recent, if acute emotional disruption is present (e.g., elevations on the Anxiety and Depression scales), and if the patient was recently hospitalized. Patients with elevations on these scales may need more immediate, intensive, or specialized treatment modalities. While there is a great deal of controversy about how to treat more severely disturbed personality disorders (Horwitz, 1985; Westen, 1991; Zetzel, 1971), elevations on the severe personality scales can be useful as a front line, "red flag" to alert clinicians that they may have a clinically difficult situation.

There is some consistent patterning of the severe personality scales in the common high-point codes. We know of no better source than the article by Retzlaff and his coworkers (1994) to elucidate this matter. Although we discussed this work above in more detail, the briefer version is that the Schizotypal scale most frequently elevates with the Schizoid, Avoidant, and Negativistic/Self-Defeating scale constellation. The Borderline scale is seen most frequently with various permutations of the Antisocial, Sadistic, Negativistic, and to a lesser extent, Avoidant scales. An elevation of the Paranoid scale is rarer, but when this occurs it is joined most often with mixtures of the Narcissistic, Sadistic, and Compulsive scales, highlighting the control and sadism of the paranoid tendency.

The remaining Axis II disorders, as assessed by scales 1 through 8B of the MCMI-III, are the central focus of Millon's model. The personality patterns as revealed by elevations on these scales are the "container" we mentioned before which gives shape and substance to symptoms and modes of coping with stressors. It is our view that the personality features assessed by most of these scales are not inherently pathological, but instead they provide the individual with a characteristic adaptive mode of negotiating the world, a style that has its strengths and weaknesses.

Based on permutations of his Polarity Model of the underlying central structures of personality (active–passive, independent–dependent, positive–negative reinforcement), these personality conceptions formed the original diagnoses of Axis II and, for the most part, they continue today within Axis II of DSM-IV. Over Millon's objections, the sadistic and self-defeating personalities have been dropped from DSM-IV, while the depressive and negativistic variants have been placed in the appendix.

While it might be simplest to approach the various elevations of the basic personality scales one at a time, in our view it is much better to understand the elevations in integrative combination. Using the example we mention in our text (Choca & Van Denburg, 1997), consider two people whose highest elevation is on Scale 8A (Negativistic). The first might have their next highest elevation on the Dependent scale (Scale 3), while the second scores highest on Scale 6A (Antisocial). In the first case, we would have a person who feels inadequate but is uncooperative because he or she feels their dependence desires will never be met by the other. In contrast, with the second case we have a combination of negativism and interpersonal conflict but with the sense that others need to be competed against, rather than depended upon, to meet one's needs.

While theoretically there are a very large number of possible permutations of the personality style scales, empirically we find there to be only about 20 high point and high-point pair codes (BR > 75) that occur at a frequency of greater than 2%, at least with the MCMI-II (Retzlaff et al., 1994). Moreover, at least with their sample, certain high-point codes never occur (e.g., Schizoid–Histrionic (1–4) and Avoidant–Histrionic (2A–4)).

Clinicians are urged to utilize the available "cookbooks" that give two- and three-point code interpretations (Choca & Van Denburg, 1997; Craig, 1993) to further flush out the NCS interpretive readout. It is also useful to have some understanding of Millon's underlying theoretical model so that one can see how certain personality combinations are understandable. It is further helpful to have an abbreviated understanding of underlying BRs of single and two-point codes. Again using data from Retzlaff and his coworkers (1994), the most frequent single point codes are the Dependent (3), and Compulsive (7). Concerning high-point pairs, the 1 and 2A (Schizoid and Avoidant) high-point code was by far the most frequent, while 2A–8A (Avoidant–Negativistic), 2A–8B (Avoidant–Self-Defeating), 3–7 (Dependent–Compulsive), and 5–6A (Narcissistic–Antisocial) all were relatively common. Of course, other high-point codes may prove more prevalent in other settings and practicing clinicians may establish data bases of their own to determine local high-point BRs.

After the Axis II picture is sculpted, one can add in the details and coloration of Axis I issues. To use an example previously discussed briefly, let us look at two patients, both of whom are markedly depressed, one of whom has a primary personality scale elevation on the Compulsive scale, while the other peaks on the Histrionic scale. While both may have elevations on Scale D (Dysthymia) and similar depressive symptoms (e.g., pessimism, problems concentrating, sad feelings), the concerns and experiences of each are vastly different because of their differing character styles. While the histrionic patient may weep about the end of a close relationship and experience a sense of emptiness, the compulsive may be more irritable, ruminative, and self-blaming. These are not irrelevant distinctions from a treatment perspective. The histrionic may need a more giving, responsive therapist to fill the interpersonal void, while the compulsive operates from a strongly "heady" perspective and may interact better with a directive, cognitive–behavioral point of view. It has become increasingly apparent that therapists need to be cognizant of character structure in tailoring their interventions, even when operating from a psychodynamic perspective (Levy, 1987).

As Retzlaff (1995) points out, one should pay particular attention to any elevations on the severe clinical syndrome scales and adjust one's interpretations accordingly. While it is highly unlikely that a profile will have one of these scales as the highest elevation, it is quite common that, if a severe clinical syndrome scale is elevated, other syndromal scales will be elevated as well. This makes conceptual and theoretical sense; if a psychotic process or deep depression manifests itself, other symptoms and psychopathology are sure to follow.

Both Millon (1987) and we (Choca & Van Denburg, 1997) have presented tables that provide expected primary and secondary MCMI-II elevations with divergent clinical syndromes. Recent empirical data (Retzlaff et al., 1994) suggest that, consistent with clinical BRs, symptom scales vary in their frequencies. For example, the Dysthymia scale (D) appears more than 20% of the time on 16 of the 20 most common MCMI-II high-point codes, whereas the Somatoform, Mania, Thought Disorder, and Delusional Disorder scales do not appear on *any* of the 20 most common high-point codes with a frequency greater than 15%. At a practical level, users of the MCMI should not be surprised to see a number of their patients obtain elevations on the Anxiety and Dysthymia scales, as these symptoms are very common in mental health settings. Moreover, for some clinicians, they may find a number of profiles with elevations on the Alcohol or Drug Dependence scales. This is, of course, due to the nature of BRs in clinical populations. An advantage of the MCMI is that the underlying psychometric structure of the test takes prevalence into account, hopefully leading to more accurate diagnoses.

Concerning the final area of the capsule summary of the NCS profile, the treatment recommendations, this section is given surprisingly extensive coverage in the NCS readout. This is perhaps the most speculative section of the report, and the least well researched. It has been recommended frequently in the literature that "intensive study of each person's personality structure or coping style is necessary for a proper match between the patient and a treatment approach" (Lovitt, 1988, p. 518). However, the average clinician often has little control over manipulating the match of therapist and patient. We often have to take patients as they are, and adjust in whatever ways we can to meet patient's personality style and symptomatic needs.

We have offered some published guidelines for altering intervention styles in supportive psychotherapy based on patient personality styles (Choca & Van Denburg, 1997). Briefly, this model encourages the therapist to adapt to the patient's underlying defensive structure, rather than trying to fight against ingrained tendencies, at least within briefer, supportive treatments. For example, with the dependent patient the therapist is likely to do best if he or she is more dominant and benignly protective; with the narcissistic patient, on the other hand, one should allow the patient to take the lead and be wary of any interpretations that have a hint of criticism, lest the narcissist feel prematurely injured and withdraw from the involvement. Such flexibility in style and manner is even more essential in these times of briefer, hopefully more efficient therapy within a managed care health environment. If one has the luxury of a more extensive therapeutic contract, at that point the therapist can move toward alterations of the underlying polarities in the personality, as Millon discusses in extensive detail for each personality type in a recently revised text (Millon, 1995).

REFERENCES

American Psychiatric Association. (1994). *Diagnostic and statistical manual of mental disorders* (4th ed.). Washington, DC: Author.

Beck, A. (1967). *Depression: Causes and treatment*. Philadelphia: University of Pennsylvania Press.

Berry, T., Baer, R., & Harris, M. (1991). Detection of malingering on the MMPI: A meta-analysis. *Clinical Psychology Review, 11*, 585–598.

Blatt, S. J. (1974). Levels of object representation in anaclitic and introjective depression. *Psychoanalytic Study of the Child, 29*, 107–157.

Blatt, S., & Shichman, S. (1983). Two primary configurations of psychopathology. *Psychoanalysis and Contemporary Thought, 6*, 187–254.

Bonato, D., Cyr, J., Kalprin, R., Prendergast, P., & Sanhueza, P. (1988). The utility of the MCMI as a DSM-III Axis I diagnostic tool. *Journal of Clinical Psychology, 44*, 867–875.

Butcher, J., Dahlstrom, W., Graham, J., Tellegen, A., & Kaemmer, B. (1989). *MMPI-2 (Minnesota Multiphasic Personality Inventory-2): Manual for administration and scoring*. Minneapolis: University of Minnesota Press.

Calsyn, D., Saxon, A., & Daisy, R. (1990). Validity of the MCMI drug abuse scale with drug abusing and psychiatric samples. *Journal of Clinical Psychology, 46*, 244–246.

Choca, J., & Bresolin, L. (1993). Affective disorders and the MCMI. In R. Craig (Ed.), *The Millon Clinical Multiaxial Inventory: A clinical research information synthesis* (pp. 111–124). Hillsdale, NJ: Erlbaum.

Choca, J., Bresolin, L., Okonek, A., & Ostrow, D. (1988). Validity of the Millon Clinical Multiaxial Inventory in the assessment of affective disorders. *Journal of Personality Assessment, 53*, 96–105.

Choca, J., Peterson, C., & Shanley, L. (1986). Factor analysis of the Millon Clinical Multiaxial Inventory. *Journal of Consulting and Clinical Psychology, 54*, 253–255.

Choca, J., Shanley, L., Peterson, C., & Van Denburg, E. (1990). Racial bias and the MCMI. *Journal of Personality Assessment, 54*, 479–490.

Choca, J., & Van Denburg, E. (1997). *Interpretive guide to the Millon Clinical Multiaxial Inventory*. Washington, DC: American Psychological Association.

Choca, J., Shanley, L. A., Van Denburg, E., Agresti, A., Mouton, A., & Vidger, L. (1992). Personality disorder or personality style: That is the question. *Journal of Counseling and Development, 70*, 429–431.

Craig, R. (Ed.). (1993a). *The Millon Clinical Multiaxial Inventory: A clinical information synthesis*. Hillsdale, NJ: Erlbaum.

Craig, R. (1993b). *Psychological screening with the MCMI-II*. Odessa, FL: Psychological Assessment Resources.

Craig, R., & Weinberg, D. (1992). Assessing drug abusers with the Millon Clinical Multiaxial Inventory: A review. *Journal of Substance Abuse Treatment, 9*, 249–255.

Derogatis, L. (1983). *The Symptom Checklist-90 Manual II*. Towson, MD: Clinical Psychometric Research.

DeWolfe, A., Larson, J., & Ryan, J. (1985). Diagnostic accuracy of the Millon test computer reports for bipolar affective illness. *Journal of Psychopathology and Behavioral Assessment, 7*, 185–189.

Divac-Jovanovic, M., Svrakic, D., & Lecic-Tosevski, D. (1993). Personality disorders: Model for conceptual approach and classification. Part I: General model. *American Journal of Psychotherapy, 47*, 558–571.

Fals-Stewart, W. (1992). Personality characteristics of substance abusers: An MCMI cluster typology of recreational drug users treated in a therapeutic community and its relationship to length of stay and outcome. *Journal of Personality Assessment, 59*, 515–527.

Goldberg, J., Shaw, B., & Segal, Z. (1987). Concurrent validity of the Millon Clinical Multiaxial Inventory depression scales. *Journal of Consulting and Clinical Psychology, 55*, 785–787.

Greenblatt, R., & Davis, W. (1993). The MCMI in the diagnosis and assessment of schizophrenia.

In R. Craig (Ed.), *The Millon Clinical Multiaxial Inventory: A clinical research information synthesis* (pp. 93–109). Hillsdale, NJ: Erlbaum.

Hamberger, L., & Hastings, J. (1992). Racial differences on the MCMI in an outpatient clinical sample. *Journal of Personality Assessment, 58,* 90–95.

Hirschfeld, R.M.A. (1993). Personality disorders: Definition and diagnosis. *Journal of Personality Disorders, 7,* 9–17.

Horwitz, L. (1985). Divergent views on the treatment of borderline patients. *Bulletin of the Menninger Clinic, 49,* 525–545.

Jackson, H., Gazis, J., Rudd, R., & Edwards, J. (1991). Concordance between two personality disorder instruments with psychiatric inpatients. *Comprehensive Psychiatry, 32,* 252–260.

Leaf, R., Alington, D., Mass, R., DiGiuseppe, R., & Ellis, A. (1991). Personality disorders, life events, and clinical syndromes. *Journal of Personality Disorders, 5,* 264–280.

Leaf, R. C., DiGiuseppe, R., Ellis, A., Mass, R., Backx, W., Wolfe, J., & Alington, D. E. (1990). "Healthy" correlates of MCMI scales 4, 5, 6, and 7. *Journal of Personality Disorders, 4,* 312–328.

Lees-Haley, P. (1992). Efficacy of MMPI-2 validity scales and MCMI-II modifier scales for detecting spurious PTSD claims: F, F–K, Fake Bad scale, ego strength, subtle–obvious subscales, DIS, and DEB. *Journal of Clinical Psychology, 48,* 681–689.

Levy, S. (1987). Therapeutic strategy and psychoanalytic technique. *Journal of the American Psychoanalytic Association, 35,* 447–466.

Lewis, S., & Harder, D. (1990). A comparison of four measures to diagnose DSM-III-R borderline personality disorder in outpatients. *Journal of Nervous and Mental Disease, 179,* 329–337.

Lovitt, R. (1988). Current practice of psychological assessment: Response to Sweeney, Clarkin, and Fitzgibbon. *Professional Psychology: Research and Practice, 19,* 516–521.

McCann, J. (1991). Convergent and discriminant validity of the MCMI-II and MMPI personality disorder scales. *Psychological Assessment, 3,* 9–18.

McCann, J., Flynn, P., & Gersh, D. (1992). MCMI-II diagnosis of borderline personality disorder: Base rates versus prototypic items. *Journal of Personality Assessment, 58,* 105–114.

McMahon, R., Kelley, A., & Kouzekanani, K. (1993). Personality and coping styles in the prediction of dropout from treatment for cocaine abuse. *Journal of Personality Assessment, 61,* 147–155.

McNeil, K., & Meyer, R. (1990). Detection of deception on the Millon Clinical Multiaxial Inventory (MCMI). *Journal of Clinical Psychology, 46,* 755–764.

Miller, H., Goldberg, J., & Streiner, D. (1993). The effects of the modifier and correction indices on MCMI-II profiles. *Journal of Personality Assessment, 60,* 477–485.

Millon, T. (1969). *Modern psychopathology: A biosocial approach to maladaptive learning and functioning.* Philadelphia: W. B. Saunders.

Millon, T. (1987). *Manual for the MCMI-II.* Minneapolis: National Computer Systems.

Millon, T., Millon, C., & Davis, R. (1994). *Millon Clinical Multiaxial Inventory—III manual.* Minneapolis: National Computer Systems.

Millon, T. (1995). *Disorders of personality: DSM-IV and beyond.* New York: Wiley.

Nakao, K., Gunderson, J., Phillips, K., Tanaka, N., Yorifuji, K., Takaishi, J., & Nishimura, T. (1992). Functional impairment in personality disorders. *Journal of Personality Disorders, 6,* 24–33.

Patrick, J. (1988). Concordance of the MCMI and the MMPI in the diagnosis of three DSM-III Axis I disorders. *Journal of Clinical Psychology, 44,* 186–190.

Patrick, J. (1993). Validation of the MCMI-I Borderline Personality Disorder scale with a well-defined criterion sample. *Journal of Clinical Psychology, 49,* 28–32.

Pfohl, B., Stangl, D., & Zimmerman, M. (1983). *Structured Interview for DSM-III Personality (SIDP)* (2nd ed.) Ames, IA: University of Iowa.

Piersma, H. (1991). The MCMI-II depression scales: Do they assist in the differential prediction of depressive disorders? *Journal of Personality Assessment, 56,* 478–486.

Retzlaff, P. (1995). Clinical application of the MCMI-III. In P. Retzlaff (Ed.), *Tactical psychotherapy of the personality disorders: An MCMI-III based approach* (pp. 1–23). Needham Heights, MA: Allyn & Bacon.

Retzlaff, P., Ofman, P., Hyer, L., & Matheson, S. (1994). MCMI-II high-point codes: Severe personality disorder and clinical syndrome extensions. *Journal of Clinical Psychology, 50,* 228–234.

Retzlaff, P., Sheehan, E., & Fiel, M. (1991). MCMI-II report style and bias: Profile and validity scales analysis. *Journal of Personality Assessment, 56,* 478–486.

Rouff, L., Van Denburg, E., Newman, A., & Choca, J. (1995, August). *Prediction of dropout in an outpatient VA psychiatric clinic.* Paper presented at the annual meeting of the American Psychological Association, New York, NY.

Schuler, C., Snibbe, J., & Buckwalter, J. (1994). The validity of the MMPI personality disorder scales (MMPI-PD). *Journal of Clinical Psychology, 50,* 220–227.

Smith, D., Carroll, J., & Fuller, G. (1988). The Millon Clinical Multiaxial Inventory and the MMPI in a private outpatient mental health clinic population. *Journal of Clinical Psychology, 44,* 165–174.

Strack, S., Lorr, M., & Campbell, L. (1989, August). *Similarities in Millon personality styles among normals and psychiatric patients.* Paper presented at the annual meeting of the American Psychological Association, New Orleans, LA.

Streiner, D., Goldberg, J., & Miller, H. (1993). MCMI-II item weights: Their lack of effectiveness. *Journal of Personality Assessment, 60,* 471–476.

Van Gorp, W., & Meyer, R. (1986). The detection of faking on the Millon Clinical Multiaxial Inventory (MCMI). *Journal of Clinical Psychology, 42,* 742–747.

Westen, D. (1991). Cognitive–behavioral interventions in the psychoanalytic psychotherapy of borderline personality disorders. *Clinical Psychology Review, 11,* 211–230.

Wetzler, S., Kahn, R., Strauman, T., & Dubro, A. (1989). Diagnosis of major depression by self-report. *Journal of Personality Assessment, 53,* 22–30.

Wetzler, S., & Marlow, D. (1993). The diagnosis and assessment of depression, mania, and psychosis by self-report. *Journal of Personality Assessment, 60,* 1–31.

Widiger, T. A. (1992). Categorical versus dimensional classification: Implications from and for research. *Journal of Personality Disorders, 6,* 287–300.

Widiger, T., & Sanderson, C. (1987). The convergent and discriminant validity of the MCMI as a measure of the DSM-III personality disorders. *Journal of Personality Assessment, 51,* 228–242.

Widiger, T., Williams, J., Spitzer, R., & Frances, A. (1986). The MCMI and DSM-III: A brief rejoinder to Millon. *Journal of Personality Assessment, 50,* 198–204.

Wiggins, J. (1982). Circumplex models of interpersonal behavior in clinical psychology. In P. Kendall & J. Butcher (Eds.), *Handbook of research methods in clinical psychology* (pp. 183–222). New York: Wiley.

Zetzel, E. (1971). A developmental approach to the borderline patient. *American Journal of Psychiatry, 128,* 867–871.

4

MCMI Assessment:
An Integrative Case Study

ROGER D. DAVIS
THEODORE MILLON

As described in Chapter 1, the methodology through which assessment instruments are created is in spirit opposed to the goal which directs their use. In tapping dimensions of individual differences, we abstract from persons only those dimensions we take as being common to all. Yet in using our instruments, we seek to build up again as a reconstructive process the very individuality we had previously distilled, so that the circle completes itself as a kind of synthesis: from rich idiographic individuality, to nomothetic commonalities, and finally, to nomothetic individuality. Apparently, we must first give up the person to ultimately understand her or him.

Integrative assessment is concerned with the last two links of this process. The fractionated person, the person who has been dispersed across scales and instruments, must be put back together again as the organic whole it once was. How is such a venture to be achieved? First and foremost, we argue that assessment is an eminently theoretical process, indeed, an evolutionary process which requires a weighing of this and a disqualifying of that across the idiosyncrasies and commonalities of methods and data sources through multiple iterations of hypothesis generation and testing. The end goal, of course, is *the* theory of the client, wherein every loose end has been tied up in a theory which follows the logic of the client's own psyche, a theory so compelling that one gets the feeling that things could not be otherwise than they have been supposed to be. Only such an eminently integrative theory allows the referral question to be addressed with confident words and concrete suggestions.

Although undoubtedly biased in our appraisal, we believe that no other inventory offers as potentially complete an integrative assessment of problematic personality styles and classical psychiatric disorders as does the Millon Clinical Multiaxial Inventory—III (MCMI). In this chapter, we refer to the MCMI-III as simply the MCMI. Moreover, perhaps no other instrument is as coordinated with the official DSM taxonomy of personality disorders as is the MCMI, or as conceptually consonant with the multiaxial logic that underlies the DSM. In fact, the MCMI is but one (essential) link in what has emerged as an integrative schema by which to conceptualize both personality and abnormal behavior (Millon, 1969, 1981, 1990).

59

Let us explain. Integrative consonance is an ideal worthy not only in the individual assessment case, but within a science as well. Rather than being developed independently as free-standing and uncoordinated structures, a mature clinical science of psychopathology should embody explicit (1) *theories*, that is, explanatory and heuristic conceptual schemas that are consistent with established knowledge, (2) *nosology*, that is, a taxonomic classification of disorders that has been logically derived from the theory, arranged to provide a cohesive organization within which major categories can be grouped and differentiated, thereby permitting the development of (3) *instrumentation*, that is, tools that are empirically grounded and sufficiently sensitive quantitatively to enable the theory's propositions and hypotheses to be adequately investigated and evaluated, and the categories comprising its nosology to be readily identified (diagnosed) and measured (dimensionalized), specifying therefrom target areas for (4) *interventions*, that is, strategies and techniques of therapy, designed in accord with the theory and oriented to modify problematic clinical characteristics (Millon, 1990).

The goals of this chapter are largely derived from the framework identified in the above paragraph. Operating on the assumption that clinicians desire "knowledge why" as much as "knowledge that," that is, clinicians want to know not only what they should do but also why they should do it, we will try to embed the "how" of the MCMI in its "why." Perhaps the test users will then feel that they are doing something more than merely following a flowchart or a chain of S–R bonds to its termination in the clinical report: One must understand the test to understand the client. Because the test is embedded in a theoretical matrix, one must understand the theory to understand the test. This requires a justification, not merely a dispensation.

Before we begin, a few reservations. In a chapter such as this, which features a particular instrument but nevertheless seeks to illuminate integrative links between the four domains of clinical science, some highly relevant issues must be greatly abbreviated or completely omitted. As a result, what otherwise might appear as a well-worn, incremental theoretical pathway contains abrupt transitions. Most of the more theoretical material presented may be found in *Toward a New Personology: An Evolutionary Model* (Millon, 1990), and *Disorders of Personality: DSM-IV and Beyond* (Millon & Davis, 1996). Other concerns have been treated at a level of abstraction more gross than their gravity requires. Here must be included the descriptions, developmental pathways (all but omitted), and specific intervention opportunities for each of the personality disorders and their more common two-point variants. Much of this information is available in *Disorders of Personality* (Millon & Davis, 1996). In an ideal world we should adopt ideal goals, but in a less than ideal world, we must often adopt pragmatic ones.

INTEGRATIVE LOGIC AND THE PROCESS OF ASSESSMENT

The word "integrative" is now used so widely as to be platitudinous: Obviously, given an equivalence of purpose, that which is more integrated is better than that which is less integrated. However, integration neither springs into being fully formed, nor is it unveiled or discovered in a single conceptual leap. Instead, integration is perhaps better understood as a dynamic process. Such a conception sees knowledge building as an ongoing activity in which internal inconsistencies are generated and resolved or transcended at successively superordinate levels of conceptualization: While reality is undoubtedly integrated, our ideas about reality must be more or less so. An inquiry into the nature of this process will be worthwhile, because, as we intend to show, essentially the same logic underlies profile interpretation, thus creating another link between theory and instrumentation.

Pepper (1942) formalized the integrative means of knowledge building as a world view which he called "organicism," one of his four relatively adequate "world hypotheses" or metaphysical world views. Pepper describes seven categories of organicism. These work in a kind of dialectical interplay between appearance and reality, one which always proceeds in the direction of increasing integration:

> These [categories] are (1) *fragments* of experience which appear with (2) *nexuses* or connections or implications, which spontaneously lead as a result of the aggravation of (3) *contradictions*, gaps, oppositions, or counteractions to resolution in (4) an *organic whole*, which is found to have been (5) *implicit* in the fragments, and to (6) *transcend* the previous contradictions by means of a coherent totality, which (7) *economizes*, saves, preserves all the original fragments of experience without any loss. (p. 283)

Translated into terms more easily recognized: (1) Observations (fragments) lead one to (2) form inchoate theoretical propositions (nexuses), which, unfortunately, do not all mesh harmoniously, automatically producing (3) aggravating and ostensibly irreconcilable inconsistencies (contradictions) which are resolved through (4) a unified theory (organic whole), which, upon reflection, is (5) found to have been implicit in the observations (fragments) all along. Thus, it (6) transcends the initial, naive inconsistencies among observations by reconceptualizing these observations in terms of a new, coherent theoretical model, one which (7) integrates or accounts for all the evidence (economizes) according to its new terms and relationships.

Undoubtedly, even this is a lot to digest in a few paragraphs. Extrapolating from the logic presented above, we might say that as a body of implicit theories is formalized, hiatuses are discovered and the theories inevitably become enmeshed in inconsistencies and contradictions. Eventually, a new theory is formulated which unifies disparate observations and inconsistencies. What was believed to have been contradictory is discovered not to have been so at all, but only to have appeared contradictory, much as special cases are transcended by more general formulations.

By this account, science cannot exist merely as a descriptive venture which consists in observing, categorizing, and cross-correlating various phenomena at face value, but instead proceeds by establishing superordinate theoretical principles that unify the manifestations of a subject domain by explaining why these particular observations or formulations obtain rather than others. The "limit of this series" (Pepper, 1942) is truth itself, what physicists have called the theory of everything, what philosophers (notably Hegel) have called the absolute. In this ultimate integration "logical necessity would become identified with ultimate fact" (Pepper, 1942, p. 301). Nothing would remain unassimilated; everything would be harmonized with everything else.

More than anything else, it is the question "Why this rather than that?" that underlies the force toward integration in this world view. By answering this question we escape what is arbitrary and capricious and move in the direction of necessity. In its most radical form, this argument holds that even if reliable observations of great or even perfect positive predictive power could be made through some infallible methodology, these indicators would stand simply as isolated facts unassimilated as scientific knowledge until unified through some theoretical basis. Predictive power alone does not make a science. Scientific explanations appeal to theoretical principles which operate above the level of superficialities, principles which are sufficient because they predict, necessary because they explain.

The process of clinical assessment follows essentially the same logic. Following Pepper (1942), we might say that: The individual scales, instruments, and other data are the (1) fragments. These possess (2) nexuses, implications, or (statistically) intercorrelations both with each other and with other clinical phenomena, leading to inchoate theories about the individual and his or her psychopathology. Inevitably these theories do not mesh, cannot be assimilated to each other exactly, leading to (3) contradictions, gaps, or inconsistencies in the assessment thus far. One then steps back, seeking (4) a more integrative theory or organic whole which makes sense of the gaps or inconsistencies. This integrative theory is then found to have been (5) implicit in the scales, observations, and other data (otherwise an integrative assessment would not be possible at all), and to (6) transcend the foregoing inconsistencies, gaps, or contradictions by means of a coherent totality, which (7) makes sense of all the observations by tying up all loose ends.

In a integrative assessment, one is required to step outside the theoretical fecundity and inevitable contradictions of a morass of scales and data domains to develop a theory of the client in which all the data somehow makes sense. This superordinate theory lies literally at a higher level of formulation than do the individual measures which constitute the "raw data" of the assessment. Thus the "loop" from idiographic individuality to nomothetic commonality to nomothetic individuality is brought to closure: Nomothetic individuality explicitly requires the reintegration of the individual, who currently lies fractionated among various scales and dimensions. An integrative assessment, then, does not come into being of its own accord, but is constructed, and its validity is linked to the mode of its construction.

The underlying assumption here is that things do not fit together equally well in all possible combinations. What exists in one personologic domain constrains what can exist in another; otherwise there would be no nexuses or implications across domains. An individual born with an active temperament, for example, is unlikely to possess a phlegmatic phenomenology as an adult; that is, biophysical construction constrains the quality of subjective realities which can evolve in the individual life. The same is true of all the domains of personality: They do not fit together equally well in all combinations. Functional and structural attributes for each of the personality prototypes have been delineated in several prior publications (Millon, 1986, 1990) and will be explored below.

Interestingly, the logic presented above finds a point of contrast with that of inventories derived through factor analysis. Orthogonal factors by definition are independent: Scores on one factor do *not* constrain what can exist on any other. The extracted traits do not influence each other in any way. Thus, while factor analysis represents a parsimonious way of looking at a particular area, it implicitly holds that the structure of reality is distinctly unintegrated and that there are a few essential underlying dimensions which determine a great variety of appearances, but these dimensions do not constrain each other. It is interesting, then, to speculate whether the methodology of factor analytic test construction might be inherently inconsistent with the epistemology of test interpretation, indeed of clinical psychology as field. The position that fundamental dimensions exist independently runs counter to the clinician's desire to put the client back together again.

A CASE INTERPRETATION

The MCMI offers several layers or levels of interpretation. Consistent with integrative logic, each level subsumes the previous one in an explanatory hierarchy, demanding a higher order of complexity and integration. At the first level, one merely examines the personality and clinical syndrome scales for single scale elevations. If these scales are sufficiently elevated, certain diagnoses may (or may not) be warranted. At the second level, the interpretive process branches to follow one of two pathways, depending upon whether any of the severe personality pathology scales are elevated, or whether elevations are confined to the less severe basic personality scales. Regardless of which branch the interpretive process follows, the goal at the second layer is to obtain an integrated picture of the client's personality functioning and dynamics. The third layer seeks to integrate the client's Axis II personality disorders and Axis I clinical syndromes according to multiaxial logic. The following sections address each of these levels in turn, and include illustrations from the featured case. We will refrain from making statements about the strengths and weaknesses of particular scales, and instead concentrate on the general interpretive logic of the instrument. In the interest of anchoring these abstract interpretive principles to concrete clinical reality, an actual case is now presented to illustrate the interpretive process. The details are as follows:

Cathy, a 31-year-old female graduate student from Venezuela majoring in English literature, presented at the outpatient center of a large psychiatric hospital with tiredness and difficulty falling asleep as her primary complaints. In her words, ". . . my mind just doesn't want to shut down, so I only get about 5 or 6 hours [of sleep] each night," a pattern she had endured for the last 5 years, and which she was at a loss to explain. Medical examination suggested no relevant physiological problems. She was referred for psychiatric impressions and treatment recommendations.

Cathy responded easily during the interview, readily offering psychologically salient information. She noted that her first graduate major was chemical engineering, from which she was forced to withdraw "when I found out I wasn't intelligent." She stated difficulty understanding some of the more abstract coursework, as well as an embarrassing incident in which an expensive apparatus in her charge was damaged. Cathy was an oldest child, with one sister 4 years younger than she. She reported that her parents at one time feared she was autistic, and that she was examined by a child psychologist at her mother's request when she was 6 years old. Her father, a physicist, passed away when she was 11 years old, and she regretted that they were not able to spend more time together. As an undergraduate, she attended a small and exclusively female liberal arts college in the Northeast. She confided that she had never had a boyfriend. When asked if she ever felt lonely, she replied "it's always been that way, you get used to it." Her family remained in Venezuela.

Diagnostic testing revealed a Wechsler Adult Intelligence Scale—Revised (WAIS-R) Verbal IQ of 128 and a Performance IQ of 115 with relative strengths in Vocabulary and Comprehension. The MCMI-III (Millon, 1994) revealed three basic personality scales in the elevated range, Schizoid (base rate [BR] = 90), Avoidant (BR = 78), and Dependent (BR = 77), with a subthreshold Axis I peak on the Dysthymia scale (BR = 74). On the Minnesota Multiphasic Personality Inventory—2 (MMPI-2), a three-point 7–8–0 profile was obtained. The Rorschach Inkblot Test, scored according to the Comprehensive System, revealed positive Schizophrenia and Depression Indices, several Level 2 special scores, many Level 1 Deviant Verbalizations, and a high $X-\%$, indicating numerous violations of the contours of the blots. Her Thematic Apperception Test (TAT) responses emphasized facial expressions and motives and featured quick and almost magical endings. Several of her responses to the Incomplete Sentences Blank (ISB) are notable: 1, "I like to lie in bed with my dog and my cat"; 2, "The happiest time I can remember is playing with my little sister"; 10, "People are not nearly as enjoyable or comfortable to be around as animals"; 11, "A mother is someone who makes you a part of herself"; 16, "Sports are wonderful except for team sports"; 28, "Sometimes I long for someone to spend my life with"; 29, "What pains me is not feeling cared for"; 32, "I am very dreamy and think more about love than a career"; and 39, "My greatest worry is the future."

Isolating Scale Elevations and Making Diagnoses

When self-report instruments consist of multiple scales, the results are usually presented in the form of a profile. Cathy's full MCMI-III profile is presented in Figure 4.1. At the first layer of interpretation we are only interested in determining which scales are elevated and their importance for making diagnostic decisions. For two reasons this must be viewed as the most basic level of interpretation: First, this layer looks only at single scales rather than at the profile as a whole, and second, it collapses continuous data down to a dichotomous level—information is first ignored, and then it is actively discarded.

Millon Clinical Multiaxial Inventory - III
CONFIDENTIAL INFORMATION FOR PROFESSIONAL USE ONLY

CATEGORY		RAW	BR	PROFILE OF BR SCORES	DIAGNOSTIC SCALES
MODIFYING INDICES	X	63	65		DISCLOSURE
	Y	8	45		DESIRABILITY
	Z	19	48		DEBASEMENT
CLINICAL PERSONALITY PATTERNS	1	9	90		SCHIZOID
	2A	12	78		AVOIDANT
	2B	10	60		DEPRESSIVE
	3	18	77		DEPENDENT
	4	5	63		HISTRIONIC
	5	4	68		NARCISSISTIC
	6A	6	61		ANTISOCIAL
	6B	3	72		AGGRESSIVE (SADISTIC)
	7	10	61		COMPULSIVE
	8A	13	72		NEGATIVISTIC
	8B	9	69		MASOCHISTIC
SEVERE PERSONALITY PATHOLOGY	S	6	65		SCHIZOTYPAL
	C	17	58		BORDERLINE
	P	3	61		PARANOID
CLINICAL SYNDROMES	A	8	64		ANXIETY DISORDER
	H	8	53		SOMATOFORM DISORDER
	N	6	59		BIPOLAR MANIC DISORDER
	D	9	74		DYSTHYMIC DISORDER
	B	4	38		ALCOHOL DEPENDENCE
	T	2	59		DRUG DEPENDENCE
	R	2	30		POST-TRAUMATIC STRESS
SEVERE SYNDROMES	SS	12	60		THOUGHT DISORDER
	CC	12	55		MAJOR DEPRESSION
	PP	10	45		DELUSIONAL DISORDER

FIGURE 4.1. Cathy's MCMI-III profile.

Base Rates

For MCMI neophytes, perhaps the first thing to notice is that, unlike other instruments, the elevation of each scale of Cathy's profile is given in terms of a BR score rather than more familiar *T*-score or percentile rank. Each is a transformation of the raw scores, and each has the purpose of putting the raw scores on a common metric. Unlike *T*-scores or percentile ranks, however, the BR scores are created such that the percentage of the clinical population deemed diagnosable with a particular disorder falls (1) either at or above a common threshold (clinical scales), or (2) at a particular rank order in the profile (personality scales). Thus, if 5% of the clinical population is deemed to possess a schizoid pattern as its primary personality style, and another 2% of the population has the schizoid pattern as a secondary feature, then the raw scores have been transformed so that the normative sample reflects these *prevalence* or *base* rates.

Obviously, the BR score implies that we are not so much interested in the "absolute quantity" of a particular trait as we are in the implications of that quantity for psychological functioning. While a certain level of narcissism is considered healthy in our society, the same level of antisocial behavior may not be; we might treat the second, but not the first. Thus, the BR concept recognizes that equal quantities of a trait or characteristic have differential pathological implications. Such scales have been equated in terms of the implications of a particular quantity for psychological functioning. The BR score simply represents the most direct way of getting at such considerations. BR scores are superior to *T*-scores, which implicitly assume the converse, that pathology varies directly with deviation from the average of one's normative group.

Conceptualization and Diagnosis

The BR score is intended to suggest positive characteristics of psychopathology. In Pepper's (1942) terms, it represents something of a fragment in that it makes a prediction in and of itself without appealing to anything immediately outside itself, such as auxiliary evidence, for corroboration. Consequently, there is a possibility of interpretive error in always diagnosing a personality disorder, or worse, multiple personality disorders, whenever BR scores equal or exceed a particular threshold. While it has become traditional to view BR = 75 and BR = 85 as indicating the presence of either significant personality traits or disorders, there are, as with every test, always false positives and false negatives. In a false positive result, the test indicates the presence of pathology where pathology does not exist. In a false negative result, the test indicates the absence of pathology where pathology in fact exists. As with most tests, false positives and false negatives derive principally from the insensitivity of any rigorous procedure, whether self-report, interview, or physiological measure, to contextual factors. Such factors must always be taken into consideration, a function of trained clinical judgment. In the featured case, three personality scales are diagnostic candidates, and we have no reason to believe that any other Axis II disorders might be applicable. As we need not worry about false negatives, our attitude in the dichotomous world of diagnostic judgment is one of culling the true positives from the set of all positives.

To elaborate on this problem, let us consider some definitions of personality pathology. Personality disorders are defined as clinical syndromes composed of intrinsic, deeply embedded, and pervasive ways of functioning (Millon, 1981). The DSM-III-R (American Psychiatric Association, 1987) states that it is "only when *personality traits* are inflexible and maladaptive and cause either significant functional impairment or subjective distress that they constitute *Personality Disorders*" (p. 335, italics original). Thus, the principal problem faced here is to separate scale elevations which have become inflexible or pervasive from those that have not. However, the degree to which a trait is problematic is not a direct function of the quantity of the trait, but instead is a function of (1) its interaction with other characteristics of the organism in which the trait is embedded, and (2) the interaction between the organism and the context in which it is embedded. Thus, not one, but two interactions separate the quantity of a trait and its flexibility or pervasiveness. Obviously, then, scale elevations which are problematic for one individual may not be pathological for another. Schizoid individuals, for example, are notable for their lack of emotional reactivity. Such individuals not only function well in, but actively seek out, environments which make few interpersonal demands. An accountant whose job requires long hours of tedious work may be well served by such characteristics. If this individual were suddenly thrust into a management position, would difficulties ensue? Quite possibly. Nevertheless, what exists can only be said to represent a vulnerability to contextual change, not a disorder per se.

This prefigures a second way of falling into error, that of viewing personality disorders as medical illnesses for which some discrete pathogen can be found, or for which there exists some underlying unitary cause, either past or present. The use of such language as "disorder" is indeed unfortunate, for personality disorders are not disorders at all in the medical sense. Instead, personality disorders are best conceptualized as disorders of the entire matrix of the person. Hence, we prefer the terms "pattern" or "style" rather than the intrinsically reifying "disorder." This misconception is more paradigmatic than diagnostic, but it leads to subsequent distortions in multiaxial logic, encouraging the view that classical clinical syndromes and personality disorders exist alongside each other in a horizontal relationship, rather than as clinical symptoms embedded in personality patterns. What threatens to undermine the interpretive process will surely undermine the intervention as well.

Configural Interpretation of MCMI Personality Scales

The quality of information that can be deduced from the profile analysis of a test is a function of several factors, including the adequacy and generativity of the theory which provides the logic underlying its various scales, the overall empirical validity of the inventory, and its internal consistency and scale generalizability. An interpretation which in fact mirrors the client's characteristic style of functioning as well as his or her current problems depends ultimately on the clinician's skill in weighing the degree to which a variety of client variables interact to corroborate, moderate, or even disqualify straightforward hypotheses, as well as to suggest ones which are more subtle. As noted by Wetzler and Marlowe (1992), even the best inventory is only as good as the clinician interpreting it. Perfect construct validity and generalizability will not make up for inadequate knowledge of the theory undergirding an inventory or ignorance of fundamental principles of psychopathology.

Although examining the elevations of single scales may be useful for making diagnostic assignments, their interpretive value is greatly amplified when viewed in the context of the remaining profile of scales. Why? The explanation of this obvious and widely accepted tenet of test interpretation can be traced back to metatheoretical assumptions addressed in the section of this chapter which dealt with what we called integrative logic. The short answer is that the process of profile interpretation is similar to that of knowledge building in the integrative world view. We are working our way toward an integrative conception of the client, what we have called nomothetic individuality. In doing so, we take distance from the individual scales and diagnoses to reconstruct the personality as an organic whole: In the context of the entire profile, the meaning of each scale becomes something other than it would have been, had that scale alone been available for interpretation. Thus we want to know more than just "avoidant" or "schizoid." In Pepper's (1942) more metaphysical terminology, each scale and even each diagnosis becomes a mere fragment to be transcended by successively more integrative formulations, the limit of the series being reality itself, here, the client. From the superordinate vista of this final product, it is little wonder that diagnoses, as such, often seem pathetic, inadequate, and next to useless, just as Ptolemy's crystal spheres must seem to modern astronomers.

In Cathy's case, the test results already suggest several diagnoses and other characteristics, each being a hypothesis about the nature of her pathology. True to Pepper's (1942) model, however, some of these diagnoses are already enmeshed in contradictions: Consulting with the various theory-derived personality prototype descriptions given above, the MCMI Schizoid (BR = 90) scale argues for an apathetic attitude and an absence of emotionality, suggesting that Cathy functions as a passive observer detached from rewards and affections as well as from the demands of human relationships. The Avoidant (BR = 78), and Dependent (BR = 77) scales and ISB findings (e.g., 34, "I wish I could find true love"), however, argue against such procrustean first-order interpretive logic, as does the elevation of MMPI-2 Scales 7 and 8. The schizoid hypothesis perhaps finds some corroboration in the elevation of the MMPI-2 social introversion scale. However, social introversion is a trait more narrow in scope than the schizoid personality, and, what is worse, both the schizoid and the avoidant personality styles often given "introverted" presentations, though for different reasons. In fact, the undergirding theory of the MCMI-III holds that both are detached types, one passively, the other actively, so. How, then, does one make sense of these ostensibly disparate findings? One means is to conceptualize the individual as a mixed type with features of each of the schizoid, avoidant, and dependent prototypes.

Such integrative configural logic is inherently nonlinear or nonmechanistic. Although it asks for a level of sophistication, in return it breaks the pattern of labeling clients and fitting them to discrete diagnostic categories: It conceptualizes diagnostic constructs as a beginning of an assessment rather than its endpoint. A narcissistic–antisocial pattern, for example, is somewhat different from either the purely prototypal narcissistic pattern or the purely prototypal antisocial pattern. Although the "two-point" pattern in part resembles these focal constructs, (nomothetic commonality), it is also more than either of these two patterns added together (nomothetic individuality), by virtue of the synergism of these elements. A narcissistic–antisocial pattern is something more than narcissism + antisocial behavior.

Interpretation of Moderate versus Severe Personality Scales

In making configural personality interpretations, a separation should be made between those scales pertaining to the *basic* clinical personality pattern (1–8B) and those pointing to the presence of more *severe* Axis II pathology, the Borderline (C), Schizotypal (S), and Paranoid (P) scales. These structural pathologies differ from the other clinical personality patterns by several criteria, notably, deficits in social competence and frequent (but readily reversible) psychotic episodes. Less integrated in terms of their personality organization and less effective in coping than their milder counterparts, they are especially vulnerable to decompensation when confronted with the strains of everyday life.

In terms of the theoretical model, these patterns are significantly less adaptable in the face of ecological vicissitudes. They are dysfunctional variants of the more moderately pathological patterns, a feature which leads to several predictions concerning these patterns and MCMI profiles. First, we noted earlier that at least two interactions mediate the role of a single personality trait for psychological functioning, and that for this reason the quantity of that trait constrains but does not determine the level of personality pathology. The elevation of S, C, and/or P may be used as a rough index of the degree to which the client's basic personality pattern has become structurally compromised. If, for example, a client receives BR = 105 on the narcissistic scale, but S, C, and P scores are low, then structurally the personality appears to be fundamentally intact, despite the elevated BR score. If, on the other hand, a client receives BR = 80 on the narcissistic scale, but scale P is also at BR = 75, this suggests a basic narcissistic pattern with paranoid tendencies, possibility an incipient structural pathology.

In Cathy's case, a somewhat elevated (BR = 69) Schizotypal scale score was achieved. This finding corroborates those obtained with the basic personality scales, that is, her schizoid–avoidant–dependent pattern. Significantly, the schizoid and avoidant personalities bracket the schizotypal personality on the circumplical model of DSM personality disorders designed by Millon (1987). This circumplex has as its axes impassive versus expressive and autonomous versus enmeshed. Cathy's pattern is located in the impassive–enmeshed quadrant. Interestingly, this appears to converge with her response to ISB item 11: "A mother is someone who makes you a part of herself." Accordingly, we may expect that in the face of severe stressors, Cathy may evidence the schizotypal's somewhat autistic ideations, mixed perhaps with personal irrelevancies and delusions of reference, depending on the nature and intensity of the stressors. The positive schizophrenia index obtained on the Rorschach with the Comprehensive System further supports this interpretation. Some authors, in fact, conceptualize the avoidant personality, the schizotypal personality, and schizophrenia as a spectrum of psychopathology.

Generating Domain Hypotheses

Not all clients with the same personality diagnosis possess the same problem(s). A single diagnostic label rarely if ever provides information specific and comprehensive enough to serve as a sound basis for intervention efforts. Not only do clients differ with respect to the magnitude of their pathology within a diagnostic kind, but also they differ in the features with which they approximate that kind. Whether diagnostic taxons are derived through clinical observation, mathematical analyses, or theoretical deduction, clients differ in *how* they meet taxonic requirements, a fact institutionalized in DSM-III (American Psychiatric Association, 1980) with the adoption of the polythetic model. In and of itself, then, a diagnosis alone *underspecifies* pathology, especially with regard to treatment considerations. Moreover, the vast majority of clients do represent so-called "mixed types." In moving toward nomothetic individuality, then, we must ask "what part of the mix" is relevant to interpreting the individual case.

One option is to systematically investigate characteristics associated with each MCMI-III high-point code in a *domain-oriented* fashion. These domains have been usefully organized in a manner similar to distinctions drawn in the biological realm, that is, by dividing them into *structural* and *functional* attributes. Functional characteristics represent dynamic processes that transpire within the intrapsychic world and between the individual's self and psychosocial environment. They represent "expressive modes of regulatory action." Structural attributes represent a deeply embedded and relatively enduring template of imprinted memories, attitudes, needs, fears, conflicts, and so on, which guide experience and transform the nature of ongoing events in accord with these imprintings. Obviously, this distinction is rooted in integrative logic. Pepper (1942), in fact, regarded both "integration" and "organism" as first approximations to the root metaphor or organicism. No organism exists which is composed exclusively of functional or exclusively of structural domains. Both are required if the organism is to exist as a self-regulating whole: Function animates structure; structure undergirds or buttresses function.

These domains are further differentiated according to their respective data level, either biophysical, intrapsychic, phenomenological, or behavioral, reflecting the four historic approaches that characterize the study of psychopathology, namely, the biological, the psychoanalytic, the cognitive, and the behavioral. The grouping of functional–structural clinical domains within the four traditional data levels of psychopathology is schematized in Table 4.1.

Several criteria were used to select and develop the clinical domains that comprise this assessment schema: (1) that they be varied in the features they embody; that is, that they not be limited just to behaviors or cognitions, but they encompass also a full range of clinically relevant characteristics; (2) that they parallel, if not correspond to, many of our profession's current therapeutic modalities, as evidenced by the four data levels; (3) that they not only be coordinated to the official DSM schema of personality disorder prototypes, as well as Millon's model of evolutionary polarities, but also that each disorder be characterized by a distinctive feature within each clinical domain. Brief descriptions of these functional and structural domains have been given in several publications (Millon, 1986, 1987, 1990), and are printed in the MCMI manual as well.

In the context of the individual case, the question then becomes: "Which functional processes and structural attributes are necessary for the client's personality pattern to exist as the organic whole represented by the code type?" Answering this question engages a synthetic process of clinical inference for which the end point is the mutual corroboration of parts and whole, a picture of the organism as a totality. If the personality assessment is to be exhaustive, then, with the guidance of the code type, a description of the client in each clinical domain should be formulated. Each domain description may be said to rep-

---

TABLE 4.1. Functional and Structural Domains of Personality

Behavioral level

(F) Expressive acts
(F) Interpersonal conduct

Phenomenological level

(F) Cognitive style
(S) Object representations
(S) Self-image

Intrapsychic level

(F) Regulatory mechanisms
(S) Morphological organizations

Biophysical level

(S) Mood/temperament

Note. F, functional domains; S, structural domains.

resent a within-domain hypothesis about client functioning in that circumscribed clinical area, and this hypothesis should be evaluated and amended as needed until it fits with auxiliary data and represents what is indeed believed to be the case. Given a two- or three-point code and a particular domain of interest, client functioning may be prototypal of the domain description for the primary code, prototypal of the domain description for the secondary code, or lie somewhere in between.

We are now in a position to advance a remarkably detailed assessment of the individual. We illustrate this process with regard to the featured case: Structural attributes and functional processes relevant to the schizoid–avoidant–dependent pattern are given in Table 4.2. We simply move down the chart from domain to domain, asking ourselves which description the client most resembles, synthesizing these descriptions when needed. *Behaviorally*, Cathy's presentation during diagnostic testing strongly suggested a dependent–avoidant behavioral style with its incumbent passivity, docility, immaturity, and heightened awareness of others' reactions to her, seen especially in her attentiveness to facial expressions on the TAT and her willingness to self-disclose in the interview. *Interpersonally*, she seems to alternate between the schizoid and the dependent–avoidant styles, perhaps as a defense against the feared rejection and helplessness which typify the latter: If what one desperately desires appears completely unobtainable, then one solution is to deny that such needs exist at all, remaining aloof from others as well as from oneself. Such an analysis conceptualizes this schizoid feature as a compromise which reflects conflictual dispositions, but has nevertheless taken on characterological pervasiveness. Her ISB responses corroborate this interpretation: Animals are more enjoyable and comfortable than people, but wouldn't true love be nice! Here one sees the avoidant's view that others are critical and humiliating, the dependent's desire to be rescued, and a blunting of affect typical of the schizoid. *Cognitively*, the intrusive and perplexing quality of Cathy's ideations appear more like the avoidant, possibly even the schizotypal, than it does the schizoid or the dependent. Cathy herself noted that her parents at one time believed she was autistic; moreover, the large number of poor form responses in her Rorschach protocol as represented by the inflated $X-\%$ argue for poor reality testing and perceptual distortion. *Defensively*, Cathy appears to combine the mechanisms of the avoidant with that of the dependent. While her TAT stories possess nearly magical endings, she seems incapable of separating her goals for herself from those of her introjected father image. Although her affective expression is blunted in an effort to avoid pain, lending her presentation a numb or flattened quality, Cathy's mood resembles more the avoidant's anguished desire for affection and constant fear of rebuff. As for her *self-image*, much like the dependent-avoidant, Cathy sees herself as weak and inadequate, belittles her own intelligence and achievements, and regards herself as a failure in her chosen profession. Her *internalizations* and *intrapsychic organization* resemble more that of the avoidant and dependent than the schizoid (e.g., ISB item 2, "The happiest time I can remember was playing with my little sister when I was a child").

Often the yield of domain hypotheses will be much richer than can be practically evaluated with data internal to the MCMI. As seen above, we have readily drawn on TAT and Rorschach data, as well as the interpersonal impressions of the examiner. Some domain hypotheses will be thoroughly corroborated, as for example by a therapist's own clinical observations, whereas others will be only partially corroborated, perhaps because the evidence simply suggests something else, but more often because not enough data exist to make an informed judgment. Evaluation of such hypotheses must await the accrual of extra-MCMI data, whether through additional testing or across therapy sessions. As with any form of clinical inference, the combination of various gauges from diverse settings provide the data aggregates (Epstein, 1979, 1983) necessary to increase the likelihood of drawing correct inferences, especially when coupled with multimethod approaches (Campbell & Fiske, 1959).

Putting Symptoms in Perspective

Because diagnoses exists as "fragments" to be transcended in successively more integrative formulations, they are, in the final analysis, somewhat trivial. We have already noted that diagnosis represents an underspecification of pathology with regard to treatment planning. In fact, as more integrative formulations are achieved, that is, as the limit of the series is reached in the necessary theory of the client, this theory becomes eminently more suitable for treatment planning than simple Axis I and Axis II diagnoses. The various diagnoses are only important for how they have been transformed, and not in themselves. Just as theoretical evolutions in a science transform the meaning of preexisting constructs, successively more integrative syntheses transform the meaning of our clinical constructs for the individual case. In this sense there are no personality a priori's, that is, clinical constructs which explain but are not themselves explained. In a pure scientific sense, clinical constructs seek their explanation in terms of an overarching theory; in an applied clinical sense, these constructs are compounded in an effort to understand the individual.

The proper question, then, in understanding the individual's pathology, is not a "whether," but rather a "how": how the interaction of individual characteristics and contextual factors, that is, the interaction of Axis II and Axis IV, produces Axis I, classic psychiatric symptomatology. Answering this "how" question requires the symptoms be put in context of the Axis II–Axis IV interaction. Consequently, determination of the level of personality pathology is secondary to a knowledge of the client's basic personality pattern. For this reason, the profile of MCMI BR scores is often more informative than is their overall elevation, arguing against the strict use of cutoff scores for the basic personality Axis II scales 1 through 8B. Thus, while the scales of interest in the current case were all elevated above the traditional MCMI-III cutting score, they need not have been to be relevant to the interpretive process. Everyone has a personality.

How do Axis II and Axis IV interact to produce the bedtime worries observed in the current case? Answering this question requires that the symptom complaint and psychosocial history and functioning be integrated with the personality style explicated above. Accordingly, Cathy emerges as a basically avoidant–dependent individual, someone who is far from home (Venezuela), feels herself to be a failure at her chosen career, is questioning her intellectual competency, and desperately longs for companionship (ISB item 34: "I wish I could find true love"). If what one desperately needs or desires is believed to be completely unattainable, too painful to pursue yet too painful to exist without, one solution is to deny that the need or desire exists at all. Thus, it appears that Cathy is socially inhibited and self-doubting, yet often secretive and intellectualizing.

Moreover, Cathy is probably less individuated and more developmentally immature than what is required for the professional life she is ostensibly seeking. Anchored in another culture, away from friends and family who could be relied upon to gratify affectionate needs and a failure at what she values most, she longs to return to the security of an earlier developmental epoch, a security which, in all likelihood, now sadly perpetuates the very immaturity and impoverishment of interpersonal abilities that it originally engendered. As noted on the ISB, "The happiest time I can remember is playing with my little sister." Given the lack of reinforcers in her current setting, Cathy may turn inward, depending excessively on imagination to achieve need gratification and conflict resolution, withdrawing

TABLE 4.2. Comparison of Schizoid, Avoidant, and Dependent Domains

	Schizoid prototype	Avoidant prototype	Dependent prototype
Expressive acts	*Expressively impassive* (e.g., appears to be in an inert emotional state, lifeless, undemonstrative, lacking in energy and vitality; is unmoved, boring, unanimated, robotic, and phlegmatic, displaying deficits in activation, motoric expressiveness, and spontaneity)	*Expressively fretful* (e.g., conveys personal unease and disquiet, a constant timorous, hesitant, and restive state; overreacts to innocuous events and anxiously judges them to signify ridicule, criticism, and disapproval)	*Expressively disconsolate* (e.g., appearance and posture conveys an irrelievably forlorn, somber, heavy-hearted, woebegone, if not grief-stricken quality; irremediably dispirited and discouraged, portraying a sense of permanent hopelessness and wretchedness)
Interpersonal conduct	*Interpersonally unengaged* (e.g., indifferent and remote, rarely responsive to actions or feelings of others, chooses solitary activities, minimal "human" interests; fades into the background, is aloof or unobtrusive, neither desires nor enjoys close relationships, and prefers a peripheral role in social, work, and family settings)	*Interpersonally aversive* (e.g., distances from activities that involve intimate personal relationships and reports extensive history of social pananxiety and distrust; seeks acceptance, but is unwilling to get involved unless certain to be liked, maintaining distance and privacy to avoid being shamed and humiliated)	*Interpersonally defenseless* (e.g., owing to feeling vulnerable, assailable, and unshielded, will beseech others to be nurturant and protective; fearing abandonment and desertion, will not only act in an endangered manner, but will seek, if not demand, assurances of affection, steadfastness, and devotion)
Cognitive style	*Cognitively impoverished* (e.g., seems deficient across broad spheres of human knowledge and evidences vague and obscure thought processes, particularly about social matters; communication with others is often unfocused, loses its purpose or intention, or is conveyed via a loose or circuitous logic)	*Cognitively distracted* (e.g., warily scans environment for potential threats and is preoccupied by intrusive and disruptive random thoughts and observations; an upwelling from within of irrelevant ideation upsets thought continuity and interferes with social communications and accurate appraisals)	*Cognitively pessimistic* (e.g., possesses defeatist and fatalistic attitudes about almost all matters, sees things in their blackest form and invariably expects the worst; feeling weighed down, discouraged, and bleak, gives the gloomiest interpretation of current events, despairing as well that things will never improve in the future)
Self-image	*Complacent self-image* (e.g., reveals minimal introspection and awareness of self; seems impervious to the emotional and personal implications of everyday social life, appearing indifferent to the praise or criticism of others)	*Alienated self-image* (e.g., sees self as socially inept, inadequate, and inferior, justifying thereby his or her isolation and rejection by others; feels personally unappealing, devalues self-achievements, and reports persistent sense of aloneness and emptiness)	*Worthless self-image* (e.g., judges one-self of no account, valueless to self or others, inadequate and unsuccessful in all aspirations; barren, sterile, impotent, sees self as inconsequential and reproachable, if not contemptible, a person who should be criticized and derogated, as well as feel guilty for possessing no praiseworthy traits or achievements)

Object representations	Meager objects (e.g., internalized representations are few in number and minimally articulated, largely devoid of the manifold percepts and memories of relationships with others, possessing little of the dynamic interplay among drives and conflicts that typify well-adjusted persons)	Vexatious objects (e.g., internalized representations are composed of readily reactivated, intense and conflict-ridden memories of problematic early relations; limited avenues for experiencing or recalling gratification, and few mechanisms to channel needs, bind impulses, resolve conflicts, or deflect external stressors)	Forsaken objects (e.g., internalized representations of the past appear jettisoned, as if life's early experiences have been depleted or devitalized, either drained of their richness and joyful elements, or withdrawn from memory, leaving one to feel abandoned, bereft, and discarded, cast off and deserted)
Regulatory mechanism	Intellectualization mechanism (e.g., describes interpersonal and affective experiences in a matter-of-fact, abstract, impersonal, or mechanical manner; pays primary attention to formal and objective aspects of social and emotional events)	Fantasy mechanism (e.g., depends excessively on imagination to achieve need gratification, confidence building, and conflict resolution; withdraws into reveries as a means of safely discharging frustrated affectionate as well as angry impulses)	Asceticism mechanism (e.g., acts of self-denial, self-punishment, and self-tormenting, believing that one should exhibit penance and be deprived of life's bounties; not only is there a repudiation of pleasures, but there are harsh self-judgments, as well as self-destructive acts)
Morphologic organization	Undifferentiated organization (e.g., given an inner barrenness, a feeble drive to fulfill needs, and minimal pressures either to defend against or resolve internal conflicts or to cope with external demands, internal morphologic structures may best be characterized by their limited framework and sterile pattern)	Fragile organization (e.g., a precarious complex of tortuous emotions depends almost exclusively on a single modality for resolution and discharge —avoidance, escape, and fantasy. Thus, when faced with personal risks, new opportunities, or unanticipated stress, few morphologic structures are available, and few backup positions can be reverted to, short of regressive decompensation)	Depleted organization (e.g., the scaffold for morphologic structures is markedly weakened, with coping methods enervated and defensive strategies impoverished, emptied and devoid of their vigor and focus, resulting in a diminished, if not exhausted, capacity to initiate action and regulate affect, impulse, and conflict)
Mood/temperament	Apathetic mood (e.g., emotionally unexcitable, intrinsically unfeeling, cold and stark; reports weak affectionate or erotic needs; rarely displays warm or intense feelings; apparently unable to experience most affects— pleasure, sadness, or anger—in any depth)	Anguished mood (e.g., describes constant and confusing undercurrent of tension, sadness, and anger; vacillates between desire for affection, fear of rebuff, embarrassment, and numbness of feeling)	Melancholic mood (e.g., is typically woeful, gloomy, tearful, joyless, and morose; characteristically worrisome and brooding, the low spirits and dysphoric state rarely remit)

into reverie to discharge occasionally overwhelming affectionate needs (and perhaps aggressive impulses as well) when these can no longer be readily denied or intellectualized. In fact, this mechanism may have achieved pathological proportions, suggesting that she may be predisposed to temporary, but readily reversible, episodes of an almost psychotic nature. Depending on the intensity of stressors, her cognitive ideational state may vary along a continuum of disruptive and irrelevant intrusions, but generally good reality testing at one (the more normal) end, to more schizotypal and schizophrenic ideations at the other. During these episodes reality testing will be poor. Given her high intellectual level, her position on this continuum at any one moment may be difficult to judge. She is intelligent enough to know what constitutes a good presentation.

No less problematic in sustaining Cathy's psychopathology is a generally inept, alienated, and devalued self-image. Her dependent style, specifically her generally fragile and inchoate intrapsychic organization, likely inclines her toward globalized beliefs of *inefficacy* rather than more realistic and differentiated appraisals of her performance in more narrow domains of competence. Her implicitly dichotomous conception of intellectual ability ("When I found out that I was not intelligent") supports this interpretation. In her eyes, her "failure" in chemical engineering likely validates her belief in her incompetence. Perhaps if she were not somewhat dependent, she could generate her own solutions and work toward realizing her possibilities. Perhaps if she were not somewhat avoidant, she could pursue whatever solutions and possibilities she envisioned. As a dependent–avoidant, however, she can do neither, creating and sustaining her dysthymic mood. Undistracted by the events of the day, a bedtime ruminative cycle begins which focuses on present unfulfilled needs and future impossibilities.

REFERENCES

American Psychiatric Association. (1980). *Diagnostic and statistical manual of mental disorders* (3rd ed.). Washington, DC: Author.

American Psychiatric Association. (1987). *Diagnostic and statistical manual of mental disorders* (3rd ed., rev.). Washington, DC: Author.

Campbell, D. T., & Fiske, D. W. (1959). Convergent and discriminant validation by the multitrait–multimethod matrix. *Psychological Bulletin, 56,* 81–105.

Epstein, S. (1979). The stability of behavior: 1. On predicting most of the people much of the time. *Journal of Personality and Social Psychology, 51,* 360–392.

Epstein, S. (1983). Aggregation and beyond: Some basic issues on the prediction of behavior. *Journal of Personality, 51,* 360–392.

Hempel, C. (1965). *Aspects of scientific explanation.* New York: Free Press.

Millon, T. (1969). *Modern psychopathology: A biosocial approach to maladaptive learning and functioning.* Philadelphia: Saunders.

Millon, T. (1981). *Disorders of personality: DSM-III, Axis II.* New York: Wiley.

Millon, T. (1986). Personality prototypes and their diagnostic criteria. In T. Millon & G. L. Klerman (Eds.), *Contemporary directions in psychopathology: Toward the DSM-IV* (pp. 671–712). New York: Guilford Press.

Millon, T. (1987). *Manual for the MCMI-II* (2nd ed.). Minneapolis: National Computer Systems.

Millon, T. (1990). *Toward a new personology: An evolutionary model.* New York: Wiley-Interscience.

Millon, T. (1994). *Millon Clinical Multiaxial Inventory—III manual.* Minneapolis: National Computer Systems.

Millon, T., & Davis, R. (1996). *Disorders of personality: DSM-IV and beyond.* New York: Wiley.

Pepper, S. P. (1942). *World hypotheses: A study in evidence.* Berkeley: University of California.

Wetzler, S., & Marlowe, D. (1992). What they don't tell you in test manuals: A response to Millon. *Journal of Consulting and Development, 70,* 327–328.

5

Clinical Integration of the MCMI-III and the Comprehensive System Rorschach

DARWIN DORR

This chapter examines the clinical use of the Millon Clinical Multiaxial Inventory—III (MCMI-III; Millon, 1994) with the contemporary Rorschach (Exner, 1986).[1] The relevant literature will be reviewed, after which I will discuss potential models for comparing information gained from the two instruments. In the final part of the chapter, two case studies will be reviewed to illustrate the advantages and difficulties when using these two instruments together clinically.

ASSUMPTIONS REGARDING PSYCHOMETRIC PROPERTIES OF THE INSTRUMENTS

One assumption of this chapter is that both instruments being discussed are psychometrically sound. This is emphasized because projective tests do not generally correlate highly with self-report measures (Archer & Krishnamurthy, 1993a). Because of this some clinicians, especially in academia, assume that the "fault" must lie with the Rorschach. For example, in 1965, Jensen (p. 238) wrote, "The rate of scientific progress in clinical psychology might well be measured by the speed and thoroughness with which it gets over the Rorschach." Further, many contemporary textbooks (e.g., Aiken, 1994), continue to diminish the psychometric quality of the Rorschach, often citing outdated negative research

---

[1]There are of course several other fine Rorschach systems such as those of Lerner (1991) and Blatt, Brenneis, Schimek, and Glick (1976). This chapter focuses primarily on the Comprehensive System because it lends itself to quantification and, thus, direct numerical comparison to MCMI-III scores.

findings. However, contemporary Rorschach research reveals an acceptable degree of statistical robustness. As this volume contains multiple chapters on the value of the MCMI-III in clinical and research assessment, I will focus solely on reviews of the technical qualities of the contemporary Rorschach.

In 1986 Atkinson reported the use of a meta-analytic procedure to assess the psychometric properties of the Minnesota Multiphasic Personality Inventory (MMPI) and the Rorschach Inkblot Test. In this paper, he asserted that researchers should be careful to distinguish between "undirected" and "conceptual" research strategies. An undirected strategy is roughly described as "shotgun" research in which multiple variables are included in the study, many or most of which may have no conceptual relationship to the phenomena being examined. A common result of this practice is an inordinate number of false negatives. In conceptual studies, variables are selected for study only when a rationale connects the selected signs/configurations to the predicted discriminations. Atkinson concluded that some of the Rorschach's early disrepute was largely attributable to undirected research strategies. Using these conceptual and empirical discriminations in his meta-analysis, Atkinson found that MMPI and Rorschach conceptual studies meet with more success than do undirected investigations. Further, he found that the conceptual validation studies of the Rorschach were as successful as the conceptual validation studies of the MMPI. Atkinson (1986) also added that the Rorschach's "questionable status may be based on sociocultural factors, rather than scientific ones" (p. 238).

Parker, Hanson, and Hunsley (1988) used meta-analysis to compare the average reliability, stability, and validity of the MMPI, Rorschach, and Wechsler Adult Intelligence Scale (WAIS) as reported in articles published in the *Journal of Personality Assessment* and the *Journal of Clinical Psychology* between 1970 and 1981. This study examined 411 studies that met their criteria for evaluability. In accordance with psychometric theory, they found that reliability values exceed stability values, which exceed validity values. They reported that validity studies based on theory, prior research, or both showed more positive effects than did studies lacking a theoretical or empirical rationale. In general, they found that the reliability and stability of all three tests were acceptable and approximately equivalent. The convergent validity estimates for the Rorschach and MMPI were not significantly different, but both were slightly lower than were the estimates for the WAIS.

Summarizing their findings, Parker et al. (1988) asserted that the Rorschach and the MMPI have acceptable and roughly equivalent psychometric properties when used appropriately. They emphasized that when the Rorschach and MMPI are used in the manner for which they were designed and validated, their psychometric properties are adequate for either clinical or research purposes. They discouraged the continued use of "shotgun" research strategies. The authors emphasized "more than anything else, the issue is to take the time and care to select the validated scale for the purpose at hand and to use that scale in a methodologically sound manner" (p. 373).

Thus, the Rorschach is psychometrically equivalent to the MMPI, and both are somewhat less efficient than the WAIS. The Rorschach, when used properly, is a useful tool for research and clinical purposes.

RESEARCH ON THE RELATIONSHIP
OF THE MILLON SCALES WITH THE RORSCHACH

I have been unable to identify more than a few empirical studies of the relationship between Rorschach variables and any of the Millon instruments. The few that have been found report modest to nil relationships. Because this research may provide some clues regarding MCMI-III/Rorschach interpretation, they will be reviewed briefly.

In 1991 Hart reported a study comparing the Rorschach Egocentricity Index (*EI* [$3r+(2)/R$]; Exner, 1986) with selected scales from the Millon Adolescent Personality Inventory (MAPI). MAPI scales selected for study included the Personal Esteem, Self-Concept, Inhibited, Peer Security, Social Tolerance, Self-Confidence, and Sociable scales. None of the correlations between the *EI* and these scales was statistically significant except the *EI*–Sociable correlation of .25. However, Hart pointed out that one component of *EI*, the total response rate (*R*), shows a significant (−.28) correlation with the Sociable scale. Hence, he performed a multiple regression analysis with Sociable as the dependent, and *EI* and *R* as the independent variables. The resulting multiple regression correlation was .43. Removing *EI* from the prediction substantially lowered the R^2. Hart concluded that *EI* contributes significantly to the prediction of Sociable scale scores.

It should be stressed that Hart (1991) utilized a relatively homogeneous sample (middle-class, white psychiatric inpatients) with a relatively small *N* (60), and that his mean *EI* at .30, is considerably below the mean that Exner (1986) reported for nonpatient adolescents. These sample factors substantially limit the power of the study to detect real covariance. Overall, we can conclude that there may be a weak relationship between the Rorschach *EI* and the MAPI Sociable scale.

Watson and Pantle (1993) reported no significant relationship between the presence of Rorschach Reflection responses (*Fr*) and MAPI Scales 5 (Confident) and 6 (Forceful). They did, however, find that in the reflection-present group, the 30 depressed subjects had lower scores on Scale 5 (*M* = 44.2, *SD* = 28.3) than did the 26 nondepressed subjects (*M* = 61.4, *SD* = 24.0). This "interaction" may suggest the need for further research on the associations between Rorschach Reflection responses and other measures of narcissism using samples less affected by acute psychiatric symptomatology.

In 1990 Trenerry and Pantle published a three-part study of MAPI code types in an inpatient crisis unit sample. As part of this study, they examined the relationship between several Rorschach variables and MAPI scales. Patients with one or more Vista (*V*) responses were more likely to have elevated scores on the Inhibited (2) Scale. Chi-square analysis revealed that the 28/82 (Inhibited–Sensitive) high-point code group had a disproportionate number of *V* responses. Further, although less striking, the 48/84 (Sociable–Sensitive) and the 45/54 (Sociable–Confident) high-point code groups also appeared to have more *V* responses associated with them, compared with other combinations. Interpretively, these results suggest that individuals with 28/82, 48/82, or 45/54 codes are more likely to harbor emotional discomfort involving negative feelings about the self and are more expressive of these feelings or demonstrate greater awareness of them through self-report measures such as the MAPI than are those with other score prefixes.

Although the number of statistically significant relationships in the Trenerry and Pantle (1990) study were modest, the presence of the *V* response is highly clinically relevant, as it suggests deep involvement in the painful process of self-assessment leading one to critically examine the negative features of the self. Hence, this finding has significant implications regarding potential response to psychotherapeutic interventions.

Hibbard (1989) published a study comparing the responses of 15 adult children of alcoholics (ACAs) with 15 children of nonalcoholics (non-ACAs) on the MCMI and the Rorschach. Hibbard used two MCMI indices of personality disorder. One consisted of the average of each individual's two high-point personality style scores. The second was the base rate (BR) score of the single highest point on the pathological personality syndromes (Schizotypal, Borderline, and Paranoid) scales.

These two MCMI indices were compared with two Rorschach measures of developmental object relations pathology. Hibbard's first Rorschach measure was Exner's Egocentricity Index (*EI* [3*r*+(2)/*R*]; Exner, 1986), a measure of self-centeredness or self-focus which in the extreme may be a form of narcissism. The second measure consisted of object concept scales *OR*+ and *OR*–) developed by Blatt, Brenneis, Schimek, and Glick (1976). These scales are believed to measure the developmental level of object complexity of human responses on the Rorschach. The two Rorschach methods were combined into a multivariate measure of object relational pathology.

The ACAs scored higher than did the non-ACAs on the combined MCMI basic personality style indices and on the MCMI severe personality pathology scales. Hibbard (1989) also found that ACAs displayed greater object relations pathology as indicated by the two Rorschach measures. In sum, both the MCMI and the Rorschach added support for the hypothesis that a greater number of personality disorders and characterological defensive problems are depicted in adult children of alcoholics.

Dougherty and Lesswing (1989) used a full battery of psychological tests to examine 100 cocaine abusers who were enrolled in a chemical dependence treatment program. Among the measures used were the MCMI and the Rorschach. The authors discovered that 88% of the sample was diagnosed by the MCMI with a DSM-III Axis II personality disorder. Diagnoses of mixed personality disorder, borderline personality disorder, and narcissistic personality disorder accounted for about half of the diagnoses. Concordantly, the Rorschach revealed narcissism, underlying anger and negativity, cognitive slippage, and problems in reality testing. Thus, the clinical picture described by the MCMI paralleled the one produced by the Rorschach.

To summarize, there are very few studies of the relationship between the Rorschach and any of the Millon instruments, and these studies report very modest relationships, indeed. Yet, meta-analyses provide convincing evidence that the contemporary Rorschach has an acceptable degree of reliability and validity. What, then, does this paucity of significant interrelationships mean?

We might turn to another, more extensively researched, self-report measure, the MMPI, to examine its relationship to the Rorschach. Perhaps an examination of MMPI–Rorschach studies will provide us with a better understanding of a possible relationship between the Rorschach and the Millon instruments.

THE RORSCHACH AND THE MMPI

Currently, the most thorough study of the Rorschach–MMPI relationship was published by Archer and Krishnamurthy (1993b). These authors pointed out that the MMPI and Rorschach are the most widely used psychological assessment instruments for both adolescents and adults. They found that more than 10,000 books and articles have been published on the MMPI since 1943, and more than 4,000 articles have been published on the Rorschach, of which over 2,000 were research writings. Yet when the authors combed the literature for articles addressing corelationships, they found fewer than 50 studies explicitly examining relationships between the MMPI and the Rorschach. Further, they discovered that only 37 of these were amenable to statistical comparison. In view of this remarkable ratio of published studies to cross-test comparison, it is not as surprising that there are so few Rorschach–Millon instrument studies. The Millon instruments are much newer and the research literature is, unfortunately, not as voluminous as it is for its two "older siblings."

Archer and Krishnamurthy (1993b) found that 19 of the 37 studies (51%) reported nonsignificant relationships between individual MMPI scales and Rorschach variables. Another 8 studies (22%) reported relatively weak associations, reflecting small effect sizes, for example, $r \geq .04$ to $r \leq .014$. They concluded that taken as an aggregate, 73% of the studies revealed either no statistically related significance or minimal associations between Rorschach and MMPI variables in these adult samples. Among the remaining 28% of the studies, most yielded moderate associations with Pearson product–moment correlations in the range of $r \geq .24$ to $r \leq .34$.

The authors noted that these findings were similar to those examining the relationship of Rorschach with MMPI patterns in adolescents (Archer & Krishnamurthy, 1993a). At the basic construct level, these authors concluded that "variables given similar labels on both instruments may, in fact, represent independent and largely non-overlapping constructs" (p. 286). They clearly discounted the possibility that either the MMPI or the Rorschach might have limited reliability or validity, citing the general reliability coefficients of $r = .84$ for the Rorschach and $r = .86$ for the MMPI. Further, the comparable convergent validity coefficients of $r = .46$ and $r = .41$, respectively, were also cited. In sum, both measures enjoy a reasonable degree of reliability and validity while apparently measuring different aspects of the personality.

In view of the low covariation between the MMPI and the Rorschach, it might be argued that it would be fruitless to examine the ways in which the Rorschach and the Millon instruments might complement each other. There are, however, additional points of view regarding test integration that suggest it may be clinically and scientifically reasonable to examine ways in which these and other instruments may be integrated to enrich our understanding of our patients as well as to design and articulate specific treatment interventions. These matters will be reviewed followed by a few comments on the concept of integration.

FRAGMENTATION AND INTEGRATION IN PSYCHOLOGY

Although this chapter focuses on the nexus of the MCMI-III and the Rorschach, we are actually attempting to address a much larger problem within psychology, which is the lack of philosophical models for helping us integrate clinical data. As psychology has grown, it has diversified. The multiplicity of models, theories, methodologies, ideologies, and/or "schools" within psychology is astonishing. There is much emphasis on how our psychologies differ and relatively little emphasis on the process of integration. In the field of psychotherapy, there has been a proliferation of different schools or approaches. Garfield (1994) writes that from the more than 60 different approaches he observed in the mid-1960s, the number grew to over 400 different techniques by 1986. In his 1994 article Garfield quotes himself from 1987, "Although I have not really computed the exponential curve (of growth) for the next 20 years . . . I am inclined to predict that sometime in the next century, there will be one form of psychotherapy for every adult in the Western world!" (Garfield, 1987, p. 98, cited in Garfield, 1994). He suggests that this is "not a very happy prospect" (1994, p. 123).

The reversal of this trend toward rapid proliferation of "different" therapies was first seen in the appearance of Wachtel's 1977 book, *Psychoanalysis and Behavior Therapy: Toward an Integration*. Since then, a number of articles and books have affirmed an integrative approach. Garfield's book *Psychotherapy: An Eclectic Approach* appeared in 1980. This book was translated into German and Japanese in 1985. Also in 1980, Marmor and Woods published *The Interface between the Psychodynamic and Behavioral Therapies*. In

1982, the International Academy of Eclectic Psychotherapists began publishing the *International Journal of Eclectic Psychotherapy*. In 1987, this journal was renamed the *Journal of Integrative and Eclectic Psychotherapy*, reflecting the growing interest in integration. In 1983, the Society for the Exploration of Psychotherapy Integration (SEPI) was formed. In 1986, Norcross edited the *Handbook of Eclectic Psychotherapy;* the *Casebook of Eclectic Psychotherapy*, also edited by Norcross, was published in 1987. The Norcross book was revised and reissued (with Goldfried) in 1992 as the *Comprehensive Handbook of Psychotherapy Integration*. In 1994, Garfield's article on psychotherapy integration, "Eclecticism and Integration in Psychotherapy: Developments and Issues," was complemented by Stricker's (1994) article, "Reflections on Psychotherapy Integration." Finally, in 1995 Garfield revised and reissued his earlier work and published it as *Psychotherapy: An Eclectic–Integrative Approach*.

There is much more to this story, but it is really beyond the scope of this chapter. The main point is that the concept of integration is relatively new to psychology and, because of this, there are few models to help us with the process. Garfield (1994) asserts that however reasonable and desirable a mature integration may be, the intellectual, academic, and clinical task of integration is difficult.

INTEGRATING TEST RESULTS: SOME IDEAS BORROWED FROM WORKS INTEGRATING THE MMPI-2 AND THE RORSCHACH[2]

In the arena of assessment we face similar problems. This is puzzling because, unlike generations of psychotherapists who promulgated their own individualistic theories, psychologists who focused on assessment have used multiple testing methods since 1896, when Lightner Witmer founded the first psychological clinic. Assessment psychologists are urged to integrate their findings (Tallent, 1993). Yet few models exist to help the practitioner in this endeavor. Lovitt (1993, p. 142) wrote, "Synthesizing contradictory data from diverse data sources is the single most difficult and critical operation fundamental to the processing of data in clinical cases. Our assessment literature devotes little attention and provides few guidelines about how to combine data from different tests."

Fortunately, in 1993 four papers were published in the *Journal of Personality Assessment* (JPA) on integrating Rorschach and MMPI in clinical assessment. Because the methodology suggested in these articles is relevant to our attempts to integrate MCMI-III and Rorschach results, these writings will be summarized herein.

Weiner (1993) argued that apparent contradictions between the MMPI and Rorschach results are generative, not invalidating. He pointed out that the two instruments assess different levels of conscious awareness with respect to the importance of what patients are being asked and the implications of how they choose to respond. Weiner asserted that the Rorschach and MMPI answers are both real phenomena, and their use depends on how skillfully assessment psychologists can determine what they mean.

Acklin (1993) observed that the Rorschach and the MMPI are among the most widely used personality instruments in existence, but there is little guidance in the literature about their combined use. He reviewed some basic assumptions in the area of personality assess-

---

[2]Since this work was completed, Ganellen (1996) has published an outstanding text on the integration of the MMPI-2 and the Rorschach. This work makes a significant contribution to our understanding of integration in personality assessment.

ment, pointing out that the use of a test battery as opposed to a single test has been a traditional practice in clinical psychology since the mid-1940s. Additionally, he advised clinicians to have a rationale for each test employed in the battery. While the recent literature suggests that the MMPI and the Rorschach represent nonoverlapping sources of data, Acklin (1993) argues that it is desirable to combine tests that are largely unrelated. He quoted Graham (1977, p. 6) stating that the MMPI, with its enormous research base, lends itself well to a "descriptive behavioral approach." However, Acklin also argued that the MMPI, in the final analysis, remains a self-report instrument. Ultimately, the responses to the questions and the resulting scales provide us with the individual's view of his or her self. Although this is a psychological reality, it is not always a behavioral reality.

On the other hand, the Rorschach is an indirect approach to the assessment of personality. Inclusion of the Rorschach in the battery provides a less structured task than the MMPI, allowing greater freedom of response and, therefore, richer clinical material. Hence, the protocol furnishes a rich sample of interactional linguistic and behavioral data. In contrast, while the MMPI categorizes symptoms and problems, the Rorschach reveals personality organization and dynamics.

Acklin (1993) summarized several methods of integration. These methods can be used singly or in concert as sequential steps toward integration. The first level of integration outlined by Acklin compares *test scales or scores*. An example would be an examination of the MMPI-2 Scale 2 (D) and the Rorschach Depression Index to determine the presence of depression.

The second approach involves integration at the *level of the test*. A test-by-test reporting technique is employed which explains the various findings of each test. This approach is more additive than truly integrative. However, in clinical practice this approach is useful.

A third approach involves integration at the level of *construct*. This is a distant cousin of the multitrait–multimethod approach. At this level, the clinician might comment on multitest evidence for any emerging themes related to such matters as affect, self-concept, interpersonal relations, and the like.

A fourth approach involves integration at the level of *theory*. This level is closely related to integration at the construct level. Data are interpreted, organized, and expressed in terms of psychological theory. Acklin notes that many writers believe the process of personality assessment necessarily involves the use of personality theory. I would add that a theory of some kind is always present, whether or not it is acknowledged by the assessor.

Finally, Acklin (1993) stressed that we *interpret persons, not tests*. He quoted Rappaport, Gil, and Schafer (1968, p. 18), who taught that the goal of assessment is an understanding and description of "uniquely organized persons." Acklin added:

> This person-centered hermeneutical focus places the emphasis where it rightly belongs, for as long as we understand that it is this unique individual in his or her unique life situation, we are able to place the test findings in the appropriate perspective. The test score or determinant has no particular meaning outside the unique life world and experience of the particular individual and the mind of the assessor, who is the integrator of the wealth of data—experiential, interpersonal, and psychometric—that personality assessment entails. (p. 129)

In the same issue of *JPA*, Archer and Krishnamurthy (1993b) examined empirical findings on the integration of the Rorschach and the MMPI for adolescents. In general, they found little covariation in this population. They concluded that these findings leave open the possibility that combining data from the two instruments may increase incremental validity. They conclude their article with a discussion of the complex process of integrating multiple test data sources with biographical and interview material.

In a third article of this *JPA* issue, Lovitt (1993) stated that our standard literature and experimental data base do not supply the necessary information practitioners need to provide integrated assessment services. According to Lovitt, "practitioners must engage in a variety of novel operations to generate an acceptable assessment product" (p. 141). He noted that the assessment literature devotes scant attention to this difficult issue and offers little guidance and even fewer methods for integrating results from diverse data sources. To remedy this, Lovitt proposed a five-stage model for integrating data from two or more sources of testing. The five guidelines are as follows:

1. Interpret each test ignoring or minimizing information from all other sources. Standard textbooks and workshops emphasize the procedures involved in this stage.
2. Bring in pertinent historical and clinical issues, and evaluate each test in light of this information.
3. Integrate all data sources (tests and history) into a complete and unified picture of the personality.
4. Account for inconsistencies between different tests by introducing clinical and personality constructs to create a meaningful synthesis. Scientific restraint must be exercised in selecting these constructs. The constructs that are introduced should be conceptually and empirically anchored to assessment data.
5. Develop hypotheses to explain inconsistencies. Retain those that have the broadest explanatory utility. Those hypotheses with limited explanatory utility should be rejected or modified.

Lovitt (1993) commented that the MMPI, as a self-report instrument, provides us with a picture of what patients are willing or able to verbalize about themselves to others. Rorschach data represent behavioral samples that describe the coping style of patients in an ambiguous and probably emotionally provoking problem situation (similar to the problems faced in life). To demonstrate his test integration model, Lovitt presented a case study of a 46-year-old female with a long history of deep dissatisfaction with her life. Her MMPI was negative for depression or any other form of emotional difficulty, despite a 7-year course of insight-oriented psychotherapy. The Rorschach, however, provided abundant evidence of the emotional and behavioral difficulties she faced, including positive Schizophrenia and Depression Indices, an *a:p* ratio of 3:9, a *Ma:Mp* ratio of 0:8, a *WSum6* of 43, 4 *C*'s, and an *X*–% of .42. The key to the interpretation was found in the high Lambda of 1.05, the total absence of any active human movement, and the low Affective Ratio of .40. Further, the patient was a pervasive introvert with an *EB* of 8:1.5.

Clearly these indices show us that she was the kind of person who was not ready or able to process psychologically and emotionally laden situations. She did not have access to vital affective cues from other people. She oversimplified her world to make it less threatening or demanding. This simplistic style made it difficult for her to use important feedback about her behavior. Because of her difficulties with perceptual accuracy and her interpersonal difficulties, it was hard for her to acquire accurate and complete information regarding herself or others from other people. Inspection of the active to passive ratios suggests that she was a rigid thinker who would rigorously hold on to her convictions— even when they were based on faulty or erroneous information.

To summarize, this 46-year-old woman's MMPI, a self-report index, provided us with a view of style of self-assessment; that is, she was not a person who was going to observe and process, psychologically speaking. Yet, behaviorally, she presented with a large array of emotional and interpersonal difficulties that were accurately measured by the Rorschach.

Lovitt's (1993) brief but seminal paper provided us with an outstanding view of the way in which we may integrate self-report methodology and Rorschach data at the individual case level, reminding us that we are, as clinicians, interested in interpreting persons— not tests.

INTEGRATING THE MCMI-III AND THE RORSCHACH

Choca, Shanley, and Van Denburg (1992) devoted a short section of their book to the relationship between MCMI indices and projective tests. They also found very few research or clinical articles on the relationship of MCMI scores to projective tests. Despite the paucity of research, Choca et al. noted that the use of multiple measures is a way to confirm, enhance, or rule out individual test results. For example, if an elevation on one of the Millon depression scales is found, the Rorschach might clarify the degree to which the depression influences thinking processes. A major contribution of their work was to establish the precept of the Millon scales as measures of enduring personality styles and the idea that these enduring personality styles may be related to the way in which subjects respond to projective tests. Consider, for example, the finding of an individual's elevations on the MCMI's Avoidance and Schizoid scales. Clinically, it would be important to know whether the individual's projective test results were lacking in human integration, as one might expect, or, conversely, they were rich with human warmth and detail. If, for example, an individual presented with a very constricted Rorschach protocol yet also appeared to be very compulsive as measured by the MCMI, we would have to wonder whether the lack of Rorschach determinants and low productivity were the result of strong compulsive tendencies or a lack of energy and enthusiasm inherent in a despondent mood. This is an excellent observation, and again highlights how the work of integration needs to occur at the level of the individual patient.

CASE STUDIES

In this section two patients' cases are presented to illustrate the advantages and difficulties one may encounter when integrating MCMI-III and Rorschach test results. Demographic variables and circumstances have been altered to protect anonymity. However, the case dynamics and data were preserved to accurately reflect the demands of the interpretive process.

It may be helpful to make a few comments on the interpretive strategy used in this section. The Comprehensive System (Exner, 1991) instructs the clinician to exhaustively review the entire set of clusters in an established sequence to maximize the amount of useful data one may extract from the System. This procedure was followed in the process of the clinical interpretation of the cases presented. However, this process yields a very large amount of data. With the addition of the three validity and 24 clinical scales of the MCMI-III, the potential interpretive combinations multiply exponentially. For these reasons, it is necessary to limit discussion of interpretive possibilities to a few general themes in each case. I am aware that this method oversimplifies the clinical picture and runs the risk of omitting clinically confirming or contradictory data. However, space limitations require parsimony. In the process of data reduction, Acklin's (1993) admonition to "interpret the person" is followed as closely as possible.

The patient cases selected for inclusion are neither "neat" nor "clean." In some instances the data cluster together effortlessly. In others, we face contradictory and challenging discrepancies. It would, however, be a disservice to the reader to report only easy cases. The day-to-day clinical work of the assessment psychologist presents many difficult patients and these difficulties must be faced and, if possible, resolved.

Case 1. Mary Steinman

Mary Steinman was a 35-year-old, never married, white female who lived with her father and worked as a bookkeeper. Her mother died when she was 7 years of age and she grew up feeling unwanted and unappreciated. She was extremely overweight and admitted to eating far too much and far too many fatty foods. She was college educated, but had a long history of problems in her social and vocational attainments. She also had a history of shoplifting, though she had since conquered this. She felt sick and tired much of the time and found her 40–hour weekly shift to be exhausting. Much of her leisure time was spent by herself resting on the couch at home. However, when she had better periods, she could be sociable and had been involved with a singles group. On occasion, she would sometimes participate in local plays and musicals.

Ms. Steinman was seen at an outpatient clinic for treatment of depression. A psychological evaluation was requested to augment the clinical picture of her personality structure and psychopathology. The test battery consisted of an intake booklet (containing social history form, human figure drawings, sentence completion tasks, and the like), the Edwards Personal Preference Schedule (1959), the MMPI-2, the MCMI-III, and the Rorschach.

For the reader's information, the MMPI-2 validity pattern was as follows: L = 43; F = 82; K = 46; and Fb = 97. On the basic clinical scales, scores are as follows: Hs = 84; D = 92; Hy = 77; Pd = 94; Mf = 40; Pa = 78; Pt = 75; Sc = 73; Ma = 45; Si = 75. Additionally, the Pk Scale (Post-traumatic Stress) T-score was 87.

Ms. Steinman's MCMI-III profile is presented in Figure 5.1.

The high Disclosure and Debasement scales, combined with a low Social Desirability scale score, indicated a general tendency to magnify the level of experienced illness or a characterological inclination to complain or to be self-pitying. Alternately, this response style may have reflected feelings of extreme vulnerability that were associated with her emotional difficulties at the time of evaluation. In any case, the scale scores may have been somewhat exaggerated, which should be considered in the process of interpretation. Of immediate concern was the elevation of 76 on the Borderline scale, one of the severe personality pathology scales. An elevation on the scale suggests that the overall personality structure and organization of this subject will be characterized by a moderate to severe level of pathology. Object representations will be incompatible, conflicted, and aborted. A failure in the development of sufficient internal cohesion suggests serious morphologic defects. As a result of this structural defect, defenses and coping strategies may be unsatisfactory. Her mechanisms for regulation of affect and conflict may have been deficient. Additionally, these structural deficits would likely have made it difficult for her to establish and maintain satisfying and relatively conflict-free relationships. Her own attitudes and feelings were likely to be capricious, contradictory, and erratic. As a result, her sense of personal consistency and the reliability of the sense of self may have been precarious. It

MILLON CLINICAL MULTIAXIAL INVENTORY - III
CONFIDENTIAL INFORMATION FOR PROFESSIONAL USE ONLY

ID NUMBER: 50760   Valid Profile

PERSONALITY CODE: 2B 2A 8B 3 ** 8A * 1 6A + 6B " 7 4 5 ' ' // - ** C * //

SYNDROME CODE: - ** A D * // CC ** - * //

DEMOGRAPHIC: 50760/ON/F/35/W/N/18/JO/OT/296/10/30186/

CATEGORY		SCORE		PROFILE OF BR SCORES					DIAGNOSTIC SCALES
		RAW	BR	0	60	75	85	115	
MODIFYING INDICES	X	137	80						DISCLOSURE
	Y	1	5						DESIRABILITY
	Z	24	83						DEBASEMENT
CLINICAL PERSONALITY PATTERNS	1	12	72						SCHIZOID
	2A	22	106						AVOIDANT
	2B	22	108						DEPRESSIVE
	3	18	89						DEPENDENT
	4	3	8						HISTRIONIC
	5	2	5						NARCISSISTIC
	6A	8	60						ANTISOCIAL
	6B	6	55						AGGRESSIVE (SADISTIC)
	7	10	34						COMPULSIVE
	8A	18	79						PASSIVE-AGGRESSIVE
	8B	17	95						SELF-DEFEATING
SEVERE PERSONALITY PATHOLOGY	S	7	59						SCHIZOTYPAL
	C	14	76						BORDERLINE
	P	6	59						PARANOID
CLINICAL SYNDROMES	A	11	79						ANXIETY DISORDER
	H	11	08						SOMATOFORM DISORDER
	N	4	44						BIPOLAR: MANIC DISORDER
	D	16	79						DYSTHYMIC DISORDER
	B	4	58						ALCOHOL DEPENDENCE
	T	4	59						DRUG DEPENDENCE
	R	15	70						POST-TRAUMATIC STRESS
SEVERE SYNDROMES	SS	10	60						THOUGHT DISORDER
	CC	19	98						MAJOR DEPRESSION
	PP	0	0						DELUSIONAL DISORDER

FIGURE 5.1. MCMI-III profile for Mary Steinman.

was likely that she had a long history of failure and disappointments in personal and family relationships. She may have repeatedly failed in establishing stable and satisfying social and vocational relationships. Her life may have been characterized by a series of failures which she had, in part, brought about by her masochistic and self-defeating tendencies.

The MCMI-III described a sad, forlorn, somber, pessimistic individual who invariably expected the worst. Routine life events were habitually interpreted as omens of doom. She viewed herself as inadequate to manage the most basic demands on her capacity to cope. She may have felt abandoned, bereft, and deserted. Life was one usually devoid of joy or lightheartedness. She may have felt empty and exhausted.

She was extremely insecure and felt vulnerable if separated from significant others, who were probably perceived as caregivers. She experienced extreme needs for affection and succorance. Perhaps as a result of such an extreme need to be dependent on others, she may also have experienced a parallel sense of resentment toward those upon whom she believed she was dependent. This extreme dependence fomented a sense of anger or even rage toward those upon whom she was dependent. Yet, she was likely to be terrified that any expression of autonomy, much less resentment, would result in abandonment, a condition that she believed she cannot possibly tolerate. Thus, there was likely to have been a chronic "stuffing" or containing of anger which further depleted her limited reservoir of energy. She probably experienced a nagging sense of fatigue, exhaustion, and heaviness. Her persistent irritability and anger may have periodically erupted directly or may have been manifested in passive–aggressive, obstinate, and contrary behaviors.

She likely experienced underlying tension and dysphoria. There would have been a distressing emotional stew of anxiety, sadness, and guilt. Insecurity and constant fear of abandonment resulted in a chronic sorrowful, dispirited world view. Though occasionally explosive, she may have presented with a weak, self-derogating, overly ascetic interpersonal style. In this way, she may have hoped at best to elicit nurturance and protection, and at the least to avoid rejection and abandonment.

Fearing abandonment, a substantial amount of energy may have been devoted to avoiding close interpersonal relationships with the very people she so desperately needed for emotional support. A classic approach–avoidance conflict characterized most or all of her close interpersonal relationships. There was likely to be an out of awareness "once-burned/twice-wary" defensive strategy in which she maladaptively compensated for early losses by defensively keeping substantial distance between her own frail self and significant others. Overall she might have been described as fragile, longing, and afraid.

In parallel fashion, the clinical and severe syndrome scales suggested a major depression interwoven with a characterological blend of dysthymic features. The depression was permeated with anxiety, tension, fatigue, and exhaustion. Anhedonia was coupled with dysthymia. This was a very depressed individual who expressed a sense of dread regarding the future. She may also have entertained thoughts of suicide coupled with a sense of hopeless resignation. There may have been vegetative signs such as motor retardation, sleep disturbances, or eating/weight difficulties.

The structural summary for Mary's Rorschach is presented in Figure 5.2.

As mentioned above, for the sake of brevity and clarity this review will focus only on variables which appear to bear directly on the patient at hand. In a few instances data from other tests and procedures will be included to enhance the clinical picture.

According to the structural summary, the interpretive search strategy should proceed through the clusters in the following order: Controls, Situational Stress, Affect, Self-Perception, Interpersonal Perception, Information Processing, Mediation, and Ideation. In the interest of space, the report of the search will not be exhaustive, although in preparation the standard Comprehensive System exhaustive search methodology was used.

In the Controls cluster, D was −1, whereas Adjusted D was 0. EA was in the low average range, but the Coping Deficit Index was positive. Thus, although she had at least minimum resources accessible to cope with most challenges, the organization of her personality was such that she was vulnerable to problems of coping with the demands of everyday living. The Situational Stress cluster indicated a substantial amount of situational stress which may have contributed to impulsiveness in thinking and affect. A review of the Affect cluster revealed affective inconsistency. That is, the patient was ambient, meaning that

ID #1,

STRUCTURAL SUMMARY

LOCATION FEATURES	DETERMINANTS BLENDS	SINGLE	CONTENTS	S—CONSTELLATION
Zf = 17	Fr.M	M = 2	H = 2, 0	NO...FV+VF+V+FD > 2
ZSum = 57.0	FT.FD	FM = 2	(H) = 1, 0	YES...Col–Shd Bl > 0
ZEst = 56.0	FT.FM	m = 0	Hd = 3, 0	YES...Ego < .31 , > .44
	Fr.m	FC = 2	(Hd) = 1, 0	NO...MOR > 3
W = 11	Fr.m	CF = 0	Hx = 0, 0	NO...Zd > +- 3.5
(Wv=0)	Fr.M	C = 0	A = 8, 1	YES...es > EA
D = 7	FM.Fr	Cn = 0	(A) = 0, 0	NO...CF+C > FC
Dd = 3	CF.YF	FC' = 1	Ad = 3, 0	YES...X+% < .70
S = 0	Fr.CF	C'F = 0	(Ad) = 0, 0	NO...S > 3
		C' = 0	An = 1, 0	NO...P < 3 or > 8
		FT = 0	Art = 0, 0	NO...Pure H < 2
DQ		TF = 0	Ay = 0, 0	NO...R < 17
............(FQ-)		T = 0	Bl = 0, 0	4......TOTAL
+ = 11 (3)		FV = 0	Bt = 0, 0	
o = 10 (2)		VF = 0	Cg = 0, 1	SPECIAL SCORINGS
w/+ = 0 (0)		V = 0	Cl = 0, 0	
v = 0 (0)		FY = 0	Ex = 0, 0	LV1 LV2
		YF = 0	Fd = 0, 0	DV = 0x1 0x2
		Y = 0	Fi = 0, 0	INC = 2x2 0x4
		Fr = 1	Ge = 0, 0	DR = 1x3 0x6
		rF = 0	Hh = 0, 2	FAB = 1x4 0x7
FORM QUALITY		FD = 0	Ls = 1, 1	ALOG = 0x5
		F = 4	Na = 1, 0	CON = 0x7
FQx FQf MQual SQx			SC = 0, 0	SUM6 = 4
+ = 0 0 0 0			Sx = 0, 0	WSUM6 = 11
o =12 4 3 0			Xy = 1, 0	
u = 4 0 0 0			Id = 0, 1	AB = 0 CP = 0
- = 5 0 1 0				AG = 1 MOR = 1
none = 0 — 0 0	(2) = 3			CFB = 0 PER = 1
				COP = 0 PSV = 0

RATIOS, PERCENTAGES, AND DERIVATIONS

R = 21	L = 0.24	FC : CF + C = 2: 2	COP = 0	AG = 1
		Pure C = 0	Food	= 0
EB = 4: 3.0	EA = 7.0 EBPer = N/A	Afr = 0.24	Isolate/R	= 0.19
eb = 6: 4	es = 10 D = -1	S = 0	H : (H)Hd(Hd)	= 2: 5
	Adj es = 9 Adj D = 0	Blends:R = 9:21	(HHd) : (AAd)	= 2: 0
		CP = 0	H + A : Hd + Ad	=12: 7
FM = 4 : C' = 1 T = 2				
m = 2 : V = 0 Y = 1				
		P = 5	ZF = 17	3r + (2) / R = 1.14
a : p = 3: 7	Sum6 = 4	X + % = 0.57	Zd = +1.0	Fr + rF = 7
Ma : Mp = 1: 3	Lv2 = 0	F + % = 1.00	W : D : Dd =11 : 7 :3	FD = 1
2AB + Art + Ay = 0	WSum6= 11	X - % = 0.24	W : M = 11 : 4	An + Xy = 2
M– = 1	Mnone = 0	S - % = 0.00	DQ+ = 11	MOR = 1
		Xu % = 0.19	DQv = 0	

SCZI = 2	DEPI = 3	CDI = 4*	S–CON = 4	HVI = No	OBS = No

FIGURE 5.2. Structural summary for Mary Steinman.

she had not developed a preferred or predictable coping strategy, be it extratensive or introversive. The low Affective Ratio suggested a tendency to avoid emotionality, even though the *FC:CF+C* ratio suggested a lack of stringency in modulating emotional discharge. *T* was elevated, suggesting a sense of loneliness or emotional deprivation. This factor is often found in the protocols of persons who have experienced significant emotional losses.

In the Self-Perception cluster, it was notable that she provided us with no fewer than seven Reflections, suggesting a narcissisticlike tendency to overvalue personal worth. At the least, we can suggest extreme self-focus. More boldly, we might wish to consider the presence of pathological narcissism. Additionally, the $H:(H)+Hd+(Hd)$ of 2:5 suggested that the self-image was based more on fantasy than reality. These persons often have very distorted notions about themselves. In the Interpersonal Perceptions and Relations cluster, it was significant that the $a:p$ ratio was 3:7, suggesting that she took a passive role in interpersonal relationships. Further, we were again drawn to the positive Coping Deficit Index and the elevated T, which implied difficulties in everyday living as well as a persistent sense of loneliness and neediness, leaving her vulnerable to the manipulations of others.

A review of the Cognitive Triad will begin with Information Processing, which describes the style with which an individual acquires information. In this cluster there was a variable that likely described a cardinal disposition. Specifically, Lambda was 0.24. Lambda is an index that reveals the proportion of pure-form determinant responses to the determinants of all other responses. When the value for Lambda is less than 0.31, it is likely that a patient becomes more involved with stimuli than is common for most people. This patient was likely to be influenced by excessive involvement with affect and/or ideation. There was very little "psychological resting." She did not simplify her world to make it less demanding. Rather, her world was likely to be unnecessarily complex. This finding was of significant import in understanding the psychological functioning of this person.

The Cognitive Mediation cluster describes the patient's manner of translating information input. The number of Popular responses was about average, suggesting that acceptable responses were likely to occur in obvious situations. However, the relatively low $X+\%$ (less than 70%) suggested a higher-than-usual frequency of behaviors that disregard social demands. There may have been a tendency to be somewhat unconventional in translating input from her environment.

The Ideation or "thinking style" cluster refocused us on the ambitency, suggesting inconsistency in ideation. Especially significant to this patient's psychodynamics was the fact that Mp was 2 points greater than Ma, suggesting that flight into fantasy has become a routine tactic for avoiding unpleasantness. In addition, this finding suggested a marked tendency to avoid responsibility and decision making. Fantasy, then, abused to excess, allowed her to deny reality. Finally, the $RawSum6$ of 4 combined with a $WSum6$ of 11 suggested slippery thinking and/or faulty conceptualizations.

Clinical Integration of MCMI-III and Rorschach

In this section an attempt will be made to integrate the findings of the MCMI-III and the Rorschach. The method of integration employs the various suggestions of Lovitt (1993) and Acklin (1993) and aims at interpreting the person, not the tests. Mindful that ours is a clinical science (Millon, 1996), the purpose of the integration is to identify themes or characteristics that may be relevant to the treatment and clinical management of the patients. The integration focuses on aggregates of data that appear to describe themes or general characteristics of the patients which may be clinically useful. In this first case, six predominant themes emerged. These six themes were: loss and defensive efforts to protect against loss, passive dependence, inadequate object representations, coping deficits, a disorder of self, and the likelihood of interpersonal difficulties.

Loss and Defense against Loss

A key feature in Ms. Steinman's life was the early loss of her mother and her continued experience of this loss. She was at once needy and avoidant. Both the MCMI-III and the

Rorschach revealed evidence of this loss theme. On the MCMI-III, the Depressive and Avoidant scales were elevated. Both depressive and avoidant individuals have often experienced a significant loss of some kind. The depressive personality style represents a sort of psychological "given up," whereas the Avoidant scale measures an active avoidance of close interpersonal relationships to protect against the pain of loss. Avoidant patients are always on guard, ready to distance themselves from life's painful experiences. Their avoidant strategy reflects their fear and mistrust of others. They maintain a constant vigil lest their impulses and longing for affection result in a repetition of the pain and anguish they have previously experienced with others. Only by withdrawing can they protect themselves. Despite their desires to relate, they have learned that it is best do to deny these feelings and to keep a good measure of interpersonal distance.

Two Rorschach variables may have been of relevance to Mary's depressive/avoidant theme. One was the presence of two Texture responses ($T = 2$). According to Exner (1986), persons with elevated T tend to have heightened needs for closeness and they apparently experience intense feelings of loneliness or stronger-than-usual needs to be dependent on others. The intensity of this neediness may have been provoked by recent emotional loss, or the intensity could represent a chronic state which perpetuates this need because an early loss was never compensated.

At the risk of being overly speculative, we may also cite Mary's low Affective Ratio of 0.24. When the Affective Ratio falls below 0.44 in adults, there is a possibility that the individual has a decided tendency to avoid emotional situations. Are there possible links among early losses, avoidance tendencies in general, and avoidance of emotional situations? Are not many close personal relationships emotional as well? Could the low Affective Ratio be related to the theme of loss and protection against further loss?

Thus, there appears to be a grouping of variables consisting of early loss (by history), a depressive "given up" personality style (Depressive scale), high dependence (Dependence scale), active avoidance (Avoidance scale), heightened needs for closeness ($T = 2$), acute need for succorance (high Edwards Succorance scale score), and avoidance of emotionality (low Affective Ratio). This aggregate of variables depicted an extremely needy, vulnerable, lonely person. We may speculate that she was so needy that it was unlikely that anyone would be able to meet all of her needs. This may have created a state of constant irritation, emptiness, dissatisfaction, and depression.

Passive Dependence

Ms. Steinman was passively dependent. The MCMI-III and Rorschach indexed this characteristic well. Persons who are high on the MCMI-III Dependent scale have learned not only to turn to others as their source of nurturance and security, but also to wait passively for their leadership in providing these emotional supplies. They are characterized by a search for relationships in which they can lean on others for affection, security, and guidance. They have learned the comfort of assuming a passive role in interpersonal relations. Indeed, the Dependence scale clearly measures tendencies toward the passive side of Millon's active–passive polarity. Although distrustful and avoidant, Mary was highly dependent, needy for the attention and affection of other people.

On the Rorschach, the *a:p* ratio was 3:7. This indicated that she was likely to assume a passive, although not necessarily submissive, role in interpersonal relationships. Further, the *Ma:Mp* ratio on the Rorschach was 1:3. This suggested an entrenched cognitive style in which flight into fantasy had become a routine tactic for managing unpleasant situations. Fantasy or escapist thinking was routine. Exner (1991) labeled this coping style the

"Snow White Syndrome" because Snow White waited passively for her prince to come. Ms. Steinman added a new twist to this concept when she told her therapist, "When my prince comes he will probably be a toad."

Finally, we must not forget that one of the interpretations of elevated T is that these persons have a driving need for closeness. The strength of this need makes them vulnerable to the manipulations of others. This is especially true for subjects who are either passive or dependent. Thus, Ms. Steinman's passivity and, to some extent, the dependence as well, suggested by the $a{:}p$ and $Ma{:}Mp$ ratios and elevated T, was not unlike the passive dependence we see in persons high on the MCMI-III Dependent scale. These persons withdraw from adult responsibilities, they act (and feel) helpless, and they wait to receive nurturance from others.

Deficient Object Representations

Ms. Steinman seemed to have a strong interest in other people as indicated by her high number of human responses, but her (H) ratio indicated that she did not understand them very well. Interpretively, she was inclined to attempt to understand others more on the basis of imagination than reality.

Millon describes the object representations of the borderline patient as incompatible. For the dependent patient, object representations are immature and unsophisticated, composed of infantile impressions of others. For the depressive, object relations are drained of their richness. For the avoidant, they are vexatious and conflict ridden. Exner (1991) does not address Rorschach indicators of object relations. However, other Rorschach systematizers (e.g., Blatt & H. Lerner, 1983; P. Lerner, 1991) have developed methods of assessing the richness and accuracy of human percepts which presumably reveal something about the subject's own object representations. Hence, a review of the human responses, even in the Comprehensive System, may yield some information about object relations. Further, when reviewing the Interpersonal Perception and Relations cluster, Exner (1991) instructs us to read the responses containing human contents.

In Ms. Steinman's case it is notable that she gave only two whole human, H, responses. The remaining seven human responses were derogated human percepts. The first H response, given to Card II, was "A mirror down the center, a person kneeling with their hands and knees against the mirror, mirror image." The other, given to Card VI was, "Somebody sitting on a bank reflecting in the water with some weeds." Thus, the only two H responses are fairly sterile, plus they were Reflections, suggesting some distortion or confusion in the relationship between self and other people. It is difficult to perpetuate the belief that one is "precious" when one is encapsulated in a social vacuum. So it would seem that there may be some accord between the MCMI-III and Rorschach with regard to describing deficiencies in this patient's object representations.

Disorder of Self

Another MCMI-III–Rorschach grouping suggested a disorder of self. The Borderline scale suggested an uncertain self-image, a wavering sense of identity, and underlying feelings of emptiness. The Self-Defeating scale implied a distorted self-image as well as a failed sense of self. Additionally, the seven Reflections on the Rorschach suggested seriously faulty perceptions of self. The lopsided $H{:}(H)+Hd+(Hd)$ ratio of 2:5 suggested that the self-image was based more on imagination than on reality. Finally, the elevated $An+Xy$ raised a question about rumination over body integrity and/or self-image.

Interpersonal Difficulties

Both the MCMI-III and Rorschach predicted interpersonal difficulties. Dependent, passive–aggressive, and borderline patients are notorious for their problems in interpersonal relationships. The Rorschach Interpersonal Perception and Relations cluster includes several predictors of proneness to interpersonal problems. The positive Coping Deficit Index, interpersonal passivity ($a:p$ = 3:7), elevated T (vulnerability to manipulation by others), and an absence of Cooperative Movement responses, coupled with one Aggressive response, described a person who did not anticipate positive social interactions.

Coping Problems

The MCMI-III also combines well with the Rorschach in describing considerable difficulties in coping. The very high elevations on Ms. Steinman's Self-Defeating, Depressive, Avoidant, and Dependent scales were darkened by the significant elevation on the Borderline scale. In the MCMI-III computer interpretive report for this profile, we see phrases such as: "... a less than satisfactory hierarchy of coping strategies"; "This woman's foundation for effective ... socially acceptable interpersonal conduct appears deficient or incompetent"; "Deficits in her social attainments ..."; "... frustrating setbacks and efforts to achieve a consistent niche in life may have failed"; "... periods of marked emotional, cognitive, or behavioral dysfunction"; "Simple responsibilities may demand more energy than she can muster." These interpretive statements, generated from descriptors within the scale domains, clearly suggested significant problems coping with the usual demands of everyday life.

Complementing the picture of coping problems suggested by the MCMI-III were the following Rorschach variables: a positive Coping Deficit Index, an EA of only 7 (modest resources), $D = -1$ (stimulus overload), too much (H) (not reality based), an $Ma:Mp$ of 1:3 (indicating passive dependence), and ambitency (inconsistency in emotions). Hence, the MCMI-III and Rorschach both suggested considerable difficulties in coping.

Now this case will be discussed at each level of Acklin's (1993) outline for integration. An exhaustive analysis using this model would, of course, be unwieldy. Hence, each level will be discussed briefly.

Integration at the scale or score level was obvious. There are several instances in which comparisons revealed meaningful covariation (even though previous research with the MMPI and Rorschach suggested that we should not expect much covariation). The passive dependence suggested by the MCMI-III Dependent scale was supported by the Rorschach $a:p$ ratio of 3:7 and by the $Ma:Mp$ ratio of 1:3. The deficient object representations suggested by the MCMI-III Borderline and Dependent scales were also implied by the small number of whole human, H, responses and their sparse quality. This was also the case for the indices of distorted sense of self, interpersonal difficulties, and coping deficits.

The test-by-test, additive approach was easily employed in this case as well. The Rorschach material generally complemented the picture described by the MCMI-III. As Weiner (1993) pointed out, self-report and projective instruments tend to assess different levels of conscious awareness regarding the importance of what patients are being asked and the implications of how they chose to respond. The test media constitute different lenses through which the person is viewed. In this case the projective material embellished the material obtained from the self-report scale. For example, the lack of emotional satisfaction in interpersonal relationships described by the MCMI-III Avoidant/Depressive/Dependent "triad" was reinforced by the Rorschach finding that the patient had two *T* responses, suggesting loneliness and a sense of emotional deprivation.

Integration at the level of the construct is more difficult. Constructs are interpretive foci that organize data at higher levels of generalization than does the individual score. In this case, as would be true of most cases, analysis of the data from the level of the construct rapidly becomes extremely complex. A construct that might be relevant to this case is Rotter's locus of control (1966). The overall MCMI-III pattern suggests that Ms. Steinman had an external locus of control. Descriptors taken from within the elevated scale domains were "helpless, passive, seeking nurturance from others, seeking protection, fearing being left to care for self, sees self as socially inept, feels vulnerable, obsequious, and accepting undeserved blame." These characteristics are not typical of an individual having high internal locus of control.

On the Rorschach the *a:p* and *Ma:Mp* ratios described a passive person who was disinclined to take responsibility for making decisions or seeking new solutions to problems. Individuals with this profile exhibit a self-imposed helplessness and they overly utilize fantasy to avoid unpleasant situations. Again, these are not typical characteristics of persons having a high internal locus of control. Though an extensive discussion of the construct of locus of control is beyond the scope of this chapter, it nevertheless seems reasonably apparent that it would be fairly easy to integrate the MCMI-III and Rorschach data around this concept.

Finally, Acklin (1993) suggests that we might integrate at the level of theory. A theory that seems especially relevant to this case is, of course, object relations theory. There appear to have been serious deficiencies in this woman's internalized representations of self and, for that matter, others. The clinical and psychometric data in this case could easily be interpreted, organized, and expressed in terms of object relations theory. It is clear that the early death of Ms. Steinman's mother, the borderline tendencies revealed by the MCMI-III, and the relatively deficient human percepts on the Rorschach are factors readily integrated within the context of contemporary object relations theory.

Dealing with Inconsistencies

Although the picture hangs together rather well, Lovitt (1993) reminded us that we should account for inconsistencies among different tests by utilizing personality constructs to facilitate synthesis. He also advises us to employ scientific restraint in this exercise. Hence, at this point, let us examine two major contradictions between the MCMI-III and the Rorschach, the issues of pathological narcissism and depression.

The eye is drawn to Ms. Steinman's seven Reflection responses on the Rorschach, a truly remarkable figure. Statistically, even one Reflection in a Rorschach record is sufficient to suggest that a nuclear element in the subject's self-image is a narcissisticlike feature marked by a tendency to overvalue personal worth. Yet the MCMI-III Scale 5 (Narcissism) is very low. How does one account for the lack of agreement between the two instruments on this dimension?

Perhaps it is best to begin by reaffirming that no test is infallible. The MCMI-III simply may have missed the presence of pathological narcissism. Alternatively, the presence of Reflection responses (one or more) on the Rorschach may not always be an indication of narcissism or even exaggerated self-focus. Further, interpretations of the Reflection response and the Egocentricity index as measures of narcissism are presently being vigorously challenged (Nezworski & Wood, 1995). Although Exner's (1995) rebuttal was sound, psychometric common sense leads us to conclude that any given sign or score, with adequate concurrent validity statistics, *may* provide evidence of any given trait or characteristic, but our interpretation must always remain inferential, not deductive. It is also important to recognize that identical terms in psychology often refer to different constructs. Further, various measures may tap differing aspects of a complex construct. It may be helpful to examine the concept of narcissism more closely.

According to Kernberg (1985), narcissistic patients exhibit an unusual degree of self-reference in their interactions with other people. They also suffer a great need to be loved and admired by others; yet, curiously, they harbor very inflated concepts of themselves and an inordinate need for tribute from others. Further, Kernberg (1986) and others (Kohut, 1977; Masterson, 1993) have all described the distinction between overt (grandiose) and covert (depleted) forms of narcissism. The *grandiose* narcissist is exhibitionistic and overt. The *depleted* narcissist is drained, depressed, and covert.

Rathvon and Holmstrom published an article in 1996 that further clarifies this issue. They performed a factor-analytic study of several measures of narcissism which revealed two orthogonal factors. They named these two factors "Narcissistic Grandiosity" and "Narcissistic Depletion." A reading of the MCMI-III Narcissism scale items reveals that these items generally describe the *grandiose* narcissist, for example, item 5: "I know I'm a superior person, so I don't care what people think." Our patient did not fit the description of the grandiose narcissist. She was much more like the depleted, depressed, covert narcissist. Also recall her first response given to Rorschach Card II: "A mirror down the center, a person kneeling with their hands and knees against the mirror, mirror image." This response seemed to be more consistent with narcissistic depletion than grandiosity. Hence, the theory combined with research clarifies the interpretation in this case.

Another possible contradiction in this case was the issue of depression. Despite the evidence of depression on the MCMI-III, Ms. Steinman's Rorschach Depression Index was not positive. In view of her tendency to overreport on the MCMI-III, the absence of the positive Depression Index on the Rorschach was clinically significant. I am not ready to conclude that Ms. Steinman was not depressed, but her Axis II problems, so clearly revealed by the MCMI-III, appeared to be of greatest import. These problems likely contributed substantially to her pervasive sense of emptiness and unhappiness and, consequently, may have provoked depressivelike affect.

This case serves to illustrate how the MCMI-III and the Rorschach can be used in tandem when making decisions regarding the relative primacy of Axis I or Axis II disorder. This sad and unfortunate woman was presenting clinically with Axis I symptomatology, but the MCMI-III revealed a crippling amount of Axis II pathology, particularly of the borderline type. She appeared to be suffering from a depression that might be in the clinical range, but the Axis II symptomatology emerged as the major difficulty. Because of this, therapy was redirected to focus on Axis II issues. Treatment included supportive psychotherapy employing a modification of Masterson's (1976) approach to focusing on issues of self, assisted by dialectical behavior therapy (Linehan, 1993) for skill development, along with antidepressant medication having an anxiolytic effect.

Case 2. Brutus McLean

Brutus McLean was a 40-year-old white male who was assessed after experiencing amnesia following a blow to the head suffered during an automobile accident. The accident occurred after Mr. McLean became enraged with another driver who allegedly pulled in front of him as he was driving home from work after his day job. The driver then stopped to make a left turn after traffic from the opposite lane had passed. Mr. McLean, in his rage, saw fit to maintain highway speed and drove into the rear of the offending vehicle (now stopped to make the left turn) under full steam. Both cars were totalled, and Mr. McLean was thrown through the windshield of his vehicle. He was taken to an emergency room for immediate treatment, and was then transferred to a psychiatric inpatient setting for 3 days' observation of his amnesiac condition. He was then released to outpatient care with the provision that he would undergo comprehensive psychological assessment of his emotional and functional deficits. A psychological test battery was administered consisting of an MCMI-III, an MMPI-2, the Rorschach, the WAIS-R, and a Wechsler Memory Scale—Revised (WMS-R). At that point further neuropsychological testing was planned, but the patient reported that his amnesiac state had cleared and insisted that he be released.

The WAIS-R revealed a Verbal IQ of 93, a Performance IQ of 98, and a Full Scale IQ of 95. There was no remarkable scatter on the Subtest scale scores except a rather low score, in comparison with his overall IQ score, of 6 on Information. On the WMS-R, his General Memory Index was 89. Verbal Memory index was 83, Visual Memory index was 111, Attention Concentration index was 108, and Delayed Recall index was 100.

Mr. McLean described himself as a "workaholic." He explained that he arrived at work at 7 A.M. Monday through Friday and worked until 3:30 P.M. He would then rush home, take a quick shower, gulp down his supper (eaten alone), and rush off to his second job, where he worked from 4:30 P.M. to midnight. He worked a third job all day Saturday and Sunday. He was described by himself and his family as "always in a rage." His wife and children were alienated from him, and the children were urging her to divorce him.

The MCMI-III profile is summarized in Figure 5.3.

The reader can see that there was a moderate tendency to exaggerate the level of emotional discomfort. However, in the context of his clinical situation, the elevations on the Disclosure and Debasement scales did not appear to be excessive. Among the clinical personality patterns there were prominent elevations on the Schizoid and Depressive scales, which suggested that he experienced life as empty and unrewarding. Few things in his life gave him pleasure. He may have attempted to be indifferent to his social environment, including his family. He was unlikely to be introspective and sensitive to the subtleties of emotional life. It is possible that he exhibited poor judgment in assessing social relationships. He was likely to be isolated and distanced from others, being unable to elicit and/or receive emotional support and kindness. Socially, he might have been described as peripheral and marginal. His depression may have had a muted quality marked by anhedonia and a sense of void. Basic emotional needs were ignored and left unmet.

Also present were clinical elevations on the Avoidant, Aggressive, Passive–Aggressive, and Self-Defeating scales. We may anticipate, then, that there was an active quality to his efforts to maintain his isolation. Aggressive tendencies may have been expressed as resentment, cynicism, and negativistic tantrums. He might have been described as irritable, contentious, touchy, belligerent, sullen, and moody. The defensive mechanism of displacement may have been used liberally, as manifested by his taking out frustration on family members and other targets somewhat removed from the real object of his rage. He masochistically inverted pleasure and pain, believing that there was merit to deprivation and suffering. He likely dwelled on past injustices and anticipated disappointment and frustration in the future. Though he was his own worst enemy, nevertheless, he blamed his troubles on others.

This sad and cranky man presented with dysthymia. He was likely to be continuously gloomy, empty, lonely, and needy. However, the schizoid, avoidant, aggressive, and passive–aggressive personality characteristics kept even loving and caring family members well at bay. Finding himself increasingly isolated, his anger and resentment increased,

MILLON CLINICAL MULTIAXIAL INVENTORY - III
CONFIDENTIAL INFORMATION FOR PROFESSIONAL USE ONLY

ID NUMBER: 82057   Valid Profile
PERSONALITY CODE: 1 2B ** 8A 2A 6B 8B * 3 + 6A 5 7 " 4 ' ' // - ** - * //
SYNDROME CODE: - ** D * // - ** - * //
DEMOGRAPHIC: 82057/ON/M/37/W/F/12/JO/MD/297/02/3017/

CATEGORY		SCORE		PROFILE OF BR SCORES					DIAGNOSTIC SCALES
		RAW	BR	0	60	75	85	115	
MODIFYING INDICES	X	128	77						DISCLOSURE
	Y	9	43						DESIRABILITY
	Z	19	76						DEBASEMENT
CLINICAL PERSONALITY PATTERNS	1	19	104						SCHIZOID
	2A	12	79						AVOIDANT
	2B	16	99						DEPRESSIVE
	3	7	63						DEPENDENT
	4	3	11						HISTRIONIC
	5	11	47						NARCISSISTIC
	6A	8	58						ANTISOCIAL
	6B	18	78						AGGRESSIVE (SADISTIC)
	7	13	44						COMPULSIVE
	8A	17	83						PASSIVE-AGGRESSIVE
	8B	8	75						SELF-DEFEATING
SEVERE PERSONALITY PATHOLOGY	S	9	67						SCHIZOTYPAL
	C	7	59						BORDERLINE
	P	11	67						PARANOID
CLINICAL SYNDROMES	A	4	73						ANXIETY DISORDER
	H	8	67						SOMATOFORM DISORDER
	N	7	62						BIPOLAR: MANIC DISORDER
	D	14	82						DYSTHYMIC DISORDER
	B	3	43						ALCOHOL DEPENDENCE
	T	3	43						DRUG DEPENDENCE
	R	6	61						POST-TRAUMATIC STRESS
SEVERE SYNDROMES	SS	8	63						THOUGHT DISORDER
	CC	12	70						MAJOR DEPRESSION
	PP	3	61						DELUSIONAL DISORDER

FIGURE 5.3. MCMI-III profile for Brutus McLean.

fueling his explosiveness, thus driving the knife of anger ever deeper into family love relationships. This man, hurt and complex, seemed unaware of ways he might break out of
this perpetual self-destruction, and he persisted in his masochistic health- and relationship-
breaking work schedule.

The results of the testing with the Rorschach are summarized in Figure 5.4.

The Schizophrenia, Depression, and Coping Deficit Indices were all negative. However, the Suicide Constellation was 7. Actuarially, we would not be able to predict lethality

TEST DATE: 14 Jul 1995   GRP: CAT: ID: FILE:
NAME: CASE #8,   AGE: 37   SEX: M   RACE: MS: Married   ED: 12

STRUCTURAL SUMMARY

LOCATION FEATURES

Zf	=	14
ZSum	=	49.5
ZEst	=	45.5
W	=	9
(Wv=0)		
D	=	13
Dd	=	1
S	=	2

DQ
.............(FQ-)
+   = 10 (1)
o   = 13 (3)
v/+ = 0   (0)
v   = 0   (0)

FORM QUALITY

	FQx	FQf	MQual	SQx
+	= 0	0	0	0
o	=15	3	4	1
u	= 4	0	1	0
-	= 4	1	0	1
none	= 0	—	0	0

DETERMINANTS

BLENDS

M.FC
Fr.M.CF
FM.CF
CF.FV
FM.FY
m.CF

SINGLE

M	=	3
FM	=	4
m	=	1
FC	=	2
CF	=	0
C	=	0
Cn	=	0
FC'	=	1
C'F	=	0
C'	=	0
FT	=	0
TF	=	0
T	=	0
FV	=	0
VF	=	0
V	=	0
FY	=	2
YF	=	0
Y	=	0
Fr	=	0
rF	=	0
FD	=	0
F	=	4

(2) = 8

CONTENTS

H	= 1,	0
(H)	= 1,	0
Hd	= 4,	1
(Hd)	= 0,	0
Hx	= 0,	0
A	=10,	0
(A)	= 0,	0
Ad	= 1,	1
(Ad)	= 1,	0
An	= 0,	0
Art	= 0,	0
Ay	= 1,	0
Bl	= 0,	1
Bt	= 1,	0
Cg	= 0,	2
Cl	= 0,	0
Ex	= 0,	0
Fd	= 1,	1
Fi	= 0,	0
Ge	= 0,	0
Hh	= 0,	1
Ls	= 1,	1
Na	= 0,	0
Sc	= 0,	0
Sx	= 0,	0
Xy	= 1,	0
Id	= 0,	0

S–CONSTELLATION

NO...FV+VF+V+FD > 2
YES...Col-Shd Bl > 0
YES...Ego < .31 , > .44
NO...MOR > 3
YES...Zd > +- 3.5
YES...es > EA
YES...CF+C > FC
YES...X+% < .70
NO...S > 3
NO...P < 3 or > 8
YES...Pure H < 2
NO...R < 17
7......TOTAL

SPECIAL SCORINGS

		LV1	LV2
DV	=	0x1	0x2
INC	=	1x2	0x4
DR	=	0x3	0x6
FAB	=	0x4	0x7
ALOG	=	0x5	
CON	=	0x7	
SUM6	= 1		
WSUM6	= 2		

AB	= 0		CP	=	0
AG	= 1		MOR	=	1
CFB	= 0		PER	=	3
COP	= 1		PSV	=	0

RATIOS, PERCENTAGES, AND DERIVATIONS

R = 23   L = 0.21

EB = 5: 5.5   EA = 10.5   EBPer = N/A
eb = 8: 5   es = 13   D = 0
               Adj es = 10 Adj D = 0

FM = 6 : C' = 1   T = 0
m = 2   : V = 1   Y = 3

a : p   = 4: 9
Ma : Mp   = 1: 4
2AB + Art + Ay = 1
M–   = 0

FC : CF + C = 3: 4   COP = 1   AG = 1
Pure C   = 0   Food   = 2
Afr   = 0.64   Isolate/R   = 0.13
S   = 2   H : (H)Hd(Hd)   = 1: 6
Blends:R   = 6:23   (HHd) : (AAd)   = 1: 1
CP   = 0   H + A : Hd + Ad   =12: 8

P	= 4	ZF	=	14	3r + (2) / R = 0.48
X + %	= 0.65	Zd	=	+4.0	Fr + rF = 1
F + %	= 0.75	W : D : Dd = 9 : 13 : 1			FD = 0
X - %	= 0.17	W : M	=	9 : 5	An + Xy = 1
S - %	= 0.25	DQ+	=	10	MOR = 1
Xu %	= 0.17	DQv	=	0	

Sum6 = 1
Lv2 = 0
WSum6= 2
Mnone = 0

SCZI = 1   DEPI = 3   CDI = 3   S–CON = 7   HVI = Yes   OBS = No

FIGURE 5.4. Structural summary for Brutus McLean.

because the index was less than 8. However, a responsible clinician would be especially sensitive to any signs of suicidal ideation or behavior.

The Structural Summary indicated that we begin our search with the Self-Perception cluster. Here we find a Reflection response suggesting, at least, an exaggerated degree of self-focus as well as the possibility of a narcissistic core with its self-centered life view. This, of course, inflated the Egocentricity Index. In addition the *H:(H)+Hd+(Hd)* ratio of 1:6

suggests that Mr. McLean's self-image was based more on imagination than reality. The presence of a Vista response suggested that this man was engaging in introspection and that this may have led him to focus on the more negative features of his self-image. As a result, he may have been experiencing some degree of negative or painful affect.

In the Interpersonal cluster, it was notable that the Hypervigilance Index was positive, suggesting the presence of a wary and mistrusting attitude. This anticipatory state has its roots in a suspicious attitude toward the environment. He may have felt vulnerable and, as a result, formulate defensive, self-protective behaviors. As "*T*"-lessness is part of the Hypervigilance Index, we may anticipate that he was not likely to experience needs for emotional closeness in ways that were similar to most people. Thus, issues of interpersonal space may have been more important to him than is emotional closeness. Interestingly, he gave three Personal responses, suggesting excessive use of a form of defensive authoritarianism. This may have been done to ward off challenges from others. Further, it may have said something about his degree of interpersonal insecurity, thus serving to fortify his personal safety zone. It is also interesting that the *a:p* ratio was 4:9, suggesting interpersonal passivity and a preference for avoiding responsibility in decision making.

The Cognitive cluster will be reviewed next. With regard to Ideation (thinking style), Mr. McLean was ambient, meaning that he had not developed a preferred style of thinking. This may have resulted in inconsistency and difficulty in reaching decisions. An examination of the *eb* indicated a ratio of 8:5. This important finding suggested that a considerable amount of thinking was outside the realm of focused attention. This can lead to distraction and difficulties in concentration. The flow of deliberate thinking may have been disrupted. Further, the *a:p* ratio of 4:9 suggested that ideational sets and values were well fixed and difficult to alter. Finally, it is of considerable note that the *Ma:Mp* ratio was 1:4, suggesting that a routine coping strategy was a flight into fantasy. This mechanism may have been used to avoid dealing with unpleasant situations. Exner (1991) designated this tendency the "Snow White Syndrome," which is characterized mainly by the avoidance of responsibility and deliberate decision-making. Here fantasy is used to excess, and the main attitude toward life is passive.

Reviewing the Information Processing cluster, we find that Mr. McLean had a "low Lambda" style of acquiring information. This suggested that he may have been more responsive, or may have reacted more strongly, to environmental stimuli than do most people. In addition, the positive Hypervigilance Index suggested that he continually monitored his environment for potential threat, thus remaining constantly wary and guarded. This style requires considerable energy to maintain. Mr. McLean also used an "over-incorporative" style, meaning that a great investment and effort was put into scanning activities. He absorbed a large amount of information from the world, perhaps too much to manage efficiently.

In the Cognitive Mediation cluster, we found some degree of unconventionality. Thus, he may have disregarded social demands or expectations. His may have been a drummer different from most. Finally, there may have been some degree of inaccuracy in perception. There may have been a subclinical but notable degree of distortion, skewing his perceptual input.

Now we turn to affect. Because he was ambient, it is possible that emotions may have been inconsistent in terms of their impact on thinking. Sometimes emotions may play a major role in problem solving and decision making, and sometimes not. Additionally, there may have been some painful affect present, as signified by the *V* response. Emotional discomfort and depression or dysphoria may also have been present. Finally, the Color-Shading blend suggested that Mr. McLean may have found emotions confusing. He may have experienced the same situation in both positive and negative terms. Hence, he may have found it difficult to attain closure in emotionally complex situations.

Clinical Integration of MCMI-III and Rorschach

There are unlimited ways to link the MCMI and Rorschach findings. In Mr. McLean's integrative analysis four predominant themes emerged. These four themes were: depression and discouragement, interpersonal problems, sadomasochism and authoritarianism, and interpersonal neediness and dependence.

Depression and Discouragement

On Mr. McLean's MCMI-III the Dysthymic and Depressive scales were both elevated. Thus, Mr. McLean likely suffered with discouragement or guilt, lack of initiative, pervasive apathy, and low self-esteem. He may have experienced a sense of futility and may have made self-deprecatory comments. These scale elevations suggested dejection, tearfulness, suicidal ideation, pessimism, withdrawal, chronic fatigue, poor concentration, marked loss of interest, and decreased effectiveness in accomplishing the usual demands of life. This sadness resided in a personality marked by gloominess, pessimism, lack of joy, and inability to experience pleasure. Motor retardation may have been present as well. This is a "given up" personality style in which the patient's life view was one of hopelessness and helplessness. Pain was seen as permanent, with pleasure no longer thought possible. The environment was perceived as barren and unforgiving.

The depressive syndrome described by the MCMI-III was supported by several Rorschach variables. One was the Suicide Constellation. This constellation measures lethality, not depression. However, several elements in it are related to depression. Mr. McLean's Suicide Constellation score of 7 did not surpass the cutoff score of 8 needed to predict with actuarial confidence that this man may have been suicidal. However, it is difficult for the clinician to ignore that Mr. McLean was so close to the cutoff of 8. This seems especially paramount in light of the event precipitating this examination—driving his car at full highway speed into the back of a stopped car that had just pulled in front of him. It seems likely that this act was impelled by suicidal or homicidal intent.

Additionally, he gave a Vista response on the Rorschach, which suggests that he was experiencing painful affect resulting from introspection. Also, there were three Y responses which suggest diffuse, painful affect. Finally, his fifth percept on the Rorschach given in response to Card II was as follows: "Could be like me looking in the mirror after the wreck. Blood on my knees, blood on my forehead." This response, scored W+ Fr.Mp.CFo H, Bl 4.5 PER, may have been considered projection. Indeed, little inference was required here, as the subject conveniently identified the percept as himself.

Interpersonal Problems

A second aggregate may be entitled interpersonal problems. His highest MCMI-III elevation on the Personality scales was on the Schizoid scale which describes an "unengaged" interpersonal style. Such persons take on a peripheral role in social, work, and family settings. The next highest score was on the Depressive scale, which suggested that he is interpersonally "defenseless." These persons feel vulnerable, assailable, and unshielded. They fear abandonment and desertion. The elevation on the Passive–Aggressive scale suggested a "contrary" interpersonal style characterized by hostile dependence coupled with feelings of envy and marked by intolerance of others. The elevation on the Aggressive–Sadistic scale suggested an "abrasive" style. The elevated Self-Defeating scale suggested that he may have been interpersonally "deferential," and the elevation on the Avoidant sale suggested that he may have been interpersonally "aversive." Thus, this interpersonally unengaged, defenseless, deferential man may also have been, at times, contrary and abrasive. He was inconsistent and vacillating. It is not surprising that he may have found interpersonal relationships aversive. His interpersonal life must indeed have been complex, complicated, and distressful for him and for others.

The Rorschach, too, suggested difficulties in the interpersonal sphere. He was positive on the Hypervigilance Index, suggesting suspiciousness and guardedness in interpersonal relationships. A component of hypervigilance is, of course, his T-lessness, suggesting considerable concern regarding interpersonal boundaries. The three Personals suggested a defensive authoritarianism in interpersonal relationships to ward off challenges. Although the $(H:H)+Hd+(Hd)$ ratio was not officially in the Comprehensive System Interpersonal cluster, the ratio of 1:6 suggested that this subject tended to base his self-image more on imagination than on real experience, which strengthened the earlier indications of difficulties in interpersonal functioning. Finally, the Reflection response, together with the accompanying high Egocentricity Index, also may have suggested some difficulties in interpersonal functioning. Narcissists do not usually enjoy smooth, satisfying interpersonal relations.

Sadomasochism/Authoritarianism

Next, there appeared to be a sadomasochistic/authoritarian theme. The Aggressive–Sadistic scale represents a reversal in the pleasure–pain polarity, as does the Self-Defeating scale. Subjects with elevations on this scale derive satisfaction from humiliating others as well as violating their rights and feelings. These subjects tend to be aggressive, hostile, and generally combative. They may even be described as abusive and brutal. Additionally, they are often found to be dogmatic, strongly opinionated, closed minded, obstinate, and authoritarian. In another vein, the Passive–Aggressive scale also suggests a contrary, discontented individual whose valences toward significant others vacillate. Hence, they are often described as negativistic, angry, and stubborn. Added to this are descriptions such as resentful, contrary, angry, whiny, hostile, irritable, and sullen. These persons are usually scornful of those in authority.

There are some variables on Mr. McLean's Rorschach that seem to have covaried with his MCMI-III findings. The positive Hypervigilance Index (which by definition involves T-lessness) suggested a hypervigilant style in which there was likely a mistrusting attitude toward others. These persons do not sustain close interpersonal relationships well. They are more concerned with issues of space and distance than they are with closeness. They are guarded and uncomfortable in close relationships. They prefer distance. They do not expect to be close to others and often are suspicious about other's overtures of friendship. Mr. McLean's three Personals suggested an excessive use of defensive authoritarianism to ward off challenges. The $a:p$ of 4:9 suggested, at the least, that his thinking patterns were well fixed (rigid?).

This troubled man, whose emotions might have been described as discordant and ambivalent, was experiencing considerable distress. Indeed, it is interesting that he presented with a Color-Shading blend ($CF.FV$), suggesting a substantial degree of ambivalence.

Interpersonal Neediness and Dependence

Mr. McLean's MCMI Passive–Aggressive scale described a discontented, grumbling, crabby, querulous, grumpy, testy, cantankerous, peevish, touchy, cranky, grouchy, petulant, irascible, gloomy, morose, sullen, temperamental, capricious, and moody individual. His meals must have been delivered on the dot, or he flew into rages. The whole family was expected to be at their battle stations to attend him when he came roaring through the house racing from one job to the other. When he did stop working, he deposited himself in his hammock in the back yard and expected to be waited on. Whatever could have been the source of his ire and discontent?

The Rorschach may help. It is, perhaps, significant that he gave us two Food responses on the Rorschach: "Radishes you get out of the garden" and "Eggs cooking." Food responses are exceedingly rare (in ambient adults $M = .16, SD = .47$, median = 0, mode = 0, range = 0–2) and suggest more dependence behaviors than are usually expected. These people tend to rely on others for direction and support. They also expect others to be tolerant of their needs and demands. This finding, together with an $a:p$ ratio of 4:9, suggested an entrenched, considerably passive–dependent character. Further, his $Ma:Mp$ was 1:4, suggesting the "Snow White Syndrome" in which he substituted fantasy for reality when coping with unpleasant situations. There may have been a tendency to avoid responsibility and decision making coupled with a self-imposed helplessness and dependence. The $H:(H)+(Hd)+Hd$ ratio of 1:6 suggested a tendency to substitute imagination for real experience. He seemed to be, on the one hand, denying pleasure and distancing himself from sources of nurturance, and on the other, craving nurturance while yearning for others to come and take care of him.

Furthermore, the picture revealed extensive conflict. On the one hand, there was abundant evidence of aggressive/sadomasochistic tendencies which suggested a "moving against" strategy as described by Horney. On the other hand, there were the schizoid, avoidant, and to some extent, depressive tendencies which suggested a detached, "moving away" strategy. Together, the MCMI-III and the Rorschach described a man in conflict with himself and the world. In conjunction, the two instruments described a "rough and tough" character with a very needy and dependent character core. We may speculate that his perception of a world without food or warmth may have been a driving force behind his rage responses.

Although the existing research literature does not predict robust covariation between the MCMI-III and Rorschach, the two instruments peering through greatly differing psychological lenses appear to be describing the same "elephant" relatively well.

Now the case will be assessed briefly from the point of Acklin's (1993) levels of integrative analysis. There were multiple examples of test scale–score covariation. For example, the painful affect suggested by elevations on the MCMI-III Dysthymic and Depressive scales seemed to be supported by the V response and three Ys, which suggested emotional irritation and negative affect. Further, the likelihood of interpersonal difficulties suggested by elevations on several of the MCMI-III scales (e.g., Passive–Aggressive) seemed to be corroborated by the Hypervigilance Index, the Personals, and the lopsided $H:(H)+Hd+(Hd)$ ratio of 1:6.

Although there was a substantial amount of covariation between the two instruments, integration at the test level method in this case reveals that each seemed to contribute salient information independent of the other. For example, the MCMI-III measured Mr. McLean's hostility and aggressiveness better than did the Rorschach. Conversively, the

Rorschach sensitized us to his (oral?) dependence and neediness. Whereas the MCMI-III identified his isolation better than did the Rorschach, the Rorschach detected his passivity better than did the MCMI-III. Thus, the test-by-test method was additive.

Integration at the construct level is complex. There seems to be an almost limitless number of constructs that might be relevant to this case. One that might be considered is the construct of authoritarianism. Adorno, Frenkel-Brunswik, Levinson, and Sanford (1950) conducted extensive work on this construct shortly after World War II. Their purpose was to investigate components of personality that make individuals open to fascist policies and practices, particularly antisemitism. Several research scales were developed in this research project including the F scale, which assessed the subject's potential for fascism. Eysenck's (1954) work on "tough mindedness" has considerable relevance to the construct of authoritarianism. Some years later, Rokeach (1960) developed a Dogmatism scale to assess authoritarianism independent of ideological commitments.

There are findings in both Mr. McLean's MCMI-III and his Rorschach that are of relevance to the construct of authoritarianism. For example, Mr. McLean had an elevation on the MCMI-III Aggressive–Sadistic scale. Some of the descriptors for this scale are: dogmatic, strongly opinionated, closed minded, obstinate, and authoritarian. According to the MCMI-III manual (Millon, 1994), the aggressive–sadistic character is akin to the competitively striving "Type A" personality, or "aggressive personalities." Further, Mr. McLean had a significant elevation on the Passive–Aggressive scale. It can be argued with some confidence that some of the characteristics of persons with an elevation on this scale fall into the realm of authoritarianism. For example, they are resistant to fulfilling the expectations of others. They are envious of the attainments of others. They are cynical and doubting, and they degrade the achievements of others. They express disdain and caustic comments toward those who experience good fortune. These characteristics are not exactly authoritarianism, but they reflect a resentment or reaction to authority which is, in effect, an authoritarian stance itself.

The Rorschach also provided some test data suggesting Mr. McLean's authoritarian characteristics. Consider the defensive authoritarianism suggested by the three Personals. Consider, also, the positive Hypervigilance Index. This index does not directly lead to the interpretation of authoritarianism. However, the paranoid manifestations that are sometimes observed in this condition are known to have an authoritarian quality. This picture is augmented by his responses to the Incomplete Sentences, not reported completely herein. A few examples will suffice:

I hate . . . my boss.
I don't like men . . . who push me around.
When the going gets rough, I . . . get mad.
When others disagree with me . . . I get mad.

In short, investigators interested in assessing the construct of authoritarianism in this case would find adequate material in both pools of data.

Integration at the level of theory is difficult in most cases, including this one. However, because Millon's theory is so inclusive and integrative, the task is made easier. Consider, for example, the interpersonal theories of Benjamin (1993) and Kiesler (1986). Millon's integrative theory encompasses interpersonal theory. There are primary and secondary descriptors of the interpersonal "stance" or "attitude" for each of the MCMI-III personality scales. Mr. McLean had marked elevations on the Schizoid, Depressive, Passive–Aggressive, Avoidant, Aggressive, and Self-Defeating scales, in that order. Primary adjectives describing the interpersonal stance for each of these personality styles listed in the above order are: unengaged, defenseless, contrary, aversive, abrasive, and deferential. This aggregate of six descriptors suggests enormous interpersonal complexity, conflict, and confusion. The interpersonal characteristics of Mr. McLean would be of considerable interest to proponents of the interpersonal school of personality and psychotherapy.

Turning to the Rorschach Interpersonal Perception and Relations cluster, we find a positive Hypervigilance Index which suggested an interpersonal anticipatory state, mistrustfulness, and feelings of vulnerability, guardedness, and even paranoid-like qualities. Mr. McLean's lack of Texture responses suggested preoccupation with issues of interpersonal space and the need to maintain distance. He would probably have been uncomfortable in close interpersonal relationships. However, he gave two Food responses, suggesting dependence. This likely resulted in conflict situations in which he wanted to take from others while remaining distant from them. The three Personals suggested an authoritarian defensiveness in interpersonal relationships. Yet the *a:p* ratio of 4:9 suggested interpersonal passivity. Again, we see remarkable complexity, confusion, and conflict in this picture of this patient's social stance that would no doubt be of some interest to investigators sympathetic to the interpersonal school of psychology and psychotherapy. An extended discussion of this matter is beyond the scope of this chapter. However, it seems rather clear that an integration of the test results at the theory level might be relatively straightforward, at least in the realm of interpersonal theory.

Dealing with Inconsistencies

Now, as Lovitt (1993) instructs, we must also account for inconsistencies. As always, there are inconsistencies. Three will be discussed briefly. The first is that although Mr. McLean's MCMI-III Schizoid and Avoidant scales suggested isolation (which was indeed present clinically), the Rorschach Isolation index was not positive. This inconsistency was not particularly troubling, especially because this was such a complex man. He would likely have been socially isolated at times and more gregarious at others. Passive–aggressive and sadistic people need others to be passive–aggressive and sadistic with!

Second, although Mr. McLean's MCMI-III Aggressive and Passive–Aggressive scales predicted overt aggression, there was only one Aggressive response on the Rorschach. Aggression is very difficult to measure. By definition, aggressiveness implies some degree of intent. Intent also is very difficult to assess. Another problem in measuring aggressiveness is that it may depend on time. Aggressiveness may be a state or a trait. In view of these difficulties, it seems best to conclude that the MCMI-III was more sensitive to Mr. McLean's aggressive tendencies than was the Rorschach. However, despite some inconsistencies, both tests provided a reasonably good picture of this man's prickliness and belligerence.

A third matter is that the Rorschach revealed a Reflection response suggesting narcissism, whereas the MCMI-III did not reveal a significant elevation on Narcissism. However, as was the case with Mary Steinman, we may argue that the narcissism measured by the Rorschach Reflection response may assess a more dynamically complex phenomenon than does the MCMI-III Narcissism scale. However, as argued above, narcissism is a very complex phenomenon. Further, it is very possible that the Rorschach and MCMI-III measure varying dimensions of the concept. Also, recall that Mr. McLean's Reflection response was, "Could be like me looking in the mirror after the wreck. Blood on my knees and forehead." As argued above, this response appears to suggest more depletion than grandiosity, and the MCMI-III Narcissism scale seems to measure the grandiose qualities of narcissism.

Overall, it is my opinion that the two instruments, interpreted in tandem, provided a rather accurate picture of Mr. McLean's personality and psychopathology as observed in an independent clinical evaluation.

SUMMARY

There are many other fascinating and challenging MCMI-III–Rorschach integrative matters to be addressed in these two case studies, but space is limited, and these matters must be left unaddressed. Although both instruments have a substantial research base, there is little in the literature about the relationship between the MCMI-III and the Rorschach. Further, there are few models available for guiding the clinician in the principles of integration. The task is difficult, but the few available models for integration are useful. Acklin (1993) made our task easier when he reminded us that basically we interpret persons, not tests. Lovitt (1993) mirrors this in emphasizing that the individual practitioner must engage in a variety of novel operations to produce the assessment product. Although there are common principles for integration, the clinician begins each case anew, weaving together idiographic and nomothetic principles in an attempt to understand the person being studied.

It seems that integrating the MCMI-III and Rorschach is no more, and no less, difficult than integrating other instruments. Further, because both instruments measure enduring personality styles, the integration and comparisons are in some ways easier for these two instruments. Finally, because both measures are style indicators, future research may reveal greater MCMI-III–Rorschach covariation than will, say, MMPI-2–Rorschach research, because many of the dimensions available for investigation clearly meet Atkinson's (1986) criteria for "conceptual" comparative research.

ACKNOWLEDGMENTS

I would like to thank Stephanie Tilden Dorr for her editorial assistance in preparing this chapter.

REFERENCES

Acklin, M. W. (1993). Integrating the Rorschach and the MMPI in clinical assessment: Conceptual and methodological issues. *Journal of Personality Assessment, 60*(1), 125–131.

Adorno, T. W., Frenkel-Brunswik, E., Levinson, D. J., & Sanford, R. N. (1950). *The authoritarian personality.* New York: Harper & Row.

Aiken, L. R. (1994). *Psychological testing and assessment* (8th ed.). Needham Heights, MA: Allyn & Bacon.

Archer, R. P., & Krishnamurthy, R. (1993a). A review of MMPI and Rorschach interrelationships in adult samples. *Journal of Personality Assessment, 61*(2), 277–293.

Archer, R. P., & Krishnamurthy, R. (1993b). Combining the Rorschach and the MMPI in the assessment of adolescents. *Journal of Personality Assessment, 60*(1), 132–140.

Atkinson, L. (1986). The comparative validities of the Rorschach and MMPI: A meta-analysis. *Canadian Psychology, 27,* 238–247.

Benjamin, L. S. (1993). *Interpersonal diagnosis and treatment of personality disorders.* New York: Guilford Press.

Blatt, S., Brenneis, D., Schimek, J., & Glick, M. (1976). *A developmental analysis of the concept of the object on the Rorschach.* Unpublished manuscript, Yale University.

Blatt, S. J., & Lerner, H. D. (1983). The psychological assessment of object representation. *Journal of Personality Assessment, 47*, 7–28.

Choca, J. P., Shanley, L. A., & Van Denburg, E. (1992). *Interpretive guide to the Millon Clinical Multiaxial Inventory.* Washington, DC: American Psychological Association.

Dougherty, R. J., & Lesswing, J. (1989). Inpatient cocaine abusers: An analysis of psychological and demographic variables. *Journal of Substance Abuse Treatment, 6*, 45–47.

Eysenck, H. J. (1954). *The psychology of politics.* London: Routledge & Kegan Paul.

Exner, J. E., Jr. (1986). *The Rorschach: A comprehensive system: Vol 1. Basic foundations* (2nd ed.). New York: Wiley.

Exner, J. E., Jr. (1991). *The Rorschach: A comprehensive system* (Vol. 2, 2nd ed.). New York: Wiley.

Exner, J. E., Jr. (1995). Comment on "Narcissism in the Comprehensive System for the Rorschach." *Clinical Psychology: Science and Practice, 2*, 200–206.

Ganellen, R. J. (1996). *Integrating the Rorschach and the MMPI-2 in personality assessment.* Mahwah, NJ: Erlbaum.

Garfield, S. L. (1980). *Psychotherapy: An eclectic approach.* New York: Wiley.

Garfield, S. L. (1987). Towards a scientifically oriented eclecticism. *Scandinavian Journal of Behavior Therapy, 16*, 95–109.

Garfield, S. L. (1994). Eclecticism and integration in psychotherapy: Developments and issues. *Clinical Psychology: Science and Practice, 1*(1), 123–137.

Garfield, S. L. (Ed.). (1995). *Psychotherapy: An eclectic-integrative approach.* (2nd ed.). New York: Wiley.

Graham, J. (1977). *The MMPI: A practical guide.* New York: Oxford University Press.

Hart, L. R. (1991). The Egocentricity Index as a measure of self-esteem and egocentric personality style for inpatient adolescents. *Perceptual and Motor Skills, 73*, 907–914.

Hibbard, S. (1989). Personality and object relational pathology in young adult children of alcoholics. *Psychotherapy, 26*(4), 504–509.

Horney, K. (1950). *Neurosis and human growth.* New York: Norton.

Jensen, A. R. (1965). Review of the Rorschach. In O. Buros (Ed.), *The sixth mental measurements yearbook* (pp. 501–509). Highland Park, NJ: Gryphon Press.

Kiesler, D. J. (1986). The 1982 interpersonal circle: An analysis of DSM-III personality disorders. In T. Millon & G. L. Klerman (Eds.), *Contemporary directions in psychopathology: Toward the DSM-IV* (pp. 571–597). New York: Guilford Press.

Kernberg, O. F. (1985). *Borderline conditions and pathological narcissism.* Northvale, NJ: Jason Aronson.

Kernberg, O. F. (1986). Narcissistic personality disorder. In A. A. Cooper, A. J. Frances, & M. H. Sachs (Eds.), *The personality disorders and neuroses* (Vol. 1, pp. 219–230.) New York: Basic Books.

Kohut, H. (1977). *The restoration of the self.* New York: International Universities Press.

Lerner, P. M. (1991). *Psychoanalytic theory and the Rorschach.* Hillsdale, NJ: Analytic Press.

Linehan, M. M. (1993). *Cognitive–behavioral treatment of borderline personality disorder.* New York: Guilford Press.

Lovitt, R. (1993). A strategy for integrating a normal MMPI-2 and dysfunctional Rorschach in a severely compromised patient. *Journal of Personality Assessment, 60*(1), 141–147.

Marmor, J., & Woods, S. M. (1980). *The interface between the psychodynamic and behavioral therapies.* New York: Plenum.

Masterson, J. F. (1976). *Psychotherapy of the borderline adult.* New York: Brunner/Mazel.

Masterson, J. F. (1993). *The emerging self: A developmental, self, and object relations approach to the treatment of the closet narcissistic disorders of the self.* New York: Brunner/Mazel.

Millon, T. (1994). *Millon Clinical Multiaxial Inventory—III manual.* Minneapolis: National Computer Systems.

Millon, T. (1996). *Disorders of personality: DSM-IV and beyond* (2nd ed.). New York: Wiley-Interscience.

Nezworski, M. T., & Wood, J. M. (1995). Narcissism in the Comprehensive System for the Rorschach. *Clinical Psychology: Science and Practice, 2*(2), 179–199.

Norcross, J. C. (1986). *Handbook of eclectic psychotherapy.* New York: Brunner/Mazel.

Norcross, J. C. (Ed.). (1987). *Casebook of eclectic psychotherapy.* New York: Brunner/Mazel.

Norcross, J. C., & Goldfried, M. R. (Eds.). (1992). *Handbook of psychotherapy integration.* New York: Basic Books.

Parker, K. C. H., Hanson, R. K., & Hunsley, J. (1988). MMPI, Rorschach, and WAIS: A meta-analytic comparison of reliability, stability, and validity. *Psychological Bulletin, 103*(3), 367–373.

Rappaport, D., Gil, M. M., & Schafer, R. (1968). *Diagnostic psychological testing* (revised by R. Holt, Ed.), New York: International Universities Press.

Rathvon, N., & Holmstrom, R. W. (1996). An MMPI-2 portrait of narcissism. *Journal of Personality Assessment, 66,* 1–19.

Rokeach, M. (1960). *The open and the closed mind.* New York: Basic Books.

Rotter, J. B. (1966). Generalized expectancies for internal versus external control of reinforcement. *Psychological Monographs: General and Applied, 80* (Whole No. 609). Washington, DC: American Psychological Association.

Stricker, G. (1994). Reflections on psychotherapy integration. *Clinical Psychology: Science and Practice, 1*(1), 3–12.

Tallent, N. (1993). *Psychological report writing* (4th ed.). Englewood Cliffs, NJ: Prentice Hall.

Trenerry, M. R., & Pantle, M. (1990). MAPI code types in an inpatient crisis-unit sample. *Journal of Personality Assessment, 55*(3&4), 683–691.

Wachtel, P. L. (1977). *Psychoanalysis and behavior therapy: Toward an integration.* New York: Basic Books.

Watson, R. A., & Pantle, M. L. (1993). Reflections on the Rorschach and the Millon Adolescent Personality Inventory. *Perceptual and Motor Skills, 77,* 1138.

Weiner, I. B. (1993). Clinical considerations in the conjoint use of the Rorschach and the MMPI. *Journal of Personality Assessment, 60*(1), 148–152.

6

Integrating the MCMI and the MMPI

MICHAEL H. ANTONI

For the better part of this century, distinctions between what are now termed clinical syndromes (DSM Axis I) and personality disorders (DSM Axis II) were not formally made, though their existence was clearly recognized. Less than two decades ago the third edition of the *Diagnostic and Statistical Manual of Mental Disorders* (DSM-III; American Psychiatric Association, 1980) made explicit the practice of differentiating longstanding patterns of behavior, mood, thinking processes, and interpersonal style (personality) from more transitory, time-limited, and obvious deviations from characteristic behaviors (clinical syndromes). This approach reflects an evolution in the understanding of psychopathological processes, namely, that the picture a patient presents will depend on his or her characteristic, longstanding perceptual and behavioral tendencies, as well as their reactions to the more transitory stressors of everyday life.

As prescribed by DSM-III-R and reiterated in DSM-IV (American Psychiatric Association, 1994), comprehensive clinical diagnostics involves a multidimensional assessment featuring at least two major sets of variables. On the one hand, there are "process" variables, including perceptions of self, others, and environmental demands and the responses to these, which occur on the behavioral, interpersonal, and emotional levels. These features, catalogued along Axis II in the DSM scheme, vary in the severity and direction (inward vs. outward) in which they are expressed and tend to perpetuate one another, creating a "loop" manifest as a pervasive personality pattern or style. On the other hand, clinical syndromes, indexed in Axis I, encompass more static, newly onset outcomes manifest in overt behaviors and phenomenological reports and are seen as "outcome" variables in reference to their genesis from the personality loop. From this standpoint, a clinical syndrome (Axis I) may result from several different loops (Axis II), or it may be one of several syndromes' output from the same loop. Knowledge of both the process and outcome variables characterizing a person is necessary (1) for comprehensive diagnostic assessment, because it simultaneously provides broad descriptive information about expected levels of current functioning and sheds light on predicted paths of decompensation after the onset of future stressors, and (2) for the person's response to specific therapeutic interventions.

Despite the potential for comprehensive case conceptualization, the ability to predict patient responses to future anticipated and unanticipated stressors, and the possibility of optimal treatment triaging that could result from such a test battery, little work has been completed which focuses on the best assessment prescription for achieving these goals at the point of screening and intake. Indeed, *combining* multiple projective assessment instruments (e.g., the TAT and the Rorschach) within a battery is a common practice; however, the ways to *integrate* the information emerging from each into a useful stratagem for addressing the goals just noted have not been laid out.

Similarly, until quite recently, little research tested the utility of integrating two or more "objective" inventories. One reasonable approach to addressing this issue is to examine the ways in which the best available instruments for measuring Axis I and Axis II phenomena covary. The Millon Clinical Multiaxial Inventory (MCMI) was designed to assess personality patterns and disorders (Axis II) specifically as established in the DSM-III. At the present time, the MCMI is the only objective, self-report inventory explicitly created to elucidate this realm of psychopathology. The MCMI also assesses levels of personality disorder severity or "organization" (i.e., borderline). The Minnesota Multiphasic Personality Inventory (MMPI) is the best documented instrument designed to assess the presence of specific clinical syndromes (Axis I). Together, the MMPI and MCMI might provide data on different domains of psychological functioning, both of which are essential to forming a complete clinical picture. Although many of the studies reported in this chapter relate to the first versions of the MCMI and the MMPI, there is good reason to assume that patterns of covariation found between these two early forms will hold true for all later forms of these instruments.

EMERGING TRENDS IN PSYCHODIAGNOSTICS: ANOTHER OFFSPRING OF THE MANAGED CARE EVOLUTION

Despite the fact that the MCMI and MMPI were each designed to focus on a different axis of functioning, it has become commonplace for clinicians to view the MCMI as a "competitor" of the MMPI (Butcher & Owen, 1978; Korchin & Schuldberg, 1981). This sort of "either/or" attitude in clinical assessment is likely to be fueled by current trends in managed health care designed to cut costs and services remunerated by third party insurers. The managed care environment that most clinicians in mental health work must operate within has brought about a greater need to justify multiple tests in a psychosocial battery. Weiss (1994) notes some of the ways in which the use of multiple psychological tests are often justified in this climate, including efforts to predict the emergence of psychotic features in major depression and to delineate characterologic versus reactive/situational difficulties precipitating current Axis I disorders. He notes one cost issue at the heart of this strategy—failing to identify characterological dynamic contributions to a currently experienced Axis I condition—could lead to extra days of hospitalization or to repeated hospitalizations (Weiss, 1994). These consequences might be due to a failure to understand the intrapsychic or interpersonal factors precipitating, exacerbating, or maintaining the current presenting problem as well as those that could increase or decrease the probability of success of a chosen treatment approach (Millon, 1988).

In a perfect world the power brokers in the health insurance industry, those case reviewers who determine the bottom-line services deemed necessary and reimbursable for a given case, would be aware of the cost risks involved in an inadequate clinical assessment which could be considerably offset with a well-chosen, if somewhat longer, clinical assessment battery. However, in the imperfect and chaotic transition period in which we currently find ourselves, it is not uncommon for the clinician to be required to obtain precertification on a "per test basis" to receive remuneration for all of the components of a clinical battery (Weiss, 1994). This might constitute a well-controlled, lean, and efficient system if it were not for the fact that the managed care system decision makers are often untrained in use of psychological tests, no less personality theory and testing.

One growing problem in this climate particularly germane to this discussion specifically involves the use of the MMPI and MCMI in clinical practice. Because both tests ostensibly provide information related to personality features and clinical syndromes, they are often deemed by managed care reviewers as interchangeable and redundant (Weiss, 1994). Weiss (1994) goes on to note that it may be clinically unwise and financially "inexpedient" for third party reviewers to disencourage clinicians from using both instruments together, because (1) the MMPI is the most widely used objective testing instrument in the world (Greene, 1991) and one which is especially adept at assessing the presence of Axis I symptoms, and (2) the MCMI is the most popular personality (Axis II) instrument of its kind (Choca, Shanley, & Van Denburg, 1992).

Weiss (1994) correctly reasons that the argument of redundancy is substantially weakened by the fact that there is overwhelming evidence suggesting that the two instruments show little, if any, direct overlap in their measurement of DSM-III-R (American Psychiatric Association, 1987) Axis I diagnoses. Based on studies comparing the MMPI with the MCMI (Patrick, 1988; Smith, Carroll, & Fuller, 1988) and with diagnostic interviews and assorted additional clinical measures (for reviews of this literature see Wetzler, 1990), it appears that there is considerable divergence in their measurement of a wide variety of commonly diagnosed conditions, including those involving signs and symptoms of anxiety and depression as well as those involving psychotic features and substance abuse symptoms.

This nonredundancy between the instruments appears to extend to personality disorders as well. Studies examining the comparability of MMPI and MCMI Axis II scales have attempted to determine the zero-order correlation between each of the MCMI and MMPI personality scales and have produced mixed results (McCann, 1989; Morey & Levine, 1988; Streiner & Miller, 1988). One study (Morey & Levine, 1988) found correlations ranging from .48 to .78 on 9 out of 11 scales, but negative correlations for the Compulsive and Antisocial scales. McCann (1989) similarly noted Pearson correlations ranging from .41 to .82 on 8 of 11 scales, with the remaining three—Compulsive, Antisocial, and Paranoid—producing negative MMPI–MCMI correlations. Finally, Streiner and Miller (1988) found overall moderate-sized correlations (r's = .29–.66) among scales and noted that 6 of 11 MMPI scales actually showed higher correlations with noncomplementary MCMI scales than with their counterpart scales. While the small samples (N's = 47–76) and low subject-to-variable ratios extant in these studies may have been responsible in part for the discrepancies observed, it is also arguable that a scale-by-scale correlational analysis of Axis II variables is not the most clinically meaningful way to examine the comparability of these instruments as they are used in clinical diagnostics. Because a code type analysis is the method most frequently used by clinicians (Butcher, Dahlstrom, Graham, Tellegen, & Kemmer, 1989; Choca et al., 1992) it seems far more useful to elucidate the code type (e.g., two-point codes) concordance between the MMPI and MCMI to evaluate the degree of overlap that the clinical "consumer" is likely to experience when using the two instruments together in practice. Once done, a reasonable decision can be made concerning the issue of redundancy and subsequent allocations of remuneration by third party reviewers. Beyond providing a test of concordance, comparing the pattern of two-point scale elevations between the two instruments may add to the richness of the clinical assessment if it can be shown that the scale scores/high-point codes from one instrument can be used to create clinically valuable subgroups subsumed under the two-point code of the other instrument. This would be particularly helpful in the case of a two-point code that has been previously associated with characteristics that appear internally inconsistent, some of which will be presented later in this chapter.

One study that tackled the issue of MMPI–MCMI code type concordance was conducted by Weiss (1994). He screened 100 patients admitted to a large, general hospital and excluded those with a primary diagnosis of organic brain syndromes, psychoses, and alcohol or drug dependence, as well as those with invalid MCMIs (more than 1 item on Validity scale endorsed) or MMPIs (F-scale scores > 100 on the MMPI), resulting in a sample of 72 patients. This sample consisted of predominantly white females with a mean age of 47 years and an average education of 12.8 years. Consistent with previous work (McCann, 1989; Morey & Levine, 1988; Streiner & Miller, 1988), Weiss noted that 9 of 11 scales showed correlations ranging from .27 to .76 with a mean of .44, and the remaining two scales—Compulsive and Antisocial—showed negative or near-zero correlations. He also found, in support of Streiner and Miller (1988), that correlations between counterpart scales (e.g., MMPI Schizoid and MCMI Schizoid) and noncomplementary scales (e.g., MMPI Schizoid and MCMI Avoidant) were not statistically different for 21 of 22 scales.

The two tests also diverged considerably on high-point code frequencies. The most common MCMI single high-point codes were for Dependent (39%) and Passive–Aggressive (18%), while the most frequently observed MMPI high-point codes were for Histrionic (22%), Narcissistic (18%), and Borderline (17%). The two-point code type analysis revealed that the most frequent MCMI two-point types were for Dependent–Passive–Aggressive (11%), Dependent–Avoidant (10%), and Passive–Aggressive–Borderline (8%), while the most frequently encountered MMPI code type patterns included the Histrionic–Narcissistic (25%), Dependent–Avoidant (11%), and Borderline–Histrionic (11%). The code type correspondence analyses for the two tests were particularly revealing and indicated a total single high-point correspondence of 19.44% and a two-point correspondence of only 9.72%! The scale with the greatest high-point convergence was Dependent (9.72%) and the two-point code with the greatest degree of correspondence was the Dependent–Avoidant code type (5.56%).

As Weiss notes, the lack of correspondence between the MMPI and MCMI in this and prior studies suggests that the scales are not measuring comparable clinical constructs and that the results emerging form the two instruments are nonredundant (Weiss, 1994). While this information may be useful in informing third party reviewers that the two tests can be viewed as nonoverlapping and deserving of separate remuneration, it still leaves open the question of how clinicians might be able to integrate MMPI and MCMI test results to arrive at the most accurate diagnosis and comprehensive understanding of the factors underlying the diagnosis for each patient who completes this test battery. Weiss (1994) concludes that because the MCMI and MMPI are not equivalent measures and appear to measure personality disorders significantly differently, using information obtained from both tests might be a useful way to gather both diagnostic (DSM-III-R) and theoretical information for formulating a treatment plan; therefore, the use of the tests concurrently should be reimbursable. Although he alludes to using the instruments in a "complementary fashion" and to synthesizing the tests' output into an "individualized, comprehensive psychological profile," there is no schematic information presented for how to do this. Thus we are back to our original question: *What are the optimal ways to integrate the information from the two most widely used objective instruments to enrich and refine data obtained from either instrument alone (1) to facilitate comprehensive case conceptualization;*

(2) *to identify factors capable of precipitating, exacerbating, or maintaining current levels of difficulties; and* (3) *to choose the most efficacious and cost-effective treatments from the resources that are available?* In this chapter we will review a series of studies we conducted over a decade ago which were designed to provide an analytic strategy for addressing this question.

A MODEL FOR INTEGRATING THE MCMI AND THE MMPI

At the time we initiated our research in this area, we were first drawn to examine the ways in which the MMPI and MCMI covaried out of a concern for the fact that MMPI two-point codes often suggest multiple interpretations, some of which contain contradictory "within-code" descriptors. We felt that many tenable hypotheses could be generated for each of the two-point codes presented which, when taken together, might cloud necessary diagnostic and therapeutic decision-making processes. We reasoned that the addition of MCMI data to the test battery might help to confirm MMPI hypotheses in some cases and resolve MMPI descriptive contradictions in others. The model that we formulated for combining information from the MCMI and MMPI was based on the assumption that many of the contradictions in the extant two-point MMPI code descriptions can be sorted out into consistent MCMI-directed subtypes of each MMPI two-point code.

We have chosen here to summarize the large collection of MMPI–MCMI subtypes identified on the basis of our extensive studies conducted in the past decade (Antoni, Tischer, Levine, Green, & Millon, 1985; Levine, Antoni, Tischer, Green, & Millon, 1985; Levine, Tischer, Antoni, Green, & Millon, 1986; Antoni, Levine, Tischer, Green, & Millon, 1986, 1987) by viewing them within the framework of a stress–coping model (Antoni, 1993). One of the most valuable benefits of personality diagnostics is that they enable us to predict a patient's course after the onset of new stressors and/or the persistence or exacerbation of extant stressors. While many different personality *styles* present on the surface as similar at regular samplings, it is likely that during periods of acute stress or throughout periods of uncontrollable, unremitting, and severe burden, the pathognomonic signs of different personality *disorders* may be more likely to present themselves. Whereas reactions to acute, short-term stressors may reach extreme levels (manifest as clinical syndromes), the resulting changes in behavior, mood, and psychosocial functioning may be relatively short lived. More long-term, uncontrollable, and unremitting stressors can be associated with more chronic changes in psychiatric status (e.g., decompensation to a borderline level of psychopathology; Millon, 1981) as well as physical status (e.g., immune system changes; Antoni et al., 1990; McKinnon, Weisse, Reynolds, Bowles, & Baum, 1989). It is plausible that the more precision one is able to develop in characterizing the personality style by, for instance, combining instruments to identify personality subtypes, the better one might be able to make predictions about a patient's response to future challenges.

A model that we have used to guide our empirical investigations is one derived from the personality theory of Millon (1981). This model characterizes reactions to acute stressors along two dimensions: reactive *currency* (or level) and *direction*. In our work we proposed that one pervasive stressor, loss (or threatened loss) of reinforcement, can lead to responses taking the form of interpersonal or emotional *currencies* or levels, expressed in an outward or inward *direction*. These dimensions taken together make up the individual's coping style—a "program" that sets into motion several strategies that can be employed in demanding situations. When an individual experiences chronic periods of burden, especially to the extent that such burdens are perceived as uncontrollable, his or her coping style will ultimately reach a point where it is relatively ineffective in regaining reinforcements and support. According to Millon (1981), the stressed individual's reactions to this loss expressed in distinct currencies and in a characteristic direction may spiral him or her into a state of self and/or social alienation, possibly followed by decompensation to a more severe level of personality pathology. Millon has defined these decompensated patterns as schizotypal, borderline, and paranoid (Millon, 1981). We have used this model to interpret the findings of our research with the MCMI–MMPI battery.

To the degree that the MMPI and MCMI can together place individuals along these dimensions they would offer clinical utility when combined as a battery. Specifically, the resulting information on personality subtypes could be used to generate testable predictions of short-term responses to acute stressors and the more decompensatory sequelae of chronic stressors. We now present a summary of our previous work with this "objective test battery" and suggest how the findings might be useful in making predictions about such stress response/outcomes. As will be seen, the personality subtypes that result from the integration of these two instruments are also useful in clarifying some of the contradictory descriptions that can result from relying on MMPI two-point codes alone.

Research Strategy

Sampling

Approximately 175 frequent users of both the MMPI and MCMI were approached to participate in the study and to administer the MMPI and MCMI to their patients. We collected data over a 16–month period from 46 of these clinicians in various professional settings at sites located across the United States. In total, 3,283 sets of MMPI and MCMI batteries were returned. Twenty-four of the clinicians responding were in private practice; 15 worked in community mental health centers, shared practices, clinics, or other group settings; and seven were in different hospital settings.

The age of the sample was widely distributed with no systematic bias, and women slightly outnumbered men. Approximately 85% of the subjects were outpatients and 15% were inpatients. Affective and anxiety disorders were predominant along Axis I, whereas Axis II primary diagnoses included a large number of dependent and borderline personality disorders.

Procedure

Raw score data were reduced to the two highest scores for each instrument, provided that at least two scale scores were above a K-corrected T-score of 70 for the MMPI and a base rate (BR) score of 65 for the first eight or "basic" personality scales of the MCMI. If no MMPI scales were elevated above $T = 70$ then the profile was listed as "flat." It was also noted whether any of the three MCMI severe personality disturbance scales (Schizotypal, Borderline, and Paranoid) were elevated. High-point codes for each subject on the MCMI were tallied and percentages of the largest and most theoretically relevant code types were computed. Code types were included only when a minimum of 10 cases were used. This cutoff point is somewhat more stringent than those employed in other research designs examining MMPI overlap with measures of psychopathology (Gilberstadt & Duker, 1965;

TABLE 6.1. Sample Sizes for Each of the Most Prevalent
MMPI Two-Point Codes Studied

MMPI code	N	% of overall	Publication
28/82	353	10.8%	Antoni, Tischer, et al. (1985)
24/42	318	9.7%	Antoni, Levine, et al. (1985)
49/94	305	9.3%	Levine, Tischer, et al. (1986)
78/87	272	8.3%	Antoni et al. (1987)
98/89	228	6.9%	Antoni, Levine, et al. (1986)
27/72	228	6.9%	Levine, Antoni, et al. (1985)

Kelly & King, 1977; Vincent et al., 1983). It was judged that this rule would reduce the possibility of subtypes emerging spuriously.

From the 3,283 MCMI–MMPI batteries, we anticipated that N's of 200 to 300 would be available for each of the more commonly observed MMPI two-point codes. To date we have published the results of six of the most prevalent MMPI two-point codes. The sample sizes and the relative proportion of the 3,283 cases collected for each of these are displayed in Table 6.1.

Here we summarize the findings from four commonly encountered, though somewhat disparate, two-point code types (28/82, 24/42, 89/98, and 78/87) with an emphasis on stress response predictions that can be made on the basis of MCMI–MMPI covariations. These four MMPI two-point codes are also those that traditionally contain a substantial number of contradictory descriptors, thus providing a demonstration of how such contradictions may be resolved with this "objective test battery" approach. Thus, before describing the results of each sets of analyses we present a sample of the MMPI two-point code description that is widely used when the MMPI is considered alone. Once the discrepancies in this code description are outlined we present the results of the MCMI–MMPI analysis as related to that MMPI two-point code. For detailed descriptions of the results of each study highlighted here, as well as those done with other MMPI two-point code types, I refer you to the primary reference (Antoni, Levine, et al., 1985; Antoni, Levine, et al., 1986; Antoni, Levine, et al., 1987; Antoni, Tischer, et al., 1985).

MMPI 28/82 (PRIMARY ELEVATIONS ON SCALES 2 AND 8 OR 8 AND 2)

Traditional Description for the MMPI 28/82 Code Type

Individuals with the MMPI 28/82 code type are basically dependent and submissive with difficulties in being assertive. They appear irritable and resentful, fear losing control, deny undesirable impulses, occasionally act-out and express guilt afterwards. Seen by some as stubborn and moody at times, they are considered peaceable and docile to others. These people are judged by some to be in a state of profound inner turmoil over highly conflictual, insoluble problems; others view them as somehow "resigned" to their psychosis. In some cases anxious, agitated depression may be seen while in others soft, reduced speech and retarded stream of thought are noted. Individuals with the 28/82 MMPI code appear most likely to receive a diagnosis of either manic–depressive psychosis or schizophrenia, schizoaffective type. A significant segment of 28/82 individuals exhibit psychotic upsets, often preceded by hypochondriacal and hysterical episodes. Psychotic symptomatology may include bizarre mentation, delusions, hallucinations, social alienation, sleep disturbance, poor family relationships, and difficulties in impulse control.

Unusual thoughts may take a specific form (hallucinations and suicidal ideation) or more diffuse symptomatology (general confusion, disorganization, and disorientation) (Dahlstrom, Welsh, & Dahlstrom, 1972; Graham, 1977). Overall, the 28/82 type appears to suffer from a heterogeneous group of disorders and syndromes characterized by disturbances of thinking, mood, and behavior. (Antoni, Levine, et al, 1985, p. 393)

This collection of descriptors presents several behavioral, interpersonal, and affective facets that at times seem to contradict one another, making clear hypotheses difficult to formulate. These contradictions appear at the *behavioral* level (denial of undesirable impulses vs. acting-out behaviors), the *interpersonal* level (withdrawn vs. hysterical), and the *emotional* level (stubborn and moody vs. peaceable and docile). While some descriptors reflect an outwardly directed response style (hostility and aggression), others portray a more inwardly directed mode (retreat into fantasy via hallucinations). Diagnostic disparities are also prevalent with the 28/82 type, including hysterical and manic syndromes on the one hand and schizoid and schizophrenic symptoms on the other.

MCMI Subtypes for the MMPI 28/82 Code Type

The results of our first MCMI–MMPI study indicated that the MCMI high-point scales that covary with the MMPI 28/82 code type yield three distinct groups of individuals differing across dimensions. To reiterate some of the aspects of the model proposed previously, the interpersonal style can be detached or ambivalent, while the reaction to loss of reinforcement is manifested in reactive currency (behavioral, interpersonal, or emotional) and direction (inward or outward). Each subtype represents a unique constellation of these dimensions. Persons with the first subtype (elevations on MCMI scales 12, 21), *the interpersonally acting-in group*, anticipate no reinforcement and therefore employ an interpersonal style of detachment or withdrawal. These people tend to react to stress with inwardly directed self-punitive responses on the behavioral and interpersonal levels. Those with the second subtype (elevations on MCMI scales 8, 82, 28), the *emotionally acting-out group*, seek reinforcement from external sources, display an ambivalent interpersonal style, and react to loss of support with outwardly directed, unpredictable, and dramatic emotional responses. Those with third subtype (elevations on MCMI scales 23, 32), the *emotionally acting-in group*, seek reinforcements from external sources, move between ambivalent and withdrawn interpersonal styles, and may react to loss of support with inwardly directed negative emotional experiences.

If stress should become excessive in any of these groups, thereby "overwhelming" their interpersonal style, these people may become ineffective in securing reinforcements and support. The reactions to this loss expressed in their distinct currencies and in characteristic direction (inward, outward) could spiral such individuals into a state of alienation followed by decompensation. In the *emotional acting-out group*, this alienation is likely to precipitate as self-alienation and identity problems. Our data suggests that decompensation appears to follow into a borderline pattern in this subtype. The *interpersonally acting-in group* may experience total alienation with decompensation to a schizotypal pattern when under unremitting stress. Finally, the *emotionally acting-in group*, possessing traits of both of the other two subtypes, may display borderline and/or schizotypal patterns of decompensation.

To summarize, it appears that the primary sources of ambiguity in the MMPI 28/82 code description—the level (emotional vs. interpersonal) and direction (inward vs. outward) on which these individuals react to stress—may be clarified by the use of MMPI–MCMI subtypes, named according to the configuration of these two dimensions.

MMPI 24/42 (PRIMARY ELEVATIONS ON SCALES 2 AND 4 OR 4 AND 2)

Traditional Description of the MMPI 24/42 Code Type

The 24/42 type, often referred to as "psychopaths in trouble," are known for their recurrent acting-out and subsequent periods of guilt and depression. They are noted as impulsive, unable to delay gratification and to have little respect for societal standards. Frustrated by their own limited achievements, resentful of the demands and expectations of others, they often experience a mixture of anger and guilt that manifests itself in agitated depression. Some are overcontrolled, avoid confrontations, and express feelings of inadequacy and self-punitive rumination. Many also engage in asocial or antisocial behaviors, such as stealing, sexual acting-out, and drug or alcohol abuse. Often described as immature and narcissistic, they appear unable to maintain deep relationships. Beneath the carefree and confident facade of many will often reside either worry and dissatisfaction, or an absence of any emotional response. Their failure to achieve life satisfactions results either in self-blame and depression or in a projection of blame and paranoid ideation. In some cases, pre-psychotic behavior and suicide attempts may be seen (Dahlstrom et al., 1972; Graham, 1977). (Antoni, Tischer, et al., 1985a, p. 509)

Some of these statements appear contradictory at the *behavioral* (asocial vs. antisocial) and *emotional* levels (worry and anger vs. absence of emotional response). Moreover, while some descriptors reflect an outwardly directed response (extrapunitive, projected blame), others indicate a more inwardly directed response (self-blame, depression).

MCMI Subtypes of the MMPI 24/42 Code Type

Analysis of the MCMI–MMPI battery for subjects classified as MMPI 24/42 produced three subtypes, with at least one of these appearing to break into two variants. For this reason we discuss our findings for this code type in somewhat more detail, emphasizing the predicted stress responses within each subtype.

Interpersonally Acting-Out Group

One of these subtypes is the interpersonally acting-out group; the tendency is to react to stress on the behavioral and interpersonal levels through impulsive, outwardly directed, and projected responses. For these patients it is possible that MMPI Scale 4 elevations approximate their personality core and Scale 2 elevations reflect a clinical outcome that is more likely to occur when they are unable to acquire the reinforcements they need. Individuals falling within this subtype (those with elevations on MCMI Scales 6; 6 and 5; 6 and 7; 5) are related in their arrogance, aggressiveness, and self-centeredness. When criticized, they may become explosive and display overtly antisocial behaviors such as brutality, alcoholism, drug addiction, and other forms of acting out.

Acute Stress Response

Persons with the first variant of this subtype (MCMI Scale 6, primary elevation) may be prone to display behavior and affect driven by fear and a mistrust of others, taking the form of hostile acting out, angry rejection of social norms and an undercurrent of inadequacy and self-dissatisfaction. This desire to provoke fear and intimidate others may come either from a need to compensate for a sense of inner weakness or from a wish to vindicate past injustices. (Millon, 1969, 1981).

Individuals who fit more into the second variant of this subtype (primary elevations on MCMI Scale 5) are more likely to be guided by their high self-esteem, leading to arrogance and a disregard for social constraints. They may come across as charming and exhibitionistic, yet manipulative. These people are rarely likely to experience self-doubt, though psychosocial stressors may trigger acting-out behaviors (addictions, sexual excesses) as a means of restoring equilibrium.

Chronic Stress Sequelae

Should the individuals with the high Scale 6 variant of this subtype meet with repeated failure in their attempts to secure support and reinforcement, paranoidlike behaviors may become evident. In support of this notion, we found that over half of the *interpersonally acting-out group* (primary elevations on MCMI Scale 6) also showed high elevations on the MCMI Paranoid scale—a scale measuring symptoms such as ideas of reference, vigilant mistrust, and grandiose self-image. It is noteworthy, however, that those people characterized by the other variant—with primary elevations on MCMI Scale 5—showed no elevations on the three, more severe syndrome scales.

Interpersonally Acting-In Group

Acute Stress Response

A second subtype of the MMPI 24/42 code type composes a more unitary group which we referred to as an *interpersonally acting-in group* to emphasize their tendency to react to stressors on the behavioral and interpersonal levels through withdrawal, self-deprecation, and self-punitive responses. Individuals in this subtype (those with elevations on MCMI scales 1 or 1, 3, and 8) may be self-belittling and possess a weak and ineffectual self-image. The intrapunitive nature of this subtype seems to be at the other end of the pole from the extrapunitive and blaming nature of the acting-out group. According to Millon (1981) this subtype may include individuals who have neither internal nor external sources of reinforcement and therefore turn neither inward nor outward to acquire psychic pleasure or support. Their high endorsement of MMPI Scale 2 items may be accounted for by the deflated self-esteem and daily experience of a pansocial isolation which are predicted by Millon's theory. Importantly, isolation for this group is likely to reflect an indifference to social interaction rather than an active disdain or rejection of others, the latter being more characteristic of the interpersonally acting-out group.

Chronic Stress Sequelae

Should individuals with this MMPI 24/42 subtype continue to experience both self- and social alienation, they may display behavioral eccentricities, ideas of reference, cognitive slippage, magical thinking, and depersonalization anxieties, symptoms in line with a schizotypal personality pattern. Not surprisingly, we found that a large proportion of patients in the interpersonally acting-in group showed distinct and frequent elevations on the Schizotypal scale of the MCMI.

Emotionally Acting-Out Group

Acute Stress Response

The two subtypes discussed thus far, both representing variations of the MMPI 24/42 type, differ in both the "direction" of their expressive functioning (acting out vs. acting in), as well as in their likely course of decompensation. Those with a third MMPI 24/42 subtype, referred to as the *emotionally acting-out group*, are best characterized by their tendencies to exhibit demodulated, labile, and outwardly expressed affect to gain attention and support. These people's coping patterns may toggle between the traits of MMPI Scales 2 and 4. In their case, the contradictory nature of the traditional MMPI 24/42 code type descriptors portray, to some extent, the intrinsically contradictory nature of ambivalent interpersonal styles (Millon, 1969, 1981). Individuals included in this subtype (those with elevations on MCMI scales 34/43, 83, 84) may vacillate between irritable, depressive moods and maniclike euphoric or hostile episodes. The unifying element in the emotional expressions is the dramatic nature. According to Millon (1981), these displays may be motivated by a desire to regain a "lost" source of reinforcement or support. Accordingly, these individuals can be characterized by both an extreme dependence and self-alienation; they display a resentful ambivalence, possibly generated by conflict between dependence needs and a desire to be autonomous.

Chronic Stress Sequelae

We hypothesized that when individuals with this subtype fail to gain and sustain attention and support, a mixed and conflicting set of emotions such as rage, guilt, and love may emerge. During these periods they may be plagued by cognitive confusions over goals and identity as well as desultory energy levels and sleep irregularities. Supportive of this notion is the fact that a significant proportion of those in the emotionally acting-out group showed marked elevations on the MCMI Borderline scale, a scale that reflects difficulties in identity confusion and physiological phenomena such as sleep patterns.

Based on the results of the MCMI–MMPI analysis just summarized, it appears that the MMPI 24/42 code represents in the *interpersonally acting-out group* an acting-out type in which Scale 4 relates to the personality, whereas Scale 2 reflects a more transient clinical outcome occurring when these individuals are unable to acquire reinforcements. High Scale 2 scores in the *interpersonally acting-in group* seem to reflect the personality style, whereas Scale 4 elevations represent the clinical outcome of withdrawal via asocial behaviors and interpersonal indifference. The contradictory descriptors of the MMPI 24/42 code appear to accurately reflect the essential ambivalent nature of the third, or *emotionally acting-out group*, whose coping style vacillates between the aspects of the MMPI Scales 2 and 4.

MMPI 89/98 (PRIMARY ELEVATIONS ON SCALES 8 AND 9 OR 9 AND 8)

Traditional Description of the MMPI 89/98 Code Type

Individuals with the 89/98 code type have been described as being self-centered and infantile in their expectations of others, demanding a great deal of attention, and responding with resentment and hostility when demands are not met. Fearing emotional involvement they avoid close relationships and tend to be socially withdrawn and isolated. Characterized as hyperactive, emotionally labile and unrealistic in self-appraisal, these individuals may impress others as grandiose, boastful and fickle. Their feelings of inadequacy and low self-esteem tend to limit the extent to which they involve themselves in competitive and achievement-oriented activities. However, these individuals usually emphasize achievement as a means of gaining status and recognition. Their affect is characterized by some as inappropriate, unmodulated, irritable and hostile, yet they may also tend to be ruminative, over-ideational and withdrawn, fearing any type of outward communication with others. Highly suspicious and distrustful of others, these individuals may display unusual and unconventional thought processes including delusions of a religious nature, feelings of grandiosity, hallucinations, poor concentration and negativism. These individuals may receive a diagnosis of either schizophrenia, stressing an interpersonal element, or manic depression, manic type, stressing the emotional features. Drug abuse is a common accompanying symptom (Dahlstrom et al., 1972; Graham, 1977). (Antoni, Levine, et al., 1986, pp. 66–67)

As we have noted previously (Antoni, Levine, et al., 1986), the phrases making up the description of this MMPI code type, taken as a whole, seem to contradict one another at the *behavioral* level (avoidance of achievement-oriented activities vs. emphasis on achievement as a means of gaining status and recognition), the *interpersonal* level (socially withdrawn and inadequate vs. grandiose and boastful), and the *emotional* level (ruminative and fearful of emotional involvement vs. overt hostility and emotional lability). Diagnostic disparities also appear possible in the 89/98 MMPI type including schizophrenia, on the one hand, and manic–depressive syndromes on the other. This range of variability seems to suggest a strong likelihood of the presence of subtypes within this code type.

MCMI Subtypes of the MMPI 89/98 Code Type

Our work integrating the MCMI and MMPI results for these individuals identified three subtypes that begin to explain the roots of these discrepancies. Because the chronic stress sequelae of the first two groups are likely to be similar, we will first list the acute stress responses of each before moving on to describing the predicted responses to more chronic burdens.

Interpersonally Acting-Out Group

Acute Stress Responses

The largest subtype, comprised of individuals with elevations on MCMI Scale 6 (Antisocial), (including 65/56, 61, 6, and 67) was referred to as the *interpersonally acting-out* group to describe their tendency to respond to stressors with impulsive, outwardly-directed, and projected responses. We hypothesized that acute stressors taking the form of criticism and assaults on their self-image may result in explosive antisocial behaviors such as substance abuse and frank brutality. The behaviors of persons of this subtype may be "driven" by a fear and mistrust of others, resulting in hostile acting out, rejection of social norms, and an avoidance of close relationships stemming from a need to compensate for an inner sense of weakness or from a wish to vindicate past injustices (Millon, 1969, 1981).

Interpersonally Grandiose Group

Acute Stress Responses

Individuals with this subtype (with primary elevations on MCMI Scale 5) (including codes other than 56) are primarily motivated by high self-esteem, feelings of grandiosity, disregard for social constraints, and interpersonal arrogance. These individuals, though charming and exhibitionistic during periods of low stress, may be prone to periods of acting out (e.g., substance abuse, sexual excesses) when they experience mounting stressors.

Chronic Stress Sequelae

Should persons of either of the two MMPI 89/98 subtypes just discussed encounter periods of unremitting stress during which they are unable to secure support and reinforcement, they may evince paranoidlike changes (e.g., magnifying the incidental remarks of others). We did indeed observe that a large proportion of individuals in both subtypes showed clear elevations on the MCMI Paranoid scale, indicating that they were experiencing symptoms such as ideas of reference, vigilant mistrust, and grandiose self-image.

Emotionally Acting-Out Group

The third MMPI 89/98 subtype, is made up of individuals with primary elevations on MCMI Scale 8 (Passive–Aggressive) and Scale 3 (Dependent), including codes 85, 86, 35, 34/43, and 83. These individuals were referred to as the *emotionally acting-out group* to describe their tendency to react to stressors with demodulated, labile, unpredictable, and intense affective responses.

Acute Stress Responses

Because these individuals actively seek reinforcers from external sources, they are susceptible to periods of extreme dependence and self-alienation and may be particularly hard hit when encountering interpersonal losses due to deaths and relocation. These individuals are also untrusting, fearful of domination, and suspiciously alert to efforts to undermine their veiled movements toward closeness and intimacy. As such, their coping style for dealing with interpersonal stressors is marked by ambivalence.

Chronic Stress Sequelae

When these individuals' attempts at securing social support and attention fail, perhaps due to self-inflicted damage to their social network or unavoidable losses, conflicting emotions of guilt, rage, and love may emerge. We hypothesized that such periods may be characterized by cognitive confusions over identity, extreme suspiciousness, and unpredictable succession of moods. In support of this notion we observed that a substantial proportion of those people in the *emotionally acting-out group* showed elevations on both the MCMI Borderline and Paranoid scales.

MMPI 78/87 (PRIMARY ELEVATIONS ON SCALES 7 AND 8 OR 8 AND 7)

Traditional Description of the MMPI 78/87 Code Type

Individuals with the 78/87 code type are often described as experiencing a good deal of psychic turmoil. Usually introspective and obsessional, they spend much of their time being worried, tense, and depressed. Often indecisive, these individuals usually show poor judgment when they do act and may appear to others as jumpy and socially inept. In interpersonal situations, the 78/87 type comes across as shy and hard to get to know at times, yet sentimental, sensitive, and softhearted on other occasions. These individuals characteristically maintain a rigid hold on affect, yet may be prone to displays of immaturity and emotionality. These people tend to deal with their psychic and social discomfort by withdrawal into a rich fantasy experience, often of a sexual nature (Dahlstrom et al., 1972; Graham, 1977). (Antoni, Levine, et al., 1987, p. 377)

What is immediately apparent in the description of the MMPI 78/87 code type is that DSM-III diagnoses can range from the neurotic to psychotic level, with primary emphasis placed on Axis I in some cases and on Axis II in others. In terms of Axis II diagnoses, these range from passive–dependent, and schizoid, to schizotypal and borderline. Several inconsistencies and ambiguities occur across interpersonal, behavioral, and emotional spheres of functioning as well. Within the *interpersonal* sphere, people with this code type are characterized as introverted and hard to get to know on the one hand, yet sentimental, sensitive, and softhearted on the other (Dahlstrom et al., 1972). We have portrayed these descriptors as presenting a simultaneous "moving away from" and "moving toward" others (Antoni et al., 1987). In the *behavioral* domain, those with the 78/87 type have been described with terms that emphasize both compulsivity and impulsivity (Dahlstrom et al., 1972; Graham, 1977). Finally, on the *emotional* level of functioning, those with 78/87 type have been characterized by some as rigid, affectively restrained, and introspective, yet by others as immature and emotional (Dahlstrom et al., 1972). The DSM-III diagnoses often associated with this code type also vary in the degree to which they emphasize behavioral (compulsive behaviors), interpersonal (schizoid, passive–dependent), and affective (depression) features. Some have utilized the relative elevations of Scales 7 and 8 for differentiating neurotic from psychotic or schizoid disorders (Graham, 1977).

MCMI Subtypes of the MMPI 78/87 Code Type

Based upon the study examining the MMPI 78/87 code type (Antoni et al., 1987) we found three MCMI subtypes including an *interpersonally acting-in group*, an *emotionally acting-out group*, and an *emotionally acting-in group*.

Interpersonally Acting-In Group

Acute Stress Responses

One subtype of the MMPI 78/87, made up of individuals with elevations on MCMI Scales 1 (Schizoid) and 2 (Avoidant), including codes 12 and 21, was termed the *interpersonally acting-in group* to describe their predicted tendency to react to stressors on the interpersonal level with indecision, withdrawal, pervasive anxiety, and obsessional thoughts. Millon (1969, 1981) theorizes that the withdrawal and acting-in quality of this group results from an inability to experience pleasure. This subtype can be seen interpersonally as a group of individuals who are often socially and self-alienated, and who experience a chronic state of psychic turmoil. Because these people are unsuccessful in reducing this chronic turmoil through interpersonal channels, they may engage in repetitive and ritualistic behaviors. Individuals who fit this subtype may be those MMPI 78/87 patients who are the most likely to receive a diagnosis of obsessive–compulsive disorder.

Chronic Stress Sequelae

Because individuals with this MMPI 78/87 subtype are isolated from social feedback, they may under periods of persistent and severe stress decompensate into a pattern of behavioral eccentricities, ideas of reference, depersonalization anxieties, cognitive slippage, and magical thinking—a schizotypal pattern. Relatedly, we observed that a large proportion of people fitting into this subtype also showed elevations on the MCMI Schizotypal scale.

Emotionally Acting-Out Group

Acute Stress Responses

Other features making up traditional descriptions of the MMPI 78/87 code type focus on a more agitated clinical picture featuring outwardly expressed affect. These features mirror a second subtype which we termed the *emotionally acting-out group* to describe the tendency to react to stressors with labile emotional responses that alternate between angry defiance and sullen moodiness. As opposed to people falling into the formerly described MMPI 78/87 subtype, these individuals actively seek reinforcement from others and are characterized by extreme dependence, self-alienation, and interpersonal ambivalence. We have hypothesized that their ambivalence over relationships could be manifest as hostility and demonstrative emotional displays, perhaps to repel the significant others that they desperately need. As such, this subtype fits the MMPI 78/87 descriptors that pertain to an immature expression of affect.

Chronic Stress Sequelae

We have reasoned that when under periods of chronic, uncontrollable demands, individuals with this subtype may become frustrated in their attempts to secure support and attention from others, especially to the extent that they have rebuffed members of their social network in the past. During such periods they may experience conflicting emotions related to others (e.g., guilt, love, rage), identity confusion, and physiological changes such as sleep irregularities. These predictions are supported by our observations that individuals in the *emotionally acting-out group* obtain elevations on the MCMI Borderline scale, which taps many of these symptoms.

Emotionally Acting-In Group

Acute Stress Response

A final subtype with the MMPI 78/87 code includes individuals with primary elevations on MCMI Scale 2 (Avoidant) and 3 (Dependent), who we have designated as the *emotionally acting-in group*. They are likely to respond to stress with inwardly directed anger and frustration which Millon (1981) has hypothesized results from an intense conflict between opposing sources of reinforcement (other, self, none) and alternating approaches to securing that support (active, passive). It could be further speculated that out of a fear of rejection by others, they may actually withdraw from their only sources of reinforcement, resulting in loneliness and mixed feelings of anxiety, sadness, anger, and guilt.

Chronic Stress Sequelae

If reinforcers are unavailable for extended periods, these individuals may become emotionally drained and may translate anger at others into self-degradation and feelings of worthlessness. Because of this relentless, downwardly spiraling conflict they may decompensate into either a schizotypal pattern, a borderline pattern, or some mixture of both, including symptoms such as acute emotional turmoil, irrational thinking, and extended periods of despondency. In support of these predictions we noted that a large proportion of individuals with this subtype also obtained elevations on both the MCMI Borderline and Schizotypal scales.

CONCLUSIONS

We believe that conceptualizing the various MMPI two-point codes as distinct MCMI-indexed subtypes will facilitate making predictions concerning the coping responses that these individuals will employ in periods of acute stress and the route of decompensation that they will take, should stressors persist and coping resources become insufficient. A pattern that runs consistently through the results of the studies that we have reviewed here is that individuals comprising a given MMPI two-point code type can display marked heterogeneity across many spheres of functioning (Antoni, Levine, et al., 1985; Antoni, Tischer, et al., 1985a). The variability described for these groups may be found across behavioral, interpersonal, and affective realms and is manifest in specific "styles" of reinforcement acquisition and decompensation. This variance describes the configurations of assorted clinical features, some describing a core issue and others representing more or less "spinoffs" of this central feature. Here we have demonstrated a format that gives a focus to the clinical picture by specifying particular spheres of psychosocial functioning and impairment (behavioral, cognitive, interpersonal, emotional), thereby establishing subtypes with distinct clusters of clinical symptoms. The goal of our work was to lay the groundwork for empirical tests of diagnostic categories assessed by an "objective" test battery made up of the most widely used and researched instruments available for addressing personality-related phenomena. This descriptive stage in this process was the aim of our previous studies. The next step (the empirical stage) necessarily involves external criteria against which these categories can be compared (e.g., clinical observations).

On a practical level, it remains uncertain, according to the set of descriptions provided for MMPI two-point code types, which axis should be considered primary and which secondary in arriving at a diagnosis. It is equally unclear as to which Axis II disorder is most likely to "coexist" with an accompanying Axis I syndrome. One consistent bias in our work has been to assign primacy to Axis II; hence, all of the subgroups identified and described had a primary label along this axis. However, this formulation allowed for the explanation of clinical syndromes that would very likely be present in each subtype and, in so doing, united the most likely Axis I–Axis II combinations. The elucidation of these combinations is essential for accurate and comprehensive diagnosis and may help predict probable clinical course and treatment prognosis. As such, the discriminations that become available with this test battery may be useful in cases in which the clinician needs to determine the salience and centrality of behavioral, interpersonal, and affective issues and observations to plan the most efficacious and cost-effective therapeutic interventions. With an understanding of the central clinical features and a clear picture of the primacy of syndrome and disorder in a given case, the clinician may be better prepared to decide on a treatment approach based on the efficacy of one intervention modality over another. Also, having available a better understanding of the spheres of functioning (e.g., interpersonal vs. emotional) that their patients tend be most comfortable operating within may help clinicians with general "rapport" and communication issues, allowing them to work more efficiently with patients in familiar ways. Ultimately, wider use of this integrated test battery approach by clinicians, supported by a more assessment-literate managed care system, will greatly facilitate the most comprehensive case conceptualizations and the ability to identify factors precipitating, exacerbating, or maintaining current levels of difficulties and the treatments that are the most efficacious and cost-effective routes to patient management, remediation, and recovery.

REFERENCES

American Psychiatric Association. (1980). *Diagnostic and statistical manual of mental disorders* (3rd ed.). Washington, DC: Author.

American Psychiatric Association. (1987). *Diagnostic and statistical manual of mental disorders* (3rd ed., rev.). Washington, DC: Author.

American Psychiatric Association. (1994). *Diagnostic and statistical manual of mental disorders* (4th ed.). Washington, DC: Author.

Antoni, M. H. (1993). The combined use of the MCMI and MMPI. In R. Craig (Ed.), *The Millon Clinical Multiaxial Inventory: A clinical research information synthesis* (pp. 279–302). Hillsdale, NJ: Erlbaum.

Antoni, M. H., Levine, J., Tischer, P., Green, C., & Millon, T. (1985). Refining MMPI code interpretations by reference to MCMI scale data. Part I: MMPI Code 28/82. *Journal of Personality Assessment, 49*(4), 392–398.

Antoni, M. H., Levine, J., Tischer, P., Green, C., & Millon, T. (1986). Refining personality assessments by combining MCMI high point profiles and MMPI codes. Part IV: MMPI code 89/98. *Journal of Personality Assessment, 50*(1), 65–72.

Antoni, M. H., Levine, J., Tischer, P., Green, C., & Millon, T. (1987). Refining personality assessments by combining MCMI high point profiles and MMPI codes. Part V: MMPI code 78/87. *Journal of Personality Assessment, 51*(3), 375–387.

Antoni, M. H., Schneiderman, N., Fletcher, M. A., Goldstein, D., Ironson, G., & LaPerriere, A. (1990). Psychoneuroimmunology and HIV-1. *Journal of Consulting and Clinical Psychology, 58*(1), 38–49.

Antoni, M. H., Tischer, P., Levine, J., Green, C., & Millon, T. (1985). Refining personality assessments by combining MCMI high point profiles and MMPI codes. Part III: MMPI Code 24/42. *Journal of Personality Assessment, 49*(5), 508–515.

Butcher, J. N., Dahlstrom, W., Graham, J., Tellegen, A., & Kemmer, B. (1989). *MMPI-2 manual for administration and scoring.* Minneapolis: University of Minnesota Research Press.

Butcher, J. N., & Owen, P. L. (1978). Objective personality inventories: Recent research and some contemporary issues. In B. B. Wolman (Ed.), *Clinical diagnosis of mental disorders: A handbook.* New York: Plenum Press.

Choca, J. P., Shanley, L., & Van Denburg, E. (1992). *Interpretative guide to the Millon Clinical Multiaxial Inventory.* Washington, DC: American Psychological Association.

Dahlstrom, W. G., Welsh, G. S., & Dahlstrom, L. E. (1972). *An MMPI handbook: Volume I. Clinical interpretation.* Minneapolis: University of Minnesota Press.

Gilberstadt, H., & Duker, J. (1965). *A handbook for clinical and actuarial MMPI interpretation.* Philadelphia: Saunders.

Graham, J. R. (1977). *The MMPI: A practical guide.* New York: Oxford University Press.

Greene, R. L. (1991). *The MMPI-2/MMPI: An interpretive manual.* New York: Allyn and Bacon.

Kelly, C., & King, G. D. (1977). MMPI behavioral correlates of spike 5 and two-point code types with scale 5 as one elevation. *Journal of Clinical Psychology, 33,* 180–185.

Korchin, S. J., & Schuldberg, D. (1981). The future of clinical assessment. *American Psychologist, 36,* 1147–1148.

Levine, J., Antoni, M. H., Tischer, P., Green, C., & Millon T. (1985). Refining MMPI code interpretations by reference to MCMI scale data. Part II: MMPI Code 27/72. *Journal of Personality Assessment, 49*(5), 501–507.

Levine, J., Tischer, P., Antoni, M. H., Green, C., & Millon, T. (1986). Refining personality assessments by combining MCMI high point profiles and MMPI codes. Part VI: MMPI code 49/94. *Journal of Personality Assessment, 51,* 388–401.

McCann, J. T. (1989). MMPI personality disorder scales and the MCMI: Concurrent validity. *Journal of Clinical Psychology, 45*(3), 365–369.

McKinnon, W., Weisse, C., Reynolds, C., Bowles, C., & Baum, A. (1989). Chronic stress, leukocyte subpopulations, and humoral responses to latent viruses. *Health Psychology, 8*(4), 389–402.

Millon, T. (1969). *Modern psychopathology: A biosocial approach to maladaptive learning and functioning.* Philadelphia: W. B. Saunders Co.

Millon, T. (1981). *Disorders of personality: DSM-III, Axis II.* New York: Wiley Interscience.

Millon, T. (1988). Personologic psychotherapy: Ten commandments for a post-eclectic approach to integrative treatment. *Psychotherapy, 25,* 209–219.

Morey, L. C., & Levine, D. (1988). Multitrait–multimethod examination of the MMPI and MCMI. *Journal of Psychopathology and Behavioral Assessment, 19*(4), 333–343.

Patrick, J. (1988). Concordance of the MCMI and MMPI in the diagnosis of three DSM-III Axis I disorders. *Journal of Clinical Psychology, 44*(2), 186–190.

Piersma, H. L. (1987). The MCMI as a measure of DSM-III Axis II diagnoses: An empirical comparison. *Journal of Clinical Psychology, 43*(5), 478–483.

Smith, D., Carroll, J., & Fuller, G. (1988). The relationship between the MCMI and MMPI in a private outpatient mental health clinic population. *Journal of Clinical Psychology, 44*(2), 165–174.

Streiner, D. L., & Miller, H. R. (1988). Validity of MMPI scales for DSM-III personality disorders: What are they measuring? *Journal of Personality Disorders, 2*(3), 238–242.

Vincent, K. R., Castillo, I., Hauser, R. I., Stuart, H. J., Zapata, J. A., Cohn, C. K., & O'Shanick, G. J. (1983). MMPI code type and DSM III diagnoses. *Journal of Clinical Psychology, 39*(6), 829–842.

Weiss, E. (1994). Managed care and the psychometric validity of the MMPI and MCMI personality disorder scales. *Psychotherapy in Private Practice, 13*(3), 81–97.

Wetzler, S. (1990). The MCMI: A review. *Journal of Personality Assessment, 55*(3 & 4), 445–464.

7

Application of the Millon Inventories in Forensic Psychology

FRANK J. DYER

In professional psychology we have two competing models of training: the pure clinical practitioner model which deemphasizes research and stresses application of skills to effect change, and the scientist–practitioner model that incorporates research methods along with applied skills training. Clinicians who graduate from many practitioner training programs tend to think like therapists, which entails a high degree of tolerance for ambiguity and an attunement to nuance and even intuitive modes of assessment and intervention. Clearly, this type of thinking is absolutely essential for therapeutic and counseling work, relying as it does on the subtleties of human interaction with multiple layers of communication, inference, innuendo, and processes associated with the unconscious. Practitioners whose professional skills were honed in this therapeutic culture typically experience a shock upon entering the world of expert testimony in the courts, for the entire *raison d'etre* of the court system is to resolve ambiguity, make all innuendo explicit, and obliterate any fuzzy, impressionistic, intuitive mental processes that come before its scrutiny. This severe process serves the ultimate purpose of making binary decisions: guilty–not guilty, liable–not liable, competent–not competent.

It is precisely because of this characteristic of the legal system that forensic psychology provides an optimal practical field of application for the scientist–practitioner model. Forensic psychologists, in accord with standards for expert testimony discussed below, must think like scientists. At the same time, they do not have the luxury of methodical exploration of abstract questions or withholding of comments on specifics until the proper experimental data are in. As good practitioners, they must be able to apply rational methods to draw conclusions about specific sets of facts on the basis of their broad knowledge of theory, general research findings, and their own clinical observations.

This chapter will review the differences between the kinds of conclusions that are acceptable in an ordinary clinical context and those that are acceptable on the witness stand. This is followed by a discussion of the current standard for scientific evidence in federal courts, standards that influence state courts as well, although the latter are not bound by them. This will be followed by a discussion of the psychological profession's current standards for psychometric instruments that are acceptable as a basis for expert testimony. The Millon Clinical Multiaxial Inventory—II (MCMI-II, Millon, 1987) and the Millon Adolescent Clinical Inventory (MACI, Millon, 1993) will be evaluated in light of these standards and additional psychometric features of the test will be discussed as they relate to the presentation of complex expert testimony before judges and lay jurors. The chapter will close with some specific applications in a variety of forensic cases.

WHAT CONSTITUTES AN EXPERT CONCLUSION AS OPPOSED TO A CLINICAL ONE?

This is an issue that was discussed at great length by a committee of the New Jersey Board of Psychological Examiners in formulating guidelines for psychological evaluations in divorce and child custody matters. It was suggested that the criterion of "reasonable psychological certainty," alternatively phrased as "reasonable professional certainty" or "reasonable scientific probability," was a viable standard by which to specify a level of rigor that differentiates expert opinion from ordinary clinical working hypotheses. The practical impact of this distinction is that the former are memorialized in the court transcript and are subject to an extremely literal analysis in the event of an appeal. The appeals court does not have the benefit of listening to the witness in person, but has only the transcript to guide it. While the words of the expert on the witness stand are etched in stone, as it were, an ordinary clinical working hypothesis can always be revised as treatment progresses. For instance, the hypothesis that a patient's display of hypermasculinity and bravado constitutes a defensive process to cope with ambiguity in core gender identity may be revised if it comes to light that the individual's subculture heavily reinforces this type of display and that, for the patient, such behavior is normative. The focus of the treatment might then shift from exploration of early subphases of development to ways in which the displays of bravado interfere with the patient's current interpersonal adjustment in a new environment where such displays are considered dysfunctional. In such a case the clinical hypothesis regarding core gender identity might have proven to be a useful guide to the treatment, had it not been tested and rejected on the basis of subsequent information. If such a conclusion were offered on the witness stand, it could conceivably continue to affect subsequent decisions in the case for years afterward.

The definition of reasonable psychological certainty adopted for purposes of the New Jersey Board's child custody evaluation guidelines (New Jersey State Board of Psychological Examiners, 1993) is that the conclusion is based on substantive clinical observations, well-grounded theory, empirical research, or an integration of these, and is clearly not speculative. As expert witnesses, psychologists are expected to be capable of demonstrating the validity of their conclusions on the basis of evidence beyond their own subjective opinion. Increasingly, psychologist expert witnesses are being viewed as part of a scientific community and their opinions subjected to scrutiny according to the dual criteria of legal requirements for scientific testimony and the profession's own standards for adequate testimony.

CHANGES IN FEDERAL RULES OF EVIDENCE

Prior to 1993, the admissibility of scientific evidence in Federal Courts was governed by the Frye test. This standard, based on a 1923 case, states, in essence, that if a scientific test or procedure has general acceptance in the relevant scientific community then it should be admitted, and procedures that have not gained such general acceptance should be excluded. Monahan and Walker (1994) state that critics of that standard argued that it was excessively conservative and vague, citing the fact that courts have had to wrestle with several questions not addressed in the Frye standard. Among these were exactly what is scientific evidence, how the particular field should be defined, and how much acceptance constitutes general acceptance.

A 1993 Supreme Court decision, *Daubert v. Merrell Dow Pharmaceuticals*, has changed the rules dramatically. In this decision, the issue before the Court was whether a lack of general acceptance was sufficient grounds to exclude testimony based on novel scientific procedures. Citing the liberalization of the Federal Rules of Evidence, the Supreme Court found that the trier of fact could appropriately determine whether scientific evidence had sufficient probative value in spite of any lack of general acceptance. This lengthy decision enumerated several criteria according to which scientific evidence might be evaluated by the trier of fact. These criteria range from abstruse standards deriving from logical positivism, such as "falsifiability," to others that are quite familiar to psychologists, including reliability, validity, and error rate.

This decision paves the way for vigorous cross-examination by attorneys, who are now presumably free to knock out even generally accepted scientific procedures if it can be demonstrated that they lack reliability and validity or have an unacceptably high error rate. This is particularly relevant to psychologists, as many well-accepted diagnostic procedures are found wanting according to such criteria.

THE PROFESSION'S OWN STANDARDS
FOR PSYCHOMETRIC INSTRUMENTS

The American Psychology–Law Society, constituted as Division 41 of the American Psychological Association, published a special issue on the use of psychometric procedures in court testimony. This issue contains an article by Heilbrun (1992) which sets forth standards for the adequacy of psychometric measures serving as a basis for expert opinion in forensic settings. Prefacing the standards, Heilbrun discusses the relevance of psychological test findings to the determination of the ultimate legal issue before the court. He stresses that test results simply provide data for a further process of inference in which the witness presents the rational connection between the pathological conditions diagnosed by the test and the behavioral particulars of the case. In other words, the test results themselves are of little value without a rational, readily comprehensible connection to the specific behaviors under consideration as to their impact on the legal issues before the trier of fact. This is a perfect illustration of Kurt Lewin's dictum that there is nothing so practical as a good theory. Clearly, in such situations, the more solid the theoretical basis of the test instrument, the greater the advantage to the witness.

Heilbrun (1992) lists seven criteria for psychometric instruments used in forensic settings. The first is that of *commercial availability*, coupled with documentation in a technical manual and professional review in one of the standard sources such as *Test Critiques* or *Buros Mental Measurements Yearbooks*.

The second criterion for psychometric adequacy is a *reliability of at least .80*. Unfortunately, Heilbrun erroneously equates reliability with test–retest stability in the case of trait measurement with objective tests. While stability is a necessary characteristic of trait scores, as opposed to state measurements, it is not a sufficient condition for adequate precision of measurement. McCann and Dyer (1996) discuss this issue at length and it is treated in more detail in the next section of this chapter.

Heilbrun (1992) stresses *relevance to the ultimate legal issue* as an important standard by which the appropriateness of a psychometric measures for use by forensic psychological experts should be assessed. He states that the constructs measured by such instruments should have direct applicability to the ultimate legal issue, in the sense of being helpful to the trier of fact in making determinations regarding that issue. Indeed, helpfulness to the trier of fact is also cited in the *Daubert* decision as a characteristic of acceptable scientific evidence.

This issue of *relevance of the constructs measured by the test* is of particular importance to users of the Millon Inventories, as it is generally recognized that their real strength is in the assessment of personality disorders. The relevance of personality disorders has frequently been disputed by attorneys, who argue, sometimes successfully, that they are not really mental disorders because they are not listed in the Axis I section of the DSM-IV and therefore should not be given any weight in determining questions such as the mental state of the accused at the time of the offense. This is no trivial matter, as the presence of the requisite mental state, or *mens rea*, can mean the difference between conviction of first degree murder with a possible life sentence and conviction on a lesser charge such as aggravated manslaughter, which exposes the defendant to significantly less prison time.

This issue was addressed in a recent New Jersey Supreme Court decision (*State v. Galloway*, 1993). In this case the defendant's stepchild presented at a hospital emergency room with Shaken Baby Syndrome. Defendant Galloway confessed to the police that he had shaken his girlfriend's baby to make the child stop crying. Further, Galloway related to police officers during his interrogation that he was aware that this child was the product of a rape by his girlfriend's previous partner and that he had been thinking about killing the child.

Despite the defense's introduction of expert testimony stating that Galloway suffered from borderline personality disorder and had suffered a severe regression in psychic functioning at the time of the offense, he was convicted of first degree murder. This is an offense that, under New Jersey law, requires a "knowing and purposeful" mental state. The lower court held that borderline personality disorder was not a "mental disorder" and that it could therefore not be regarded as a factor in producing a diminished capacity to form the requisite *mens rea*. This was also the opinion of the appeals court. The New Jersey Supreme Court found that testimony as to borderline personality disorder was clearly relevant to the legal determination of *mens rea*. The Court explicitly stated that borderline personality disorder is a mental disorder and that it is capable of affecting an individual's "cognitive capacities" and therefore the capacity to form the knowing and purposeful mental state required under New Jersey law for first degree homicide.

Other criteria that appear in the Heilbrun (1992) list include *standardization of the test on groups that are similar to the litigants* being assessed, *objective test format with actuarial basis for diagnosis and prediction* rather than subjective, impressionistic methods, and *explicit assessment of response style*. Remarkably, Heilbrun asserts that the only psychological test with extensive empirical support for response style assessment is the MMPI. It is noted that the MCMI-II has substantial data on the effectiveness of the four modifier indices, with generally favorable results (Choca, Shanley, & Van Denburg, 1992).

PSYCHOMETRIC ADEQUACY OF THE MILLON INVENTORIES FOR FORENSIC USE

This discussion will focus primarily on the MCMI-II and secondarily on the MACI. Advantages and limitations of the MCMI-III will be discussed in a separate section.

Reliability

Internal consistency statistics for the MCMI-II are reported in terms of K-R 20 coefficients on page 129 of the test manual (Millon, 1987). Values for all of the basic personality disorder scales, basic clinical scales, and severe clinical scales exceed the .80 reliability criterion cited by Heilbrun (1992). All of the severe personality disorder scales have K-R 20 coefficients of .90 and above. Technically, the internal consistency statistics for all of these weighted score scales should have been computed with coefficient alpha rather than with the K-R 20, as the latter is a special case of coefficient alpha applicable only when scoring is dichotomous. However, as Retzlaff, Sheehan, and Lorr (1990) have demonstrated that the results of weighted and unweighted scoring of these scales are essentially the same, the distortions associated with the use of K-R 20 are negligible.

Stability coefficients for all of the above scales are generally above the .80 criterion, according to a study reported in the MCMI-II manual (Millon, 1987) of nonclinical subjects tested at 3- to 5-week intervals. Stability coefficients for psychiatric outpatients and inpatients are lower, ranging from .59 to .75 for basic personality disorder scales and from .49 to .64 for severe personality disorder scales. As many of these subjects were tested at intake and discharge, it is to be expected that their MCMI-II scale scores would be less stable; they underwent a presumably successful intervention to address their personality and other problems during this interval.

A study of the stability of two-point MCMI-II codes reported in the test manual (Millon, 1987) indicates that 45% of the subjects had the same first and second highest scales, either in the same or reverse order. This is a respectable finding, given the fact that subjects were tested at various phases of their treatment.

The MACI manual presents internal consistency data for the 12 personality pattern and 15 clinical syndrome and expressed concern scales. The median value for the personality pattern scales is .84 and for the clinical syndrome and expressed concern scales it is .79. Coefficient alpha was used for these calculations.

The reliability of the Millon Inventories compares favorably with that of other objective personality measures. This is especially true of the scales' internal consistency. As noted above, stability, while a necessary condition for the precision of measurement of a personality inventory that purports to measure traits rather than transient mental states, is not a sufficient condition. Internal consistency is absolutely essential for a measure of this type. Generalizability theory, originally formulated by Cronbach, Gleser, Nanda, and Rajaratnam, (1972), provides some insights into why this is so. Shavelson and Webb (1991), in their primer on generalizability theory, point out that what is of interest to consumers of psychological test data is not the examinee's performance on any particular set of items comprised by a single form of the test, but a generalized performance that would have been the result of examining the individual with a very large number of items from the particular content domain. The entire content domain for a particular measure is termed the universe of test items in generalizability theory. Shavelson and Webb state "Ideally, test users want to know each person's universe score. Because this ideal datum is unknown, we want to know how accurate the generalization is from the particular set of items" (1991, p. 4). Further, generalizability theory divides the test situation into a number of facets, each of which is responsible for a certain amount of variance. Facets may include occasions, raters, test administrators, items, and other features of the test procedure. In presenting the advantages of generalizability theory over classical procedures, Shavelson and Webb state, "Classical test theory can estimate separately only one source of error at a time (e.g., variation in scores across occasions can be assessed with test-retest reliability)" (1991, p. 2).

The true test of generalizability from a single test form to the entire content domain is the items facet, which in classical test theory is assessed by internal consistency methods. Knowing the percentage of variance in test scores attributable to occasions does not provide an adequate answer to the question of how accurately the finite set of items on a particular form of the test estimates the subject's universe score, or standing on the underlying trait. Nunnally (1967) points out that a test with extremely high stability, as measured by retest procedures, can have zero internal consistency. In other words, if subjects simply give the same responses on test and retest, the high stability coefficient will make it appear as though the test is accurately measuring some trait, whereas in fact the test is simply an agglomeration of items of extremely heterogeneous content that does not provide an estimate of any universe score.

Currently the MCMI-II is the only major clinical personality inventory with internal consistency for all scales above the .80 criterion judged essential for forensic psychometric instruments. The MMPI-2 manual (Butcher, Dahlstrom, Graham, Tellegen, & Kaember, 1989), for example, lists coefficient alpha values in the .50s for 5 of the 10 basic scales (D, Hy, Pd, Mf, and Ma). For Scale Pa the tabled value is .3366 for males and .3924 for females. This is hardly a fluke attributable to inadequate sampling, as all of the reported sample sizes on which these values were computed are above 1000. Nor do the MMPI-2 supplementary scales fare much better. In fact, for a sample of 1,402 females, the tabled coefficient alpha value for Scale O–H was .2433. All of these coefficients appear in Appendix D-7 on page 91 of the manual (Butcher et al., 1989). However, there is no hint that such statistics even exist if one goes by the text on page 31 of the manual, under the heading "Reliability of the Basic Scales."

Validity

The centerpiece of the MCMI-II manual (Millon, 1987) is a series of figures and tables presenting validity information on the test gathered in a well-designed study employing samples of psychotherapy patients whose treating clinicians rated them using the Millon Personality Diagnostic Checklist and draft DSM-III-R criteria. Rather than employing the more usual Pearson product–moment correlation coefficient to assess the relationship between MCMI-II scores and the criterion ratings, the test manual presents the study results in terms of operating characteristics, or as they are alternatively known, classification efficiency statistics. The advantages of this mode of presentation of validity evidence for forensic work are discussed by McCann and Dyer (1996). In essence, operating characteristics make validity results accessible to lay jurors by answering a series of probability questions. These include:

1. What are the chances that someone who has X disorder will be identified as having this disorder on the test? (*sensitivity*)
2. What are the chances that someone who does not have X disorder will be correctly classified by the test as not having it? (*specificity*)

3. What are the chances that someone who is found by the test to have *X* disorder actually does have it? (*positive predictive power*, the "bottom line" of test effectiveness for many clinicians)

4. What are the chances that someone who is found by the test not to have *X* disorder actually does not have it? (*negative predictive power*)

5. What are the chances that an individual being evaluated for *X* disorder (including both those who do and do not have the disorder) will be correctly classified by the test? (*overall hit rate*)

The MACI manual includes correlational studies of scale scores against clinicians' ratings and scores on other personality measures. Correlations between the 10 personality pattern scales and clinicians' ratings ranged from .08 to .27, with a median value of .18 for a sample of 74 males and 65 females. Validities for the expressed concerns and clinical syndrome scales ranged from .00 to .43, with a median value of .14. Validity results employing other clinical measures as criteria are somewhat more impressive and provide a moderate degree of support for the construct validity of several MACI scales.

PRESENTING CLASSIFICATION EFFICIENCY STATISTICS ON THE WITNESS STAND

Taking into account the frequencies of the various disorders measured by the MCMI-II, the overall results presented in the operating characteristics, or classification efficiency statistics, tables of the test manual are impressive. However, a special word of caution is in order for forensic psychologists whose testimony incorporates this type of evidence. There is an old maxim that states that the best sword fighter in France will not duel with the worst sword fighter in France. This is because the worst sword fighter will randomly slash and wave the sword around in unanticipated ways, completely violating all of the conventions on which the best sword fighter's style is based. The following is an illustration of how this can play out in cross-examination.

Table 3-15 of the MCMI-II manual (Millon, 1987, p. 174) presents operating characteristics of the test for 703 male and female subjects for highest-diagnosed Axis II disorders. The positive predictive power for paranoid personality disorder is 40%. It is also noted that the prevalence of this disorder is 2%. The expert has testified on direct examination that the subject suffers from paranoid personality disorder, based on the MCMI-II results. On cross-examination the opposing counsel presents the expert with a copy of the MCMI-II manual and elicits an acknowledgment that the expert accepts this as an authoritative treatise. The attorney then asks the expert to read the positive predictive power figure of 40% for paranoid personality disorder. The attorney then elicits from the expert a statement that this represents the percentage of true positives. The attorney then asks, "If 40% is the true positive percentage, then is not the false positive percentage 60%?" The expert acknowledges that this is accurate. This is immediately followed by the question "So, Doctor, wouldn't you do better by just flipping a coin?." Taking advantage of the expert's hesitance in answering the question, the attorney adds, "I mean, I don't have a Ph.D. in psychology, but if I flipped a coin I would get fifty-fifty, wouldn't I? And isn't it better to have 50% false positives than 60% false positives?" Taking advantage of the expert's further hesitance in responding, the attorney quickly excuses the expert from answering the question and leaves the jury to consider the apparent superiority of the coin-flipping method of diagnosis over the worse-than-chance results achieved by psychometric methods.

Backing up to the midpoint of this exchange, it is possible to do in print what the expert cannot do on the stand, that is, reverse the outcome by analyzing these figures that have been run by the jury so quickly and supplying the right answer. To the question "Wouldn't you do better by flipping a coin?" the correct answer is an immediate and emphatic "No!" What the attorney has cleverly done is to equate the sample of paranoid subjects with the total sample. In actuality, the paranoid personality disorder subjects are only 2% of the entire sample; therefore, the true and false positive percentages on that scale of the MCMI-II are computed on a rather highly selected subsample of the total group. The highly touted coin-flipping procedure, rather than producing a false positive rate of 50%, would yield 98% false positives. A chance method utilizing a preselected subsample is not random. Chance procedures by definition involve the group as it occurs normally, without any preselection, which would introduce a nonrandom distortion.

The expert would explain, if pressed, that with a prevalence rate of 2%, a fair coin would diagnose 50 out of every 100 subjects as having paranoid personality disorder. Thus, out of every 100 subjects, 50 would be either true or false positives and 50 would be either true or false negatives. If it is assumed that out of every 100, the 2 paranoid subjects are evenly split between positive and negative diagnoses by the coin flip, then in the positive group, containing 50 subjects, 49 would be false positives and 1 would be a true positive. Converting these into percentages, we find a 2% true positive rate and a 98% false positive rate, exactly corresponding to the prevalence figure of 2%. Therefore, with the 40% true positive rate and a prevalence rate of 2%, the MCMI-II does 20 times better than chance. While classification efficiency evidence can be much more persuasive than correlational validity evidence in court (try explaining shared variance to a lay jury), experts who incorporate it into their testimony should be well acquainted with its subtleties.

APPLICATIONS

McCann and Dyer (1996) cite 22 court opinions through 1994 in which one of the Millon inventories was mentioned. Several of these were disability cases in which individuals had petitioned the court to award benefits. Several cases involved assessment of defendants accused of sexual abuse. Two involved motions for transfer of juvenile defendants to adult court. One involved determining mental state at the time of the offense, and three involved termination of either visitation rights or full parental rights. Applications of the Millon inventories in specific types of cases are discussed below.

Criminal Confessions

In many criminal trials the most important and compelling piece of evidence is the confession of the defendant. While "third degree" methods of eliciting criminal confessions have been categorically rejected by the United States Supreme Court, Wrightsman and Kassin (1993) report that overstatement or falsification of evidence is permitted in most states as an interrogation technique. They also describe a number of "emotional appeal" techniques recommended in police manuals in which the objective is for one of the interrogators to develop a personal rapport with the suspect as a means of coercing a confession. These methods include showing sympathy with the suspect, offering food and drink, flattery, and the fabled "good cop–bad cop" routine.

Despite the fact that there has been a great deal written on the subject of police interrogation procedures and the voluntariness of criminal confessions, the area of personality disorders as they relate to a subject's vulnerability to coercive interrogation is a relatively new area in which there is not as yet any definitive research. This does not mean that the possibility that a criminal suspect may have given an involuntary statement because of being incapacitated by a personality disorder should go unexplored in such cases. The American Bar Association's Criminal Justice Mental Health Standards state: "The increased vulnerability of a mentally disabled suspect and his or her naivete, ignorance, confusion, extraordinary susceptibility to pressure, and similar considerations may make it possible for law enforcement officers to induce an involuntary statement by using techniques that would be acceptable in cases involving mentally typical suspects" (American Bar Association, 1988). Wrightsman and Kassin (1993) cite studies by Gudjonsson (1984, 1988, 1990) that demonstrate that suggestibility, anxiety, and compliance are critical factors in determining whether a suspect can be coerced or manipulated into making a false confession. These three field studies by Gudjonsson were conducted on actual criminal suspects who had either allegedly made false confessions or who had resisted police pressure to confess. Suggestibility was found to be the deciding factor in these cases.

Based on this research, Gudjonsson (1990) has developed a Compliance scale associated with what Wrightsman and Kassin (1993) term "coerced–compliant" confessions. Many items of this Compliance scale resemble those of the MCMI-II dependent scale. Indeed, the hallmark characteristics associated with dependent personality disorder include a surrendering of one's autonomy and a tendency to avoid displeasing others by assuming a position of unquestioning compliance. Similarly, the diffuse sense of personal identity and faulty reality contact in the schizotypal personality disorder and temporary regressions to less organized modes of psychic functioning in borderline personality disorders may also contribute to the inducing of an involuntary confession by means of police interrogation methods that would not be deemed coercive in the case of psychologically normal defendants. Here, as in other areas of forensic psychology where there is an absence of directly applicable research, the advantages of a psychometric instrument that is solidly grounded in a coherent theory, such as the MCMI-II, are obvious.

Use of the MCMI-II in the Penalty Phase of a Capital Murder Trial

In many states capital murder trials are bifurcated into a guilt phase and a penalty phase. In the latter, which is held if the accused is convicted of charges carrying exposure to the death penalty, the jury typically hears testimony concerning aggravating and mitigating factors and then, according to the criterion of whether the aggravating factors outweigh the mitigating factors, decide whether the defendant should be executed or given a life sentence. In cases where a conviction on the capital charges is highly likely, attorneys often forgo any use of psychological testimony during the guilt phase. This avoids a situation in which the jury rejects the testimony of the expert in the first phase, only to be asked to find the same expert credible in the second phase.

It is often the case that a psychological examination of the defendant is of little help during the penalty phase, as the results indicate that the individual has an antisocial personality disorder or aggressive–sadistic personality disorder. Here the prosecutor merely has to read the diagnostic criteria for the diagnosed conditions to convince "death-qualified" jurors that the defendant, rather than suffering from a psychological disorder that mitigates the severity of the offense, is simply a bad person who should be eliminated from society. However, there are many cases in which the defendant suffers from either a personality disorder or a clinical syndrome that, while not rising to the level of a defense to the crime, does have mitigating value.

Martin T., a 25-year-old former security guard, was convicted of the double homicide of a 60-year-old woman and her 6-year-old grandson for the purpose of stealing the woman's income tax refund money. After bludgeoning the victims to death with a hammer, the defendant turned on the gas jets of the stove in the apartment in an attempt to cause a subsequent explosion that would cover up the crime. This defendant caused a commotion on the opening day of the trial by getting up from the defense table and striking the prosecutor in the jaw as the latter was making his opening statement before the jury, an act that did not make him a very sympathetic defendant.

Martin T.'s MCMI-II record was as follows: 2 3 1** 8B * 4 6A 7 + 8A 5 6B"–"// –**–* //–** T * //–**–*//. Looking at the clinical syndrome scales portion of the record first, there is significant elevation on Scale T, Drug Dependence. This is consistent with the subject's admission that he had been addicted to cocaine for several years. Turning to the Axis II section of the record, the pattern is 2–3–1, indicating that there are severe elevations of the Avoidant, Dependent, and Schizoid scales. There is an elevation on the Self-Defeating scale as well. While not included by convention in the summary scoring, it should be noted that the record contained a base rate (BR) score of 74 for the Schizotypal scale and a BR score of 73 for the severe syndrome scale of Thought Disorder.

The MCMI-II manual states that elevations on Scales 2 (Avoidant) and S (Schizotypal) may be as good a diagnostic gauge of schizophrenia as is Scale SS (Thought Disorder). Thus, the subject's MCMI-II record, containing elevations of those two personality scales and an elevation on Scale SS as well, strongly suggests a psychotic core to the defendant's ego organization, although he had never undergone an overt psychotic break with reality. Taking all MCMI-II scales into account, the picture that emerges is one of an isolated, emotionally immature individual who has low self-esteem and fears other people. Lacking effective interpersonal skills and coping mechanisms, he tends to set himself up for humiliation and failure. His thought processes tend to be infantile, eccentric, and unrealistic. His already tenuous ego controls are further weakened by his habitual use of cocaine.

Divorce/Child Custody Evaluations

This area has generated new practice opportunities for psychologists, with increasing judicial recognition of the expertise that psychologists can contribute in such matters. At the same time, child custody cases have become one of the largest sources of complaints against psychologists. This is primarily due to two factors: first, it is typical for there to be at least one "loser" in every such evaluation; second, it appears to have become a routine practice among many matrimonial attorneys to encourage their clients file a complaint against the psychologist expert witness if the results do not favor them. There is absolutely nothing to lose and everything to gain by this action. In the worst case the licensing board will simply find the complaint to be without merit. There is always the possibility that close scrutiny of the psychologist's evaluative methods or testimony will turn up some violation of professional standards, in which case the litigant will rush back to the courtroom waving the board's consent order to ask that the judicial decision based on the examination results or testimony be reconsidered in light of the board's findings.

It is particularly important for psychologists who perform child custody assessments in divorce cases to be aware of the pitfalls involved in using psychometric instruments in such cases. Most importantly, it is essential for the psychologist to have an adequate understanding of the instrument's characteristics. This includes an independent capacity to interpret any scores generated by the instrument apart from the computerized narrative report. A well-known case in New Jersey in which a practitioner made recommendations based extremely literally on the computerized narrative report of a personality inventory other than the MCMI resulted in a total of 22 complaints filed against him with the New Jersey State Board of Psychological Examiners. The licensee was unable to demonstrate even a rudimentary knowledge of scale interpretation for this instrument and was found guilty of gross malpractice, resulting in revocation of his license.

In general, it is desirable to avoid using a computer-generated narrative report in forensic work, as it provides an opportunity for opposing counsel to hold witnesses accountable for any slight contradiction between their testimony and the content of the report. Most reports of this nature, including those of the Millon Inventories, are written broadly in such a manner as to generate a maximum number of clinical hypotheses. In contrast, optimal expert testimony is narrowly focused upon the psycholegal issues specific to the case, with the limits of conclusions very clearly delineated. Witnesses have enough difficulty in defending their own conclusions under cross-examination, let alone dozens of extraneous computer-generated clinical hypotheses.

Many attorneys object to the use of the MCMI-II in child custody evaluations because of the statement in the manual that the instrument should not be used with normals. Since 1993 Millon trainers have been stating in workshops that the test author explicitly permits use of the Inventories in these types of evaluations. The rationale is that if child custody litigation progresses to the point where a judge orders the litigants to submit to an evaluation, then this constitutes a significantly serious degree of interpersonal difficulty to label the evaluation as a clinical case. Dr. Millon's comment concerning the use of the MCMI-II with normals is a caution against the routine use of the test as an employee selection device and any use by individuals for purposes of self-exploration. In cases in which litigants are accusing each other of gross personality flaws that would cause harm to their children if custody were awarded to them, the MCMI-II is perfectly appropriate as an assessment device.

A related concern is the objection by attorneys that a client's extreme defensiveness on the Inventory is merely a null result that is not interpretable. It is not unusual for individuals who are undergoing psychological evaluation in forensic contexts, especially child custody assessments, to display some defensiveness on personality inventories. However, if one encounters an extremely low Disclosure score, low Debasement score, or high Desirability score on the MCMI-II, it is perfectly legitimate to state that the test subject is exhibiting defensiveness and the findings should not simply be considered as a null result. Invariably, in bitterly fought child custody actions each party attempts to present him- or herself as being a paragon of good adjustment and accommodation, while portraying the other party as extremely pathological. If ever such a situation were actually encountered in psychological practice, it would warrant the attention of every major clinical journal. Custody battles that reach the point of requiring psychological evaluation of the litigants are typically the product of a history of complementary neurotic needs on the part of both parties.

In contrast to a parental fitness evaluation, in which the question is whether the subject is capable of discharging parental responsibilities adequately, a child custody evaluation assists the court in making relative determinations. The usual task before the court is to decide which of the litigants should be granted custody and how much contact with the other litigant is in the best interests of the children. There is a temptation in such cases to employ an assessment model that resembles an employee selection model in the sense that the evaluator attempts to make decisions and recommendations based on which of the parties achieves better scores on the assessment instruments. Speaking here specifically of personality assessment instruments and not of specialized custody assessment devices, the employee selection model in which recommendations are based on which party has better scores relative to the other party is inappropriate. Clinical assessment instruments were not designed for this purpose and the MCMI-II is certainly no exception. While statements such as "Parent A's MCMI-II protocol indicates a great deal of psychopathology, whereas Parent B's MCMI-II indicates currently adequate interpersonal adjustment" are perfectly appropriate, statements such as "Parent C scored 10 BR points higher than did Parent D on several scales, suggesting that Parent D is better equipped to raise the children" represent the kind of pseudoscience that has caused the legal system to be skeptical of behavioral science data.

Finally, in response to attorneys' questions as to what a genuinely well-adjusted individual would look like on the MCMI-II, the best explanation is to reference the statistics provided in the manual. A BR score of 35 designates the median for normal subjects on all personality disorder and clinical syndrome scales, with the exception of Scale N (MCMI-II manual, Millon, 1987, p. 100). Normals admit to some degree of pathology, and any deviation from that is to be considered as defensive. In response to a further objection advanced by some attorneys that Mother Theresa would not be expected to look at all pathological on the MCMI-II, it should be conceded that such personages would not look pathological on the Inventory, but that it is highly unlikely that they would be going for their mate's jugular in a child custody action either.

Use of the MCMI-II in Parental Fitness Assessment

In contrast to child custody evaluations in the context of a divorce action, a parental fitness assessment has as its chief referral question whether the individual is capable of caring for a child. There are usually subsidiary referral questions involving the individual's prognosis and need for services to enable them to discharge parental responsibilities appropriately.

Edith Z, who was referred by the state Child Protective Services department, was a 34-year-old woman whose children were removed on several occasions because of neglect due to her homelessness, drug abuse, and repeated incarcerations. The subject resided with her father at the time of the examination and the children were all in foster care. Edith satisfactorily completed a drug rehabilitation program, and for several months had lived an organized lifestyle that included successful biweekly visits with the children. The caseworker from Child Protective Services noted that this client appeared to be rather dependent on her father and that it was his close supervision that seemed to be keeping her together. Edith petitioned the court for return of the children, asserting that her current stability clearly indicated that she was ready to parent them appropriately.

Edith Z's MCMI-II record contained BR scores exceeding 100 on the Self-Defeating, Borderline, Passive–Aggressive, Avoidant, and Dependent personality scales. The subject also had BR scores above 75 on both Dysthymia and Anxiety scales. Her BR scores were 95 for Disclosure, 90 on the Debasement scale, and 63 on Desirability. This is quite unusual in a parental fitness assessment record. Here, as with divorce/child custody assessments, it is normal to attempt to project a maximally positive impression. That type of response set would result in a high Desirability score and low Debasement, as well as a midrange Disclosure score.

Turning to the Axis I portion of the record, Edith Z suffered from psychic distress in the form of mild anxiety and depression. She was in adequate contact with reality most of the time; however, her highest BR score scale, Borderline, indicated that she tended to regress to transient disorganized mental states in which her reality testing suffered. She presented as a socially inept individual who was uncomfortable around others and who avoided social situations unless she could fortify herself with heroin or cocaine. She tended to set herself up for humiliation, exploitation, and punishment. She was irritable, negativistic, and oppositional in response to efforts to correct her behavior. Lacking autonomy and mature boundaries, for which the negativism appeared to be an infantile substitute, Edith sought out competent partners on whom she developed an intense dependence. Invariably she ended up exploited, abused, and rejected by these figures. Given her borderline level of ego organization, these rejections led to brief psychotic regressions. This is a typical trigger for individuals with borderline personality disorder to fall apart psychologically. In the past, heroin and cocaine had provided buffers against such experiences for Edith.

The report advised intensive individual psychotherapy for Edith. Child Protective Services was advised to seek out responsible relatives with whom to place the children on a long-term basis while the client recovered. Edith's superficially good adjustment while residing with her father was attributable in large measure to the father's supervision and support, as the caseworker had suspected. Given her low level of ego organization, resistant attitude, self-defeating tendencies, and long history of reliance on drugs to dull her psychic suffering, the prognosis for this client was listed as guarded.

Use of the MCMI-II with Impaired Professionals

Professional boards are invested with a quasi-judicial function in that they are empowered to hold hearings for the purpose of processing disciplinary charges against their licensees. In cases where the board is unable, because of either time constraints or the complexity of the case, to hear the matter itself, it can refer it out to a court of administrative law for disposition. Very often either professional boards or counsel for their licensees facing disciplinary action refer the licensee to a psychologist for evaluation. These cases present special problems and challenges, as the professionals undergoing assessment are typically highly intelligent and somewhat sophisticated about the psychological evaluation process. For example, it is not uncommon for the evaluator to receive a telephone call beforehand from the client requesting the names of all of the psychological tests that will be part of the evaluation. Also, extremely defensive test records are very frequent among this examinee population.

George J was a 50-year-old oral surgeon whose partner complained to the Sate Board of Dentistry after an incident in which he appeared to be under the influence of drugs while performing oral surgery on a patient. The subject allegedly left the operatory in the middle of a surgical procedure to answer a telephone call. George J's partner further alleged that he had bloodied gloves on while answering the telephone, stumbled across the office to the telephone, had slurred speech, and dropped the telephone receiver six times while continuing to speak. The partner also complained that George J then left the office abruptly and that one-half hour later the partner discovered the fully anesthetized patient in the operatory where he had been abandoned in the middle of a procedure. Nurses in the office reported too that this problem had occurred on a prior occasion as well and stated that they would no longer assist George J, whom they perceived as a danger to his patients. When his partners in the oral surgery practice confronted him about this incident, George J reacted by completely denying any problems with drugs. An investigation by the Board of Dentistry disclosed that George J had purchased for his own personal use controlled dangerous substances including Tylenol with codeine, Percocet, and Percodan.

George J's MCMI-II record was as follows: -**-*1 7 + 6B 6A 5 " 8A 2 4 8B 3 " // _-**-*//-**-*//-**-*//. The BR scores were as follows: for Disclosure, 15; Desirability, 20; and Debasement, 12. This is a typically defensive record with no clinically significant elevations. The only clue in this test record to the extent of the subject's personality problems is found in his positive endorsement of the item "Frankly, I lie quite often to get out of trouble," an accurate reflection of his overall posture regarding his drug problems.

Victor S was a 53-year-old general dentist who was picked up by the Dental Board when a routine check of pharmacies in his area disclosed that there had been an enormous number of controlled dangerous substance (CDS) prescriptions written to the subject by physicians. Further investigation indicated that two of the physicians under whose names prescriptions for Valium and Fiorinol had been issued to the subject had never prescribed these drugs for him.

During the interview prior to psychological testing, Victor S admitted that he had obtained a supply of 500 Fiorinol from a pharmacist by telephone, who told him that he would mark the bottle "for office use." It is ironic that the subject admitted to using these drugs in the office, on himself rather than his patients, "all day long." When asked if he felt that his dental patients had ever been put in danger by his constant use of Valium and Fiorinol, he categorically denied any risk. He rationalized that the "downer" effects of the Valium were offset by the "upper" effects of the Fiorinol, which contains caffeine in addition to a barbiturate. While he stated that he never felt "overmedicated" in the office, he admitted that he once had to cancel his last patient of the day because he was throwing up in the office as a result of his drug use. He dated the beginning of his drug problem to a boating accident in which he injured his hand and had to undergo surgery. After the operation his hand was placed in what he described as a large disfiguring cast that made him feel as though he were no longer a "superman" who was invulnerable and could tackle any challenge successfully.

Victor S's MCMI-II record was as follows: 7** 5 3 * 4 + 6B 8B " 1 6A 2 8A // −**−*// _-**-*//-**-*//. The BR score for Disclosure was 40, for Desirability, 85, and for Debasement, 35.

Again, this was a defensive record, although in this case the subject permitted some insights into his personality style. On the Axis I side of the record he denied all pathological conditions, including drug abuse. Remarkably, in spite of his admissions that he took Valium and Fiorinol all day while working on patients and that he obtained large quantities of these drugs by illicit means, the BR score for Scale T was only 51. The elevation on Scale 7 (Compulsive) on the personality pattern side of the record presented the subject as a rigid, hard-driving, perfectionistic individual with a great deal of repressed hostility. The elevation on Scale 5 (Narcissistic) was consistent with the subject's description of himself as a "superman" who was invulnerable and successful in all undertakings. Indeed, many impaired practitioners who run afoul of various professional boards have a narcissism about them that is associated with contempt for the efforts of the state or their professional association to regulate their behavior. The simply feel as though they are above such authority. The elevation on Scale 3 (Dependent) suggested that the subject's narcissistic facade is actually a defensive effort against feelings of low self-worth and incompetence. This hypothesis is consistent with the subject's self-reported precipitous loss of self-esteem when he was fitted with a "disfiguring" cast after surgery on his hand.

Use of the MCMI-III in Forensic Contexts

The MCMI-III constitutes a major revision of the MCMI-II, with more than half of the item content changed to conform to specific diagnostic criteria in the recently published

DSM-IV (American Psychiatric Association, 1994). This change confers an enormous advantage on the MCMI-III over any other major diagnostic instrument: the Inventory has excellent content validity against the current DSM. An additional advantage of the MCMI-III specific to forensic cases involving personal injury is that it includes a new clinical syndrome scale measuring posttraumatic stress disorder. In terms of the standards for reliability, the MCMI-III holds up fairly well, although there has been some sacrifice of internal consistency as a result of the elimination of item overlap, which had been a frequently heard criticism of the MCMI-II.

Although at the time of publication of the MCMI-III it had not accumulated a sufficient number of criterion-related validity studies to be considered adequately supported for forensic use, it currently has such a basis. A recent study by Davis, Wenger, and Guzman (Chapter 17, this volume) describes a well-designed validity study of the MCMI-III employing a reliable criterion. Criterion reliability was achieved through providing participating clinicians with detailed instructions in making the criterion diagnoses of clients. As with the excellent clinician rating criterion study presented in the manual of the MCMI-II (Millon, 1987), these diagnoses provided the basis for calculation of classification efficiency statistics. The present MCMI-III statistics are comparable to, or exceed, those contained in the MCMI-II study. These findings bear out Millon's observations in the MCMI-III manual (Millon, 1994, p. 30) that the clinician diagnoses in the original validity study conducted at the time of the construction of the MCMI-III were not as reliable as they needed to be to support this type of validity research. Millon (personal communication, 1994) indicated that these data were collected chiefly for the purposes of construction of BR scores and item analysis. Their relationships to subjects' test performance were added to the MCMI-III manual for informational purposes and were not intended to serve as the primary validity support for the instrument; this function is now performed by the current study (Davis, Wenger, & Guzman, Chapter 17, this volume).

Thus, the MCMI-III's DSM-IV-keyed content validity is now complemented by the new criterion-related study. With an adequately demonstrated empirical validity basis and content validity that is superior to any other major clinical personality instrument, the MCMI-III should be relatively resistant to attorneys' attacks upon its scientific adequacy. The one area that still requires extensive study is the factor structure of the test. In contrast to the MCMI-II, which has been extensively factor analyzed, the factor structure of the MCMI-III has not been investigated. However, this defect should pose little difficulty for forensic use, where empirically demonstrated relationships of individual scales to specific behaviors are the focus of attention rather than patterns of statistical clustering of scales.

REFERENCES

American Bar Association. (1988). *Criminal justice mental health standards*. Standard 7-5.8.

American Psychiatric Association. (1994). *Diagnostic and statistical manual of mental disorders* (4th ed.). Washington, DC: Author.

Butcher, J. N., Dahlstrom, W. G., Graham, J. R., Tellegen, A., & Kaember, B. (1989). *Minnesota Multiphasic Personality Inventory (MMPI-2) manual for administration and scoring*. Minneapolis: University of Minnesota Press.

Choca, J. P., Shanley, L. A., & Van Denburg, E. (1992). *Interpretative guide to the Millon Clinical Multiaxial Inventory*. Washington, DC: American Psychological Association.

Cronbach, L. J., Gleser, G. C., Nanda, H., & Rajaratnam, N. (1972). *The dependability of behavioral measurements: Theory of generalizability of scores and profiles*. New York: Wiley.

Daubert v. Merrell Dow Pharmaceuticals, 2786 L.Ed.2d (U.S. 113 S.Ct. 1993).

Gudjonsson, G. H. (1984). Interrogative suggestibility comparison between "false confessions" and "deniers" in criminal trials. *Medicine, Science, and the Law, 24,* 56–60.

Gudjonsson, G. H. (1988). Interrogative suggestibility and its relationship with assertiveness, social anxiety, fear of negative evaluation, and methods of coping. *British Journal of Clinical Psychology, 27,* 159–166.

Gudjonsson, G. H. (1990). One hundred alleged false confession cases: Some normative data. *British Journal of Clinical Psychology, 29,* 249–250.

Heilbrun, K. (1992). The role of psychological testing in forensic assessment. *Law and Human Behavior, 16*(3), 257–272.

McCann, J. T., & Dyer, F. J. (1996). *Forensic assessment with the Millon Inventories.* New York: Guilford Press.

Millon, T. (1987). *Manual for the Millon Clinical Multiaxial Inventory—II.* Minneapolis: National Computer Systems Assessments.

Millon, T. (1993). *Manual for the Millon Adolescent Clinical Inventory.* Minneapolis: National Computer Systems.

Millon, T. (1994). *Manual for the Millon Clinical Multiaxial Inventory—III.* Minneapolis: National Computer Systems Assessments.

Monahan, J., & Walker, L. (1994). *Social science in law: Cases and materials* (3rd ed.). Westbury, NY: Foundation Press.

New Jersey State Board of Psychological Examiners. (1993). *Specialty guidelines for psychologists in custody/visitation evaluations.* Newark, NJ: Author.

Nunnally, J. C. (1967). *Psychometric theory.* New York: McGraw-Hill.

Retzlaff, P. D., Sheehan, E. P., Lorr, M. (1990). MCMI-II scoring: Weighted and unweighted algorithms. *Journal of Personality Assessment, 55,* 219–223.

Shavelson, R. J., & Webb, N. M. (1991). *Generalizability theory: A primer.* Newbury Park, CA: Sage.

State v. Galloway, 133 N.J. 631, 628 A.2d 735 (1993).

Wrightsman, L. S., & Kassin, S. M. (1993). *Confessions in the courtroom.* Newbury Park, CA: Sage.

8

Using the MCMI in Correctional Settings

CARRIE M. MILLON
THEODORE MILLON

The MCMI has had a Correctional Form since the early years of the first version of the MCMI, first published some 20 years ago. Considerable research and theoretic work has been done since then, resulting in a series of updatings for the MCMI-II and MCMI-III (Millon, 1987, 1994). This chapter attempts to summarize some of the new features relevant to correctional settings that are included in the most recent form of the instrument.

We will attempt to characterize persons who are incarcerated in America's prisons and to specify a number of clinical and personality features that are of special interest to psychologists who work in this setting. In addition, we will illustrate the most recent Preliminary Report available to correctional psychologists who wish to use the MCMI-III for purposes of personality screening, but desire a specialized report fashioned to meet the particular needs they have for characterizing inmate populations.

We will begin with a historical review of concepts regarding those who are variously referred to as having antisocial, psychopathic, and criminal personalities. Next we will describe inmate personality types, both salient varieties (e.g., pure official DSM disorders), as well as mixed personality types (the more common personality composites seen in prison settings). Third, we will record a number of special features of the correctional form of the MCMI-III, possible item rephrasings, normative comparison groups, and the increased relevance of a prisoner-oriented interpretive report. Last, we will present an illustrative report of the Correctional Form of the MCMI-III.

HISTORICAL REVIEW OF ANTISOCIAL BEHAVIOR AND CRIMINAL CHARACTERISTICS

The threads of this historical review begin with the descriptions provided by Emil Kraepelin at the turn of the century. The successive editions of his important texts reflect the changing emphases given these disorders. In the second edition of his major work (1887), Kraepelin identified the "morally insane" as suffering congenital defects in their ability to restrain the "reckless gratification of . . . immediate egotistical desires" (p. 281). The fifth edition, in 1896, referred to these conditions as "psychopathic states" for the first time, asserting that these constitutional disorders display themselves as lifelong morbid personalities. The next edition, published in 1899, referred to psychopathic states as one of several forms of degeneration along with syndromes such as obsessions, impulsive insanity, and sexual perversions. Retaining the theme of degeneration in his seventh edition of 1903–1904, Kraepelin now referred to these states as "psychopathic personalities," by which he meant: "Those peculiar morbid forms of personality development which we have grounds for regarding as degenerative. The characteristic of degeneration is a lasting morbid reaction to the stresses of life" (p. 547).

In 1905, Kraepelin identified four kinds of persons who had features akin to what we speak of today as antisocial personalities. First were the "morbid liars and swindlers" who were glib and charming, but lacking in inner morality and a sense of responsibility to others; they made frequent use of aliases, were inclined to be fraudulent con men, and often accumulated heavy debts that were invariably unpaid. The second group included "criminals by impulse," individuals who engaged in crimes such as arson, rape, and kleptomania, and were driven by an inability to control their urges; they rarely sought material gains for their criminal actions. The third type, those essentially referred to as "professional criminals," were neither impulsive nor undisciplined; in fact, they often appeared well mannered and socially appropriate but were inwardly calculating, manipulative, and self-serving. Those of the fourth type, the "morbid vagabonds," were strongly disposed to wander through life, never taking firm root, lacking both self-confidence and the ability to undertake adult responsibilities.

By the fourth volume of the eighth edition of his work (1909–1915) Kraepelin described psychopaths as deficient in either affect or volition. He separated them into two broad varieties, those of morbid disposition, consisting of obsessives, impulsives, and sexual deviants, and those exhibiting personality peculiarities. The latter group was differentiated into seven classes: the excitable (*Erregbaren*), the unstable (*Haltlosen*), the impulsive (*Triebmenschen*), the eccentric (*Verschobenen*), the liars and swindlers (*Luegner und Schwindler*), the antisocial (*Gesellschaftsfeinde*), and the quarrelsome (*Streitsuechtige*). Only the latter three possess features similar to current notions of a criminal type. As noted previously, liars and swindlers are "naturally cheats and occasionally thieves"; sexual offenses are common to them, and they are "uncertain and capricious in everything." Those with quarrelsome personalities are "in constant trouble"; they think others are always against them and their judgment is "warped and unreliable." Last, those with antisocial personalities, the explicit and prime forerunners of our contemporary nomenclature, are "the enemies of society . . . characterized by a blunting of the moral elements. They are often destructive and threatening . . . [and] there is a lack of deep emotional reaction; and of sympathy and affection they have little. They are apt to have been troublesome in school, given to truancy and running away. Early thievery is common among them and they commit crimes of various kinds" (Partridge, 1930, pp. 88–89).

The details characterized by Kraepelin in the final edition of his monumental text (1909–1915) are almost identical to the diagnostic criteria spelled out for the younger antisocial in the DSM-III (American Psychiatric Association, 1980). Were Kraepelin's views the final word? Apparently many of his contemporaries thought not. K. Birnbaum (1914), writing in Germany at the time of Kraepelin's final edition, was the first to suggest that the term *sociopathic* might be the most apt designation for the majority of these cases. To him, not all delinquents of the degenerative psychopathic type were either morally defective or constitutionally inclined to criminality. Birnbaum asserted that antisocial behavior only rarely stems from inherent immoral traits of character; rather, it reflects most often the operation of societal forces that make the more acceptable forms of behavior and adaptation difficult to acquire. This social conditioning thesis did not become a prominent alternative in psychiatric circles until the later 1920s, largely gaining serious consideration through the writings of Healy and Bronner (1926) and Partridge (1930) in the United States. In the interim decades, psychopathy was conceived internationally in the manner most explicitly stated in the British Mental Deficiency Act of 1913; still wedded to Prichard's conception of moral insanity developed some 80 years earlier (Prichard, 1835, pp. 91–92), it was judged a constitutional defect that manifested "strong vicious or criminal propensities on which punishment has had little or no deterrent effect."

Kraepelin's prime disciple in German psychiatry, Kurt Schneider (1923, 1950), reinforced his mentor's thesis, stressing the observation that many were delinquent in youth and largely incorrigible. However, he stated that we should be mindful that in addition to those who progress into criminal activity, many of this type may also be found in society-at-large. Moreover, Schneider observed that many of these individuals were unusually successful in positions of either political or material power.

As the novel concepts and theories of psychoanalysis took root in the 1920s, preliminary and scattered notions concerning the "character" of psychopaths began to be published by clinicians oriented by this school of thought. Most were prompted to this task by an intriguing paper of Freud's (1915/1925) entitled "Some Character Types Met with in Psychoanalytic Work"; here Freud described "peculiar acts" that appear out of character for the individual. In exposing the dynamics of a subgroup of these cases, referred to as "criminality from a sense of guilt," Freud wrote, "Analytic work then afforded the surprising conclusion that such deeds are done precisely because they are forbidden, and because by carrying them out the doer enjoys a sense of mental relief. He suffered an oppressive feeling of guilt, of which he did not know the origin, and after he had committed a misdeed the oppression was mitigated" (1915/1925, p. 342).

This paper served as the impetus for a number of subsequent clinical reports by other analysts. Among those written in the early to mid-1920s was Aichhorn's (1935) *Wayward Youth*, and Reich's (1925) study, *Impulse Ridden Character*.

Perhaps the first analytically based examination of delinquent behavior was that formulated by Aichhorn (1925/1935). Stressing the observation that surface controls imposed by treatment are rarely sufficient to withstand the unconscious forces of the patient, Aichhorn wrote:

> When we look at dissocial behavior, or symptoms of delinquency, as distinct from delinquency, we see the same relation as that between the symptoms of a disease and the disease itself. This parallel enables us to regard truancy, vagrancy, stealing, and the like as symptoms of delinquency, just as fever, inflammation, and pain are symptoms of disease. If the physician limits himself to clearing up symptoms, he does not necessarily cure the disease. The possibility of a new illness may remain; new symptoms may replace the old . . . When a psychic process is denied expression and the psychic energies determining it remain undischarged, a new path of discharge will be found along the line of least resistance, and a new form of delinquency will result. (pp. 38–39)

Particularly sensitive to variations in the background of delinquent behaviors, Aichhorn (1925/1935) asserted that either extreme indulgence and overvaluation or excessive harshness and deprecation can set the groundwork for the child's renunciation of social values. Viewing these as defects of the superego, Aichhorn notes that these children are not disposed to internalize parental norms and will be inclined to seek immediate gratification through impulsive behaviors.

Writing also in 1925/1927, Abraham articulated his view of the development of antisocials in his analysis of "an impostor." In the following brief quote, he appears to have joined Aichhorn (1925/1935) in recognizing conditions that give rise to narcissistic personality traits, on the one hand, and those of the antisocial, on the other:

> We often come across the results of early pampering, which intensifies the child's demands for love to an extent which can never be adequately satisfied (narcissistic). Among delinquents (antisocial) we are more likely to come across a different fate of the libido in early childhood. It is the absence of love, comparable to psychological under-nourishment, which provides the pre-condition for the establishment of dissocial traits. An excess of hatred and fury is generated which, first directed against a small circle of persons, is later directed against society as a whole. (p. 304)

In what he first termed "instinct-ridden characters" and later revised as the "impulsive character," Reich (1925) asserted that the "superego" of these personalities failed to gain expression under the ego's unyielding controls, and subsequently could not adequately restrain the id's seduction when faced with instinctual temptations, hence resulting in the free expression of impulses.

A nonanalytic, yet incisive and thorough clinical characterization of the antisocial was provided by Cleckley in his book *The Mask of Sanity*, first published in 1941. Attempting to clarify problem terminologies and seeking to counter the trend of including ever more diverse disorders under the rubric of "psychopathy," Cleckley proposed replacing the term with the label "semantic dementia" to signify what he viewed to be the syndrome's prime feature, the tendency to say one thing and to do another. More important than his proposal of a new nomenclature, which attracted little following, was the clarity of Cleckley's description of the psychopath's primary traits—guiltlessness. incapacity for object love, impulsivity, emotional shallowness, superficial social charm, and an inability to profit from experience. No less significant was Cleckley's assertion that these personalities are found not only in prisons but in society's most respected roles and settings. Cleckley (1941) illustrated this thesis with several examples of "successful" businessmen, scientists, physicians, and psychiatrists. He wrote as follows:

> In these personalities . . . a very deep seated disorder often exists. The true difference between them and the psychopaths who continually go to jails or to psychiatric hospitals is that they keep up a far better and more consistent outward appearance of being normal. . . . The chief difference . . . lies perhaps in whether the mask or facade of psychobiologic health is extended into superficial material success. (pp. 198–199)

The work of Hare and his associates (Hare, 1985) has drawn upon Cleckley's formulation of the "psychopathic" personality, reconceptualizing his descriptive texts in the form of a Psychopathy Checklist (PCL). Two correlated factors have emerged from this work. The first factor appears to represent a narcissistic personality variant of the psychopathic pattern, evidencing tendencies toward selfishness, egocentricity, superficial charm, and a lack of remorse and empathy. The second factor appears more directly related to those with an overtly antisocial lifestyle, evidencing early periods of delinquency, low frustration tolerance, frequent substance abuse, a parasitic lifestyle, impulsivity, and frequent illegal or criminal behaviors.

Hare's (1985) work appears to support the ideas of both Kernberg (1992) and Millon (1981) concerning the two major features of the psychopathic lifestyle. It represents Millon's view that psychopathy has at its core a *deficiency* in concerns for "others," manifesting on the one hand the *passively entitled* variant in the narcissistic's self-focus and, on the other, the *actively aggrandizing* variant as seen in the self-focus of the antisocial. Similarly, these data reflect Kernberg's recognition that the antisocial and the narcissist share essential and major features in common, despite aspects of dissimilarity in their overt behaviors, notably the prominent lack of conscience or morality in the antisocial.

Reference to the biogenic origins of the antisocial has been made by many investigators seeking to uncover the underlying biophysical correlates of the disorder. However equivocal these results may be, biologic theorists continue to explore its potential substrates. Thus, Siever and Davis (1991) have formulated the following thesis regarding the antisocial syndrome. With other associates of his (Siever, Klar, & Coccaro, 1985), Siever writes:

> In antisocial personality disorder (APD), the impulsive characteristics take the form of repetitive behaviors that conflict with social constraints, for example, stealing, lying, and fighting behaviors that are normally suppressed or inhibited in the service of societal rules. Clinically, these behaviors are often conceptualized in terms of a failure of social learning or internalization of societal constraints in the course of development—that is, a faulty superego or capacity for experiencing guilt. A number of studies suggest that such individuals may demonstrate lowered cortical arousal and more disinhibited motoric responses to a variety of stimuli. Thus, patients with antisocial personality disorder may be considered to be more likely to act than to reflect prior to their taking action, so that internalization of societally sanctioned controls may be more problematic. (p.43)

INMATE PERSONALITY TYPES

The following pages describe several "pure" or DSM criminal personalities, followed by the characteristics of the more common mixed personalities found in prison settings.

Salient or "Pure" DSM-III-R and DSM-IV Types

What we are referring to as salient types are the classic personality disorders as described in the DSM-III-R and -IV (American Psychiatric Association, 1987, 1994). These "pure" varieties are not as frequent as one might expect; rather, most inmates exhibit mixed clinical pictures, partly antisocial, partly histrionic, and partly borderline, *or* partly sadistic and partly narcissistic, and so on. What we are highlighting in the few paragraphs of this next section are just a few of these salient types as they are occasionally seen in prison settings.

The DSM *schizoid* inmate shows little affect—he or she is not happy, sad, or angry. He or she is socially indifferent and isolated, appears most comfortable when alone, and is viewed by others as quiet, colorless, apathetic, and retiring; many seem lost in fantasy.

The DSM *avoidant* inmate is behaviorally guarded, socially pananxious, and withdrawn. He or she is fearful and mistrustful, overreacts to innocuous events, and scans the environment for potential threats. Many feel alienated, isolated, and rejected by others.

The DSM *dependent* inmate is gullible, naive, and dependent. He or she may be functionally incompetent, ill-equipped to assume adult roles and responsibilities, and may act helpless, weak, and conciliatory. Many seek guidance from stronger figures, lack self-confidence, are self-belittling, and timidly avoid social conflict.

The DSM *histrionic* inmate seems intolerant of inactivity, is restless, seeks momentary excitements, and is often glib and superficially charming. He or she gets easily enthused and then quickly bored and is temperamentally fickle and socially shallow and dramatic.

The DSM *narcissistic* inmate acts proud and self-assured, is egocentrically arrogant, and flouts conventional rules. He or she feels entitled, expects special favors, and is facile in devising plausible rationalizations for his or her irresponsible conduct.

The DSM *antisocial* inmate is untrustworthy and unreliable and actively violates established social codes through repeated duplicitous and criminal behavior. He or she acts in a restless and impulsive manner, is often contemptuous and devious, has few personal loyalties, and disregards the safety of self or others.

The DSM-III-R *sadistic* inmate is mean-spirited and fractious, if not overtly hostile, displaying an excitable and pugnacious temper that flares quickly into belligerence. He or she often intimidates others with verbally abusive and physically brutal behaviors and views his or her destructiveness in a cold-blooded manner.

The DSM *compulsive* inmate is dutiful, conscientious, and respectful of authority. He or she seeks to engage in commendable behaviors, adhering to prescribed regulations and rules. Most have self-discipline and are socially formal and correct, keeping emotions under control, but are often tense and grim.

The DSM *depressive* and *masochistic* inmate is self-demeaning and melancholic and acts in a submissive, if not servile manner, allowing (if not encouraging) others to take advantage and be exploitative of him or her. He or she anticipates disappointments, sabotages good opportunities, and seeks to justify his or her suffering, guilt, and shame.

The DSM *negativistic* (passive–aggressive) inmate is persistently discontented, touchy, obstinate, and resentful. His or her outlook is cynical, skeptical, and untrusting; he or she is often sulky and moody, begrudging others their good fortune. Many resist doing expected tasks by being contrary and irksome.

The DSM *schizotypal* inmate is notably insensitive to feelings. He or she experiences a strange sense of nonbeing or nonexistence, as if his or her floating conscious awareness carried with it a depersonalized or identityless human form. He or she tends to be drab, sluggish, and inexpressive, possesses a marked deficit in affectivity, and appears bland, indifferent, unmotivated, and insensitive to the external word. Cognitive processes are obscure, vague, and tangential.

The DSM *borderline* inmate exhibits extreme unpredictability and is restless, irritable, impatient, and complaining. He or she acts defiant, disgruntled, and discontent, as well as stubborn, sullen, pessimistic, and resentful. He or she is easily disillusioned or slighted and is envious and feels unappreciated and cheated.

The DSM *paranoid* inmate finds that his or her efforts to abuse and tyrannize others has prompted them to reciprocate, to inflict hostility and punishment in return. The strategy of arrogance and brutalization has backfired too often. He or she now seeks retribution not in action, but in fantasy.

Mixed Personality Types

In this section we shall attempt to highlight prisoner varieties that are commonly seen in institutions of incarceration, but which reflect the complex characteristics of several personality types as they blend and are found among prisoners. Although not complete in the varieties we find or include in the several MCMI narrative reports, we will describe a significant number of these mixed types in the following paragraphs (Millon & Davis, 1996).

1. In what we term the *covetous* criminal type we see, in its most distilled form, the essential feature characterizing the DSM antisocial personality, the element of aggrandizement. Here we observe inmates who feel that life has not given them their due, that they have been deprived of their rightful level of emotional support and material rewards, that others have received more than their share, and that they personally never were given the bounties of the good life. What drives these prisoners is envy and a desire for retribution. These goals can be achieved by the assumption of power, best expressed through avaricious greed and voracity. To usurp that which others possess is their highest reward. Not only can they gain retribution, but they thereby fill the emptiness within themselves. More pleasure comes from taking than in merely having. Like a predatory animal after its prey, these criminal types have an enormous drive, a rapacious outlook in which they manipulate and treat others as possessions in their power games. Although they have little compassion for the effects of their behaviors, feeling little or no guilt for their actions, they remain at heart quite insecure about their power and their possessions, never feeling that they have acquired enough to make up for their earlier deprivations. They are pushy and greedy, anxious lest they lose the gains they have achieved. Their life has been openly materialistic, characterized by both conspicuous consumptions and ostentatious displays. Regardless of their voracious desires and achievements, they remain ever jealous and envious.

2. Not all criminal types desire to fill their sense of emptiness by pursuing material acquisitions. It is their reputation and status that they wish to defend or enlarge. For some, their behaviors are primarily defensive, designed to ensure that others recognize them as persons of substance, people who should "not be trifled with." These persons, whose personalities we term *reputation-defending* types (Toch, 1992), need to be thought of as invincible and formidable persons, indomitable and inviolable; moreover, others should be aware that they possess qualities of strength and invulnerability. Inmates of this type wish to convey to others that they are tough and potent persons, that they cannot be pushed around readily, and that others cannot get away with anything that slights the prisoners' "true" status. These prisoners react with great intensity when their status and capabilities are questioned. Most are perpetually on guard against the possibility that others will denigrate or belittle them.

3. These inmates, whose personalities we label the *risk-taking* type, often carry out dangerous action for its own sake, for the excitement it provides, for the sense of feeling alive and engaged in life, rather than for purposes such as material gain or reputation defending. These are prisoners who respond before thinking and act impulsively, behaving in an unreflective and uncontrolled manner. Beyond the inability to control their behaviors and feelings, these inmates appear to be substantially fearless, unblanched by events that most people experience as dangerous or frightening. They give evidence of a venturesomeness that appears blind to the potential of serious consequences. Their risk taking seems foolhardy, not courageous. Yet, they persist in a hyperactive search for hazardous challenges and for gambling with life's dangers.

4. In what has been termed the *nomadic* type we find persons who seek to run away from a society in which they feel unwanted, cast aside, and abandoned. Instead of reacting antagonistically to this rejection by seeking retribution for having been denied the normal benefits of social life, these inmates drift to the periphery of society, scavenging what little remains they can find of what they could not achieve through acceptable social means. These criminals are angry at the injustices to which they were exposed, but now feel sorry for themselves and have distanced from conventional social affairs because they feel they have little influence on others and are fearful of being further rejected. These peripheral

drifters and vagrants feel jinxed, ill-fated, and doomed in life. They are gypsy-like in their roaming, itinerant vagabonds and wanderers who have become misfits or dropouts from society. Their isolation, however, is not benign. Beneath their social withdrawal are intense feelings of resentment and anger. Under minor provocation, or as a consequence of alcohol or substance abuse, these persons may act out impulsively, precipitously discharging their pent-up frustrations in brutal assaults or sexual attacks upon those weaker than themselves.

5. These persons, whose personalities we term the *malevolents*, epitomize the least attractive of criminals because they include individuals who are especially vindictive and hostile. Their impulse toward retribution is discharged in a hateful and destructive defiance of conventional social life. Distrustful of others and anticipating betrayal and punishment, they have acquired a coldblooded ruthlessness, an intense desire to gain revenge for the real or imagined mistreatment to which they were subjected earlier in life. Here we see a sweeping rejection of tender emotions and a deep suspicion that the goodwill efforts expressed by others are merely ploys to deceive and undo them. They assume a chip-on-the-shoulder attitude, a readiness to lash out at those whom they distrust or those whom they can use as scapegoats for their seething impulse to destroy.

6. It is the unpredictability and sudden emergence of hostility that differentiates what we term the *explosive* type from other variants of the criminal population. The explosive criminal manifests adult-like tantrums, uncontrollable rages, and fearsome attacks upon others, most frequently in a nonincarcerated period against members of their own family. Before its intense nature can be identified and constrained there is a rapid escalation of fury in which unforgivable things are said and unforgettable blows are struck. Explosive behaviors erupt precipitously. Feeling thwarted or threatened, this person responds in a volatile and hurtful way, bewildering others by the abrupt change that has overtaken him or her.

7. Along with the malevolent type, what we label the *tyrannical* inmate stands among the most frightening and cruel of the criminal personality types. Both relate to others in an attacking, intimidating, and overwhelming way, frequently accusatory and abusive, and almost invariably destructive. There is a verbally or physically overbearing character to their assaults, and minor resistances or weaknesses seem to stimulate forceful action, encouraging attack rather than deterring it and slowing them down. It is the forcefulness, the unrestrained character, and the indiscriminate anger that is most notable in the tyrannical type. Inmates of this type appear to relish the act of menacing and brutalizing others; forcing them to cower and submit seems to provide them with a special sense of satisfaction. Many intentionally heighten and dramatize their surly, abusive, inhumane, and unmerciful behaviors.

8. The next type, the *disingenuous* criminal, is typified by a veneer of friendliness and sociability. Although making a superficially good impression upon acquaintances, more characteristic unreliability, an impulsive tendency, resentment, and moodiness are seen among close associates. A socially facile lifestyle may be noted by a persistent seeking of attention and excitement, often expressed in seductive behaviors. Relationships are shallow and fleeting, frequently disrupted by caustic comments and impulses that are acted upon with insufficient deliberation. Those with this personality are frequently seen as irresponsible and undependable, exhibiting short-lived enthusiasms and immature stimulus-seeking behaviors. Notable also among these criminals is a tendency to be contriving and plotting, to exhibit a crafty and scheming approach to life, and tendencies to be insincere, calculating, and occasionally deceitful.

9. The behavior of the *unprincipled* criminal type is characterized by an arrogant sense of self-worth, an indifference to the welfare of others, and a fraudulent and deceptive social manner. There is a desire to exploit others and to expect special recognitions and considerations without assuming reciprocal responsibilities. A deficient social conscience is evident in the tendency to flout conventions, to engage in actions that raise questions of personal integrity, and to disregard the rights of others. Achievement deficits and social irresponsibilities are justified by expansive fantasies and frank prevarications. More than merely disloyal and exploitative, these individuals may be found among society's conmen and -women and charlatans, many of whom are vindictive and contemptuous of their victims. The unprincipled inmate displays an indifference to truth that, if brought to his or her attention, is likely to elicit an attitude of nonchalant indifference. He or she is skillful in the ways of social influence, is capable of feigning an air of justified innocence, and is adept in deceiving others with charm and glibness. Lacking any deep feelings of loyalty, he or she may successfully scheme beneath a veneer of politeness and civility.

10. The *borderline* criminal type is capricious and evasive, has always resented any dependence on others, and hates those to whom he or she has turned to for support. In contrast to other criminal types, borderlines are not likely to have had even a small measure of consistency in support from others; most have never had their needs satisfied on a regular basis and have never felt secure in relationships. The borderline openly registers his or her disappointments, is stubborn and recalcitrant, and vents his or her angers only to recant and feel guilty and contrite. He or she is erratic and continues to vacillate between apologetic submission on the one hand and stubborn resistance and contrariness on the other. Unable to get hold of themselves and unable to find a comfortable niche with others, these prisoners may become increasingly testy, bitter, and discontent. Resigned to their fate and despairing of hope, they oscillate between pathological extremes of behavior. Many express feelings of worthlessness and futility, act in a highly agitated or deeply depressed manner, develop delusions of guilt, and become self-condemnatory, even self-destructive.

SPECIAL FEATURES OF THE MCMI-III FORM C

There are two major areas in which the Correctional Form of the MCMI-III (MCMI-III-C) differs from the standard MCMI-III instrument and its interpretive report. We will attend to each separately. The first pertains to the characteristics of the MCMI-III test itself, including its norms; the second pertains to specific realms of information contained in the correctional interpretive report that are not part of the basic MCMI-III narratives.

Features of the Instrument Itself

Relevant Normative Population

The original MCMI-III was based on normative data gathered with patients involved in psychological assessment and treatment. A small proportion of this normative group, perhaps less than 15%, included individuals appraised in prisons. By contrast, the new norms developed for Form C of the MCMI-III will be based entirely on incarcerated individuals. They participated in psychological assessment at intake points in the course of incarceration. About two-thirds of this incarcerated population was seen at an early phase of prisoner screening. Another segment of the normative population includes prisoners seen during their initial year or two. A third segment of the prisoner normative population, perhaps 10% to 20%, are individuals who were appraised for special consideration in rehabilitation programs or mental health judgments. The key point, however, is that norms for the correctional version of the test are based completely on prison rather than psychiatric populations. A modest proportion of those in the prisoner normative group, however, were inmates being evaluated for possible psychiatric disorders.

Appropriate Reading Level

The standard MCMI-III items are suitable for those who can read at the seventh to eighth grade level. This level is too demanding for a large number of inmates in prisons and accounts for the high proportion of invalid results that are found with several self-report instruments. To reduce this high level of invalidity and to make the items more readable and understandable by prisoners who are given the instrument, standard MCMI-III items are being substantially rewritten so as to be usable for those prisoners whose reading levels are at the third or fourth grade. Every MCMI-III-C item has been reviewed and modified to achieve these ends while still representing the same psychological traits as found in the original MCMI. To illustrate:

MCMI-III Item 15. "Things that are going well today won't last very long."
MCMI-III-C Item 15. "Good things don't last."
MCMI-III item 29. "People usually think of me as a reserved and serious-minded person."
MCMI-III-C Item 29. "People see me as a serious person."
MCMI-III Item 40. "I guess I'm a fearful and inhibited person."
MCMI-III-C Item 40. "I'm a fearful and shy person."

Scale correlations between the MCMI-III and MCMI-III-C items range from .74 to .87. These averaged results derive from several populations retested approximately 7 to 10 days apart, some with MCMI-III-C first and others with the MCMI-III first. These reliability data are modestly lower than same-test repeat results.

Features of the MCMI-III-C Interpretive Report

The concerns of psychologists working in prison settings are special; they must deal with persons possessing attributes that differ from general psychiatric patients, and their evaluations must prove useful in settings that call for psychological and behavioral considerations other than those found in most mental health contexts. It is these prison-relevant attributes and considerations that are "added" to the more-or-less standard interpretive narrative of the MCMI-III-C report, as will also be illustrated in Figure 8.1, later in this chapter.

Reaction to Authority

This paragraph of the MCMI-III-C report seeks to identify prisoners who will exhibit cooperative or confrontational attitudes in response to prison staff. Some inmates evidence a willingness to ride roughshod over those who frustrate them, whereas others choose isolation, apathy, or social indifference. Whether of the tough, the conforming, or the insulated type, characteristics of authority reactivity have been judged of value in appraising prisoners.

Potential for Violence

There are few characteristics more relevant to the management of prison behavior than inmate proclivities to act out violently. Tendencies toward rage and brutality are among the more important pieces of general information recorded with the MCMI-III-C Interpretive Report, in addition to the standard personality characterizations. Potentials for frequent displays of brutality, domination, and cruelty are noted in this special section.

Impulsivity Proneness

The inability to restrain one's urges and momentary desires is another major area of psychological concern. Thoughtless, spur-of-the-moment, impulsive acts result in precipitous and reckless behaviors which may set off explosive outbursts. If paired with tendencies toward violence, impulsivity proneness may result in frenzied brawls and riotous behaviors.

Sexual Predation/Victimization

Homosexual behavior has become all too commonplace in prison settings. This clinical paragraph of the MCMI-III-C Interpretive Report, however, is concerned with heterosexual inclinations of a predatory or ravenous character that are enacted in extraprison life. The intent is to identify inmates who have either engaged in prior acts of heterosexual abuse (e.g., rape, molestation) or who are potentially so inclined.

Suicidal Potential

A continuum exists among inmates ranging from diffuse and periodic thoughts of intentional self-injury or death (suicidal ideation), intentional self-injury (self-destruc-tive behavior), unsuccessful suicidal behavior (suicidal attempts) and finally, successful attempts (suicide). Although inmates facing their bleak prospects or their feelings of worthlessness or guilt often think of suicide as a way out, few act or are able to act while incarcerated. Nevertheless, indications of such potentials are important for prison psychologists.

Amenability to Treatment/Rehabilitation

A major consideration in working with inmates relates to their readiness and receptivity to efforts to rehabilitate them psychologically and/or vocationally. No less significant is their preparedness and fitness for parole. Difficult as it may be to predict, as opposed to diagnose, an effort will be made in this section of the report to appraise the likelihood that the inmate is willing and equipped to take advantage of such rehabilitative and reformative steps.

A sample of the Preliminary MCMI-III Form C interpretive report is shown in Figure 8.1.

DSM-IV Diagnostic Characterization

The MCMI-III-Form C profile of this inmate suggests that he is driven by a desire to display an image of daring and defiance, which may be characterized by outspokenness, brusqueness, impudence, and cheekiness. Particularly notable may be inclinations to exploit and intimidate others and to expect, if not demand, recognition without assuming reciprocal responsibility. Actions that raise questions about his personal integrity, such as a ruthless indifference to the rights of others, are likely present and may be indicative of a deficient social conscience. He is likely to be disdainful of traditional ideals and contemptuous of conventional values.

Personal displays of brashness and unsentimentality are viewed with pride. This prisoner may also court danger and punishment, display a rash willingness to risk personal harm, and react fearlessly to threats and punitive action. Punishment appears only to reinforce this convict's rebellious and hostile feelings. Malicious tendencies seen in others may be used to justify his own aggressive inclinations and may lead not only to frequent personal and family difficulties but also to a history of legal entanglements, antisocial behavior, alcoholism, or drug problems. The clinical staff may wish to corroborate these hypotheses.

When his life is under reasonable control, he may be adept at enticing the goodwill of others. More characteristically, he may be envious of others and wary of their motives. This inmate is likely to feel unfairly treated and can be easily provoked to irritability and anger. His limited facade of sociability may give way to antagonistic and caustic comments, and gratification may often be obtained by humiliating others. A marked suspicion of guards and others in authority may cause him to feel secure only when he has the upper hand. Socially repugnant impulses may not be refashioned in sublimated forms but may be directly discharged, usually with minimal guilt.

Deficient in deep feelings of loyalty and displaying an occasional indifference to truth, he may scheme beneath a veneer of charm. A guiding principle is that of outwitting others, exploiting them before they exploit him. Carrying a chip-on-the-shoulder attitude, he may exhibit an energy and readiness to attack those who are distrusting. If he is unsuccessful in channeling these aggressive impulses, resentments may mount into episodes of manic activity or into overt acts of hostility.

Testy and demanding, this inmate may currently evince an agitated depression, as seen in a daily moodiness and vacillation. He is likely to display a rapidly shifting mix of disparaging comments about himself, anxiously expressed suicidal thoughts, and outbursts of bitter resentment interwoven with a demanding irritability toward others. Feeling trapped by constraints imposed by his circumstances and upset by emotions and thoughts he can neither understand nor control, he may periodically turn his reservoir of anger inward, voicing severe self-recrimination and self-loathing. These signs of contrition may serve to induce guilt in others, an effective manipulation in which he can give a measure of retribution without further jeopardizing what he sees as his currently precarious, if not hopeless, situation.

Failing to keep deep and powerful sources of inner conflict from overwhelming his controls, this characteristically difficult and conflicted man may also be experiencing signs of an anxiety disorder. He is unable to rid himself of preoccupations with his fearful presentiments as well as recurring headaches, fatigue, and insomnia, currently upset by their uncharacteristic presence in his life. Feeling at the mercy of unknown and upsetting forces that seem to well up within him, he is at a loss as to how to counteract them, but he may exploit them to manipulate others or to complain at great length.

Periods of manic hyperactivity and excitement may also be probable in the history of this inmate. During these periods he is likely to exhibit a sequence of hostile periods that are marked by pressured speech, lessened need for sleep, hyperdistractibility, and a general restlessness. Periods of restraint may be manifested for brief spans of time, only to be suddenly and unpredictably replaced by temper tantrums, belligerence, and explosive anger.

(continued)

FIGURE 8.1. Sample MCMI-III Form C interpretive report for a 34-year-old male inmate in prison for murder committed in a "drug war." He is poorly adjusted in the institution and described by guards as "violence prone, amoral, and undependable."

Prison-Relevant Characteristics

Reaction to Authority: This man may evidence transient controls, but is likely to be different and confrontational. This irritability or lack of conformity should be kept in mind in plans for cell assignment.

Potential for Violence: There is strong evidence that this inmate may act out in an aggressive and hostile manner. Care should be taken to anticipate precipitous anger and potential brutality. Inasmuch as he lacks controls to restrain his violent inclination, he should be isolated from weaker inmates who will be readily victimized by him.

Impulsivity Proneness: Although controlled much of the time, this inmate can suddenly and capriciously vent his impulses, especially those of a hostile nature.

Sexual Predation/Victimization: There is evidence that this inmate may have engaged in destructive sexual behaviors in the past; also notable are strong urges of a sexual character that may manifest themselves in prison life. Preparatory counseling may be wise.

Suicidal Potential: There are clear signs of a marked though transient period of depression in this man that calls for clinical attention and observational alertness to the potential of suicide behavior.

Amenability to Treatment/Rehabilitation: This inmate is not likely to be a willing participant in rehabilitation efforts, most probably agreeing, if ever, under the pressure of further incarceration or punitive action. His tendency to attribute his problems to the malice of others will be evident and even when accepting some measure of responsibility, resentment may be felt toward those who try to point these out. Given his proneness to violence and his orientation to raw power, efforts are best directed to an anger management program, rather than to general personal counseling and rehabilitation.

This person will probably seek to bluff or outwit staff efforts. These oppositional actions will call for the staff to restrain the impulse to react with harsh disapproval. On the other hand, warmth and understanding will only be interpreted as weakness. An important step in building some rapport is to attempt to see his past history from his experience of it.

Although the staff can attempt to develop a constructive alliance with him, he probably will do best in peer groups composed of like-minded inmates. Unlikely to accept assistance, or even to admit deficiencies, only fellow inmates of a similar propensity may be able to break through his resistance and arrogance. Approaches that focus on present behaviors and which accept no excuses for past misconduct may be responded to with respect rather than cynicism. Any infraction of rules or brutalizing actions should be responded to unequivocally and swiftly, lest he see that such behaviors go unpunished.

FIGURE 8.1. *cont.*

REFERENCES

Abraham, K. (1925). Character-formation on the genital level of the libido. In *Selected papers on psychoanalysis* (English translation, 1927). London: Hogarth Press.
Aichhorn, A. (1935). *Wayward youth*. New York: Viking. (Original work published 1925)
American Psychiatric Association. (1987). *Diagnostic and statistical manual of mental disorders* (3rd ed., rev.). Washington, DC: Author.
American Psychiatric Association. (1994). *Diagnostic and statistical manual of mental disorders* (4th ed.). Washington, DC: Author.
Birnbaum, K. (1914). *Die psychopathischen Verbrecher* (2nd ed.). Leipzig: Thieme.
Cleckley, H. (1941). *The mask of sanity*. St. Louis: Mosby.
Freud, S. (1925). Some character types met with in psychoanalytic work. In *Collected papers* (Vol. 4). London: Hogarth Press. (Original work published 1915)

Hare, R. D. (1985). *The Psychopathy Checklist*. Unpublished manuscript, University of British Columbia, Vancouver, Canada.

Healy, W., & Bronner, A. (1926). *Delinquents and criminals: Their making and unmaking*. New York: Macmillan.

Kernberg, O. F. (1992). *Aggression in personality disorders and perversions*. New Haven, CT: Yale University Press.

Kraepelin, E. (1896). *Psychiatrie* (5th ed.). Leipzig: J. A. Barth Verlag.

Kraepelin, E. (1887). *Psychiatrie: Ein lehrbuch* (2nd ed.). Leipzig: Abel.

Kraepelin, E. (1899). *Psychiatrie: Ein lehrbuch* (6th ed.). Leipzig: Barth.

Kraepelin, E. (1903–1904). *Psychiatrie* (7th ed.). Leipzig: Barth.

Kraepelin, E. (1905). *Psychiatrie* (7th ed. Vol. 2). Leipzig: Barth.

Kraepelin, E. (1909–1915). *Psychiatrie* (8th ed., Vol. 4). Leipzig: Barth.

Millon, T. (1977). *Millon Clinical Multiaxial Inventory Manual*. Minneapolis: National Computer Systems.

Millon, T. (1981). *Disorders of personality: DSM-III, Axis II*. New York: Wiley-Interscience.

Millon, T. (1987). *Millon Clinical Multiaxial Inventory II Manual*. Minneapolis: National Computer Systems.

Millon, T., Million, C., & Davis, R. D. (1994). *Millon Clinical Multiaxial Inventory—III Manual*. Minneapolis: National Computer Systems.

Millon, T., & Davis, R. D. (1996). *Disorders of personality: DSM-IV and beyond*. New York: Wiley-Interscience.

Partridge, G. E. (1930). Current conceptions of psychopathic personality. *American Journal of Psychiatry*, *10*, 53–99.

Prichard, J. C. (1835). *A treatise on insanity*. London: Sherwood, Gilbert, and Piper.

Reich, W. (1925). *Der Triebhafie Charakter*. Leipzig: Internationaler Psychoanalytischer Verlag.

Schneider, K. (1923). *Die psychopathischen Personlichkeiten*. Vienna: Deuticke.

Schneider, K. (1950). *Psychopathic personalities* (Trans., 9th ed.). London: Cassell. (Original work published 1923)

Siever, L. J., & Davis, K. L. (1991). A psychobiological perspective on the personality disorders. *American Journal of Psychiatry*, *148*, 1647–1658.

Siever, L. J., Klar, H., & Coccaro, E. (1985). Biological response styles: Clinical implications. In L. J. Siever & H. Klar (Eds.), *Psychobiological substrates of personality* (pp. 38–66). Washington, DC: American Psychiatric Press.

Toch, H. (1992). *Violent men: An inquiry into the psychology of violence*. Washington DC: American Psychological Association.

9

Using the MCMI in Neuropsychological Evaluations

SALLY L. KOLITZ RUSSELL
ELBERT W. RUSSELL

Objective measures of personality and emotional status make an indispensable contribution to any thorough neuropsychological examination. The Millon Clinical Multiaxial Inventory—III (MCMI-III; Millon, 1994) provides such a contribution with its relationship to the DSM-IV. It also provides the best measure of personality characteristics as well as an examination of types of psychopathology. Although such objective measures of personality are neither designed nor intended to be a method of assessing the cognitive abilities that are affected by brain damage, this type of information is essential for a thorough neuropsychological examination.

THE PURPOSE OF THE
NEUROPSYCHOLOGICAL EVALUATION

A neuropsychological assessment is conducted for the purpose of determining the cognitive status of an individual. Prior to the advent of computerized tomographic scans (CT) and magnetic resonance imaging (MRI), diagnosis and localization were the major factors examined in neuropsychology. There are certain conditions which still warrant the need for such information, such as mild to moderate head trauma and dementia of the Alzheimer's type, which often are not demonstrated on neurological tests. However, neuropsychological assessment now makes its contribution by providing information concerning a patient's cognitive or psychological condition. Such information is essential for rehabilitation, vocational or educational planning, disability ratings, forensic compensation in personal injury cases, and differential diagnosis between neurological and psychiatric conditions. Neuropsychological assessment is also crucial for research in our continually expanding knowledge of the brain, as well as in the development and efficacy of neurological and psychiatric medications.

154

No matter how accurate the measures of cognition may be in the neuropsychological evaluation, if a deficit in cognition is primarily the result of an emotional problem, the cognitive evaluation is useless. No neuropsychological evaluation is valid without an accurate measure of emotional and personality functioning. Yet, it is disturbing how often a neuropsychological report does not include an objective psychological test. This omission is tantamount to excluding information concerning one of the areas most necessary for a thorough evaluation of brain functioning.

The Functional Examination

Almost 20 years ago there were attempts to study the correlation of psychological measures with neuropsychological conditions. No significant correlation was found between the MMPI and any of the subtests of the Halstead–Reitan battery (Wiens & Matarazzo, 1977).

The effect of schizophrenia is especially vexing. It is now a universal understanding that schizophrenia and some other emotional conditions will impair performance on neuropsychological tests (Goldstein, 1986; Watson, Thomas, Anderson, & Felling, 1968). Neuropsychological examinations themselves cannot distinguish schizophrenia from brain damage. As such, neuropsychological measures are blind to those emotional factors that may impair such measures. This means that "functional" factors must be measured and taken into account when assessing brain damage.

Utility of an Objective Test

There are many neuropsychologists who attack objective testing and then advocate for an interview to assess the emotional condition of a neuropsychological patient. Lezak's (1995) approach to this problem is typical. In her recent book the critique of objective testing used to evaluate functional pathology is primarily leveled at the MMPI because research relating all versions of the MCMI to organic conditions is lacking. Nevertheless, the same criticisms would have been leveled at any version of the MCMI.

First, Lezak (1995) accepts the universal finding (pp. 324–325) that neuropsychological measures will not distinguish brain damage from schizophrenia. The critique discusses the various studies that have been done with the MMPI and concludes that the MMPI will not diagnosis brain damage (p. 785). This is not surprising because personality and emotional status examinations were not designed and were never intended to assess the existence of brain damage any more than the neuropsychology battery was designed to assess the existence of emotional problems. While psychopathology examinations were not designed to determine the existence of brain damage, they were designed to determine the existence of schizophrenia and other functional conditions.

Subsequently, she examines the studies concerning differential diagnosis between brain damage and emotional problems and the utility of an objective test of schizophrenia in particular. Her selective analysis concludes that these tests, the MMPI in particular, are not accurate enough to be useful in a neuropsychology examination.

However, if these studies are carefully examined they demonstrate that while these objective measures (primarily the MMPI) cannot diagnose brain damage, they can separate schizophrenia from organic conditions at an acceptable rate (Golden, Sweet, & Osman, 1979; Russell, 1975, 1977; Ryan & Southeaver, 1977; Watson, 1977; Watson & Plemel, 1978; Watson, Plemel, & Jacobs, 1978). The rate of correct separation of schizophrenia from brain damage falls between 75% and 80%. This level of accuracy approaches that of neuropsychological batteries in assessing the existence of brain damage when there are no emotional factors involved (Russell, 1995).

At this point Lezak (1995) commits the fallacy of nonrefutation. This fallacy states that if a test or battery has not been shown to be invalid, it must be valid. Lezak's book presents research studies that show that the MMPI is not completely valid, that is, 100% accurate, and concludes that therefore one should not use it. Elsewhere, the book advocates using an interview and history method (pp. 319–331; pp. 791–792) which has never been shown to be invalid (or valid). There is not one study referenced in the entire book concerned with the validation of the interview–history method. History includes all of the neurological examination studies that the patient has received. Although undemonstrated, the interview–history method is undoubtedly relatively accurate, as that is the method used by neurologists and psychiatrists. However, is it more accurate than the combination of the interview–history and an objective psychopathology test? Or more broadly, does objective measurement, including both cognition and personality attributes, confer anything to the patient's total examination beyond that which neurology and psychiatry have already contributed?

The procedure for making a differential diagnosis when a brain condition is involved has been delineated by Watson (1977). Apparently, Lezak (1995) does not understand this method, a pattern analysis method. Her critique emphasizes the fact that the MMPI cannot diagnose brain damage (p.785), but this method does not utilize the MMPI to detect brain damage.

The method is to administer both a neuropsychological battery and an objective test or tests of psychopathology. Comparison of these will produce a more accurate assessment between normals, schizophrenics, and organic subjects than is possible with either the neuropsychology battery or the psychopathology test alone. If the neuropsychology battery indicates impairment and the psychopathology tests are relatively benign then the patient probably has an organic condition. If the neuropsychology battery is not impaired and the psychopathology test indicates an emotional condition then the problem is probably emotional. If the neuropsychological battery is impaired and the psychopathology tests indicate an emotional condition, especially a severe one, such as schizophrenia, then the diagnosis is functional and probably schizophrenia. If neither is impaired then the patient is probably normal.

A preliminary study by Brown (1987), which was designed to use an algorithm based on the preceding method, has been completed. When the most accurate cutting points were used the algorithm's overall separation of normal, organic, and psychiatric (largely schizophrenic) cases was 73%. In terms of separate categories, 69% of the organics, 94% of the psychiatric subjects, and 89% of the normal subjects were correctly identified.

This procedure as presented here may be termed superficial; however, it is basically correct in that it is based on research. In going beyond this basic method, in each individual case the specific test findings will help determine the type and severity of the brain condition along with other aspects of the case. The following case histories in this chapter will demonstrate how this procedure, using versions II and III of the MCMI in particular, operates with regard to various conditions.

The Utility of the MCMI-III

The MCMI-III is quite valuable in a neuropsychological evaluation. With the advent and inclusion of the MCMI-III the efficacy of the test battery has increased. The addition of the Post-Traumatic Stress Disorder scale is a welcome advance, as much of the neuropsychological population comes from a head trauma group. This dimension will be elaborated upon later in the chapter. Additionally, now that the DSM-IV has been published, the new items on the MCMI-III provide a description of personality styles congruent with the updated diagnostic guide.

Although a personality test cannot be used to assess cognitive functioning, differentiating between long-existing personality styles and current or transient emotional dysfunction is essential, particularly in the forensic arena. The MCMI-III provides this information, which of course has to be evaluated in light of background information and clinician judgment. While there has not been much research directly relating the MCMI to organic conditions, there has been considerable research into personality pathology, particularly in the areas of schizophrenia and the borderline personality.

The severity of psychopathology is quite important to assess because the results of a neuropsychological examination can be influenced by an individual who may be seriously emotionally compromised. Particularly in the area of a thought disorder such as schizophrenia, the neurobiological health of the brain may be affected. An organic personality disorder may occur as a result of head trauma or neurological disease and for this diagnostic entity, an objective psychological test is a necessity.

Many chronic and congenital organic problems such as attention deficit disorders (ADD) and learning disabilities (LD) are often accompanied by emotional problems which must be fully assessed. Much research has concentrated on the increased incidence of emotional problems in children who are diagnosed with ADD and LD. These children are often labeled with multiple diagnoses (Biederman, Gillis, Toner, & Goldberg, 1991). The increased interest in adult ADD has resulted in a need for accurate assessment for this disorder in this population as well. Neuropsychologists have experienced an increase in referrals reflecting this entity. It is important to be able to distinguish ADD from a psychological condition and to assess accurately personality style. The MCMI-III can help to accomplish this.

One of the major advantages of the MCMI-III over other objective tests of psychopathology is that it specifically examines personality characteristics. No other test provides such personality information as this objective test.

It is perhaps the "user-friendliness" of the test which is one of the MCMI's best strong points. In a neuropsychological evaluation, all brain functions must be assessed. "If the set of tests in a battery is to be an adequate representation of the brain, then coverage is an essential concern" (Russell, 1994. p. 229). Furthermore, this complete coverage of the brain must include the redundancy factor as well. That is, several tests must be administered for each brain function to assess the possibility and extent of brain damage. It is standard practice that a complete neuropsychological evaluation may take 6 or more hours of testing, exclusive of the clinical interview and psychological testing. Thus, a test which accurately assesses personality with the least number of questions necessary for accurate diagnosis is certainly preferable.

Although the MMPI is often administered as part of a battery, its length and the fact that the short versions are not as reliable as is the complete test makes it difficult to include in a neuropsychological evaluation. The reliability and validity of MMPI short forms are compromised and their use is not considered advisable (Pope, Butcher, & Seelen, 1993, p. 24).

This attribute of the shorter length of the MCMI-III cannot be underestimated. In our experience of administering neuropsychological evaluations, almost no patients have balked when given the MCMI-III; but there have been more than several instances in which administration of the MMPI has been met with a disgruntled attitude by a patient. Because the attitude of the examinee can affect the outcome of the test results, this is no small matter. Furthermore, a person's attitude can influence the entire neuropsychological battery of test results.

The MCMI-III in general has good concurrent validity (Craig & Olson, 1992) as well as temporal stability (Overholser, 1990). The results of the latter study showed that similar symptom patterns were displayed over time. This finding held true whether these patterns were part of personality traits or patterns of responding when patients were symptomatic.

The audiotaped version of the MCMI-III is particularly useful for patients who have either some type of organic damage or a low reading level. Additionally, the incidence of visual impairments or difficulties with attention and concentration are fairly common in this population and an audiotaped version of a shorter personality test is more feasible.

The Spanish version of the MCMI-III brings with it added cultural fairness and is a welcome addition to a neuropsychologist's armamentarium. There are relatively few tests which are offered in Spanish and this audiotaped version is administered to our patients, as it is difficult to assess the reading level of the Spanish-speaking individual unless the examiner him- or herself is a fluent Spanish speaker.

Because a literature search uncovered almost no published research on the Millon Inventories directly related to neuropsychological entities, the bulk of this chapter will be based on clinical experience and actual case studies in the use of the MCMI-II and -III. Topics concerned with strictly clinical as well as forensic issues will be covered. We have been working with the MCMIs in our practice for over 10 years as part of the neuropsychological evaluation process and are familiar with how they aid the neuropsychological assessment.

EMOTIONAL COMPONENTS OF BRAIN INJURY

The Effect of Brain Damage on the MCMI-II and the MCMI-III

The research on the effect of neurological conditions on the MCMI-II and -III has been minimal, to this point. The only study that directly examined the relationship between aspects of the MCMI and types of brain damage was completed by Chitwood (1989)as a doctoral dissertation. The effect of lateralized brain lesions on MCMI-II indices of personality disorders was studied. When subjects' irritative lesions were removed, lateralized differences were found. These differences showed more characteristics of the avoidant personality in patients with left hemisphere damage. In right-hemisphere-damaged subjects, more histrionic features were found. Chitwood points out that the MCMI-II differentiated lateralized effects better than did the MMPI. However, the MMPI was found to be somewhat more effective in differentiating psychiatric from brain-damaged subjects.

The MCMI-II was one of the measures used in diagnosing the borderline personality in a study that explored subtle organic deficits accompanying borderline personality disorder (Swirsky-Sacchetti et al., 1993). Such defects were found in patients assessed as having a borderline disorder by the MCMI-II.

However, in an area such as violent behavior, neuropsychological measures have been found to delineate behavioral characteristics more accurately than do personality measures (Spellacy, 1977). Using the MMPI and neuropsychological tests, the author indicated that neuropsychological assessment had greater power to predict group membership of violent and nonviolent adolescents than did the personality measure alone. It would be interesting to conduct research on the MCMI-III on this topic.

Postconcussion Syndrome

This syndrome consists of many of the following symptoms: headaches, concentration deficits, memory problems, irritability, increased anxiety, emotional lability, loss of perceived self-worth, and depression. A fair number of people with mild head traumas report all or some of the above symptoms. The more subtle effects of mild head injury (duration of loss of consciousness less than 15 minutes) are sometimes difficult to detect with standard neuropsychological tests. Because a closed head injury more commonly affects the frontal, temporal, and midbrain areas, the limbic system is often involved. These are the areas of the brain that are concerned with emotional reactions. Emotional sequelae are thus often demonstrated in the postconcussion syndrome, whereas cognitive deficits are not always seen. The medical profession and the public at large are often insensitive to the needs and problems of the mildly head-injured patient, even though they represent the greatest percentage of the head injured. Psychological assessment is one way of focusing attention on this most important area and referring patients for psychological help where indicated. Indeed, sometimes cognitive deficits are the direct result of emotional problems experienced by head-injured patients.

Organic Mood Disorder

While the expected problem is to differentiate functional from organic conditions, both can coexist in the case of an organic mood disorder. Moderate to severe head trauma can produce this condition. The degree of brain injury is best assessed on the basis of length of loss of consciousness, the rating of the Glasgow Coma Scale (Teasdale & Jennett, 1974), and the presence and duration of retrograde or anterograde amnesia. Recommendations for treatment are extremely important in the case of an organic mood disorder and the amount of compensation will be increased in the forensic area if this condition is diagnosed. Additionally, as has been mentioned, brain damage itself can produce depression, so that accurate psychological assessment is a necessity.

Recently we saw a case of a 43-year-old man who had been working on a construction site when over 50 pounds of steel beams fell from the ceiling, trapping him underneath. He sustained not only multiple physical injuries but also brain damage. Organic damage was diffuse, with significant dysfunction of frontal lobe functioning. This type of frontal brain damage typically results in intense mood swings, lack of impulse control, and aggressive behavior. The MCMI-III demonstrated a pattern of high SS and PP scale scores (Schizophrenic and Delusional Disorder). There had been no premorbid history for personality problems and the quite severe brain damage was consistent with a person who showed bizarre thought patterns, regressive behavior, patchy hallucinatory experiences, and delusions of a persecutory nature. Thus the diagnosis of an organic mood disorder was made and inpatient psychiatric treatment was recommended.

Because this was a forensic case, the defense had attempted to discredit the findings in both the neurological areas of impairment and the psychological findings. The use of the MCMI-III findings strongly supported our contentions of an organic mood disorder. An objective psychological test is mandatory in a court case because it provides objective evidence to support a contention. The MCMI-III is gaining such recognition in the forensic arena. In fact, in this particular case the actual graph was replicated in the form of an exhibit so that the neuropsychologist could explain its significance to the jury.

DIFFERENTIAL DIAGNOSIS
Dementia versus Depression

Perhaps the most frequent referral for neuropsychological assessment is for differentiating organic from functional conditions. An example of a differential diagnosis case was that of a 62-year-old married woman who had worked as an executive secretary for a major company for 20 years. She had been reporting increasing memory problems and an inability to concentrate. Her neurologist had sent her for a neuropsychological evaluation to rule out a dementing process. An MRI had not detected significant atrophy and the electroencephalogram (EEG) was within normal limits.

Her neuropsychological testing found her to have above-average intellectual functioning as based on the Wechsler Adult Intelligence Scale—Revised (WAIS-R; Full Scale IQ = 118) (Wechsler, 1981). Memory and executive functioning tests were all above average when normed for her age and educational level. The only area in the neuropsychological testing which was found to be below average was for psychomotor speed and motor functions, and because she had an arthritic condition in her hands, this finding was not thought to be related to problems with her brain.

The MCMI-III indicated an individual who may have a tendency to magnify symptomatology and who appeared to be experiencing a period of acute turmoil. One of the Axis I diagnoses was indicated as that of a major depression with a personality disorder noted as a depressive personality disorder with dependent personality traits. Interestingly, within the clinical interview, this woman described her marital relationship as tenuous and reported feeling extreme rejection from her husband. Profile analysis revealed that in addition to the elevated Dysthymia scale score, the dependent–avoidant personality pattern was evident. Because dementia had been ruled out on the basis of her neuropsychological tests, the MCMI-III and clinical history were consistent with a depressive condition which was obviously compromising her work performance. The psychomotor retardation found in the neuropsychological test results was also consistent with depression.

Cognitive functioning tends to be preserved under the pressure of the testing situation even in seriously depressed individuals. Gass and Russell in their 1986 article wrote "One should probably be conservative in attributing poor verbal memory performance to depression, particularly when there is evidence of organicity or when other factors are present that might account for the memory deficit" (p. 262).

Another differential diagnostic case with a different conclusion was that of a 67-year-old man who had been referred by his neurologist for neuropsychological testing because he reported memory and word-finding problems. Complicating the diagnosis of possible dementia was the fact that his wife of 46 years had died 1 year previously. In the clinical interview this gentleman appeared rather stoic and guarded with his feelings. He described his memory problems in an understated manner and only displayed minimal word-finding problems. Although he described the death of his wife as a significant loss to him, he did not evidence much emotionality.

The neuropsychological test results demonstrated a clear left parietal problem. That is, he was found to have significant anomia (word-finding problems) as well as memory deficits for verbal material, both rote (in the form of word lists) and semantic (stories). Right hemisphere tests such as spatial relations tasks indicated that this hemisphere was intact.

The MCMI-III showed base rate (BR) scores which were all below 75. The profile was constricted and described a man who endorsed no psychosocial or environmental problems. The audiotaped version had been administered to him because of his left hemisphere problems and resulting difficulties with reading. He had scored within the average range on the Comprehension subtest of the WAIS-R and had understood all the directions given to him during the testing. Additionally, he had understood the examiner's questions during the clinical interview. It was decided that this man's test results were unfortunately consistent with a dementia of the Alzheimer's type more prominent in left hemisphere functioning.

It is a characteristic of Alzheimer's patients that they often do not suffer with much depression. Emotional problems and stress are more characteristic of the families of such patients. In this case, the MCMI-III had been extremely helpful in showing the typical picture of the Alzheimer patient's emotional status and the neuropsychological testing had served to corroborate a cognitive pattern found in patients with dementia.

Organic Brain Damage versus Schizophrenia

The pattern of neuropsychological test results of a schizophrenic or schizophreniform patient often resembles a brain-damage pattern (Goldstein, 1986; Watson et al., 1968). Because schizophrenia is often thought to be a "brain condition," one would expect neuropsychological deficits in the test results. Nevertheless, it is important to distinguish an acquired organic condition such as head injury from the schizophrenic "organic condition." In a practical situation, it is extremely important to differentiate a preexisting psychiatric condition from traumatic brain injury. This can best be exemplified by a forensic case which, in fact, was settled in favor of the defense based on the use of the MCMI-II (Millon, 1987).

A 28-year-old male who worked as a laborer on a construction site fell off the back of a truck as he was being transported to the site. He broke his left arm but there was no report in the medical records or in the patient's own self-report of his having hit his head. However, the plaintiff was suing for brain damage on the basis of a whiplash-type injury which supposedly caused an axonal shearing, resulting in brain damage.

The plaintiff performed in the brain-damaged range on tests of memory, executive functioning, and language functions. His Verbal IQ on the WAIS-R was equal to 75. His answers to some of the questions on the Comprehension subtest were somewhat bizarre. For example, he said "people needed a license to get married because they might need to put the other person in jail." His reading level, as determined by an achievement test, was at the tenth grade, so he was able to complete the MCMI-II. His personality code was noted as schizoid, avoidant, and dependent with the Schizotypal scale extremely elevated.

His premorbid history was consistent with his MCMI results, as he had never married, had not formed close relationships with anyone (including his own family), and had an inconsistent work history with more periods of being unemployed than employed. He presented in the clinical interview as devoid of affect, never making eye contact, displaying ideas of grandeur, and being tangential in his responses. The conclusions of the neuropsychological evaluation were not consistent with the pattern of test results found in head trauma and were more consistent with a schizoaffective disorder. Additionally, the possibility of secondary gain could not be ruled out. Needless to say, this condition would have preexisted the alleged mild head trauma.

Confirmation of this diagnosis was obtained prior to the trial, but after the neuropsychological report was issued. Depositions taken of various employers and acquaintances who had known the plaintiff before the accident had confirmed that this person had been considered as having had rather severe personality problems before the accident.

Organic Damage versus Hysteria or Conversion Reaction

While there is no iron-clad rule or definitive test to distinguish hysteria from malingering, neuropsychological testing along with reliable and valid objective psychological tests can usually rule out brain damage. Premorbid history as well as experienced clinician judgment must also be utilized in the determination. The neuropsychologist needs to assess whether or not the neuropsychological test results are consistent with a neurological condition; in other words, do the results make neuro*psychological* or neuro*logical* sense? To determine this factor, the clinician needs to have not only a knowledge of neuroanatomy but also an understanding of the neurological entities and the various patterns each typically produces in neuropsychological protocols. Objective personality tests, especially the MCMI-III, are often helpful (if not necessary) in making this separation.

Hysteria

In a relatively typical case, a 52-year-old woman was evaluated for brain damage 2 years postaccident. She had fallen in an elevator which had malfunctioned, causing it to jolt rather strongly when it arrived at the first floor. There had been no physical indication that this woman had hit her head (no loss of consciousness, no cuts or bruises on the head). However, 2 years later, she was still experiencing severe headaches and backaches, an inability to concentrate, and a decreased libido. Her performance on the battery of neuropsychological tests was all in the average to above average range as normed for her age and educational level. Although she was only a high school graduate, her IQ testing placed her in the Superior range on the WAIS-R. Based on her high cognitive test performance, there was obviously no indication for malingering.

Administration of the MCMI-II revealed elevations of the Histrionic, Dependent, and Narcissistic personality scales. It was surprising and significant that in the history session, she spoke about a situation earlier in her life in which she was hospitalized for 5 days in a psychiatric unit because she had "lost her voice after her divorce." In sending for her medical records, it was learned that she had been hospitalized at least four additional times for various physical problems for which no organic cause was ever found. One of the authors had to appear in court to describe to the jury the characteristics of a histrionic personality style. Utilizing the results from the MCMI-II, the jury was better able to understand the personality dynamics involved and, in fact, the plaintiff was not awarded any compensation. It was obvious that her personality dynamics had been long standing.

Pseudoseizure Activity

Two of the more fascinating patients were referred by neurologists for evaluation of pseudoseizure activity in one patient and episodic cluster headaches which resulted in dissociative states in the other patient.

In the first case, a 21-year-old woman had been experiencing seizurelike activity for 2 years. These "seizures" manifested themselves in the form of sleepwalking in which she would be aware of her surroundings but was in a dreamlike state, unable to speak. She would clench her jaw and hands during these episodes, shake, and have difficulty breathing. Her parents had witnessed these "seizures" which would awaken them during the night. They would occur on an average of once a week.

An MRI was noted to be negative but, adding to the mystery, the EEG showed nonspecific signs which could either point in the direction of a neurological problem or be interpreted as a normal variation.

This young woman presented herself at the first testing session as guarded, with a depressed affect. She responded to questions during the clinical interview in a highly defensive and constrained manner. Projective testing was administered and the Rorschach (Klopfer & Davidson, 1962) produced a paucity of responses for someone of her age and intellectual level, which was average. She responded to many of the cards by stating "I have no idea" or "I have no imagination."

Neuropsychological testing was negative in that there was no temporal lobe pattern which may be found in seizure patients, nor were there any signs of focal or diffuse impairment. Her neurologist had placed her on an antiseizure medication as both a precautionary and diagnostic measure, but the medication had not reduced her "seizure" activity.

Both the MMPI-2 and the MCMI-III were administered. Consistent with the information found in the technical manual (Millon, 1994) describing the test pattern related to hysteria, the Hysteria scale (Hy) on the MMPI-2 was elevated to a *T*-score of 90; the scales on the MCMI-III which were elevated were those of Somatoform and Major Depression. It was concluded that this young woman was suffering from a conversion disorder and it was recommended that she seek psychiatric treatment.

Dissociative States

In the second case, a 54-year-old divorced woman had been experiencing migrainous headaches along with dissociation for several months. Following the headaches she would regress to a childlike state and call to her mother, who had been dead for 10 years. Her adult children had witnessed this phenomena and had described her behavior, as she herself had no memories of the episodes. Her neurologist had hospitalized her and administered several EEGs. While undergoing one of the EEG tests she began dissociating, but the EEG had been unremarkable.

Neuropsychological testing results did not indicate any cognitive deficits. In fact, her performance was well above the average range for all brain functions. Her WAIS-R Full Scale IQ was equal to 127. Objective and projective psychological testing were administered. The Rorschach demonstrated a protocol consistent with an individual who tended to internalize concerns which were more likely to be expressed through overt physical symptoms. There was shown to be a considerable degree of anger and negativism as well as depression.

The MCMI-II revealed a histrionic personality pattern as well as the clinical syndrome of an anxiety and somatoform disorder. The pattern of results indicated a woman who needed extreme attention as well as approval from others. However, due to her problems with self-assertion it was difficult for her to obtain approval and she most often went with her needs unmet. Desirability on the Modifier Indices was elevated to a BR of 85. Additionally, she was shown to lack insight and to avoid introspection. Hostile urges were denied and as a result, her constrained feelings tended to produce psychosomatic problems. Consistent with the MCMI-II was this woman's past medical history. She had suffered from severe bouts of gastrointestinal problems as well as extreme periods of fatigue. No physical causes had been documented for her problems, despite consistent medical attention.

Psychotherapy along with psychopharmacological medications were suggested under the MCMI-II's Prognostic and Therapeutic Implications reports. Consistent with the narrative, this woman did consider therapy as a threat to her self-image and withdrew from counseling after her second session. Interestingly and perhaps predictably, she was unhappy with the neuropsychological test results and refused to believe that she did not have a neurological problem. Upon follow-up with her neurologist it was learned that her cluster headaches with the accompanying dissociative states had disappeared. However, several months later it was learned that she was now being evaluated medically for heart palpitations of unknown etiology.

Adult Attention Deficit Disorder and Learning Disabilities

Increasing attention is being paid to the diagnosis of attention deficit disorder (ADD) in adults. In many instances, a parent recognizes his or her own ADD problem after having had a child diagnosed with this disorder. Although the heritability factor is prominent in this disorder, a systematic diagnosis must be made of the adult, as in the case of the child. One of the important facets of this evaluation is to rule out a primary emotional problem as the cause of the adult's distractibility and/or hyperactivity. Information from the MCMI-II and -III has been essential in many cases in which we diagnosed ADD as well as in cases in which this entity was ruled out.

A 42-year-old gentleman was referred by his physician because of problems with attention. The patient was a college-educated business executive who had considerable difficulty following through on projects, organizing his work, and focusing on conversations both at work and at home. He described himself as always feeling bored and needing to participate in risk-taking behaviors to make life interesting. His latest escapade had resulted in his losing a considerable amount of money from his wife's inheritance.

His neuropsychological test results indicated memory, executive, psychomotor, and attentional deficits. However, all of these functions are sensitive to psychological problems as well as to ADD. The MCMI-III portrayed a man who viewed his emotional adjustment as adequate, with endorsement for a mild depression concerned with an inability to concentrate, difficulty with organization, and frequent periods of restlessness. He presented his history as being in a stable and loving marriage with strong ties to family and close friends. Because there were no apparent significant problems, the diagnosis of ADD was made. He was placed on Ritalin, which helped him considerably. Therefore, the combination of the abnormal neuropsychological markers as well as the relatively normal MCMI-III profile proved essential in this determination.

Adults who have difficulty with learning despite the fact that their intellectual capacity is normal are considered as LD. ADD and LD often coexist. This disability may relate to verbal or nonverbal (spatial–perceptual) abilities. Dyslexia is the most common of the learning problems. However, research has now begun to focus on the so-called "right hemisphere" problems as well. In fact, where problems in the verbal area have often created frustration and a feeling of low self-worth, the emotional problems connected with a nonverbal LD can be even greater. There may be a lack of social awareness and difficulty with understanding nonverbal communication as a result of a nonverbal LD. Thus, an objective psychological test is an important part of an evaluation for a LD as well as for ADD.

Posttraumatic Stress Disorder

In forensic cases posttraumatic stress disorder (PTSD) is one of the most common sequelae claimed to be the result of accidents. Assessing people who have undergone a trauma requires knowledge of PTSD so as not to confuse these symptoms with brain injury. The DSM-IV (American Psychiatric Association, 1994) lists 21 symptoms or behaviors of PTSD, with specified numbers which have to be present in certain categories, to make this diagnosis. There has been considerable controversy over whether someone who has amnesia for an event because of organic memory problems can suffer from PTSD, as memory is important in this psychological condition. It is beyond the scope of this chapter to pursue this controversy.

Further research may tell us if there is a representative pattern of neuropsychological test results in these patients. For the present, the neuropsychologist should be aware that the PTSD patient may resemble a brain-damaged patient. Cognitive and emotional variables are all too closely intertwined. The administration of accurate neuropsychological measures, along with the psychological measures, is essential for a definitive diagnosis.

Thus, an accurate psychological test which assesses PTSD is essential in providing a differential diagnosis. Scale R (Post-Traumatic Stress Disorder) on the MCMI-III is a welcome addition to this test. Dysfunctional cognitions were found in a group of 31 Vietnam veterans with PTSD (Muran & Motta, 1993). This group was compared with a group of patients with anxiety or depression disorders and a nonclinical group of college students. One of the measures the subjects completed was the MCMI-II. There was supporting evidence for the uniqueness of the PTSD group in thought processing.

In our practice we examined a 31-year-old fireman who had been on duty when a light fixture in the fire station fell, grazing his head. Fortunately, he was not cut by the shattered glass. Several months later he was sent by his neurologist for a neuropsychological evaluation, as he was continuing to experience memory and concentration problems. He was also suffering from headaches and extreme fatigue. He reported in the clinical interview that each time he got a headache he thought about the accident and got upset but did not feel angry, as he said he had no one with whom to be angry. His neuropsychological test results were all within the normal range or above when normed on his age and educational levels; even his memory testing was basically above average.

The MCMI-III described an individual who, as the narrative read, "was inclined to view psychological problems as a sign of emotional or moral weakness." However interestingly, the Post-Traumatic Stress Disorder scale reached a BR of 81, which indicated the presence of a disorder. This gentleman was referred to a psychologist and was able to understand that all of his past traumas (including having been stationed in Vietnam), which he had previously stoically endured, had resurfaced due to this accident.

Factitious Disorders or Malingering

Factitious Disorder

The factitious disorder may look like malingering because the person is aware that he or she is pretending to have a condition. Nevertheless, it is a separate entity. In the absence of external incentives such as monetary gain or a determination of disability, a person who pretends to be suffering from physical or emotional problems can be said to have a factitious disorder. This category is different from malingering, in which there is an intentional purpose to feign symptoms for economic or some other tangible gain. It is very difficult to diagnose this disorder, as it is easily confused with malingering, somaticizing, or hysteria.

The following case of a woman with a factitious disorder was misdiagnosed by us. We knew that this was not a case of brain damage and diagnosed the person with a somatoform disorder and a posttraumatic stress disorder. In this case, the MCMI-II had been consistent with schizophrenia as well as a paranoid personality disorder. However, schizophrenia was ruled out on the basis of this woman's history, as she had been married, had children, and had been steadily employed. Clinical judgment of her behavior in the interview also ruled out this diagnosis. The paranoid personality disorder was also found not to fit by history, as she was a black, uneducated person from the deep South who had strong fundamentalist religious beliefs coupled with an understandable distrust of people based on her life experience of discrimination.

This 55-year-old woman had been preparing to go to work in the housekeeping department of the hospital where she had been employed as a janitor for 15 years. She was sitting by a window in her house eating her lunch when a hammer crashed through the window, hitting her on the forehead. A workman had been repairing a neighbor's roof and had thrown the hammer to a coworker in jest.

The results of the neuropsychological tests showed mild to moderate deficits across many brain functions. It was felt that the emotional sequelae brought on by her accident were interfering in her cognitive processing. Additionally, her low level of premorbid academic and intellectual functioning was an important factor compromising her performance. Because there had been a question in our minds about possible monetary gain factors, there was the possibility of malingering.

As it turned out, unbeknownst to us, her legal case had been settled months before the evaluation. She was referred to a psychologist for supportive and behavior modification counseling after the testing. The therapy uncovered the fact that this woman had always been responsible for taking care of family members since she was 8 years old and first had to take care of three younger siblings. This caretaker pattern had been predominant from then on, culminating with her nursing both of her parents the past few years until their deaths. She admitted to the psychologist that she had wanted to be cared for herself by her live-in boyfriend whom she had helped through a crisis with drug addiction. Her goal had been achieved, as she was now dependent on him both physically and financially.

We decided to include this example of a factitious disorder as a caution concerning any objective psychological test. Clinical judgment and detailed history are extremely important. The MCMI-II could not have assessed the parameters surrounding this individual's life.

Malingering

Perhaps there is no greater challenge in the forensic area than in detecting a true malingerer. This is always a possibility in a forensic case. There are multiple factors which can be operating other than a patient's intent to purposefully deceive. One of the most cogent articles in this area was written in the journal *Behavioral Sciences and the Law* by Weissman (1990). This article spoke to the fact that we often underestimate the influence of litigation on a person's psychological and physical condition. The stress upon the individual who has been ordered to be examined by multiple expert witness physicians and psychologists takes its toll. The plaintiff may feel angered at the process and believe that he or she is not trusted and the defense expert witnesses thus can appear as professionals to deceive and outwit. Dr. Weissman makes the important point that often the plaintiff is not sent to defense expert witnesses for several years from the date of the accident and thus has had an extended period of time to experience the stressors, which often exacerbate preexisting personality styles such as those found in individuals with histrionic, narcissistic, or antisocial traits. Thus, evaluating a malingerer is an involved and multifactorial challenge. Objective and subjective information must be carefully gathered.

To complicate the situation, malingering and conversion disorder are often confused. It is also important to keep in mind that conversion disorder and malingering are not mutually exclusive; people with conversion disorders can also malinger. The behaviors of individuals with a diagnosis of a conversion disorder or malingering are also similar in nature, as they both may attempt to be declared disabled and both may be reporting atypical symptomatology. Both of these conditions can be subsumed under the category of a functional disorder.

It is generally easier to determine that the patient does not have significant brain damage than to separate malingering from a hysterical, somatic, or conversion reaction. Especially in forensic cases, the determination of the existence of brain damage takes priority. There are several effects on neuropsychological tests which may help separate functional problems from organic damage. In the functional case, psychological factors can have the effect of overwhelming a person over time so that the person may appear to be regressing. In neuropsychological assessment, serial testings on an individual often show a pattern of lowered performance on cognitive tasks over time. This type of pattern is not one produced by brain damage. It is almost inevitably the result of an emotional regression or secondary gain.

The neuropsychological test profile itself provides information which helps the clinician detect malingering. Variable and inconsistent test results which make neither neurological nor neuropsychological sense are a major clue. Unless the examinee is neurologically sophisticated it is difficult to fake successfully the entire test battery. For example, a test profile is suspect when the memory tests are performed so poorly that a person who has dementia could do better, but tests that are highly sensitive to brain damage are within normal limits. Additionally, missing easier items and then answering more difficult items may also indicate motivational problems.

In his book on malingering, Rogers (1988) wrote, "Nearly all psychological measures are susceptible to dissimulation. The notable exception is defensiveness on intellectual and neuropsychological testing, since patients cannot perform better than their organic impairment will allow" (p. 295). Clearly, someone cannot perform better than his or her own best effort but it is important to realize that they can perform poorly for reasons other than brain damage.

There are also tests in neuropsychology specifically designed to help detect malingering. In these tests, missing more items than would be expected by chance alone provides important information. The objective personality tests are often of great help in separating the functional from the organic case. The validity scales can be helpful.

Along the same line of reasoning, a study was conducted to measure the degree to which there was a relationship between the validity scales on the MMPI-2 and personality disorders as determined by the MCMI-II (Grillo, Brown, Hilsabeck, Price, & Lees-Haley, 1994). The authors concluded that there was a relationship between the validity scales and the personality disorder scales. Whether the effect on the MCMI-II personality scales indicated a malingering type of person was not completely clear, as there was also the possibility that the elevations on the personality scales themselves may have been exaggerated.

Hysteria includes both conversion reactions and functional somatic reactions; consequently, these conditions can be treated as types of hysteria. Such hysterical problems and malingering are often difficult to separate. It is important for the diagnostic decision not to confuse them. The personality test itself must have the ability to discriminate among different testing styles. In one study of the MCMI-II, eight different test-taking styles were analyzed to determine if clinically relevant separation of the profiles was found (Retzlaff, Sheehan, & Fiel, 1991). Good statistical and clinically relevant separation of the profiles was found for normal, fake good, fake bad, and randomly generated profiles. However, the percentage of profiles identified by validity scales was not as good. In a related study, the effectiveness of three validity scales from the MCMI-II were analyzed (Bagby, Gillis, Toner, & Goldberg, 1991). The overall rate of classification was found to be quite high. It will be interesting to learn of the accuracy in this regard of the MCMI-III when more research has been completed.

A clear case of malingering is represented by a 40-year-old man who claimed to have sustained a head trauma when he slipped and fell at his place of work. He presented a fluent narrative during the clinical interview without any word-finding problems or aphasias. When questioning him about the period directly before and after his fall, he gave a lengthy and detailed description. There was no evidence of retrograde or anterograde amnesia. He presented a list of approximately 40 problems which he believed were the direct result of this accident 4 years previous to the assessment. Additionally, when asked questions which indicated exaggeration for effect, he answered all of these in the affirmative. These were questions such as "Do you notice that you have difficulty remembering events from your childhood since the accident?," "Does soap burn your face where it had not before?," and "Do you sometimes forget your age since the accident?" Of course, these questions alone do not indicate malingering, but they do represent deviant response sets.

On the neuropsychological testing he could not repeat more than two numbers forward, and all the memory scores were in the profoundly impaired range. In fact, a children's memory test was administered to him and he performed worse than the average 5-year-old. Yet, on tests of executive functioning, which are measures of complex functions utilizing planning and organization skills, his performance was in the average range. These are tests sensitive to brain damage and one would not expect a person with profound memory impairment due to an accident to even remember the directions given to him, much less be able to perform the functions successfully. On tests of sensory perceptions, he demonstrated anesthesia for both hands. Neurological examinations had not indicated any problems with sensation. Interestingly, on a test which measures level of motivation, he performed in the motivated range on the Dot Counting Test (Lezak, 1995, pp. 800–801). The test did not have anything to do with memory functions.

The MCMI-III was administered in the audiotaped version. Although the profile was considered to be valid, there was a warning to consider the scales as possibly exaggerated and to be cautious in interpretation. The MCMI-III narrative read "This patient's response style may indicate a tendency to magnify illness, an inclination to complain, or feelings of extreme vulnerability associated with the current episode of acute turmoil." Needless to say, we chose the hypothesis that fit with the exaggerated pattern. Interestingly, the MCMI-III BR scores were 95 for a thought disorder as well as for a delusional disorder. The individual with this protocol was portrayed as probably experiencing a psychotic state. One of the Axis I clinical syndromes, schizophrenia, was indicated. If there had been indication on the basis of the neuropsychological testing for brain damage, the MCMI-III might have been showing the picture of an organic personality disorder. However, such was not the case. In our experience patients who show a schizophrenic or severe psychotic pattern on the MMPI or MCMI-II and -III and are obviously not psychotic according to their history and the interview behavior are probably malingering. The conclusion of the neuropsychological assessment was that this individual's test results indicated secondary gain. In fact, it was indicated in the report that if he had truly been so incapacitated in his memory functioning, he would have needed constant supervision.

Interestingly, subsequent to the report being issued, the insurance company had asked for surveillance on this man. The videotapes revealed that he had been participating in sailing, dancing, and gambling—all activities which required mobility and a fair amount of memory.

Another case involved a woman who had fallen off of a chair at work and was complaining of severely reduced cognitive functioning. She was even found to have forgotten the alphabet when administered the mental status portion of the neuropsychological evaluation. She turned out to be so "deranged" on the testing that she could not even understand many of the directions and thus the administration of some of the tests had to be aborted. However, quite ironically, she was easily able to follow the questions on the audiotaped MCMI-III. Her best Axis II diagnosis fit was a schizoid personality disorder.

The MCMI-III narrative read "The pattern of scores achieved by this woman typically signifies emotional impoverishment, social introversiveness, and a discouraged, dependent, and timid way of relating to others." This woman had been married for over 25 years, had several grown children, and had been employed steadily over the years. Her behavior in the 8 hours of testing demonstrated her to be sociable, garrulous, and generally socially interactive. Obviously this woman had been exaggerating her responses on the MCMI-III as well as on the neuropsychological tests. This is another example of how a schizophrenic pattern on the MCMI-III in light of a normal history and interview can indicate malingering. This case actually was tried in court and the plaintiff was awarded nothing.

REHABILITATION

Neuropsychology and rehabilitation are closely allied as parts of an interdisciplinary entity, as neuropsychology journals and professional organizations share a common science. Rehabilitation experts depend on a neuropsychological assessment to provide them with the information necessary to perform their work. A person's emotional functioning and personality style influence the course of remediation for brain injury. Thus, an objective personality inventory is essential for the complete assessment of a patient. The MCMI-II and -III are making their contribution in this area. It is necessary to assess patients psychologically both in the acute stage of neurological problems as well as in the chronic stage. In rehabilitation planning, knowledge of personality and character traits is as important as types of psychopathology. Just as neuropsychological measures are important in determining the success of a rehabilitation program, so are psychological measures vital to complete an assessment providing for the most optimal functioning of the brain-injured patient as well as ensuring compliance with treatment.

SUGGESTIONS FOR FUTURE RESEARCH

As was mentioned in the beginning of this chapter, there has been little research on any of the versions of the MCMI in relation to neuropsychological variables. This is unfortunate, as the complex and vital interrelationship between emotional and cognitive functioning is only beginning to be understood.

The study by Swirsky-Sacchetti et al. (1993) demonstrates how the MCMI-II can be used in neuropsychological investigations. This study used the MCMI-II as one of the major measures used in diagnosing borderline personality disorder. The study investigated the question of whether borderline personality disorder might be a subtle organic condition, or at least have an organic component. Such defects which impaired neuropsychological tests were found in patients assessed as having a borderline personality pattern by the MCMI.

The area of differential diagnosis is one in which the MCMI-II and -III may make a significant contribution. The psychosis scales as well as the personality scales on the MCMI may be able to separate certain types of schizophrenia from brain damage better than any other test. Case histories in this chapter demonstrate that both Alzheimer's and malingering patients may have particular patterns on the MCMI. Considering the gravity of their disease, Alzheimer's patients appear to have a remarkably bland pattern on the MCMI. They show little of the expected depression or other emotional disturbances. This could reinforce the typical pattern found for the Halstead–Reitan battery (Russell & Polakoff,

1993). The finding of a schizophrenic-like pattern in a person who has no historical or interview characteristics typical of schizophrenia, in our experience, is a strong indication of malingering. If this could be verified in a research study, it would greatly enhance the ability to detect malingerers in neuropsychology cases.

Substance abuse and its influence on brain functioning has produced considerable and controversial research. The relationship between psychopathology and neuropsychological deficits needs to be explored further. Using the MCMI-II and -III to discover the degree to which depression, anxiety, and personality style influence neuropsychological performance is another fertile research field.

An area in neuropsychology which is continually expanding is the influence of toxins on our neuropsychological processes. The neurotoxic effects of pollutants is an expanding field and the interaction of emotional and neurological factors is obvious. Biochemical explanation for neuropsychological deficits and psychological deficits needs to be explored.

Currently, the relationship between emotions and our health is being explored in the exciting field of psychoimmunology. In the same manner, we must continue to explore how our psychological functioning relates to our mental abilities/functioning. The MCMI-II and -III are valuable personality instruments to use in conducting this research because of its reliance on personality theory.

Frontal and temporal lobe damage have been researched from both neurological and psychological vantage points. However, we are discovering that these syndromes cannot be considered as single entities and that there appears to be a wide spectrum of emotional and cognitive changes which occur with such damage both bilaterally and with only one affected hemisphere (Chitwood, 1989). The MCMI-II and -III would be useful in conducting such studies. The whole area of lateralized brain damage and depression needs additional research to understand more thoroughly the specialized hemispheric functions as well as those functions shared by both hemispheres. The differences in psychological problems incurred because of damage to a particular hemisphere are still not fully understood.

Return-to-work as it relates to neuropsychological deficits and psychological status is another important research area, as it relates to successful rehabilitation of brain-injured patients. In the area of closed head injury there are indications that patients with more optimal psychological functioning perform better cognitively and rehabilitate more quickly. Discovering markers for which individuals are at the highest risk for a lifetime of disability is crucial for the whole field of rehabilitation and for society's productivity. Personality variables as assessed by the MCMI-II and -III can increase the likelihood of achieving a predictive model.

Thus in clinical cases, forensic cases, and issues of treatment and rehabilitation, the MCMI is making a considerable impact. Continued research with this personality instrument may open even more vistas for the field of neuropsychology.

REFERENCES

American Psychiatric Association. (1994). *Diagnostic and statistical manual of mental disorders* (4th ed.). Washington, DC: Author.

Bagby, M. R., Gillis, J. R., Toner, B. B., & Goldberg, J. (1991). Detecting fake-good and fake-bad responding on the Millon Clinical Multiaxial Inventory—II. *Psychological Assessment: A Journal of Consulting and Clinical Psychology, 3,* 496–498.

Biederman, J., Gillis, J. R., Toner, B. B., & Goldberg, S. (1991). Comorbidity of attention deficit hyperactivity disorder with conduct, depressive, anxiety and other disorders. *American Journal of Psychiatry, 148,* 564–567.

Brown, J. (1987). *A screening key to differentiate normals from organics and patients with functional disorders.* Unpublished doctoral dissertation, Nova University, Fort Lauderdale, FL.

Chitwood, R. P. (1989). *Objective assessment of personality characteristics related to cerebral lesions and cognitive deficits in persons with unilateral brain damage.* Unpublished doctoral dissertation, Florida State University, Tallahassee, FL.

Craig, R. J., & Olson, R. E. (1992). Relationship between MCMI-II scales and normal personality traits. *Psychological Reports, 71,* 699-705.

Gass, C. S., & Russell, E. W. (1986). Differential impact of brain damage and depression on memory test performance. *Journal of Consulting and Clinical Psychology, 54,* 261-263.

Golden, C. J., Sweet, J. J., & Osman, D. C. (1979). The diagnosis of brain-damage by the MMPI: A comprehensive evaluation. *Journal of Personality Assessment, 43,* 138–142.

Goldstein, G. (1986). The neuropsychology of schizophrenia. In I. Grant & K. M. Adams (Eds.), *Neuropsychological assessment of neuropsychiatric disorders* (pp. 147–171). New York: Oxford University Press.

Grillo, J., Brown, R. S., Hilsabeck, R., Price, J. R., & Lees-Haley, P. R. (1994). Raising doubts about claims of malingering implications of relationships between MCMI-II and MMPI-2 performances. *Journal of Clinical Psychology, 50,* 651–655.

Klopfer, B., & Davidson, H. H. (1962). *The Rorschach technique, an introductory manual.* New York: Harcourt, Brace & World.

Lezak, M. D. (1995). *Neuropsychological assessment* (3rd ed.). New York: Oxford University Press.

Millon, T. (1982). *Millon clinical multiaxial inventory manual* (2nd. ed.). Minneapolis: National Computer Systems.

Millon, T. (1987). *Manual for the MCMI-II* (2nd ed.). Minneapolis: National Computer Systems.

Millon, T. (1994). *Millon Clinical Multiaxial Inventory—III manual.* Minneapolis: National Computer Systems.

Muran, E. M., & Motta, R. W. (1993). Cognitive distortions and irrational beliefs in post-traumatic stress, anxiety, and depressive disorders. *Journal of Clinical Psychology, 49,* 166–176.

Overholser, J. C. (1990). Retest reliability of the Millon Clinical Multiaxial Inventory. *Journal of Personality Assessment, 55,* 202–208.

Pope, K. S., Butcher, J. N., & Seelen, J. (1993). *The MMPI, MMPI-2 & MMPI-A in court.* Washington, DC: American Psychological Association.

Retzlaff, P., Sheehan, E., & Fiel, A. (1991). MCMI-II report style and bias: Profile and validity scales analyses. *Journal of Personality Assessment, 56,* 466–477.

Rogers, R. (1988). Current status of clinical methods. In R. Rogers (Ed.), *Clinical assessment of malingering and deception* (pp. 293–308). New York: Guilford Press.

Russell, E. W. (1975). Validation of a brain-damage versus schizophrenia MMPI key. *Journal of Clinical Psychology, 31,* 659–661.

Russell, E. W. (1977). MMPI profiles of brain-damaged and schizophrenic subjects. *Journal of Clinical Psychology, 33,* 190–193.

Russell, E. W. (1994). The cognitive–metric, fixed battery approach to neuropsychological assessment. In R. D. Vanderploeg (Ed.), *Clinician's guide to neuropsychological assessment* (pp. 211–258). Hillsdale, NJ: Erlbaum.

Russell, E. W. (1995). The accuracy of automated and clinical detection of brain damage and lateralization in neuropsychology. *Neuropsychology Review, 5,* 1–68.

Russell, E. W., & Polakoff, D. (1993). Neuropsychological test patterns in men for Alzheimer's and Multi-infarct dementia. *Archives of Clinical Neuropsychology, 8,* 327–343.

Ryan, J. J., & Southeaver, G. T. (1977). Further evidence that concerns the validity of an MMPI key for separation of brain-damaged and schizophrenic patients. *Journal of Clinical Psychology, 33,* 753–754.

Spellacy, F. (1977). Neuropsychological differences between violent and nonviolent adolescents. *Journal of Clinical Psychology, 33,* 966–969.

Swirsky-Sacchetti, T., Gorton, G., Samuel, S., Sobel, R., Genetta-Wadley, A., & Burleigh, B. (1993).

Neuropsychological function in borderline personality disorder. *Journal of Clinical Psychology*, *49*, 385–396.

Teasdale, G., & Jennett, B. (1974). Assessment of coma and impaired consciousness. *Lancet*, *ii*, 81–84.

Watson, C. G. (1977). Brain damage tests in psychiatric settings. *The INS Bulletin*, March 10–12.

Watson, C. G., & Plemel, D. (1978). An MMPI scale to separate brain damaged from functional psychiatric patients in neuropsychiatric settings. *Journal of Clinical Psychology*, *46*, 1127–1132.

Watson, C. G., Plemel, D., & Jacobs, L. (1978). An MMPI sign to separate organic from functional psychiatric patients. *Journal of Clinical Psychology*, *34*, 398–401.

Watson, C. G., Thomas, R. W., Anderson, D., & Felling, J. (1968). Differentiation of schizophrenics from organics at two chronicity levels by use of Reitan–Halstead organic test battery. *Journal of Consulting and Clinical Psychology*, *32*, 679–684.

Wechsler, D. (1981). *WAIS-R, Wechsler Adult Intelligence Scale—Revised, Manual*. San Antonio, TX: Psychological Corporation.

Weissman, H. N. (1990). Distortions and deceptions in self presentation: Effects of protracted litigation in personal injury cases. *Behavioral Sciences and the Law*, *8*, 67–74.

Wiens, A. N., & Matarazzo, J. D. (1977). WAIS and MMPI correlates of the Halstead–Reitan Neuropsychology Battery in normal male subjects. *Journal of Nervous and Mental Disease*, *164*, 112–121.

10

MCMI Applications in Substance Abuse

PATRICK M. FLYNN
ROBERT C. McMAHON

Those receiving treatment for substance abuse show evidence of high rates of psychiatric disorder (Flynn, Craddock, Luckey, Hubbard, & Dunteman, 1996; Slaby, 1991). The importance of systematically evaluating coexisting psychiatric problems among substance abusers has been clearly shown in studies that demonstrate (1) higher relapse rates among dual diagnosis substance abusers, (2) that those with certain forms of psychopathology profit from the addition of psychotherapy to the standard drug treatment package, and (3) that matching substance abusing patients with treatments tailored to address their particular needs may enhance treatment effects (Kadden, Cooney, Getter, & Litt, 1989).

Recent versions of the Millon Clinical Multiaxial Inventory (MCMI) have become increasingly popular differential diagnostic instruments which may facilitate the evaluation of the substance abusing patient (Millon, 1982, 1994).[1] Millon (1981) has been among the most prolific theorists committed to defining clinically relevant dimensions of personality and in articulating their relationships with clinical symptom syndromes, including substance abuse disorders. The original and revised versions of the MCMI were developed as measures of the basic constructs outlined in Millon's theory of personality and psychopathology (Millon, 1981, 1994). Ongoing efforts have been made to enhance correspondence between the personality and symptom scales of the instrument and various Axis I and Axis II syndromes outlined in the *Diagnostic and Statistical Manual of Mental Disorders* of the American Psychiatric Association (1980, 1987, 1994). MCMI profile interpretation involves the integration of characteristics measured by various personality and symptom scales with other relevant demographic and life history information to achieve a meaningful clinical synthesis. In this process, characteristics associated with clinically elevated basic and pathological personality scales and those measured by clinical symptom

---

Note. Drs. Flynn and McMahon contributed equally to this chapter. Authors are listed in alphabetical order.

[1]Three editions of the MCMI have been published (MCMI-I, MCMI-II, and MCMI-III). Throughout the chapter, we use the label MCMI when the discussion applies to all versions of the test. In all other instances, we refer specifically to the MCMI-I, MCMI-II, or the MCMI-III.

syndrome scales are evaluated in a theoretically coordinated manner. Basic personality styles may be seen as precursors to severe personality disorders. Clinical symptom syndromes may reflect disturbances in underlying personality patterns which emerge under conditions of stress. Symptoms are described in a way which reflects their distinctiveness in relation to the undergirding personality configuration (McMahon, 1993).

A number of researchers have drawn upon Millon's theory of personality and psychopathology as a unifying framework for studying relations among theoretically derived dimensions of personality and psychopathology and various substance dependence disorders. This chapter reviews studies involving use of various versions of the MCMI in diverse substance-abusing groups. These studies provide a view of theoretically and clinically meaningful dimensions of psychopathology and serve as a basis for understanding differences among substance abusers, which may allow for more effective treatment planning. Attention is also paid to studies in which the MCMI has been used to understand relationships among maladaptive personality patterns, symptom syndromes, and important dimensions of clinical status relevant to substance dependence. Emphasis is given to studies which examine relationships among personality, substance abuse patterns, depression, and such critical clinical outcomes as treatment dropout and relapse. Finally, MCMI-III scales which gauge drug dependence and alcohol dependence are examined in a manner which reveals their distinctive features and elements which reflect their overlap with personality disorder scales.

MCMI CLUSTER STUDIES OF SUBSTANCE ABUSERS

Bartsch and Hoffman (1985) used the 20 clinical scales of the MCMI-I in a cluster analysis involving male veterans admitted to an alcohol treatment unit. The five clusters which emerged were described in terms of the highest MCMI-I elevations for each cluster. The first cluster was defined by elevations on the Compulsive and Antisocial scales. Alcohol use for this group was hypothesized to permit escape from feelings of responsibility and/or to enable expressions of anger. The second and fourth clusters involved elevations on the Narcissistic, Histrionic, and Antisocial scales. Those in the second cluster had scores in the clinically elevated range on these scales. Members of these clusters were thought to be initially recreational drug users who manifested lifestyles of self-indulgence and thrill seeking. The third cluster was defined by elevations on the Passive–Aggressive, Borderline, Paranoid, Anxiety, and Dysthymic scales. This group was considered likely to use alcohol for self-medication purposes. The final cluster involved elevations on the Dependent, Avoidant, Schizotypal, Schizoid, Anxiety, and Dysthymic scales. For members of this cluster, alcohol use was hypothesized to be motivated by an effort to cope with feelings of loneliness and to reduce social anxiety to a level that enabled more comfortable social involvement.

Donat (1988) also used the 20 MCMI-I clinical scales and conducted a hierarchical cluster analysis involving a sample that included both male and female alcohol abusers. A five-cluster solution was derived that generally replicated Bartsch and Hoffman's (1985) findings. In a follow-up investigation, Donat and associates derived a similar five-cluster solution and compared the clusters on the basis of perceived benefits and adverse consequences of drinking (Donat, Walters, & Hume, 1991). Members of clusters with peaks on the MCMI-I Compulsive scale and on the Narcissistic, Antisocial, and Histrionic scales scored relatively low on most Alcohol Use Inventory (AUI) scales reflecting the tendency to deny the impact of alcohol use in their lives (Wanberg, Horn, & Foster, 1985). In the case of members of the compulsive cluster, this tendency toward denial is thought to be associated with sensitivity to, and efforts to avoid, the disapproval of others. Alcohol use for members of this cluster is hypothesized to be negatively reinforced by escape from distress. In contrast, members of the narcissistic/antisocial cluster are assumed to view themselves as highly self-reliant and to resist judgments that they have problems with alcohol they cannot control. Their denial of significant motivation for alcohol use is associated with a pervasive tendency to deny personal weaknesses. Patients in the remaining three clusters scored relatively high on the AUI scales measuring perceived benefits and drawbacks of alcohol use. Members of these clusters tended to be less able to inhibit interpersonal anxieties, frustrations, and discouragements than were those in the narcissistic/antisocial cluster. One other notable finding was that those in the cluster characterized by elevations on the Avoidant and Schizotypal scales were most likely to engage in solitary drinking. For these individuals, drinking is assumed to be motivated by attempts to cope with self-criticism, feelings of discouragement, and social withdrawal.

Corbisiero and Reznikoff (1991) used the 20 clinical scales of the MCMI-I in a cluster analysis involving male alcoholics. The first cluster was characterized by mean scores in the subclinical range on all scales. The second cluster was defined by significant elevations on the Antisocial, Narcissistic, Paranoia, Alcohol Abuse, and Drug Abuse scales. The third cluster revealed mean elevations on the Avoidant, Passive–Aggressive, Schizoid, Dependent, Anxiety, Dysthymic, and Alcohol Abuse scales of the MCMI-I. The subclinical cluster reported fewest perceived benefits and adverse consequences associated with alcohol use on the AUI. They also revealed less compulsive alcohol use and fewer disruptive effects of alcohol use than did those in the other two clusters. Members of the second (antisocial) and third (passive–aggressive/avoidant) clusters reported serious and widespread alcohol problems. Members of the passive–aggressive/avoidant cluster had more overall alcohol involvement than was found in the other two clusters. They had particularly high scores on the AUI Life Disruption scale, considered characteristic of severe alcoholics, and reported significantly more distress about their problem drinking than did those in the other two clusters.

Retzlaff and Bromley (1991) canonically correlated the 20 MCMI-I scales and 11 Basic Personality Inventory (BPI, Jackson, 1989) scales and cluster analyzed the canonical variates. The six clusters which emerged are described in terms of clinically elevated MCMI-I scales. The first cluster was defined by highly elevated scores on the Passive–Aggressive, Avoidant, Schizoid, Anxiety, Dysthymia, Alcohol Abuse, and Drug Abuse scales. This cluster was characterized by a high level of general distress, self-deprecation, social introversion, interpersonal problems, and depression. The second cluster had a single clinical elevation on the Histrionic scale and few associated problems. The third cluster had high mean scores on the Dependent, Anxiety, Dysthymia, and Alcohol Abuse scales. This cluster was characterized by high anxiety and depression scores on the BPI. The fourth cluster had a single elevation on the MCMI-I Narcissistic scale and was characterized as particularly low on BPI scales measuring hypochondriasis, depression, anxiety, and impulse expression. The fifth cluster was defined by significant clinical elevations on the Passive–Aggressive, Dependent, Avoidant, Anxiety, Dysthymic, Somatoform, and Hypomania scales. High levels of hypochondriasis and moderately high levels of depression, anxiety, thought disorder, self-deprecation, and impulse expression were revealed on the BPI in this cluster. The sixth cluster was characterized by high scores on the Schizoid, Dysthymia, Anxiety, and Alcohol Abuse. Scores on the BPI confirm social introversion and low impulse expression in this cluster.

Matano, Locke, and Schwartz (1994) conducted separate cluster analyses for male and female alcoholics using the 11 MCMI-I personality scales. Clusters were then compared on the basis of scores on research measures of alcohol use and interpersonal problems. The first clusters for both males and females involved scores in the subclinical range on all MCMI-I personality scales. The second cluster for the male sample involved elevations on the Avoidant, Schizoid, Passive–Aggressive, and Borderline scales. The second cluster for females involved clinical elevations on the Passive–Aggressive and Borderline scales. The third clusters involved elevations on the Narcissistic and Antisocial scales for males and on the Histrionic and Narcissistic scales for females. Males demonstrated more alcohol consumption than females. High alcohol consumption was particularly noteworthy in the male narcissistic/antisocial cluster. Both male and female "subclinical" clusters were characterized by later onset of both drinking and alcohol problems than was seen in the "clinical" clusters.

Craig, Verinis, and Wexler (1985) conducted separate hierarchical cluster analyses of MCMI-I profiles on groups of opiate addicts and alcoholics. Two clusters emerged in the analysis of opiate addicts. The first included MCMI-I profile peaks on the Narcissistic and Antisocial scales and moderately high scores on the Drug Abuse and Alcohol Abuse scales. The second cluster was defined by high scores on the Passive–Aggressive and Avoidant personality scales and by elevations on the Anxiety and Dysthymia scales. The analysis involving alcoholics led to the identification of four clusters. The first cluster was defined by elevations on the Passive–Aggressive, Borderline, Paranoid, and Anxiety scales and might be defined as a severe personality pathology group. The second was characterized by elevations on the Dependent, Avoidant, Passive–Aggressive, and Schizoid personality scales and on the Anxiety and Dysthymic symptom scales and might be described as a neuroticism cluster. The third cluster included a peak on the Compulsive scale with scores within the normal range on most other scales. The final cluster had high scores on the Narcissistic, Antisocial, and Paranoid personality scales and on the Drug Abuse and Dysthymia symptom scales. Thus, although similar clusters emerged in analyses involving alcoholics and opiate addicts, there was more evidence of diversity in the analysis involving alcoholics. In addition to the antisocial/narcissistic and passive–aggressive–avoidant clusters found in both substance abusing groups, a cluster defined in terms of severe personality pathology, and one which might be called a "normal limits" cluster, emerged in the analysis involving alcoholics.

In a cluster study involving separate analyses of heroin addicts and cocaine-dependent subjects, Craig and Olson (1990) found evidence for two MCMI-I clusters in each group. In both the cocaine- and heroin-dependent groups, clusters emerged which were defined in terms of elevations on the Narcissistic, Antisocial, and Drug Abuse scales. The second cocaine cluster involved elevations on quite a number of personality (Passive–Aggressive, Antisocial, Narcissistic, Paranoid) and symptom (Alcohol Abuse, Drug Abuse, Anxiety, and Dysthymia) scales. The second MCMI-I cluster identified in the heroin group reflected less evidence of personality pathology (i.e., no personality scales in the clinically elevated range) but distinctively high scores on Drug Abuse, Alcohol Abuse, and Anxiety.

In summary, in the majority of studies of alcoholics and drug-dependent individuals, a cluster type emerged in which members might be described in terms of a dominating, manipulative, and exploitive interpersonal pattern. Drug use by members of this cluster type may be associated with a self-indulgent and thrill-seeking lifestyle. These individuals are considered poor candidates for psychotherapy because their fierce sense of independence clashes with externally imposed expectations for attitude and behavior change inherent in treatment for substance abuse. A second cluster type which emerged with considerable consistency involved substance abusers with evidence of rather severe personality pathology. Craig and Olson (1990) have described this type as characterized by pessimistic attitudes, unstable moods, and erratic behavior. Paranoid features involving feelings of being misunderstood, unappreciated, and exploited may be associated with edgy irritability and interpersonal acting out. A third cluster type, which was found with particular frequency among alcoholics, involves those who experience self-deprecatory cognitions, excessive social dependence and/or avoidance, anticipation of failure in interpersonal relations, and high levels of depression and anxiety. For members of the second and third cluster types, substance use may be associated with attempts to manage interpersonal anxieties, frustrations, and critical attitudes about self and others. Finally, a "normal limits" or "subclinical" cluster, which emerged in a series of studies, was found to be associated with relatively fewer overall problems associated with substance use than those seen in other cluster types.

MCMI SCALE LEVEL COMPARISONS OF SUBSTANCE USE SUBTYPES

Craig, Verinis, and Wexler (1985) compared groups of alcoholics and opiate addicts using the MCMI-I (Millon, 1983). In age-controlled comparisons, alcoholics were found to have higher scores on the Avoidant, Dependent, Schizotypal, Borderline, and Paranoid scales than did opiate addicts. The opiate group scored significantly higher on the Narcissistic scale. Craig and Olson (1990) also used the MCMI-I in a comparison of groups of African American males who abused either cocaine or opiates. Significant univariate differences revealed that the opiate group had higher MCMI-I Anxiety, Somatoform, and Alcohol Abuse scale scores than did the cocaine group. The cocaine group scored significantly higher on the Antisocial personality scale than did the opiate group.

A more recent study by Flynn and colleagues (1995) included the use of the MCMI-II (Millon, 1987) to examine clinical differences in groups of substance abuse treatment clients who exhibited a preference for either heroin or cocaine. Univariate analyses showed that, in comparison with the heroin preference group, the cocaine group had more subjects who were younger, never married, involved with the criminal justice system, and psychologically impaired. All mean MCMI-II scale scores for the cocaine group were higher than for the heroin group, with the exception of the Compulsive scale. A discriminant function analysis classified approximately 75% of the subjects into their respective drug preference groups. The dimension that discriminated between groups revealed that the cocaine group had more avoidant and self-defeating personality characteristics than did the heroin group after controlling for age, gender, marital status, and length of illicit drug use. An analysis of MCMI-II scores showed both groups to be considerably distressed. However, the authors noted that the higher levels of distress in the cocaine group, and the shorter durations between onset of cocaine use and admission to treatment, suggests that cocaine may have greater negative effects than does heroin. They also concluded that their results supported the clinically held belief about the intensely harmful effects of cocaine and that cocaine users consume this substance for relatively short periods before they enter treatment (Tims & Leukefeld, 1993).

In comparing groups of alcohol- and cocaine-dependent inpatients, Lesswing and Dougherty (1993) used a psychological test battery that included the MCMI-II to determine group differences. They found that alcoholics were older, entered treatment later, and had higher levels of education, socioeconomic status, and intellectual functioning than did cocaine users. Group differences in psychopathology were evident and included evidence of more severe personality patterns in the cocaine group as measured by the MCMI-II. Despite the differences, the authors noted significant levels of personality disorder in both groups and expressed uncertainty about whether the disturbances were due to the transient effects of substances or reflected more ingrained and stable patterns of maladjustment.

PERSONALITY, CLINICAL STATUS, AND TREATMENT OUTCOMES

One of the most important features of the MCMI is that it is anchored to a comprehensive theory of personality and psychopathology. A number of investigators have made explicit use of Millon's (1969, 1981) theory as the basis for examining relationships between MCMI personality measures and important dimensions of clinical status and treatment outcomes. McMahon and colleagues conducted a series of studies which examined associations between personality and depression in alcoholics (McMahon & Davidson, 1985a, 1985b, 1986; McMahon & Tyson, 1990; McMahon, Schram, & Davidson, 1993). Many cases of clinical depression exhibited by alcoholics entering treatment are assumed to be associated with the effects of ethanol ingestion and withdrawal (Schuckit, 1983). Remission of depressive symptoms occurs within several weeks after completion of detoxification. However, a significant number of alcoholics experience a more enduring depression which does not abate by the time of substance abuse treatment completion. McMahon and colleagues provide evidence that this more enduring depression may be associated with underlying personality disorder (McMahon & Davidson, 1985b; McMahon & Tyson, 1990). Indeed, McMahon and Tyson (1990) argued that personality styles revealed by alcoholics at treatment intake could be useful in distinguishing between alcoholics who would be likely to show an early remission of depressive symptoms and those who have enduring patterns of perceiving and relating to self and others that predispose to various enduring depressive syndromes (Millon, 1981).

For example, those with avoidant personalities were assumed to be vulnerable to enduring depression because of their alienated and devalued self-images and hypersensitivity to social rejection. Similarly, for passive–aggressive personalities enduring depression was assumed to be associated with both discontented self-images and with unstable, conflictual, and fault-finding interpersonal behaviors leading to low rates of positive reinforcement and high rates of punishment. It was hypothesized that the depression associated with these two personality styles would be unlikely to respond to short-term drug treatment interventions.

In contrast, those with narcissistic, histrionic, and compulsive personalities were assumed to have characteristics associated with less vulnerability to enduring clinical depression. Millon (1981) suggests that enduring depression is not consistent with the narcissist's highly developed sense of self-assurance and self-worth. Failures to live up to inflated self-estimations are typically rationalized and externalized and infrequently lead to enduring depression. Those with histrionic personalities may experience transient depressions associated with predictable disruptions in social attachments. Such depressive reactions often reflect the histrionic's dramatic but superficial emotionality, and should dissipate rather quickly as supportive social relationships are established in the residential drug treatment community. Finally, those with compulsive personalities may be vulnerable to depression when they have failed to live up to self-imposed performance standards or when they receive negative evaluations from those upon whom they depend for guidance and approval. However, their depressions are considered likely to be transient because they have been punished for signs for vulnerability and inadequacy and are likely to respond to structured and supportive residential treatment.

McMahon and Tyson (1990) found that approximately two-thirds of their sample of alcoholic women demonstrated significant clinical depression at intake into treatment. Slightly more than half were classified as having met criteria for enduring depression. The remainder met criteria for transient depression. Discriminant analysis was used to examine associations between MCMI-I personality measures based on both intake and discharge administrations and depression subgroup membership. Separate analyses of intake and discharge MCMI-I records revealed strong and moderate positive associations, respectively, between scores on the Passive–Aggressive and Avoidant scales, and membership in the enduring depression group. Moderate positive associations were found in both analyses between scores on the Compulsive scale and membership in the transient depression group.

A moderate association was also found between scores on the Narcissistic scale and transient depression in the follow-up analysis.

Findings in the McMahon and Tyson (1990) study of alcohol-dependent women are generally consistent with the results of an earlier investigation (McMahon & Davidson, 1985b) of male alcoholics in revealing that personality factors are useful in differentiating between transient and enduring depression. However, there appear to be differences in the characteristics which led to this differentiation. In the study of alcoholic women, the passive–aggressive personality style was most clearly associated with enduring depression. In the earlier study of men, MCMI-I scales associated with clinical features including irrational, confused, and disorganized thinking and behavior and an avoidant personality pattern were more strongly predictive of enduring depression. McMahon and Tyson (1990) pointed out the conceptual similarities between defining cognitive and interpersonal features of the passive–aggressive and avoidant personalities, and influential cognitive and interpersonal models of depression (Beck, 1967; Klerman & Weissman, 1986).

These findings raise interesting questions about the nature of the link between various personality styles and depression in alcoholics. McMahon, Schram, and Davidson (1993) used the MCMI-II to examine the relationship between personality and depression among alcoholics in three personality groups. The first group was defined by peak MCMI-II personality scale elevations on the Schizoid or Avoidant scales (detached styles) and a secondary elevation on the Passive–Aggressive scale (ambivalent style). The second group was characterized by elevations on the Dependent scale. The third group had significant elevations on the Narcissistic and/or Antisocial scales (independent styles). It was hypothesized that because those with prominent avoidant and passive–aggressive characteristics have disturbing cognitions, limited interpersonal coping skills, and a tendency to withdraw from actually or potentially supportive relationships, they were likely to report higher levels of depression than were those in the other two groups. Individuals with these personality styles have characteristics similar to those that cognitive (e.g., Beck, 1967) and interpersonal (e.g., Klerman & Weissman, 1986) theorists assume lead directly to depression. Consistent with expectations, those in the detached/ambivalent group reported significantly greater depression than did those in either dependent or independent groups.

Of even greater interest in this investigation was the hypothesis that the relationship between maladaptive personality styles and depression may be mediated by vulnerability to negative life events or responsiveness to the effects of social support. McMahon, Schram, and Davidson (1993) point out that although there has been great interest in direct effects models of stress and direct and stress-buffering effects models of social support in relationship to depression, little has been done to examine these models within theoretically coherent personality subgroups. Millon's (1981) theory provides a useful framework for such an analysis because it provides detailed descriptions of differences among personality types in terms of stress and coping vulnerabilities and capacity to profit from supportive social relationships.

Consistent with hypotheses derived from Millon's (1981) theory, the detached/ambivalent group reported significantly more depression under conditions of high stress than low stress and no evidence consistent with having benefited from either direct or stress-buffering effects of supportive social relationships (McMahon, Schram, & Davidson, 1993). The dependent group reported significantly more depression under high stress than low stress conditions, as predicted. However, anticipated directly beneficial, and beneficial stress-buffering, effects of social support were not found. In the independent group, no significant relationships were found between stress or support levels and depression. However, an unanticipated stress by support interaction was found which was consistent with the possibility that, when stress is low, independent types in treatment for substance abuse may experience social support as unwanted pressure for attitude and behavior change, which leads to depression. The authors point out that although study results are consistent with hypothesized effects of stress on depression in detached/ambivalent and dependent personality groups, care must be taken in the interpretation of these relationships (McMahon, Schram, & Davidson, 1993). Although subjects reported about stressors which occurred during the year prior to their treatment admission, the possibility that depression preceded the reported life stressors must be considered. Further, a current depression may lead to overreporting of life events. Prospective designs would allow for more confidence in uncovering critical temporal relationships among personality, life stressors, supportive social relationships, and depression.

McMahon, Kelley, and Kouzekanani (1993) argued that these same detached, dependent, and independent personality styles could be useful in predicting dropout from residential therapeutic community treatment for cocaine abuse. Because those with detached personality features (schizoid and avoidant) have few interpersonal coping skills, they receive little reinforcement from social participation and are likely to find pressures for group involvement in the residential therapeutic community aversive. Treatment dropout was predicted. Independent (narcissistic and antisocial) personalities tend to be self-oriented, manipulative, and exploitative in social interactions. Those with this style were expected to resist pressure for attitude and behavior change inherent in therapeutic community-oriented drug treatment and to eventually drop out. In contrast, those with significant passive–dependent characteristics seek guidance and approval from caretakers who are viewed as more competent than themselves. They were expected to find the structured and supportive therapeutic community appealing. Engagement and retention in treatment would be likely and dropout was expected to be unlikely for this group. Discriminant analysis was used to differentiate between treatment dropouts and completers based upon scores on the MCMI-II personality scales from an intake assessment. Dropouts were differentiated from completers by a discriminant function defined, in part, by scores on MCMI-II personality scales which tap a ruggedly independent orientation with dominating, exploitative, and manipulative features. McMahon, Kelley, and Kouzekanani (1993) suggest that pressures for attitude and behavior change within the therapeutic-oriented treatment environment were likely difficult to tolerate for those with this orientation. MCMI-II scales measuring opposing characteristics, such as a strong need for social approval and a compliant, respectful, and conscientious interpersonal pattern, also contributed to the function. Those with this pattern demonstrated a greater likelihood of treatment completion.

Results of the McMahon, Kelley, and Kouzekanani (1993) investigation are consistent with a trend in the literature in suggesting that psychopathic characteristics are associated with treatment dropout in diverse populations of substance abusers (Craig, 1984; Stark, 1992). Further, Craig and Olson (1988) found that dropouts had lower needs for affiliation and nurturance and higher needs for autonomy and aggression than did drug abuse treatment completers. However, although Stark and Campbell (1988) found that drug treatment completers showed more evidence of interpersonal dependence on the MCMI-I, no differences between dropouts and completers were found on MCMI-I scales measuring independent personality features. Interestingly, Craig (1984) found that histrionic features predicted treatment completion, whereas passive–dependent features were associated with dropout. Craig (1984) suggests that results vary depending upon mode of treatment (therapeutic community, methadone maintenance, detoxification), duration of treatment, and the type of substance abuse for which treatment is sought.

Fals-Stewart (1992) used hierarchical agglomerative cluster analysis of intake MCMI-II personality scales to identify homogeneous subgroups among drug abusers in therapeutic community residential treatment. He then compared these clusters in terms of length of stay in treatment and in proportions of who remained abstinent during the follow-up period. Consistent with his predictions, those in clusters defined by elevations on the Antisocial scale and on the Schizoid and Avoidant scales had substantially shorter stays in treatment and significantly smaller proportions of subjects who were abstinent during the follow-up interval than did clusters with those characterized by peaks on MCMI-II Narcissistic, Dependent, and Histrionic scales. Members of the antisocial cluster were most likely to be removed from treatment for rule infractions, whereas those in the schizoid/avoidant cluster were most likely to leave against staff advice. Members of these two clusters not only relapsed in greater percentages, but also did so more quickly than did those in other clusters. Fals-Stewart (1992) concluded that those with personality features associated with membership in these clusters are not as appropriate for traditional therapeutic community-oriented treatment as are those in the other clusters.

MCMI ALCOHOL AND DRUG DEPENDENCE SCALES

Over the past several decades the MCMI scales designed to assess alcoholism and drug abuse problems have evolved from those in the original MMCI through several revisions to the current MCMI-III format. Scale titles have changed from Alcohol Misuse and Drug Misuse to Alcohol Abuse and Drug Abuse, and most recently to Alcohol Dependence and Drug Dependence. The number and composition of items in the drug and alcohol scales have varied from version to version; however, the clinical features and interpretive descriptions of the scales have changed little over time. Item weights based upon the prototypic item concept were incorporated into the MCMI-II and there have been further refinements to weights and prototypic alignments with the release of the MCMI-III. Researchers have examined the MCMI alcohol and drug scales (e.g., Craig & Weinberg, 1992a, 1992b), but studies using the MCMI-III substance dependence scales have not yet appeared in the literature. This section of the chapter presents an overview of the MCMI-III Alcohol and Drug Dependence scales (Scales B and T), scale item composition, association with DSM-IV criteria for dependence and abuse, and practical applications of these scales as screening indices to assess drug and alcohol problems in clinical populations. The intent of this section is to supplement the information provided in the MCMI-III manual, to describe the distinguishing features of the Alcohol Dependence and Drug Dependence scales, and to illuminate the interrelatedness of these scales with the personality and other clinical and severe syndrome scales.

MCMI-III Scale B: Alcohol Dependence

Millon (1994) described the clinical characteristics assessed by Scale B as related to alcoholism. High-scoring patients are likely to have a history of alcohol misuse, little success in controlling their use, and negative alcohol-related social, familial, and occupational consequences. The scale is composed of 15 true/false items, 14 keyed true. Prototypic items are weighted at 2 points each. Other items receive 1 point. Prototypic items are those considered most central to the construct measured by the scale. Six of the scale's fifteen items are closely related to DSM-IV substance dependence and abuse criteria and are assigned weights of 2. The remaining nine items are related to DSM-III-R or DSM-IV personality disorder criteria (antisocial, four items; aggressive, two items; and narcissistic, self-defeating, and borderline, one item each). Items from Scale B are also included on eight other MCMI-III scales. Table 10.1 shows the item content for the MCMI-III Alcohol

TABLE 10.1. MCMI-III Alcohol Dependence Scale Items, Weighting, DSM Disorder Criteria, and Other Scale Overlap (Total Items = 15)

DSM criteria	Criterion items on MCMI-III Scale B: Alcohol Dependence (weighting)	Other scale loading/overlap (weighting)
Substance dependence[a]		
A maladaptive pattern of substance use, leading to clinically significant impairment or distress, as manifested by three (or more) of the following, occurring at any time in the same 12-month period:	131 Drinking alcohol helps when I'm feeling down. (2)	
(3) the substance is often taken in larger amounts over a longer period than was intended	100 I guess I'm no different from my parents in becoming somewhat of an alcoholic. (2)	
(4) there is a persistent desire or unsuccessful efforts to cut down or control substance use	77 I have a great deal of trouble trying to control an impulse to drink to excess. (2)	
	152 I have a drinking problem that I've tried unsuccessfully to end. (2)	
Substance abuse[a]		
(1) recurrent substance use resulting in a failure to fulfill major role obligations at work, school, or home (e.g., repeated absences or poor work performance related to substance use; substance-related absences, suspensions or expulsions from school; neglect of children or household)	23 Drinking alcohol has never caused me any real problems in my work. (2F)	
(4) continued substance use despite having persistent or recurrent social or interpersonal problems caused or exacerbated by the effects of the substance (e.g., arguments with spouse about consequences of intoxication, physical fights)	52 I have an alcohol problem that has made difficulties for me and my family. (2)	Antisocial (1)
Aggressive (sadistic) personality disorder[b]		
(3) has treated or disciplined someone under his or her control unusually harshly (e.g., a child, student, prisoner, or patient)	14 Sometimes I can be pretty rough and mean in my relations with my family. (1)	Aggressive (2) Antisocial (1) Compulsive (1F)
(4) is amused by, or takes pleasure in, the psychological or physical suffering of others (including animals)	64 I don't know why, but I sometimes say cruel things just to make others unhappy. (1)	Aggressive (2)

Antisocial personality disorder[a]

(1)	113	failure to conform to social norms with respect to lawful behaviors as indicated by repeatedly performing acts that are grounds for arrest	I've gotten into trouble with the law a couple of times. (1)	Antisocial (2) Drug Dependence (1)
(2)	139	deceitfulness, as indicated by repeated lying, use of aliases, or conning others for personal profit or pleasure	I'm very good at making up excuses when I get into trouble. (1)	Antisocial (2) Compulsive (1F) Drug Dependence (1)
(3)	166	impulsivity or failure to plan ahead	I act quickly much of the time and don't think things through as I should. (1)	Antisocial (2) Aggressive (1) Compulsive (1F) Passive–Aggressive (1) Borderline (1) Bipolar (1)
(6)	101	consistent irresponsibility, as indicated by repeated failure to sustain consistent work behavior or honor financial obligations	I guess I don't take many of my family responsibilities as seriously as I should. (1)	Antisocial (2) Schizoid (1) Compulsive (1F) Drug Dependence (1)

Narcissistic personality disorder[a]

(7)	93	lacks empathy: is unwilling to recognize or identify with the feelings and needs of others	There are members of my family who say I'm selfish and think only of myself. (1)	Narcissistic (2) Antisocial (1) Aggressive (1)

Self-defeating personality disorder[b]

(6)	122	fails to accomplish tasks crucial to his or her personal objectives despite demonstrated ability to do so (e.g., helps fellow students write papers, but is unable to write his or her own)	I seem to make a mess of good opportunities that come my way. (1)	Self-Defeating (2) Antisocial (1) Passive–Aggressive (1) Borderline (1)

Borderline personality disorder[a]

(4)	41	impulsivity in at least two areas that are potentially self-damaging (e.g., spending, sex, substance abuse, reckless driving, binge eating)	I've done a number of stupid things on impulse that ended up causing me great trouble. (1)	Borderline (2) Antisocial (1) Aggressive (1) Compulsive (1F) Bipolar (1) Drug Dependence (1)

[a]DSM-IV criteria.
[b]DSM-III-R criteria.

Dependence scale, associated DSM criteria, and the other MCMI-III scales on which these items are found. Table 10.2 shows the MCMI-III Alcohol Dependence scale loadings and item content related to DSM disorder criteria.

MCMI-III Scale T: Drug Dependence

High scores on the Drug Dependence scale indicate patients with drug abuse histories or current drug abuse problems (Millon, 1994). The Drug Dependence scale is composed of 14 true/false items, all keyed true. Six of the scale's items correspond to DSM-IV substance dependence or abuse criteria and are assigned weights of 2. The remaining eight weight-1 items are primarily related to DSM personality disorder criteria (Antisocial, five items; and Passive–Aggressive, Histrionic, and Borderline, one item each). One (1)-weight items from Scale T also contribute to nine other MCMI-III scales tapping disorders other than substance abuse or dependence. Table 10.3 shows the item content for the MCMI-III Drug Dependence scale, corresponding DSM criteria, and the other MCMI-III scales on which these items are found. Table 10.4 shows the MCMI-III Drug Dependence scale loadings and item content related to DSM disorder criteria.

PRACTICAL APPLICATIONS

When using the MCMI to screen for clinical problems among drug and alcohol patients, it is important to recognize several operating characteristics of the Inventory. Gibertini, Brandenburg, and Retzlaff (1986) provided an excellent overview of psychometric characteristics associated with the MCMI. In addition, they discuss both positive and negative predictive power which are useful to clinicians when using the MCMI to screen for disorders. Because the predictive power of a test is dependent on several factors, including prevalence rates, it may prove necessary for clinicians to develop local norms and use available prevalence data to calculate the probability that a patient has a particular disorder given

TABLE 10.2. MCMI-III Alcohol Dependence Scale Prototypic Item Loadings (Weight = 2) and Secondary Item Loadings (Weight = 1) and Content Related to DSM Disorder Criteria

DSM disorder criteria	Prototypic item loadings		Secondary item loadings	
	n	%	n	%
Substance Dependence[a]	4	27	—	—
Substance Abuse[a]	2	13	—	—
Antisocial[a]	4	27	5	21
Narcissistic[a]	1	7	—	—
Aggressive (Sadistic)[b]	2	13	3	13
Self-Defeating[b]	1	7	—	—
Borderline[a]	1	7	2	8
Compulsive[a]	—	—	5(F)	21
Passive–Aggressive[a]	—	—	2	8
Schizoid[a]	—	—	1	4
Drug Dependence[a]	—	—	4	17
Bipolar[a]	—	—	2	8
Total	15	101%	24	100%

[a]Related to DSM-IV criteria.
[b]Related to DSM-III-R criteria.

TABLE 10.3. MCMI-III Drug Dependence Scale Items, Weighting, DSM Disorder Criteria, and Other Scale Overlap (Total Items = 14)

DSM criteria	Criterion items on MCMI-III Scale T: Drug Dependence (weighting)	Other scale loading/overlap (weighting)
Substance dependence[a]		
A maladaptive pattern of substance use, leading to clinically significant impairment or distress, as manifested by three (or more) of the following, occurring at any time in the same 12-month period:	13 My drug habits have gotten me into a good deal of trouble in the past. (2)	Antisocial (1) Aggressive (1)
	39 Taking so-called illegal drugs may be unwise, but in the past I found I needed them. (2)	Aggressive (1)
	118 There have been times when I couldn't get through the day without some street drugs. (2)	
	136 I know I've spent more money than I should buying illegal drugs. (2)	Antisocial (1)
(6) important social, occupational, or recreational activities are given up or reduced because of substance use	66 My habit of abusing drugs has caused me to miss work in the past. (2)	
Substance abuse[a]		
(4) continued substance use despite having persistent or recurrent social or interpersonal problems caused or exacerbated by the effects of the substance (e.g., arguments with spouse about consequences of intoxication, physical fights)	91 My use of so-called illegal drugs has led to family arguments. (2)	
Passive–aggressive personality disorder[a]		
(1) passively resists fulfilling routine social and occupational tasks	7 If my family puts pressure on me, I'm likely to feel angry and resist doing what they want. (1)	Passive–Aggressive (2) Antisocial (1) Aggressive (1) Compulsive (1F) Borderline (1)
Histrionic personality disorder[a]		
(2) interaction with others is often characterized by inappropriate sexually seductive or provocative behavior	21 I like to flirt with members of the opposite sex. (1)	Histrionic (2) Narcissistic (1) Antisocial (1)

(continued)

185

TABLE 10.3. (*continued*)

DSM criteria		Criterion items on MCMI-III Scale T: Drug Dependence (weighting)	Other scale loading/overlap (weighting)
Antisocial personality disorder[a]			
A. There is a pervasive pattern of disregard for and violation of the rights of others occurring since age 15 years, as indicated by three (or more) of the following:	53	Punishment never stopped me from doing what I wanted. (1)	Antisocial (2) Aggressive (1)
(1) failure to conform to social norms with respect to lawful behaviors as indicated by repeatedly performing acts that are grounds for arrest	113	I've gotten into trouble with the law a couple of times. (1)	Antisocial (2) Alcohol Dependence (1)
(2) deceitfulness, as indicated by repeated lying, use of aliases, or conning others for personal profit or pleasure	139	I'm very good at making up excuses when I get into trouble. (1)	Antisocial (2) Compulsive (1F) Alcohol Dependence (1)
(6) consistent irresponsibility, as indicated by repeated failure to sustain consistent work behavior or honor financial obligations	101	I guess I don't take many of my family responsibilities as seriously as I should. (1)	Antisocial (2) Schizoid (1) Compulsive (1F) Alcohol Dependence (1)
(7) lack of remorse, as indicated by being indifferent to or rationalizing having hurt, mistreated, or stolen from another	38	I do what I want without worrying about its effect on others. (1)	Antisocial (2) Schizoid (1) Narcissistic (1) Delusional (1)
Borderline personality disorder[a]			
(4) impulsivity in at least two areas that are potentially self-damaging (e.g., spending, sex, substance abuse, reckless driving, binge eating).	41	I've done a number of stupid things on impulse that ended up causing me great trouble. (1)	Borderline (2) Antisocial (1) Aggressive (1) Compulsive (1F) Bipolar (1) Alcohol Dependence (1)

[a]DSM-IV criteria.

186

TABLE 10.4. MCMI-III Drug Dependence Scale Prototypic Item Loadings (Weight = 2) and Secondary Item Loadings (Weight = 1) and Content Related to DSM Disorder Criteria

DSM disorder criteria	Prototypic item loadings		Secondary item loadings	
	n	%	*n*	%
Substance Dependence[a]	5	36	—	—
Substance Abuse[a]	1	7	—	—
Antisocial[a]	5	36	5	20
Passive–Aggressive[a]	1	7	—	—
Histrionic[a]	1	7	—	—
Borderline[a]	1	7	1	4
Aggressive[b]	—	—	5	20
Compulsive[a]	—	—	4(F)	16
Narcissistic[a]	—	—	2	8
Schizoid[a]	—	—	2	8
Delusional[a]	—	—	1	4
Bipolar[a]	—	—	1	4
Alcohol Dependence[a]	—	—	4	16
Total	14	100%	25	100%

[a]Related to DSM-IV criteria.
[b]Related to DSM-III-R criteria.

a base rate (BR) cutoff indicating the presence of such a disorder (Gibertini, Brandenburg, & Retzlaff, 1986). Gibertini and colleagues provide a formula that can be used with specific MCMI scales when prevalence estimates are available. This approach would prove useful with substance-abusing populations or in private practices in which a majority of the patients are substance abusers.

Prevalence data show high rates of specific personality disorders (i.e., antisocial personality) in substance abusing populations. This information may be of considerable value when using the MCMI in the diagnostic decision-making process. For example, using the Gibertini formula, a BR score of 85 on the Antisocial Personality scale in a psychiatric patient population similar to the MCMI-II standardization sample would indicate a probability of .88 that the patient had the disorder. However, a BR score of 85 on the same scale in a drug-abusing population that had a prevalence of 55% for antisocial personality disorder (cf. Kosten, Rounsaville, & Kleber, 1982) would indicate a probability of .99, reflecting a high degree of clinical certainty. This example shows the benefit of having access to local norms or known prevalence estimates when using the MCMI to screen for psychological disorders.

SUMMARY

A review of cluster analytic studies of various versions of the MCMI in substance-abusing populations led to the identification of a series of rather distinctive personality-based clusters. Differences among these cluster types in terms of severity of alcohol and drug abuse problems, possible motivations for substance use, and responsiveness to treatment were discussed. Cluster studies involving alcoholics typically led to the identification of a greater number of clusters than did those involving drug abusers. Studies that involved MCMI-I and -II scale-level comparisons of groups classified according to preferred substance of abuse are difficult to interpret. There is a clear need for additional investigations in which sub-

stance preference characteristics are clearly defined and in which the background characteristics of groups compared are carefully controlled. A series of interesting studies was
reviewed in which the MCMI-I and -II were used to examine relationships among personality, substance abuse patterns, depression, and clinical outcomes, including treatment
dropout and relapse. Personality patterns were found to be useful in differentiating between transient and enduring depression among alcoholics in several studies. The relationship between stress and depression in defined personality subgroups was explored in
another. In several studies, MCMI-II-based personality patterns were found to be useful
in predicting treatment dropout. In one of these, MCMI-II personality clusters were found
useful in predicting relapse to drug abuse. Finally, the MCMI-III scales which tap alcohol
dependence and drug dependence were described in a way which shows their distinctive
elements and their features which overlap with other MCMI-III scales.

REFERENCES

American Psychiatric Association. (1980). *Diagnostic and statistical manual of mental disorders*
(3rd ed.). Washington, DC: Author.
American Psychiatric Association. (1987). *Diagnostic and statistical manual of mental disorders*
(3rd ed., rev.). Washington, DC: Author.
American Psychiatric Association. (1994). *Diagnostic and statistical manual of mental disorders*
(4th ed.). Washington, DC: Author.
Bartsch, T. W., & Hoffman, J. J. (1985). A cluster analysis of Millon Clinical Multiaxial Inventory
(MCMI) profiles: More about a taxonomy of alcoholic subtypes. *Journal of Clinical Psychol-
ogy, 41*, 707–713.
Beck, A. T. (1967). *Depression: Clinical, experimental, and theoretical aspects*. New York: Harper
& Row.
Corbisiero, J. R., & Reznikoff, M. (1991). The relationship between personality type and style of
alcohol use. *Journal of Clinical Psychology, 47*, 291–298.
Craig, R. J. (1984). Can personality tests predict treatment dropouts? *International Journal of the
Addictions, 23*, 115–124.
Craig, R. J., & Olson, R. E. (1988). Differences in psychological need hierarchy between program
completers and dropouts from a drug abuse treatment program. *American Journal of Alcohol
Abuse, 14*(1), 89–96.
Craig, R. J., & Olson, R. E. (1990). MCMI comparisons of cocaine abusers and heroin addicts.
Journal of Clinical Psychology, 46, 230–237.
Craig, R. J., Verinis, J. S., & Wexler, S. (1985). Personality characteristics of drug addicts and al-
coholics on the Millon Clinical Multiaxial Inventory. *Journal of Personality Assessment, 49*,
156–160.
Craig, R. J., & Weinberg, D. (1992a). Assessing alcoholics with the Millon Clinical Multiaxial
Inventory: A review. *Psychology of Addictive Behaviors, 6*, 200–208.
Craig, R. J., & Weinberg, D. (1992b). Assessing drug abusers with the Millon Clinical Multiaxial
Inventory: A review. *Journal of Substance Abuse Treatment, 9*, 249–255.
Donat, D. C. (1988). Millon Clinical Multiaxial Inventory (MCMI) clusters for alcohol abusers:
Further evidence of validity and implications for medical psychotherapy. *Medical Psycho-
therapy, 1*, 41–50.
Donat, D. C., Walters, J., & Hume, A. (1991). Personality characteristics of alcohol dependent
inpatients: Relationship of MCMI subtypes to self-reported drinking behavior. *Journal of
Personality Assessment, 57*, 335–344.
Fals-Stewart, W. (1992). Personality characteristics of substance abusers: An MCMI cluster typology of recreational drug users treated in a therapeutic community and its relationship to length
of stay and outcome. *Journal of Personality Assessment, 59*, 515–527.

Flynn, P. M., Craddock, S. G., Luckey, J. W., Hubbard, R. L., & Dunteman, G. H. (1996). Comorbidity of antisocial personality and mood disorders among psychoactive substance-dependent treatment clients. *Journal of Personality Disorders, 10,* 56–67.

Flynn, P., Luckey, J., Brown, B., Hoffman, J., Dunteman, G., Theisen, A., Hubbard, R., Needle, R., Schneider, S., Koman, J., Atef-Vahid, M., Karson, S., Palsgrove, G., & Yates, B. (1995). Relationship between drug preference and indicators of psychiatric impairment. *American Journal of Drug and Alcohol Abuse, 21,* 153–166.

Gilbertini, M., Brandenburg, N. A., & Retzlaff, P. D. (1986). The operating characteristics of the Millon Clinical Multiaxial Inventory. *Journal of Personality Assessment, 50,* 554–567.

Jackson, D. N. (1989). *Basic Personality Inventory Manual.* Port Huron, MI: Research Psychologists Press.

Kadden, R. M., Cooney, N. L., Getter, H., & Litt, M. D. (1989). Matching alcoholics to coping skills or interactional therapies: Posttreatment results. *Journal of Consulting and Clinical Psychology, 57*(6), 698–704.

Klerman, G. L., & Weissman, M. M. (1986). The interpersonal approach to understanding depression. In T. Millon & G. L. Klerman (Eds.), *Contemporary directions in psychopathology: Toward the DSM-IV.* New York: Guilford Press.

Kosten, T. R., Rounsaville, B. J., & Kleber, H. D. (1982). DSM-III personality disorders in opiate addicts. *Comprehensive Psychiatry, 23,* 572–581.

Lesswing, N. J., & Dougherty, R. J. (1993). Psychopathology in alcohol- and cocaine-dependent patients: A comparison of findings from psychological testing. *Journal of Substance Abuse Treatment, 10,* 53–57.

Matano, R. A., Locke, K. D., & Schwartz, K. (1994). MCMI personality subtypes for male and female alcoholics. *Journal of Personality Assessment, 63,* 250–264.

McMahon, R. (1993). The Millon Clinical Multiaxial Inventory: An introduction to theory, development, and interpretation. In R. Craig (Ed.), *The Millon Clinical Multiaxial Inventory: A clinical research information synthesis* (pp. 3–22). Hillsdale, NJ: Erlbaum.

McMahon, R., & Davidson, R. (1985a). An examination of the relationship between personality patterns and symptom/mood patterns. *Journal of Personality Assessment, 49,* 552–556.

McMahon, R., & Davidson, R. (1985b). Transient versus enduring depression among alcoholics in inpatient treatment. *Journal of Psychopathology and Behavioral Assessment, 7,* 317–328.

McMahon, R., & Davidson, R. (1986). An examination of depressed versus non-depressed alcoholics in inpatient treatment. *Journal of Clinical Psychology, 42,* 177–184.

McMahon, R., Kelley, A., & Kouzekanani, K. (1993). Personality and coping styles in the prediction of dropout from treatment for cocaine abuse. *Journal of Personality Assessment, 61,* 147–155.

McMahon, R., Schram, L., & Davidson, R. (1993). Negative life events, social support, and depression in three personality types. *Journal of Personality Disorders, 7,* 241–254.

McMahon, R., & Tyson, D. (1990). Personality factors in transient versus enduring depression among inpatient alcoholic women: A preliminary investigation. *Journal of Personality Disorders, 4,* 150–160.

Millon, T. (1969). *Modern psychopathology.* Philadelphia: Saunders.

Millon, T. (1981). *Disorders of personality.* New York: Wiley.

Millon, T. (1983). *Millon Clinical Multiaxial Inventory Manual* (3rd ed.). Minneapolis: National Computer Systems.

Millon, T. (1987). *Manual for the MCMI-II* (2nd ed.). Minneapolis: National Computer Systems.

Millon, T. (1994). *Millon Clinical Multiaxial Inventory—III manual.* Minneapolis: National Computer Systems.

Millon, T., & Davis, R. (1995). *Disorders of personality: DSM-IV and beyond.* New York: Wiley.

Retzlaff, P. D., & Bromley, S. (1991). A multi-test alcohol taxonomy: Canonical coefficient clusters. *Journal of Clinical Psychology, 47,* 299–309.

Schuckit, M. (1983). Alcoholic patients with secondary depression. *Archives of General Psychiatry, 140,* 711–714.

Slaby, A. E. (1991). Dual diagnosis: Fact or fiction? In M. Gold & A. Slaby (Eds.), *Dual diagnosis in substance abuse* (pp. 3–28). New York: Marcel Decker.

Stark, M. J. (1992). Dropping out of substance abuse treatment: A clinically oriented review. *American Journal of Drug and Alcohol Abuse, 12*(4), 475–486.

Stark, M. J., & Campbell, B. K. (1988). Personality, drug use, and early attrition from substance abuse treatment. *American Journal of Drug and Alcohol Abuse, 14*, 475–485.

Tims, F. M., & Leukefeld, C. G. (1993). Treatment of cocaine abusers: Issues and perspectives. In F. M. Tims & C. G. Leukefeld (Eds.), *Cocaine treatment: Research and clinical perspectives* (NIDA Research Monograph 135, NIH Publication No. 93–3639, pp. 1–14). Rockville, MD: National Institute on Drug Abuse.

Wanberg, K. W., Horn, J. L., & Foster, F. M. (1985). *Manual for the Alcohol Use Inventory*. Denver, CO: Multivariate Measurement Consultants.

11

The MCMIs and Posttraumatic Stress Disorder

LEE HYER
JEFFREY BRANDSMA
STEPHANIE BOYD

In recent years an explosion of awareness of clinical problems due to trauma has emerged. In a most insidious form, a nonresilient response (as a result of a major stressor) results in posttraumatic stress disorder (PTSD). Even this relatively new construct does not do justice to the oftentimes total devastation of the person, described by Lifton (1993) as a "transformation of the self." Because it can be so impactful on and chronic for the person, over its 15-year existence the construct of PTSD has proven to be anything but simple in composition or cure (Hyer & Associates, 1994).

One problem has been the almost exclusive focus on the profile of symptoms of PTSD as well as the nature of the stressor itself. Looking at the PTSD construct itself, it is generally agreed that the (three) symptom categories cluster independently, and that no one-to-one relationship exists between a symptom and the stressor or between this disorder and its resultant symptom(s). That may be "good news" for the construct, but it bypasses or downplays the pervasiveness of the disorder, its resistance to change, and the role of other factors.

It is our belief that one truth above all others emerges in the dissection of the trauma response: Trauma sequelae or symptoms are responses, the result of a sequential destructuring process whose principal pilot is the person. In this formulation the person(ality) is the most important element in the equation of the "trauma catching" process (Hyer & Associates, 1994). The individual conducts and orchestrates the residual impact of the trauma, even if largely unconsciously. The transition, then, of the trauma survivor's torturing event to a (chronic) trauma memory involves the central dynamic of the expression of psychopathology in PTSD. This transcoding process is prepotent in understanding PTSD.

If our interest is the person of the victim, then *trauma as response* is emphasized instead of *trauma as stressor*. Logically, three components are involved: the stressor, the role

191

of the long-standing characteristics of the individual, and the mediating influences of the recovery process. Often the stressor is polymorphous in presentation and has multiple trajectories, including PTSD (but not limited to this disorder). And, because PTSD has a distinct and common symptom grouping, knowledge of typical "maladaptive resolutions" (Epstein, 1990) is helpful to the clinician. But again, we argue that the poor trauma response is best understood by examining the personality of the survivor.

We divide this chapter into three parts: (1) the importance of personality from the perspective of trauma in the calculus of care; (2) a review of PTSD highlighting the findings of the Millon Clinical Multiaxial Inventories (MCMIs) (Millon, 1977, 1987, 1994) in light of these arguments; and (3) the connection of personality to the core of PTSD (intrusive memory). One word of caution is given: Our data sets involve PTSD survivors of combat, groups of veterans with chronic trauma problems. This is a limitation in one sense, as problems will appear homogenized. It is also a strength, as differences will mean something because they are harder to obtain. Since studies on the victims of World War II, no satisfactory answer has been developed to the most logical question regarding trauma: "Why some and not others?" Our argument is that trauma is but a starting point for inquiry into the symptom picture. This information provides only "prototypical," clinical help and no sanctuary for complete understanding. For that we need something more, a knowledge of personality.

THE ROLE OF PERSONALITY AND MODERATORS IN TRAUMA

Only recently has it been safe to say that an awareness of the personality is relevant in the formation of the trauma response. Only recently too has it been "fashionable" to discuss PTSD in ways similar to discussions of personality, for example, the dimensional versus categorical diagnostic determinants of PTSD (Weiss, 1993). In one recent publication (Wolfe & Keane, 1993, p. 166) an endorsement for "enhancing the sophistication of these (personality) assessment methods" was even made. In the past several studies have punctuated the relevance of personality without using the term. Weisaeth (1984), for example, followed victims of a Norwegian fire over time. Results showed that the prevalence of acute PTSD was related mostly to the initial intensity of the exposure. But after 4 years, pre-accident psychological functioning was a higher predictor of adjustment than was accident intensity. McFarlane (1990) as well found that in an acute group of fire victims, no vulnerability factors of importance were noted, but in a chronic group several of these (including a concurrent psychiatric disorder, a positive family history of problems, avoidance as a personality trait, being older, and having panicked during the disaster itself) were related.

In the trauma literature the process of evolution from acuteness to chronicity (of combat-related PTSD) has tended to rest conceptually on combat exposure alone (Kulka et al., 1990). This has been labeled the "extreme event" hypothesis, and it asserts that posttrauma maladjustment is largely a consequence of the inherent nature of the stressor. Research examining the influence of other contenders now is more popular, including age of onset of symptoms (Gibbs, 1989), receptivity to social support (Lyons, 1991), ethnicity (Penk & Allen, 1991), and comorbidity, especially with substance abuse (Abueg & Fairbank, 1992). This "personal characteristics" hypothesis maintains that persistent adverse psychological reactions after exposure to trauma represent exacerbations of preexisting psychopathology (e.g., neurosis or character disorder) or are manifestations of a predisposition to such reactions (Boulanger & Kadushin, 1986; Hendin & Haas, 1984).

An attempt to integrate both types of explanations is the "person–event interaction model." In this formulation the individual's variability (in response to extreme stressors) is viewed as a function of the dynamic interaction of both internal and external factors (Keane, 1989). Advocates argue that severity and persistence of adverse psychological reactions will vary depending on the magnitude of the event *relative* to the individual's coping resources. In an important way the person–event interaction model better explains the chronic expression of PTSD than do other models, as it consistently highlights variables different from those responsible for an acute episode of PTSD. Parson (1993) proposed a two-part model of trauma stress, noting that PTSD develops in response to the traumatic stressor, but a posttraumatic self disorder (PTsfD) develops in response to a "sanctuarial stress," the failure of the environment to meet the needs of the survivor. It might also be said that the learning model (an unconditioned response results from an intense, unconditioned stimulus) applies for acute PTSD, but for chronic PTSD other mediating (conditioned, symbolic) variables must enter into the equation (Foy, Osato, Houskamp, & Neumann, 1992).

Research using prospective or longitudinal designs to assess the effects of trauma has fostered this position. Using early grade school (Card, 1987) or premorbid college data (Schnurr, Friedman, & Rosenberg, 1991), for example, early "personality problems" were noted with (Vietnam combat) victims with a lifetime prevalence of PTSD symptoms relative to those who had no symptoms. Two additional studies (Foy et al., 1992; McCranie, Hyer, Boudewyns, & Woods, 1991) have confirmed the person–event interaction or "threshold model" of PTSD etiology. In addition, the psychodynamic literature (e.g., Emery & Emery, 1989; Emery, Emery, Shama, Quiana, & Jassani, 1991; Horowitz, 1986; Hendin, 1983; Hendin, Pollinger, Singer, & Ulman, 1981; McFarlane, 1990; Wilson, 1988) and a handful of studies addressing traditional personality problems (Hyer & Boudewyns, 1985), especially antisocial and borderline traits (Lipkin, Scurfield, & Blank, 1983; Wilson & Zigelbaum, 1983; Berman, Price, & Gusman, 1982), have been supportive. Most notable among this grouping is the work of Horowitz et al. (1984), who developed a method of treatment for PTSD based on the information processing of the stressors and character structure of the person. Finally, Perry, Lavori, Pagano, Hoke, and O'Donnell (1992), using a "mini-longitudinal" design, showed that the pathogenicity of interpersonal exit events was not by itself related to problems, but rather to the type of personality psychopathology.

Just as people with personality disorders have more trouble negotiating life's options (according to the personality research), so too do "vulnerable" victims respond poorly after the trauma (e.g., Benedek, 1985; Black, 1982). This is the true unfolding of the person–event model. The ability to request social support, for example, is related both to adjustment and to one's personality (Boyd, Hyer, Summers, & Litaker, 1995). In fact, certain types of personalities (ambivalent–detached and dependent) report higher levels of depression under conditions of high stress than they do under low stress (McMahon, Schram, & Davidson, 1993). Furthermore, if a victim is in turmoil (or for that matter if any person experiences psychiatric symptoms), the likelihood of an Axis II disorder being present is high, whether as a "real" premorbid condition or an artifact of a current intense emotion (Choca, Shanley, & Van Denberg, 1992). Interestingly, what is not known is whether responses that predict the reoccurrence or course of this disorder are the same as those present at onset (Monroe, Bromet, Connell, & Steiner, 1986).

It is implied as well that a subgroup of victims exists that is more resilient or that has a high level of self-complexity that prevents or modulates the influence or mood shifts due to stress (Morgan & Janoff-Bulman, 1992). Leaf, Alington, Mass, DiGuiseppe, and Ellis (1991) evaluated the MCMI and its relationship to stress. These authors found that some

scales are associated with less distress (Histrionic, Narcissistic, Antisocial, and Compulsive) and some with more (e.g., Passive–Aggressive, Avoidant, Schizoid, and Dependent).
They speculate that those with the former group of personalities may be associated with
hardiness (attitudinal toughness). Once again, person factors dictate the stressor experience—both amount and type.

    PTSD is complex. At a symptom level we argue that this disorder is often virulent and
pernicious, providing sanctuary only for nosological order. We have argued further that
the "real" understanding of the residuals of trauma occur best from the perspective of
personality. Below we even argue that the actual character of the PTSD survivor may change
over time. We now turn to its measurement.

PTSD AND THE MCMI

PTSD Composition

A look at personality demands one more brief review of the composition of PTSD. *No
other disorder in the DSM-IV appears to share more symptoms with other disorders or is
more conceptually related to other disorders than is PTSD* (American Psychiatric Association, 1994); on the one hand, being more intense than other anxiety disorders (Foa, Steketee,
& Rothbaum, 1989) and, on the other, consisting of many varieties (Horowitz et al., 1984).
In practical, "clinical" fact, PTSD vies for a "place" in the smorgasbord of disorders. For
this diagnosis to be made the clinician validates that a stressor has happened and assesses
if a threshold of suffering is passed, checking this against a listing of symptoms. In the
deliberation of this process the worst problem (group of symptoms) is called the primary
diagnosis. In the "real world" of trauma victims, a heterogeneity of symptom possibilities
can be present with no pathognomonic signs (other than trauma history) to identify the
disorder. This overlap highlights the inherent variability among trauma victims and, by
implication, the need for the importance of another, more analytic taxonomy for an
understanding of this disorder.

    The DSM-IV criteria for PTSD, 17 symptoms in addition to the trauma (American
Psychiatric Association, 1994), is formed around three symptom categories: reexperiencing, avoidance, and arousal, with a centerpiece of a trauma. Interestingly, all correlate highly
with PTSD as a whole, indicating each's contribution (Hyer & Associates, 1994). Category
B, reexperiencing, and Category D, increased arousal, have received the most attention, as
these symptoms are considered central to PTSD and are considered more important than
"avoidance/numbing" (Category C; Pitman, Orr, Forgue, deJong, & Claiborn, 1987;
Weisenberg, Solomon, Schwarzwald, & Mikulincer, 1987). But it is Category C that perpetuates the trauma state, and it is this area that appears most related to the personality
style (Hyer & Associates, 1994). In fact, the style of avoidance and constriction represents
adaptation and continuance of the trauma response(s): Sufferers avoid–escape in the way
most related to habitual patterns, that is, personality (see below for patterns).

The MCMIs' Similarities Criteria

Over the years the MCMIs have attempted to improve on pathology bias, base rate (BR)
issues, item overlap, weighting problems, the paucity of evidence for validity, and diagnostic decision rules for scales or profiles (Dana & Cantrell, 1988; Millon, 1994; Widiger,
Williams, Spitzer, & Francis, 1985). All three MCMIs have attempted to apply the Axis II

multiaxial formulations, with scales being reasonably anchored to the DSM-III (American Psychiatric Association, 1980; Choca et al., 1992), DSM-III-R (American Psychiatric Association, 1987; Craig, 1993), and now the DSM-IV (Millon, 1994).

Figure 11.1 presents a profile of the MCMIs of PTSD combat veterans taken at different points in time by mostly different subjects. Several conclusions appear evident. First, the profiles are rather similar. The high scales are the Avoidant and Passive–Aggressive as we have discussed, as well as the Schizoid and Self-Defeating. The structurally deficient scales are also high. Second, the MCMI-II BR scores are slightly higher than on other MCMIs. This is noted because the MCMI-II was developed to reduce spurious overlap and overreporting by groups with acute turmoil (Millon, 1987). Third, although slight, scores on the Schizoid scale on the MCMI-III are higher than the other modal scales noted. It may be that chronic victims are not adapting (are indeed chronic) and are increasingly detached as a result of a lack of desire in life. The MCMI-III was, of course, taken last. Fourth, for that small group of subjects who completed all three MCMIs, intercorrelations (not shown) between the various MCMIs are lower, especially on the symptom scales, but they are still significant and respectable. This too follows other research.

One other feature is noteworthy. Scores on the Self-Defeating and Aggressive personality scales are both high for this population and appear to provide new clinical information. In a separate study on the MCMI-II (Hyer, Davis, Woods, Albrecht, & Boudewyns, 1992) these two personality styles proved important, as they provided extra (incremental) information on this group of veterans. The Self-Defeating scale, especially, predicted problems in treatment, early dropout, and compliance problems. Subjects who scored higher

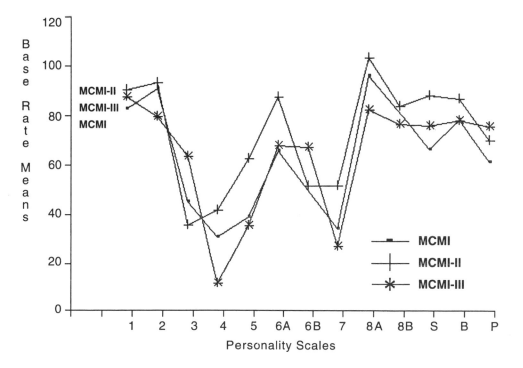

FIGURE 11.1. PTSD personality profiles on the MCMIs.

on this scale also had increased overreporting, a greater number of suicidal gestures, and lower adjustment potential and ego strength. The addition of the aggressive style alone does not appear as pathological. Rather, when high scores on the Aggressive scale are combined with high scores on the Self-Defeating personality scale, the resultant profile tends to be nosologically complex (other personalities are high also) and to augment the effect of the Self-Defeating style. These two personalty styles, now removed from the DSM-IV, add information to PTSD victim profiles: Victims with high scores on the Self-Defeating style particularly are resistant to change.

Another way to evaluate these patterns is to look at the high-point pairs of the MCMI-II (Table 11.1). These data are from a sample of veterans, most of whom had combat experience and had PTSD or PTSD problems. It is noteworthy that the combinations are heavily represented with 1–2, 2–8A, 2–8B, 7–3, and 8A-7 combinations. The detached and the ambivalent–discordant personalities are most represented. We shall revisit the influence of these personalities on PTSD shortly.

The MCMI-III is new in several ways. It has substantially fewer item keyings, has cut the number of items on most scales by half, has a reduced weighting procedure, and has a PTSD scale. With only a few subjects ($n = 25$), data from the *MCMI-III Manual* (Millon, 1994) show that the PTSD scale is correlated significantly with the Impact of Events scale (.61), as well with several MMPI scales (notably D, Pt, Sc, and Pa; correlations >.5). The positive predictive power of the scale, however, has not been determined. Data from our medical center show that the MCMI-III PTSD scale, along with other personality scales (e.g., Schizoid, Avoidant, and Self-Defeating) had significant correlations with standard self-report PTSD scale (Hyer, Boyd, Stanger, Davis, & Walters, in press).

One other table is presented in this section. Table 11.2 presents correlations between the MCMI-II and the three PTSD categories from the interviewer-rated Clinician Administered PTSD Scale (CAPS) (Blake, Weathers, et al., 1995). The correlations are generally low. Nonetheless, some significance is present in this group with little variance. For the intrusion symptoms only, the Self-Defeating and Compulsive (negative) personality scales are significant; for Avoidance, the detached personality scales, including Schizotypal (structurally-deficient personality), and once again the Self-Defeating personality scales, are significant; and for arousal, the Borderline, Schizotypal, Aggressive, Avoidant, and Self-Defeating scales are significant. Interestingly, PTSD ratings as a whole correlate significantly with the two detached personality scales and the Schizotypal, as well as the Self-Defeating and Borderline scales. In sum, the Self-Defeating and the Avoidant personality scales, as

TABLE 11.1. Percentage of Profiles as High-Point Pairs on MCMI-II

	1	2	3	4	5	6A	6B	7	8A
					Scales				
1									
2	13								
3	1	3							
4	0	0	2						
5	<1	1	1	2					
6A	1	2	0	1	4				
6B	1	<1	0	0	3	3			
7	2	1	5	<1	3	<1	2		
8A	2	5	1	<1	1	3	5	5	
8B	<1	5	1	0	<1	0	<1	<1	1

TABLE 11.2. Correlation of MCMI-II and PTSD Ratings

MCMI-II	CAPS			
	Intrusion	Avoidance	Arousal	Total
Schizoid	.19	.33	.15	.26
Avoidant	.17	.33	.22	.30
Dependent	.10	.14	−.05	.11
Histrionic	−.13	−.22	−.16	−.16
Narcissistic	−.04	−.08	.12	−.00
Antisocial	−.11	−.18	.00	−.13
Aggressive	−.00	.01	.22	.08
Compulsive	−.26	−.00	.05	−.05
Passive–Aggressive	.05	.17	.20	.18
Self-Defeating	.30	.39	.33	.43
Schizotypal	.16	.29	.27	.34
Borderline	.16	.23	.35	.29
Paranoid	−.07	−.04	.20	.04

Note. CAPS, Clinician Administered PTSD Scale. If $r \geq .2$, then $p > .05$

do the Borderline and Schizotypal scales, correlate well with the PTSD ratings and each of the symptom clusters; the Passive–Aggressive scale does not.

Taxonomy

In 1991, Hyer and colleagues (Hyer, Woods, & Boudewyns, 1991) developed a three-tier model of PTSD. Tier 1 involves the lifestyle of the survivor and was wholly idiographic. This tier was conceived as a dynamic formulation of the person, an idiosyncratic, ever-evolving characterization that captures the "true core" of the person. Obviously, this is a heuristic ideal that is never quite reached and is difficult to measure. Tier 2 involves the personality of the survivor, and was measurable and helpful in the treatment of the person. Tier 3 includes symptoms divided into psychosocial and trauma-specific (intrusions). Among PTSD victims, psychosocial symptoms include all DSM criteria (American Psychiatric Association, 1994) and correlated symptoms characteristic of this disorder. These symptoms are often the notable "squeaky wheels" in treatment. The trauma-specific symptoms include just the trauma memory and its intrusions, the heart of PTSD.

Special note was given to Tier 2, from which a typology of PTSD was developed on the basis of personality. Initially, based on a procedure outlined by Millon (1983), eight basic personality codes were sorted on the MCMI among a group of PTSD combat veterans. A code was arrived at by prominence of a style; that is, any of the eight mild personality style scales with BR scores above 84 were included in that code. Next, each veteran's profile was sorted into additional codes based on presence (BR>74). As a result of these two procedures, a parent code, the 8–2 (traumatic personality), was identified. Despite the fact that this code (8–2) is one reflective of general psychopathology (Retzlaff, 1993) or response style distortion in selected groups such as PTSD (McNeil & Meyer, 1990), it is argued that these two styles become "crystalized" in trauma victims and are representative of the trauma patterns of the victim.

In the extant literature a handful of studies now exist that have used the MCMI in the evaluation of PTSD (combat-related) and the Passive–Aggressive–Avoidant code (8–2 or 2–8) (Hyer et al., 1991; Hyer et al., 1992; McDermott, 1986; Robert et al., 1985; Sherwood,

Funari, & Piekorski, 1990) and there are also studies using the MCMI-II to examine these high-point codes (Hyer & Associates, 1994). Bryer, Nelson, Miller, and Krol (1987) replicated this pattern also with sexually abused women (using the MCMI). Using the MCMI-II Dutton (1994) even saw this pattern characteristic of abusers and labeled it an abusive personality. Interestingly, in all of these studies the borderline personality was in evidence, suggesting the intense nature and increased pathogenesis of problems. Sherwood et al. (1990) noted that the Passive–Aggressive and Avoidant pattern was surprisingly homogeneous and may represent adaptive patterns developed to cope with the traumas (of Vietnam). Munley, Bains, Bloem, Busby, and Pendziszewski (in press) also found this profile on the MCMI-II, controlling for response bias (overreporting).

Conceptually, the components of avoidance and ambivalence (Millon, 1969, 1983) are related to the symptoms of PTSD. Criterion C involves avoidance. The combination of this criterion along with Criteria B and D (intrusions and hyperactivity) connotes ambivalence. Choca et al. (1992) indicated that this profile is noteworthy for its intense emotional conflict (dependence and avoidance) characteristically being moody and angry and then guilty and contrite, features associated with the borderline personality. Given these descriptors, it is not difficult to see that the Self-Defeating scale relating so strongly to the PTSD criteria. There appears to be a kind of dance in action here between PTSD and common personality styles, a topic about which we shall return.

In the Tier 2 formulation, three additional codes were also identified: schizoid influence (Scale 1), dependent influence (Scale 3), and the antisocial influence (Scale 6) (follow Table 11.3 for discussion in this section). A subsequent study with the MCMI-II added the self-defeating influence (Scale 8B; Hyer, Gratton, & Melton, 1993). The severe personality styles also are present and their influence was noted, but not formally evaluated. The importance of this typology, therefore, rests in the incremental information provided by the additional codes (Scales 1, 3, 6A, and 8B; see Hyer et al., 1993) for clinical explanation). All codes possess the 8–2 pattern plus an added style(s).

This is, however, a "clinical" taxonomy and it represents anything but perfect classification. Actuarially, the typing of PTSD has not been done until recently. Cluster analysis represents a way to assess this issue of typing. This technique has been employed for diagnostic classification purposes and has been reviewed elsewhere (Aldenderfer & Blashfield, 1984). The application of a cluster analysis is especially useful, then, in identifying natural groupings in a heterogeneous group and in constructing a useful conceptual schema for

TABLE 11.3. PTSD Typology Based on MCMI-II High-Point Codes

Code	Label	Code	Label	Code	Label
8–2	Traumatic personality	8–2	Traumatic personality	6A–6B–8A	Antisocial influence
1	Schizoid influence	8–2–1	Schizoid influence	1–2–8A–8B	Self-Defeating influence
3	Dependent influence			1–2–6A–8B	Global subclinical
6A	Antisocial influence	8–6	Antisocial influence		
8B	Self-Defeating influence				

classification (Lorr & Strack, 1990). Any subsequent "meaning" for the desired clusters would depend on the external validators applied to the various clusters, and ultimately on cross-validation.

A cluster analysis was used to identify groups of inpatients with confirmed PTSD due to combat (Hyer, Davis, Albrecht, Boudewyns, & Woods, 1994). In Study 1, the MCMI-I was given to 256 subjects along with the MMPI, PTSD measures, and interviews for background variables. Three clusters resulted: a traumatic personality (8–2 profile), schizoid influence (Scale 1), and antisocial influence (Scale 6). Comparison on the MCMI symptom scales, MMPI, and PTSD scales showed that members of the antisocial influence cluster were "healthier" on all measures. Members of the schizoid influence cluster were most psychopathological. Interestingly, these clusters appear similar to factors noted by Retzlaff and Gibertini (1990) and have been found in over 10 studies. The schizoid influence (Cluster 2) shows a generalized pathology and is a marker of the aloof/social factor; the traumatic personality (Cluster 1) seems representative of the contradictory lability/restrained factor discussed above; and the antisocial influence (Cluster 3) appears most characterized by the submissive–aggressive factor.

In Study 2 the MCMI-II was given to 136 new subjects who met the same criteria as did those in Study 1. Four clusters resulted: global (1–2–6A–6B–8A–8B profile), subclinical (having elevations on none or one scale), aggressive (6A–6B–8A profile), and detached–self-defeating (1–2–8A–8B profile). Comparisons of these four clusters revealed two healthier groups, the subclinical and aggressive, and two groups that were more pathological (Hyer et al., 1994).

It is difficult to draw one-to-one similarities with Study 1, but what began as a clinical taxonomy, "traumatic personality" (the 8–2 profile) and three variants (schizoid, antisocial, and dependent [MCMI] later with the addition of self-defeating influence (on MCMI-II), has changed in some predictable ways. In using the MCMI, clinical interest is directed to the traumatic personality, as well as the schizoid and antisocial influences, the latter often appearing "healthy." In using the MCMI-II, on the other hand, different groups were extracted. At a simple level there were two clusters that represented high levels of psychopathology (Clusters 2 and 4) and two where this was less so (Clusters 1 and 3). The former two clusters cannot be differentiated well without further study; the latter two appear to be distinct—Cluster 3 is more classically PTSD (fewer character issues), and Cluster 1, more characterological and given to acting out. Regarding the high levels of psychopathology, Retzlaff (1993) has identified a "distress clinical convergence" factor. This is an overreporting, "cry for help" response by the person. It includes those labeled as avoidant, passive–aggressive, borderline, anxious, dysthymic, and psychotically depressed. He noted that this is an interpretable profile, perhaps a "pathology profile," and should be useful clinically. Clusters 2 and 4, then, can be considered in this light.

Factor Analysis

Empirical findings regarding the lack of connections of the first and second versions of the MCMIs to their matching DSMs (APA, 1980, 1987) and concordance of different personality measures (e.g., Widiger & Corbitt, 1993) legitimized concerns about factorial solutions. Choca, Peterson, and Shanley (1986) identified over 15 factor-analytic studies of the Millon instruments using BR scores, item overlap correlations, or items on both the MCMI and MCMI-II. Perhaps the most important of these is Retzlaff and Gibertini's (1990) study in which three personality factors (aloof–social, submissive–aggressive, and labile–restrained) and five symptom factors (detached, submissive, suspicious, high social energy, and general distress) were found to best account for the variance of the MCMI. This study and others produced remarkable consistency for both the MCMI and MCMI-II, even when using "better" procedures, such as an item-level factor analysis (see Lorr, 1993).

One group (Retzlaff, Lorr, Hyer, & Ofman, 1991) used a population of mostly PTSD combat veterans; this group performed a standard factor analysis on the items of the MCMI-II, separating the scales by personality and symptoms. Results showed that nine personality factors were extracted which closely matched the scales on the MCMI-II itself. These included Schizoid/Histrionic, Self-Defeating, Antisocial–Hostility, Dependent, Narcissistic, Antisocial–Aggressive, and Impulsivity factors. Most of the items for each of the factors were from the parent scales or related ones. Interestingly, the nine factors that resulted from the symptom scales also were anchored to symptom scales themselves—Depression, Alcohol Abuse and Substance Abuse, Fatigue, Crying (Psychotic Depression), Mania, Paranoia and Somatization, and the Validity scales. Again, all factors were highly consistent with the MCMI-II scale keyings.

One other study used a PTSD population. Stewart, Hyer, Retzlaff, and Ofman (in submission) performed a factor analysis on the MCMI-II scales themselves, something rarely done. Again, using a sample of mostly PTSD combat victims, this group performed a factor analysis on the non-structurally deficient personalities (Millon, 1995). Results of data on the two personalities most akin to PTSD, the avoidant and passive–aggressive, as well as the other personalities most related to PTSD (i.e., schizoid, antisocial, and self-defeating), are presented in Table 11.4. The passive–aggressive personality has two factors: emotionally impulsive and resentful, and the avoidant personality has two also: isolation and aimlessness. These factors are conceptually close to the construct of PTSD itself. The other factors that make up the incremental personalities provide additional information regarding PTSD (for that personality). Of note are the dysthymia factor of self-defeating personality, a depressive component influencing this style, and factors that are distinctive for the schizoid and avoidant personalities.

TABLE 11.4. MCMI-II Factors on Key PTSD Scales

Scale	Factor	No. of items	% Variance
Central			
Passive–Aggrssive	Resentful	5	4
	Aimlessness	4	5
Avoidant	Isolation	7	16
	Aimlessness	4	5
Influencing			
Schizoid	Introversion	9	15
	Lack of conation	4	6
	Unspecified	4	5
Antisocial	Behavioral act out	6	9
	Resistance to authority	4	5
	Unspecified	4	4
Self-Defeating	Dysthymia	11	14
	Agreeable	5	6
	Self-abasement	6	5

Coping and the MCMI

The relationship between personality and coping has rarely been evaluated using any of the personality scales. Perhaps this is because conceptual confusion exists between the two. The MCMIs were designed to represent a theoretical model that emphasizes personality styles as central in the determination and expression of the patterns and styles of the person in both positive coping and psychopathology (Millon, 1969, 1983, 1987). Millon, as well as other personologists (Costa & McCrae, 1992), have always considered personality to be "causally prior" to coping and stressors: that is, personality represents the themes or traits that comprise the person, and coping is a method of operation in the service of these traits.

Hyer, McCranie, Boudewyns, and Sperr (1996) assessed just under 100 PTSD combat veterans, applying the MCMI and the Ways of Coping—Revised (WOC-R) scale. The frame of reference for the coping scale was usual experiences with trauma memories. A special scoring system was employed to provide the percentage of all coping responses for a particular person. For each survivor, therefore, the percentage of each coping style added to 100. The relative frequency of the coping strategies and the relationship between the two measures constituted the central questions.

Results indicated that the relative frequency of each coping style followed a predictable form (percentage of use) for PTSD: escape–avoidance, 23.7%; self-controlling, 16.8%; distancing, 13.6%; confrontative coping, 12.3%; planful problem solving, 9.3%; accept responsibility, 8.6%; seeking social support, 8.3%; and positive reappraisal, 7.3%. As expected, the PTSD mechanism of avoidance was most frequently used and positive reappraisal was least utilized.

Importantly, results also showed that PTSD victims cope with trauma memories in ways conceptually related to their personality style (Table 11.5). In the *detached* personality only the avoidant style is significantly related to any coping style, that is, escape–avoidance. Whereas those with the avoidant personality are interested in avoiding stress, those with schizoid personalities choose no particular coping style and are unaffected by stress. The *dependent* person copes by holding their self responsible, avoiding confrontation, and, surprisingly, by use of planful problem solving. Like schizoid persons, the histrionic shows no preferences in coping style.

For the *independent* and *ambivalent* patterns predictable coping profiles result also. Those with narcissistic personalities tend to problem solve, to be confrontative, and do not avoid. Those with antisocial personalities, on the other hand, have several styles of coping—being confrontative, actively problem solving, and being unavoidant and unaccepting of responsibility. With the ambivalent styles, WOC-R coping patterns reveal striking understandable differences: Compulsives tend to avoid confrontation and to positively reappraise self, and those with passive–aggressive personalities paradoxically combine confrontation with avoidance and a lack of problem solving. Predictably, this latter personality type does not positively regard self.

Finally, those with structurally deficient personalities also perform in expected ways, having fewer positive problem-solving strategies or more confusing strategies. Those with a schizotypal style cope by avoidance, those with a borderline style by confusion—accepting responsibility but also avoiding, not problem solving, and not positively reappraising self; and those with a paranoid style manage by action—confrontation, problem solving, and an absence of avoidance. These results are noteworthy, as the WOC-R coping patterns were coincident with the personality coping patterns. Implied is that the personality pattern dictates the necessary "survival" strategy for the PTSD victim. Once again, the argument holds that the person(ality) of the victim dictates the trauma response.

TABLE 11.5. Pearson Correlations between MCMI Personality Scales and WOC-R Relative Coping Scores ($N = 110$)

MCMI Scale	WOC-R							
	Confrontive coping	Distancing	Self-control	Seeking social support	Accepting responsibility	Escape–avoidance	Planful problem solving	Positive reappraisal
Schizoid	.05	-.04	-.02	-.04	.01	.05	.04	-.06
Avoidant	.09	-.05	-.06	-.12	.13	.19*	-.06	-.18
Dependent	-.30**	-.02	.05	.03	.24*	.14	-.20*	.03
Histrionic	.09	.14	.05	-.09	-.11	-.04	-.03	.00
Narcissistic	.19*	.02	-.12	.06	-.18	-.27*	.20*	.15
Antisocial	.38**	-.01	-.11	-.08	-.20*	-.23*	.30**	.01
Compulsive	-.40**	-.11	.12	.15	.11	-.14	.06	.28**
Passive–Aggressive	.23*	.05	.01	-.14	.01	.22*	-.19	-.26**

Note. WOC-R, Ways of Coping—Revised.
*$p < .05$, two-tailed; **$p < .01$, two-tailed.

202

Concurrent Validation

Some construct confusion exists in the "borderland" between personality measures and PTSD constructs or measures. Often in the disorder PTSD, it is hard to discern what is the measure and what is the construct (Morey, 1993). It may also be that Blashfield (1992) is correct in asserting that a single factor accounts for the comorbidity of people with several problems (severe personality disorder). Already it was noted that the traumatic experience seems to evolve into a personality profile characterized by the passive–aggressive and avoidant personalities at least for combat veterans. In data not presented, the average number of personality disorders (BR > 84) from subjects in the MCMI and MCMI-II data sets noted above (from our center) had an average number of personality disorders of greater than four. Hirshfield (1986) also elaborated on the "scar" and pathoplastic problem of the Axes I and II connection, the virtual impossibility of teasing apart the variance between Axis I and Axis II pathology.

Surprisingly little convergent and discriminant validation on personality with PTSD victims has occurred. While efforts at criterion validation (PTSD versus non-PTSD) have been attempted, data on the relationship among personality scales has been in short supply. We will focus on our own data (based on PTSD victims), utilizing several scales: the NEO Personality Inventory (NEO-PI; Costa & McCrae, 1992), the Personality Adjective Checklist (PACL; Strack, 1990), and Cattell's Sixteen Personality Factor Questionnaire (16PF; Cattell, Eber, & Tatsouka, 1970), as well as the Minnesota Multiphasic Personality Inventory (MMPI).

Starting with the NEO-PI, studies by Wiggins and Pincus (1989) among others have suggested that this measure is reflective of personality disorder pathology in this clinical group. Hyer et al. (1994) studied the relationship of the domains and facets of the NEO-PI to personality disorders (MCMI-II) using a PTSD population. Eighty subjects with PTSD were given these two measures. Results supported the above-mentioned previous studies (using a clinical population): The NEO-PI domains and facets correlated in expected ways with the MCMI-II. The use of the five-factor model of personality in this clinical population was supported.

From the perspective of each of the personality disorders, results reflect what may be expected from an understanding of each style (Table 11.6—facets not shown). The schizoid personality pattern follows the results of Costa and McCrae (1990), with low O (Openness) and E (Extroversion) as well as "expected" facets of these domains, including high Vulnerability. For the avoidants, in addition to the above two domains, N (Neuroticism) was present (but not as a result of the facet Anxiety). For the detached personalities, then, results were as expected.

The dependent and independent personality styles also are represented in a predictable way. The Dependent scale was not low on O (as in Costa & McCrae, 1990), but it was high on A (Agreeableness) and C (Conscientiousness). The Histrionic personality was highly related to E and O, with a low N. There was no low C (as in Costa & McCrae, 1990). The MCMI-II Narcissistic scale has a low A and high O (with low Hostility and high Ideas and Excitement facets). No high E or C was found. For the Antisocial scale, high E and O resulted. The aggressive style was absent any relationship to the domains (but was high on Hostility and low on Warmth facets).

The compulsive personality was most predictable—with a high relationship to C. Interestingly, the compulsives were low on the facet values, perhaps reflecting an inner confusion. Passive–Aggressive and Self-Defeating appear to be "neurotic-like" scales, being high on N (for facets, the former was low on Warmth, Gregariousness, and Positive Emotions, and the latter was high on Self-Confidence and Activity).

TABLE 11.6. Correlations of NEO-PI Domains with the MCMI-II

Personality	N	E	O	A	C
Schizoid		L	L		
Avoidant	H	L	L		
Dependent			L	H	H
Histrionic	L	H	H		
Narcissistic		H		L	
Antisocial		H	H		
Aggressive					
Compulsive					H
Passive–Aggressive	H				
Self-Defeating	H			L	
Schizotypal	H				
Borderline	H				
Paranoid					

Note. N, Neuroticism; E, Extroversion; O, Openness; A, Agreeableness; C, Conscientiousness; L, a negative correlation that is significant; H, a positive correlation that is significant.

Finally, for the structurally deficient personalities the domain N was high and positive for schizotypal and borderline personalities. No significant relationship was present for the paranoid personality. This too corresponds to other studies. Unfortunately, the amount of variance accounted for is small, predictably with N and E being most representative of the various personality disorders. This study punches a hole in one myth, however: that the Axis II disorders and the factor analytic conception of personality disorders are "worlds apart." As no personality instrument represents the gold standard, perhaps it may be best to consider the NEO-PI and all of the MCMIs as instruments that provide incremental information, hopefully helping "the clinician understand the patient, select appropriate treatments, and anticipate the course and outcome of therapy" (Costa & McCrae, 1992, p. 5). Of all the studies that precede or follow, these two scales may be the most important combination for clinical use with PTSD victims.

Next, the Personality Adjective Check List (PACL; Strack, 1990) was applied to a group of older combat veterans with and without PTSD. To our knowledge this is the first time a personality scale has been applied to an older group with a carefully defined diagnoses of PTSD. Results of the PACL indicate that older veterans with PTSD are similar to the younger veterans: the PTSD subjects differ from non-PTSD veterans on two of the personalities especially: Sensitive and Inhibited. This should not be strange to the reader, as it is the equivalent to the MCMI "8–2" profile or the traumatic personality previously found in younger PTSD victims. Elevation was also found on the Pathological Index (PI—a scale of pathology) of the PACL. In addition, the trauma-related scales of the MMPI-2 (PS and PK) and other PTSD measures were significantly related to the two PACL–PTSD personality scales. While reduced, the partial correlation between the two PACL–PTSD scales and a self-report measure of PTSD accounting for PI was still significant. These data suggest that the older PTSD veterans, like their younger counterparts, have considerable problems, not "just" PTSD.

The PACL is a "clone" of the MCMI-I and appears to have utility for use with older veterans in detecting PTSD pathology. Also, as was the case with the MCMI, over time the effects of severe stressors may "result" in a pattern of interaction that reflects the Inhibited and the Sensitive styles. As noted above, these styles also are similar to the disorder PTSD itself.

The 16 PF has been a time-honored scale used heuristically for three decades (Cattell et al., 1970). Again, a carefully defined group of combat veterans with PTSD was given the MCMI and the 16 PF (Hyer, Woods, Boudewyns, Bruno, & Tamkin, 1990). The 16 PF pattern of PTSD included low scores on Warmth, Emotional Stability, Happy-Go-Lucky, Boldness, Self-Discipline, and Extroversion. High scores were found on Suspiciousness, Insecurity, Self-Sufficiency, and Anxiety. When each MCMI scale was inspected for its relationship to the 16 PF scales, the concurrent validation was striking. On the two modal MCMI scales, for example, matches were highly understandable—Avoidant was low on Emotional Stability, Assertive, Happy-Go-Lucky, Conformity, Self-Sufficiency, and Extroversion; Passive–Aggressive was low on Warmth, Emotional Stability, Happy-Go-Lucky, Conformity, Boldness, and Self-Discipline, and high on Tension and Anxiety. As the 16 PF has been extensively factor analyzed and is so face valid, the MCMI represents a close connection to trait expectations in this group of PTSD survivors.

Finally, the MMPI has been applied to this population in several studies. Focusing on only the key MMPI scales related to PTSD, including the PS and PK scales, and the MCMI-II personality scales, Table 11.7 provides data on the relationships using groups of PTSD combat veterans. Noteworthy are the high correlations between the detached (including schizotypal) personalities and the MMPI. The avoidant personality correlates at over .5 with the PTSD scales on the MMPI, as does the self-defeating personality. These two personalities relate to PTSD indices on the MMPI better than does the passive–aggressive personality. The borderline personality also has a high relationship with the MMPI PTSD-specific scales and indices.

In sum, it appears that the MCMI-II-specific personalities avoidant and passive–aggressive, as well as borderline and schizotypal, continue to show the conceptual closeness to PTSD indicators on the MMPI. The surprise is the robust relationship with the self-defeating personality.

TABLE 11.7. Correlation of MCMI-II and MMPI-2 Key Scales

MCMI-II	MMPI-2						
	F	D	PT	PA	SC	PK	PS
Schizoid	.38	.38	.41	.29	.42	.30	.30
Avoidant	.42	.52	.60	.36	.56	.60	.56
Dependent	.08	.14	.15	.25	.11	.10	.08
Histrionic	−.08	−.39	−.35	−.11	−.26	−.18	−.17
Narcissistic	.03	−.44	−.40	−.09	−.11	−.12	−.14
Antisocial	.11	−.24	−.20	−.10	−.03	.13	.10
Aggressive	.25	−.17	−.07	.05	.13	.21	.20
Compulsive	−.05	−.05	−.11	−.09	−.17	−.06	−.08
Passive–Aggressive	.33	.20	.16	.13	.32	.46	.44
Self-Defeating	.58	.38	.51	.49	.64	.72	.68
Schizotypal	.46	.29	.33	.39	.45	.44	.38
Borderline	.39	.20	.22	.21	.37	.50	.46
Paranoid	.19	−.29	−.19	.07	.02	.14	.12

Chronicity as Reality in the Clinical World

A new reality has become apparent in the PTSD literature: chronicity. Although trauma can have a symptomatic impact upon everyone exposed, current data are showing that the impact of this stress is more enduring, more pervasive, and more destructive than originally estimated. Even subthreshold effects have become important (Weiss et al., 1992). In addition, comorbidity is the rule (Boudewyns, Albrecht, & Hyer, 1992), and basic physiological responses are altered (van der Kolk & Saporta, 1993).

Through the decades it has been held that early or severe trauma results in an ego contraction (e.g., Kardiner, 1959; see Millon & Davis, 1995) or "frozen imprint" (Lifton, 1993), but it has only recently been argued that trauma can lead to enduring dysfunctions in basic character structure (Herman, 1992; Horowitz, 1993). In fact, over time a person may adapt to the chronicity of the symptoms in a way that establishes a sense of "normalcy" to the psychopathology (Epstein, 1990), making it very difficult to treat. And, as noted above, trauma creates secondary effects within the family and social systems of the victim that can extend across generations in the form of secondary trauma.

Different attempts to define this chronic form of PTSD have led to creative speculation; labels have been generated such as "complicated or reactivated trauma" (Catherall, 1991; Hiley-Young, 1992; Solomon, 1993), as well as our own "traumatic personality." Three formulations of the chronicity related to the combat-related PTSD process have been especially noteworthy. Hiley-Young (1992) labeled these PTSD veterans "complicated reactivators": Veterans do not feel understood, they feel intense mistrust and hostility, and they sense indignation perpetually.

In the similar characterization, Cohen (1992) identified two recovery styles of victims of combat-related problems, "integration" and "sealing over." Integration is a style that involves a curiosity about one's reactions and the ability to accommodate these into a continuous sense of self. The integrator is intellectually curious about self, tries to attach struggles to an internal locus of control and sense of self, and sees choice in trauma as part of an ongoing struggle across one's own life. Sealing-over victims, on the hand, will have none of this. A lack of curiosity about self (in growth), feelings that life dealt them a hard hand, a belief that they are passive victims of circumstances, and a penchant to blame others or externalize problems are common fare. McCranie and Hyer (1995) and Southwick, Yehuda, and Giller (1991) measured one component of this state, self-critical guilt, a depressionlike quality that persists and remains chronic. Finally, Johnson, Feldman, Southwick, and Charney (1994) went one step further and viewed these men as having an impaired sense of self, often with an expectation of secondary gain. In effect, these authors argue that it is time to treat the "second generation" issues of PTSD. The conclusion is that "persistent mental illness" seems to characterize the veteran population, and that these men cannot be cured in any traditional sense.

It should be no surprise to the reader that in the studies above, PTSD victims can only be considered chronic. To represent this subcategory, DSM-IV work groups initially considered use of the label "Disorders of Extreme Stress, Not Otherwise Specified (DESNOS)." In this context the MCMI and MCMI-II studies cited above parsed apart differences in a sea of pathology. To clinicians and researchers alike who work with these patients, they do not change on any traditional scale after treatment (Hyer, Woods, Bruno, & Boudewyns, 1989). Not only did these PTSD combat veterans have substantial problems, but they were treated in a system that many consider reinforcing for psychopathology. Findings of the MCMIs, then, are all the more relevant because they point to useful differences in this population where few exist. On other scales (e.g., the MMPI), excessive pathology and overreporting on any scale are the rule (Hyer et al., 1988). The MCMIs provide a way to view differences among chronic survivors which will lead to different treatments.

PERSONALITY AND MEMORY

PTSD, the legacy of trauma, can also be conceived as an attempt at providing some semblance of organization after abuse shatters assumptions. In this sense, a maladaptive reorganizing response occurs to a chaotic event (Epstein, 1990). The reexperiencing symptoms are then a symbolic representation of needed information for a completion of the troubling event, and the numbing symptoms are necessary outlets of this whole process of "reasonable" maladaptation. It is a way of providing a reconciliation for the horrible realization that one's identity will never be quite the same. It is the organism's attempt to bridge living with death. This inner level is a compromise, the best the person can do to adapt and make sense of their new handicapped "being."

The core of victimization is the trauma memory and its intrusions. For chronic trauma sufferers this process is a complex adaptive system on autopilot. The fear network caused by trauma is chronically aroused, avoided, and reconditioned, and the patterns used for accommodation are congealed. The PTSD research literature data now substantiate the postulate that distinct networks of trauma meanings exist and are involuntarily activated when there are definite internal or external cues (Wolfe & Charney, 1991). Information is "screwed up"; orienting responses, habituation modes, psychophysiological reactivity, selective processing of threat-perceived cues, recall abilities, and, of course, the symptom-influenced process of data gathering are altered. Even given opportunities for exposure (treatment), chronic victims show a failure of extinction or habituation. In effect, information processing is not only compromised, but it becomes "comfortable" with patterns of approach/avoidance that reinforce the status quo. Over time these patterns become "hard wired," producing conditioned emotional responses, neurological damage (Kolb, 1987), and hormonal dysregulation (van der Kolk & Saporta, 1993). Given this condition, an important question is posed: Is there a pattern to the interconnections of the person(ality) and the trauma memory, even if "screwed up"? In other words, can we still say that the personality is an influence in this process?

Memories as Exemplars

We have not intentionally ignored symptoms. Our three-tier model (and the Millon model) posits that the symptoms are contextualized in the person by the "rules" of the personality. They take the form that the personality provides. The therapeutic goal is to reframe the psychosocial and trauma symptoms (Tier 3) in the context of the personality style of the person (Tiers 1 and 2).

The trauma symptoms are the heart of PTSD and are represented by the trauma memory. This memory is *the* reason for the disorder. Although not concerned with the mechanisms of this process, several authors have posited a symbiotic relationship between memory (content) and personality styles. In this context memories are the products or exemplars of abused schemas in personality. Kramer, Schoen, and Kinney (1984) noted that traumatic dreams reflect past and current life events of the individual: Kardiner (1959) noted the theme of helplessness, and Wilmer (1982), danger. In addition, Ulman and Brothers (1988) speculated that "empathic influences" are appropriate in therapy to address the match of the trauma experience and its unconscious expression of the person. This applies most especially to personality styles. Dependent trauma victims tend to cringe with ineffectual performance and guilt; independent trauma victims develop anger and pain memories around helplessness, or, in the case of combat veterans, recollections of atrocities. And finally, in an interesting book on Vietnam veterans, Hendin and Haas (1984) developed the idea that the form of the symptoms of PTSD is determined by the meaning of the stressor to the person.

At our treatment center ratings of trauma memories were requested on nine dimensions. Ratings were done by two raters blind to the personality code of the victim. Personality codes were established using a hand-sorting system that placed PTSD combat veterans with an MCMI 8–2 high-point code for personality plus dependence, schizoid, or antisocial "influences." There were then four groups of different personality types *and* independent ratings of the trauma memories. How did they match? Figure 11.2 provides the results (Hyer & Associates, 1994). Note the high degree of compatibility between the trauma content and the particular personality code that was obtained. Trauma memories appear related to the personality of the victim. Victims who have a dependent style, for example, had trauma memories reflective of more withdrawal, passiveness, cooperation, dependence, and the like; antisocial styles reflected more active and acting out ratings; and schizoid styles tended to have memories characterized by withdrawal, passivity, and more negative features. Perhaps trauma memories are indeed exemplars of the personality. Safran and Segal (1990) wrote:

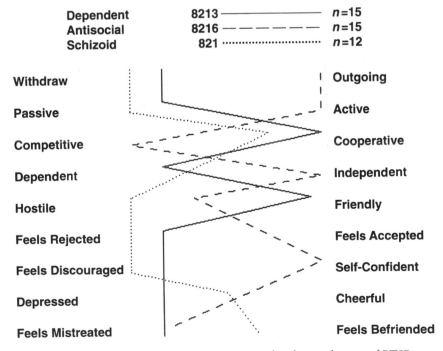

FIGURE 11.2. Ratings of trauma memories for three subtypes of PTSD.

We hypothesize, therefore, that memories that emerge spontaneously when an interpersonal issue is being explored in an emotionally immediate way, are often prototypical exemplars of the interpersonal experience that contributed to the development of the interpersonal schema being activated. It may also be that some memories accessible in therapy do not correspond to the events that actually took place, but may instead be prototypical constructions that capture the essential features of a class of relevant events. (p. 113)

What is going on in this complex connection of self narrations of the past? Beyond the scope of this book is discussion of the linkage among the trauma memories, the "important question" of memory (Neisser, 1978) and the person(ality). In a highly relevant book, Singer and Salovey (1993) have described the memory part of this process, labeling it a "middle-level unit" of analysis, the self-defining memory. These authors hold that each person has a unique collection of autobiographical memories that can be studied to see who the person is. In effect, each of us has a core set of "slides in our carousel" amidst others. At key moments we return to this special set that represent who we are. Each consists of a single episode in the person's life and a personal summary of such incidents. It is in fact this combination of the "white heat of relevance" of the moment and the reflexive meaning-making that provide the defining importance of these recollections. They are autobiographical for the person and are "responsible" for influencing individual differences. They are so important that they keep the person on course in the present (and future), and even determine which retrospective memories are accessed. In time, these memories even can be altered to fit present demands—in fact, current demands of the person are considered more influential than the past.

But more exists. Something must provide order here. Given that trauma occurs frequently in life, the self-defining memories of the person are products of the personality, the life story of the person. Even with PTSD victims who are chronic, this implicit theory of the self is at work. The personality somehow organizes knowingly in the background as a friendly deity, savoring and reconstructing the memories of critical events in ways that are consistent with one's life story. The personality provides the "right amount" of remembered and misremembered features of the self to encode or decode the information for consistency. This coheres into the narrative of the self, the personality.

We, as others, believe that a larger organization is in place. Memories are linked by affect and by the goals of the person; perhaps in the way Adler opined—man is teleologically "determined," as goals present the only appealing path the person can take. Memories may be the "appropriate" level for content of this organization. As memories become attached by the fire of affect and the glue of goal direction, a template forms, a personality. Quickly the editing and organizing of these memories involves the personality, the script process. We do this in the way that a compulsive or a histrionic would prototypically organize information. Tomkins (1987) referred to this outline of the person's patterns as a script; McAdams (1990) labeled this a life story. Regardless of the label, the personality is *the* overarching and organizing framework that provides unity and purpose to thoughts, feelings, and behaviors.

With the existence of trauma a true traumatogenesis model may exist wherein Axis II marries with Axis I problems. If so, this process does not occur randomly. Each person's personality develops through some combination of biopsychosocial components that quickly become ordered. Even the negative affectivity factor present in all mood states (Watson & Clark, 1984) is expressed in individual differences as a function of the person's personality domains (Millon, 1995). Perhaps a few self-defining memories give rise to a personality template that provides direction to our acts. With the presence of trauma or chronic trauma, something changes in the person. But what changes does so in an orderly way, at the dictates of the personality. Wiggins and Schwartz (1992) suggest that, as this occurs, as we go deeper into the person, the result is complexity and chaos, requiring a new metascientific method for understanding this human process. But even here many "surface-level" components in the complexity of the person are measurable, again according to the dictates of the personality.

CONCLUSION

The role of personality in PTSD is just now unfolding. Our argument is that this construct is not the "bane of diagnosis," as has been alleged. In fact, it appears that this is the one construct that can (and has) applied some order to otherwise "noise" in the expression and care of PTSD, especially the chronic variety. We have made the point further that personality acts as a predisposing or perhaps a pathoplastic (or scar) influence on PTSD, "leading to" and modifying its symptomatology. From an information-processing perspective, personality at times acts in a punctuated equilibrium sense, lying dormant for an event to occur, and at times, as an emergent property, defining the issues in the chaotic system of living. Finally, at the end we argued that personality asserts direction over the narrative that is stuck, the content of the trauma. We see this as good news in the eventual treatment of this disorder.

One final issue has been a discomforting presence in the background: psychotherapy. Psychotherapy with this chronic group is a sobering act that produces little in the way of "managed care" change. In fact, to the serious student of psychotherapeutic outcome research with trauma victims, the need for extended discussion does not exist, as only a few carefully controlled outcome studies have been done. Fortunately, most clinicians know that outcome research on psychotherapy is flawed, and people are never really cured in any absolute sense. Therapists know, too, that the work of psychotherapy is more extensive than can be captured in evaluation.

It is true that victims with personality disorders, as with other treatment outcomes, are more resistant to change. This is so often because of the nature of the inflexibility involved in care and one other factor: Outcomes are poor because personologic and integrationist psychotherapy (Millon & Davis, 1995) is not applied. All outcome studies on PTSD have involved symptoms. For the clinician who works with trauma victims it is known that treatment involves more the strategies of trench warfare and less the quick-strike mentality of a commando raid. So too, as we have argued in this chapter, the importance of the information of the dynamics of the personality(ies) appears a necessary component for treatment.

A trauma victim may not always be a "trauma victim." In a review study on treatment of trauma victims, Solomon, Gerrity, and Muff (1992, p. 637) noted that the "assumption that all traumatized populations share important similarities that allow for meaningful generalizability of findings" may not apply. In this most messy of disorders (PTSD), "specific" treatments intended for selected symptoms apply only to the truly acute stressor time. Even here a good deal of individuality exists in how this process unfolds. After the early window of treatment opportunity passes, personality kicks in and this, along with the current realities of the person, result in an altered reality of the stress response.

Mahoney (1991) holds that all psychotherapies are psychotherapies of the self. For the trauma victim, psychotherapy involves a deep healing process with efforts directed at change in the self, in the personality. Psychotherapy must at some level be modulated through the self and the person must be affected for change to occur. The victim "cured" by a technique such as self-management is the product of a different cure than one who has experienced true psychotherapy at the level of the self, personologic psychotherapy. This can best be done by the integrationist therapist (Millon & Davis, 1995) guided by the dictates of the organization of the personality.

REFERENCES

Abueg, F., & Fairbank, J. (1992). Behavioral treatment of posttraumatic stress disorder and co-occurring substance abuse. In P. A. Saigh (Ed.), *Posttraumatic stress disorder* (pp. 111–146). New York: MacMillan.

Aldenderfer, M., & Blashfield, R. (1984). *Cluster analysis.* Beverly Hills, CA: Sage.

American Psychiatric Association. (1980). *Diagnostic and statistical manual of mental disorders* (3rd ed.). Washington, DC: Author.

American Psychiatric Association. (1989). *Diagnostic and statistical manual of mental disorders* (3rd ed., rev.). Washington, DC: Author.

American Psychiatric Association. (1994). *Diagnostic and statistical manual of mental disorders* (4th ed.). Washington, DC: Author.

Benedek, E. P. (1985). Children and disaster: Emerging issues. *Psychological Annuals, 15*(3), 168–172.

Berman, S., Price, S., & Gusman, F. (1982). An inpatient program for Vietnam combat veterans in a Veterans Administration Hospital. *Hospital and Community Psychiatry, 33,* 919–927.

Black, D. (1982). Children and disaster. *British Medical Journal, 285,* 989–990.

Blake, D., Weathers, F., Nagy, L., Kaloupek, D., Gusman, F., Charney, D., & Keane, T. (1995). The development of the Clinician-Administered PTSD Scale. *Journal of Traumatic Stress, 8,* 75–90.

Blashfield, K. (1992). [LISREL analyses of diagnoses of personality disorder using the SIDP-R]. Unpublished raw data.

Boudewyns, J. Albrecht, W., & Hyer, L. (1992, August). *Long-term effects of direct therapeutic exposure in PTSD.* Poster session presented at the annual meeting of the American Psychological Association. Washington, DC.

Boulanger, G., & Kadushin, C. (1986). *The Vietnam veteran redefined: Fact and fiction.* Hillsdale, NJ: Erlbaum.

Boyd, S., Hyer, L., Summers, M., & Litaker, M. (1995). *PACL personality profiles of older combat veterans with PTSD and the influence of social support.* Manuscript submitted for publication.

Bryer, J. B., Nelson, B. A., Miller, J. B., & Krol, P. A. (1987). Childhood sexual and physical abuse as factors in adult psychiatric illness. *American Journal of Psychiatry, 144*(11), 1426–1430.

Card, J. J. (1987). Epidemiology of PTSD in a national cohort of Vietnam veterans. *Journal of Clinical Psychology, 43,* 6–17.

Catherall, D. C. (1991). Aggression and projective identification in the treatment of victims. *Psychotherapy, 28,* 145–149.

Cattell, R., Eber, J., & Tatsuoka, M. *Handbook for the 16-PF.* Champaign, IL: Institute for Personality and Ability Testing.

Choca, J., Shanley, L., & Van Denburg, E. (1992). *Interpretive guide to the Millon Clinical Multiaxial Inventory.* Washington, DC: American Psychological Press.

Choca, J., Peterson, S., & Shanley, L. (1986). Factor analysis of the MCMI. *Journal of Consulting and Clinical Psychology, 44*(5), 760–763.

Cohen, R. (1992, August). *Psychodynamic theories of recovery from adult trauma: An empirical study.* Paper presented at the annual meeting of the American Psychological Association. Washington, DC.

Costa, P., & McCrae, R. (1990). Personality disorders and the five-factor model of personality. *Journal of Personality Disorders, 4*, 362–371.

Costa, P., & McCrae, R. (1992). Normal personality assessment in clinical practice: The NEO Personality Inventory. *Psychological Assessment, 4*, 5–13.

Craig, R. J. (1993). The MCMI/MCMI-II with substance abusers. In R. Craig (Ed.), *The Millon Clinical Multiaxial Inventory: A clinical research information synthesis* (pp. 125–145). Hillsdale, NJ: Erlbaum.

Dana, R., & Cantrell, J. (1988). An update on the Millon Clinical Multiaxial Inventory (MCMI). *Journal of Clinical Psychology, 44*, 760–763.

Dutton, D. (1994). The origin and structure of the abusive personality. *Journal of Personality Disorders, 8*, 181–191.

Emery, P., & Emery, V. (1989). Psychoanalytic considerations on post-traumatic stress disorders. *Journal of Contemporary Psychotherapy, 19*, 19–53.

Emery, V., Emery, P., Shama, D., Quiana, N., & Jassani, A. (1991). Predisposing variables in PTSD patients. *Journal of Traumatic Stress, 4*(3), 325–344.

Epstein, S. (1990). The self-concept: The traumatic neurosis of the structure of personality. In D. Ozer, J. M. Healy, & A. J. Stewart (Eds.), *Perspectives on personality* (Vol. 3, pp. 63–98). London: Jessica Kingsley, Publishers.

Foa, E., Steketee, G., & Rothbaum, B. (1989). Behavioral/cognitive conceptualizations of post-traumatic stress disorder. *Behavior Therapy, 20*, 155–176.

Foy, D. W., Osato, S. S., Houskamp, B. M., & Neumann, D. A. (1992). Etiology of posttraumatic stress disorder. In A. P. Goldstein, L. Krasner, & S. L. Garfield (Eds.), *Posttraumatic stress disorder* (pp. 28–49). New York: MacMillan.

Gibbs, M. (1989). Factors in the victim that mediate between disaster and psychopathology: A review. *Journal of Traumatic Stress, 2*(4), 489–514.

Hendin, H. (1983). Psychotherapy for Vietnam veterans with PTSD. *American Journal of Psychotherapy, 37*, 86–99.

Hendin, H., & Haas, A. (1984). Combat adaptation of Vietnam veterans without posttraumatic stress disorders. *American Journal of Psychiatry, 141*, 8, 956–960.

Hendin, H., Pollinger, A., Singer, P., & Ulman, R. B. (1981). Meaning of combat and the development of posttraumatic stress disorder. *American Journal of Psychiatry, 138*, 1490–1493.

Herman, J. L. (1992). Complex PTSD: A syndrome in survivors of prolonged and repeated trauma. *Journal of Traumatic Stress, 5*, 377–392.

Hiley-Young, B. (1992). Trauma reactivation assessment and treatment. *Journal of Traumatic Stress, 5*(4), 545–555.

Hirshfield, R. M. A. (1986). Personality disorders: Foreword. In A. Francis & R. Hales (Eds.), *Annual review of psychiatry* (pp. 233–257). Washington, DC: American Psychiatric Press.

Horowitz, M. J. (1986). Stress-response syndromes: Post-traumatic and adjustment disorders. In A. Cooper, A. Francis, & M. Sacks (Eds.), *The personality disorders and neuroses* (pp. 409–424). New York: Lippincott.

Horowitz, M. J. (1993). Stress-response syndromes: A review of posttraumatic stress and adjustment disorders. In J. P. Wilson & B. Raphael (Eds.), *International handbook of traumatic stress syndromes* (pp. 11–23). New York: Plenum Press.

Horowitz, M. J., Marmar, C., Krupnick, J., Wilmer, N., Kaltreider, M., & Wallestein, R. (1984). *Personality styles and brief psychotherapy.* New York: Blair Books.

Hyer, L., & Associates (1994). *Trauma victim: Theoretical issues and practical suggestions.* Muncie, IN: Accelerated Development, Inc.

Hyer, L., & Boudewyns, P. (1985). The 8–2 code among Vietnam veterans. *PTSD Newsletter, 4*, 2.

Hyer, L., Boudewyns, P., Harrison, W. R., O'Leary, W. C., Bruno, R. D., Saucer, R. T., & Blount, J. B. (1988).Vietnam veterans: Overreporting versus acceptable reporting of symptoms. *Journal of Personality Assessment, 52*, 475–486.

Hyer, L., Boyd, S., Stanger, E., Davis, H., & Walters, P. (in press). Validation of the MCMI-III PTSD scale among older combat veterans. *Psychological Reports.*

Hyer, L., Davis, H., Albrecht, J., Boudewyns, P., & Woods, M. (1994). Cluster analysis of MCMI and MCMI-II on chronic PTSD victims. *Journal of Clinical Psychology, 50*(4), 502–515.

Hyer, L., Davis, H., Woods, G., Albrecht, W., & Boudewyns, P. (1992). Relationship between the MCMI and MCMI-II and value of aggressive and self-defeating personalities in posttraumatic stress disorder. *Psychological Reports, 71,* 867–879.

Hyer, L., Gratton, C., & Melton, M. (1993). Assessment and treatment of PTSD: Understanding the person. In R. Craig (Ed.), *Readings of the MCMI and MCMI-II* (pp. 159–172). Hillsdale, NJ: Erlbaum.

Hyer, L., McCranie, E., Boudewyns, P., & Sperr, E. (1996). Modes of long-term coping with trauma memories: Relative use and associations with personality among Vietnam veterans with chronic PTSD. *Journal of Traumatic Stress, 9,* 299–317.

Hyer, L., Woods, M., & Boudewyns, P. (1991). A three tier evaluation of posttraumatic stress disorder. *Journal of Traumatic Stress, 4*(2), 165–194.

Hyer, L., Braswell, L., Albrecht, W., Boyd, S., Boudewyns, P., & Talbert, S. (1994). Relationship of NEO-PI to personality styles and severity of trauma in chronic PTSD victims. *Journal of Clinical Psychology, 50,* 699–707.

Hyer, L., Woods, M., Boudewyns, P., Bruno, R., & Tamkin, A. (1990). MCMI and 16-PF with Vietnam veterans: Profiles and concurrent validation of MCMI. *Journal of Personality Disorders, 4*(4), 391–402.

Hyer, L., Woods, M., Bruno, R., & Boudewyns, P. (1989). Treatment outcomes of Vietnam veterans with PTSD and consistency of MCMI. *Journal of Clinical Psychology, 45,* 547–552.

Johnson, D. R., Feldman, S. C., Southwick, S. M., & Charney, D. S. (1994). The concept of the second generation program in the treatment of post-traumatic stress disorder among Vietnam veterans. *Journal of Traumatic Stress, 7*(2), 217–236.

Kardiner, A. (1959). Traumatic neuroses of war. In S. Arieti (Ed.), *American handbook of psychiatry* (pp. 245–257). New York: Basic Books.

Keane, T. (1989). Post-traumatic stress disorder: Current status and future directions. *Behavioral Therapy, 20,* 149–153.

Kramer, M., Schoen, L. S., & Kinney, L. (1984). Psychological and behavioral features of disturbed dreamers. *Psychiatric Journal of the University of Ottawa, 9*(3), 102–106.

Kolb, L. C. (1987). A neuropsychological hypothesis explaining post traumatic stress disorders. *The American Journal of Psychiatry, 144,* 989–995.

Kulka, R., Schlenger, W., Fairbank, J., Hough, R., Jordan, K., Marmar, C., & Weiss, D. (1990). *Trauma and the Vietnam generation.* New York: Brunner/Mazel.

Leaf, R. C., Alington, E. E., Mass, R., DiGuiseppe, R., & Ellis, A. (1991). Family environment characteristics and dependent personality disorder. *Journal of Personality Disorders, 5,* 264–280.

Lifton, J. (1993). From Hiroshima to the Nazi doctors: The evolution of psychoformative approaches to understanding traumatic stress syndromes. In J. P. Wilson & B. Raphael (Eds.), *International handbook of traumatic stress syndromes* (pp. 11–23). New York: Plenum Press.

Lipkin, J. O., Scurfield, R. M., & Blank, A. S. (1983). Post-traumatic stress disorder in Vietnam veterans: Assessment in a forensic setting. *Behavioral Sciences and the Law, 1,* 51–67.

Lorr, M. (1993). Dimensional structure of the Millon Clinical Multiaxial Inventory. In R. J. Craig (Ed.), *The Millon Clinical Multiaxial Inventory: A clinical research information synthesis* (pp. 81–92). Hillsdale, NJ: Erlbaum.

Lorr, M., & Strack, S. (1990). Profile clusters of the MCMI-II personality disorder scales. *Journal of Clinical Psychology, 46,* 606–612.

Lyons, J. A. (1991). Strategies for assessing the potential for positive adjustment following trauma. *Journal of Traumatic Stress, 4*(1), 113–122.

Mahoney, M. C. (1991). *Human change processes: The scientific foundations of psychotherapy.* Delran, NJ: Basic Books.

McAdams, D. (1990). Unity and purpose in human lives: The emergence of identity as a life story. In I. Rabin, R. Zucker, R. Emmons, & S. Frank (Eds.), *Studying persons and lives* (pp. 148–200). New York: Springer.

McCranie, E., Hyer, L., Boudewyns, P., & Woods, M. (1991). Negative parenting, combat exposure, and PTSD symptom severity: Test of a person/event interaction model. *Journal of Nervous and Mental Disease, 16,* 70–74.

McCranie, E., & Hyer, L. (1995). Self-criticism and guilt in combat-related posttraumatic stress disorder. *Psychological Reports, 77,* 880–882.

McDermott, W. (1986, March). *The influence of Vietnam combat on subsequent psychopathology.* Paper presented at the Conference on the Millon Clinical Inventory, Miami, FL.

McFarlane, A. (1990). Vulnerability to posttraumatic stress disorder. In M. Wolf & A. Mosnaim (Eds.), *Posttraumatic stress disorder: Etiology, phenomenology, and treatment* (pp. 2–21). Washington, DC: American Psychiatric Press.

McMahon, F., Schram, L., & Davidson, R. (1993). Negative life events, social support, and depression in three personality types. *Journal of Personality Disorders, 7,* 241–254.

McNeil, K., & Meyer, R. G. (1990). Detection of deception on the Millon Clinical Multiaxial Inventory (MCMI). *Journal of Clinical Psychology, 46,* 755–764.

Millon, T. (1969). *Modern psychopathology.* Philadelphia: Saunders.

Millon, T. (1977). *Millon Clinical Multiaxial Inventory.* Minneapolis: National Computer Systems.

Millon, T. (1983). *Modern psychopathology.* Prospect Heights, IL: Waveland Press.

Millon, T. (1987). *Manual for the Millon Clinical Multiaxial Inventory—II.* Minneapolis: National Computer Systems.

Millon, T. (1994). *Millon Clinical Multiaxial Inventory—III manual.* Minneapolis: National Computer Systems.

Millon, T., & Davis, R. (1995). *Disorders of personality: DSM-IV and beyond.* New York: Wiley.

Monroe, S. M., Bromet, E. J., Connell, M. M., & Steiner, S. C. (1986). Social support, life events, and depressive symptoms: A 1-year prospective study. *Journal of Consulting and Clinical Psychology, 54,* 424–431.

Morey, L.C. (1993). Psychological correlates of personality disorder. *Journal of Personality Disorders* (7, Suppl.), 149–166.

Morgan, H. J., & Janoff-Bulman, R. (1992). *Positive self-complexity and reactions to traumatic events.* Paper presented at the 100th annual convention of the American Psychological Association. Washington, DC.

Munley, P., Bains, D., Bloem, W., Busby, R., & Pendziszewski, S. (in press). Post-traumatic stress disorder and the MCMI-II. *Psychological Reports.*

Neisser, U. (1978). Memory: What are the important questions? In M. M. Gruneburg, P. E. Morris, & R. N. Sykes (Eds.), *Practical Aspects of memory* (pp. 3–24). London: Academic Press.

Parson, E. R. (1993). Posttraumatic narcissism: Healing traumatic alterations in the self through curvilinear group psychotherapy. In J. P. Wilson & B. Raphael (Eds.), *International handbook of traumatic stress syndromes* (pp. 25–33). New York: Plenum Press.

Penk, W. E., & Allen, I. (1991). Clinical assessment of posttraumatic stress disorder as a diagnostic category: Problems and proposals. *Journal of Traumatic Stress, 4*(1),41–66.

Perry, C., Lavori, C., Pagano, P., Hoke, L., & O'Connell, M. (1992). Life events and recurrent depression in borderline and antisocial personality disorders. *Journal of Personality Disorders, 6,* 394–407.

Pitman, R. K., Orr, S. P., Forgue, D. F., de Jong, J. B., & Claiborn, J. M. (1987). Psychophysiologic assessment of posttraumatic stress disorder imagery in Vietnam combat veterans. *Archives of General Psychiatry, 44*(11), 970–975.

Retzlaff, P. (1993). Special scales for the MCMI: Theory, development, and utility. In R. Craig (Ed.), *The Millon Clinical Multiaxial Inventory: A clinical research information synthesis* (pp. 237–251). Hillsdale, NJ: Erlbaum.

Retzlaff, P., & Gibertini, M. (1990). Factor-based special scales for the MCMI. *Journal of Clinical Psychology, 46,* 47–52.

Retzlaff, P., Lorr, M., Hyer, L., & Ofman, P. (1991). An MCMI-II item level component analysis: Personality and clinical factors. *Journal of Personality Assessment, 57,* 323–334.

Robert, J., Ryan, J., McEntyre, W., McFarland, R., Lipps, O., & Rosenburg, S. (1985). MCMI characteristics of DSM-III posttraumatic stress disorders in Vietnam veterans. *Journal of Personality Assessment, 49,* 226–230.

Safran, J., & Segal, Z. (1990). *Interpersonal processing in cognitive therapy.* New York: Basic Books.

Schnurr, P., Friedman, M., & Rosenberg, S. (1991, August). *Premilitary MMPI scores as predictors of combat-related PTSD symptomatology.* Poster proposal submitted to Division 18 for the annual meeting of the American Psychological Association, Washington, DC.

Sherwood, R., Funari, D., & Piekorski, A. (1990). Adapted character styles of Vietnam veterans with posttraumatic stress disorder. *Journal of Traumatic Stress, 2*(2), 199–223.

Singer, J. A., & Salovey, P. (1993). *The remembered self: Emotion and memory in personality.* New York: The Free Press.

Solomon, Z. (1993). *Combat stress reaction: The enduring toll of war.* New York: Plenum Press.

Solomon, S., Gerrity, E. T., & Muff, A. M. (1992). Efficacy of treatments for posttraumatic stress disorder. *Journal of the American Medical Association, 268,* 633–638.

Southwick, S. M., Yehuda, R., & Giller, E. L. (1991). Characterization of depression in war-related posttraumatic stress disorder. *American Journal of Psychiatry, 148*(2), 179–183.

Stewart, A., Hyer, L., Retzlaff, P., & Ofman, P. (1995). MCMI-II personality scales: Factors and latent traits. *Journal of Personality Disorders.* Manuscript submitted for publication.

Strack, S. (1990). *Manual for Personality Adjective Check List (PACL)—Revised.* South Pasadena, CA: 21st Century Assessment.

Tomkins, S. (1987). Script theory. In J. Aranoff, A. I. Rabin, & R. A. Zucker (Eds.), *The emergence of personality* (pp. 147–216). New York: Springer.

Ulman, R. B., & Brothers, D. (1988). *The shattered self: A psychoanalytic study of trauma.* Hillsdale, NJ: Analytic Press.

van der Kolk, B., & Saporta, J. (1993). Biological response to psychic trauma. In J. P. Wilson & B. Raphael (Eds.), *International handbook of traumatic stress syndromes* (pp. 25–33). New York: Plenum Press.

Watson, D., & Clark, L. (1984). Negative affectivity: The disposition to experience aversive emotional states. *Psychological Bulletin, 96,* 465–490.

Weisaeth, L. (1984). *Stress reactions in an industrial accident.* Unpublished doctoral dissertation, University of Oslo, Oslo, Norway.

Weisenberg, M., Solomon, Z., Schwarzwald, J., & Mikulincer, M. (1987). Assessing the severity of posttraumatic stress disorder: Relation between dichotomous and continuous measures. *Journal of Consulting and Clinical Psychology, 55,* 432–434.

Weiss, D. (1993). Structured clinical interview techniques. In J. P. Wilson & B. Raphael (Eds.), *International handbook of traumatic stress syndromes* (pp. 179–187). New York: Plenum Press.

Weiss, D. S., Marmar, C. R., Schlenger, W. E., Fairbank, J. A., Jordan, B. K., Hough, R. L., & Kulka, R. A. (1992). The prevalence of lifetime and partial post-traumatic stress disorder in Vietnam theater veterans. *Journal of Traumatic Stress, 5,* 365–376.

Widiger, T. A., Williams, J. B. W., Spitzer, R. L., & Frances, A. (1985). The MCMI as a measure of DSM-II. *Journal of Personality Assessment, 49,* 366–378.

Widiger, T. A., & Corbitt, E. M. (1993). The MCMI-II personality disorder scales and their relationship to DSM-III-R diagnosis. In R. J. Craig (Ed.), *The Million Clinical Multiaxial Inventory: A clinical research information synthesis* (pp. 181–201). Hillsdale, NJ: Erlbaum.

Wiggins, J. S., & Pincus, A. L. (1989). Conceptions of personality disorders and dimensions of personality. *Psychological Assessment, 1,* 305–316.

Wiggins, O., & Schwartz, M. (1992). Research into personality disorders: The alternatives of dimensions and ideal types. *Journal of Personality Disorders, 5,* 69–81.

Wilmer, H. A. (1982). Vietnam and madness: Dreams of schizophrenic veterans. *Journal of the American Academy of Psychoanalysis, 10*(1), 47–65.

Wilson, J. P. (1988). Understanding the Vietnam veteran. In F. Ochberg (Ed.), *Posttraumatic therapy and victims of violence* (pp. 227–294). New York: Brunner/Mazel.

Wilson, J. P., & Zigelbaum, S. D. (1983). The Vietnam veteran on trial: The relation of posttrau-
    matic stress disorder to criminal behavior. *Behavioral Sciences and the Law, 1,* 25–50.
Wolfe, J., & Charney, D. (1991). Use of neuropsychological assessment in posttraumatic stress
    disorder. *Journal of Consulting and Clinical Psychology, 3,* 573–580.
Wolfe, J., & Keane, T. (1993). A new perspective in the assessment and diagnosis of combat-
    related posttraumatic stress disorder. In P. Wilson & B. Raphael (Eds.), *International hand-
    book of traumatic stress Syndromes* (pp. 165–177). New York: Plenum Press.

12

The MCMI as a Treatment Planning Tool

PAUL RETZLAFF

The purpose of this chapter is to delineate for the reader an approach to psychotherapy using the Millon Clinical Multiaxial Inventory—III (MCMI-III; Millon, 1994). While the test may be used in a number of ways to plan treatment, the focus of this chapter will be primarily on the treatment itself of the personality disorders. To that end, the importance of the personality disorders will be discussed. Specifically, their highly varied use by clinicians and their potential in understanding and treating Axis I disorders will be examined. The second half of the chapter will focus on the treatment of the personality disorders as suggested by the MCMI-III. This treatment will include options for practioners of behavioral, interpersonal, cognitive, object relations, self-image, defense mechanism, psychic morphology, and temperamental perspectives.

The MCMI-III offers an exceptional opportunity to integrate assessment with treatment. It seems all too often within the clinical sciences and psychology in particular that assessment and diagnostics are artificially separated from treatment planning and its accomplishment. This is most probably an artifact of the methods associated with the two aspects of patient care. There are diagnostic methods and there are treatment methods. We learn them individually and practice them in isolation. While some areas of clinical psychology, such as behavioral and psychoanalytic schools, use the methods of treatment as the methods of diagnosis, most schools do little to integrate the two. The usual psychological tests are given to assess and then the most comfortable mode of therapy is called upon.

The MCMI-III offers an integrated approach not only across assessment and treatment but also inclusive of the DSM nosology. The test fits, to a great degree, the diagnoses we find in the fourth edition of the *Diagnostic and Statistical Manual of Mental Disorders* (DSM-IV; American Psychiatric Association, 1994) and offers, for the personality disorders, treatment approaches consistent with the majority of the philosophical schools within clinical psychology. As such, it is a rare assessment instrument. Practitioners are afforded an opportunity to integrate most aspects of clinical practice while being given the flexibility to choose the type of therapy most suited to both patient and therapist.

217

THE IMPORTANCE OF THE PERSONALITY DISORDERS
IN TREATMENT PLANNING

The reason to use the MCMI-III for treatment planning is not specific to the test itself, but rather it has to do with the personality disorders, and the MCMI-III is simply the best way to assess the personality disorders (Retzlaff, 1995a; Choca, Shanley, & Van Denburg, 1992).

The personality disorders are given insufficient emphasis in our training, politics, and practice. In graduate school, there is generally one course in psychopathology. Within that one course, there is usually little more than 1 week devoted to the personality disorders. Depressions and the schizophrenias are seemingly more important and, as such, each are given 2 or 3 weeks. What we are left with is a feeling that while the personality disorders exist, they certainly aren't very important and probably should only be diagnosed occasionally.

The politics of diagnostics primarily are manifest in the DSMs (American Psychiatric Association, 1968, 1980, 1987, 1994). One chapter out of 18 clinical chapters in the DSM-IV is devoted to the personality disorders. While the personality disorders make up many of the Axis II disorders, there is still a sense that one shouldn't really use these diagnoses. Perhaps simply chalk up the difficulties to "traits" or "features."

Finally, the personality disorders are diagnosed in highly varied ways across clinical practice. Some clinicians never diagnose a personality disorder while others may diagnose most patients with one or more. The problem is that these two clinicians will often work in the very same clinic taking patients by almost random assignment. How can one see personality disturbance so rarely and the other so often? The other common clinical error in the diagnosis of the personality disorders occurs when a clinician fails to utilize the majority of the personality disorders but instead has a favorite one or two. It is unfortunately all too common for a clinician to see narcissistic personality disorder in all referrals. Issues of projection aside, this is probably inconsistent with the underlying epidemiology. The other common example of this is reserved for "difficult" patients. They, of course, are "borderlines." A more appropriate view of the personality disorders is probably that they deserve more attention than is given in training and the DSMs, and that they are probably distributed clinically in logical patterns.

The personality disorders deserve more clinical attention because they are often the true chief complaint and/or they often cause the treatment of an Axis I condition to go poorly. There is a clinical bias toward Axis I diagnoses. When we wonder what is wrong with a patient, our first thoughts and rule outs go to the Axis I disorders. Is this a psychosis? Is this a depression? Is this an anxiety disorder? Patients additionally bias us toward Axis I disorders in the presentation of their symptoms. Patients never come in and complain of a life-long characterological problem. They complain of depression, anxiety, marital problems, or occupational dysfunction. The true nature of many chief complaints is a personality disorder, not an Axis I disorder. Indeed, many personality disorders are misdiagnosed as Axis I disorders. A patient will come in and complain of cycling mood, one minute happy, the next sad, the next angry. Too many of these patients are misdiagnosed as bipolar. Rapidly shifting moods more likely ensue from a negativistic or a borderline personality disorder. Other common errors include the affective chief complaints of borderline personality disorders. The patient reports dysphoria, difficulty concentrating, and suicidal ideation. This, depending upon the history, is just as likely a borderline personality disorder as a major depression. We, however, make the major depression diagnosis, refer for medication, and engage in lengthy and unrewarding psychotherapy. Proper diagnoses must be made to properly treat patients.

The second reason the personality disorders deserve more attention is that they often make the treatment of true Axis I disorders very difficult. Not all paranoid schizophrenics are the same, and the differences are largely due to the comorbid personality disorders. A paranoid schizophrenic who is also schizoid and dependent is much different than one who is sadistic and negativistic. The first will appear, at least, to be a model patient and cause little concern for inpatient staff. That patient will be compliant with medications and generally will enjoy a successful treatment outcome. The sadistic and negativistic paranoid schizophrenic, however, will be quite different. That patient will be a source of untold difficulty for the treatment team and nursing staff. The patient will be not only unpleasant, but possibly dangerous for staff and other patients. Medication regimes will not be followed and the patient will overutilize inpatient treatment. In short, regardless of the Axis I disorder, the personality disorders will often impact treatment far more than the Axis I focus of treatment.

Not only do the personality disorders deserve more attention, but that attention should be given in a logical fashion. As mentioned above, the distribution of the personality disorders should have little to do with the clinician. The distribution does have a great deal to do with the catchment of a particular program, clinic, or inpatient facility. Prisons have a very high prevalence of personality disorders, perhaps as high as 90%. Further, those personality disorders are probably concentrated among antisocial, narcissistic, sadistic, and paranoid types. Drug and alcohol programs probably have a prevalence of those disorders as high as 70%, with a broader mix of disorders (Retzlaff & Bromley, 1991). Finally, a college counseling center probably has a prevalence of these disorders of perhaps 10% to 20%, with a preponderance of avoidant, dependent, and borderline diagnoses. It is unfortunate that so little research is done on the prevalence of disorders and their distribution not only nationally but at the program/ clinic level. The importance of this is that without knowing the types of personality disorders likely to be the true chief complaint or the comorbid disturbance, it is difficult to make accurate diagnoses and to effectively plan treatment.

The MCMI-III goes a long way toward resolving the difficulties of a lack of attention to the personality disorders, the misdiagnosis of the personality disorders, the existence of comorbid personality diagnoses, and the problems with clinical prevalence. The diagnosis of Axis I disorders is not difficult. Psychoses, major depressions, and bipolar disorders are relatively obvious. The difficulty lies with the accurate assessment of the personality disorders. This is where lack of training, clinical bias, and subtle symptoms cause trouble. In summary, the first step toward using the MCMI-III in treatment planning is to understand the importance of the personality disorders.

The Personality Disorders as Psychic Autoimmune System

Comorbid Axis I and Axis II disorders do not represent a static or orthogonal system. The various disorders as well as stressors act as a dynamic system. Millon (1990) has suggested that the system is akin to the biological autoimmune system. There are three elements in this system, which include the Axis IV stressor (environment), the Axis II personality, and any Axis I clinical disturbance. The important element of this triad is actually the personality or its disorder. The reason for this is that the personality mediates the interaction between the stressor and the clinical response.

Two patients can be faced with the same stressor but will develop two completely different Axis I disorders. The only logical reason for this would be the existence of a mediating force such as the personality. By way of example, two patients might get divorced. One patient will fall into a depression and the other will end up apparently happy and out on the town. The first patient may have a personality which predisposes that patient to a depression in the face of interpersonal loss such as a dependent personality disorder. The other patient may end up seeking treatment for alcohol dependence as a result of the interpersonal loss ("new-found freedom") and comorbid antisocial personality disorder. Two patients, same stressor, two personality disorders, and two Axis I complaints are seen as the outcome (Retzlaff, Ofman, Hyer, & Matheson, 1994).

As we have discovered over recent years with AIDS, cancer, and heart disease, autoimmune systems can be both friend and foe. So it is with the personality disorders; a personality disorder in one situation will result in an Axis I disorder and significant distress. In another situation, the very same personality disorder will not result in a problem. In yet a third situation, the personality disorder will actually be adaptive and prevent the development of a clinical syndrome. A patient who is antisocial and sadistic will have marital problems and will be distressed if any abuse has come to the attention of the authorities. The same patient will probably be oblivious to any financial problems of an employer and as such will not be clinically impacted by a slowdown at work. Finally, the same patient may find employment where the personality disorder is adaptive. Whole life insurance sales comes to mind. The personality disorders should be viewed within this system when planning treatment.

Treatment Planning with Comorbidities

Along this autoimmune line, the personality disorders can be the reason for treatment, they can be a relatively neutral element of the diagnostic picture, or they can be used to further the treatment of an Axis I disorder. The same is surprisingly true of the Axis I disorders.

Given that something will be treated, Table 12.1 presents the six possible options for the treatment of a patient with comorbid Axis I and Axis II disorders. The possible approaches to both the Axis I and II disorders include being unaware of the disorder, being aware of the disorder so as not to be confused by it, treating the disorder, and, finally, using the disorder in the service of the treatment of the other axis's disorder.

The first of the six options is the most typical found in clinical practice. It is the treatment of the Axis I disorder without knowledge of the comorbid personality disorder. This may seem parsimonious, but it indeed leaves the clinician open to not understanding the entire symptom picture and confusing Axis I and Axis II symptoms and treatment. This is not recommended.

The second option is the converse. It includes the treatment of a perceived Axis II disorder without an understanding of the comorbid Axis I disorder. While less common

TABLE 12.1. Psychotherapy Decisions
with Comorbidities

Axis I clinical syndrome	Axis II personality disorder
Treat	Unaware
Unaware	Treat
Treat	Aware
Aware	Treat
Treat	Use to help
Use to help	Treat

than the first option, there is a small but galvanized group of therapists who believe that all difficulties are personality-based and view Axis I clinical syndromes as part of personality. This approach is also not recommended. The simple use of the MCMI-III will preclude the selection of either of these first two therapeutic options.

The third option is to treat the Axis I disorder in light of the personality disorder. Here simple awareness of the Axis II disorder will largely prevent the misattribution of personality symptoms to the Axis I disorder as well as prevent outright misdiagnosis. Awareness of the comorbid personality disorder allows for a number of suboptions. The personality disorder can be simply ignored, used to clarify the diagnosis, guarded against while treating the Axis I disorder, and used to limit the prognosis for outcome. The last of these is of particular interest. A patient whose underlying personality is depressive will have a more limited outcome from the treatment of a major depression than will a patient whose underlying personality is histrionic.

The fourth option includes the treatment of the personality disorder with awareness of the Axis I disorder. An example may be a patient who presents with both narcissistic personality disorder and alcohol abuse. A decision could be made that the cause of the alcohol abuse and other problems is the personality. Because the alcohol abuse is not life threatening, only the narcissism is treated. Indeed, the alcohol abuse may be used as an outcome variable in the personality disorder treatment. Here, if the personality is causing the alcohol abuse and the alcohol abuse is not the focus of therapy but it decreases, then there is good evidence of the success of the personality psychotherapy. Here too, the other uses of "awareness" can be brought to bear on a case, such as diagnostic clarity, therapeutic intrusion, and outcome portense (Retzlaff & Bromley, 1994).

The fifth option is rarely well developed in treatment planning. It is the use of the personality disorder to better treat the Axis I disorder. Here there is no desire to change the personality disorder, only to use it in the service of the Axis I treatment. It is the use of autoimmune leverage against the chief complaint. While rarely done, it is obvious that different personalities will respond to different approaches to the treatment of a single Axis I complaint. Those with dependent personality disorder and those with a paranoid personality disorder need differential treatment for a major depression. The dependent elements of the first patient can be used to make the usual treatment for depression more effective. Here, allowing the dependence on the therapist to deepen will allow the therapist to maximize therapeutic compliance. Meeting the dependence needs will hasten the effect of the therapeutic components aimed at the depression. A paranoid personality disorder, on the other hand, would terminate therapy if treated like a dependent. Here it would be useful to "encourage" the suspiciousness of this patient, perhaps by suggesting or providing readings on the medication or psychotherapy regime. One could also suggest careful therapeutic trials to determine if therapy elements were "truly" useful or simply "further exploitation." Regardless of the Axis I disorder, its treatment is within the context of the personality of the patient and as such the personality can go a long way to aid the therapy of the Axis I disorder.

The final and sixth option in the treatment of comorbid disorders is the treatment of the personality disorder while using the Axis I disorder to maximize the therapy. Here a decision is made to not directly address the clinical syndrome such as anxiety, but to use it to aid in the amelioration of the Axis II disorder. Traditionally, this is viewed as whether patients are "motivated" for therapy. A marital partner in for therapy who is anxious is probably motivated. Here it would be inappropriate to reduce the anxiety directly, as this would result in reduced motivation to work on personality issues. Similarly, depression may be used as a break in the armor of a histrionic or narcissist who otherwise would see little reason to change. Obviously, syndromes such as psychosis or mania do not lend themselves as well to this approach.

In summary, there are six therapeutic options for the therapist given a case with comorbid Axis disorders. The MCMI-III allows the therapist to make an informed decision regarding the focus of therapy. In general, when treating only the Axis I or Axis II disorder, the other disorder should be in therapeutic awareness or be used to aid in the treatment of the target Axis.

The Domains of the Personality Disorders

It is beyond the scope of this chapter and my expertise to posit therapeutic techniques for all Axis I, Axis II, and comorbid pathologies. A case has been made that it is the personality disorders that result in poor diagnoses and limited therapeutic outcome. As such, the remainder of the chapter will focus on domain-specific psychotherapy of the personality disorders.

Millon (1990, 1994) has assembled and hypothesized the existence of eight domains of interest. These include Expressive Acts, Interpersonal Conduct, Cognitive Style, Object Representations, Self-Image, Regulatory Mechanisms, Morphologic Organization, and Mood/Temperament. These represent an organized and comprehensive qualification of the personality disorders across most of the popular theoretical foci.

Millon primarily put these descriptors to use in the factorial delineation of the personality disorders diagnostics. The desire was to go beyond the criteria of the DSMs to encompass a broad range of clinical phenomena to better understand each of the personality disorders.

The domains are defined (Millon, 1994) in Table 12.2. Expressive Acts are seen as the overt behaviors of the patient. This include physical actions as well as verbalizations. They are quite obvious and accessible. Interpersonal Conduct is the interactions of a patient with others. This includes the style of interaction as well as content of the interactions. It can also be the outcomes of the interactions, including the impression left on others.

Internal phenomena include Cognitive Style which is the perception, interpretation, and conclusions made by the patient about the world. It is both the manner in which these occur and the content of the cognitions. Object Representations are another internal phenomena. The personality disorders all have distinct process and content of the object relation. The memories, experiences, and significant others all form an internal structure. Finally, the Self-Image is seen as the patient's sense of self. "Who" they are is made up of attributes which may or may not be realistic.

Intrapsychic dimensions include the Regulatory Mechanisms. These are the classic defense mechanisms. These internal processes work to ameliorate anxiety and conflict. Each personality disorder manifests a primary defense mechanism. The structure of these intrapsychic processes is the Morphologic Organization. This organization may be strong or weak, flexible or rigid, and consistent or inconsistent. It is the psychic "house" and its construction.

The sole biological dimension delineated by Millon is the Mood/Temperament dimension. Here specific affects are seen in the personality disorders. While there has been a lack of affect attributed to the personality disorders since the DSM-II (American Psychiatric Association, 1968), here a full emotional dimension is seen in all the personality disorders.

Table 12.3 provides an example of this multidimensional approach to diagnostics. Here the avoidant personality disorder is seen as expressively *fretful* and interpersonally *aversive*. Also, the patient is cognitively *distracted*, objects are *vexatious*, and the self is *alienated*.

TABLE 12.2. Clinical Definitions of the Domains

Expressive Acts

The observables of physical and verbal behavior can be readily identified by clinicians. Through inference, these data enable us to deduce either what the patient unknowingly reveals about him- or herself or, conversely, what he or she wishes us to think or to know about him or her. The criteria for this clinical attribute consist of both of these presented behavioral variants.

Interpersonal Conduct

A patient's style of relating to others may be captured in a number of ways, such as the manner in which his or her actions impact on others, intended or otherwise; the attitudes that underlie, prompt, and give shape to these actions; the methods by which he or she engages others to meet his or her needs; or his or her way of coping with interpersonal tensions and conflicts.

Cognitive Styles

The cognitive styles domain includes some of the most useful indices in identifying the patient's distinctive way of functioning. This is how the patient perceives events, focuses his or her attention, processes information, organizes his or her thoughts, and communicates his or her reactions and ideas to others. The criteria for this clinical attribute represent some of the more notable styles in this functional realm.

Object Representations

Significant experiences from the past leave an inner imprint, a structural residue composed of memories, attitudes, and affects that continue to serve as a substrate of dispositions for perceiving and reacting to life's ongoing events. Both the character and content of these internalized representations of the past are evaluated.

Self-Image

Each person builds a perception of him- or herself as an identifiable being, an "I" or "me." Most people have a consistent sense of "who they are," but do differ in the clarity of their introspections into self and/or in their ability to articulate the attributes comprising this image. Clinical ratings, therefore, are likely to be somewhat speculative.

Regulatory Mechanisms

This clinical attribute represents internal and often unconscious processes that are difficult to discern and evaluate. Nevertheless, they are important in that they show how the patient denies or distorts painful feelings or incompatible thoughts, often setting into motion a sequence of events that intensifies the very problems he or she may have sought to circumvent.

Morphologic Organization

The overall configuration of elements comprising the mind's interior world may display weakness in organizational cohesion, exhibit deficient balance and coordination, or possess rigidities or pressures. It is the structural strength, interior congruity, and functional efficacy of this intrapsychic system to which this clinical attribute pertains.

Mood/Temperament

The "meaning" of extreme affective states are easy to decode. Not so with persistent moods and subtle feelings that have colored and continue to insidiously color a wide range of the patient's relationships and experiences. No matter how clear the criteria for this clinical attribute may be, the database for their deduction may call for more information than may be available observationally, especially during acute emotional periods.

TABLE 12.3. Domains of the Avoidant Personality

Expressively fretful (e.g., conveys personal unease and disquiet, a constant timorous, hesitant, and restive state; overreacts to innocuous events and anxiously judges them to signify ridicule, criticism, and disapproval)

Interpersonally aversive (e.g., distances from activities that involve intimate personal relationships and reports extensive history of social pananxiety and distrust; seeks acceptance, but is unwilling to get involved unless certain to be liked, maintaining distance and privacy to avoid being shamed and humiliated)

Cognitively distracted (e.g., warily scans environment for potential threats and is preoccupied by intrusive and disruptive random thoughts and observations; an upwelling from within of irrelevant ideation upsets thought continuity and interferes with social communications and accurate appraisals)

Vexatious objects (e.g., internalized representations are composed of readily reactivated, intense and conflict-ridden memories of problematic early relations; limited avenues for experiencing or recalling gratification, and few mechanisms to channel needs, bind impulses, resolve conflicts, or deflect external stressors)

Alienated self-image (e.g., sees self as socially inept, inadequate, and inferior, justifying thereby his or her isolation and rejection by others; feels personally unappealing, devalues self-achievements, and reports persistent sense of aloneness and emptiness)

Fantasy mechanism (e.g., depends excessively on imagination to achieve need gratification, confidence building, and conflict resolution; withdraws into reveries as a means of safely discharging frustrated affectionate and angry impulses)

Fragile organization (e.g., a precarious complex of tortuous emotions depends almost exclusively on a single modality for its resolution and discharge, that of avoidance, escape, and fantasy; hence, when faced with personal risks, new opportunities, or unanticipated stress, few morphologic structures are available to deploy and few back-up positions can be reverted to, short of regressive decompensation)

Anguished mood (e.g., describes constant and confusing undercurrent of tension, sadness, and anger; vacillates between desire for affection, fear of rebuff, embarrassment, and numbness of feeling)

Intrapsychically, the avoidant uses the *fantasy* mechanism within a *fragile* organization. Finally, the mood of the avoidant is *anguished*. Unlike the rather fragmented approach of the DSMs, this approach is both rich and multidimensional.

DOMAIN-SPECIFIC PSYCHOTHERAPY OF THE PERSONALITY DISORDERS

While the usual presentation of these domains is for the purpose of better understanding the full dimensionality of each of the personality disorders, it is the intent of this chapter to view the dimensions from a treatment perspective. While a particular personality may engender particular expressive acts, interpersonal interactions, and cognitive styles, this does little to help the therapist treat the patient. Therapists usually have been trained in, believe in, and practice one or two therapies which are along the lines of the domains. Behavioralists will be more interested in the expressive acts domain, interpersonalists in the interpersonal domain, and cognitivists in the cognitive domain. Therefore, I suggest that the domain-specific criteria become the domain-specific targets of treatment (Retzlaff, 1995b).

Everly (1995) suggested a number of therapies (see Table 12.4) which lend themselves to the specific domains. While in theory any type of psychotherapy could be used to treat any of the domain-specific symptoms, some therapies simply lend themselves to closer concordance with the symptom. As such, the traditional therapies and techniques of behaviorism are probably best suited to the expressive acts domain. Counterconditioning and social skills training would be examples which may help the *fretfulness* of the avoidant, for instance. Group and family therapies would lend themselves to the interpersonal conduct domain. Cognitive–behavioral approaches would work well with the cognitive style problems. Object relations-oriented psychotherapies will work best with the pathological object representations. The self-image is best treated through self-oriented therapies. Both regulatory mechanisms and morphologic organization domains seem best suited to variants of psychoanalytic psychotherapy. Finally, the mood domain is appropriately attacked through a number of approaches including psychopharmacology as well as experiential therapies. While single approaches to individual domain targets are suggested here, more complex multimodal (Lazarus, 1981) or integrative (Millon, Everly, & Davis, 1993; Norcross & Goldfried, 1992) approaches may be used.

TABLE 12.4. Domain-Targeted Interventions

Expressive Acts

Counterconditioning; social skills training; assertiveness training; behavioral rehearsal; operant conditioning

Interpersonal Conduct

Group therapy; family therapy; social skills training; humanistic therapy approaches; anger management; interpersonal therapy

Cognitive Style

Reframing methods; cognitive–behavioral approaches; existential therapies

Object Representations

Dream analysis; object-relations analysis

Self-Image

Client-centered therapy; self-oriented analysis; assertiveness

Regulatory Mechanisms

Ego-oriented analysis; hypnotherapy; psychoanalytic psychotherapy

Morphologic Organization

Transference; classical psychoanalysis; psychoanalytic psychotherapy

Mood/Temperament

Psychopharmacological agents; relaxation training; counterconditioning; experiential therapy

The application of these techniques to the specific domain symptoms follows. Due to space limitations, only a few examples of the personality disorders are included under each domain.

Expressive Acts

Donat (1995) brings together the traditional work in classical and operant conditioning with the more recent work in self-management to suggest very specific behavioral therapy for the personality disorders. From this perspective, Millon's (1994) expressive acts symptoms become the targets of therapy (see Table 12.5).

TABLE 12.5. Expressive Acts

Schizoid Personality

Expressively impassive (e.g., appears to be in an inert emotional state, lifeless, undemonstrative, lacking in energy and vitality; is unmoved, boring, unanimated, robotic, phlegmatic, displaying deficits in activation, motoric expressiveness, and spontaneity)

Avoidant Personality

Expressively fretful (e.g., conveys personal unease and disquiet, a constant timorous, hesitant, and restive state; overreacts to innocuous events and anxiously judges them to signify ridicule, criticism, and disapproval)

Depressive Personality

Expressively disconsolate (e.g., appearance and posture conveys and irrelievably forlorn, somber, heavy-hearted, woebegone, if not grief-stricken, quality; irremediably dispirited and discouraged, portraying a sense of permanent hopelessness and wretchedness)

Dependent Personality

Expressively incompetent (e.g., withdraws from adult responsibilities by acting helpless and seeking nurturance from others; is docile and passive, lacks functional competencies, and avoids self-assertion)

Histrionic Personality

Expressively dramatic (e.g., is overreactive, volatile, provocative, and engaging, as well as intolerant of inactivity, resulting in impulsive, highly emotional, and theatrical responsiveness; describes penchant for momentary excitements, fleeting adventures, and short-sighted hedonism)

Narcissistic Personality

Expressively haughty (e.g., acts in an arrogant, supercilious, pompous, and disdainful manner, flouting conventional rules of shared social living, viewing them as naive or inapplicable to self; reveals a careless disregard for personal integrity and a self-important indifference to the rights of others)

Antisocial Personality

Expressively impulsive (e.g., is impetuous and irrepressible, acting hastily and spontaneously in a restless, spur-of-the-moment manner; is short-sighted, incautious and imprudent, failing to plan ahead or consider alternatives, no less to heed consequences)

(*continued*)

TABLE 12.5. (*continued*)

Aggressive (Sadistic) Personality

Expressively precipitate (e.g., is disposed to react in sudden, abrupt outbursts of an unexpected and unwarranted nature; recklessly reactive and daring, attracted to challenge, risk, and harm, as well as unflinching, undeterred by pain, and undaunted by danger and punishment)

Compulsive Personality

Expressively disciplined (e.g., maintains a regulated, highly structured, and strictly organized life; perfectionism interferes with decision making and task completion)

Negativistic Personality

Expressively resentful (e.g., resists fulfilling expectancies of others, frequently exhibiting procrastination, inefficiency, and obstinance, as well as contrary and irksome behaviors; reveals gratification in demoralizing and undermining the pleasures and aspirations of others)

Self-Defeating Personality

Expressively abstinent (e.g., presents self as nonindulgent, frugal, and chaste; is reluctant to seek pleasurable experiences, refraining from exhibiting signs of enjoying life; acts in an unpresuming and self-effacing manner, preferring to place self in an inferior light or abject position)

Schizotypal Personality

Expressively eccentric (e.g., exhibits socially gauche and peculiar mannerisms; is perceived by others as aberrant and disposed to behave in an unobtrusively odd, aloof, curious, or bizarre manner)

Borderline Personality

Expressively spasmodic (e.g., displays a desultory energy level with sudden, unexpected, and impulsive outbursts; abrupt, endogenous shifts in drive state and inhibitory controls; not only places activation and emotional equilibrium in constant jeopardy, but engages in recurrent suicidal or self-mutilating behaviors)

Paranoid Personality

Expressively defensive (e.g., is vigilantly guarded, alert to anticipate and ward off expected derogation, malice, and deception; is tenacious and firmly resistant to sources of external influence and control)

Here, for example, the techniques of social skills training are suggested for the schizoid and avoidant personality disorders. The former is viewed as *impassive* and the latter as *fretful*. These symptoms become the targets of both the ongoing assessment process within behavior therapy and the therapeutic interventions. Role playing, for instance, involving these specific behaviors could be the method of the skills training.

Self-management and monitoring is suggested for the *incompetence* of the dependent, the *haughtiness* of the narcissist, and the *impulsiveness* of the antisocial. While behavioral techniques will work with many types of symptoms, the choice of symptoms is of particular concern with the personality disorders. The MCMI-III allows for the assessment of the disorder and the theory provides the appropriate target symptom.

Interpersonal Conduct

Craig (1995) provides a comprehensive approach to interpersonal psychotherapy. He suggests that the process of the therapy is time limited, focused on one or two major issues, and deals primarily with present interpersonal behavior. Finally, he sees the personality of the patient within the context of others. The technique of the therapy is very active, involving advice, suggestion, limit setting, education, and direct help.

Craig suggests that Millon's (1994) interpersonal issues of concern (see Table 12.6) provide a good initial set of treatment issues for the personality disorders. The *submissive* dependent, for example, is encouraged to analyze encounters with others, their roles and reactions, and other ways of dealing with people. More active means may include the en-

TABLE 12.6. Interpersonal Conduct

Schizoid Personality

Interpersonally unengaged (e.g., seems indifferent and remote, rarely responsive to the actions or feelings of others; chooses solitary activities, possesses minimal "human" interests; fades into the background, is aloof or unobtrusive, neither desires nor enjoys close relationships; prefers a peripheral role in social, work, and family settings)

Avoidant Personality

Interpersonally aversive (e.g., distances from activities that involve intimate personal relationships and reports extensive history of social pananxiety and distrust; seeks acceptance, but is unwilling to get involved unless certain to be liked, maintaining distance and privacy to avoid being shamed and humiliated)

Depressive Personality

Interpersonally defenseless (e.g., owing to feeling vulnerable, assailable, and unshielded, will beseech others to be nurturant and protective; fearing abandonment and desertion, will not only act in an endangered manner, but will seek, if not demand, assurances of affection, steadfastness, and devotion)

Dependent Personality

Interpersonally submissive (e.g., needs excessive advice and reassurance, as well as subordinates self to stronger, nurturing figure, without whom may feel anxiously alone and helpless; is compliant, conciliatory and placating, fearing being left to care for oneself)

Histrionic Personality

Interpersonally attention-seeking (e.g., actively solicits praise and manipulates others to gain needed reassurance, attention, and approval; is demanding, flirtatious, vain, and seductively exhibitionistic, especially when wishing to be the center of attention)

Narcissistic Personality

Interpersonally exploitive (e.g., feels entitled, is unempathic and expects special favors without assuming reciprocal responsibilities; shamelessly takes others for granted and uses them to enhance self and indulge desires

(continued)

TABLE 12.6. (*continued*)

Antisocial Personality

Interpersonally irresponsible (e.g., is untrustworthy and unreliable, failing to meet or intentionally negating personal obligations of a marital, parental, employment, or financial nature; actively intrudes upon and violates the rights of others; transgresses established social codes through deceitful or illegal behaviors)

Aggressive (Sadistic) Personality

Interpersonally abrasive (e.g., reveals satisfaction in intimidating, coercing, and humiliating others; regularly expresses verbally abusive and derisive social commentary, as well as exhibiting vicious, if not physically brutal, behavior)

Compulsive Personality

Interpersonally respectful (e.g., exhibits unusual adherence to social conventions and proprieties, as well as being scrupulous and overconscientious about matters of morality and ethics; prefers polite, formal, and correct personal relationships, usually insisting that subordinates adhere to personally established rules and methods)

Negativistic Personality

Interpersonally contrary (e.g., assumes conflicting and changing roles in social relationships, particularly dependent and contrite acquiescence and assertive and hostile independence; conveys envy and pique toward those more fortunate, as well as being actively concurrently or sequentially obstructive and intolerant of others, expressing either negative or incompatible attitudes)

Self-Defeating Personality

Interpersonally deferential (e.g., distances from those who are consistently supportive, relating to others where one can be sacrificing, servile, and obsequious, thus allowing, if not encouraging, them to exploit, mistreat, or take advantage, renders ineffectual the attempts of others to be helpful and solicits condemnation by accepting undeserved blame and courting unjust criticism)

Schizotypal Personality

Interpersonally secretive (e.g., prefers privacy and isolation, with few highly tentative attachments and personal obligations; has drifted over time into increasingly peripheral vocational roles and clandestine social activities)

Borderline Personality

Interpersonally paradoxical (e.g., although needing attention and affection is unpredictably contrary, manipulative, and volatile, frequently eliciting rejection rather than support; frantically reacts to fears of abandonment and isolation, but often in angry, mercurial, and self-damaging ways)

Paranoid Personality

Interpersonally provocative (e.g., not only bears grudges and is unforgiving of those of the past, but also displays a quarrelsome, fractious, and abrasive attitude with recent acquaintances; precipitates exasperation and anger by a testing of loyalties and an intrusive and searching preoccupation with hidden motives) couragement of more independent interpersonal interactions. The narcissist is seen as *exploitive* interpersonally. Therefore, therapy should focus on the result of these exploitive interpersonal encounters on others. The reanalysis of relationships is encouraged to focus on the mutual benefits which are lost and may be recovered.

Cognitive Style

The cognitive approach as synthesized by Will (1995) includes a number of tenets. First, the process of perceiving and experiencing the environment is active. Second, cognitions are integrations of internal and external stimuli. Third, the approach the patient takes to the analysis of a problem is best seen through the cognitions. Fourth, this approach is colored by the past, present, and future. Fifth, it is believed that changes in cognitions will manifest themselves in changes in behavior and affect. Finally, cognitive distortions cause pathology and they can be changed through psychotherapy. Specific techniques may include a psychoeducational component showing linkage between thought and action, a visualization procedure illustrative of distortion or change, and a homework assignment recording automatic thoughts.

The avoidant, by way of example, is seen as having *distracted* thoughts (see Table 12.7). The thought process is defective and as Will (1995) points out, the thought content is condemning and automatic. Common thoughts will include, "I don't fit in anywhere." It is probable that the distracted process forces from consciousness the pain of the content

TABLE 12.7. Cognitive Style

Schizoid Personality

Cognitively impoverished (e.g., seems deficient across broad spheres of human knowledge and evidences vague and obscure thought processes, particularly about social matters; communication with others is often unfocused, loses its purpose or intention, or is conveyed via a loose or circuitous logic)

Avoidant Personality

Cognitively distracted (e.g., warily scans environment for potential threats and is preoccupied by intrusive and disruptive random thoughts and observations; an upwelling from within of irrelevant ideation upsets thought continuity and interferes with social communications and accurate appraisals)

Depressive Personality

Cognitively pessimistic (e.g., possesses defeatist and fatalistic attitudes about almost all matters, sees things in their blackest form and invariably expects the worst; feeling weighed down, discouraged, and bleak, gives the gloomiest interpretation of current events, despairing as well that things will never improve in the future)

Dependent Personality

Cognitively naive (e.g., rarely disagrees with others and is easily persuaded, unsuspicious, and gullible; reveals a Pollyanna attitude toward interpersonal difficulties, watering down objective problems and smoothing over troubling events)

Histrionic Personality

Cognitively flighty (e.g., avoids introspective thought, is overly suggestible, attentive to fleeting external events, and speaks in impressionistic generalities; integrates experiences poorly, resulting in scattered learning and thoughtless judgments)

(continued)

TABLE 12.7. (*continued*)

Narcissistic Personality

Cognitively expansive (e.g., has an undisciplined imagination and exhibits a preoccupation with immature and self-glorifying fantasies of success, beauty, or love; is minimally constrained by objective reality, takes liberties with facts, and often lies to redeem self-illusions)

Antisocial Personality

Cognitively deviant (e.g., construes events and relationships in accord with socially unorthodox beliefs and morals; is disdainful of traditional ideals, fails to conform to social norms, and is contemptuous of conventional values)

Aggressive (Sadistic) Personality

Cognitively dogmatic (e.g., is strongly opinionated and closed-minded, as well as unbending and obstinate in holding to one's preconceptions; exhibits a broad-ranging authoritarianism, social intolerance, and prejudice)

Compulsive Personality

Cognitively constricted (e.g., constructs world in terms of rules, regulations, schedules, and hierarchies; is rigid, stubborn, and indecisive and notably upset by unfamiliar or novel ideas and customs)

Negativistic Personality

Cognitively skeptical (e.g., is cynical, doubting, and untrusting, approaching positive events with disbelief and future possibilities with pessimism, anger, and trepidation; has a misanthropic view of life, is whining and grumbling, voicing disdain and caustic comments toward those experiencing good fortune)

Self-Defeating Personality

Cognitively diffident (e.g., hesitant to interpret observations positively for fear that, in doing so, they may not take problematic forms or achieve troublesome and self-denigrating outcomes; as a result, repeatedly expresses attitudes and anticipations contrary to favorable beliefs and feelings)

Schizotypal Personality

Cognitively autistic (e.g., capacity to "read" thoughts and feelings of others is markedly dysfunctional; mixes social communications with personal irrelevancies, circumstantial speech, ideas of reference, and metaphorical asides; often ruminative, appearing self-absorbed and lost in daydreams with occasional magical thinking, bodily illusions, obscure suspicion, odd beliefs, and a blurring of reality and fantasy)

Borderline Personality

Cognitively capricious (e.g., experiences rapidly changing, fluctuating, and antithetical perceptions or thoughts concerning passing events, as well as contrasting emotions and conflicting thoughts toward self and others, notably love, rage, and guilt; vacillating and contradictory reactions are evoked in others by virtue of one's behaviors, creating, in turn, conflicting and confusing social feedback)

Paranoid Personality

Cognitively suspicious (e.g., is unwarrantedly skeptical, cynical, and mistrustful of the motives of others, including relatives, friends, and associates, construing innocuous events as signifying hidden or conspiratorial intent; reveals tendency to read hidden meanings into benign matters and to magnify tangential or minor difficulties into proofs of duplicity and treachery, especially regarding the fidelity and trustworthiness of a spouse or intimate friend) of the thoughts. Cognitive therapy would look to improve the quality of the thought process through focusing on the stream of thought. As well, it would attempt to change the underlying schema which results in the negative and condemning cognitions.

The compulsive style is another that is amenable to the use of cognitive therapy. Here the cognitions are seen as *constricted*. The goal of cognitive therapy is to reduce the tendency of the patient to view the world in black or white terms and to explore the shades of gray. The perfectionism is also ripe for reconstruction; anything less than perfect is not failure.

Object Representations

The etiology of internal objects has a lengthy and interesting history. Van Denburg (1995) covers the current thinking well, including the notions of splitting, rewarding object relation units, withdrawing object relation units, and self-objects. Therapy is seen as a variant of analytic work with an emphasis on transference interpretation. Van Denburg (1995) sees the patient as placing the therapist into an object "template." Millon's descriptors of the objects (see Table 12.8) are particularly interesting, if not entertaining.

TABLE 12.8. Object Representations

Schizoid Personality

Meager objects (e.g., internalized representations are few in number and minimally articulated, largely devoid of the manifold percepts and memories of relationships with others, possessing little of the dynamic interplay among drives and conflicts that typify well-adjusted persons)

Avoidant Personality

Vexatious objects (e.g., internalized representations are composed of readily reactivated, intense, and conflict-ridden memories of problematic early relations; limited avenues for experiencing or recalling gratification, and few mechanisms to channel needs, bind impulses, resolve conflicts, or deflect external stressors)

Depressive Personality

Forsaken objects (e.g., internalized representations of the past appear jettisoned, as if life's early experiences have been depleted or devitalized, either drained of their richness and joyful elements or withdrawn from memory, leaving one to feel abandoned, bereft, discarded, cast off, and deserted)

Dependent Personality

Immature objects (e.g., internalized representations are composed of infantile impressions of others, unsophisticated ideas, incomplete recollections, rudimentary drives, and childlike impulses, as well as minimal competencies to manage and resolve stressors)

Histrionic Personality

Shallow objects (e.g., internalized representations are composed largely of superficial memories of past relations, random collections of transient and segregated affects and conflicts, and insubstantial drives and mechanisms)

Narcissistic Personality

Contrived objects (e.g., internalized representations are composed far more than usual of illusory and changing memories of past relationships; unacceptable drives and conflicts are readily refashioned as the need arises; often simulated and pretentious)

(continued)

TABLE 12.8. (*continued*)

Antisocial Personality

Debased objects (e.g., internalized representations comprise degraded and corrupt relationships that spur revengeful attitudes and restive impulses which are driven to subvert established cultural ideals and mores, as well as to devalue personal sentiments and to sully, but intensely covet, the material attainments of society denied them)

Aggressive (Sadistic) Personality

Pernicious objects (e.g., internalized representations of the past are distinguished by early relationships that have generated strongly driven aggressive energies and malicious attitudes, as well as by a contrasting paucity of sentimental memories, tender affects, internal conflicts, and shame or guilt feelings)

Compulsive Personality

Concealed objects (e.g., only those internalized representations with associated inner affects and attitudes that can be socially approved are allowed conscious awareness or behavioral expression; as a result, actions and memories are highly regulated, forbidden impulses are sequestered and tightly bound, and personal and social conflicts are defensively denied, kept from awareness, and maintained under stringent control)

Negativistic Personality

Vacillating objects (e.g., internalized representations of the past comprise a complex of countervailing relationships setting in motion contradictory feelings, conflicting inclinations, and incompatible memories that are driven by the desire to degrade the achievements and pleasures of others without necessarily appearing to do so)

Self-Defeating Personality

Discredited objects (e.g., object representations are composed of failed past relationships and disparaged personal achievements, of positive feelings and erotic drives transposed into their least attractive opposites, of internal conflicts intentionally aggravated, and of mechanisms for reducing dysphoria which are subverted by processes which intensify discomfort)

Schizotypal Personality

Chaotic objects (e.g., internalized representations consist of a piecemeal jumble of early relationships and affects, random drives and impulses, and uncoordinated channels of regulation that are only fitfully competent for binding tensions, accommodating needs, and mediating conflicts)

Borderline Personality

Incompatible objects (e.g., internalized representations comprise rudimentary and extemporaneously devised, but repetitively aborted learnings, resulting in conflicting memories, discordant attitudes, contradictory needs, antithetical emotions, erratic impulses, and clashing strategies for conflict reduction)

Paranoid Personality

Unalterable objects (e.g., internalized representations of significant early relationships are a fixed and implacable configuration of deeply held beliefs and attitudes and are driven by unyielding convictions which, in turn, are aligned in an idiosyncratic manner with a fixed hierarchy of tenaciously held but unwarranted assumptions, fears, and conjectures)

For example, the depressive personality disorder is seen as having *forsaken* objects. The objects have been left behind or killed off. In so doing, though, the patient has lost much of the richness and complexity of life. It is the purpose of therapy here to revitalize those objects. This can be done by emphasizing the interpretations of the positive and healthy elements of those objects.

The histrionic has *shallow* objects. The therapist can easily be taken off course by the initial positive transference. The sad fact of the matter is that the histrionic is empty and alone under those shallow objects. The therapist may become a new, whole, complex, and healthy object on which the patient may draw.

Finally, the person with borderline personality disorder has *incompatible* objects. The objects conflict and result in swings from idealization to devaluation. Hence, the experience of the therapist working with a borderline patient is intense. Here the therapist must become a positive and stable object among the other objects to effect change. Only after this occurs can the therapist interpret the complex conflicts among the other objects.

Self-Image

Across development a sense of the self is developed through introspection and coalesces into a fairly stable structure. McCann (1995) suggests an analytic self psychotherapy which requires the therapist to empathically understand the patient's experience of self. This empathic attunement will allow for the two major goals of this therapy, understanding and explaining. The answer to "Who are you?" is found in Table 12.9 for each of the personality disorders.

TABLE 12.9. Self-Image

Schizoid Personality

Complacent self-image (e.g., reveals minimal introspection and awareness of self; seems impervious to the emotional and personal implications of everyday social life, appearing indifferent to the praise or criticism of others)

Avoidant Personality

Alienated self-image (e.g., sees self as socially inept, inadequate, and inferior, justifying thereby his or her isolation and rejection by others; feels personally unappealing, devalues self-achievements, and reports persistent sense of aloneness and emptiness)

Depressive Personality

Worthless self-image (e.g., judges oneself of no account, valueless to self or others, inadequate and unsuccessful in all aspirations, barren, sterile, and impotent; sees self as inconsequential and reproachable, if not contemptible, a person who should be criticized and derogated, as well as one who should feel guilty for possessing no praiseworthy traits or achievements)

Dependent Personality

Inept self-image (e.g., views self as weak, fragile, and inadequate; exhibits lack of self-confidence by belittling own attitudes and competencies, and hence not capable of doing things on one's own)

Histrionic Personality

Gregarious self-image (e.g., views self as sociable, stimulating and charming; enjoys the image of attracting acquaintances by physical appearance and by pursuing a busy and pleasure-oriented life)

(continued)

TABLE 12.9. (*continued*)

Narcissistic Personality

Admirable self-image (e.g., believes self to be meritorious, special, if not unique, deserving of great admiration, and acting in a grandiose or self-assured manner, often without commensurate achievements; has a sense of high self-worth, despite being seen by others as egotistic, inconsiderate, and arrogant)

Antisocial Personality

Autonomous self-image (e.g., sees self as unfettered by the restrictions of social customs and the constraints of personal loyalties; values the image and enjoys the sense of being free, unencumbered, and unconfined by persons, places, obligations, or routines)

Aggressive (Sadistic) Personality

Combative self-image (e.g., is proud to characterize self as assertively competitive, as well as vigorously energetic and militantly hardheaded; values aspects of self that present pugnacious, domineering, and power-oriented image)

Compulsive Personality

Conscientious self-image (e.g., sees self as devoted to work, industrious, reliable, meticulous, and efficient, largely to the exclusion of leisure activities; fearful of error or misjudgment; hence, overvalues aspects of self that exhibit discipline, perfection, prudence, and loyalty)

Negativistic Personality

Discontented self-image (e.g., sees self as misunderstood, luckless, unappreciated, jinxed, and demeaned by others; recognizes being characteristically embittered, disgruntled, and disillusioned with life)

Self-Defeating Personality

Undeserving self-image (e.g., is self-abasing, focusing on the very worst personal features, asserting thereby that one is worthy of being shamed, humbled, and debased; feels that one has failed to live up to the expectations of others and hence, deserves to suffer painful consequences)

Schizotypal Personality

Estranged self-image (e.g., exhibits recurrent social perplexities and illusions as well as experiences of depersonalization, derealization, and dissociation; sees self as forlorn, with repetitive thoughts of life's emptiness and meaninglessness)

Borderline Personality

Uncertain self-image (e.g., experiences the confusions of an immature, nebulous, or wavering sense of identity, often with underlying feelings of emptiness; seeks to redeem precipitate actions and changing self-presentations with expressions of contrition and self-punitive behaviors)

Paranoid Personality

Inviolable self-image (e.g., has persistent ideas of self-importance and self-reference, perceiving attacks on one's character not apparent to others, asserting as personally derogatory and scurrilous, if not libelous, entirely innocuous actions and events; is pridefully independent, reluctant to confide in others, highly insular, but experiencing intense fears, of losing identity, status, and powers of self-determination)

Those with negativistic personality disorder see the self as *discontented*. From the beginning of therapy they are discontented with the therapist, technique, time, and cost. It is also obviously difficult for many therapists to empathically attune to such feelings for very long or in a very genuine manner. Should the patient remain in therapy, an analysis of the needs being met in therapy are indicated, especially in light of the verbalized discontent. Finally, the successful development of a therapeutic relationship will lead to the examination of the global discontent.

The *undeserving* self-image of those with self-defeating personality disorder is probably at the root of much of the interpersonal difficulty of this type of patient. Here the patient will focus on the negative elements of the self, making empathy difficult. Exploration of the events of life will result in a more thorough understanding of the self and its development as well as allowing for the opportunity to explain the current self-image.

Regulatory Mechanisms

The regulatory mechanisms are the traditional defense mechanisms. As such, many of the analytic techniques will work well. Kubacki and Smith (1995) suggest the extension of these techniques to better encompass the therapist as well as the patient. The MCMI-III is used as an augmentation of traditional psychoanalytic assessment procedures. The personality patterns as seen in the MCMI-III are tied to the personality organization, self/other development, and the defense mechanisms. Further, the defense mechanisms are grouped at neurotic, borderline, and psychotic levels of organization.

TABLE 12.10. Regulatory Mechanisms

Schizoid Personality

Intellectualization mechanism (e.g., describes interpersonal and affective experiences in a matter-of-fact, abstract, impersonal, or mechanical manner; pays primary attention to formal and objective aspects of social and emotional events)

Avoidant Personality

Fantasy mechanism (e.g., depends excessively on imagination to achieve need gratification, confidence building, and conflict resolution; withdraws into reveries as a means of safely discharging frustrated affectionate as well as angry impulses)

Depressive Personality

Asceticism mechanism (e.g., engages in acts of self-denial, self-punishment, and self-tormenting, believing that one should exhibit penance and be deprived of life's bounties; not only is there a repudiation of pleasures, but there are harsh self-judgments, as well as self-destructive acts)

Dependent Personality

Introjection mechanism (e.g., is firmly devoted to another to strengthen the belief that an inseparable bond exists between them; jettisons one's own views in favor of those of others to preclude conflicts and threats to relationship)

Histrionic Personality

Dissociation mechanism (e.g., regularly alters and recomposes self-presentations to create a succession of socially attractive but changing facades; engages in self-distracting activities to avoid reflecting on and integrating unpleasant thoughts and emotions)

(continued)

TABLE 12.10. (*continued*)

Narcissistic Personality

Rationalization mechanism (e.g., is self-deceptive and facile in devising plausible reasons to justify self-centered and socially inconsiderate behaviors; offers alibis to place oneself in the best possible light, despite evident shortcomings or failures)

Antisocial Personality

Acting-out mechanism (e.g., inner tensions that might accrue by postponing the expression of offensive thoughts and malevolent actions are rarely constrained; socially repugnant impulses are not refashioned in sublimated forms, but are discharged directly in precipitous ways, usually without guilt or remorse)

Aggressive (Sadistic) Personality

Isolation mechanism (e.g., can be cold-blooded and remarkably detached from an awareness of the impact of own destructive acts; views objects of violation impersonally, as symbols of devalued groups devoid of human sensibilities)

Compulsive Personality

Reaction formation mechanism (e.g., repeatedly presents positive thoughts and socially commendable behaviors that are diametrically opposite one's deeper contrary and forbidden feelings; displays reasonableness and maturity when faced with circumstances that evoke anger or dismay in others)

Negativistic Personality

Displacement mechanism (e.g., discharges anger and other troublesome emotions either precipitously or by employing unconscious maneuvers to shift them from their instigator to settings or persons of lesser significance; vents disapproval by substitute or passive means, such as acting inept or perplexed or behaving in a forgetful or indolent manner)

Self-Defeating Personality

Exaggeration mechanism (e.g., repetitively recalls past injustices and anticipates future disappointments as a means of raising distress to homeostatic levels; undermines personal objectives and sabotages good fortunes so as to enhance or maintain accustomed level of suffering and pain)

Schizotypal Personality

Undoing mechanism (e.g., bizarre mannerisms and idiosyncratic thoughts appear to reflect a retraction or reversal of previous acts or ideas that have stirred feelings of anxiety, conflict, or guilt; ritualistic or magical behaviors serve to repent for or nullify assumed misdeeds or "evil" thoughts)

Borderline Personality

Regression mechanism (e.g., retreats under stress to developmentally earlier levels of anxiety tolerance, impulse control, and social adaptation; among adolescents, is unable to cope with adult demands and conflicts as evident in immature, if not increasingly infantile, behaviors)

Paranoid Personality

Projection mechanism (e.g., actively disowns undesirable personal traits and motives and attributes them to others; remains blind to one's own unattractive behaviors and characteristics, yet is overalert to, and hypercritical of, similar features in others)

Intellectualization is the defense mechanism of schizoid individuals. While cognitively impoverished, they tend to describe experiences in matter-of-fact ways without affect. Affectively oriented exploration may frighten these patients initially. Analytically, they fear intimacy to the point that they do not socialize. Slowly, however, the intellectualization must be broken down to reveal the fear of intimacy. Therapists may miss the asociality of the usual patient and react inappropriately.

The *projection* of those with paranoid personality disorder is obvious. The attribution of this patient's own problems onto others, including the therapist, makes for difficult therapy. The level of organization for this patient is severely impaired. The therapist must spend a good deal of time developing a trusting relationship with this patient while at the same time remaining empathically neutral.

Morphologic Organization

Again, some form of psychoanalytic psychotherapy is probably best for the treatment of the morphologic organization domain (see Table 12.11). Here the focus of attention is neither the objects nor the defenses of the psyche, but rather the construction qualities of the structure. Dorr (1995) suggests that the goal of therapy here is not to unlock the underlying conflicts, but to stop the destructive behavior. This can be stopped through "healthy" repression and sublimation. He believes that with personality-disordered patients the techniques of clarification and confrontation are particularly useful along with the traditional transference and countertransference interpretation.

The sadistic individual, for example, has an *eruptive* organization. While typically all elements of regulation are intact and the structure is cohesive and adequate, surges of aggression will break through. Therapy should be directed at the further detection and control of these impulses. Confrontation may be used to help the patient gain a sense of the effect of the eruptive affect on others. Additionally, the encouragement of secondary process thinking and the constraint that may bring to the aggression is indicated.

The *fragmented* organization of the schizotype requires an exercise in rebuilding. Ego boundaries are weak and permeable and the general condition of the organization is haphazard and incomplete. Therapy focuses on the development of basic ego functioning, including reality testing and judgment. What few resources are available morphologically should be reinforced and used to complete more regulatory and perceptual defenses. Like the schizophrenic, the morphology is weak and too many demands will be counterproductive.

Mood/Temperament

Mood within the personality disorders is again not well understood and often is the source of misdiagnosis. The moods can involve either the process of the affect or its content. Hyer, Brandsma, and Shealy (1995; Hyer & Associates, 1994) have used the treatment of mood and temperament as a tool in the treatment of personality disorders. They propose an experiential therapy which includes as its underlying theory and technique five elements. The first is the natural completion of unfinished affective business through Gestalt techniques such as two-chair procedures. The second is an active, empathic, client-centered reflection of feelings. The third is an evocative unfolding of the affective material through corrective emotional experiences. The fourth is focusing the expressive therapy on unearthing the unfinished anger. Finally, there is a schematic restructuring of the person by finishing the affective business.

TABLE 12.11. Morphologic Organization

Schizoid Personality

Undifferentiated organization (e.g., given an inner barrenness, a feeble drive to fulfill needs, and minimal pressures either to defend against or to resolve internal conflicts or cope with external demands, internal morphologic structures may best be characterized by their limited framework and sterile pattern)

Avoidant Personality

Fragile organization (e.g., a precarious complex of tortuous emotions depends almost exclusively on a single modality for its resolution and discharge: that of avoidance, escape, and fantasy; hence, when faced with personal risks, new opportunities, or unanticipated stress, few morphologic structures are available to deploy and few back-up positions can be reverted to short of regressive decompensation)

Depressive Personality

Depleted organization (e.g., the scaffold for morphologic structures is markedly weakened, with coping methods enervated and defensive strategies impoverished, emptied, and devoid of their vigor and focus, resulting in a diminished, if not exhausted, capacity to initiate action and regulate affect, impulse, and conflict)

Dependent Personality

Inchoate organization (e.g., owing to entrusting others with the responsibility to fulfill needs and to cope with adult tasks, there is both a deficient morphologic structure and a lack of diversity in internal regulatory controls, leaving a miscellany of relatively undeveloped and undifferentiated adaptive abilities, as well as an elementary system for functioning independently)

Histrionic Personality

Disjointed organization (e.g., there exists a loosely knit and carelessly united morphologic structure in which processes of internal regulation and control are scattered and unintegrated, with ad hoc methods for restraining impulses, coordinating defenses, and resolving conflicts, leading to mechanisms that must of necessity be broad and sweeping to maintain psychic cohesion and stability and, when successful, only further isolate and disconnect thoughts, feelings, and actions)

Narcissistic Personality

Spurious organization (e.g., morphologic structures underlying coping and defensive strategies tend to be flimsy and transparent, appear more substantial and dynamically orchestrated than they are in fact, regulating impulses only marginally, channeling needs with minimal restraint, and creating an inner world in which conflicts are dismissed, failures are quickly redeemed, and self-pride is effortlessly reasserted)

Antisocial Personality

Unruly organization (e.g., inner morphologic structures to contain drive and impulse are noted by their paucity, as are efforts to curb refractory energies and attitudes, leading to easily transgressed controls, low thresholds for hostile or erotic discharge, few subliminatory channels, unfettered self-expression, and a marked intolerance of delay or frustration)

Aggressive (Sadistic) Personality

Eruptive organization (e.g., despite a generally cohesive morphologic structure composed of routinely adequate modulating controls, defenses, and expressive channels, surging powerful and explosive energies of an aggressive and sexual nature threaten to produce precipitous outbursts which periodically overwhelm and overrun otherwise competent restraints)

(continued)

TABLE 12.11. (*continued*)

Compulsive Personality

Compartmentalized organization (e.g., morphologic structures are rigidly organized in a tightly consolidated system that is clearly partitioned into numerous, distinct, and segregated constellations of drive, memory, and cognition, with few open channels to permit interplay among these components)

Negativistic Personality

Divergent organization (e.g., there is a clear division in the pattern of morphologic structures such that coping and defensive maneuvers are often directed toward incompatible goals, leaving major conflicts unresolved and full psychic cohesion often impossible by virtue of the fact that fulfillment of one drive or need inevitably nullifies or reverses another)

Self-Defeating Personality

Inverted organization (e.g., owing to a significant reversal of the pain–pleasure polarity, morphologic structures have contrasting and dual qualities, one more or less conventional, the other its obverse, resulting in a repetitive undoing of affect and intention, a transposing of channels of need gratification with those leading to frustration, and engaging in actions which produce antithetical, if not self-sabotaging, consequences)

Schizotypal Personality

Fragmented organization (e.g., possesses permeable ego boundaries; coping and defensive operations are haphazardly ordered in a loose assemblage of morphologic structures, leading to desultory actions in which primitive thoughts and affects are discharged directly, with few reality-based sublimations and significantly further disintegrations, into a psychotic structural level, likely under even modest stress)

Borderline Personality

Split organization (e.g., inner structures exist in a sharply segmented and conflictful configuration in which a marked lack of consistency and congruence are seen among elements; levels of consciousness often shift and result in rapid movements across boundaries that usually separate contrasting percepts, memories, and affects, all of which lead to periodic schisms in what limited psychic order and cohesion may otherwise be present, often resulting in transient, stress-related psychotic episodes)

Paranoid Personality

Inelastic organization (e.g., systemic constriction and inflexibility of undergirding morphologic structures, as well as rigidly fixed channels of defensive coping, conflict mediation, and need gratification create an overstrung and taut frame that is so uncompromising in its accommodation to changing circumstances that unanticipated stressors are likely to precipitate either explosive outbursts or inner shatterings)

New to the DSM-IV is the depressive personality disorder. Millon (1994) sees the mood of the depressive as *melancholic*. The focus of the therapy should therefore focus on the melancholia with the expectation that it is caused by an unfinished affect. Should anger be found to be the root of this, the anger can be played out to its natural conclusion and the patient can reintegrate whatever experience has caused this.

The person with borderline personality disorder evidences a *labile* mood. Here the content changes often, with the only common core being change. As an emotional expres-

TABLE 12.12. Mood/Temperament

Schizoid Personality

Apathetic mood (e.g., is emotionally unexcitable, exhibiting an intrinsic unfeeling, cold, and stark quality; reports weak affectionate or erotic needs, rarely displaying warm or intense feelings, and is apparently unable to experience most affects (pleasure, sadness, or anger) in any depth)

Avoidant Personality

Anguished mood (e.g., describes constant and confusing undercurrent of tension, sadness, and anger; vacillates between desire for affection, fear of rebuff, embarrassment, and numbness of feeling)

Depressive Personality

Melancholic mood (e.g., is typically woeful, gloomy, tearful, joyless, and morose; characteristically worrisome and brooding, the low spirits and dysphoric state rarely remit)

Dependent Personality

Pacific mood (e.g., is characteristically warm, tender, and noncompetitive; timidly avoids social tension and interpersonal conflicts)

Histrionic Personality

Fickle mood (e.g., displays rapidly shifting and shallow emotions; is vivacious, animated, and impetuous and exhibits tendencies to be easily enthused and as easily angered or bored)

Narcissistic Personality

Insouciant mood (e.g., manifests a general air of nonchalance, imperturbability, and feigned tranquility; appears coolly unimpressionable or buoyantly optimistic, except when narcissistic confidence is shaken, at which time either rage, shame, or emptiness is briefly displayed)

Antisocial Personality

Callous mood (e.g., is insensitive, irritable, and aggressive, as expressed in a wide-ranging deficit in social charitableness, human compassion, or personal remorse; exhibits a coarse incivility as well as an offensive, if not reckless, disregard for the safety of self or others)

Aggressive (Sadistic) Personality

Hostile mood (e.g., has an excitable and irritable temper which flares readily into contentious argument and physical belligerence; is cruel, mean-spirited, and fractious, willing to do harm or even persecute others to gets one's way)

Compulsive Personality

Solemn mood (e.g., is unrelaxed, tense, joyless, and grim; restrains warm feelings and keeps most emotions under tight control)

Negativistic Personality

Irritable mood (e.g., frequently touchy, temperamental, and peevish, followed in turn by sullen and moody withdrawal; is often petulant and impatient, unreasonably scorns those in authority, and reports being annoyed easily or frustrated by many)

(continued)

TABLE 12.12. (*continued*)

Self-Defeating Personality

Dysphoric mood (e.g., experiences a complex mix of emotions: at times anxiously apprehensive, at others forlorn and mournful, to feeling anguished and tormented; intentionally displays a plaintive and wistful appearance, frequently to induce guilt and discomfort in others)

Schizotypal Personality

Distraught or insentient mood (e.g., excessively apprehensive and ill at ease, particularly in social encounters; agitated and anxiously watchful, evincing distrust of others and suspicion of their motives that persists despite growing familiarity; *or* manifests drab, apathetic, sluggish, joyless, and spiritless appearance; reveals marked deficiencies in face-to-face rapport and emotional expression)

Borderline Personality

Labile mood (e.g., fails to accord unstable mood level with external reality; has either marked shifts from normality to depression to excitement, or has periods of dejection and apathy interspersed with episodes of inappropriate and intense anger, as well as brief spells of anxiety or euphoria)

Paranoid Personality

Irascible mood (e.g., displays a cold, sullen, churlish, and humorless demeanor; attempts to appear unemotional and objective but is edgy, envious, jealous, and quick to take personal offense and react angrily)

sion deficit, it is reflective of such things as fear of abandonment. Experiential therapy can focus on any of the affects and follow them to the core. This core may unfortunately be a fear of change (change of the lability). Here, due to the morphological problems, restructuring is much more difficult.

The preceding is meant to show the application of a number of therapeutic techniques to the personality disorders. While a number of authors have been referenced with specific techniques, the importance of the exercise is to show the specific symptoms and treatment targets for each of the personality disorders across a wide range of domains.

SUMMARY

It has been the intent of this chapter to do two things. First, the personality disorders were presented as important in the diagnosis and treatment of patients. They or Axis I disorders may be (1) the focus of treatment, (2) ignored, (3) guarded against, or (4) used to further the treatment of a comorbid disorder. The second half of the chapter provided Millon's domains of diagnosis from a therapeutic perspective. Indeed, the very symptom of a disorder should probably be the target of the treatment. Eight therapy approaches were provided to elucidate the eight domain-specific targets. The MCMI-III is the best available method to bring together assessment and therapy. While at first blush this may appear limiting, it in actuality opens to many schools of thought the use of objective testing.

REFERENCES

American Psychiatric Association. (1968). *Diagnostic and statistical manual of mental disorders* (2nd ed.). Washington, DC: Author.

American Psychiatric Association. (1980). *Diagnostic and statistical manual of mental disorders* (3rd ed.). Washington, DC: Author.

American Psychiatric Association. (1987). *Diagnostic and statistical manual of mental disorders* (3rd ed., rev.). Washington, DC: Author.

American Psychiatric Association. (1994). *Diagnostic and statistical manual of mental disorders* (4th ed.). Washington, DC: Author.

Choca, J., Shanley, L., & Van Denburg, E. (1992). *Interpretive guide to the Millon Clinical Multiaxial Inventory*. Washington, DC: American Psychological Association.

Craig, R. (1995). Interpersonal psychotherapy and MCMI-III-based assessment. In P. Retzlaff (Ed.), *Tactical psychotherapy of the personality disorders: An MCMI-III based approach*. Needham Heights, MA: Allyn & Bacon.

Donat, D. (1995). The use of the MCMI-III in behavior therapy. In P. Retzlaff (Ed.), *Tactical psychotherapy of the personality disorders: An MCMI-III based approach*. Needham Heights, MA: Allyn & Bacon.

Dorr, D. (1995). Psychoanalytic psychotherapy of the personality disorders toward morphologic change. In P. Retzlaff (Ed.), *Tactical psychotherapy of the personality disorders: An MCMI-III based approach*. Needham Heights, MA: Allyn & Bacon.

Everly, G. (1995). Domain oriented personality theory. In P. Retzlaff (Ed.), *Tactical psychotherapy of the personality disorders: An MCMI-III based approach*. Needham Heights, MA: Allyn & Bacon.

Hyer, L., & Associates. (1994). *Trauma victim: Theoretical issues and practical suggestions*. Muncie, IN: Accelerated Development.

Hyer, L., Brandsma, J., & Shealy, L. (1995). Experiential mood therapy with the MCMI-III. In P. Retzlaff (Ed.), *Tactical psychotherapy of the personality disorders: An MCMI-III based approach*. Needham Heights, MA: Allyn & Bacon.

Kubacki, S., & Smith, P. (1995). An intersubjective approach to assessing and treating ego defenses using the MCMI-III. In P. Retzlaff (Ed.), *Tactical psychotherapy of the personality disorders: An MCMI-III based approach*. Needham Heights, MA: Allyn & Bacon.

Lazarus, A. (1981). *The practice of multimodal therapy*. New York: McGraw-Hill.

McCann, J. (1995). The MCMI-III and treatment of the self. In P. Retzlaff (Ed.), *Tactical psychotherapy of the personality disorders: An MCMI-III based approach*. Needham Heights, MA: Allyn & Bacon.

Millon, T. (1990). *Toward a new personology*. New York: Wiley.

Millon, T., Millon C., & Davis, R. (1994). *Millon Clinical Multiaxial Inventory—III manual*. Minneapolis: National Computer Systems.

Millon, T., Everly, G., & Davis, R. (1993). How can knowledge of psychopathology facilitate psychotherapy integration. *Journal of Psychotherapy Integration*, 3(4), 331–352.

Norcross, J., & Goldfried, M. (1992). *Handbook of psychotherapy integration*. New York: Basic Books.

Retzlaff, P., Ofman, P., Hyer, L., & Matheson, S. (1994). MCMI-II highpoint codes: Severe personality disorder and clinical syndrome extensions. *Journal of Clinical Psychology*, 50, 228-234.

Retzlaff, P. (1995a). Clinical application of the MCMI-III. In P. Retzlaff (Ed.), *Tactical psychotherapy of the personality disorders: An MCMI-III based approach*. Needham Heights, MA: Allyn & Bacon.

Retzlaff, P. (Ed.). (1995b). *Tactical psychotherapy of the personality disorders: An MCMI-III based approach*. Needham Heights, MA: Allyn & Bacon.

Retzlaff, P., & Bromley, S. (1991). A multi-test alcoholic taxonomy: Canonical coefficient clusters. *Journal of Clinical Psychology*, 47, 135-145.

Retzlaff, P., & Bromley, S. (1994). The counseling of personality disorders. In J. L. Ronch & W. Van Ornum (Eds.), *The Continuum encyclopedia of counseling*. New York: Continuum/Crossroads Publishing.

Retzlaff, P., Ofman, P., Hyer, L., & Matheson, S. (1994). MCMI-II highpoint codes: Severe personality disorder and clinical syndrome extensions. *Journal of Clinical Psychology, 50*, 228-234.

Van Denburg, E. (1995). Object relations theory and the MCMI-III. In P. Retzlaff (Ed.), *Tactical psychotherapy of the personality disorders: An MCMI-III based approach*. Needham Heights, MA: Allyn & Bacon.

Will, T. (1995). Cognitive therapy and the MCMI-III. In P. Retzlaff (Ed.), *Tactical psychotherapy of the personality disorders: An MCMI-III based approach*. Needham Heights, MA: Allyn & Bacon.

13

Using the MCMI in Treating Couples

A. RODNEY NURSE

Some of the most frequent complaints of clients asking for psychological help have to do with their marriage or their couple relationship. People are regularly questioning the quality of their relationships. The extent of this questioning and the solutions couples reach are reflected in statistics indicating that the number of divorces doubled annually from the early 1960s until the 1980s (Schwartz & Kaslow, 1997) and in demographers' predictions that 40–60% of all current marriages will end in divorce (Ahrons, 1994).

While these complaints about relationship difficulties are sometimes dealt with only in individual therapy because of a spouse's or partner's lack of cooperation or unavailability, and although some spouses (such as those with extreme battering problems) may need to be seen initially individually (Martin, 1995), overall research findings and clinical experience indicate that most couples should be seen as couples when there are couple relationship problems. For example, a recent review of research findings concludes that for depressed persons marital therapy aimed at enhancing marital satisfaction in a discordant marriage is more effective than is individual therapy (Beach & Anderson, 1995).

Given that couple therapy for a couple problem is thus often the treatment of choice, in planning treatment strategy it is to the advantage of the clinician to quickly determine not only the personality styles or disorders of the individual partners, but also how the meshing of their personalities is likely to meet or fail to meet the needs of the individuals (Nurse, in press). These needs are reflected in the various domains of personality, which in turn supply hypotheses on which to plan psychological interventions.

It is also of help to the clinician to scan for the presence of symptoms or problem mood states such as anxiety or depression. While these are often mentioned in an initial evaluative contact, some symptom or mood state problems may be out of awareness or denied, such as alcoholism or manic episodes. The sooner the clinician is aware of these possibilities, the better, to plan interventions and anticipate possible pitfalls on the therapeutic road.

To all of these concerns MCMI-III findings have something to say, and in many instances the MCMI provides truly salient information. It is the purpose of this chapter to present an approach for interpreting MCMI-III profiles of couples together with descriptions of treatment planning and interventions with typical complementary couple styles or disorders. MCMI-III results taken from treated couples are discussed. Examples reflect both intrapersonal problems and interlocking couple interpersonal dynamics. These are considered in the context of pertinent individual and family life cycle developmental issues.

COUPLE INTERPRETATIONS

After having examined the MCMI-III profile of each partner for validity, response style, and overall meanings of significant scores, perhaps using approaches described elsewhere (Millon, Millon, & Davis, 1994; Retzlaff, 1995), the individual profile information should be compared for consistencies or inconsistencies with other available information, such as presenting complaints, socioeconomic levels, and occupational and general personal histories (including paying particular attention to individual life cycle issues). With couples it is especially important to have obtained fairly detailed information about the functioning of the family of origin. Many adults are only dimly aware or are even unaware of the impact of unresolved family of origin issues on their relationships. Perhaps it should go without saying that a careful history of the couple relationship itself should be obtained.

While the general functionality of the individual's personality style or disorder may well have been considered when each individual profile was first inspected, it is important to look at the two profiles together to determine if there has been or is now a functionality of personality patterns in their relationship. As an example, an actor's histrionic–narcissistic disorder may be quite functional occupationally, or even career-enhancing. The compulsive style or even disorder of the actor's partner may be occupationally helpful in the field of accounting. While initially the couple's styles might have drawn them together (him to her excitement, she to his stability), later, well into their marriage, their styles may no longer be functional. Instead they may prove most problematic and conflictual in household management and parenting responsibilities. What was originally an attraction now serves to repel and erode the marriage.

Couple therapists and counselors commonly report this seemingly paradoxical observation that what initially was most attractive in a marriage relationship may turn out to repel. What was her exciting (histrionic) style or disorder (in the example above) turns into a series of annoying crises; his comfortable stability turns into boring (compulsive) sameness.

It may also be that one partner's personality pattern has, over time and life experience, become significantly modified so that the first partner's personality pattern needs are not met. Serial monogamy is now one of the acceptable and common marital patterns throughout the life cycle (Ahrons, 1994). Or it may be that a change in living context, such as the arrival of the first baby, will change the valence of energy forces in the couple relationship in even the most functional of marriages (Cowan & Cowan, 1992). The marital and family systems have thereby become unbalanced.

Having inspected the individual profiles and considered their overall possible functional relationships in the context of their marital history and family of origin information, a more in-depth analysis of each partner's relationships is made possible by referring to the clinical domains of the prototype of the highest significant personality pattern score(s) present. These clinical domains are categorized through four levels: *behavioral, phenomenological, intrapsychic,* and *biophysical* (Millon, Millon, & Davis, 1994; Millon, 1996).

With couple interpretations it is particularly important to consider first the behavioral level, divided into *expressive behavior* and *interpersonal behavior*. That level is available for therapist observation and ordinarily is the focus of the couple's complaints. From that level, inferences can be drawn about linkages with features of domains falling in the other levels. This analysis permits the development of more detailed descriptions of the interacting personality patterns of the couple and provides a basis for psychotherapeutic planning and intervention.

When two or more scores are significant in one or both profiles, as is frequently the case, special attention needs to be paid as to how they blend. Millon (1996) provides a framework for considering blends. In addition, Choca, Shanley, and Van Denburg (1992) present useful 3-point code descriptions based on their concept that all iterations of the MCMI may best be thought of as measuring styles.

For those profiles indicating more severe personality disorders (schizotypal, borderline, and paranoid) a more generally dysfunctional pattern is anticipated. These may require a more complex, in-depth evaluation using additional methods (such as the Rorschach), and, more than likely, a more involved pattern of multimethod treatment.

Couple Therapy

In the intake session with the couple the therapist can hear the complaints of the partners, observe the interaction, and make an initial contract for therapy which includes an agreement to take the MCMI-III. Next an individual session is conducted with each partner, during which the MCMI-III results are discussed with particular relevance to complaints presented in the conjoint session, and treatment planning and forming an individual alliance with each partner occur. The therapist undertakes in the next conjoint session to have them share with each other their understandings about themselves as reflected in the MCMI-III discussions with the therapist. The therapist helps with clarification of the content of the communication and is alert to the occasional behavioral acting out of the content with the partner even as that person tries to verbally convey personal information. MCMI-III results form a basis for setting priorities with the couple for the therapeutic work in subsequent sessions. As therapy continues the therapist makes references as appropriate back to the original goals set for therapy as impacted by the MCMI-III findings.

As with individual therapy, Millon's theoretical formulation may be usefully applied to couple therapy. Whether planning long-range strategy or designing tactics for specific sessions, a primary aim is to balance the polarities—pain–pleasure, passive–active, and self–other. These polarities are discussed in relation to each personality disorder in Millon's recent book (1996). Using this reference, the therapist can intervene to strengthen the weaker polarities and lessen the impact of the stronger ones. With this concept in mind the therapist can reinforce any spouse's action that helps balance the weaker polarities of his or her partner, in addition to the therapist directly helping a spouse to strengthen their own weaker polarity. For example, when the partner of the histrionic does not respond immediately to an impulsive statement, but instead asks the histrionic to stop and think and really pay attention to what he needs, the therapist can point out how helpful this calm, nonjudgmental spouse's comment can be. The histrionic's self polarity becomes reinforced. The partner does not blame the histrionic.

With couples, when one partner has a personality pattern score suggesting a disorder (base rate [BR] = 85+) accompanied by a second score indicating a trait (BR = 75–84), and the other partner has a highest personality pattern score which is identical to the secondary score for the first partner, an interesting phenomena may occur. In the couple sessions what may appear as a blatant display of the highest characteristic of the one partner seems not to be observed or confronted by the other. For example, if a wife has a second high score indicating narcissistic traits and her spouse peaks on narcissistic disorder, what appear to the therapist to be arrogant statements of entitlement by the husband may simply be accepted as a given by the wife. Presumably, were the wife to challenge him on these statements, she would have to look at those same aspects in herself. A comparison of the profiles and an alertness by the therapist in the couple session will reveal the importance in the couples interaction of the narcissism dimension, which for the wife might be of only minor importance in interactions with others. The unsuspecting couple therapist, unaware of this collusive dynamic, may attempt to directly challenge this couple's narcissistic dynamic, only to be turned against by both partners! With foreknowledge, however, the therapist can work around this collusion and intervene subtly with this strong couple relationship dimension.

The remainder of this chapter presents MCMI-IIIs for couples often found in outpatient practices. They are presented with the aim of providing a pattern for interpreting MCMI-III couple profiles in general and for designing specific therapeutic tactics and longrange strategies. The first example models carrying through the entire analytical process in detail. Each example thereafter focuses increasingly on the couple interaction and couple therapy and less on the intricacies of individual profile interpretation.

EXAMPLES OF THREE COUPLES

Bud and Nancy: Avoidant/Histrionic

Bud, age 45, was in a corporate, technical, middle-level position. Nancy, 30, did receptionist/clerical work part time. After an exciting courtship and later the birth of their son, Bud and Nancy engaged in an increasing number of fights and a series of outright separations. They came to therapy as a last-ditch effort to see if they could reconcile and learn to live together "for the sake of our son." Bud complained that Nancy was no longer interested in him, but instead seemed energized to flirt (if not more, he suspected) with other men. "Bud is just a bore," stated Nancy. She said that he seemed insanely jealous (but, though complaining, she sounded subtly pleased).

Bud's MCMI Profile

The Validity or response style scores in Bud's MCMI-III, given in Figure 13.1, were within acceptable guidelines. He had no severe personality pathology significant score. Clearly, his Avoidant score placed him just within a level predicting that he suffered from an avoidant personality disorder. Thus, one would anticipate "a pattern of social inhibition, feelings of inadequacy, and a hypersensitivity to negative evaluation" (American Psychiatric Association, 1994, p. 629).

The prediction was that, given his avoidant dynamic, at a behavioral level Bud was *expressively fretful*. Italic type refers to domain descriptors (Millon, Millon, & Davis, 1994, 1996). He conveyed a hesitant, worried appearance. He constantly scanned to detect clues signaling potential dangers so that he may have responded adequately to Nancy. He was *interpersonally aversive*; thus, he kept an anxious personal distance from Nancy, becoming involved only when he was sure of her acceptance. When the relationship was going well his clues were constantly positive and he could, being sure of acceptance, approach Nancy more directly.

At a phenomenological level Bud experienced many distracting thoughts and was well aware of his feelings of social inadequacy and his sense of limited satisfactions in life. Nancy could have helped provide him with more satisfactions. Sometimes, when the relationship was difficult, he withdrew into fantasy (intrapsychic level), yet his personality organiza-

CATEGORY		SCORE		PROFILE OF BR SCORES					DIAGNOSTIC SCALES
		RAW	BR	0	60	75	85	115	
MODIFYING INDICES	X	81	52						DISCLOSURE
	Y	12	55						DESIRABILITY
	Z	5	49						DEBASEMENT
CLINICAL PERSONALITY PATTERNS	1	5	60						SCHIZOID
	2A	15	85						AVOIDANT
	2B	5	68						DEPRESSIVE
	3	8	70						DEPENDENT
	4	10	38						HISTRIONIC
	5	8	37						NARCISSISTIC
	6A	5	38						ANTISOCIAL
	6B	12	65						AGGRESSIVE (SADISTIC)
	7	12	44						COMPULSIVE
	8A	2	15						PASSIVE-AGGRESSIVE
	8B	2	40						SELF-DEFEATING
SEVERE PERSONALITY PATHOLOGY	S	2	40						SCHIZOTYPAL
	C	4	40						BORDERLINE
	P	2	24						PARANOID
CLINICAL SYNDROMES	A	3	60						ANXIETY DISORDER
	H	1	30						SOMATOFORM DISORDER
	N	6	62						BIPOLAR: MANIC DISORDER
	D	2	40						DYSTHYMIC DISORDER
	B	2	30						ALCOHOL DEPENDENCE
	T	3	45						DRUG DEPENDENCE
	R	1	15						POST-TRAUMATIC STRESS
SEVERE SYNDROMES	SS	3	45						THOUGHT DISORDER
	CC	1	20						MAJOR DEPRESSION
	PP	0	0						DELUSIONAL DISORDER

FIGURE 13.1. Bud's MCMI-III profile.

tion remained unstable and was accompanied by a regular experience of an *anguished mood* (biophysical level). He continued to be caught on the horns of dilemma: needing her, yet fearing to approach her out of fear of rejection. The presumption was that this dynamic was a core aspect of his relationship with Nancy. Nancy, it will be seen, had a pattern such that she could allay many of his fears, bolster his sense of self, and provide a stimulus that kept him out of his anguished state, at least early in their relationship.

Nancy's MCMI Profile

In surveying Nancy's profile, presented in Figure 13.2, her Desirability scale score was elevated, probably reflective of an other-directed personality needing to be accepted and

CATEGORY		SCORE		PROFILE OF BR SCORES					DIAGNOSTIC SCALES
		RAW	BR	0	60	75	85	115	
MODIFYING INDICES	X	56	30						DISCLOSURE
	Y	17	80						DESIRABILITY
	Z	3	42						DEBASEMENT
CLINICAL PERSONALITY PATTERNS	1	0	4						SCHIZOID
	2A	1	13						AVOIDANT
	2B	4	31						DEPRESSIVE
	3	1	11						DEPENDENT
	4	20	93						HISTRIONIC
	5	15	72						NARCISSISTIC
	6A	1	16						ANTISOCIAL
	6B	0	4						AGGRESSIVE (SADISTIC)
	7	17	71						COMPULSIVE
	8A	2	17						PASSIVE-AGGRESSIVE
	8B	0	4						SELF-DEFEATING
SEVERE PERSONALITY PATHOLOGY	S	0	3						SCHIZOTYPAL
	C	0	3						BORDERLINE
	P	1	18						PARANOID
CLINICAL SYNDROMES	A	3	39						ANXIETY DISORDER
	H	1	12						SOMATOFORM DISORDER
	N	2	27						BIPOLAR: MANIC DISORDER
	D	1	10						DYSTHYMIC DISORDER
	B	0	3						ALCOHOL DEPENDENCE
	T	1	28						DRUG DEPENDENCE
	R	2	23						POST-TRAUMATIC STRESS
SEVERE SYNDROMES	SS	2	20						THOUGHT DISORDER
	CC	0	3						MAJOR DEPRESSION
	PP	2	63						DELUSIONAL DISORDER

FIGURE 13.2. Nancy's MCMI-III profile.

liked; this high score was consistent with a histrionic personality dynamic. While her significantly low Disclosure score raised the question of profile validity, if reasonably valid, her profile may have indicated an attitude of extreme openness to others. One hypothesis was that, if Nancy was so extraordinarily open, it may mean that she had a simplistic view of herself as without inner conflict, allowing her to share (with unusual ease) extensively with others. It may mean, too, that she was simply not reflective on her own psychological state. She may not have acknowledged that there could be aspects of herself that were out of her own awareness.

If the conclusion is reached that Nancy's profile had a degree of validity sufficient to permit interpretation of the clinical personality pattern and clinical pathology scales, analysis continues (see Figure 13.2). No severe personality pathology scales were significant. As to clinical personality patterns, one scale, Histrionic, was high enough (BR = 93) to propose a personality disorder, in her case a histrionic personality disorder. This personality disorder would point to "a pattern of excessive emotionality and attention seeking" (American Psychiatric Association, 1994, p. 629).

With her apparent disorder, it was important to look first at behavioral level manifestations. At this level her behavior was seen as *expressively dramatic*. She tended to be overreactive and volatile. While engaging, she was at the same time provocative. Intolerant of inactivity, she was emotional, seeking excitement in a pursuit of pleasure. She was a "dancing girl" in her relationship with Bud, or at least she was in the beginning. She could experience Bud's anxious attention, focusing on her every aspect, which she interpreted as his being intrigued with her, which of course he was. She did not understand initially that his focus on her had a defensive quality wherein he had an underlying fear of rejection, and so he was driven to be attentive.

At the behavioral level, she also *sought attention interpersonally*. Bud could provide this in abundance. She actively elicited praise and manipulated him into responding positively to her. An important aspect of this dynamic was that she could be demanding, flirtatious, and seductive, particularly when she needed to be the center of attention. Bud loved this aspect, and she felt needed and not in danger of abandonment.

Considering her phenomenological level, she was *cognitively flighty*, externally focused. She integrated poorly and was scattered in learning. In attending to others she was overly suggestible and overly attended to fleeting events. Her thinking was global and impressionistic; therefore, her speech was overly general; this lack of exactness confused the couple's communication. Thoughtless judgments could result from these combinations of characteristics. She correctly viewed herself as sociable, but may not have understood that she was actually somewhat ineffective interpersonally in that her relationships were rather superficial. Her relationship with Bud did not need to be anything other than superficial initially because in-depth demands were not placed on her as the relationship was in its early stages.

At an intrapsychic level Nancy's internal psychological organization was disjointed and disorganized. A major defense was *dissociation*. She was busy distracting herself by her high level of activity, which helped her avoid coming to grips with repressed or excluded memories and conflicts. When there were disquieting aspects to her relationship with Bud, she could take her mind off of them and focus on other things, such as entertaining him or flirting with somebody else to reassure herself. From a biosocial level standpoint Nancy was characterized by *fickle moods* ever changing in keeping with her ungrounded psychological state.

Bud and Nancy's Relationship

In reconstructing the beginning of the relationship of Bud and Nancy, an initially strong mutual attraction was clear. Bud, although hesitant and very fearful of rejection, was at the same time very needy. Nancy was dramatic, expressive, entertaining, sexual, and focused strongly (literally and figuratively) on seducing Bud. He was reassured by her manipulative efforts to control him. She must really want him, he believed, not being aware that she went into high gear in all relationships, focusing so much on the other person.

Nancy found his constant attention to her filling her own sense of self. She didn't realize that he was scanning anxiously for clues that related to acceptance and rejection; she simply experienced the attention. Even though she was very sensitive to the behavior of others, her lack of introspectiveness did not allow for a very complex construction of human behavior, either hers or others'. She successfully entertained him, thereby allaying her fears of abandonment.

In their interaction Nancy's pleasure-seeking orientation provided for Bud something of the pleasure he tended to deny himself, making Nancy very special for him, as well as reinforcing his dependence on her. Nancy experienced this increased connection in their relationship, furthering her sense of security, helping to balance her shifting feelings and thoughts.

In the case of Bud and Nancy the difference in age provided an initial reinforcement of coquettish childlike behavior in Nancy and solid, parentlike caregiving behavior on the part of Bud. In fact, Nancy felt rescued (like a princess) and Bud experienced being the rescuer, (the knight), thus reinforcing the somewhat shaky gender identity of both partners. From this relationship came more confidence to face the world and hence more success, which could in part be attributed to this buttressing of their personality dynamics by their relationship.

When their son was born, however, the supportive dyad changed to a triangle. As the partners refocused their attention on the new arrival, they both experienced losing attention from the other. While this is a necessary adjustment for all couples who are new parents, for this couple it was devastating. Nancy was no longer the princess; she had to be the mother. Her primary activity was no longer to entertain. Although she provided significant nurturance for her baby, she lacked reinforcement for her sense of self. Bud experienced his protecting side with the baby. However, lacking the security of experiencing Nancy's constant attention focused on him, he retreated. Nancy experienced feeling abandoned, confirming her worst fears. Periodically, out of her hurt and anger, she exploded. This drove Bud further away and he scanned ever more closely in an effort to pick up clues with which to sense Nancy's even more rapidly changing moods. His anger built as he experienced rejection. Their once happy, "idyllic" relationship had changed to a field of resentments, overt spats, remorse, reconciliation, and buildup of resentments, etc. As a last ditch effort to recover their relationship, Bud and Nancy sought marital therapy.

Strategy and Tactics for Couple Therapy

Given the interlocking nature of the personality disorders of Bud and Nancy, couples therapy conducted by a male/female cotherapist team was an ideal mode of approach for helping both, regardless of the future of their marital relationship. A joint intake provided the therapists with a first-hand experience of their interaction and their complaints and they set a contract for their therapeutic work.

In the next step the male cotherapist met individually with Bud and the female cotherapist with Nancy, focusing on discussing the results of their MCMI-IIIs. Separate reactions to the inventory results were obtained without direct influence of the partner, thus underlining their individuality. It was particularly important for Bud and Nancy to have this individual contact to give the same-sex therapist the opportunity to experience each in relationship to the therapist without their need to be so attuned to the threat of either abandonment or rejection. The therapists had then the braking force of calling on a more mature Nancy and Bud when, in the course of couple therapy, accusations and generally immature behaviors appeared. The therapist in this inventory interpretation session also collected necessary background information and worked to deepen the therapeutic relationship with each partner.

An emphasis was placed on the double-edged nature of their personality patterns (the word disorders was not used). In Nancy's case her social, gregarious qualities were underscored as providing her with good initial contact with people, such as in her receptionist activities and the ability to quickly engage men. At the same time, it was stressed that she seemed to have lost sight of her own needs in her marriage, and a major task was for her to learn to be less focused on her spouse and more on herself (addressing the self–other balance).

For Bud the discussion of MCMI-III results centered on his lifelong pattern of needing reassurance to enter and stay with a relationship. While this pattern provided time to avoid looking before he might leap, certainly sometimes a positive, his withdrawal pattern had made for isolation, compounding the general lack of satisfaction in his life. He was encouraged to risk in the relationship (addressing the pain–pleasure polarity).

After the inventory interpretation session, came a couple session in which Nancy and Bud were asked to share what had struck them as important from discussing their inventory results in the interpretation session. This tactic helped draw attention to their individual characteristics while at the same time focusing on their relationship. Nancy shared about her overemphasis on others, her fear of abandonment, and her avoidance of paying attention to her self. Bud talked about his incessant worry of being accepted or rejected. They were encouraged to confront their own neediness with awareness of the problems of abandonment and rejection. During this exchange the therapist picked up on tying elements of their style (or disorder) into the difficulties in their relationship, confirming their individual responsibilities for this two-edged nature of their personality patterns and helping them to avoid concentrating on the other person too frequently. This process analysis assisted in setting specific goals such as learning to identify and halt their escalation of behaviors into nonproductive fights. This included for Nancy, paying more attention to herself and for Bud, not withdrawing automatically.

The female cotherapist, during the early sessions, actively helped Nancy with her overreactivity and her overfocus on Bud. Thus, the therapist assisted her in becoming more tolerant of how he "pushes her buttons" in the couple's sessions. She was encouraged to be less automatically active and, in effect, to be more passive. The therapist actively intervened with her in session by saying "Stop, think what you want." The therapist also pointed out how she needed to pay more attention to herself and less to Bud. The attention of both therapists in the session and her need to please she enabled her to respond with beginning attempts at self-reflection. She learned to internalize the "stop" signal so that she could more readily depend on herself and not the therapist.

As Bud felt this withdrawal of attention from himself, the male co-therapist helped him understand that Nancy's movement was not intended as rejection (despite his experience of it as rejection), but rather it was simply Nancy's need to attend to herself. As both therapists accepted Bud's concerns and anxiety and were not rejecting, Bud developed more tolerance for being with himself positively and not feeling hurt when Nancy paid attention to herself. When Nancy did dramatically strike out, both therapists said to Bud,"that's just Nancy," which kept him from personalizing her comment, giving an angry retort and withdrawing. Bud also learned to give himself internal instructions, reminding himself at times that "that's just Nancy."

During these couple sessions the therapists made use of the couple's interaction to avoid rigidly aligning with one or the other spouse. The therapists were careful to be very precise so as to counteract global thinking for Nancy and problems of ambiguity for Bud. The therapist stopped the couple from hurling verbal complaints at each other. This served to protect Bud so that his tendency for hurt withdrawal was lessened. It also short-circuited Nancy's tendency to restimulate herself by dramatic, angry accusations. In the sessions this led to a search for ways to stop the escalation at home and save the issues for discussion in therapy sessions.

They gradually began to join forces in planning for and actively sharing the parenting of their baby. They both gained satisfaction and reinforcement from the other for sacrificing some needs to provide a consistent, close, and less agitated home for their baby. Their disorders were at least modestly modified, and they were on their way across "the great divide," as Cowan and Cowan (1992) have described that journey from being a couple to becoming a family.

Bob and Kim: Compulsive/Narcissistic

Bob, 52, and Kim, 50, had been married for more than 25 years. They had one older daughter living away from home and a younger daughter who was a sophomore at a college at the other end of their state. Kim arrived at an initial interview out of breath, hurrying, and indicated that her family physician referred her for help with her "worries." She acknowledged her uneasiness and discouraged feelings, apologizing that she is usually more poised.

She stated that she returned to teaching grade school when her youngest went off to college. The more the interview progressed, the more she complained about her husband, a financial investor, who, she said, always assumed his work and sports interests should have priority over her activities. She accepted this when the children were young, but with them both employed she had grown increasingly "frustrated," (actually angry) at the continuance of his assumptions that she manage the homemaking role alone, as she had in the past. She agreed to try to get him to come in, although she was not sure if he would.

As it turned out, Kim easily gained Bob's (passive) cooperation. He presented as pleasant, self-assured, quiet, and nonanxious, in contrast to Kim. He spoke carefully, deliberately, and slowly. He was not quite sure why his wife wanted him to attend sessions, but he was willing to cooperate any way he could. Perhaps he could help her. He did acknowledge that Kim "has been more irritable lately" and has a "shorter fuse" than before, but he attributed it to her adjusting to no longer being an active "mom" and to her menopause. He opined that she would adjust with time.

Kim's MCMI-III Profile

Figure 13.3 shows Kim's MCMI-III profile. Modifying indices showed nothing unusual. Her "worries" were reflected in the significantly high Anxiety scale score, which calls for attention early on in the treatment. Of major interest was the very significant Narcissistic clinical personality pattern score (BR = 96). By DSM-IV definition, this score indicates "a pattern of grandiosity, a need for admiration, and a lack of empathy"(American Psychiatric Association, 1994, p. 629).

For a thorough look at Kim's personality pattern, as with Bud and Nancy's, reference is made to the four levels organized as eight domains (Millon, Millon, & Davis, 1994; Millon, 1996). At a behavioral level Kim may have been described as *expressively haughty*. This presentation may not have distinguished her from some others of a privileged background, however. Her background was consistent, also, with her tendency to be *interpersonally exploitive*; this was true in the sense that she felt entitled to special favors and took others for granted, although she was in no way malicious in her attitude and behavior. In her past 25-year-long career as "housewife" and "mom" she believed that she was (somewhat resentfully) deliberately submissive to her husband's wishes, playing second fiddle to his activities (he did not totally agree). His orderliness and organization (to be noted below) was a help in raising two children. Now she wanted her due, presented in the form of an equal marriage partnership in which her needs were more prominently considered— certainly an appropriate stance, despite being driven in part by her need to see herself as special (an aspect of her *phenomenological level*).

CATEGORY		SCORE		PROFILE OF BR SCORES					DIAGNOSTIC SCALES
		RAW	BR	0	60	75	85	115	
MODIFYING INDICES	X	91	58						DISCLOSURE
	Y	14	65						DESIRABILITY
	Z	10	63						DEBASEMENT
CLINICAL PERSONALITY PATTERNS	1	1	10						SCHIZOID
	2A	6	50						AVOIDANT
	2B	9	59						DEPRESSIVE
	3	5	33						DEPENDENT
	4	16	70						HISTRIONIC
	5	19	96						NARCISSISTIC
	6A	3	36						ANTISOCIAL
	6B	6	61						AGGRESSIVE (SADISTIC)
	7	18	69						COMPULSIVE
	8A	9	60						PASSIVE-AGGRESSIVE
	8B	5	59						SELF-DEFEATING
SEVERE PERSONALITY PATHOLOGY	S	2	29						SCHIZOTYPAL
	C	1	7						BORDERLINE
	P	3	45						PARANOID
CLINICAL SYNDROMES	A	9	80						ANXIETY DISORDER
	H	3	26						SOMATOFORM DISORDER
	N	5	60						BIPOLAR: MANIC DISORDER
	D	4	27						DYSTHYMIC DISORDER
	B	5	63						ALCOHOL DEPENDENCE
	T	1	25						DRUG DEPENDENCE
	R	5	50						POST-TRAUMATIC STRESS
SEVERE SYNDROMES	SS	3	26						THOUGHT DISORDER
	CC	3	22						MAJOR DEPRESSION
	PP	2	60						DELUSIONAL DISORDER

FIGURE 13.3. Kim's MCMI-III profile.

Kim's MCMI-III profile also included Histrionic and Compulsive scores sufficiently high to consider them as possible features of Kim's personality, although they were not at the level of being considered as traits. Kim had been unusually pretty all her life and exhibited charm and somewhat seductive behavior. Despite questioning society's rules, she paid attention to them and demonstrated an ability to work hard for what she wanted, taking refurbishing courses in education to facilitate her return to teaching.

Bob's MCMI-III Profile

Bob's profile, shown in Figure 13.4, evidenced a defensive style (Desirability BR = 100), suggesting that he was unwilling to admit to many shortcomings; this was consistent with his interview presentation. Nor was he likely admit to any problems; the majority of his

CATEGORY		RAW	BR	PROFILE OF BR SCORES	DIAGNOSTIC SCALES
MODIFYING INDICES	X	69	43		DISCLOSURE
	Y	21	100		DESIRABILITY
	Z	0	0		DEBASEMENT
CLINICAL PERSONALITY PATTERNS	1	1	12		SCHIZOID
	2A	0	0		AVOIDANT
	2B	0	0		DEPRESSIVE
	3	0	0		DEPENDENT
	4	22	73		HISTRIONIC
	5	19	75		NARCISSISTIC
	6A	1	8		ANTISOCIAL
	6B	5	43		AGGRESSIVE (SADISTIC)
	7	24	83		COMPULSIVE
	8A	3	22		PASSIVE-AGGRESSIVE
	8B	0	0		SELF-DEFEATING
SEVERE PERSONALITY PATHOLOGY	S	2	40		SCHIZOTYPAL
	C	1	10		BORDERLINE
	P	4	48		PARANOID
CLINICAL SYNDROMES	A	0	0		ANXIETY DISORDER
	H	0	0		SOMATOFORM DISORDER
	N	3	36		BIPOLAR: MANIC DISORDER
	D	0	0		DYSTHYMIC DISORDER
	B	0	0		ALCOHOL DEPENDENCE
	T	1	15		DRUG DEPENDENCE
	R	0	0		POST-TRAUMATIC STRESS
SEVERE SYNDROMES	SS	1	15		THOUGHT DISORDER
	CC	0	0		MAJOR DEPRESSION
	PP	1	25		DELUSIONAL DISORDER

FIGURE 13.4. Bob's MCMI-III profile.

syndrome raw scores were 0! Bob's profile indicated compulsive personality traits, almost at the level of disorder. In the DSM-IV the compulsive personality disorder is described as "a pattern of preoccupation with orderliness, perfectionism and control" (American Psychiatric Association, 1994, p. 629). It was safe to assume that he had a compulsive style, which probably is an asset in his financially related occupation. His ability to organize and need for predictability was likely an advantage in raising two children. He had probably been seen by others as a dutiful husband and father.

He was most likely not only duty bound, hard working, and meticulous with his family, but perhaps even more so in his professional work. Underlings and peers were likely to experience him as officious, high handed, and closed minded, as judged by his just-significant Narcissistic score with reference to his Compulsive score. With his histrionic features, he tended to push away discordant emotions, underlining his lack of psychological insightfulness in general, and with the family in particular.

At a behavioral level Bob was expressively disciplined, leading an organized life. He was not known as a "people person" at work. At home he had seemed like an insensitive stonewall at times to his wife and children, despite their experience that he loved them.

He was interpersonally respectful and expected family members and others to be as well. Ordinarily he was not predisposed to novelty. His phenomenological world was behaviorally constricted. In his conscientiousness he was punctual and perfectionistic. Professionally these qualities led to professional success, although his tendency to look down on others made him an irritant at times. At home with Kim he expected to keep the routine that they had always had, which made her furious, a surprise to him. Changed circumstances, such as Kim working outside the home and the children being out of the house, did not really phase Bob. From his standpoint husband and wife role relationships needed to remain the same because they had always been comfortable (for him). He saw no need for change, or at most very minor modifications might have been considered.

Bob and Kim's Relationship

As with all couples, it is important to at least briefly reconstruct the sweep of their relationship through time. In their case after being members of the "right" fraternity and sorority and graduating from "good" universities, they engaged in a conservative, conventional dating pattern. He was getting started in business and she in teaching. It was never that exciting, but they were good "catches" for each other, with lots of friends and acquaintances as well as clubs in common. His stolidity and even temper, coupled with a "good background" and hardworking style, were attractive to her. For him, her beauty, intelligence, and charm made her seem like someone it would be good for him to "settle down with." Actually, he'd never "sown his wild oats" as had some of his classmates during the 1960s; he'd been busy studying for his B.S. and his master's in business.

After the marriage, children arrived fairly soon. He focused on work and she on making a home and being a "mom." They had their relationship difficulties along the way, especially because she felt so often that she was treated by him as a live-in maid, but they got through their ups and downs focusing on the children and doing what society expected of them. On occasion they obtained family therapy to help them deal with their children, who their therapist claimed were acting out some of their needs. Their relationship was seriously ruptured only when the children left home and Kim began to work outside the home again, precipitating the couple's entrance into therapy.

Strategy and Tactics for Couple Therapy

After her initial contact and his later appearance, separate discussions were held with the couple therapist about the MCMI-III profiles. These were useful for this couple in different ways. For him, despite his skepticism about social science, it provided an orderly structure and the measurements meant that some scientific, organized, thoughtful planning by the therapist was under way; this was reassuring for him. He could certainly agree that he was a conscientious, steady husband who seldom became perturbed. He saw his self-focus in his work as necessary, as was his paying attention to his athletic needs off work to have the sort of breaks that would allow for his concentration at work. He still appreciated her charm and warmth, but he did not "understand her problems." He was satisfied with life.

Kim acknowledged her anxiety. She still worried about her children, but she was more concerned that she could not stay in the marriage unless "something changed." He needed to be more attentive, less of a "grind," and more willing to acknowledge the power imbalance between them and the energy she was expending in her work outside the home. She did not see anything that she needed to change in herself, although she was interested in finding new approaches to use with him. From her perception she assumed that these new approaches needed to be indirect (perhaps manipulative) because of the power imbalance in the marriage.

As a primary stance, particularly because of the narcissistic aspect to their relationship, it was very important for the therapist to be supportive and respectful of Kim and Bob in the individual test interpretation interview, accepting them for themselves and gaining an alliance with them. The alliance sought was not one to ally with Bob to deal with the "problems of Kim," nor was it to reinforce Kim's perception of Bob's weaknesses. The therapist could not be taken over by Bob's authority or by Kim's superior attitude. Both were initially resistant to any truly personal exploration in the couple sessions. Instead, carefully reviewing their couple history and what they had done together to successfully raise their children provided the therapist with significant information to reinforce the couple's true successes in their life together. The therapist stressed that they need not change, but that circumstances had changed, and they could use some of their same (cognitively focused) personal resources that had brought them success so far to apply to the present.

With this sort of couple it was especially useful to help them talk with each other during the session. This action directly focused on the self–other polarity. The therapist helped Kim become more empathetic by assisting her in listening to Bob. Bob was encouraged to share more personally in the session about the stresses he actually felt at work. As she understood his personal experiences apart from her and as he gained personal knowledge by virtue of his risking expressing these personal experiences with her, they developed more ability to discuss their problems, including the one they experienced almost every night upon his arrival home, usually after her teaching day had ended. On arrival, he was often abrupt and distant, which she interpreted as rejection of her—he should focus on her now that he was through with work. He, in turn, was miffed, believing he had done his duty for the family in the cold world of business and needed some space to relax and then receive the warmth and appreciation he deserved. The therapist led the couple through a negotiation of an agreement whereby he would have 30 minutes in his study and then appear for discussions about the day for both of them. Both were reassured by this structure. These and other specific relationship opportunities were worked through in therapy. The result was that their typical day, formerly filled with many negative interchanges with each other, included many more mutually positive experiences. Working in this specific way helped the couple move toward the goal of a 5-to-1 balance of positive versus negative interactions with each other that Gottman found in his research characterized more stable couples (1994).

In assisting the couple to walk through everyday problems the therapist helped them learn to avoid major obstacles to communication: criticism of each other, defensiveness, contempt, and stonewalling. These are four processes that most significantly sabotage couple relationship (Gottman, 1994). The therapist actively intervened when these four features arose, helping to train them for more effective discussions at home.

Bob's compulsiveness could be explained in part by the fact that Bob had a parent who was cold and domineering. In a parallel fashion, Kim had a parent who assumed perfection on her part, neglecting her and not helping her with real peer problems as a child because it was not acceptable for this perfect child to have mundane relationship problems. There was always the threat of not being emotionally supported when she could not carry off her role of being special. Thus, as couple therapy progressed to discussions of how they treated each other by acting out the same style as their parents, they began to joke a bit and the therapist framed a goal to get these parents out of their marriage. Occasionally role playing themselves and their partner furthered this process. This process also assisted in developing more playfulness.

Overall the therapist kept in mind the need to reinforce the polarity of activeness in the couple engagement. He helped them build in rewards in the interaction so that not only did they continue through couple therapy, but more important of course, they found that being more active in their relationship at home had its rewards. They, to their surprise, were less lonely and more playful and continued to find it easier to negotiate the day-to-day couple interchanges. Indeed, they would not say they had changed much if asked, but their behavior had; so, consequently, had the original power imbalance, their couple system—their marriage, and the quality of their lives.

Jackie and Wirt: Compulsive/Histrionic

Jackie, 35, was an administrative assistant to a top financial executive in a traditional, multilayered corporation. She was in the process of divorcing Wirt, 40, a successful whole-sale salesman. After a whirlwind, exciting courtship and a brief marriage, Jackie found Wirt irresponsible and suspected his fidelity on his lengthy sales trips. They had been unable to negotiate an agreement as to how they would share parenting of their daughter, age 2. Through their attorneys they had stipulated to time-limited couples counseling with a male/female co-therapist team, designed not to bring them back together in marriage, but instead to develop a shared parenting agreement so that they would have the basis for becoming an effective binuclear family (Ahrons, 1994). In this family form each parent has a different household and the marriage relationship is concluded, but the parenting under a joint custody agreement is cooperative and conflicts can ordinarily be resolved without marked angry disputes (Ahrons, 1994).

Jackie's MCMI-III Profile

Validity scores on Jackie's MCMI-III were within usual ranges, as may be seen in Figure 13.5, which presents her profile. Not surprisingly, given the legal pressure and the restricted nature of the therapy's goals, her Disclosure score was somewhat low, suggesting some unwillingness to be personally open. This close-to-the-vest approach may also have been an aspect of her ongoing personality pattern. Her profile reveals a compulsive clinical personality pattern, at least a major trait, if not a disorder. The DSM-IV characterizes the obsessive–compulsive disorder as "a pattern of preoccupation with orderliness, perfectionism, and control" (American Psychiatric Association, 1994, p. 629).

Thus, as with Bob in the previous couple pattern, Jackie was expressively disciplined and interpersonally respectful (behavioral level). She was most comfortable in hierarchies wherein she could be concerned with order, rules, and set procedures, reflecting her cognitive constriction (phenomenological level). She was conscientious and stressed morality. It was easy to understand why she was a highly prized employee and leaned on by her church for volunteer activities. A slim, but potentially useful hypothesis to be checked out was that she may have had a very secondary narcissistic quality to her personality.

CATEGORY		SCORE		PROFILE OF BR SCORES					DIAGNOSTIC SCALES
		RAW	BR	0	60	75	85	115	
MODIFYING INDICES	X	57	31						DISCLOSURE
	Y	11	65						DESIRABILITY
	Z	5	49						DEBASEMENT
CLINICAL PERSONALITY PATTERNS	1	2	23						SCHIZOID
	2A	5	46						AVOIDANT
	2B	5	36						DEPRESSIVE
	3	6	43						DEPENDENT
	4	10	49						HISTRIONIC
	5	12	65						NARCISSISTIC
	6A	0	3						ANTISOCIAL
	6B	0	3						AGGRESSIVE (SADISTIC)
	7	19	83						COMPULSIVE
	8A	1	10						PASSIVE-AGGRESSIVE
	8B	1	15						SELF-DEFEATING
SEVERE PERSONALITY PATHOLOGY	S	1	17						SCHIZOTYPAL
	C	0	2						BORDERLINE
	P	0	2						PARANOID
CLINICAL SYNDROMES	A	4	50						ANXIETY DISORDER
	H	1	11						SOMATOFORM DISORDER
	N	0	2						BIPOLAR: MANIC DISORDER
	D	2	15						DYSTHYMIC DISORDER
	B	0	2						ALCOHOL DEPENDENCE
	T	0	2						DRUG DEPENDENCE
	R	2	22						POST-TRAUMATIC STRESS
SEVERE SYNDROMES	SS	0	2						THOUGHT DISORDER
	CC	2	17						MAJOR DEPRESSION
	PP	0	2						DELUSIONAL DISORDER

FIGURE 13.5. Jackie's MCMI-III profile.

Wirt's MCMI-III Profile

Although all Validity scores fell within normal ranges, Wirt had a low Disclosure score, as did Jackie, suggesting that he was avoiding self-disclosure, as may be seen Figure 13.6. As noted with Jackie, this was appropriate to the situation.

Wirt's profile indicated histrionic personality traits. The DSM-IV refers to this pattern, when it becomes a disorder, as reflecting "excessive emotionality and attention seeking" (American Psychiatric Association, 1994, p. 629).

Wirt's pattern could be seen as a style that served him well in selling. His strong feelings, possibly excessive drama at times, and constant need for positive response from others made his behavior appealing to his clients and social gatherings (behavioral level). His tendency to be shallow and his avoidance of problem affects were congruent with work

CATEGORY			SCORE	PROFILE OF BR SCORES					DIAGNOSTIC SCALES
			RAW	BR	0	60	75	85	115	
MODIFYING INDICES	X	48	14						DISCLOSURE
	Y	14	65						DESIRABILITY
	Z	1	34						DEBASEMENT
CLINICAL PERSONALITY PATTERNS	1	0	10						SCHIZOID
	2A	1	22						AVOIDANT
	2B	0	10						DEPRESSIVE
	3	1	20						DEPENDENT
	4	20	78						HISTRIONIC
	5	14	67						NARCISSISTIC
	6A	3	32						ANTISOCIAL
	6B	2	27						AGGRESSIVE (SADISTIC)
	7	12	54						COMPULSIVE
	8A	0	10						PASSIVE-AGGRESSIVE
	8B	0	10						SELF-DEFEATING
SEVERE PERSONALITY PATHOLOGY	S	0	6						SCHIZOTYPAL
	C	2	26						BORDERLINE
	P	0	6						PARANOID
CLINICAL SYNDROMES	A	0	6						ANXIETY DISORDER
	H	0	6						SOMATOFORM DISORDER
	N	6	68						BIPOLAR: MANIC DISORDER
	D	2	46						DYSTHYMIC DISORDER
	B	1	21						ALCOHOL DEPENDENCE
	T	2	36						DRUG DEPENDENCE
	R	1	21						POST-TRAUMATIC STRESS
SEVERE SYNDROMES	SS	0	6						THOUGHT DISORDER
	CC	0	6						MAJOR DEPRESSION
	PP	0	6						DELUSIONAL DISORDER

FIGURE 13.6. Wirt's MCMI-III profile.

demands, although not a characteristic helpful in deepening a marital relationship. As with Jackie, a secondary hypothesis was that he had some narcissistic traits. An additional conjecture was that he may have had hypomanic episodes stemming from his histrionic style.

Jackie and Wirt's Relationship

Jackie, ordinarily tied into her work and church-related activities, met Wirt on a vacation. She was more open than usual away from her comfortable routine and felt swept off her feet by Wirt. He, in turn, having ended a long and childless marriage, felt a need for conquering and a need for someone to reinforce his maleness. Jackie seemed to fit the bill so he focused his charms on her, not reflecting on the qualities he needed in a partner. In his "selling" himself to her, he "sold" the idea to himself that she would be good for him. They were good for each other—very briefly. Even before she became pregnant they began having trouble. She would not tolerate a disorderly household and he became a rebellious teenager.

After the baby's birth, they floundered on feelings of possession of the child. Both spent time parenting, becoming rivalrous for the child's attention as she grew. With the "terrible 2s" the daughter's need for independent exploration became very anxiety provoking to Jackie, who responded by controlling, training, and discipline. By contrast, Wirt related in a loving fashion, but not providing any limits at all. In the intake session their present dislike of each other's divergent parenting style was focused on. Both needed to be "the primary parent" even though they each recognized the "unfortunate" necessity of sharing parenting, at least to some extent.

Strategy and Tactics for Couple Therapy

The goal of couple therapy was to help them achieve the basis for establishing a binuclear family (Ahrons, 1994). Practically, the first step meant working out an agreement for parenting. They were at loggerheads. Jackie had presented an elaborate set of rules and procedures for his acquiescence. Wirt had overreacted to what he believed was primarily an effort to control him, and he yelled that he was not going along with her every wish. She indicated that her detailed procedures were necessary because he did not pay sufficient attention to the child's health and her meals. He said that he could be as good a parent as she, and that the child was not going to be harmed or become ill.

In the test interpretation session the female cotherapist reassured Jackie that her efforts to do right by her daughter would continue to be of importance as the daughter matured. What could help Jackie in guiding (modified rigid control of) her daughter would be Jackie's learning to relax. She could see that if the parental tension was reduced and agreements were reached, her child was less likely to be psychologically damaged. Her daughter might in fact flourish, doing better than had the couple stayed maritally together. Jackie had to learn to accept that Wirt could provide some useful, spontaneous fathering for their daughter.

For Wirt, in the interpretive session the male cotherapist reinforced how his warm, fun-loving parenting style would benefit his daughter, but that he needed to work to set limits and routines because children need those. The therapist stressed that for his daughter's sake he must let Jackie know about his responsible actions to alleviate her anxiety. He had to accept Jackie as she was. He was encouraged to pay strong attention to what his daughter was really like as she developed. By joining a parenting group, he could learn to think with more depth about his daughter, and perhaps his life, too.

In couple sessions the therapists, in an effort to lessen the parents' guilt (especially Jackie's), told the parents that half of U.S. children were then raised in nonnuclear families, and that if the parents could lessen their conflict, their daughter could do well. The therapists stressed the need to mesh their different parenting styles so that their daughter could benefit from both, however. Jackie's orderly lifestyle would provide stability if she could become mildly more flexible, building on her daughter's spontaneous play. Wirt's enthusiasm for life could be an advantage if he could see that his daughter was less agitated when he set limits and maintained an orderly schedule for her. By repeating with the couple what had been said individually, acknowledging principles of behavior on both their parts became an underpinning for developing the specific parenting agreements as to time-sharing, transfer processes, etcetera, focusing on what was best for a child almost 3 years old, thus sidestepping the adult conflicts. Because their goal was to parent, not to renew their marital relationship, they was no attempt to work through the fact that their original attraction to the other was to those aspects that were undeveloped in themselves.

SUMMARY

This chapter presented an approach for using the MCMI-III with couples who are seeking therapeutic help for their relationship problems. After a joint intake interview the therapist discusses with each partner the probable meaning of their MCMI-III scores for themselves as individuals. Then the therapist and client consider the implications of these results for their relationship. Next, in a conjoint session with the therapist, the partners mutually share their sense of the most pertinent findings; the therapist helps with clarifications, reminders, and confrontations. The couple and the therapist establish therapeutic goals jointly based on this shared information as it pertains to the problems experienced by the couple.

The therapist uses the MCMI-III findings to intervene quickly if marked symptom or mood state problems exist, such as alcoholism or potentially debilitating depression. Most importantly, the therapist applies knowledge of the personality styles or disorders present to design therapeutic interventions consistent with knowledge of these styles and their probable impact on the couple's behavior. Three couple cases were presented: avoidant/histrionic, compulsive/narcissistic, and compulsive/histrionic. Not only did each represent a different couple dynamic interaction, but also each couple faced a different common stress point in the present-day population: changing from a dyadic family relationship to a triadic one with the arrival of the first baby, returning to a dyadic relationship when children leave home, and reshaping the nuclear family to a binuclear family when a divorce occurs. The MCMI-III, monetarily very inexpensive with the therapist interpreting the profile, and very economic of patients' and therapists' time, provides an extremely cost-effective basis for accurately intervening with couple problems.

REFERENCES

Ahrons, C. R. (1994). *The good divorce*. New York: HarperCollins.

American Psychiatric Association. (1994) *Diagnostic and statistical manual of mental disorders* (4th ed.). Washington, DC: Author.

Beach, R. H., & Anderson, P. (1995). Marital therapy for depression: When should the marriage be the focus of therapy? *Psychotherapy, 30*, 40–43.

Choca, J. P., Shanley, L. A., & Van Denburg, R. (1992). *Interpretive guide to the Millon Clinical Multiaxial Inventory*. Washington, DC: American Psychological Association.

Cowan, P. C., & Cowan, P. A. (1992). *When partners become parents: The big life change for couples*. New York: Basic Books.

Gottman, J. (1994). *Why marriages succeed or fail*. New York: Simon & Schuster.

Martin, S. (1995). Psychologists may spark violence by using inappropriate couples therapy. *APA Monitor, 26*(11), 35.

Millon, T., Millon, C., & Davis, R. (1994). *Millon Clinical Multiaxial Inventory—III manual*. Minneapolis: National Computer Systems.

Millon, T. (1996). *Disorders of personality: DSM-IV and beyond*. New York: Wiley.

Nurse, A. R. (In press). *Psychological testing with families*. New York: Wiley.

Retzlaff, P. D. (Ed.). (1995). *Tactical psychotherapy of the personality disorders: An MCMI-III based approach*. Needham Heights, MA: Allyn & Bacon.

Schwartz, L. L., & Kaslow, F. W. (1997). *Painful partings*. New York: Wiley.

14

The Millon Inventories: Sociocultural Considerations

LUIS A. ESCOVAR

This chapter looks at the Millon inventories from a sociocultural perspective. It is guided by the principle that a true clinical science must address theoretical and nosological issues before developing instrumentation to test theoretical propositions and hypotheses (Millon & Davis, 1996). Instruments should evolve from theory as tools for its enhancement and empirical validation. From this perspective, examination of the cross-cultural utility of psychological tests should be a secondary step taken only after more fundamental considerations have been addressed. Issues such as backtranslations, cross-cultural psychological equivalence of items, and factorial structures should take a back seat to theoretical considerations regarding the nature of psychopathology cross-culturally. The fundamental concern should be to figure out the role of sociocultural factors in the development of psychopathology. Only after theoretical inroads have been established in answering this question should attention be diverted to the construction, improvement, and testing of psychological devices. The field must move away from the current practice of taking a test developed in this country, bringing it to another culture, "validating" it, and using it for diagnostic assessment. Dustbowl empiricism does not have a place in the study of psychopathology cross-culturally. Instead, tests should be selected because of their theoretical soundness and their potential to clarify cross-cultural issues.

A major distinguishing feature of the Millon inventories—the first, second, and third versions of the Millon Clinical Multiaxial Inventory and the Millon Index of Personality Styles—is that they are linked systematically to a comprehensive clinical theory (Millon, 1977, 1987a, 1994; Millon, Weiss, Millon, & Davis, 1994). This feature makes them unique among psychometric devices currently available to clinical practitioners and ideally suited for the study of psychopathology cross-culturally. This chapter focuses on the theoretical foundations of the Millon inventories and their promise for use in cross-cultural assessment. The material of the chapter is organized into three major sections. The first addresses the issue of determining which of the many possible differences between cultures are relevant to the study of psychopathology. Rather than emphasizing the endless possibilities cultural diversity presents, this chapter narrows the focus by examining a current model of psychopathology (Millon, 1990) and extending it for use cross-culturally. The second section focuses on sociocultural transactions and conceptualizes them as consisting of essentially three types of variables. The emphasis in this section is on looking at the functional mechanisms that underlie human behavior within culture. Principles from social judgment theory are used to examine the role of culture as an anchor for social judgment within and across cultures. A third and final section looks at the programmatic use of the Millon inventories cross-culturally.

EXTENSION OF MILLON'S MODEL TO THE SOCIOCULTURAL LEVEL

Culture, Personality, and Evolutionary Biology

Culture is the product of human activity. Accordingly, cultural patterns reflect the principles that govern individual human behavior. In 1954 American anthropologist Florence Kluckhohn said that culture is to society what memory is to the person (Kluckhohn, 1954). Culture represents the accumulation of all behavioral patterns, ideas, attitudes, and symbols that have worked in the past as individuals strived to adapt to a particular ecological milieu. Cultural products are the shared outcomes of multiple individual acts and interactions. This accumulation of cultural elements takes the form of cultural structures (e.g., symbols) and cultural functions (e.g., cultural worldviews) so that truly one could paraphrase Kluckhohn and state that culture is to society what *personality* is to the person. Culture and personality share many features in common; both represent the accumulation of human striving to adapt, both are highly integrated such that change in one of its elements can produce change in all others, and both have evolutionary significance. A key distinction between the two is that cultural patterns are shared, whereas personality traits are private. "To the extent such aspects are *shared* by people who speak a common language and who are able to interact because they live in adjacent locations during the same historical period, we can refer to all of these elements as a cultural group's *subjective culture*" (Triandis, 1989, p. 507). It is this similarity of elements among members of a cultural group that makes it possible to speak of modal personalities defined as the most prevalent personality style in a cultural group.

If human beings had to start from scratch at birth, they would have to engage in many tasks to adapt successfully to a particular ecological milieu, perhaps endlessly repeating mistakes and serendipitously hitting upon solutions. Culture simplifies the adaptation process by providing tried and proven formulas. In this sense, culture has preeminence because it has temporal precedence. A person is born, utterly dependent and with a few potential traits and skills, into a preexisting culture. The unfolding of those traits and skills and their relative salience is determined partially by cultural norms and the person's relative position in them. Although the number of prescribed cultural tasks in this developmental process is potentially very large, the fundamental goals for all humans in all cultures must be finite due to limitations inherent in the person and the environment. The key to understanding the relationship between personality and culture is to identify the principles that are important in the formation and functioning of both. The same fundamental principles that give rise to personality must also be at work in the development of culture. Otherwise, culture and personality would behave independently of each other. That, however, is not so, and earlier writers have described relationships between these two constructs.

Mental Health and Parsimony

Cultures differ in countless ways, not all of which are important to mental health. Part of the task of the cross-cultural mental health theorist is to narrow down the differences to those few that truly affect psychopathology and its manifestation across cultures. The question emerges "How best to accomplish this parsing?" Evidently, the impact of those factors that make up the sociocultural foundation of psychopathology should be extensive and pervasive. In other words, the manifestations of their influence must be discernible in all cultures—a criterion of universality. Additionally, because of their universality, they must be detectable by researchers from different disciplines working with data at different levels of analysis. A strict application of these two criteria would quickly eliminate many culture-specific behaviors and leave for examination universal principles. Accordingly, a model of cross-cultural psychopathology would only include factors whose manifestation was not easily altered by immediate environmental circumstances. Clinical syndromes, as defined in Axis I of the DSM nosologies, and specific trait manifestations that may be highly culture bound would probably not yield satisfying results because by their very nature their presentation is more likely affected by circumstantial and temporal factors. Which cultural factors to include as relevant for such a model may be insurmountable, given the large diversity of cultural groups in existence at any point in time. Prior thinking on this issue has focused on the relationship between personality and culture, and looking at personality as the construct that would link culture and psychopathology seems appropriate. After all, as indicated above, personality and culture share many characteristics in common. Culture may be easily regarded as the reflection of personality at the sociocultural level.

What are, then, these principles, so basic, so fundamental, yet so powerful that they affect in essentially linear fashion constructs at different levels of analysis? In a brilliant piece of scholarly sleuthing, Millon (1990) has identified three "motivating aims" that prompt, energize, and direct human behavior (Millon, 1994). These aims, set as bipolar dimensions, have been variously called "pleasure–pain," "active–passive," and "self–other" (Millon, 1981) or "existence," "adaptation," and "replication" (Millon, 1990). Anchoring his deductions firmly on evolutionary and ecological theory, Millon uses these three principles to explicate the development of personality as a process analogous to the phylogenetic evolution of species.

> At any point in time, a species will possess a limited set of genes that serve as trait potentials. Over succeeding generations the frequency distribution of these genes will likely change in their relative proportions depending on how well the traits they undergird contribute to the species' "fittedness" within its varying ecological habitats. In a similar fashion, individual organisms begin life with a limited subset of their species' genes and the trait potential they subserve. Over time the *salience* of these traits potentials—not the proportion of genes themselves—will become differentially prominent as the organism interacts with its environments. It "learns" from these experiences which of its traits "fit" best, that is, most optimally suited to its ecosystem. In phylogenesis, then, actual gene *frequencies* change during the generation-to-generation adaptive process, whereas in ontogenesis it is the *salience* or prominence of gene-based traits that changes as adaptive learning takes place. Parallel evolutionary processes occur, one within the life of a species, the other within the life of an organism. (Millon, 1990, p. 22)

In an analogous fashion the thinking underlying Millon's model can be extended beyond the personologic to the cultural—a task that would require identifying manifestations of the three dimensions at a broader level of analysis. This expanded theoretical framework would make it possible to cross levels of analysis, from the biological to the personologic to the cultural, without losing explanatory power. Table 14.1 is a depiction of the proposed extension of Millon's model. The advantage of this framework for the construction of a cross-cultural model of psychopathology should be evident. In the next few sections

TABLE 14.1. Evolutionary Model of Personality Dimensions

Level/dimension	Selective diversification	Existence	Mode of adaptation
Evolutionary mechanisms	r-Strategy versus K-strategy in biological reproduction	Enhancement/ preservation of life	Ecological accommodation versus ecological modification
Psychological mechanisms	Self versus other Internal versus external controls of learning Self-structures versus object relations Competitive versus cooperative dispositions of motivation Neurobiological substrates of gender	Pain versus pleasure Positive versus negative reinforcers Pleasant/unpleasant valences of emotions Instinctual aims of the ID Neurological substrates of mood	Passive versus active Respondent versus operant learning Reality apparatuses of the ego Low/high intensity of activation Neurological substrates of arousal
Sociocultural mechanisms	Individualism versus collectivism (Triandis)	Malevolence versus benevolence (Marianismo)	Industrious versus sedentary (n-Ach, McClelland; I-E, Rotter)

each of the polar dimensions identified by Millon is reviewed, paying particular attention to empirical evidence on its manifestation at the sociocultural level.

Self versus Other

The distinction between self and other reflects the subject–object polarity and refers to a person's source of reinforcement—the preferred locus where the person turns to when in need of reinforcement (Millon, 1981). From a different perspective Millon has called these polar opposites, tendencies to enhance either one's own interests or the interests of another. "Humans can be both self-actualizing and other-encouraging, although most persons are likely to lean toward one or the other side. A balance that coordinates the two provides a satisfactory answer to the question of whether one should be devoted to the support and welfare of others or fashion one's life in accord with one's own needs and desires" (Millon & Davis, 1996, p. 39). This disparity in orientation emerges from differences in reproductive strategies seen at the biological level. "Designated the r-strategy and K-strategy in population biology, the former represents a pattern of propagating a vast number of offspring, but exhibiting minimal attention to their survival, the latter typified by the production of few progeny, followed by considerable effort to assure their survival" (Millon, 1990, p. 39). Millon and other theorists (Rushton, 1985), have come to regard this asymmetry in replication strategies as the fundamental distinction between the genders with males, who generally employ the r-strategy, being more inclined toward egotistic self-orientation and females, for whom the K-strategy is the most prevalent, toward a nurturant other orientation. At the psychological level of analysis the distinction finds a manifestation in constructs such as competition versus cooperation, self-structures versus object relations in psychoanalytic theory, and certain aspects of Rotter's internal versus external locus of control (Millon, 1990).

Sociocultural Evidence

Shifting to a sociocultural level of analysis, one finds striking evidence that the very same distinction (biological differentiation) that manifests itself in varied forms at the psychological level (Millon, 1990) also is at work at this level. Triandis (1994) has identified a dimension of cultural variation that parallels Millon's self–other dimension, which he regards as perhaps "the most important worldview that differentiates cultures" (p. 286). Labeled *individualism–collectivism*, it refers to the extent to which persons in given cultural groups give priority to personal goals over the goals of collectives and vice-versa. Individuals in collectivist cultures either "make no distinctions between personal and collective goals, or if they do make such distinctions, they subordinate their personal goals to the collective goals" (Triandis, 1989, p. 509). Contrasting the two ends of this variable, Triandis notes that the individualistic pattern emphasizes "that the views, needs, and goals of the self are most important . . . [that] behavior can be explained by the pleasure principle and the computation of personal profits and losses . . . [that] beliefs distinguish the individual from the in-group, allowing the individual to be an autonomous entity . . . [and that] social behavior is independent of and emotionally detached from the collective" (Triandis, 1994, p. 287).

The collectivist pattern represents almost a mirror image by emphasizing ". . . the views, needs, and goals of some collective . . . shared beliefs, that is, what the individual and the collective have in common. . . . [that] social behavior is dependent, emotionally attached, and involved with the collective . . . [and that] behavior is a function of norms and duties imposed by the collective" (Triandis, 1994, p. 287). The impact of these cultural distinctions is quite powerful and Triandis, in a line of research that spans a lifetime, has documented their effects on different aspects of human functioning.

Among the most salient findings, Triandis identifies consistent differences in the definition of the self, in social behavior, in social communication, and in types of attributions made. In collectivist cultures individuals tend to be identified by group membership, thus *teknonyms* are used more frequently than are personal names. *Teknonyms* refer to ways of referring to a person that emphasize their status within a group. Triandis (1994, p. 289) uses as an example of a *teknonym* "the second son of the Brown family." This collectivist self-identity is also reflected in a higher tendency to use "common fate" responses to complete the sentence "I am" (Triandis, McCusker, & Hui, 1990) and on a similarly higher tendency to give more "social responses" to the question "What do you have in common with your family and friends?" (Trafimow, Triandis, & Goto, 1991).

Social behavior is affected by individualism–collectivism. Collectivists seem to restrict their social interactions to members of the in-group and, hence, overvalue intimacy and develop few skills for meeting strangers. In contrast, individualists have good skills for dealing with strangers but not for developing close relationships (Triandis, 1994). Collectivists perceive role relationships as more nurturant, respectful, and intimate (Triandis, Vassiliou, & Nassiakou, 1968), and appear to be more enmeshed with other in-group members (Hui & Triandis, 1986). Lest the reader think that a collectivist mentality is good because of its emphasis on intimate relationships, one must be reminded that the social behavior of collectivists is very different when the other person is a member of the in-group as opposed to an out-group member. Individualists do not make this sharp distinction (Triandis, 1994). In fact, collectivists engage in a form of ethnocentrism by believing that norms of their own groups are universally valid (Shweder & LeVine, 1984).

Because they are other oriented, collectivists tend to focus more on the person than on the content of social communication. They pay attention to paralinguistic cues (Gudykunst, 1991) and are more concerned with the other person's emotional reaction to the communication. In fact, this emphasis on the other person during communication leads to some interesting consequences: "Because maintaining relationships is very important to them, they prefer to suppress negative communications and tell others what they want to hear, rather than tell the truth and create bad feelings. Thus, collectivists are more likely to lie and less likely to say "no" than are individualists. Individualists, by contrast, have no difficulties in "telling it like it is" (Triandis, 1994, p. 293). In making attributions about the causes of behavior, collectivists tend to emphasize the importance of norms, customs, and traditions, whereas individualists emphasize personal elements such as attitudes and expectations of personal gain or loss (Triandis, 1994).

Cross-cultural classification of groups along the individualism–collectivism dimension yields consistent findings with Latin American, Asian, and African cultures leaning more toward collectivism and North American and Northern and Western European cultures more toward individualism (Triandis, 1989). Hofstede (1984, 1991) reports similar findings in the ranking of 40 countries with the United States, Australia, Great Britain, and Canada having the highest individualism scores and Colombia, Venezuela, Panama, Ecuador, and Guatemala having the lowest scores (higher collectivism; Hofstede, 1991, Table 3.1, p. 53). In the United States, Hispanics display much more collectivism than do persons from Northern and Western European traditions (Marin & Triandis, 1985).

Pain versus Pleasure

A second bipolar dimension in Millon's model pertains to phenomena that enhance life, experienced as "pleasurable," contrasted with those whose aim is the preservation of life, experienced as "painful." As was the case with self versus other in elaborating on the importance of this dimension, Millon's reasoning is based on principles of evolutionary biology:

> More complicated organic structures, such as plants and animals, also have mechanisms to counter entropic dissolution, that is, maintain the existence of their "life." Two intertwined strategies are required, one to achieve existence, the other to preserve it. The first aim is the *enhancement* of life, that is, creating or enriching ecologically survivable organisms; the second is oriented to the *preservation* of life, that is, avoiding events that might terminate it. (1990, p. 31; italics in the original)

The most prominent constructs reflecting this dimension in contemporary psychological theory are those of the positive and negative reinforcers of learning which speak to the strengthening or weakening of the association between responses and their consequences. In the erudite presentation of his evolutionary model, Millon (1990) finds parallels between this dimension and a number of constructs from other theoretical orientations, including psychoanalytic instinctual aims of the id and Eysenck's (1967, 1981) pioneering work on the neurologic substrates of mood.

Sociocultural Evidence

It is evident, and history can attest, that some cultural groups use pain as the primary mechanism to control the behavior of its members. These groups harbor a malevolent inclination bent on suppressing and limiting the manifestation of behavior. On the other hand, there are other cultural groups whose benevolent practices are directed to the enhancement and fostering of behaviors by their members. The two polar extremes, malevolence versus benevolence, refer to cultural patterns regarding the preferred manner of controlling human behavior and may reflect distinct ideologies about human nature. There is abundant evidence that many cultures have acknowledged the functions of pain and pleasure as inextricably related motivating mechanisms for the control of behavior. In ancient

Greek and Roman cultures the infliction of pain was believed to have medicinal and curative powers. Accordingly, insanity, female infertility, fever, constipation, lockjaw, smallpox, rheumatism, and male impotence were all treated in exactly the same way, with flogging. Some theorists believe that ancient thinking regarding the curative effectiveness of pain may have originated in an incorrect inference based on observing the usually ennervating effect of pain on the sufferer (Scott, 1938/1974). The ancients may have mistaken momentary arousal with permanent healing. Yet this belief in the restorative powers of pain has persisted through the history of Western medicine. According to a statement attributed to Seneca (Scott, 1938/1974, p. 120), "Medicine begins to have an effect on insensible bodies when they are so handled as to feel pain." Lest we believe that our thinking has come a long way in this regard, we should listen to the pitch of purveyors of exercise programs nowadays who admonish us with phrases such as "No pain, no gain." Similar thinking is behind our beliefs that a medicine, to be most effective, has to be bitter.

Western cultural thinking about pain and pleasure has been heavily influenced by the Judeo-Christian tradition and therefore shares its ambivalence.

> In modern American and Western European culture, the social orientation toward pain is characterized by two opposite attitudes. According to one, pain is considered to be bad, and as such it is to be combated and, if possible, removed. The other orientation toward pain is perhaps less openly recognized but is nevertheless conscious and clearcut. According to it, pain and suffering indicate . . . that we are good or trying to be good. . . . The whole complex concept of masochism, and particularly so called moral masochism, deals with this aspect of pain and is familiar to psychoanalysts. (Szasz, 1975, pp. 248–249)

In religious life, belief in the restorative powers of pain often took the form of flagellation and self-flagellation, either as punishment for transgressions or to undo evil deeds. Nevertheless, pain also bestowed a special status, a virtuous state, on the sufferer and brought with it the admiration of others.

> One must not overlook the fact that in many cases the priests genuinely believed that self-punishment, being a form of sacrifice, would propitiate the god they worshipped. This provides one of the explanations of all forms of asceticism; from the chastity of Roman Catholic priests to the extreme self-tortures practised [sic] by the yogis of Tibet and the fakirs of India. Also, and often coincident with this propriation of their god, the arousing of the sympathy or compassion of the public, which, inevitably, is connected with any form of martyrdom, was no doubt in the minds of those indulging in self-flagellation. (Scott, 1938/1974, p. 123)

Accordingly, the attainment of virtue through the endurance of pain is an idea that has deep roots in the historical and religious heritage of many groups and that, not surprisingly, manifests itself in different cultural practices. In the Hispanic culture the antithetical gender-related norms for marianismo and machismo contain a pain versus pleasure component. Men are free to enjoy life (*divertirse*) while women are expected to play a subordinate, yet virtuous, role.

> In counterpoint to the macho ideal among Hispanic peoples is the cultural idealization of femininity embodied in the concept of marianismo. The marianismo stereotype, which derives its name from the Virgin Mary, refers to the ideal of the virtuous woman as one who "suffers in silence," submerging her needs and desires to those of her husband and children. With the marianismo stereotype, the image of a woman's role as a martyr is

raised to the level of a cultural ideal. . . . The feminine ideal is one of suffering in silence and being the provider of joy, even in the face of pain. (Javier, 1995, p. 317)

Hispanic cultures, as indicated in the previous section, tend to be more collectivistic and an ideal based on subordination and suffering may be more easily accepted by its members. At the other extreme of the pain–pleasure, malevolent–benevolent polarity is the European American United States population, one of the most individualistic peoples in the world, which emphasizes the rights of individuals and has gone as far as codifying the idea of the *pursuit of happiness* as one of those rights. No other country in the world has gone this far in promoting pleasure to the level of an individual right.

Cultural malevolence versus benevolence refers to the manifestation of the pain versus pleasure dimension at the sociocultural level. It is a world view which reflects the extent to which human nature is seen as more apt to respond to painful rather than to pleasurable consequences and as such it must affect diverse cultural elements in areas such as preferred disciplining techniques in childrearing practices, the severity and cruelty of punishment for violations of law in the penal code, and the treatment of prisoners during wartime. Although history tells us that there are cultural differences in this and other areas concerning this dimension, more cross-cultural studies are needed in this area.

Passive versus Active

The third dimension in Millon's model pertains to the manner in which organisms adapt to their surroundings. He identifies two modes; the first refers to an accommodating style that emphasizes "fitting" into the environment, and the second, to a more energetic style that is bent on actively modifying existing conditions. At the biological level these modes of adaptation are best illustrated in the distinction between plants and animals.

> Plants best characterize the mode of ecologic *accommodation*, an essentially *passive* style which disposes them to locate and remain securely anchored in a niche where the elements comprising their environment . . . furnish both the nourishment and protection requisite to sustaining individual homeostatic balance and promoting species survival. Animals, in contrast, typify what has been termed adaptation via ecologic *modification*, an essentially active style which intervenes and transforms the surrounds, a versatile mobility that enables the organism not only to seek out its needs and to escape threats to its survival, but also to reconstruct or shift from one niche to another as unpredictable events arise. (Millon, 1990, p. 65; italics in the original)

Millon (1990) extends this dimension to the psychological level of analysis to encompass the human experience.

> Often reflective and deliberate, those who are passively oriented manifest few overt strategies to gain their ends. This display a seeming inertness, a phlegmatic lack of ambition or persistence, a tendency toward acquiescence, a restrained attitude in which they initiate little to modify events, waiting for the circumstances of their environment to take their course before making accommodations. . . . Descriptively, those who are at the active end of the polarity are best characterized by their alertness, vigilance, liveliness, vigor, forcefulness, their stimulus-seeking energy, and drive. Some plan strategies and scan alternatives to circumvent obstacles or avoid the distress of punishment, rejection, and anxiety. Others are impulsive, precipitate, excitable, rash, and hasty, seeking to elicit pleasures and rewards. (pp. 65–66)

Millon finds parallels between this dimension and a number of psychological constructs which include respondent versus operant modes of learning, with the former referring to passive orientation and the latter, to an active one.

Sociocultural Evidence

Some cultural groups prefer to live a sedentary existence, adapting to change gradually and slowly. Others are more dynamic and appear to generate change at a rapid pace. In dealing with primitive cultures anthropologists have made the distinction between hunter–gatherer groups and agriculturalists as reflecting these differences. The passive versus active dimension at the sociocultural level appears to reflect differences between a preference for a sedentary orientation versus an industrious, dynamic approach to existence. McClelland's (1961) need achievement motivation (n-Ach), which incorporates this notion of adaptation to the environment in either an active, modifying manner or a passive, accommodating one, has been shown to influence economic development in countries around the world. Need achievement refers to an "affectively toned associative network" (McClelland & Winter, 1969, p. 43) of cognitions related to achievement. People who score high on need achievement are goal oriented and concerned with doing things well and with doing them better than others, and when blocked either because of their own deficits or because of environmental constrains they try to overcome those obstacles rather than giving up. These people travel a great deal more than the average person and constantly search for ways of improving whatever it is they are doing. They are also more likely to migrate if conditions in their current locale are not conducive to success. Unmistakably, high need achievers are action-oriented persons who would fall in the modifying end of the active versus passive dimension. McClelland (1961) and his colleagues (Child, Storm, & Veroff, 1958) were able to demonstrate systematic differences in the achievement motivation of 45 preliterate cultures by analyzing the content of their folk tales. As they predicted, those differences were related to the level of economic development of the groups, with those high in n-Ach showing a more advanced level of entrepreneurial activity and greater economic achievement. A subsequent study by McClelland (1961) of 40 contemporary societies showed similar results. Here the level of need achievement was obtained by analyzing the content of children's elementary school readers in 1925. The correlation between need achievement and economic growth 25 years later was positive and significant.

In summary, extending Millon's model to the sociocultural level has the advantage of narrowing the focus of interest to only those cultural elements important to the development of psychopathology. No longer is it necessary to study endless lists of differences between cultures. All that is necessary is to ascertain cultural worldviews regarding individualism versus collectivism, malevolence versus benevolence, and industriousness versus a preference for sedentary adaptation. These cultural elements provide the structure (content) of interest but reveal very little about how members of different cultural groups use them. For that one must turn to the functional aspects of these elements. The next sections review functional characteristics of culture.

A MODEL OF SOCIOCULTURAL TRANSACTIONS

Whenever a clinical practitioner deals with a patient from a cultural group different from his or her own, the situation is greatly complicated by a set of factors that are not immediately evident. The face-to-face interaction between therapist and patient constitutes but the tip of a number of different factors at work in that situation. Three types can be identified as important: (1) factors that pertain to the relationship between the person and his or her native culture, (2) factors that define the links between native and host cultures, and (3) factors that characterize the functioning of the person in the host culture. These factors can be conceptualized as a model of interlocking components and are depicted in Figure 14.1. Following a contextualist perspective (Szapocznick & Kurtines, 1993) the person is viewed as embedded within any number of primary reference groups (e.g., family, professions, gangs) which in turn are embedded within a native cultural context. Primary reference groups are shown as broken lines in the figure. The larger cultural context has been drawn as a separate ellipse to show more clearly the relationship between the native culture and the person. In this fashion a set of linkages is established between the elements of the model. The relationship between the person and his or her native culture is said to consist of *intracultural factors*. The relationship between the native culture and other cultures, depicted as a separate ellipse in Figure 14.1, yields a set of *cross-cultural factors*. Finally, the interaction of the person with elements of another culture generates a set of *xenocultural factors*. Testing a minority person with an instrument constructed in a dominant culture is an example of xenocultural interaction. Another example of *xenocultural interaction* is having a psychotherapist from a dominant culture work with a minority patient or conversely, having a minority psychotherapist work with a person from a dominant culure.

Functional Aspects of Intracultural and Xenocultural Interactions

Social judgment theory (Sherif & Sherif, 1969) is instructive in understanding cultural interactions. A person's native culture—the set of intracultural elements—constitutes a frame of reference consisting of categorizations of important components of the culture

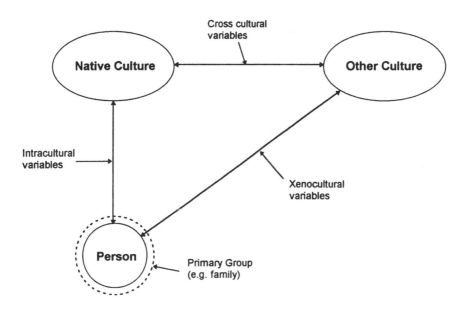

FIGURE 14.1. Model of xenocultural interactions.

which serve as standards (anchors) for judgment which provide guidelines for action. The influence of this cultural frame may be mediated by any number of reference groups (family, friends, gangs, etc.) that provide the day-to-day interpretation of the culture for the individual. In other words, a person's own culture provides the definition of the situation for him or her and because people tend to remain within the same social milieu for extended periods of time, the frame of reference provided by the culture stays valid and useful. Problems emerge when the person must deal with elements of other cultural groups and is thus forced outside of the guidelines provided by the cultural frame of reference. Under these ambiguous circumstances the person may try to use the familiar frame of reference provided by his or her native culture when a different one is required. This "forcing" of the situation into the "wrong" frame of reference may lead to errors in judgment by the individual.

Assimilation and Contrast Effects

When confronted with a previously unknown stimulus, for example, an element from a foreign culture—a person, an object, an instance of behavior—individuals will assess it using their own positions in their intracultural frame of reference as anchors. In xenocultural situations the frame of reference is given by their native culture and the anchor for judgment is the person's own position in that frame. If the new element is close to the person's own position, it will be assimilated; if not, it will be contrasted. The closer or farther away the element is judged to be, the stronger will be the tendencies to assimilate or contrast it relative to the person's own position. This principle from social judgment theory has clear implications for the behavior of persons in xenocultural interactions. Accordingly, it is easier for someone to assimilate and by that accept an element from a different culture if it is judged to be closer to his or her own position. Similarly, contrasting and by that rejecting such elements becomes easier, the more they are judged as farther away from that anchor. Clearly, if the foreign element is so distant that it falls outside the intracultural frame of reference it will certainly be contrasted and rejected.

Distance from the person's own position is not the only factor affecting assimilation and contrast effects. Assimilation and by that, acceptance, will be more likely in those situations in which the person does not have culturally provided elements for judgment. In these ambiguous situations the person will be more susceptible to external influences, *including those that come from a different culture*. On the other hand, assimilation will be more difficult if the cultural frame of reference is well established and strong. Under circumstances where clear guidelines for judgments exist the person will be more intolerant of even small deviations from his or her own position within the culturally provided frame of reference.

Clinical practice is fraught with opportunities for using the "wrong" frame of reference. Diagnosis, after all, indicates judgment. The clinical practitioner defines diagnostic or treatment situations with the cultural frame of reference provided by his or her own culture and "distorted" by years of training within a Western European clinical tradition. Patients, on the other hand, bring their own cultural ideas about what ails them and the role they expect the clinical practitioner to play in the diagnostic and healing process. Because it is likely that the cultural groups to which they—practitioners and patients—belong, have interacted in the past, there will be a history of these encounters that influence the judgments being made. This second set of factors pertaining to the relationship between cultural groups constitutes yet another source of influence in sociocultural situations. Put in the terminology of social judgment theory, what this means is that the cultures of other participants in a social situation also constitute anchors that affect judgments being made within that situation. This point is discussed in the next section.

Cross-Cultural Considerations

The nature of the relationship between the two cultures—historical and current—can have an anchoring effect in social judgment. Perhaps the single most important variable in this regard is the existence of power differentials between the two cultures. The concept of power distance (Mulder, 1976) can inform our understanding of the impact of cross-cultural factors in interpersonal relationships. Hofstede (1984) defines power distance as the difference between the extent to which one person can determine the behavior of another and the extent to which the second can determine the behavior of the first. Although this recipro-cal influence can be easily observed in small groups, Hofstede's (1984) research demon-strates that it is culturally determined as well. In a cross-cultural comparison he was able to rank 40 countries in a Power Distance Index (PDI) with countries such as the Philip-pines, Mexico, Venezuela, and India having the highest PDI indices and countries such as New Zealand, Denmark, Israel, and Austria, the lowest. A number of factors, including cultural ones, seemed to account for the between-countries differences. Perusal of Hosftede's data (1984, Figure 3.1, p. 77) reveals that of the 10 countries with the highest PDI scores, 8 were Latin or Asian. Of the 10 countries with the lowest PDI scores, eight were Euro-pean. People in high-PDI countries emphasized obedience and conformity and were more fearful to disagree with those in authority. They also preferred to be closely supervised and to have those in authority make decisions while those in authority, in turn, saw them-selves as "benevolent decision makers." Interestingly, in high-PDI countries people seemed more reluctant to trust each other. Clearly, power distance is a cross-cultural variable that can have significant impact on interpersonal relations, particularly in xenocultural inter-actions. The United States ranked below the mean of the 40 countries in Hosftede's study. Because the amalgamatio of subcultural groups in this country has not always been a smooth one, and because there is a history of aggression and tension between these subgroups, it is not surprising to find marked discrepancies in the power orientation of members of dif-ferent subcultural groups. These different orientations affect xenocultural interactions— that is, diagnostic testing—regardless of whether the participants are aware of them.

In summary, the proposed model uses principles from social judgment theory to con-ceptualize functional aspects of sociocultural transactions. Intracultural factors consist of the person's native culture and provide a frame of reference for judgment and action. Xenocultural factors emerge when a person interacts with elements of a foreign culture and makes judgments about accepting (assimilating) or rejecting (contrasting) those ele-ments using his or her own position as an anchor. Cross-cultural factors, particularly power differentials, can also affect xenocultural relations. The principal idea of this model is that a full explanation of any xenocultural interaction requires studying cross-cultural and also intracultural dynamics. Xenocultural variables cannot be understood without knowledge of the intracultural and cross-cultural factors that affect them. In practical terms this means that the assessment of psychopathology across cultures must take into consideration factors that go beyond those usually considered as relevant in clinical practice, namely, cultural frames of reference, anchoring effects, assimilation and contrast effects, and historical and current power differentials between cultural groups. Viewed from this perspective the task appears daunting.

Which of the myriad cultural elements constitutes a frame of reference relevant to psychopathology? Obviously, not all cultural elements are important. When dealing with issues of mental health the important elements of the cultural frame are those reviewed in the previous section pertaining to the extension of Millon's model. They refer to the culture's worldview regarding individualism–collectivism, its view regarding human nature as primarily responsive to pain or to pleasure, and its preference for sedentary adaptation or for industrious activity.

Structural and Functional Elements in Item Response and Selection

Figure 14.2 illustrates a hypothetical xenocultural situation involving the individualism–collectivism (self versus other) dimension. The role of both structural and functional elements—the person's own position within a culturally provided frame of reference elements, and the tendency to assimilate or contrast stimuli in social judgment—are depicted. Person A can be regarded as self-oriented and functioning within an individualistic culture. Person B, on the other hand, is other-oriented and functioning within a collectivist culture. Their responses to several items will differ depending on their relative positions within their cultural frames. Item 1 in Figure 14.2, a critical item in the Nurturing scale of the Millon Index of Personality Styles (MIPS, item 154), will be readily accepted by person B because it will be perceived as close to that person's own position. Person A, on the other hand, will perceive that item as farther from his or her own position, although still within the cultural frame of reference, prompting that person to reject it. Item 2 in Figure 14.2—an item suggested by Triandis (1994, p. 292)—would most likely be outside the individualistic frame and would certainly be rejected by a self-oriented person. The same item would still be within the collectivist frame of reference and close to person's B own position, making it easier for him or her to accept it. Finally, item 3 in Figure 14.2, a critical item in the Dependent scale of the Millon Clinical Multiaxial Inventory—III, (MCMI-III, item 135; Millon, 1994) falls outside both the individualistic and collectivist frames of reference and would probably be regarded as abnormal by both persons A and B, although the latter would be more inclined to endorse it than would the former.

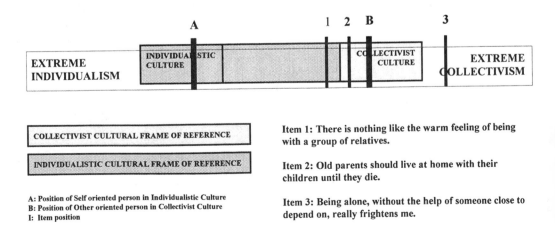

Item 1: There is nothing like the warm feeling of being with a group of relatives.

Item 2: Old parents should live at home with their children until they die.

Item 3: Being alone, without the help of someone close to depend on, really frightens me.

FIGURE 14.2. Using a cultural frame of reference to modulate assessment information.

Item Selection

Figure 14.2 is instructive in making determinations about the cultural suitability of items in test construction. It seems logical to assume that the population distribution in the collectivist culture would be skewed toward individualism (to the left in Figure 14.2), and toward collectivism (to the right in Figure 14.2) for the individualistic culture. The modal personality for each culture is represented by the positions of persons A and B, respectively. When making judgments about the other culture, persons A and B will regard as "normal" only those cultural elements that fall within their own cultural frame of reference. Anything beyond and outside that cultural frame will be regarded as abnormal. In Figure 14.2, this area of "normality" refers to the overlap between the two cultural frames of reference. This tendency to judge as normal only those things included within one's own cultural frame leads to a *restriction in the range of normality* in xenocultural interactions. Given the way social judgment works, then, there will be a marked tendency and a greater probability to regard as abnormal cultural elements that are foreign to us.

In the construction of tests to assess psychopathology cross-culturally, care must be exercised to ensure that the universe of items considered for inclusion represents items that are regarded as "truly" abnormal by the other culture, namely, those outside the frame of reference of the other culture as well as one's own. Equal care must be exercised in the opposite situation when judgments of normality are called for. For instance, therapists should not judge as abnormal behaviors that are outside their own frame of reference but regarded as quite normal by other cultures.

Cultural Considerations on Normality and Abnormality

The products of biological evolution are different species; the products of adaptive learning are different personality types and the cultural environments that reflect and sustain them. At the biological level the evolutionary process is Darwinian; at the psychological and cultural levels, it is Lamarckian. Psychological traits and cultural norms learned by an individual can be transmitted directly to its descendants or to others in the cultural group. Consequently, the rate of change at the psychological and cultural levels is much faster, and failures and successes are more evident, than in biological evolution. Whereas the demise of a species is a portentous and definitive event, it occurs in the relative obscurity of biological time. Although not as drastic as extinction, failures to adapt psychologically and culturally can appear to have far more immediate urgency. This latter point is important in that it has significance for the development of concepts such as normality and abnormality.

Intraculturally, normality is defined by the relation of the individual to his or her culture. This notion is analogous to that of the "fit" of an organism to its habitat. In evolutionary biology the closest idea to a concept of normality is the notion of "fitness" indexed by individual survival and reproductive success. It is a relational concept in that it can be influenced by changes in the environment so that "fitness" is always in reference to the immediate, present circumstances. Whatever genetic traits allow an organism to adapt to a particular habitat may become liabilities if the environment changes. Failure to "fit" into a habitat at the biological level can lead to extinction. At the psychological level, failure to adapt can lead to psychopathology. Normality, then, refers to the adaptive functioning of a person within a given cultural milieu.

The definition of normality as adaptive functioning within a given culture implies the existence of an optimum level of congruence or relatedness between the individual and his or her culture. The relative "fit" of the person to the culture would be given by the congruence between the person's habitual ways of functioning—his or her personality—and the modal cultural pattern. In Figure 14.2, both persons A and B could be said to have congruent relationships with their cultural groups and thus, to enjoy "normality" in their respective cultures. Examining this dimension from an intracultural perspective shows that a good fit between the person and his or her culture occurs for self-oriented individuals in individualist cultures; or, vice-versa, for other-oriented persons in collectivist cultures. A relatively high degree of congruence can be expected between the person and his or her cultural environment provided that his or her habitual ways of functioning fall within the ranges provided by cultural norms. Marked deviations from these ideals would lead to conflict and possibly psychopathology. Of course, the closer an individual's personality comes to reflecting the modal personality of the culture, the more congruent he or she will be to that culture. This type of congruence is reflected, for example, by beliefs such as "*Primero, sangre*" (literally, "First, blood.") held by Hispanic American and Latino persons whose cultures are primarily collectivist. The expression refers to the cultural norm of giving preference to blood relatives rather than to outsiders. Thus, for example, a spouse will have a lower priority than a child. Beliefs such as this provide a reference point or anchor for the person. To the extent that there is a lack of congruence there will be tension and conflict. If the discrepancy is small, there may be attempts on both parts to resolve the differences. If, however, the discrepancy is large, cultural norms may call for severe sanctions or rejection and isolation of the individual. At this exteme point the person will probably suffer some symptoms and may be labeled as deviant by others.

Things would remain simple for a definition of normality, or abnormality, for that matter, if individuals remained stationary in their native cultures. A relative degree of permanence would confer stability to the relatedness between the person and the culture. Change, if any, would be gradual and easily assimilated into existing cultural and psychological structures. However, this is not so. In the span of a lifetime a person comes into contact with many and varied cultures. Sometimes this contact is initiated by the individual. In other instances cultural groups try to impose their own set of structures on others. It is at this point that sets of xenocultural interactions enter the picture and judgments of normality or abnormality must then be defined not only by adaptive behavior within the native culture but also as the person mingles in the new culture. There are any number of factors that can disturb the relatedness of the individual and his or her cultural milieu. Although not an exhaustive list, four appear relevant to our current discussion: *migration*, *marginality*, *cultural subjugation*, and *social change*.

Migration and Marginality

Sometimes xenocultural contact is initiated when the lack of congruence with his or her culture prompts the person to escape to more congenial environments. Migration and marginality are two modes of escape. Cultural migrants are motivated by the desire to find cultural environments different from the native one. In this quest they are not to be confused with economic refugees whose motives are financial and who, unlike cultural migrants, tend to maintain a strong attachment to the culture of origin. Economic refugees adopt new cultural patterns to the extent that they are instrumental to attaining financial goals. Having a somewhat different set of motivations are political exiles who have been forcibly expelled from their native culture and who may harbor the hope of returning home someday. Similar to economic refugees, they maintain a strong attachment to the native culture but perhaps tend to idealize it because of the distressing conditions of the separation.

Marginality is another way in which to resolve the conflict created by a lack of congruence between the person's style and cultural patterns. Whether they are American expatriates in Paris in the 1920s, counterculture hippies of the 1960s, or current migrants to this multicultural society, some people live in the interstitial spaces between cultures. These interstitial denizens may be so by choice or through a historical accident, but they are best characterized, as Perez Firmat suggests in "Life On the Hyphen" (1994), by their ability to navigate in both cultures without truly being of any one.

> The [marginal] individual is unique in that, unlike younger and older compatriots, he or she may actually find it possible to circulate within and through both the old and the new cultures. . . . While [they] may never feel entirely at ease in either one, they are capable of availing themselves of the resources—linguistic, artistic, commercial—that both cultures have to offer. (pp. 4–5)

Cultural migrants, economic refugees, political exiles, and marginals are all moved by different motives and develop different ways of relating to the native and to the host culture. Accordingly, what constitutes psychopathology from a xenocultural perspective will differ for persons in each of these circumstances. For example, cultural migrants may try to accelerate their acculturation to the host culture and experience considerable distress if rejected. For economic refugees acculturation may consist more of a series of pragmatic decisions based on the relative utility of the outcome. The impact of rejection by the host culture would be attenuated by the economic refugee's continuing attachment to the native culture. Political exiles, on the other hand, may confront the process of acculturation quite differently. They may actively resist it for fear of losing ties to the native culture. From their vantage point rejection by the host culture may strengthen their resolve to return to the native culture at some future point.

The experience of culturally marginal persons may be quite different. One could speculate that "life on the hyphen" (Perez Firmat, 1994) would be a more desirable experience for persons of the detached interpersonal pattern (Millon, 1981), who would want to distance themselves from their native culture either as a protective maneuver or because of a genuine lack of motivation to remain in it.

Cultural Subjugation

How much dominance one cultural group has over another—a cross-cultural variable—also has implications for a definition of psychopathology. Whether it is through war, colonialism, slavery, or economic subordination, the aims of the dominant cultural group are generally twofold: the eradication of elements of the native culture and the imposition of its own cultural patterns. Psychologically this process forces members of the subservient cultural group not only to adapt to a new set of standards but to do so under conditions of helplessness and degradation. The devastating psychological effects of helplessness (Abramson, Garber, & Seligman, 1980; Seligman, 1975) and degradation are well documented.

Cultural subjugation creates a power differential between cultural groups that affects intergroup behavior. Motivated by self-preservation, the behavior of members of the subordinate culture may be guarded and distrustful when dealing with dominant culture members. In time their wariness may become normative and will manifest itself readily in xenocultural interactions. It should not be surprising then that psychometric research with these populations yields consistent results in which members of historically oppressed cultural groups score in what are considered deviant patterns. Their deviant scores depend on the long-standing cross-cultural power differential between subcultural groups (Gynther, 1972; Gynther, 1981).

Social Change

Cultures are dynamic. They change and that change may in itself be pathogenic, depending on its speed and magnitude. Paradoxically, under conditions of rapid social change those who had a firm and secure fit to the original culture may find themselves more vulnerable. Equally at risk are those who have not secured a firm anchoring and find themselves adrift because of the pace and complexity of cultural transformations. Millon (1987) has cogently described the role of changing sociocultural factors in the pathogenesis of the borderline personality disorder:

> Recent cultural changes have led to a loss of key cohering experiences that once protected against problematic parent–child relationships. Traditional societies provided ameliorative and reparative relationships (grandparents, aunts, older siblings, neighbors) and institutions (church, school) that offered remedies for parental disaffiliation; such societies provided a backup, so to speak, that insured that those who had been deprived or abused would be given a second chance to gain love and to observe models for developmental coherence. . . . Whereas the cultural institutions of most societies have retained practices that furnish reparative stabilizing and cohering experiences, thereby remedying disturbed parent–child relationships . . . the changes of the past two to three decades (in Western societies) have not only fostered an increase in intrapsychic diffusion and splintering, but have also resulted in the discontinuation of psychically restorative institutions and customs, contributing thereby to both the incidence and exacerbation of features that typify borderline pathology. Without the corrective effects of undergirding and focusing social mentors and practices, the diffusing or divisive consequences of unfavorable earlier experience take firm root and unyielding form. (p. 367)

In summary, the link to study psychopathology cross-culturally rests with the study of personality, and from this perspective psychopathology arises from a lack of fit between the person and the culture, from changes in the environment which render previously adaptive traits maladaptive.

PROGRAMMATIC USE OF THE MILLON INVENTORIES CROSS-CULTURALLY

Evidently, attempts to study psychopathology cross-culturally must be guided by knowledge of the elements that make up a cultural group's frame of reference and of the functional mechanisms that underlie social judgment at the cultural level. In most groups it will be the case that behaviors which fall within the cultural frame of reference will be regarded as normal and will serve as anchors for judgment. Behaviors that fall outside the cultural frame will be regarded as increasingly pathological the farther away they are from culturally accepted anchors and from the judge's own position. As we have seen in this chapter, extending Millon's evolutionary model provides the theoretical underpinnings for work at the sociocultural level. Research must be guided by the definition of normality as a "good fit" or congruence between the individual's personality and the modal cultural patterns. Instrumentation to assess personality styles already exists with the Millon inventories in their different presentations (the MCMI-II and MCMI-III, the Millon Adolescent Personality Inventory [MAPI] and the Millon Adolescent Clinical Inventory [MACI], and the Millon Index of Personality Styles [MIPS]), allowing for testing both abnormal and normal variants. Measurement of cultural differences may be more complicated and fewer instruments exist for this purpose. Triandis's work (Triandis, 1995) offers the most systematic treatment of the measurement of individualism and collectivism. He suggests a variety of approaches ranging from observations on "sociability"—indexed by whether people generally walk alone or with others in a given cultural group—to the use of standardized instruments (see Triandis, 1995, Appendix). Content analysis of cultural products (e.g., children's stories) can be used to assess cultural variation in the other dimensions of the model. Atkinson's research on n-Ach (Atkinson, 1958) represents a good example of this type of work. Whatever the method of measurement used, the strategy for crosscultural research remains the same. Judgments on normality and abnormality can only be made within the context provided by the cultural frame of reference.

The Millon Index of Personality Styles

This is a true/false questionnaire designed to measure normal personality styles in adults between the ages of 18 and 65+. It provides scores on 24 separate scales. Six of these—the Motivating Aims—are of particular interest because they represent measurements of the bipolar constructs of Millon's evolutionary model. In the MIPS the evolutionary principles of existence, adaptation, and replication are measured not as bipolar constructs but as unipolar variables with each pole represented by a different scale: Enhancing, Preserving, Modifying, Accommodating, Individuating, and Nurturing. These six scales of the MIPS can be used in what Triandis has called an "intracultural" approach to measure modal personality, defined as the most prevalent personality orientation, of different cultural groups. This would establish the parameters of the frame of reference for each group and allow clinical practitioners to make judgments about what traits would be considered most adaptive by a cultural group. For example, a group whose modal personality was pleasure oriented (enhancing), active (modifying), and self-oriented (individuating) would probably regard as highly adaptive traits such as popularity, superficiality in interpersonal relations, competitiveness, and denial. In such a group, the prevalence of outgoing (histrionic), controlling (aggressive), and asserting (narcissistic) styles would be relatively high and admired. On the other hand, the pleasure-deficient personalities—retiring (schizoid), hesitating (avoidant), and depressive—would be poorly tolerated and probably ostracized.

In Chapter 5 of the MIPS manual (Millon et al., 1994) descriptions of several applied research studies are offered. Invariably, these studies show the ability of the MIPS to identify the personality characteristics of individuals who will do well in a variety of settings ranging from the military to managerial positions in business. The logic of this type of research can be extended to the cultural level by identifying a priori the cultural dimensions of given groups and determining the personality characteristics most suited for those groups. For example, a monastery would require from its members a passive withdrawal from the pleasures of the world. Within this type of setting individuals who are high in the Preserving (pain) and Accommodating (passivity) dimensions and who load weakly on the self–other dimension would do well. More active or pleasure-seeking persons would not do well.

A potentially profitable line of research is the study of the marital satisfaction of intercultural couples. In this type of union there are potentially four different elements to deal with: each spouses' personality characteristics and their respective cultural orientations. One would expect the greatest harmony in those marriages where the spouses have compatible personality characteristics and they come from similar cultural backgrounds, and the greatest marital strife in those couples who do not have compatible personalities and come from very dissimilar cultural backgrounds.

Another use of the MIPS is in the area of acculturation. Systematic study of different cultural groups can be carried out to obtain typologies of cultures according to the dimensions of the evolutionary model. Issues of acculturation could then be discussed in terms of movement along the dimensions of the model. A person could be said to become more acculturated to a new group if he or she changed on some or all of the key dimensions, for example from individualism to collectivism, regardless of whether he or she had adopted the superficial aspects of the culture (preferences in language, dress, foods, etc.). A truly acculturated person would be one who adopted those superficial aspects of the culture *and* changed the orientation of the key dimensions.

The Millon Clinical Multiaxial Inventory

Surprisingly, in spite of the considerable care exercised in making the MCMI sensitive to cross-cultural issues (Millon, 1977), it has not been used extensively for work in that area. A few studies using the MCMI compared African Americans and European Americans and yielded the customary results, with African Americans scoring higher on those scales that reflect "mistrust, alienation, vigilance, and impulsivity, as well as cynicism" (Hamberger & Hastings, 1992, p. 94). A similar pattern of results was obtained in a previous study by Choca, Shanley, Peterson, and Van Denburg (1990). These patterns of results may reflect the history of subjugation that minorities have suffered in this country and in effect constitute a cross-cultural phenomenon more than a psychological one.

Cross-culturally, psychotherapy can be conceptualized as an attempt to bring the patient back into congruence with the prevailing cultural pattern. Conceived this way the process requires that the therapist have very good knowledge about two sets of variables; on the one hand, the therapist has to know the modal personality of the culture and the parameters that constitute the frame of reference for that group. On the other, the therapist must know the personality dynamics of the patient to decide how and why there has been a deviation from the culturally expected. An example may help to illustrate this point. A male, Hispanic patient, born and raised in a South American country but living in the United States, presented with panic disorder with agoraphobia. A simplistic approach to this case would have attempted to reduce the anxiety provoking the panic attacks. A more culturally sensitive approach would have taken into consideration the patient's own personality and the cultural elements that define a set of expectations for him. Testing with the MCMI-II revealed a mildly narcissistic personality. The patient was the youngest male in a large family and had been the center of his mother's attention all of his life. Upon coming to the United States the patient met and married an American woman from the Midwest. Both the patient and his wife professed to love each other and there were no signs of marital strife. However, the patient did complain about the lack of "caring" that his wife showed toward him (e.g., "married all these years and she has never even ironed a shirt for me") and about her not getting along well with his relatives, particularly his older brothers. Upon hearing of his panic attacks his mother came to the United States to live with him. Also, his older brothers took turns to fly to this country and spend a week or 2 with him. Additionally, whenever the patient visited his home country he did not suffer from panic attacks. With his brothers' visits, the frequency of his panic attacks decreased.

This patient who came from a strong collectivist culture, defined his sense of self from his relationship to his family. His wife, who came from an individualistic orientation, unwittingly failed to provide for his "needs" and by that contributed to his attacks. The panic attacks were a desperate, yet successful attempt to recreate those cultural patterns that had always given him a sense of well-being, namely his own family. This type of analysis offers several therapeutic options. One approach would be making the patient's wife more sensitive to her husband's culturally determined way of defining himself as an integral part of a collective, that is, his family. Another alternative would be to reassure the husband that his wife's "coldness" should not be viewed as a rejection of him personally but as a cultural characteristic. In any event, either or both alternatives applied simultaneously would probably yield better results than would a simplistic attempt to desensitize the anxiety felt by the patient.

CONCLUSION

This chapter proposed to extend Millon's evolutionary model of personality to the sociocultural level to complete the progression from the biological to the social for the three polarities—existence, adaptation, and replication. As extended, the model provides solid support for examining the influence of culture on psychopathology, allowing clinicians to focus only on the important aspects of this influence—namely, the polarities—rather than being overwhelmed by the bewildering array of cultural diversity. Extending the model also makes it possible to define normality based on the congruence between the individual's personality and the set of expectations provided by the cultural frame of reference. Set this way, the task of the clinician should become relatively simple. Psychological assessment provides the data about the individual; cultural assessment provides data about the cultural frame of reference. Psychotherapy can then be guided by the congruency principle—a matter of finding the "fittedness" of the patient and the culture. In practice, of course, the process is far from simple. Fortunately, there are instruments based on Millon's theoretical model that are ideally suited for cross-cultural work. Obviously what is needed now is more research that explores the cultural foundations of psychopathology using Millon's evolutionary model.

REFERENCES

Abramson, L., Garber, J., & Seligman, M. (1980). Learned helplessness in humans: An attributional analysis. In J. Garber & M. E. Seligman (Eds.), *Human helplessness: Theory and applications* (pp. 33–34). New York: Academic Press.

Atkinson, J. W. (1958). *Motives in fantasy, action, and society.* Princeton, NJ: Van Nostrand.

Child, I. L., Storm, T., & Veroff, J. (1958). Achievement themes in folk tales related to socialization practice. In J. W. Atkinson (Ed.), *Motives in fantasy, action, and society* (pp. 479–492). Princeton, NJ: Van Nostrand.

Choca, J. P., Shanley, L. A., Peterson, C. A., & Van Denburg, E. (1990). Racial bias and the MCMI. *Journal of Personality Assessment, 54,* 470–490.

Eysenck, H. J. (1967). *The biological basis of personality.* Springfield, IL: Thomas.

Eysenck, H. J. (Ed.). (1981). *A model of personality.* New York: Springer-Verlag.

Gudykunst, W. B. (1991). *Bridging differences.* Newbury Park, CA: Sage.

Gynther, M. D. (1972). White norms and black MMPI's: A prescription for discrimination? *Psychological Bulletin, 78,* 386–402.

Gynther, M. D. (1981). Is the MMPI an appropriate assessment device for blacks? *Journal of Black Psychology, 7*, 67–75.

Hamberger, L. K., & Hastings, J. E. (1992). Racial differences on the MCMI in an outpatient clinical sample. *Journal of Personality Assessment, 58*(1), 90–95.

Hofstede, G. (1984). *Culture's consequences.* Beverly Hills: Sage.

Hofstede, G. (1991). *Cultures and organizations: Software of the mind.* London: McGraw-Hill.

Hui, C. H., & Triandis, H. C. (1986). Individualism and collectivism: A study of crosscultural researchers. *Journal of Cross-Cultural Psychology, 17*, 225–248.

Javier, R. A. (1995). Machismo/marianismo: Stereotypes and Hispanic culture. In S. Rathus & J. Nevid (Eds.), *Adjustment and growth: The challenges of life* (p. 317). New York: Harcourt Brace College Publishers.

Kluckhohn, F. (1954). Culture and behavior. In G. Lindzey (Ed.), *Handbook of social psychology* (Vol. 2, pp. 921–976). Reading, MA: Addison-Wesley.

Marin, G., & Triandis, H. C. (1985). Allocentrism as an important characteristic of the behavior of Latin Americans and Hispanics. In R. Diaz-Guerrero (Ed.), *Cross-cultural and national studies in social psychology* (pp. 85–104). Amsterdam: North Holland.

McClelland, D. C. (1961). *The achieving society.* New York: Free Press.

McClelland, D. C., & Winter, D. G. (1969). *Motivating economic achievement.* New York: Free Press.

Millon, T. (1977). *Millon Clinical Multiaxial Inventory manual.* Minneapolis: National Computer Systems.

Millon, T. (1981). *Disorders of personality: DSM-III, Axis II.* New York: Wiley.

Millon, T. (1987a). *Millon Clinical Multiaxial Inventory manual II.* Minneapolis: National Computer Systems.

Millon, T. (1987b). On the genesis and prevalence of the borderline personality disorder: A social learning thesis. *Journal of Personality Disorders, 1*, 354–372.

Millon, T. (1990). *Toward a new personology: An evolutionary model.* New York: Wiley.

Millon, T., & Davis, R. (1996). *Disorders of personality: DSM-IV and beyond.* New York: Wiley.

Millon, T. (1994). *Millon Clinical Multiaxial Inventory—III manual.* Minneapolis: National Computer Systems.

Millon, T., Weiss, L., Millon, C., & Davis, R. (1994). *MIPS: Millon index of personality styles manual.* San Antonio: Psychological Corporation.

Mulder, M. (1976). Reduction of power differences in practice: The power distance reduction theory and its applications. In G. Hofstede & M. Kassem (Eds.), *European contributions to organization theory.* Assen, Netherlands: Van Gorcum.

Perez Firmat, G. (1994). *Life on the hyphen: The Cuban-American way.* Austin: University of Texas Press.

Rushton, J. P. (1985). Differential K theory: The sociobiology of individual and group differences. *Personality and Individual Differences, 6*, 441–452.

Scott, G. R. (1974). *The history of corporal punishment.* Detroit: Gale Research Company. (Original work published 1938)

Seligman, M. E. (1975). *Helplessness: On depression, development, and death.* San Francisco: Freeman.

Sherif, M., & Sherif, C. (1969). *Social psychology.* New York: Harper & Row.

Shweder, R. A., & LeVine, R. A. (1984). *Cultural theory: Essays on mind, self and emotion.* New York: Cambridge University Press.

Szapocznick, J., & Kurtines, W. (1993). Family psychology and cultural diversity. *American Psychologist, 48*(4), 400–407.

Szasz, T. S. (1975). *Pain and pleasure: A study of bodily feelings.* New York: Basic Books.

Trafimow, D., Triandis, H. C., & Goto, S. (1991). Some tests of the distinction between private self and collective self. *Journal of Personality and Social Psychology, 60*, 649–655.

Triandis, H. C. (1989). The self and social behavior in differing cultural contexts. *Psychological Review, 96*, 506–520.

Triandis, H. C. (1994). Major cultural syndromes and emotion. In S. Kitayama & H. R. Markus (Eds.), *Emotion and culture: Empirical studies of mutual influence* (pp. 285–306). Washington, DC: American Psychological Association.

Triandis, H. C. (1995). *Individualism and collectivism.* Boulder, CO: Westview Press.

Triandis, H. C., McCusker, C., & Hui, C. H. (1990). Multimethod probes of individualism and collectivism. *Journal of Personality and Social Psychology, 59,* 1006–1020.

Triandis, H. C., Vassiliou, V., & Nassiakou, M. (1968). Three crosscultural studies of subjective culture. *Journal of Personality and Social Psychology, 8*(Suppl.), 1–42.

15

Issues and Procedures in MCMI Translations

HEDWIG V. SLOORE
JAN J. L. DERKSEN

The translation of a psychological test into another language is only part of the broader process of adaptation of an instrument to another language and culture. Professionally developed and validated guidelines for adapting tests are being developed at this moment (Hambleton, 1994). So far the technical literature for guiding the test adaptation process has been incomplete and scattered through many international journals, reports and books. In the last 2½ years the following organizations have been active in producing guidelines for instrument adaptation: the International Test Commission (ITC), the European Association of Psychological Assessment (EAPA), the European Test Publishers Group (ETPG), the International Association for Cross-Cultural Psychology (IACCP), the International Association of Applied Psychology (IAAP), the International Association for the Evaluation of Educational Achievement (IEA), the International Language Testing Association (ILTA), and the International Union of Psychological Science (IUPsyS). They have developed a set of guidelines for instrument adaptation, the final version of which they hope to publish late in 1996.

The following guidelines recommended by the ITC are relevant for the MCMI project in the Netherlands and Belgium.

1. Instrument developers/publishers should ensure that the adaptation process takes full account of the linguistic and cultural differences among the populations for whom adapted versions of the instrument are intended.

2. Instrument developers/publishers should provide evidence that the language used for the items and in the manual is appropriate for all cultural and language populations for whom the instrument is intended.

3. Instrument developers/publishers should provide evidence that the choice of testing techniques, item formats, test conventions, and procedures are familiar to all intended populations.

4. Instrument developers/publishers should provide evidence that item content and stimulus materials are familiar to all intended populations.

5. Instrument developers/publishers should implement systematic judgmental evidence, both linguistic and psychological, to improve the accuracy of the adaptation process and compile evidence on the equivalence of different language versions.

6. Instrument developers/publishers should ensure that the data collection design permits the use of appropriate statistical techniques to establish item equivalence between the different language versions of the instrument.

7. Instrument developers/publishers should apply appropriate statistical techniques to (a) establish the equivalence of the different versions of the instrument, and (b) identify problematic components or aspects of the instrument which may be inadequate to one or more of the intended populations.

8. Instrument developers/publishers should provide information on the evaluation of validity in all target populations for whom the adapted version is intended.

9. Instrument developers/publishers should provide statistical evidence of the equivalence of questions for all intended populations.

10. Nonequivalent questions between versions intended for different populations should not be used in preparing a common scale or in comparing these populations. However, they may be useful in enhancing content validity of scores reported for each population separately.

Two common errors in the translation process are frequently mentioned: (1) the selection of easily available translators or individuals familiar to the instrument developer (i.e., friends), simply because they are bilingual, has shown to be an unsuccessful practice (Brislin, 1986); and (2) there has been a failure to ensure that translators selected are familiar with the content area of the questionnaire under study, as well as experienced in instrument development in general.

With these internationally developed guidelines in mind we started working on the translation of the Millon Clinical Multiaxial Inventory—III (MCMI-III; Millon, 1994). In this project Hedwig Sloore, Jan Derksen, Hubert de Mey, and Greet Hellenbosch used their recent experience with the adaptation of the Minnesota Multiphasic Personality Inventory—2 (MMPI-2) as a starting point (Derksen, Sloore, de Mey, & Hellenbosch, 1993). Special attention was paid to the fact that the adaptation was developed for two countries at the same time: The Netherlands and Belgium. Although the languages look very similar, there are specific differences which could be very important in such a project (see above point 4). To avoid the most important pitfalls, the committee approach to translation was used. At the start two teams of bilingual translators were installed: the Dutch team was composed of two psychologists who independently made a translation of all MCMI-III items (Drs. Derksen and de Mey). In the end they tried to reach a consensus on the basis of discussion. In Belgium the same procedure was followed; three psychologists (Drs. Sloore, Hellenbosch, and Van Alboom) first made a translation in an independent way and then they integrated their work into one single Flemish version on the basis of discussion. Some of the general principles used by both teams during this work were as follows: (1) try to stick as close as possible to the original English formulation; (2) if two or more formulations are possible, choose the most simple one; (3) clarity of the formulation is important; and (4) the items should be written in a fluent and readable style (points 2 and 5 mentioned above). At this stage of the translation process we had at our disposal Dutch and Flemish versions which had to be integrated. This was the moment of confrontation of two "different" cultures. If we take into account the number of mutual jokes on the two countries, we could expect quite some differences! The two Dutch psychologists and two Flemish psychologists (without Dr. Van Alboom) formed a new committee to discuss the final formulation for all items.

All four can be considered as true bilinguals; they are all familiar with the psychological language as well as with everyday language, they all have experience with potential respondents to the MCMI-III (between 4 years and more than 20 years of clinical experience), and they are familiar with the procedures of test development. Two of them had some extensive bicultural experience due to repeated visits to the United States as well.

It took many hours of discussion for the committee of four psychologists to find a consensus. When they had any doubts on the exact meaning of an item or when different interpretations were possible, Theodore Millon was contacted by fax or e-mail to be sure about the intended meaning of the original item. For instance, the use of the American word "family" can have different meanings in Belgium: it can refer to the small, nuclear family ("gezin") or to the broader family, including grandparents, uncles, etcetera ("familie"). A second example of intercultural differences in word use: several items in the MCMI-III refer to the use of "illegal drugs." The word "drug" is common in our language too, but it always refers to the illegal hard and soft drugs and never to medication prescribed by doctors or to over-the-counter medication. However, we were able to solve all of these problems and even to remain friends afterwards.

The backtranslation (point 7) was done by a native Englishman who received his basic training in the United Kingdom; he received his language training at the university level in English and Dutch at a Belgian University. For the last 15 years he had lived and worked in Belgium. A style review was also conducted by a specialist in Dutch. The results of both of these activities were nine suggestions concerning the translation and three suggestions related to the style of the Dutch. All suggestions had to do with details, mostly using a different Dutch word for an English concept, except for item 60; for this item the style reviewer suggested a different Dutch sentence. All suggestions were reviewed by the Dutch–Flemish committee and most of them were integrated into the final version.

The Dutch–Flemish MCMI-III and the original English version were subjected to a research project to detect different answer patterns of bilinguals. Thirty students of English, all in their final stages of study, were willing to fill in the English and the Dutch versions. One-half of the subjects first received the Dutch version, and the second half did it viceversa. Between the two conditions a time period of 2 weeks existed. The results were as follows: of the 175 items, the percentages of answers that were in agreement varied from 56.67 to 100. The mean stability percentage according to the formula (equal / [equal + unequal]) × 100 was 90.04. Twenty-seven items scored 100 percent. The three items with lowest agreement were item 50 (56.67%) (this item had caused us considerable translation difficulties), item 114 (60%), and item 23 (70%).

THE MCMI-III AS ASSESSMENT INSTRUMENT

Adaptation of an existing questionnaire to another language and culture means more than just making a correct translation on the basis of the internationally approved rules. We needed the basic validation research to verify the test's characteristics and we also had to construct proper norms or base rates (BRs) based on a representative sample of patients from The Netherlands and Belgium. This common Dutch–Flemish project should result in the marketing of the questionnaire, which should in turn lead to a much broader use in clinical practice than was the case in the past.

In the early 1980s, shortly after the publication of the original MCMI, I (H. S.) translated the MCMI-II (Millon, 1982) and started to do research with the instrument. As a clinical psychologist doing research at the university and having clinical practice at the state prison, I was always looking for "new" and "better" instruments. The apparent advantages of the MCMI were: it was an "objective" technique with a limited number of questions; it made use of almost the same labels as did the DSM-III taxonomy (American Psychiatric Association, 1980); and it was one of the few self-report instruments for the assessment of personality disorders (Derksen, 1995).

In addition to the already mentioned clinical and pragmatic reasons to start research with the MCMI at that moment, there were some more profound and theoretical reasons as well. The domain of the study of psychopathology has some very traditional roots in Europe combining observables, phenotypic aspects, and theoretical concepts. As an example, some of the historically most important names are Hippocrates, Galen, Kraepelin, Kretschmer, Heymans, Jaspers, etcetera, and I think we can state that the MCMI-III and especially Millon's theory (Millon, 1969, 1981, 1990) are much closer to this European tradition than are most other objective questionnaires. We must agree with Millon (1990) that in the field of psychopathology, just as much as in other domains of personality psychology in general, we need (1) a firm theoretical basis, (2) diagnostic instruments derived from that theory, and (3) intervention techniques which are also based on the theory. The MCMI measures syndromes derived from a comprehensive clinical theory and the results obtained can better be integrated into the clinical data and the clinical process.

The MCMI, as a self-report questionnaire, was also attractive due to the fact that the test introduced a rather different principle of construction, or at least made appeal to principles which were not used in most other techniques: the use of actuarial base rates (BRs) instead of *T*-scores or other forms of normalized scores. On the basis of previous research with different tests we had already noticed that the distribution curves obtained do not always approximate the normal distribution, especially when we measure pathology. The introduction of the BR scores which take into account the prevalence of particular characteristics in clinical populations seemed attractive to us. Some of the most frequently used questionnaires in the field of clinical psychology were constructed in the first place to differentiate patients from normal people. In many situations these tests have proved to be very useful. However, in many clinical settings we are also interested in comparing the results obtained by "our" patient with results of other patients, and not with normal individuals. Here, too, the MCMI offered a new perspective because the test was constructed to differentiate between pathological syndromes on the basis of BRs in clinical populations.

In 1984 we decided to translate the MCMI to construct our own BRs and to do clinical validation studies. Although at that moment the requirements for translations were not as strict as they now are, great care was given to the process of translation. Four psychologists made a translation of the questionnaire in an independent way. These four translations were then discussed to come to one version agreed upon by the independent translators. If necessary, the advice of a linguist was sought. Then the questionnaire was repeatedly administered to different patients, not with the aim of obtaining their results and scores, but with the only aim to check the way they understood the different questions. We were very conscious of the fact that language is not unequivocal and that it is absolutely crucial that potential users of the questionnaire can give their views on the meaning of the different questions. Making a grammatically correct translation does not automatically mean that you have an equivalent version as far as meaning is concerned.

RESEARCH WITH THE MCMIs IN BELGIUM

The first part of the research project started in the mid-1980s: the collection of clinical information necessary to construct adapted BRs. The first, second, and third versions of the MCMI were administered to 427 patients in different clinical settings all over the Flemish-speaking part of Belgium. The great majority (78%) were patients of private and public psychiatric institutions. The remaining 22% were private practice patients, in- and outpatients of psychiatric departments in general hospitals, and prisoners of prisons for mental patients. It is important to stress the fact that a total of 22 different psychiatric or psychological institutions were prepared to collaborate and to gather the clinical data necessary to do the initial research. Thirty-seven percent of the patients were females, while 63% were males. The mean age of the males was slightly higher than that of the females; the range was between 17 and 77 years of age.

We tried to find as many clinicians as possible who were prepared to make a clinical judgment or evaluation of the patient; this resulted in a total of 358 clinical evaluations. The clinicians participating in this part of the research had been in direct contact with the patient for at least 4 hours. The clinical evaluation was done on the same basis as it was done in the original Millon study, as published in the manual for the MCMI (1982). Short descriptions of the eight basic personality styles, the three pathological personality syndromes, and the nine current symptom disorders were given to the clinicians. The most prominent personality style was rated on a 10-point scale. The same was done for a second or third personality style, if present. The part on the pathological personality syndromes had to be completed only if the clinician judged that the patient's personality pathology was of moderate to severe nature. Again, a rating on a 10-point scale was given if any of these syndromes was present. If necessary, a second characteristic syndrome could be rated. The last part of the clinical evaluation, the current clinical symptoms, was to be filled out only if the patient actually displayed some of the symptoms. The same 10-point rating system was used but clinicians were free to rate as many symptoms as they judged to be descriptive for the patient under study.

By means of Mann–Whitney tests, the differences between subgroups (patients, prisoners, age groups, etc.) were tested. Most tests revealed no statistical differences; only sex differences were important. Six out of the twenty scales revealed no statistical differences between the sexes at the .05 level: Scale 7 (Compulsive), Scale P (Paranoid), Scale N (Hypomanic), Scale B (Alcohol Abuse), Scale T (Drug Abuse) and Scale PP (Psychotic Delusions). The median values for the females were in general higher than for the male population, except for Scale 4 (Histrionic), Scale 5 (Narcissistic), and Scale 6 (Antisocial). These sex differences have been confirmed by studies using the Morey Personality Disorder Scales (Morey, Waugh, & Blashfield, 1985), developed from the MMPI-item pool. On a large sample of 2,514 in- and outpatients (933 females, 1,581 males) the only mean values which were higher for males were on the Histrionic, Narcissistic, and Antisocial scales (Sloore, Rouckhout, & Hellenbosch, 1993).

The scale reliability was examined solely on the basis of a homogeneity measure, the Kuder–Richardson Formula 20. The internal consistency was rather satisfactory; the median K-R 20 coefficient for all clinical scales was .82 (.88 in the original Millon study), with a range from .62 to .94. Five scales had K-R 20 values in the .90s, while only three scales fell below .70 (Histrionic, Antisocial, and Psychotic Delusions). Although most of the values obtained are smaller than for the original American data, they are very similar.

As we were in the possession of a standardized clinical evaluation for 358 patients in terms of Millon's theory, we tried to construct our own BRs. Two types of information are used to determine the 75 and 85 BR: the total prevalence rate of each personality type or syndrome disorder, and the most salient prevalence rate, respectively. The former was the percentage of patients who were judged by the clinicians to display some of the characteristics of the syndrome, regardless of the fact if the syndrome was ranked as most important or only in second or third order. The latter was the percentage of patients who were judged to present the syndrome under study as the most prominent one. To use the same example as in the MCMI-manual: 29.61% of our total patient sample were judged by the clinicians to present some characteristics of the histrionic personality pattern, while only 18.16% were judged to have a histrionic personality disorder as the most predominant disorder. As described in the manual (Millon, 1982), we calculated the median values for the different scales for the groups of patients mentioned above.

This procedure proved to be problematic, at least applied to our clinical data: for 13 of the 20 scales, the median values of the BR 85 group were lower than the median values of the BR 75 group. Here we find probably the major reason why the MCMI and the MCMI-II have been used mostly for research purposes in Belgium and The Netherlands rather than in clinical practice. The phenomenon was less pronounced in the female subsample (8 out of 20 scales), although this group was smaller ($N = 153$) than our male group ($N = 267$). It is hard to speculate on the possible causes of these astonishing results:

1. In the first place, it could have been due to the fact that our research sample was too small, although we had patients from different settings and a rather large number of clinicians making clinical evaluations.

2. A second possible reason could be our clinicians, although they all had been in contact with the patient for at least 4 hours. Nevertheless, using clinical descriptions for the evaluation should have avoided the tricky problem of important differences among clinicians in familiarity with diagnostic systems.

3. A third possible reason was possibly the most fundamental one: the discrepancy reported in most studies (Oldham, 1991) between self-report data and clinical evaluations, or the overreporting on self-report questionnaires compared with clinical judgments. The main reason for this discrepancy was probably the difference in standards used by the patients and by the clinicians. It could be that the patient was more evaluating her- or himself compared with previous situations and "normal" people, while the clinician compared the patient under study with other patients and other pathologies. Moreover, the patient was answering the questionnaire question by question and at the end, the answers on the different questions are added to obtain scale values. On the contrary, the clinician, in addition to taking into account the different criteria, was probably also judging the degree of pathology on a more global and integrated level.

FACTOR STRUCTURE OF THE MCMIs

An important step in the preliminary research when making translations of existing questionnaires into other languages and in adapting instruments to other cultures is the comparison of the factor structures obtained in both cultures. The intercorrelations were calculated on the Belgian sample and were compared with the American values. As there is quite some item overlap between the scales, some high intercorrelations can be expected. Most of the correlations obtained for the Belgian sample were higher than were the American values. Although we know from Millon's theoretical model (Millon, 1981) and from clinical practice that the patterns and syndromes can not be conceived as independent and that some aspects are shared over different forms of pathology, some of the scale intercorrelations are extremely high. For example, in the MCMI more than 30 correlations were over .80, but they confirm the anticipated pattern of covariation. Eleven correlations are over .90. Just as an example, the three most important correlations at the level .96 are: Scale 2 (Avoidant) and Scale S (Schizotypal); Scale C (Borderline) and Scale A (Anxiety); and Scale D (Dysthymic) and Scale C (Borderline).

The matrix of intercorrelations was factor analyzed by the method of principal components and rotated to a varimax criterion (see Table 15.1). We obtained four factors with eigenvalues over 1.0. These factors accounted for 86.8% of the variance. On the basis of this MCMI factor analysis, no clear distinction was found between personality styles, pathological personality disorders, and clinical syndromes. The first factor had important loadings on a large number of scales: Scales 8, Passive–Aggressive (.94); D, Dysthymia (.93); C, Borderline (.92); CC, Psychotic Depression (.91); A, Anxiety (.89); 2, Avoidant (.88); S, Schizotypal (.84); and H, Somatoform (.78). A substantial negative loading was obtained on Scale 7, Compulsive (–.78). This factor is very similar to the one obtained by Millon (1982). When factors are defined by a large number of high loadings it is always difficult to label the common aspects or the central theme. Millon (1982) describes this factor as "depressive and labile emotionality expressed in affective moodiness and neurotic complaints" (p. 49).

The second factor was characterized by a high loading on Scales N, Hypomanic (.82); 4, Histrionic (.81); T, Drug Abuse (.79); and 5, Narcissistic (.65). This factor corresponds to a certain degree to the negative pool of Millon's Factor 2. This second factor portrays a cluster of excitement, social acting out, and extraversion. Factor 3 has an important loading on Scales PP, Psychotic Delusions (.93); P, Paranoid (.79); and SS, Psychotic Thinking (.55). This seems to be a factor of delusional cognitions and is only partly similar to Millon's second factor. The fourth factor is defined on the positive pole by Scale 3, Dependent (.81); and on the negative pole by Scale 6, Antisocial (–.69). Factor 4 seems to represent a dimension defined by submissiveness, social restraint, and conformity on one side and dominance, rebellious behavior, and independence on the other.

Choca, Shanley, and Van Denburg (1992) reported on more than 15 factor analytic studies using all scales of the MCMI. The number of factors extracted varies between three and five. Only a small number of studies analyzed a heterogeneous group of psychiatric patients. Despite some differences, the factorial solutions are rather similar. Three of

TABLE 15.1. Factor Loadings for the Belgian Sample

Factor 1		Factor 2		Factor 3		Factor 4	
8	.94	N	.82	PP	.93	3	.81
D	.93	4	.81	P	.79	4	.42
C	.92	T	.79	SS	.55		
CC	.91	5	.65	1	.41	6	–.69
A	.89	B	.52				
2	.88	6	.51				
S	.84						
H	.78						
SS	.75						
1	.70						
B	.58						
7	–.78						
5	–.53						
Eigenvalue	10.41		4.04		1.76		1.15
% var.	52.0		20.2		8.8		5.8

Note. 1, Schizoid; 2, Avoidant; 3, Dependent; 4, Histrionic; 5, Narcissistic; 6, Antisocial; 7, Compulsive; 8, Passive–Aggressive; S, Schizotypal; C, Borderline; P, Paranoid; A, Anxiety; H, Somatoform; N, Hypomanic; D, Dysthymic; B, Alcohol Abuse; T, Drug Abuse; SS, Psychotic Thinking; CC, Psychotic Depression; PP, Psychotic Delusions.

the factors were identified as (general) maladjustment, acting out or impulsiveness, and psychoticism.

We labeled our first factor to correspond with Millon's (1982) first factor: Depression and Anxiety. A label of "General Maladjustment," however, could also fit this factor. The negative pole is perhaps more problematic to explain. Would defining the positive pole as "Maladjustment" mean that the other pole should be labeled as "Adjustment"?

The Acting Out or Impulsiveness factor, as identified by Choca, Peterson, and Shanley (1986), Piersma (1986), and Lewis and Harder (1990), is very similar to our second factor. Our third factor could also be labeled "Psychoticism," a factor identified by Choca et al. (1986), Greenblatt, Modzierz, Murphy, and Trimakas (1986), and Piersma (1986), who labeled this factor as "Paranoid Distrust." Most studies identified just three factors; Piersma (1986), however, identified five facets, his first factor being "Dependence" versus "Dominance." This factor is identical to our fourth factor. This short overview of the results of factor analysis illustrates how difficult it is to define adequate labels for factors, but at the same time there seems to be a certain stability even over different groups of patients and different cultures. As noted by Wetzler (1990), the factor stability found is a positive aspect of the MCMIs, assuming that this stability is not an artifact resulting from the item overlap.

EXTERNAL CORRELATES

We administered the MCMI and the MMPI to a small group of patients ($N = 52$) to look at the relationships of the questionnaire under study with other diagnostic inventories. Of course it is impossible to discuss all correlations; we will only present a short overview of some of the most important ones. The correlations between the MCMI scales and the clinical scales of the MMPI are presented in Table 15.2.

It is amazing to see how the correlation pattern of the different MCMI scales with MMPI Scales Pt (Psychasthenia) and Sc (Schizophrenia) are very similar. It is also apparent that Scale 4 (Histrionic) and Scale Hy (Hysteria) measure two different syndromes ($r = .30$), as do Scales 6 (Antisocial) and Pd (Psychopathic Deviate; $r = -.13$). Scale P (Paranoid) correlates only at .39 with Scale Pa (Paranoia). Moderate correlations are found between Scales H (Somatoform) and Hs (Hypochondriasis; $r = .59$) and between Scales N (Hypomanic) and Ma (Hypomania; $r = .59$). These results are confirmed by the Smith, Carroll, and Fuller's (1988) study of 106 outpatients.

A rather striking fact is that Scale 1 (Schizoid) shows the highest correlation with Scale Si (Social Introversion), .60, while Scale S (Schizotypal) shows the highest correlation with Scale Pt (Psychasthenia), .68, instead of with Scale Sc (Schizophrenia), .64. The MMPI Schizophrenia scale correlates in the first place with Scale D (Dysthymic), .73, with Scale 2 (Avoidant), .72, with Scale A (Anxiety), .71, and Scale H (Somatoform), .70. The correlations between Scale Sc (Schizophrenia) and two of the MCMI "psychotic" scales (SS and CC) are lower than could be expected: .67 and .65, respectively. Rather unexpected is the very weak correlation between Scale PP (Psychotic Delusions) and Scale Sc (Schizophrenia), .13. Again, the majority of these results are confirmed by the study published by Smith, Carroll, and Fuller (1988), although most of the correlations in our study are higher. If these results are confirmed by further research, it would indicate that the instruments or questionnaires measure quite different aspects of pathology and could be used in a complementary way in clinical practice.

In the next step all correlations were calculated between the MCMI scales and the MMPI subscales, the Wiggins content scales, and some supplementary scales. We will present a se-

TABLE 15.2. Correlation Matrix, MCMI–MMPI (*N* = 52)

MCMI scale	MMPI scale								
	Hs	D	Hy	Pd	Pa	Pt	Sc	Ma	Si
1	.35	.62	.22	.14	.47	.55	.56	.14	.60
2	.54	.64	.46	.20	.65	.75	.72	.26	.58
3	.32	.14	.12	−.03	.57	.41	.42	.21	.10
4	−.31	−.59	−.30	.05	−.09	−.41	−.32	.21	−.61
5	−.45	−.61	−.37	−.03	−.40	−.65	−.56	.23	−.69
6	−.30	−.29	−.28	−.13	−.23	−.39	−.29	.26	−.36
7	−.32	−.25	−.22	−.34	−.43	−.40	−.46	−.43	−.15
8	.49	.49	.40	.36	.53	.61	.64	.50	.27
S	.50	.64	.37	.07	.60	.68	.64	.17	.58
C	.54	.52	.45	.30	.62	.66	.67	.51	.24
P	.08	.10	.00	.14	.39	.09	.19	.53	−.11
A	.57	.56	.43	.30	.58	.68	.71	.46	.28
H	.59	.48	.48	.15	.64	.68	.70	.50	.20
N	.07	−.20	.06	.13	.28	−.02	.08	.59	−.39
D	.62	.62	.52	.31	.59	.76	.73	.37	.38
B	.09	−.02	.04	.34	.36	.18	.24	.58	−.24
T	−.07	−.19	−.09	.18	.24	−.05	.05	.68	−.41
SS	.43	.51	.30	.16	.71	.60	.67	.35	.43
CC	.54	.53	.48	.29	.61	.67	.65	.41	.33
PP	.10	.20	.03	−.06	.29	.13	.13	.27	.07

Note. 1, Schizoid; 2, Avoidant; 3, Dependent; 4, Histrionic; 5, Narcissistic; 6, Antisocial; 7, Compulsive; 8, Passive–Aggressive; S, Schizotypal; C, Borderline; P, Paranoid; A, Anxiety; H, Somatoform; N, Hypomanic; D, Dysthymic; B, Alcohol Abuse; T, Drug Abuse; SS, Psychotic Thinking; CC, Psychotic Depression; PP, Psychotic Delusions; Hs, Hypochondriasis; D, Depression; Hy, Hysteria; Pd, Psychopathic Deviate; Pa, Paranoia; Pt, Psychasthenia; Sc, Schizophrenia; Ma, Hypomania; Si, Social Introversion.

lection of some of the most important correlations. Scale 1 (Schizoid) shows the highest correlations with some of the subscales of Scale D (Depression): .69 with Subjective Depression (D1), .65 with Mental Dullness (D4), and .65 with Brooding (D5). The correlation with the Wiggins depression scale is .62. The only subscale of Scale Sc (Schizophrenia) which shows an important correlation (.65) with Scale 1 is the scale Emotional Alienation (Sc2).

Scale 2 (Avoidant) shows an important number of correlations with a large number of MMPI-I -subscales, experimental, and Wiggins scales: Dependence (.84), Anxiety (.81), Wiggins Depression (.78), Brooding (D5; .78), Wiggins Poor Morale (.76), Wiggins Psychotism (.74), Inferiority–Personal Discomfort (Si1; .72), Physical/somatic Concerns (Si6; .72), and an important negative correlation with ego strength (−.78).

The correlations with Scale 3 (Dependent) and Scale 4 (Histrionic) are all rather weak. Scale 5 (Narcissistic) correlates significantly in a positive way with only one scale, Social Imperturbability (Pd3), .71, but it correlates in a negative way with the following scales: Wiggins Social Maladjustment (−.69) and Inferiority–Personal Discomfort (Si1; −.65).

The correlation of Scale 6 (Antisocial) with the MMPI Scale 4 (Psychopathic Deviate) is only .13, as mentioned in Table 15.2. Two of the correlations with the subscales, however, are more important, namely .54 with Authority Problems (Pd2) and .50 with Social Imperturbability (Pd3). The correlation with the Wiggins Authority Conflict scale points in the same direction (.49). The most important correlations of Scale 7 (Compulsive) are negative correlations with scales such as Self-Alienation (Pd5; −.67, Wiggins Manifest Hostility (−.67), Prejudice (−.61), and Wiggins Family Problems (−.61).

Scale 8 (Passive–Aggressive) shows some quite important correlations with a great number of MMPI scales. Three of the subscales of the Depression scale correlate over .60 with Scale 8: Brooding (D5; .70), Mental Dullness (D4; .65), and Subjective Depression (D1; .63). Other important correlations with subscales in decreasing order are: Self-alienation (Pd5; .71), Lack of Ego Mastering–Cognitive (Sc5; .70), Psychomotor Acceleration (Ma2; .67), Social Alienation (Pd4; .66), Lassitude–Malaise (Hy3; .65), and Bizarre Sensory Experiences (Sc6; .65). The high correlations with some of the schizophrenia subscales are perhaps "bizarre," but could point in the direction of the deficient regulatory controls. Scale 8 correlates also highly with Welsh's Anxiety scale (.74), Wiggins Depression scale (.72), Wiggins Poor Morale scale (.71), the Prejudice scale (.67), Dependence (.66), Wiggins Psychotism scale (.66), and Wiggins Manifest Hostility scale (.66).

The correlation pattern of the pathological personality disorders and the MMPI looks very similar for Scales S (Schizotypal) and C (Borderline), while Scale P (Paranoid) shows only moderate correlations with the MMPI scales. Scales S and C both correlate highly with Subjective Depression (D1), Mental Dullness (D4), Brooding (D5), Lack of Ego Mastery–Cognitive (Sc3), Anxiety, Dependence, Wiggins Psychotism, Wiggins Depression, and Wiggins Poor Morale. There is an important negative correlation for both scales with the ego strength scale (–.75 and –.67). The main differences between the two scales are Scale C (Borderline) having also high correlations with Self-Alienation (Pd5), Lack of Ego Mastery–Defective Inhibition (Sc5), Bizarre Sensory Experiences (Sc6), Psychomotor Acceleration (Ma2), and Wiggins Hypomania.

The correlations of the different Axis I scales or clinical symptom syndromes with the MMPI scales are, as could be expected, very dissimilar. Scale PP (Psychotic Delusions) does not show significant correlations with any of the MMPI scales or subscales and Wiggins content scales. In terms of MMPI aspects measured, some of the most common aspects of the different syndromes represented in the MCMI are: lack of ego mastery–cognitive (import correlations with A, SS, D, H, and CC), bizarre sensory experiences (high correlations with H, SS, CC, A, and D), anxiety (important correlations with CC, D, SS, A, and H), dependence, psychotism, depression, and poor morale. The highest correlations are always found with the same scales: A (Anxiety), D (Dysthymic), H (Somatoform), SS (Psychotic Thinking), and CC (Psychotic Depression). A common theme could be the anxiety.

Scale A (Anxiety) correlates with Welsh's anxiety scale at .73 and with many other scales. Just to mention some of the more important ones not already mentioned: Psychomotor Acceleration (.71), Hypersensitivity (.65), and Lack of Ego Mastery–Defective Inhibition (.67). Scales H (Somatoform) and N (Hypomanic) show very few important correlations; Scale D (Dysthymic) seems to measure in the first place the subjective impression of depression (subjective depression, mental dullness, brooding, lassitude–malaise, poor morale) and some somatic complains. The correlation between Scale D and the Wiggins Depression scale is.79. The correlations of Scales B (Alcohol Abuse) and T (Drug Abuse) and the McAndrew Alcohol scale are, respectively, .51 and .58. Drug abuse, more than alcohol abuse, seems to be associated with the Wiggins Manifest Hostility and Hypomania scales.

The three other scales represent disorders of marked severity and emphasize three different aspects of these disorders: Psychotic Thinking (SS), Psychotic Depression (CC), and Psychotic Delusions (PP). As already mentioned, Scales SS and CC manifest very similar correlations with the different MMPI scales, while Scale PP does not correlate with MMPI scales in a significant way. Important correlations are found with the Schizophrenia scale and all of the subscales (the majority are higher than .60), with Dependence, Wiggins Psychotism (.81 for Scale SS, .68 for Scale CC), Wiggins Depression (.72 and .77) and

Wiggins Poor Morale (.72 and .80). Most of the correlations are in the expected direction, although some could be expected to be higher while other correlations are relatively important and should be expected to be lower. This is, of course, inevitable when correlations are calculated between a large number of scales. However, the research concerning external validity is a necessity to define the exact meaning of the different scales.

As Campbell and Fiske (1959) indicated, it is important to have information on the convergent and discriminant validity of the questionnaires or assessment techniques used. Morey, Waugh, and Blashfield (1985) developed 11 personality disorder scales starting from the MMPI item pool. In a separate study we developed our own norms for the personality pattern scales on a sample of 324 patients. As mentioned above, we had a sample of 52 patients who were administered both questionnaires (the MCMI and the MMPI), so it was possible to calculate the monotrait–heteromethod correlations. These correlations vary between .60 (avoidant–avoidant) and –.49 (compulsive–compulsive). No particularly high correlations were found; some were even under .40. The weaker correlations were .32 (schizoid–schizoid), .31 (dependent–dependent) and .25 (antisocial–antisocial). The correlations in the McCann (1989) study varied between .82 (avoidant) and –.30 (compulsive), also with very low correlations for antisocial (.15) and paranoid (.08). Although both studies point in the same direction, differences could have been due to the small size of both samples or to a different sex ratio. Green and Farr (1987) demonstrated, at least for certain scales (for instance Narcissistic, Antisocial, Avoidant) that the correlations for both sexes can be quite different. A relatively important number of heterotrait–heteromethod correlations are larger or of the same magnitude as are the monotrait–heteromethod correlations. Although we know that the MCMI-III is not conceived as a measure of the DSM-III personality disorders, but rather as an operationalization of Millon's theory, higher correlations could be expected. For instance, there are clear discrepancies between the DSM-III criteria for antisocial personality disorder and Millon's (1981) description of this disorder. This could partly explain the low correlation between the two scales (.15). It is always confusing for clinicians to have two different questionnaires at their disposal which seem to measure the same aspcts—at least as far as the scale names are concerned—while in clinical practice, each instrument seems to measure quite different things.

THE MCMI AS A MEASURE OF PERSONALITY DISORDERS

Another part of our research centered on Axis II of DSM, or the personality disorders. In a comparative study we incorporated the original Millon data (Millon, 1982), the data published by Choca et al. (1986), and our own sample of 427 patients. We reanalyzed the data from the MCMI-III manual (Millon, 1982) by means of a principal axis factor analysis (PAF); only the eight basic personality patterns and three severe personality patterns were incorporated in the analysis. Two factors were identified, explaining 72% of the variance (Table 15.3). In the same way, we reanalyzed the data published by Choca et al. (1986) on a sample of 478 patients. Two factors had eigenvalues greater than 1.0, and 62% of the variance was explained by these two factors (Table 15.4). The third set of data was our Belgian sample of 427 in- and outpatients. The same method of analysis (PAF) was used and we obtained two factors with eigenvalues greater than 1.0, explaining 73% of the variance (Table 15.5).

The results obtained on the three sets of data reveal broadly the same structure; in particular, the factor structures obtained on the Millon sample and our Belgian sample are very similar. The first factor loaded high on Passive–Aggressive, Borderline, and Avoidant

TABLE 15.3. Original MCMI Sample (*N* = 744)

MCMI scale	Factor 1	Factor 2
SZD	.399	.754
AVD	.711	.615
DEP	.567	.338
HST	.146	−.911
NAR	−.140	−.804
ANT	.077	−.340
CPS	−.818	.127
PAG	.946	.058
STY	.682	.665
BDL	.896	.309
PAR	.451	.274

Note. SZD, Schizoid; AVD, Avoidant; DEP, Dependent; HST, Histrionic; NAR, Narcissistic; ANT, Antisocial; CPS, Compulsive; PAG, Passive–Aggressive; STY, Schizotypal; BDL, Borderline; PAR, Paranoid.

with an important negative loading on Compulsive. This factor could be labeled "Emotional Versus Restrained." The second factor, Introversion–Extroversion, has positive weights for Schizotypal, Schizoid, and Avoidant (and in the Belgian sample, also for Dependent) and negative loadings for Histrionic, Narcissistic, and Antisocial. We notice a difference between the results obtained for Millon's sample and our sample: we are missing an important negative loading on the Narcissistic scale. Although the results presented in the literature are difficult to compare (different sample sizes, different populations, different scales incorporated in the analysis, etc.), some of our results are confirmed (Strack, Lorr, Campbell, & Lamerin, 1992).

Multidimensional scaling (MDS) is an alternative to factor analysis. In most published studies different psychological questionnaires or methods are used, but the use of statistical methods is astonishingly constant. As we know already on the basis of the results of the factor analysis, two factors were obtained on the three data sets. We used on the same sets of data a KYST MDS method (Kruskal & Wish, 1978) to determine the position of the personality pattern scales on two dimensions. Figures 15.1, 15.2, and 15.3 are the plots

TABLE 15.4. Factor Reanalysis of Choca et al.'s (1986) Data (*N* = 478)

MCMI scale	Factor 1	Factor 2
SZD	.653	−.262
AVD	.934	−.235
DEP	.484	−.247
HST	−.241	.696
NAR	−.292	.928
ANT	−.019	.463
CPS	−.717	−.230
PAG	.300	.121
STY	.828	−.339
BDL	.885	−.078
PAR	.410	.558

Note. SZD, Schizoid; AVD, Avoidant; DEP, Dependent; HST, Histrionic; NAR, Narcissistic; ANT, Antisocial; CPS, Compulsive; PAG, Passive–Aggressive; STY, Schizotypal; BDL, Borderline; PAR, Paranoid.

TABLE 15.5. Factor Reanalysis on Belgian Sample (N = 427)

MCMI scale	Factor 1	Factor 2
SZD	.447	.758
AVD	.665	.711
DEP	.290	.602
HST	.103	−.725
NAR	−.350	−.107
ANT	.140	−.428
CPS	−.912	−.014
PAG	.899	.343
STY	.385	.928
BDL	.822	.480
PAR	.430	.263

Note. SZD, Schizoid; AVD, Avoidant; DEP, Dependent; HST, Histrionic; NAR, Narcissistic; ANT, Antisocial; CPS, Compulsive; PAG,
Passive–Aggressive; STY, Schizotypal; BDL, Borderline; PAR, Paranoid.

of the results of MDS on the 1982 Millon sample, the Choca et al. (1986) data, and our
Belgian sample. The results for the three sets of data are very similar: the first dimension
always seems to be the introversion–extroversion dimension, with scales such as Narcissistic, Histrionic, and Antisocial on one side and scales Schizoid, Schizotypal, and Avoidant
on the other. The second dimension is much more difficult to interpret and seems to vary
more over the three sets of data.

To compare in a more strict way the three solutions obtained, a Pindis analysis was

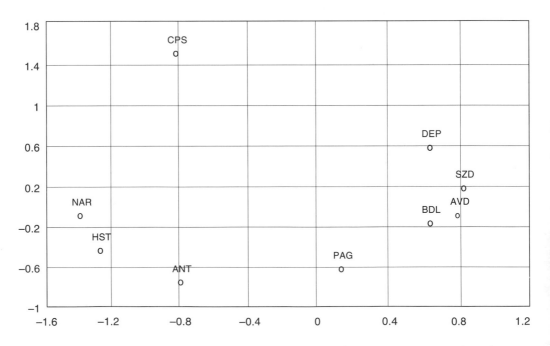

FIGURE 15.1. Multidimensional scaling, Millon (1982) sample (N = 774). SZD, Schizoid; AVD,
Avoidant; DEP, Dependent; HST, Histrionic; NAR, Narcissistic; ANT, Antisocial; CPS, Compulsive;
PAG, Passive–Aggressive; BDL, Borderline.

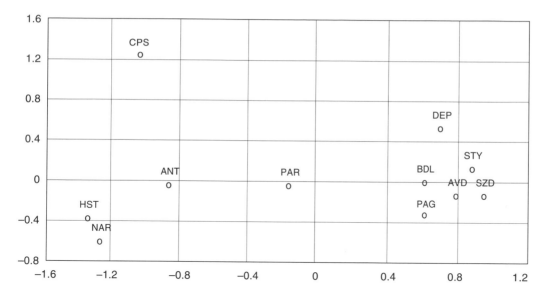

FIGURE 15.2. Multidimensional scaling, Choca et al. (1986) sample (N = 478). SZD, Schizoid; AVD, Avoidant; DEP, Dependent; HST, Histrionic; NAR, Narcissistic; ANT, Antisocial; CPS, Compulsive; PAG, Passive–Aggressive; STY, Schizotypal; BDL, Borderline; PAR, Paranoid.

used. The Pindis analysis revealed that even with minimal transformations (the so called "admissible" transformations), the general fit between the three configurations is excellent. In terms of similarities (communalities) between the centroid configuration and each individual configuration, there was excellent internal agreement. On average, 97% of the variation between the configurations was attributable to admissible transformations, with the three groups equally well fit. On the basis of this data it is impossible to conclude if the

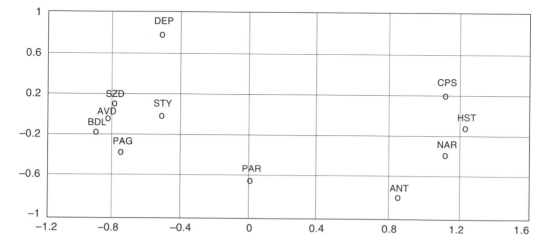

FIGURE 15.3. Multidimensional scaling, Belgian sample (N = 427). SZD, Schizoid; AVD, Avoidant; DEP, Dependent; HST, Histrionic; NAR, Narcissistic; ANT, Antisocial; CPS, Compulsive; PAG, Passive–Aggressive; STY, Schizotypal; BDL, Borderline; PAR, Paranoid.

minor differences (the largest distances were observed for Antisocial, Narcissistic, and Histrionic) were due to intercultural differences or to differences in sample composition. At least on the basis of our analyses, there does not seem to be a systematic larger distance between the Belgian sample and the two American samples.

It is important to notice that the structures found on the basis of factor analysis and on the basis of MDS are all very similar. The results of our research point in the direction of a rather robust structure as far as one dimension or factor is concerned: the dimension introversion–extroversion. The second dimension or factor is much more difficult to identify.

The theoretical clusters as proposed in the DSM-III are only partly confirmed: a cluster which always shows up is Cluster II, the Dramatic, Emotional, and Erratic cluster. The scales measuring the narcissistic, histrionic, and antisocial personality patterns always cluster together. The borderline personality pattern, however, seems to be part of Cluster III, the Anxious and Fearful cluster, and/or Cluster I, the Odd and Eccentric cluster. At least on the basis of our analyses, we were not able to make a clear distinction between Clusters I and III. Scale 7 (Compulsive) of the MCMI seems to take a separate position and does not seem to cluster with any of the other personality pattern scales.

CONCLUSION

The major part of this chapter treats the research done in Belgium on the basis of the MCMI-I. As the MCMI-III has recently been translated into Dutch/Flemish and has been adapted for use in both countries, we will start new research projects in the coming months and we will organize some clinical trials. We hold great hopes for the new questionnaire, both as a research instrument and as a tool in clinical practice. The MCMI-III has changed quite a lot compared with the MCMI. Already in the previous version, numerous adaptations of the inventory were introduced on the basis of technical aspects or refinements of the underlying theory. It is a matter of course that, in planning the new research projects, we will try to avoid some of the mistakes in our previous research. We will, for instance, pay greater attention to the selection of our patients and to the composition of our sample. In the domain of clinical psychology or psychopathology it is nearly impossible to speak of representative samples. However, the test will be administered to as large as possible a number of in- and outpatients selected in a large number of clinical settings. This is an absolute necessity because the different categories of patients are unequally distributed over the different settings. Although we do not have reasons to suppose that there could be significant differences between Belgian patients and patients from The Netherlands, we plan to have samples of patients of both countries in our research. In the same way, whenever possible, the research will be coordinated so that data can be treated as a large single sample of patients.

As discussed above, to calculate solid BRs we need to have a good sample but also reliable and correct clinical evaluations. As Faraone and Tsuang (1994) have illustrated, diagnostic reliability tells us something about the degree to which different clinicians are likely to make the same diagnoses, but it does not tell anything about the diagnostic accuracy or about whether or not the judgments are correct. In the absence of a "gold standard," we have been looking for at least a standardized way to obtain the clinical judgments: we intend to offer to the clinicians a computer program based on the DSM-IV (American Psychiatric Association, 1994) criteria which should guide them in a systematic way through the diagnostic program. For the moment it is difficult to predict what the results of our research projects with the MCMI-III will be; however, we personally are convinced that the questionnaire could be a very useful tool in clinical practice.

REFERENCES

American Psychiatric Association. (1980). *Diagnostic and statistical manual of mental disorders* (3rd ed.). Washington, DC: Author.

American Psychiatric Association. (1994). *Diagnostic and statistical manual of mental disorders* (4th ed.). Washington, DC: Author.

Brislin, R. (1986). The wording and translation of research instruments. In W. Lonner & J. Berry (Eds.), *Field methods in cross-cultural psychology* (pp. 137–164). Newbury Park, CA: Sage.

Campbell, D., & Fiske, D. (1959). Convergent and discriminant validity in the multitrait–multimethod matrix. *Psychological Bulletin, 56,* 81–105.

Choca, J. P., Peterson, C. A., & Shanley, L. A. (1986). Factor analysis of the Millon Clinical Multiaxial Inventory. *Journal of Consulting and Clinical Psychology, 54,* 253–255.

Choca, J. P., Shanley, L. A., & Van Denburg, E. (1992). *Interpretive guide to the Millon Clinical Multiaxial Inventory.* Washington, DC: American Psychological Association.

Derksen, J. (1995). *Personality disorders: Clinical and social perspectives.* New York: Wiley.

Derksen, J., Sloore, H., de Mey, H., & Hellenbosch, G. (1993). *MMPI-2: Handleiding bij afname, scoring en interpretatie.* Nijmegen: Pen Tests Publisher.

Faraone, S., & Tsuang, M. (1994). Measuring diagnostic accuracy in the absence of a "Gold Standard". *American Journal of Psychiatry, 151*(5), 650–657.

Green, R. L., & Farr, S. P. (1987). *Concordance among the MCMI and MMPI personality disorder scales.* Paper presented at the annual meeting of the American Psychological Association, New York.

Greenblatt, R. L., Modzierz, G. J., Murphy, T. J., & Trimakas, K. (1986). *Nonmetric multidimensional scaling of the MCMI.* Paper presented at the annual conference on the Millon Clinical Inventories, Miami, FL.

Hambleton, R. (1994). Guidelines for adapting educational and psychological tests: A progress report. *European Journal of Psychological Assessment, 10,* 229–244.

Kruskal, J. B., & Wish, M. (1978). *Multidimensional scaling.* Beverly Hills: Sage.

Lewis, S. J., & Harder, D. W. (1990). Factor structure of the MCMI among personality disordered outpatients and in other populations. *Journal of Clinical Psychology, 46,* 613–617.

McCann, J. T. (1989). MMPI personality disorder scales and the MCMI: Concurrent validity. *Journal of Clinical Psychology, 45,* 365–369.

Millon, T. (1969). *Modern psychopathology: A biosocial approach to maladaptive learning and functioning.* Philadelphia: Saunders.

Millon, T. (1977). *Millon Clinical Multiaxial Inventory manual* (1st ed). Minneapolis: National Computer Systems.

Millon, T. (1981). *Disorders of personality: DSM-III Axis II.* New York: Wiley.

Millon, T. (1982). *Millon Clinical Multiaxial Inventory manual* (2nd ed.). Minneapolis: National Computer Systems.

Millon, T. (1990). *Toward a new personology: An evolutionary model.* New York: Wiley.

Millon, T. (1994). *Millon Clinical Multiaxial Inventory—III manual.* Minneapolis: National Computer Systems.

Morey, L. C., Waugh, M. H., & Blashfield, R. K. (1985). MMPI scales for the DSM-III personality disorders: Their derivation and correlates. *Journal of Personality Assessment, 49,* 245–251.

Oldham, J. M. (Ed.). (1991). *Personality disorders: New perspectives on diagnostic validity.* Washington, DC: American Psychiatric Press.

Piersma, H. L. (1986). The factor structure of the Millon Clinical Multiaxial Inventory (MCMI) for psychiatric inpatients. *Journal of Personality Assessment, 50,* 578–584.

Sloore, H., Rouckhout, D., & Hellenbosch, G. (1993). *An epidemiological study of personality disorders.* Paper presented at the 28th annual Symposium on Recent Developments in the Use of the MMPI-2 and MMPI-A. St. Petersburg Beach, FL.

Smith, D., Carroll, J. L., & Fuller, G. B. (1988). The relationship between the Millon Clinical Multiaxial Inventory and the MMPI in a private outpatient mental health clinic population. *Journal of Clinical Psychology, 44,* 165–174.

Strack, S., Lorr, M., Campbell, L., & Lamerin, A. (1992). Personality disorders and clinical syndrome factors of MCMI-II scales. *Journal of Personality Disorders, 6,* 40–52.

Wetzler, S. (1990). The Millon Clinical Multiaxial Inventory (MCMI): A review. *Journal of Personality Assessment, 55,* 445–464.

Wiggins, J. S. (1966). Substantive dimensions of self-report in the MMPI item pool. *Psychological Monographs, 80*(22, Whole No. 630).

16

A Selected Review of the MCMI Empirical Literature

ROBERT J. CRAIG

This chapter presents a selected review of the Millon Clinical Multiaxial Inventory (the MCMI and the MCMI-II; Millon, 1983, 1987) empirical literature. Through late 1996, there have been over 450 papers published on the MCMIs. The sheer volume of this knowledge base and space limitations defy simple elucidation of this material. Readers wishing more comprehensive coverage of this literature should consult the major books on the MCMIs (Choca & Van Denberg, 1997; Craig, 1993a) or the many reviews of this test (Dana & Cantrell, 1988; Fleishauer, 1987; Greer, 1984; Haladyna, 1992; Hess, 1985; Lanyon, 1984; McCabe, 1984; Reynolds, 1992; Wetzler, 1990; Widiger, 1985).

This chapter is generally directed to clinicians and presents information that should be useful to practitioners. Meta-analysis and effect size statistics have been sacrificed to focus on the clinical utility of the instrument. No doubt, other researchers will continue to address the scientific underpinnings of the instrument. This chapter presents literature pertaining to psychometric features emphasizing factor analysis, test reliability, the effects of moderator variables on MCMI test scores, and content validity. The chapter then focuses on studies pertaining to the test's validity indices (i.e., modifier indices), the efficacy of the MCMI as a diagnostic instrument for personality disorders and clinical syndromes, and its utility with special populations including use with alcoholics, drug addicts, posttraumatic stress disorder (PTSD) sufferers, those with eating disorders, spouse abusers, and correctional inmates.

PSYCHOMETRIC FEATURES

Factor Analysis

Craig and Weinberg (1993) found 20 studies containing published factor analysis results on the MCMI or the MCMI-II. In general, five main factors have been isolated: (1) general maladjustment, (2) schizoid/asocial, (3) narcissistic/antisocial/acting out, (4) submission/ aggression, and (5) paranoid thinking and behavior. The major point of contention in this research has been the question of item overlap, which introduces a forced similarity between

303

scores which artificially elevates the intercorrelations, thus leading to factor loadings which are also artificially elevated. The factor invariance found in the literature may be a function of this built-in structure and may be controlling the outcome of factor studies rather than subject response patterns (Gibertini & Retzlaff, 1988). Millon persuasively argues that such overlap reflects the reality of the constructs measured by the test. For example, many patients with an antisocial personality disorder also have narcissistic features and abuse drugs. The fact that some items on the MCMI-III (Millon, 1994) are keyed on all three scales reflects this reality, which also results in "item redundancy." Millon has reduced the amount of item redundancy in the MCMI-III and there is no report of MCMI-III factor studies in the test manual.

Test–Retest Reliability

Estimates of test reliability are somewhat confounded by the effects of treatment and by fluctuating clinical states, as well as by the length of the retest interval and perhaps by different populations. Stability estimates of the personality disorder (PD) scales should be higher than those of the clinical syndrome scales and nonclinical groups should have higher stability estimates than do clinical populations. Craig and Weinberg's (1993) literature review supported this general expectation. Table 16.1 presents median stability estimates for MCMI scales across the three versions of the test based on 11 data sets for MCMI personality pattern scales and on 9 to 13 data sets for the MCMI clinical syndrome scales, three data sets for MCMI-II scales, and one for MCMI-III scales (Flynn & McMahon, 1983; Hyer, Woods, Bruno, & Boudewyns, 1989; Libb, Stankovic, Sokol, Houck, & Switzer, 1990; McCormack, Barnett, & Wallbrown, 1989; McMahon & Davidson, 1985a; McMahon, Flynn, & Davidson, 1985; Millon, 1983, 1987, 1994; Murphy, Greenblatt, Modzierz, & Trimakas, 1991; Overholser, 1990, 1991; Piersma, 1986a, 1989a; Wheeler & Schwartz, 1989).

Median stability estimates for the MCMI personality disorder scales ranged from .63 to .82 with a median of .70 for clinical populations. For MCMI-II personality pattern scales estimates ranged from .51 to .75, with a median of .70. For the clinical syndrome scales, MCMI studies ranged from .45 to .68 with a median of .61, and ranged from .44 to .72 with a median of .53 for the MCMI-II. Millon (1994) reported test–retest reliability coefficients for MCMI-III scales generally in the high .80s and low .90s over a short retest interval. MCMI and MCMI-II reliability studies generally reported stability coefficients lower than those presented in the test manuals, but the median correlations reported here suggest that these scales are generally reliable.

Moderator Variables

There has been little research attention devoted to the effect of moderator variables on MCMI scale scores. We do have some preliminary data on the effects of *race* and *gender*. Results of these studies have not been consistent, with some researchers finding differences between blacks and whites and between males and females on certain scales, while others report no difference between these groups on the same scales. Scales for which no racial differences between blacks and whites have consistently been found include scales 3, 7, 8A, and A. Blacks consistently score higher on Scales 5, 6A, P, T, and PP, while whites consistently score higher on Scale D. No gender differences are consistently found on Scales 2 and 8A. Males consistently score higher on Scale 6A, while females consistently score higher on Scales H and CC. The remaining scales show no consistent pattern by race or

TABLE 16.1. Overview of Median Stability Estimates for MCMI Scales

MCMI scale	MCMI		MCMI-II		MCMI-III
	Clinical population[a]	Nonclinical population[b]	Clinical population[c]	Nonclinical population	Clinical population[d]
Schizoid	.71	.54	.74	.84	.89
Avoidant	.70	.56	.71	.86	.89
Dependent	.63	.63	.73	.85	.89
Depressive	XX[f]	XX	XX	XX	.93
Histrionic	.82	.62	.75	.91	.91
Narcissistic	.71	.53	.64	.83	.89
Antisocial	.79	.60	.73	.91	.93
Aggressive (Sadistic)	XX	XX	.75	.81	.88
Compulsive	.70	.61	.70	.89	.92
Passive–Aggressive	.64	.54	.69	.85	.89
Self-Defeating	XX	XX	.72	.86	.91
Schizotypal	.70	.49	.64	.89	.87
Borderline	.54	.41	.51	.79	.93
Paranoid	.63	.37	.59	.87	.85
Anxiety	.61	.42	.47	.80	.84
Somatoform	.45	.35	.44	.85	.96
Bipolar manic	.67	.64	.71	.78	.93
Dysthymia	.58	.40	.53	.78	.91
Alcohol dependence	.57	.54	.66	.88	.92
Drug dependence[e]	.68	.59	.72	.85	.91
PTSD	XX	XX	XX	XX	.91
Thought disorder	.63	.38	.47	.91	.92
Major depression	.55	.45	.57	.78	.95
Delusional disorder	.66	.39	.60	.91	.86

[a]N = 11 data sets for personality pattern scales and 9 for clinical scales.
[b]N = 1 data set, 3-year retest interval.
[c]N = 3 data sets for clinical populations and 1 data set for nonclinical group.
[d]N = 1 data set in test manual.
[e]N = 13 data sets.
[f]XX = Scale not on the MCMI.

gender (Choca, Shanley, Peterson, & Van Denberg, 1990; Davis, Greenblatt, & Pochyly, 1990; Dillon, 1988; Donat, Walters, & Hume, 1992; Gabrys et al., 1988; Hamberger & Hastings, 1992; Piersma, 1986b; Matano, Locke, & Schwartz, 1994).

How is this data to be interpreted? First, merely demonstrating that two groups have unequal mean base rate (BR) scores on a given scale does not establish test bias. A reasonable alternative explanation is that the scales reflect true differences in the populations. For example, the fact that males score higher on the Antisocial scale probably reflects true prevalence rates in the disorder favoring males. Higher scores on Scale T by blacks might also reflect proportionally higher prevalence rates among blacks for substance abuse compared with whites. Second, while these studies report statistical differences in means on some scales, these scores were in BR ranges which would not change a person's diagnostic category. For example, one study found that black psychiatric patients (N = 235) scored higher (average BR = 64) than did white psychiatric patients (N = 471; average BR = 50) on MCMI Scale N (Choca et al., 1990). However, the magnitude of the BR scores were such that a bipolar disorder would have been ruled out for both black and white patients. This has often been the case in studies in which racial differences were reported. Third,

MCMI scales predicted equally well for black and white psychiatric patients despite some differences on individual scales (Davis et al., 1990).

Content Validity

An early content evaluation of certain MCMI scales concluded that the MCMI was a poor reflection of DSM-III diagnoses, except for those scales where the criteria closely resembled that of Millon's theory, that is, Avoidant (Widiger & Sanderson, 1987; Widiger, Williams, Spitzer, & Frances, 1985). Millon (1985) argued that not every symptom in a criteria set needs to be assessed to adequately assess the syndrome, and that the MCMI is an operational measure of his biopsychosocial theory of personality pathology and is not intended to be isomorphic with the DSM-III (American Psychiatric Association, 1980). The MCMI-III test manual provides an appendix that lists each DSM-IV (American Psychiatric Association, 1994) personality disorder criterion and the MCMI-III test item that assesses it. This should make the test more consonant with DSM-IV, but there still are differences so that we should not expect perfect correlations between MCMI-III personality pattern scales and similar measures of DSM-IV personality disorders.

CLINICAL STUDIES: MODERATOR INDICES

Twelve studies have been published on the MCMI and the MCMI-II validity and/or adjustment indices. Little support has been found for the differential weighting of prototype items, as correlations between weighted and unweighted BR scores approach unity (Retzlaff, Sheehan, & Lorr, 1990; Streiner, Goldberg, & Miller, 1993), and adjustment indices have little effect on MCMI-II profiles (Miller, Goldberg, & Streiner, 1993). The Validity index (VI) appears effective (Langevin et al., 1988; Bagby, Gillis, & Dickens, 1990; Bagby, Gillis, & Rogers, 1991; McNeil & Meyer, 1990), but the use of subtle–obvious items discriminated faked from nonfaked profiles more often than did the VI (Wierzbicki, 1993). The test has been able to detect faked-bad profiles with more effectiveness than it can faked-good profiles (Bagby et al., 1990; McNeil & Meyer, 1990; Retzlaff, Sheehan, & Fiel, 1991; Van Gorp & Meyer, 1986). While the Debasement index works well to identify intentional faking, elevated scores may also reflect severity of psychopathology (Wetzler & Marlowe, 1990). The Disclosure and Debasement indices were also effective in detecting exaggeration of PTSD for insurance purposes (Lees-Haley, 1992).

MCMI AS A DIAGNOSTIC INSTRUMENT OF PERSONALITY DISORDERS AND CLINICAL SYNDROMES

At its heart, the MCMI is an instrument to diagnose personality patterns and disorders and major clinical syndromes. Millon has raised the standard of measurement by developing BR scores, which are transformed scores based on known prevalence rates of the disorder. Millon found that point in the distribution of scores in the standardization sample above which the patient had the disorder and below which the patient did not. He arbitrarily set the BR above 85 for the presence of the most prominent traits that define the disorder, and between 75 and 84 for the presence of features or traits of the disorder. This specificity has allowed researchers to compare MCMI (all versions) test scores with other criteria, usually clinician or discharge diagnosis, DSM criteria, a personality disorder clinical psychiatric interview schedule, or another personality disorder inventory. Because there is no "gold standard," discrepancies could be as much the result of inaccurate criteria as they could be an inaccurate MCMI. Also, measurement in this field is complicated by problems inherent in self-report methodology, covariation of Axis I and II disorders, mood state distortions, trait versus situational behaviors, effects of gender, culture, and ethnicity on test scores, discrepancies between reports of informants and patient self-reports, and treatment effects.

With these facts in mind, research has focused primarily on those disorders which are more directly observable, such as psychotic disorders and affective disorders (dysthymia, major depression, mania), alcohol abuse, and drug abuse. This section of the chapter presents a selected review of research that pertains to diagnostic accuracy of selected personality disorders and selected clinical syndromes. The accuracy in detecting substance abuse is presented later in the chapter in the section on alcohol- and drug-abusing populations. I only provide information on selected scales for illustrative purposes and only include scales where there is sufficient data which provides evidence to formulate preliminary findings.

Personality Pattern Scales

Correlations of MCMI, MCMI-II, and MCMI-III scales with similar measures can provide evidence of convergent validity. Evidence is presented on the MCMI-I and -II correlations with a personality inventory, a structured clinical interview, and two specific personality disorders for which the evidence is sufficient to generate reasonable conclusions.

Several studies have correlated the MCMI and MCMI-II with Minnesota Multiphasic Personality Inventory (MMPI) personality disorder (PD) scales. Table 16.2 summarizes this data. Using the MMPI and MMPI-II PD scales as the criterion, there is convergent validity for MCMI and MCMI-II scales 1, 2, 3, 4, 5, 8A, and S; the evidence is mixed for Scales B and

TABLE 16.2. Correlations between MCMI and MMPI and MMPI-II Personality Scales

	MCMI version C					
	I	I	I	I	I	II
	Study[a]					
MCMI scale	1	2	3	4	5	6
Schizoid	.74	.67	.35	.87	X[b]	.73
Avoidant	.79	.82	.65	.86	X	.87
Dependent	.67	.50	.68	.89	X	.56
Histrionic	.69	.68	.66	.85	X	.74
Narcissistic	.73	.78	.55	.68	.66	.65
Antisocial	.25	.15	.14	.30	X	.57
Aggressive (Sadistic)	X	X	X	X	X	X
Compulsive	−.27	−.30	−.42	X	X	−.04
Passive–Aggressive	.46	.57	.50	.59		.70
Self-Defeating	X	X	X	X	X	X
Schizotypal	.53	.74	.51	.92	X	.32
Borderline	.37	.42	.28	.70	X	.68
Paranoid	.32	.08	.44	.83	X	.50

[a](1) Schuler, Snibbe, & Buckwalter (1994); (2) McCann (1991); (3) McCann (1989); (4) Dubro & Wetzler (1989); (5) Morey & Levine (1988); (6) Chatham, Tibbals, & Harrington (1993).
[b]X = Scale not on the MCMI.

P; and there is a lack of convergent validity for scales 6A and 7. There is insufficient data for Scale 8B and MMPI and MMPI-II PD does not assess aggressive/sadistic disorder.

The MCMI scale Antisocial measures something quite different than does the MMPI Antisocial scale. Part of the difference is based on the fact that the MCMI scale development was theory driven as to item selection. Millon's theory on the antisocial style includes the belief that antisocial personality is characterized by a fiercely independent style that is motivated to control others before they themselves are controlled (i.e., malevolent projection). Thus there are several items that tap this dimension of the construct, whereas MMPI PD assessment contains no such items and more closely resembles DSM-III (American Psychiatric Association, 1980) concepts of the antisocial style characterized by delinquency and criminality. Thus, based on this difference in theory and differences in corresponding item selection in scale development, we would not expect high correlations between these measures. Similarly, MMPI compulsive PD scales measure obsessive thinking and indecisiveness, while the item content on MCMI, MCMI-II, and MCMI-III Scale 7 pertains to traits such as serious, organized, moralistic, routinized, lack of impulsive behavior, and obedience to rules. Thus, these scales measure compulsivity quite differently and hence show negative correlations.

I believe that Scale 7 does not measure obsessive–compulsive clinical syndrome or the disorder, but rather it measures a compulsive *style*. The evidence is as follows: (1) Scale 7 negatively correlates with similar measures of compulsivity (see Table 16.3), (2) patients with an obsessive–compulsive disorder do not evidence spikes on Scale 7 MCMI-I, -II, and -III profiles (Fals-Stewart & Lucente, 1993), (3) Scale 7 positively correlates with mea-

TABLE 16.3. Correspondence of MCMI Scale 7 with Similar Measures

Authors (year)	Instrument	MCMI	r'
Morey & Levine (1988)	MMPI PD	I	.00
Dubro & Wetzler (1989)	MMPI PD	I	−.42
McCann (1989)	MMPI PD	I	−.30
Zarella, Schuerger, & Ritz (1990)	MMPI PD	I	−.50
		I	−.49
McCann (1991)	MMPI PD	II	−.04
Schuler et al. (1994)	MMPI PD	I	−.27
Hogg, Jackson, Rudd, & Edwards (1990)	SIDP	I	−.04
Torgersen & Alnaes (1990)	SIDP	I	−.05
Renneberg, Chambless, Dowdall, Fauerbach, & Gracely (1992)	SCID	II	.06
Klein et al. (1993)	Wisconsin PD Inventory	I	−.32
Coolidge & Merwin (1992)	Coolidge Axis II Inventory	II	.56
Soldz, Budman, Demby, & Merry (1993)	PDE	II	−.05
Hart, Dutton, & Newlove (1993)	PDE symptom count	II	−.01
Chick, Schaeffer, & Goggin (1993)	DSM-III-R Checklist	I	.05
Lehne (1994)	NEO Extroversion	I	.58
Wise (1994)	MBHI Respectful	II	.34
Millon (1994)	SCL-90-R O/C	III	−.37
	MMPI Pt	III	−.47

Note. MMPI PD, Minnesota Multiphasic Personality Inventory Personality Disorder indices (Morley, Blashfield, Webb, & Jewell, 1988); SIDP, Structured Interview for DSM-III-R Personality (Pfohl, Blum, Zimmerman, & Stangl, 1989); SCID, Structured Clinical Interview for DSM-III-R (Spitzer, Williams, Gibbon & First, 1990); Wisconsin PD Inventory, Wisconsin Personality Disorder Inventory (Klein et al., 1993); Coolidge Axis II Inventory (Coolidge & Merlin, 1992); PDE, Personality Disorder Examination (Loranger, 1988); DSM-III-R checklist (American Psychiatric Association, 1987); NEO, Neuroticism, Extroversion, Otherness (Costa & McCrae, 1992); MBHI, Millon Behavioral Health Inventory (Millon, 1982); SCL-90-R O/C, Symptom Checklist 90—Revised, obsessive–compulsive (Derogatis, 1983); MMPI Pt, Minnesota Multiphasic Personality Inventory Psychasthenia (Hathaway & McKinley, 1943).

sures of positive mental health, and (4) normal persons often have peak scores on Scale 7. I believe that this scale measures traits of efficiency, productiveness, organization, endurance, and energy, but not a clinical personality disorder.

Correlations with the Structured Inventory for DSM-III Personality Disorders (SIDP)

The previous section presented results comparing the MCMI to the MMPI. In this section I compare the MCMI with a frequently used structured clinical interview for DSM PDs, the Structured Interview for DSM-III-R Personality (SIDP; Pfohl, Blum, Zimmerman, & Stangl, 1989). The level of agreement between these two measures of personality disorder has uniformly been poor, with generally low intercorrelations (Alnaes & Torgersen, 1991; Hogg, Jackson, Rudd, & Edwards, 1990; Miller, Streiner, & Parkinson, 1992; Overholser, 1991; Patrick, 1993; Torgersen & Alnaes, 1990; Turley, Bates, Edwards, & Jackson, 1992). These two ways of assessing personality disorders (i.e., self-report inventory and clinical interview) produce different results. The low intercorrelation may be the result of poor validity of the criterion test.

Narcissism

In this section we look at a specific personality disorder and its relationship to similar measures using several different criteria. Table 16.4 presents the results of studies that have correlated MCMI and MCMI-II Scale 5 with similar measures of narcissism. Inspection of the data suggests that there is convergent validity of narcissism with MMPI PD (Morey, Blashfield, Webb, & Jewell, 1988), with the Narcissistic Personality Inventory (NPI; Raskin & Hall, 1979), and with measures of extroversion, but the scale poorly correlates with the narcissistic personality scales from the SIDP, the Structured Clinical Interview for DSM-III-R Personality Disorders (SCID; Spitzer, Williams, Gibbon, & First, 1990), the Wisconsin Personality Disorder Inventory (Klein, Benjamin, Rosenfeld, Treece, Husted, & Greist, 1993), and the Coolidge Axis II Inventory, and it shows unreliable correlations with the Personality Disorder Examination (PDE; Lorranger, 1988).

Psychosis

Both versions of the MCMI have done poorly in diagnosing psychosis and they tend to underestimate it compared with clinician-generated DSM diagnosis (Bonato, Cyr, Kalpin, Prendergast, & Sanhueza, 1988; Inch & Crossley, 1993; Jackson, Greenblatt, Davis, Murphy, & Trimakas, 1991; Patrick, 1988; Sexton, McIlwraith, Barnes, & Dunn, 1987). The first version of the test was more sensitive to detecting psychosis among a group of schizophrenics with low evoked potentials (Josiassen, Shagass, & Roemer, 1988), and when discriminant function analysis was employed instead of only one or two scales (Sexton et al., 1987).

Depression

All studies have found that the MCMI and MCMI-II Scale CC (Major Depression) was insensitive to diagnosing major depression (i.e., psychotic depression; Choca, Bresolin, Okonek, & Ostrow, 1988; Goldberg, Shaw, & Segal, 1987; Patrick, 1988; Wetzler, 1990;

TABLE 16.4. Correspondence of MCMI Scale 5 with Similar Measures

Authors (year)	Instrument	MCMI	r'
Morey & Levine (1988)	MMPI PD	I	.68
Dubro & Wetzler (1989)	MMPI PD	I	.55
McCann (1989)	MMPI PD	I	.78
Zarella, Schuerger, & Ritz (1990)	MMPI PD	I	.70
		I	.49
McCann (1991)	MMPI PD	II	.65
Chatham et al. (1993)	MMPI PD	I	.66
	NPI	I	.75
Schuler et al. (1994)	MMPI PD	I	.73
Hogg et al. (1990)	SIDP	I	.34
Torgersen & Alnaes (1990)	SIDP	I	.18
Turley et al. (1992)	SIDP	II	.02
Prifitera & Ryan (1984)	NPI	I	.66
Auerback (1984)	NPI	I	.55
Emmons (1987)	NPI	I	.27
Klein et al. (1993)	Wisconsin PD Inventory	I	.16
Morey (1985)	ICL Narc	I	.51
Coolidge & Merwin (1992)	Coolidge Axis II Inventory	II	−.05
Renneberg et al. (1992)	SCID	II	.16
Soldz et al. (1993a)	PDE	II	.41
Hart et al. (1993)	PDE symptom count	II	.22
Chick et al. (1993)	DSM-III-R Checklist	I	.09
Lehne (1994)	NEO Extroversion	I	.57
Wise (1994)	MBHI Confident	I	.69

Note. MMPI PD, Minnesota Multiphasic Personality Inventory Personality Disorder indices (Morey, Blashfield, Webb, & Jewell, 1988); NPI, Narcissistic Personality Inventory (Raskin & Hall, 1979); SIDP, Structured Interview for DSM-III-R Personality (Pfohl, Blum, Zimmerman, & Stangl, 1989); ICL Narc (Morey, 1985); SCID, Structured Clinical Interview for DSM-III-R (Spitzer, Williams, Gibbon, & First, 1990); PDE, Personality Disorder Examination (Loranger, 1988); NEO, Neuroticism, Extroversion, Openness (Costa & McCrae, 1992); DSM-III-R Checklist (American Psychiatric Association, 1987); MBHI, Millon Behavioral Health Inventory (Millon, 1982); Coolidge Axis II Inventory (Coolidge & Merlin, 1992); Wisconsin PD Inventory, Wisconsin Personality Disorder Inventory (Klein et al., 1993).

Wetzler, Kahn, Strauman, & Dubro, 1989; Wetzler & Marlowe, 1993). The reason for this is that MCMI and MCMI-II CC contained no vegetative items that forms the basis of the diagnosis in DSM-III and -III-R. The MCMI-III CC now contains vegetative items such that the diagnostic accuracy of this scale should improve over its earlier versions.

The scale Dysthymia (D) was sensitive to major depression (Choca et al., 1988; Goldberg et al., 1987; Libb, Murray, Thurstin, & Alarcon, 1992; Patrick, 1988; Piersma, 1991; Wetzler et al., 1989; Wetzler & Marlowe, 1993) and identified 50% of euthymic patients with a history of major depression (Choca et al., 1988). The elevations in the personality disorders that appear among patients with depressive disorders (i.e., Scales 3, 8A, and C; Joffe & Regan, 1988; Joffe, Swinson, & Regan, 1988; Wetzler, Kahn, Cahn, Van Praag, & Asnis, 1990) generally disappear when clinical depression abates (Joffe & Regan, 1988; Libb et al., 1990; Reich & Noyes, 1987).

Mania

The first and second versions of test, based on Scale N BR scores, show poor sensitivity to mania, diagnosing only 15% (Wetzler & Marlowe, 1993), 27% (DeWolfe, Larsen, & Ryan, 1985), and 56% (Choca et al., 1988) of true cases. Wetzler and Marlowe (1993) concluded that the MCMI and MCMI-II does not identify recovered bipolar patients but is able to describe features of these patients during the manic phase.

USE WITH SPECIAL POPULATIONS

Alcoholics

Craig and Weinberg (1992a) presented a literature review on the use of the MCMI and MCMI-II with alcoholics. They reported on 26 studies and since their publication, an additional six studies have been published using the MCMI with alcoholics. Millon (1987) initially reported that the modal MCMI profile of an alcoholic was associated with peak scores on the Antisocial (6A) and Aggressive/Sadistic (6B) scales with secondary elevations on the Passive–Aggressive (8A) and Borderline (C) scales. Female alcoholics had a similar modal profile but also had clinical elevations on the Dependent scale (McMahon & Tyson, 1990). The clinical syndrome scales peaked on Scales B (Alcohol Dependence) and T (Drug Dependence). Subsequent studies among alcoholic patients have found that the modal profile of the alcoholic is generally consistent with that reported by Millon, except that scores have peaked on Scale 8A with mild elevations on Scale 6A (Craig & Weinberg, 1992a). While a modal MCMI and MCMI-II alcoholic profile exists, there are too many variables that interact with alcoholism and too many subpopulations of alcoholics to suggest that only one profile would tap the many variations of the disorder. An early indication of this was provided through cluster analysis of 106 alcoholics, which found four basic types: (1) the modal type, (2) a group with elevated scores on Scales 3, 2, and 8A–1, (3) a group with normal scores and peaking on Scale 7 in subclinical ranges, and (4) group with high scores on Scales 5 and 6A (Craig, Verinis, & Wexler, 1985).

The most recent study provided a literature review of cluster analysis studies ($N = 8$) with alcoholics, concluded that seven subtypes have been identified, and provided median rates of occurrence for each type: (1) a subclinical profile peaking on Compulsive (18%); (2) a subclinical profile peaking on Narcissistic and Histrionic (10%), (3) a histrionic/ narcissistic type (3%), (4) a narcissistic/antisocial type (17%), (5) a negativistic/borderline type (24%), (6) a negativistic/avoidant/schizoid/dependent/borderline type, and (7) a dependent/avoidant/schizoid/negativistic type (Matano et al., 1994). These findings were also replicated with female alcoholics (McMahon & Tyson, 1990). External correlates of these subtypes are beginning to appear in the literature (Donat, 1994; Donat, Walters, & Hume, 1991) and these subgroups may have prognostic implications. For example, preliminary research suggests that alcoholics with a compulsive personality style frequently are associated with high social functioning and episodic drinking, whereas alcoholics with elevated scores on Psychotic Thinking (SS) and Scales 8A and 2 were associated with low social functioning, continuous drinking, and depression (McMahon, Davidson, & Flynn, 1986; McMahon, Davidson, Flynn, & Gersh, 1991; McMahon, Davidson, Gersh, & Flynn, 1991; McMahon, Gersh, & Davidson, 1989). Alcoholics with dependent personality styles, detached/ambivalent types, and independent styles differed in terms of severity of stress, levels of depression, and degree of social support (McMahon, Schram, & Davidson, 1993).

Clinical syndrome scales also seem to have some predictive validity with alcoholics, particularly Scale D. For example, alcoholics whose initial depression remained after 6 weeks of treatment, compared with alcoholics whose depression was transient, were characterized more by irrational, confused, and disorganized thinking and behavior and by an avoidant interpersonal style (McMahon & Davidson, 1985b). The MCMI and MCMI-II had moderate correlations with the MacAndrews Alcoholism Scale (Millon, 1983; McCann, 1990), with the Alcohol Abuse Scale of the Diagnostic Inventory of Personality and Symptoms (Leroux, Vincent, McPherson, & Williams, 1990), and with the Alcohol Scale of the COPE, a coping styles inventory (Carver, Scheier, & Weintraub, 1989; Vollrath, Alnaes, & Torgersen, 1994). Millon (1994) reported that MCMI-III Scale B correlated .36 with the Michigan Alcohol Screening Inventory.

Posttreatment scores among alcoholics did decrease across most scales except for Scales 4, 6A, and 7, suggesting that these tap stable personality traits (McMahon & Davidson, 1985b; McMahon et al., 1986).

While preliminary evidence suggests that the MCMI and MCMI-II profiles have clinical and predictive utility with alcoholics, the Alcohol Dependence scale (B) is expressly designed to detect alcoholism so that its concurrent validity is of central interest to the MCMI and MCMI-II as a diagnostic instrument. In this section, I review the scale's content, stability, relationship with similar instruments, and diagnostic power.

Scale B has two kinds of item content: those admitting problematic behaviors associated with excessive drinking, and those personality traits often seen with alcoholics. Stability estimates indicate that Scale B is moderately stable (see Table 16.1). The MCMI and MCMI-II's Scale B is moderately correlated with the MacAndrews Alcoholism Scale (Millon, 1983; McCann, 1990), the Alcohol Abuse Scale of the Diagnostic Inventory of Personality and Symptoms (Leroux et al., 1990), and with the Alcohol Abuse scale of the COPE, a coping styles inventory (Vollrath et al., 1994). Millon (1994) reported that MCMI-III Scale B is correlated .36 with the Michigan Alcohol Screening Test, perhaps because the latter is primarily symptom oriented whereas Scale B covers a broader content of the disorder.

Six studies have been published on the diagnostic power of Scale B. By diagnostic power we mean the ability to detect the disorder when the disorder is present (i.e., sensitivity), and to rule out the disorder when it is absent (i.e., specificity). Four of these studies pertained to MCMI-I Scale B and results indicated that sensitivity ranged from .22 (low) to .75 (moderately high). Specificity ranged from .46 to .97 (extremely high), with most reports in the .90s (Gibertini, Brandenberg, & Retzlaff, 1986; Streiner & Miller, 1991; Miller & Streiner, 1990; Bryer, Martines, & Dignan, 1990). Differences in diagnostic power may be attributed to differences in criteria (i.e., BR > 74, BR > 84; other personality disorder instruments; current diagnosis versus lifetime diagnosis; admitting versus discharge diagnosis [where treatment effects interact with outcome criterion]; and populations studied [i.e., pure alcohol samples or diagnosing alcoholism among general psychiatric patients]). Also, diagnostic power varies with prevalence rate and prevalence rates have varied with each study. Millon (1987) reported an overall diagnostic power of .97 for MCMI-II Scale B and .84 for MCMI-III Scale B (Millon, 1994).

To date, research has found that the sensitivity level of Scale B is lower than its specificity. However, Craig and Weinberg (1992a) reported that the average Scale B scores among alcoholics across all populations of alcoholics was 92, which attests to the scale's concurrent validity.

Drug Addicts

A comprehensive review on assessing drug addicts with the MCMI and MCMI-II reported that the tests have been used with over 2,000 drug abusing patients in the published literature from 19 studies (Craig & Weinberg, 1992b). Since then, an additional seven studies have appeared that used the MCMI with drug addicts. The modal addict profile consists of character-disordered traits (i.e., elevations on Scales 5, 6A, and 6B) with little subjective distress. The initial MCMI cluster analysis study with drug addicts found two basic types, a narcissistic/antisocial type and a passive–aggressive/avoidant type (Craig et al., 1985). However, subsequent cluster analysis studies have found at least four subtypes: (1) a narcissistic/antisocial type (the modal profile), (2) a passive–aggressive/withdrawn style (with elevations on Scales 8A,1, and 2), (3) a dependent type (elevated Scale 3 score), and a high-ranging profile of addictive patients with significant underlying psychopathology who would be considered psychiatric patients (Calsyn & Saxon, 1988, 1990; Craig & Olson, 1990; Craig et al., 1985; Craig & Weinberg, 1992b; Fals-Stewart, 1992). No studies to date have reported on the use of any MCMI with female addicts.

Also, few differences have appeared on MCMI and MCMI-II scales between heroin and cocaine abusers, such that drug of choice seems to have little effect on scale scores (Calsyn & Saxon, 1990; Craig & Olson, 1990). Male alcoholics scored higher on Scales 2, 8A, S, C, and P, while heroin addicts scored higher on Scale 5 (Craig et al., 1985). When age, race, and gender were controlled, differences between alcoholics and cocaine addicts disappeared (Donat et al., 1992).

The content of Scale T (Drug Dependence) contains items pertaining to problematic use of drugs and personality traits often associated with drug abuse. Median stability estimates for Scale T are .68, .72, and .91 for the MCMI, MCMI-II, and MCMI-III, respectively (See Table 16.1). However, Scale T has shown reduced sensitivity levels in detecting drug addicts in treatment. Sensitivity levels for addicts on methadone maintenance were 49% (Marsh, Stile, Stoughton, & Trout-Landen, 1988), 39% (Calsyn & Saxon, 1990), and 49% (Calsyn, Saxon, & Daisy, 1991) for a mixed group of opiate and cocaine addicts, and 49% for adult psychiatric patients with drug abuse problems (Bryer et al., 1990).

Millon (1994) reports the sensitivity level for MCMI-III Scale T at .52. The scale's specificity is excellent, with most studies reporting values in the mid- to high .90s (Bryer et al., 1990; Calsyn et al., 1991; Gibertini et al., 1986; Millon, 1987, 1994; Streiner & Miller, 1991). However, my review of the literature found 13 studies with 28 data sets which published BR scores for Scale T with drug abusing populations (excluding alcoholics). Median BR scores for a variety of drug addict samples was 81. Using BR > 74 as the criterion, only three samples (11%) met this threshold, and one of those studies used addicts who were cognitively impaired. Using a criteria of BR > 84, only six samples (21%) met the threshold. This data suggests that using the criterion of BR > 74 would most accurately diagnose known drug addicts.

MCMI and MCMI-II studies of substance abuse have all used alcoholics and drug addicts in treatment, who would have no reason to distort their substance abuse. A more common clinical question is whether the test can detect substance abuse in addicts motivated to deny their abuse, which is more of a diagnostic issue for outpatient clinicians who see patients in the early stages of the disorder. A recent study asked addicts to respond honestly to the MCMI-II until they faced a question which, if answered honestly, would reveal their substance abuse. The patients were instructed to lie to those items and to mark on the answer sheet those items on which there was a lie. Results showed that about 50% of the patients were able to successfully avoid detection of substance abuse on the MCMI-II. On the other hand, the test was able to detect substance abuse in about 50%, even when the motivational set was to mask their addiction. Generally, patients whose substance abuse was rated as mild were more able to conceal their abuse than were addicts whose abuse was rated as moderate or severe (Craig, Kuncel, & Olson, 1994).

Little work has been done on the predictive validity of Scale T. No MCMI differences were found between treatment dropouts and treatment completers in a hospital-based program (Craig, 1984), while another study found that program completers scored higher on seven scales and had more psychopathology than did program dropouts (Stark & Campbell, 1988). Dropouts from a residential therapeutic community (TC) were found to have a fiercely independent interpersonal style characterized by manipulative, exploitive and confrontive features (elevations on Scales 6A and 6B; McMahon, Kelley, & Kouzekanani, 1993) and they relapsed sooner than did program completers (Fals-Stewart, 1992). Patients with an antisocial personality style along with cognitive impairments who were in a TC also stayed in the program for shorter periods of time and were given more disciplinary discharges (Fals-Stewart & Lucente, 1994). Jaffe and Archer (1987) found that scores on Scale T were mildly associated with a variety of drug-using categories among college students, but Scale B actually was a better predictor of drug use than was Scale T. Prevalence rates of personality disorders established by MCMI and MCMI-II scores were quite similar to those established by structured psychiatric interviews and did not differ by drug of choice (Craig, 1988; Craig & Olson, 1990; De Jong, van der Brink, Harteveld, & van der Wielen, 1993).

Five studies reported on Scale T changes after treatment. Patients with PTSD showed no significant changes on Scale T after 35 days of inpatient treatment (Hyer et al., 1989) or 140 days of treatment (Funari, Piekarski, & Sherwood, 1991). Patients with major depression ($N = 28$), after 3 months of treatment, showed no significant differences on T (Libb et al., 1990), whereas Piersma (1989b) found that patients with major depression ($N = 98$) significantly reduced their scores on Scale T after inpatient treatment. Patients ($N = 16$) who underwent gastric stapling for morbid obesity showed no significant changes in their scores on Scale T postsurgically (Chandarana, Conlon, Holliday, Deslippe, & Field, 1990). These same studies also found no changes on Scale B. No study has reported on changes on Scale T or B scores pre- and posttreatment of substance abuse, which would be a more important outcome measure than these scale scores in non-drug-using populations.

Posttraumatic Stress Disorder

MCMI research in this area has primarily focused on male Vietnam Veterans with PTSD, although one study reported on PTSD in addicted, pathological gamblers (McCormick, Taber, & Kruedelback, 1989). Table 16.5 presents results of all published studies that have reported BR scores on PTSD populations. Since Hyer and Boudewyns (1985) initially reported that PTSD patients have an 8A–2 MCMI codetype, subsequent research has consistently reported similar findings. Patients with PTSD generally have an MCMI codetype of 8A–2 or 8A–2–1. Other studies, which did not report actual scores, have found nearly identical results (McCormick et al., 1989; Sherwood, Funari, & Piekarski, 1990), and German-held World War II prisoners of war had an MCMI codetype similar to their Vietnam counterparts (Miller, Martin, & Spiro, 1991). This personality style is characterized by negativistic behaviors, erratic emotionality, and petulant, quarrelsome, and demanding behavior. The patient's ambivalence is expressed in personality as acting disruptively and argumentatively at one moment (the passive–aggressive component) and withdrawn and contrite at the next moment (the detached component). The elevations on Scale C in these studies reflects the quixotic emotionality seen in PTSD patients. Also extant are problems with anxiety, depression, and substance abuse. Alexithymia has also been reported to be part of the clinical picture (Hyer, Woods, Summers, Boudewyns, & Harrison, 1990). Cluster analysis of 100 Vietnam veterans with PTSD revealed four subtypes associated with the parent code, including 8A–2 (the parent code), 8A–2–1, 8A–2–1–3, and 8A–2–1–6

TABLE 16.5. MCMI Scores for PTSD Patients

Authors (year)	Robert et al. (1985)	Hyer et al. (1988)	Hyer et al. (1989)		McCormick et al. (1989)	Hyer et al. (1990)	Funari et al. (1991)		Hyer et al. (1991)
N =	25	60	50		17	60	45		100
Population	Vietnam vets	Vietnam vets	Vietnam vets		Gamblers w/PTSD	Vietnam vets	Vietnam vets		Vietnam vets
Codetype	8A-2	8A-2-1	8A-2-1 Pre	8A-2-1 Post	Not available	8A-2-1	8A-2 Pre	6A-2 Post	8A-2-1
Schizoid	66	c80	80	82	X[a]	c81	84	68	c76
Avoidant	81	c86	88	93	66	c91	93	75	c86
Dependent	54	c50	42	44	X	c50	52	48	c61
Histrionic	52	c34	30	31	X	c33	42	47	c50
Narcissistic	54	c40	40	38	X	c40	52	67	c61
Antisocial	63	c62	66	69	X	c60	72	80	c50
Compulsive	28	c34	34	25	X	c34	32	47	c50
Passive–Aggressive	91	c95	93	96	X	c90	95	71	c95
Schizotypal	61	c65	64	68	X	c62	65	58	c62
Borderline	78	c77	76	80	X	c90	73	60	c76
Paranoid	64	c62	63	66	X	c62	63	78	c56
Anxious	94	c96	98	99	77	c92	90	65	c94
Somatoform Disorder	72	c71	69	71	X	c67	66	55	c58
Hypomania	63	c40	43	46	X	c58	49	49	c61
Dysthymic Disorder	87	c92	92	95	58	c90	86	67	c88
Alcohol Dependence	81	c80	77	71	48	c80	83	77	c60
Drug Dependence	77	c70	66	69	63	c72	76	76	c50
Thought Disorder	66	c71	69	71	X	c73	71	64	c60
Major Depression	70	c77	75	78	X	c74	71	59	c76
Delusional disorder	58	c58	60	59	X	c59	59	65	c70

[a]X = Scale not on the MCMI.

(Hyer, Woods, & Boudewyns, 1991). Thus, the MCMI and MCMI-II provide a very accurate assessment of the known characteristics of many patients with PTSD. There is evidence that the MCMI-II can distinguish between actual and pseudo-PTSD patients (Lees-Haley, 1992).

The consistency of the findings in this area, validated with other instruments (Hyer et al., 1994; Hyer, Woods, Boudewyns, Harrison, & Tamkin, 1990), has led some authors to conclude that the 8A-2(1) codetype is a traumatogenic profile and/or is unique to PTSD patients (Hyer, Melton, & Stratton, 1993; Hyer, Woods, Boudewyns, Bruno, & O'Leary, 1988; Robert et al., 1985). However, this codetype appears in many other populations and is not specific to PTSD (Craig, 1995).

Eating Disorders

Twelve studies have been published concerning the use of the MCMI with eating disorders (Chandarana et al., 1990; Chandarana, Holliday, Conlon, & Deslippe, 1988; Garner, Olmstead, Davis, Rocket, et al., 1990; Head & Williamson, 1991; Kennedy, McVey, & Katz, 1990; Lepkowsky, 1987; Lundholm, Pelegreno, Wolins, & Graham, 1989; Norman, Blais, & Herzog, 1993; Sansone & Fine, 1992; Tisdale, Pendelton & Marler, 1990; Tisdale & Pendelton, 1993; Tracy, Norman, & Weisberg, 1987). Table 16.6 presents the results of all published studies that have reported MCMI BR scores on bulimic and anorexic populations, representing four studies from seven independent samples, totaling 204 patients

TABLE 16.6. MCMI Scores among Different Eating-Disordered Populations

	Studies[a]							
	1		2	3	4			
MCMI scale	(N = 17) Good outcomes	(N = 19) Poor outcomes	(N = 44)	(N = 37)	(N = 58) Bulimics	(N = 17) Anorexics	(N = 12) Both	Average (N = 204)
Schizoid	50	60	75	58	c48	c65	c74	61.43
Avoidant	59	72	81	69	c63	c73	c83	71.43
Dependent	60	66	82	75	c72	c65	c78	71.14
Histrionic	62	59	42	52	c65	c51	c43	53.43
Narcissistic	52	46	40	47	c53	c50	c40	46.86
Antisocial	51	48	44	45	c45	c51	c42	46.57
Compulsive	58	49	58	55	c46	c51	c43	51.43
Passive–Aggressive	62	77	73	67	c73	c66	c81	71.28
Schizotypal	55	61	60	62	c52	c61	c70	60.14
Borderline	73	75	81	70	c71	c70	c81	74.28
Paranoid	47	52	71	51	c49	c58	c56	54.86
Syndromes								
Anxiety Disorder	88	91	X[b]	X	X	X	X	89.50
Somatoform Disorder	73	70	X	X	X	X	X	71.50
Bipolar Disorder	47	44	X	X	X	X	X	45.50
Dysthymia	87	87	X	X	X	X	X	87.00
Alcohol Dependence	44	58	X	X	X	X	X	51.00
Drug Dependence	50	51	X	X	X	X	X	50.50

[a](1) Garner et al. (1990) (bulimics); (2) Kennedy et al. (1990) (bulimics and anorexics); (3) Tisdale et al. (1990) (bulimics); (4) Norman et al. (1993) (bulimics, anorexics, and combined sample).
[b]X = Scale not on the MCMI.

with bulimia, anorexia, or bulimia and anorexia. Inspection of Table 16.6 indicates that eating disordered patients have personality characteristics associated with dependent, avoidant, and borderline traits of varying degrees of severity. Also, anxiety, dysthymia, and, to a lesser extent, somatoform are the clinical syndromes most prevalent across all samples. However, the basic MCMI codetypes are not specific to eating-disordered patients and have been found in patients with other psychopathologies (Craig, 1995). These results are quite similar to those contained in the MMPI literature as well as research using other instruments which demonstrates that social withdrawal and depression are part of the eating disorder syndrome (Lundholm et al., 1989).

There is early evidence on the predictive validity of the MCMI with eating-disordered populations. Females who scored high on MCMI Scale B reported more episodes of bulimia and reduced confidence to recognize emotions and sensations of hunger and satiety (Lundholm et al., 1989). Scale C scores predicted poor response to treatment outcome in women with eating disorders (Sansone & Fine, 1992), while Scales C and D significantly declined among successfully treated bulimics (Garner et al., 1990). However, one study found that Scale C scores remained unchanged while scores on D were significantly reduced following treatment (Kennedy et al., 1990). Patients who underwent gastric stapling for morbid obesity showed significant reductions postsurgically on Scales A, H, and D (Chandarana et al., 1990; Chandarana et al., 1988). Eating-disordered patients with elevated scores on Scales 2 and D were associated with a restricted and conflicted family environment, while elevated scores on Scales 4, 7, and P were associated with having a stimulating, achievement-oriented family environment (Head & Williamson, 1991).

While these general findings are limited by a small number of studies, small sample sizes, and an overrepresentation of bulimic samples compared with pure anorexics, these preliminary findings suggest that the MCMI can validly assess personality characteristics, disorders, and syndromes among this population.

Spouse Abusers

Eight studies have been published using the MCMI and MCMI-II with spouse abusers. The primary emphasis of these studies has been to assess personality disorders within this population and the findings indicate that the majority of wifebeaters have personality characteristics consistent with diagnoses of personality disorders, particularly antisocial, aggressive, narcissistic, borderline, and passive–aggressive (negativistic). Spouse abusers are a heterogeneous population and there is a subset who have problematic personality traits but who would not meet the criteria of a personality disorder (Beasley & Stoltenberg, 1992; Dutton, 1994; Hamberger & Hastings, 1986, 1988, 1989, 1992; Hart, Dutton, & Newlove, 1993; Lohr, Hamberger, & Bonge, 1988). MCMI and MCMI-II BR scores for spouse abusers in published studies appear in Table 16.7.

Correctional Inmates

Seven studies report on the clinical use of the MCMI with an inmate population and the results are quite consistent. Surprisingly, there is a preponderance of dependent personality traits among child molesters, (Barnett & McCormack, 1988; Chantry & Craig, 1994a) adult rapists and aggressive felons (Chantry & Craig, 1994b), forensic inpatients (McNeil & Meyer, 1990), and general prison inmates (Ahrens & Evans, 1990; Ownby, Wallbrown, Carmin, & Barnett, 1990), but at subclinical levels. Only one study reported antisocial personality styles among an inmate population using the MCMI-II (Hart, Forth, & Hare, 1991). One explanation of these results is that much of the research has been on sexual offenders, who may have personality characteristics which differ from the general prison population. Cluster analysis of MCMI profiles of child molesters ($N = 202$), adult rapists ($N = 195$), and nonsexually aggressive felons ($N = 206$) found the personality styles of dependent and narcissistic–antisocial appeared across all groups. A third type was also found with relatively subclinical scores for narcissism and compulsivity (Chantry & Craig, 1994a).

CONCLUSION

The MCMI has made impressive gains in the literature on personality and personality pathology. No other personality pattern and disorder instrument or psychiatric clinical interview schedule has generated so much research. The instrument is in use in hospitals, medical centers, psychiatric clinics, counseling centers, residential treatment centers, community mental health clinics, and private practice settings. While this paper has focused on empirical studies with the MCMIs, certainly the value of a test can also be assessed by the frequency with which clinicians regard it as useful for assessment and treatment planning (Craig, 1993b; Retzlaff, 1995). We can have no fewer expectations for the MCMI-III as well.

TABLE 16.7. BR Scores for Spouse Abusers

Study 1

MCMI scale	Grp. 1		Grp. 2		Grp. 3		Grp. 4		Grp. 5		Grp. 6	
	(N = 12)	(N = 10)	(N = 14)	(N = 13)	(N = 12)	(N = 16)	(N = 12)	(N = 12)	(N = 10)	(N = 14)	(N = 10)	(N = 14)
Schizoid	76	63	23	17	43	56	37	33	80	77	17	18
Avoidant	80	73	27	28	46	54	47	57	93	79	37	32
Dependent	49	45	46	50	87	77	46	50	93	91	76	83
Histrionic	53	63	66	68	56	60	73	75	53	57	73	73
Narcissistic	63	73	80	83	55	63	85	85	55	59	75	79
Antisocial	76	78	76	83	36	66	86	87	63	53	56	57
Aggressive	X[a]	X	X	X	X	X	X	X	X	X	X	X
Compulsive	37	38	66	70	70	71	35	37	45	44	66	73
Passive–Aggressive	77	80	43	47	25	33	77	73	95	83	36	33
Code type	2–8A–6A	8A–6A	5–6A	5–6A	3	3	5–6A–8A	5–6A–4	8A–2–3	3–8A–2	3–5	3–5

	Study 1 (cont.)				Study 2			Study 3		Study 4
	Grp. 7		Grp. 8		Grp. 1	Grp. 2	Grp. 3	Completers	Dropouts	
MCMI scale	(N = 14)	(N = 11)	(N = 15)	(N = 12)	(N = 66)	(N = 74)	(N = 48)	(N = 77)	(N = 57)	(N = 49)
Schizoid	57	43	47	40	71	31	30	40	60	X
Avoidant	58	60	45	42	76	43	33	52	62	X
Dependent	86	77	44	36	73	42	61	55	61	52
Histrionic	74	70	55	60	54	73	62	68	65	64
Narcissistic	74	70	66	70	58	82	68	28	71	72
Antisocial	64	60	67	72	62	83	58	68	73	77
Aggressive	X	X	X	X	X	X	X	X	X	85
Compulsive	43	42	73	74	43	48	67	15	54	X
Passive–Aggressive	84	83	48	54	82	68	31	64	75	X
Code type	3–8A	8A–3	'7	'7	8A–2	6A–5	'–7			6B–6A

Note. No study has provided BR scores for the Self-Defeating scale. Study 1: Hamberger & Hastings (1986) (MCMI; *N* = 99); Study 2: Lohr et al. (1988) (MCMI; *N* = 188); Study 3: Hamberger & Hastings (1989) (MCMI; *N* = 156); Study 4: Beasley & Stoltenberg (1992) (MCMI-II; *N* = 49).
[a] X = Scale not on the MCMI.

318

REFERENCES

Ahrens, J. A., & Evans, R. G. (1990). Factors related to dropping out of school in an incarcerated population. *Educational and Psychological Measurement, 50*, 61–67.

Alnaes, R., & Torgersen, S. (1991). Personality and personality disorders among patients with various affective disorders. *Journal of Personality Disorders, 5*, 107–121.

American Psychiatric Association. (1980). *Diagnostic and statistical manual of mental disorders* (3rd ed.). Washington, DC: Author.

American Psychiatric Association. (1987). *Diagnostic and statistical manual of mental disorders* (3rd ed., rev.). Washington, DC: Author.

American Psychiatric Association. (1994). *Diagnostic and statistical manual of mental disorders* (4th ed.). Washington, DC: Author.

Auerback, J. S. (1984). Validation of two scales for narcissistic personality disorder. *Journal of Personality Assessment, 48*, 649–653.

Bagby, R. M., Gillis, J. R., & Dickens, S. (1990). Detection of dissimulation with the new generation of objective personality measures. *Behavioral Sciences and the Law, 8*, 93–102.

Bagby, R. M., Gillis, J. R., & Rogers, R. (1991). Effectiveness of the Millon Clinical Multiaxial Inventory Validity index in the detection of random responding. *Psychological Assessment: A Journal of Consulting and Clinical Psychology, 3*, 285–287.

Barnett, R. W., & McCormack, J. K. (1988). MCMI child molester profiles. *Corrective and Social Psychiatry and Journal of Behavior Technology, Methods, and Therapy, 34*, 14–16.

Beasley, R., & Stoltenberg, C. D. (1992). Personality characteristics of male spouse abusers. *Professional Psychology: Research and Practice, 23*, 310–317.

Bonato, D., Cyr, J., Kalpin, R., Prendergast, P., & Sanhueza, P. (1988). The utility of the MCMI as a DSM-III Axis I diagnostic tool. *Journal of Clinical Psychology, 44*, 867–875.

Bryer, J. B., Martines, K. A., & Dignan, M. A. (1990). Millon Clinical Multiaxial Inventory Alcohol Abuse and Drug Abuse Scales and the identification of substance-abuse patients. *Psychological Assessment: A Journal of Clinical and Consulting Psychology, 4*, 438–441.

Butcher, J. N., Dahlstrom, W. G., Graham, J. R., Tellegen, A., & Kaemmer, B. (1989). *MMPI-2: Manual for administration and scoring.* Minneapolis: University of Minnesota Press.

Calsyn, D. A., & Saxon, A. J. (1988). Identification of personality disorder subtypes among drug abusers using the Millon Clinical Multiaxial Inventory. *National Institute on Drug Abuse: Research Monograph Series, 49*, 299. Rockville, MD.

Calsyn, D. A., & Saxon, A. J. (1990). Personality disorder subtypes among cocaine and opioid addicts using the Millon Clinical Multiaxial Inventory. *International Journal of the Addictions, 25*, 1037–1049.

Calsyn, D. A., Saxon, A. J., & Daisy, F. (1991). Validity of the MCMI Drug Abuse scale varies as a function of drug choice, race, and Axis II subtypes. *American Journal of Drug and Alcohol Abuse, 17*, 153–159.

Carver, C. S., Scheier, M. F., & Weintraub, J. K. (1989). Assessing coping strategies: A theoretically based approach. *Journal of Personality and Social Psychology, 56*, 267–283.

Chandarana, P. C., Conlon, P., Holliday, M. D., Deslippe, T., & Field, V. A. (1990). A prospective study of psychosocial aspects of gastric stapling surgery. *Psychiatric Journal of the University of Ottawa, 15*, 32–35.

Chandarana, P. C., Holliday, R., Conlon, P., & Deslippe, T. (1988). Psychosocial considerations in gastric stapling surgery. *Journal of Psychosomatic Research, 32*, 85–92.

Chantry, K., & Craig, R. J. (1994a). MCMI typologies of criminal sexual offenders. *Sexual Addiction and Compulsivity, 1*, 11–33.

Chantry, K., & Craig, R. J. (1994b). Psychological screening of sexually violent offenders with the MCMI. *Journal of Clinical Psychology, 50*, 430–435.

Chatham, P. M., Tibbals, C. J., & Harrington, M. E. (1993). The MMPI and the MCMI in the evaluation of narcissism in a clinical sample. *Journal of Personality Assessment, 60*, 239–251.

Chick, D., Sheaffer, C. I., & Goggin, W. C. (1993). The relationship between MCMI personality scales and clinician-generated DSM-III-R personality disorder diagnoses. *Journal of Personality Assessment, 61,* 264–276.

Choca, J. P., Bresolin, L., Okonek, A., & Ostrow, D. (1988). Validity of the MCMI in the assessment of affective disorders. *Journal of Personality Assessment, 52,* 96–105.

Choca, J. P., Shanley, L. A., Peterson, C. A., & Van Denburg, E. (1990). Racial bias and the MCMI. *Journal of Personality Assessment, 54,* 479–490.

Choca, J. P., & Van Denburg, E. (1997). *Interpretive guide to the Millon Clinical Multiaxial Inventory* (2nd ed.). Washington, DC: American Psychological Association.

Coolidge, F. L., & Merwin, M. M. (1992). Reliability and validity of the Coolidge Axis II Inventory: A new inventory for the assessment of personality disorders. *Journal of Personality Assessment, 59,* 233–238.

Costa, P. T., & McCrae, R. R. (1992). *Revised NEO Personality Inventory: Professional manual.* Odessa, FL: Psychological Assessment Resources.

Craig, R. J. (1984). Can personality tests predict treatment dropouts? *International Journal of the Addictions, 19,* 665–674.

Craig, R. J. (1988). A psychometric study of the prevalence of DSM-III personality disorders among treated opiate addicts. *International Journal of the Addictions, 23,* 115–124.

Craig, R. J. (Ed.). (1993a). *The Millon Clinical Multiaxial Inventory: A clinical and research information synthesis.* Hillsdale, NJ: Erlbaum.

Craig, R. J. (1993b). *Psychological assessment with the Millon Clinical Multiaxial Inventory (II): An interpretive guide.* Odessa, FL: Psychological Assessment Resources.

Craig, R. J. (1995). Clinical diagnosis and MCMI codetypes. *Journal of Clinical Psychology, 51,* 352–360.

Craig, R. J., Kuncel, R., & Olson, R. E. (1994). Ability of drug addicts to avoid detection of substance abuse on the MCMI-II. *Journal of Social Behavior and Personality, 9,* 95–106.

Craig, R. J., & Olson, R. E. (1990). MCMI comparisons of cocaine abusers and heroin addicts. *Journal of Clinical Psychology, 46,* 230–237.

Craig, R. J., Verinis, J., & Wexler, S. (1985). Personality characteristics of drug addicts and alcoholics on the Millon Clinical Multiaxial Inventory. *Journal of Personality Assessment, 49,* 156–160.

Craig, R. J., & Weinberg, D. (1992a). Assessing alcoholics with the Millon Clinical Multiaxial Inventory: A review. *Psychology of Addictive Behaviors, 6,* 200–208.

Craig, R. J., & Weinberg, D. (1992b). Assessing drug abusers with the Millon Clinical Multiaxial Inventory: A review. *Journal of Substance Abuse Treatment, 9,* 249–255.

Craig, R. D., & Weinberg, D. (1993). MCMI: Review of the literature. In R. Craig (Ed.), *The Millon Clinical Multiaxial Inventory: A clinical and research information synthesis* (pp. 23–70). Hillsdale, NJ: Erlbaum.

Dana, R., & Cantrell, J. (1988). An update on the Millon Clinical Multiaxial Inventory (MCMI). *Journal of Clinical Psychology, 44,* 760–763.

Davis, W. E., Greenblatt, R. L., & Pochyly, J. M. (1990). Test of MCMI black norms for five scales. *Journal of Clinical Psychology, 46,* 175–178.

De Jong, C. A., van der Brink, W., Harteveld, F. M., & van der Wielen, G. M. (1993). Personality disorders in alcoholics and drug addicts. *Comprehensive Psychiatry, 34,* 87–94.

Derogatis, L. R. (1983). *SCL-90-R: Administration, scoring, and procedures manual-II.* Towson, MD: Clinical Psychometric Research.

DeWolfe, A., Larsen, J., & Ryan, J. (1985). Diagnostic accuracy of the Millon test computer reports for bipolar affective disorder. *Journal of Psychopathology and Behavioral Assessment, 7,* 185–189.

Dillon, S. K. (1988). Narcissism and embellishments of signature. *Psychological Reports, 62,* 152–154.

Donat, D. C. (1994). Empirical groupings of perceptions of alcohol use among alcohol dependent persons: A cluster analysis of the alcohol use inventory (AUI) scales. *Assessment, 1,* 103–110.

Donat, D. C., Walters, J., & Hume, A. (1991). Personality characteristics of alcohol dependent inpatients: Relationship of MCMI subtypes to self-reported drinking behavior. *Journal of Personality Assessment, 57,* 335–344.

Donat, D. C., Walters, J., & Hume, A. (1992). MCMI differences between alcoholics and cocaine abusers: Effects of age, sex, and race. *Journal of Personality Assessment, 58,* 96–104.

Dubro, A. F., & Wetzler, S. (1989). An external validity study of the MMPI personality disorder scales. *Journal of Clinical Psychology, 45,* 570–575.

Dutton, D. G. (1994). The origin and structure of the abusive personality. *Journal of Personality Disorders, 8,* 181–191.

Emmons, R. A. (1987). Narcissism: Theory and measurement. *Journal of Personality and Social Psychology, 52,* 11–17.

Fals-Stewart, W. (1992). Personality characteristics of substance abusers: An MCMI cluster typology of recreational drug users treated in a therapeutic community and its relationship to length of stay and outcome. *Journal of Personality Assessment, 59,* 515–527.

Fals-Stewart, W., & Lucente, S. (1993). An MCMI cluster typology of obsessive–compulsives: A measure of personality characteristics and its relationship to treatment participation, compliance and outcome in behavior therapy. *Journal of Psychiatric Research, 27,* 139–154.

Fals-Stewart, W., & Lucente, S. (1994). Effect of neurocognitive status and personality functioning on length of stay in residential substance abuse treatment: An integrative study. *Psychology of Addictive Behaviors, 8,* 179–190.

Fleishauer, A. (1987). The MCMI-II: A reflection of current knowledge. *Noteworthy Response, 3,* 7.

Flynn, P., & McMahon, R. C. (1983). Stability of the drug misuse scale of the Millon Clinical Multiaxial Inventory. *Psychological Reports, 52,* 536–538.

Funari, D. J., Piekarski, A. M., & Sherwood, R. J. (1991). Treatment outcomes of Vietnam veterans with post-traumatic stress disorder. *Psychological Reports, 68,* 571–578.

Gabrys, J. B., Untendale, K. A., Schumph, P., Phillips, K., Robertson, E., Sherwood, G., O'Haire, T., Allard, I., & Clark, M. (1988). Two inventories for the measurement of psychopathology: Dimensions and common factorial space on Millon's clinical and Eysenck's general personality scales. *Psychological Reports, 62,* 591–601.

Garner, D. M., Olmsted, M. R., Davis, R., Rockct, W. (1990). The association between bulimic symptoms and reported psychopathology. *International Journal of Eating Disorders, 9,* 1–15.

Gibertini, M., Brandenberg, N., & Retzlaff, P. (1986). The operating characteristics of the Millon Clinical Multiaxial Inventory. *Journal of Personality Assessment, 50,* 554–567.

Gibertini, M., & Retzlaff, P. (1988). Factor invariance of the Millon Clinical Multiaxial Inventory. *Journal of Psychopathology and Behavioral Assessment, 10,* 65–74.

Goldberg, J. O., Shaw, B., & Segal, Z. V. (1987). Concurrent validity of the MCMI depression scales. *Journal of Consulting and Clinical Psychology, 55,* 785–787.

Greer, S. (1984). Testing the test: A review of the Millon Multiaxial Inventory. *Journal of Counseling and Development, 63,* 262–263.

Haladyna, T. M. (1992). Review of the Millon Clinical Multiaxial Inventory—II. In J. J. Kramer & J. C. Conoley (Eds.), *Eleventh mental measurement yearbook* (pp. 532–533). Lincoln: University of Nebraska Press.

Hamberger, L. K., & Hastings, J. E. (1986). Personality correlates of men who abuse their partners: A cross-validational study. *Journal of Family Violence, 1,* 323–341.

Hamberger, L. K., & Hastings, J. E. (1988). Characteristics of male spouse abusers consistent with personality disorders. *Hospital and Community Psychiatry, 39,* 763–770.

Hamberger, L. K., & Hastings, J. E. (1989). Counseling male spouse abusers: Characteristics of treatment completers and dropouts. *Violence and Victims, 4,* 275–286.

Hamberger, L. K., & Hastings, J. E. (1992). Racial differences on the MCMI in an outpatient clinical sample. *Journal of Personality Assessment, 58,* 90–95.

Hart, S. D., Dutton, D. G., & Newlove, T. (1993). The prevalence of personality disorder among wife assaulters. *Journal of Personality Disorders, 7,* 329–341.

Hart, S. D., Forth, A. E., & Hare, R. D.(1991). The MCMI-II and psychopathy. *Journal of Personality Disorders, 5,* 318–327.

Hathaway, S. R., & McKinley, J. C. (1943). *The Minnesota Multiphasic Personality Inventory.* Minneapolis: University of Minnesota Press.

Head, S. B., & Williamson, D. A. (1991). Association of family environment and personality disturbances in bulimia nervosa. *International Journal of Eating Disorders, 9,* 667–674.

Hess, A. (1985). Review of Millon Clinical Multiaxial Inventory. In J. Mitchell, Jr. (Ed.), *Ninth mental measurements yearbook* (Vol. 1, pp. 984–986). Lincoln: University of Nebraska Press.

Hogg, B., Jackson, H. J., Rudd, R. P., & Edwards, J. (1990). Diagnosing personality disorders in recent-onset schizophrenia. *Journal of Nervous and Mental Disease, 179,* 194–199.

Hyer, L., & Boudewyns, P. (1985). The 8–2 MCMI personality profile among Vietnam veterans with PTSD. *PTSD Newsletter, 4,* 2.

Hyer, L., Braswell, L., Albrecht, B., Boyd, S., Boudewyns, P., & Talbert, S. (1994). Relationship of NEO-PI to personality styles and severity of trauma in chronic PTSD victims. *Journal of Clinical Psychology, 50,* 699–707.

Hyer, L., Melton, M., & Gratton, C. (1993). Posttraumatic stress disorders and MCMI-based assessment. In R. Craig (Ed.), *Millon Clinical Multiaxial Inventory: A clinical and research information synthesis* (pp. 159–172). Hillsdale, NJ: Erlbaum.

Hyer, L., Woods, M. G., & Boudewyns, P. A. (1991). A three tier evaluation of PTSD among Vietnam combat veterans. *Journal of Traumatic Stress, 4,* 165–194.

Hyer, L., Woods, M. G., Boudewyns, P. A., Bruno, R., & O'Leary, W. C. (1988). Concurrent validation of the Millon Clinical Multiaxial Inventory among Vietnam veterans with posttraumatic stress disorder. *Psychological Reports, 63,* 271–278.

Hyer, L., Woods, M. G., Boudewyns, P. A., Harrison, W. R., & Tamkin, A. S. (1990). MCMI and 16PF with Vietnam veterans: Profiles and concurrent validation of MCMI. *Journal of Personality Disorders, 4,* 391–401.

Hyer, L., Woods, M. G., Bruno, R., & Boudewyns, P. (1989). Treatment outcomes of Vietnam veterans with PTSD and consistency of the MCMI. *Journal of Clinical Psychology, 45,* 547–552.

Hyer, L., Woods, M. G., Summers, M. N., Boudewyns, P., & Harrison, W. R. (1990). Alexithymia among Vietnam veterans with posttraumatic stress disorder. *Journal of Clinical Psychiatry, 51,* 243–247.

Hyler, S. E., Reider, R., Spitzer, R. L., & Williams, J. B. (1993). *Personality Disorder Questionnaire (PDQ).* New York: New York State Psychiatric Institute.

Inch, R., & Crossley, M. (1993). Diagnostic utility of the MCMI-I and MCMI-II with psychiatric outpatients. *Journal of Clinical Psychology, 49,* 358–366.

Jackson, J. L., Greenblatt, R. L., Davis, W. E., Murphy, T. T., & Trimakas, K. (1991). Assessment of schizophrenic inpatients with the MCMI. *Journal of Personality Assessment, 51,* 243–253.

Jaffe, L., & Archer, R. (1987). The prediction of drug use among college students from the MMPI, MCMI and Sensation Seeking Scales. *Journal of Personality Assessment, 51,* 243–253.

Joffe, R. T., & Regan, J. J. (1988). Personality and depression. *Journal of Psychiatric Research, 22,* 279–286.

Joffe, R. T., Swinson, R. P., & Regan, J. J. (1988). Personality features of obsessive-compulsive disorder. *American Journal of Psychiatry, 145,* 1127–1129.

Josiassen, R. C., Shagass, C., & Roemer, R. A. (1988). Somato-sensory evoked potential correlates of schizophrenic subtypes identified by the Millon Clinical Multiaxial Inventory. *Psychiatry Research, 23,* 209–219.

Kennedy, S. H., McVey, G., & Katz, R. (1990). Personality disorders in anorexia nervosa and bulimia nervosa. *Journal of Psychiatric Research, 24,* 259–269.

Klein, M. H., Benjamin, L. S., Rosenfeld, R., Treece, C., Husted, J., & Greist, J. H. (1993). The Wisconsin Personality Disorders Inventory: Development, reliability, and validity. *Journal of Personality Disorders, 7,* 285–303.

Langevin, R., Lang, R., Reynolds, R., Wright, P., Garrels, D., Marchese, V., Handy, C., Pugh, G., & Frenzel, R. (1988). Personality and sexual anomalies: An examination of the Millon Clinical Multiaxial Inventory. *Annals of Sex Research, 1,* 13–32.

Lanyon, R. (1984). Personality assessment. *Annual Review of Psychology, 35,* 667–701.

Lees-Haley, P. R. (1992). Efficacy of MMPI-2 validity scales and MCMI-II modifier scales for detecting spurious PTSD claims: F, F–K, Fake Bad scale, Ego Strength, Subtle–Obvious subscales, DIS, and DEB. *Journal of Clinical Psychology, 48,* 681–688.

Lehne, G. K. (1994). The NEO-PI and the MCMI in the forensic evaluation of sex offenders. In P. T. Costa & T. A. Widiger (Eds.), *Personality disorders and the five-factor model of personality* (pp. 175–188). Washington, DC: American Psychological Association.

Lepkowsky, C. M. (1987). Personality pathology in eating disorders. In C. Green (Ed.), *Conference on the Millon clinical inventories (MCMI, MBHI, MAPI)* (pp. 215–220). Minneapolis: National Computer Systems.

Leroux, M. D., Vincent, K. R., McPherson, R. H., & Williams, W. (1990). Construct validity of the Diagnostic Inventory of Personality and Symptoms: External correlates. *Journal of Clinical Psychology, 46,* 285, 291.

Libb, J. W., Murray, J., Thurstin, H., & Alarcon, R. D. (1992). Concordance of the MCMI-II, the MMPI, and Axis I discharge diagnosis in psychiatric inpatients. *Journal of Personality Assessment, 58,* 580–590.

Libb, J. W., Stankovic, S., Sokol, A., Houck, C., & Switzer, P. (1990). Stability of the MCMI among depressed psychiatric outpatients. *Journal of Personality Assessment, 55,* 209–218.

Lohr, J. M., Hamberger, L. K., & Bonge, D. (1988). The nature of irrational beliefs in different personality clusters of spouse abusers. *Journal of Rational–Emotive and Cognitive Behavior Therapy, 6,* 273–285.

Loranger, A. (1988). *Personality Disorder Examination (PDE) manual.* New York: Cornell University Medical College, Department of Psychiatry.

Lundholm, J. K., Pelegreno, D. D., Wolins, L., & Graham, S. L. (1989). Predicting eating disorders in women: A preliminary measurement study. *Measurement and Evaluation in Counseling and Development, 22,* 23–30.

Marsh, D. T., Stile, S. A., Stoughton, N. L., & Trout-Landen, B. L. (1988). Psychopathology among opiate addiction: Comparative data from the MMPI and MCMI. *American Journal of Drug and Alcohol Abuse, 14,* 17–27.

Matano, R. A., Locke, K. D., & Schwartz, K. (1994). MCMI personality subtypes for male and female alcoholics. *Journal of Personality Assessment, 63,* 250–264.

McCabe, S. (1984). Millon Clinical Multiaxial Inventory. In D. Keyser & R. Sweetland (Eds.), *Test critiques* (Vol. 1, pp. 455–456). Kansas City, MO: Westport.

McCann, J. T. (1989). MMPI personality disorder scales and the MCMI: Concurrent validity. *Journal of Clinical Psychology, 45,* 365–369.

McCann, J. T. (1990). A multitrait–multimethod analysis of the MCMI-II clinical syndrome scales. *Journal of Personality Assessment, 55,* 465–476.

McCann, J. T. (1991). Convergent and discriminant validity of the MCMI-II and MMPI personality disorder scales. *Psychological Assessment: A Journal of Consulting and Clinical Psychology, 3,* 9–18.

McCormack, J. K., Barnett, R. W., & Wallbrown, F. H. (1989). Factor structure of the Millon Clinical Multiaxial Inventory with an offender sample. *Journal of Personality Assessment, 53,* 442–448.

McCormick, R. A., Taber, J. I., & Kruedelback, N. (1989). The relationship between attributional style and post-traumatic stress disorder in addicted patients. *Journal of Traumatic Stress, 2,* 477–487.

McMahon, R. C., & Davidson, R. S. (1985a). An examination of the relationship between personality patterns and symptom/mood patterns. *Journal of Personality Assessment, 49,* 552–556.

McMahon, R. C., & Davidson, R. S. (1985b). Transient versus enduring depression among alcoholics in inpatient treatment. *Journal of Psychopathology and Behavioral Assessment, 7,* 317–328.

McMahon, R. C., Davidson, R. S., & Flynn, P. M. (1986). Psychological correlates and treatment outcomes for high and low social functioning alcoholics. *International Journal of the Addictions, 21,* 819–835.

McMahon, R. C., Davidson, R. S., Gersh, D., & Flynn, P. (1991). A comparison of continuous and episodic drinkers using the MCMI, MMPI, and Alceval–R. *Journal of Clinical Psychology*, *47*, 148–159.

McMahon, R. C., Davidson, R. S., Flynn, P., & Gersh, D. (1991). A comparison of continuous and episodic drinkers using the MCMI. *Journal of Clinical Psychology*, *47*, 148–159.

McMahon, R. C., Flynn, P. M., & Davidson, R. S. (1985). Stability of the personality and symptom scales of the Millon Clinical Multiaxial Inventory. *Journal of Personality Assessment*, *49*, 231–234.

McMahon, R. C., Gersh, D., & Davidson, R. S. (1989). Personality and symptom characteristics of continuous vs. episodic drinkers. *Journal of Clinical Psychology*, *45*, 161–168.

McMahon, R. C., Kelley, A., & Kouzekanani, K. (1993). Personality and coping styles in the prediction of dropout from treatment for cocaine abuse. *Journal of Personality Assessment*, *61*, 147–155.

McMahon, R. C., Schram, L. L., & Davidson, R. S. (1993). Negative life events, social support, and depression in three personality types. *Journal of Personality Disorders*, *7*, 241–254.

McMahon, R. C., & Tyson, D. (1990). Personality factors in transient versus enduring depression among inpatient alcoholic women: A preliminary analysis. *Journal of Personality Disorders*, *4*, 150–160.

McNeil, K., & Meyer, R. G. (1990). Detection of deception on the Millon Clinical Multiaxial Inventory (MCMI). *Journal of Clinical Psychology*, *46*, 755–764.

Miller, H. R., Goldberg, J. O., & Streiner, D. L. (1993). The effects of the modifier and correction indices on MCMI-II profiles. *Journal of Personality Assessment*, *60*, 477–485.

Miller, H. R., & Streiner, D. L. (1990). Using the Millon Clinical Multiaxial Inventory's Scale B and the MacAndrew's Alcoholism Scale to identify alcoholics with concurrent psychiatric diagnosis. *Journal of Personality Assessment*, *54*, 736–746.

Miller, H. R., Streiner, D. L., & Parkinson, A. (1992). Maximum likelihood estimates of the ability of the MMPI and MCMI personality disorder scales and the SIDP to identify personality disorders. *Journal of Personality Assessment*, *59*, 1–13.

Miller, T. W., Martin, W., & Spiro, K. (1991). Traumatic stress disorder: Diagnostic and clinical issues in former prisoners of war. *Comprehensive Psychiatry*, *30*, 139–148.

Millon, T. (1982). *Millon Behavioral Health Inventory manual*. Minneapolis: National Computer Systems.

Millon, T. (1983). *Millon Clinical Multiaxial Inventory manual* (3rd ed.). New York: Holt, Rinehart & Winston.

Millon, T. (1985). The MCMI provides a good assessment of DSM-III disorders: The MCMI-II will prove even better. *Journal of Personality Assessment*, *49*, 379–391.

Millon, T. (1987). *Millon Clinical Multiaxial Inventory—II: Manual for the MCMI-II*. Minneapolis: National Computer Systems.

Millon, T. (1994). *Millon Clinical Multiaxial Inventory—III manual*. Minneapolis: National Computer Systems.

Morey, L. C. (1985). An empirical approach of interpersonal and DSM-III approaches to classification of personality disorders. *Psychiatry*, *48*, 358–364.

Morey, L. C., Blashfield, R. K., Webb, W. W., & Jewell, J. J. (1988). MMPI scales for DSM-III personality disorders: A preliminary study. *Journal of Clinical Psychology*, *44*, 47–50.

Morey, L. C., & Levine, D. J. (1988). A multitrait–multimethod examination of Minnesota Multiphasic Personality Inventory (MMPI) and Millon Clinical Multiaxial Inventory (MCMI). *Journal of Psychopathology and Behavioral Assessment*, *10*, 333–344.

Murphy, T. J., Greenblatt, R. L., Modzierz, G. J., & Trimakas, K. A. (1991). Stability of the Millon Clinical Multiaxial Inventory among psychiatric inpatients. *Journal of Psychopathology and Behavioral Assessment*, *12*, 143–150.

Norman, D., Blais, M. A., & Herzog, D. (1993). Personality characteristics of eating-disordered patients as identified by the Millon Clinical Multiaxial Inventory. *Journal of Personality Disorders*, *7*, 1–9.

Ownby, R. L., Wallbrown, F. H., Carmin, C. N., & Barnett, R. W. (1990). A combined factor analysis of the Millon Clinical Multiaxial Inventory and the MMPI in an offender population. *Journal of Clinical Psychology, 46,* 89–96.

Overholser, J. C. (1990). Retest reliability of the Millon Clinical Multiaxial Inventory. *Journal of Personality Assessment, 55,* 202–208.

Overholser, J. C. (1991). Categorical assessment of the dependent personality disorder in depressed inpatients. *Journal of Personality Disorders, 5,* 243–255.

Patrick, J. (1988). Concordance of the MCMI and the MMPI in the diagnosis of three DSM-III Axis I disorders. *Journal of Clinical Psychology, 44,* 186–190.

Patrick, J. (1993). Validation of the MCMI-I borderline personality disorder scale with a well-defined criterion sample. *Journal of Clinical Psychology, 49,* 29–32.

Pfohl, B., Blum, N., Zimmerman, M., & Stangl, D. (1989). *Structured interview for DSM-III-R personality (SIDP-R).* Iowa City: University of Iowa, Department of Psychiatry.

Piersma, H. L. (1986a). The stability of the Millon Clinical Multiaxial Inventory for psychiatric inpatients. *Journal of Personality Assessment, 50,* 193–197.

Piersma, H. L. (1986b). The Millon Clinical Multiaxial Inventory (MCMI) as a treatment outcome measure for psychiatric inpatients. *Journal of Clinical Psychology, 42,* 493–499.

Piersma, H. L. (1989a). The stability of the MCMI-II for psychiatric inpatients. *Journal of Clinical Psychology, 45,* 781–785.

Piersma, H. L. (1989b). The MCMI-II as a treatment outcome measure for psychiatric inpatients. *Journal of Clinical Psychology, 45,* 87–93.

Piersma, H. L. (1991). The MCMI-II depression scales: Do they assist in the differential prediction of depressive disorders? *Journal of Personality Assessment, 56,* 478–486.

Prifitera, A., & Ryan, J. J. (1984). Validity of the Narcissistic Personality Inventory (NPI) in a psychiatric sample. *Journal of Clinical Psychology, 40,* 140–142.

Raskin, R. N., & Hall, C. S. (1979). A narcissistic personality inventory. *Psychological Reports, 45,* 590.

Reich, J. H., & Noyes, R. (1987). A comparison of DSM-III personality disorders in acutely ill panic and depressed patients. *Journal of Anxiety Disorders, 1,* 123–131.

Renneberg, B., Chambless, D. L., Dowdall, D. J., Fauerbach, J. A., & Gracely, E. J. (1992). The Structured Clinical Interview for DSM-III-R, AXIS-II and the Millon Clinical Multiaxial Inventory: A concurrent validity study of personality disorders among anxious patients. *Journal of Personality Disorders, 6,* 117–124.

Retzlaff, P. D. (Ed.). (1995). *Interpersonal psychotherapy and MCMI-based assessment.* Needham Heights, MA: Allyn & Bacon.

Retzlaff, P. D., Sheehan, E. P., & Fiel, A. (1991). MCMI-II report style and bias: Profile and validity scales analyses. *Journal of Personality Assessment, 56,* 466–477.

Retzlaff, P. D., Sheehan, E. P., & Lorr, M. (1990). MCMI-II scoring: Weighted and unweighted algorithms. *Journal of Personality Assessment, 55,* 219–223.

Reynolds, C. R. (1992). Review of the Millon Clinical Multiaxial Inventory—II. In J. J. Kramer & J. C. Conoley (Eds.), *Eleventh mental measurement yearbook* (pp. 533–535). Lincoln: University of Nebraska Press.

Robert, J. A., Ryan, J. J., McEntyre, W. L., McFarland, R. S., Lips, O. J., & Rosenberg, S. J. (1985). MCMI characteristics of DSM-III posttraumatic stress disorder in Vietnam veterans. *Journal of Personality Assessment, 49,* 226–230.

Sansone, R. A., & Fine, M. A. (1992). Borderline personality disorder as a predictor of outcome in women with eating disorders. *Journal of Personality Disorders, 6,* 176–186.

Schuler, C. E., Snibbe, J. R., & Buckwalter, J. G. (1994). Validity of the MMPI personality disorder scales (MMPI-Pd). *Journal of Clinical Psychology, 50,* 220–227.

Selzer, M. L. (1971). The Michigan Alcoholism Screening Test: The quest for a new diagnostic instrument. *American Journal of Psychiatry, 127,* 1653–1658.

Sexton, D., McIlwraith, R., Barnes, G., & Dunn, R. (1987). Comparison of the MCMI and MMPI-168 as psychiatric inpatient screening inventories. *Journal of Personality Assessment, 51,* 388–398.

Sherwood, R. J., Funari, D. J., & Piekarski, A. M. (1990). Adapted character styles of Vietnam veterans with posttraumatic stress disorder. *Psychological Reports, 66,* 623–631.

Soldz, S., Budman, S., Demby, A., & Merry, J. (1993). Representation of personality disorders in circumplex and five-factor space: Explorations with a clinical sample. *Psychological Assessment, 5*, 41–52.

Spitzer, R. L., Williams, J. B., Gibbon, M., & First, M. B. (1990). *SCID user's guide for the structured clinical interview for DSM-III-R.* Washington, DC: American Psychiatric Association.

Stark, M. J., & Campbell, B. K. (1988). Personality, drug use, and early attrition from substance abuse treatment. *American Journal of Drug and Alcohol Abuse, 14*, 475–485.

Streiner, D. L., & Miller, H. R. (1991). Maximum likelihood estimates of the accuracy of four diagnostic techniques. *Educational and Psychological Measurement, 50*, 653–662.

Streiner, D. L., Goldberg, J. O., & Miller, H. R. (1993). MCMI-II item weights: Their lack of effectiveness. *Journal of Personality Assessment, 60*, 471–476.

Tisdale, M. J., & Pendelton, L. (1993). The use of the MCMI with eating disorders. In R. Craig (Ed.), *The Millon Clinical Multiaxial Inventory: A clinical and research information synthesis* (pp. 147–157). Hillsdale, NJ: Erlbaum.

Tisdale, M. J., Pendelton, L., & Marler, M. (1990). MCMI characteristics of DSM-III-R bulimics. *Journal of Personality Assessment, 55*, 477–483.

Torgersen, S., & Alnaes, R. (1990). The relationship between the MCMI personality scales and DSM-III, Axis II. *Journal of Personality Assessment, 55*, 698–707.

Tracy, H., Norman, D., & Weisberg, L. (1987). Anorexia and bulimia: A comparison of MCMI results: In C. Green (Ed.), *Conference on the Millon clinical inventories (MCMI, MBHI, MAPI)* (pp. 195–197). Minneapolis: National Computer Systems.

Turley, B., Bates, G. W., Edwards, J., & Jackson, H. J. (1992). MCMI-II personality disorders in recent-onset bipolar disorders. *Journal of Clinical Psychology, 48*, 320–329.

Van Gorp, W. G., & Meyer, R. G. (1986). The detection of faking on the Millon Clinical Multiaxial Inventory (MCMI). *Journal of Clinical Psychology, 42*, 742–747.

Vollrath, M., Alnaes, R., & Torgersen, S. (1994). Coping and MCMI-II symptom scales. *Journal of Clinical Psychology, 50*, 727–736.

Wetzler, S. (1990). The Millon Clinical Multiaxial Inventory: A review. *Journal of Personality Assessment, 55*, 445–464.

Wetzler, S., Kahn, R. S., Cahn, W., Van Praag, H. M., & Asnis, G. M. (1990). Psychological test characteristics of depressed and panic patients. *Psychiatry Research, 31*, 179–192.

Wetzler, S., Kahn, R. S., Strauman, T. J., & Dubro, A. (1989). Diagnosis of major depression by self-report. *Journal of Personality Assessment, 53*, 22–30.

Wetzler, S., & Marlowe, D. (1990). "Faking bad" on the MMPI, MMPI-2, and Millon-II. *Psychological Reports, 67*, 1117–1118.

Wetzler, S., & Marlowe, D. B. (1993). The diagnosis and assessment of depression, mania, and psychosis by self-report. *Journal of Personality Assessment, 60*, 1–31.

Wheeler, D. S., & Schwartz, J. C. (1989). Millon Clinical Inventory (MCMI) scores with a collegiate sample: Long term stability and self–other agreement. *Journal of Psychopathology and Behavioral Assessment, 11*, 339–352.

Widiger, T. A. (1985). Review of the Millon Clinical Multiaxial Inventory. In J. Mitchell Jr. (Ed.), *Ninth mental measurements yearbook* (Vol. 1, pp. 986–988). Lincoln: University of Nebraska Press.

Widiger, T., & Sanderson, C. (1987). The convergent and discriminant validity of the MCMI as a measure of the DSM-III personality disorders. *Journal of Personality Assessment, 51*, 228–242.

Widiger, T., Williams, J., Spitzer, R., & Frances, A. (1985). The MCMI as a measure of DSM-III. *Journal of Personality Assessment, 49*, 366–380.

Wierzbicki, M. (1993). Use of the MCMI subtle and obvious subscales to detect faking. *Journal of Clinical Psychology, 49*, 809–814.

Wise, E. A. (1994). Personality style codetype concordance between the MCMI and MBHI. *Journal of Clinical Psychology, 50*, 367–380.

Zarella, K. L., Schuerger, J. M., & Ritz, G. H. (1990). Estimation of MCMI DSM-III Axis II constructs from MMPI scales and subscales. *Journal of Personality Assessment, 55*, 195–201.

17

Validation of the MCMI-III

ROGER D. DAVIS
ANDREW WENGER
ALEXANDRA GUZMAN

Any given psychological construct may be operationalized in a variety of ways. Narcissism, for example, might be measured with a self-report scale as the proportion of time spent looking in a mirror, or as the proportion of conversation spent in self-referential commentary. Each gauge is related, yet different, containing its own measurement biases. Reminiscent of the prototype construct, we might say that these measures neither singly nor collectively exhaust the narcissism construct as an ideal, for which an almost infinite number of intervening variables is possible, limited only by the imagination and ingenuity of psychologists.

How can the validity of an instrument be assessed in the absence of an objectively defined and consensual criterion? Without an absolute reference point or objective standard, not only does no rigorous feedback loop exist that might directly quantify and therefore guarantee the validity of an instrument, but no such feedback loop *can* exist. Psychological constructs, especially those relating to personality traits, are by definition diverse and largely inferential and therefore not anchored to any absolute criterion. This fact requires a different conception of validity than that used with simple and objective observables. Where the constructs are multireferential and hierarchical, validity must be acknowledged as being multireferential and hierarchical as well. Just as any single behavioral act not only will, but must, fail as an unequivocal measure of the construct of interest simply because its bandwidth is too narrow to represent the construct in its totality, a single study, conducted as it is in the particularities of time, circumstance, and sample characteristics, must also be viewed as inadequate to establish the construct validity of an instrument.

How then, is the construction of diagnostic and personality assessment instruments possible at all? Without a construct validity coefficient and the rigorous feedback it would make possible, we have only our expectations concerning what an instrument should do to guide us, both in construction and evaluation. Two general principles apply.

First, our expectations, whether explicit or not, really are theories about relationships between different gauges of a construct. Accordingly, because all we have with which to evaluate construct validity is our expectations and not some single, external, and absolute criterion, the content of the constructs to be included in the inventory and the relations between them should be specified as precisely as possible. Otherwise, we will be left, despite our time and effort, with something the quality of which can only be determined after the fact, by delineating post hoc what should have been specified from the beginning.

Second, we must distinguish between variables which are internal and external to those of a diagnostic inventory, and specify these internal–external relationships as well. If our inventory is intended to assess personality disorders, we might expect, for example, that those classified as having dependent personalities will also be classified as experiencing depressive episodes more often than will, say, antisocials, simply because dependents are likely to feel helpless and hopeless more often than antisocials, who are more likely to take matters into their own hands and change the world around them, albeit in a self-aggran-dizing fashion. Together, these internal–internal and internal–external expectations form a set of constraints that our inventory must be constructed to satisfy. The larger this set of constraints, the better, for if the inventory can satisfy many such constraints at the outset, then validity has been built into the instrument from the beginning. In general, the more such constraints the test has been shown to satisfy, the better the instrument, and the greater confidence we can have that it will meet whatever challenges are put to it in the future. Each constraint is an additional point through which the pattern of findings which emerge from the instrument are triangulated with reality as it is assumed to exist in theory.

Sometimes, after the instrument has been constructed, certain variables about which we had no preformed ideas show a significant relationship. Perhaps in the beginning we believed that antisocial personalities should also report high family distress and a high incidence of alcoholism. Perhaps we also believed that dependent persons should report overprotective parents and an inability to end relationships, and these expectations were built into the instrument. About the relationship between dependent personality and inci-dence of alcoholism, however, we may have no a priori notions at all, so that, with regard to the expectations we held in the context of constructing the instrument, the magnitude of this relationship was "free to vary," simply because we did not know much about it, how it should be evaluated, or whether it should even exist. How do we evaluate this ob-served, but unexpected, relationship? Having constructed our instrument to satisfy mul-tiple constraints in the form of theoretically-driven expectations, we are no longer work-ing with just any item pool, but with a system of scales of demonstrated validity. The more the tests satisfies these constraints, the greater our expectations of the generalizability of the entire system of instrumentation. Demonstrated validity in diverse areas of the nomologi-cal network becomes a promissory note that observed relationships between intervening variables elsewhere are not peculiar to their mode of operationalization, but are instead representative of nature's structure and, so, are worthy of genuine scientific interest. In addition to their shortcomings in comprehensiveness and comparability, one of the prob-lems of the DSM-IV (American Psychiatric Association, 1994) criteria is that they have not been subjected to such a process of refinement, but were instead constructed through committee consensus.

In their thoughtful article some 40 years ago on the concept of construct validity in psychological tests, Cronbach and Meehl (1955) wrote that it is the nomological network of relationships among internal concepts and external observables that provides the basis of an instrument's undergirding theory. The value and interpretability of a test's scores are, in large measure, a function of the comprehensiveness of this network of supporting observables and concepts. No single observable or concept can serve as *the* ultimate criterion, the so-called "gold standard" against which all other parts of the network are to be judged as deficient. The more the instrument is grounded in a range of minicriteria, internal and external, the more likely is it to possess a solid level of generalizable validity and reliability. Such con-struct validity will, in effect, be likely to be more substantial than would any single criterion.

To complicate matters further in test validation, whatever gauge or criterion may be employed must demonstrate a high level of correlation with other established criteria and must be coordinated with the theory's conceptual network. In addition, as Retzlaff (1996) has pointed out, preliminary validation studies of an instrument, such as the Millon Clinical Multiaxial Inventory—III (MCMI-III; Millon, 1994) often prove inadequate to the validation task owing to methodological deficiencies, for example, the adequacy of the diagnostic criteria employed; the level and frequency of contact between clinical judges and patients; the extent to which clinicians know their patients' traits and difficulties; the diversity in, if not conflicting purposes of, the study, and so on.

We may find it useful to illustrate how detailed knowledge of the characteristics of both specific patients and knowledge of the nomological network of the theory (science?) are necessary to achieve accurate or valid judgments. We shall use a six-sided die to discuss the pros and cons of this analysis.

Each die has six sides. If we were to roll the die and guess the result, our accuracy level would be approximately 16.67%. However, if we had considerable experience with a particular die and had learned that the number 3 showed up 40% of the time (and the others less than 16%) we would gradually modify our guesses so that the number 3 would be chosen more frequently than any of the others. That is, our base rate (BR) for guessing would change form some expected chance number in which all possibilities are equally likely to one in which the number 3 would be guessed more frequently, probably until it reached roughly 40% of the time.

We can shift from the preceding example to one in which different die proportions emerge over time. Experience teaches us to approximate what those proportions are. In the case just noted, the number 3 was guessed roughly 40% of the time. In another situation, we might find that the number 5 shows up roughly 50% of the time. In time, the judgments we made for each number would approximate the actual BR for that particular die. Note, however, that the specific individual judgments for each throw in a series might be wrong, although the overall BRs would gradually approximate reality. We do not need to guess any single case correctly for the *overall* BR of our judgments to be quite accurate. Single judgments can remain as erroneous as ever (except by selecting high BR die numbers, our results are more likely to be a little bit better than chance).

This die example approximates what occurs when clinicians make their diagnostic judgments about patients whom they *do not* know well. Clinicians who work in a particular setting may be very good at estimating that setting's *overall* BRs but may not be very good at making *specific* diagnostic judgments. How do we improve the accuracy of these judgments? Let us go back to the die. If one has plenty of time to study an individual die, to look at its scratches, chips, and so on, so that one can assess its distinctive characteristics, and if one understands enough about the physics of what happens to dice when they are chipped here or marred there, this knowledge should enhance the accuracy of individual judgments—not merely the overall BR proportions. Likewise, if a clinician knows a particular patient very well and can identify his or her traits, features, history, etc., *and* if the clinician has studied personality pathology in great detail, he or she then has both general knowledge of the way pathological personality traits interrelate and the distinctive features of the specific patient in question. Consequently, the clinician's judgments should be appreciably better than chance.

Not untypically, most clinical judges in the exploratory MCMI-III validation study saw the subjects only once, and usually without the benefit of clinical interviews or extensive readings of their histories. It was like picking up a die, glancing at it, guessing, and then throwing it. They did not know the subjects well. Nor do we know the level of sophistication the clinicians had concerning personality disorders. If they had time to study the subjects, and if they had studied the personality disorder literature extensively, then we would have considerable confidence in the accuracy of their individual judgments. Without such background information, their judgments are likely to be suitable only for estimating overall BRs. For making individual clinical diagnoses, their lack of familiarity with the subjects and perhaps with the clinical literature on personality disorders would likely lead them to make judgments that are less than satisfactory.

The unreliability inherent in these exploratory clinical ratings create an upper bound for diagnostic efficiency statistics. Any differences between these preliminary statistics and those reported for the MCMI-II (Millon, 1987) were likely due to differences in the reliabilities of the respective clinical judgments and not to changes in the quality of the scales themselves (Retzlaff, 1996). In the MCMI-II study, all clinicians were well acquainted with the patients they rated and they had attended workshops or seminars on personality disorders conducted by the test's author.

The conditions under which the original MCMI-II study was conducted have now been replicated with the MCMI-III. It is this properly executed study that is reported here. The following section reports on the methods of this project, the diagnostic efficiency results they achieve, and comparisons with both the MCMI and the MCMI-II.

METHOD

Some 75 clinicians who were well acquainted with a systematic theory of personality and psychopathology, notably the theory formulated by Millon (1990), who were frequent users of the MCMI-III, (the theory's operational gauge), and who had participated in earlier MCMI research projects were contacted to inquire as to whether they would be interested in participating in an MCMI-III validation study. Informed as to the general features of the study as well as to their responsibilities in executing their segment of the project, approximately 30 expressed a willingness to participate; most indicated that they had several associates (group practice or clinic colleagues) who would join in the clinical judgment task. In all, 67 primary clinicians and associates participated in rating patients in accord with the instruction booklet reproduced below.

In contrast to the exploratory study reported in the first edition of the MCMI-III manual, all of these clinicians reported having substantial direct contact with the patients they treated. The minimum contact time required was "at least three therapeutic or counseling sessions"; inform inquiries indicated that seven sessions was modal and the number of hours of contact ranged from 3 to 60+.

The following Instruction Booklet was distributed to each clinical participant.

Instruction Booklet

Thank you for participating in the current project concerning the MCMI-III. You will be playing a key role in the refinement of one of the most widely used objective diagnostic instruments in the mental health field. To ensure the validity and clinical utility of the MCMI-III, we have included sites such as yours from settings across the country to assist in gathering a large and representative clinical sample. Such careful test validation and refinement is a major undertaking that could not succeed without the participation of psychologists such as yourself and your associates—we thank you for the time, the interest, and the effort that you and your associates will be investing.

The purpose of this packet is to provide details about participation in this project. If you have any questions or would like to discuss any aspect of the research process, please call either Ted Millon, Roger Davis, or Andrew Wenger at [phone number], or email us at [email address].

Inclusion and Exclusion Criteria

As an integral party of this research project, it is assumed (1) that the patients chosen for this study have already taken (or will soon take) and produced a valid MCMI-III (not the MCMI-II), (2) that the rater has personally seen the patient for *at least three* therapeutic or counseling sessions, (3) that the rater has a good understanding of the patient's clinical features and personality characteristics, and (4) that the rater has reviewed the DSM-IV clinical syndrome summaries and DSM-IV personality disorder summaries, as well as the Millon Clinical Domain Descriptions given in this booklet. These are the inclusion criteria for the study.

Ideally, your Axis I syndrome and Axis II personality ratings should be made blind to MCMI-III results. To ensure a sample of adequate size, we are encouraging the inclusion of patients whose MCMI-III results have already been obtained. *Do not*, however, include patients for whom you have a clear recollection of their MCMI-III scores before completing the Clinical Rating Form. This is the exclusion criterion for the study.

Clinician's Ratings

We ask that you and your associates complete a separate Clinician's Rating Form for each patient evaluated. Detailed information regarding the criteria of each of the Clinical Syndromes and Personality Style or Disorders to be evaluated is included in the latter part of this instruction packet. This information is to serve to standardize all clinical ratings.

Completion of study consists of five steps: First, you and your associates should review descriptions of the clinical syndromes and personality features in this booklet. You should feel free to refer to these descriptions at any point while making your ratings. Second, you are asked to evaluate each patient with respect to a number of the Axis I disorders included in the DSM-IV and assessed by the MCMI-III, and then to rate the severity of these disorders. Third, you are asked to select up to three personality patterns that characterize the patient, and to rate the severity of these patterns. Fourth, you are asked to record your confidence in each of the preceding ratings. Fifth, after completing the above, you are asked to locate the MCMI-III BR scores achieved by this patient, and to record ALL of them in the boxes at the bottom of the Clinical Rating Form. To assure uniformity in procedure, we will detail these steps in the following sections.

Step 1: Review the Descriptions of the Axis I Syndromes and Axis II Disorders Given in This Booklet

Clinicians differ in their interpretation of the various Axis I clinical syndromes and Axis II personality disorders. What one clinician considers a depressive personality may be interpreted by another as the characteristics of a masochistic personality. Accordingly, it becomes necessary to define or operationalize each of the disorders more precisely. Consequently, while each clinician may continue to hold his or her own pet notions about the various disorders, his or her conceptions are given a measure of standardization for research purposes. For the Axis I clinical syndromes, we suggest that you closely follow the listed criteria from the DSM-IV, summarized in the lists of Part B of this booklet. For the Axis II personality patterns, however, we have provided both the list of DSM criteria for each disorder, as well as descriptions for each of eight Clinical Domains of personality, derived from Millon's theory. Our view here is that personality is not expressed only in the cognitive, or behavioral, or psychodynamic, or interpersonal realms, but is instead manifested across all these clinical domains, and that the DSM is markedly incomplete with regard to its sampling of many domains of clinical expression. You should attempt to use both DSM and Millon criteria when making your personality rating decisions.

Step 2: Rate Up to Three of This Patient's Axis I Clinical Syndromes and Their Severity

All clinical syndromes included in the MCMI-III are listed in the upper left column of the Clinician's Rating Form. Fill in the encircled number under the *first* column for the Clinical Syndrome that calls for greatest professional concern or treatment. Note that two syndromes cannot both be rated as 1; the first column will contain only one darkened circle. Next, fill in the encircled number that is aligned with the *second* most clinically significant syndrome. Note that two syndromes cannot both be rated as 2; the second column should contain only one darkened circle. If a *third* syndrome is present, however slight, fill in its appropriate number under the third column as well.

Next, rate the *severity* of those clinical syndromes that you judged above as 1st, 2nd, and 3rd; these severity ratings are to be placed in the middle section of the grid. Note that severity judgments are not exclusive; that is, two clinical syndromes may both be judged marked, for example. Use the following definitions as a guide when making your judgments:

> *Slight*: Symptoms are *present*, but modest and only on occasion. They usually are of no clinical concern. Clinical intervention is *not* called for on the basis of these symptoms alone.
>
> *Mild* (Subsyndrome): These symptoms are not sufficiently problematic to require active treatment in and of themselves. However, they are *troublesome* to the patient and/ or others, usually in a more-or-less transient way. These symptoms may occasionally be associated with minor social, occupational, or family difficulties. *Treatment* should be viewed as *optional*.
>
> *Syndrome*: Symptoms are sufficiently problematic to *justify* a clinical syndrome *diagnosis*. Difficulties in social, occupational, and/or family functioning are *clearly present* and *treatment* is *advisable*.
>
> *Marked syndrome*: Signifies the presence of *serious* and/or *prolonged* clinical symptoms that markedly *impair* all *psychosocial functions*. They call for careful professional assessment and determination as to whether *treatment* should be in an *inpatient* or *outpatient* setting.
>
> *Extreme syndrome*: Symptoms are *intense* and *dysfunctional*, as well as socially and occupationally *debilitating*. They generally necessitate treatment in an *inpatient/ residential* setting.

Step 3: Rate Up to Three of This Patient's Most Prominent Personality Features and Their Severity

Next, turn to the Personality grid in the upper right column. Identify the *one* personality pattern that most closely "fits" or captures the patient's characteristic way of functioning according to the descriptions given in this booklet. Typically, few patients fit only one personality type; they often possess features or domain characteristics of two or three patterns. As you have seen on the Ratings section for the Clinical Syndromes, there are columns for a second and third choice. The *second* best fit can be recorded under the second column. If a *third* "close fit" also seems applicable, fill in the appropriate circle under the third column.

Next, rate the severity of these personality patterns in the bottom part of the grid. Note that severity judgments are not exclusive; that is, two patterns may both be judged as being disorders or traits, for example.

Use the following definitions as a guide when making severity judgments:

Trait: The presence of *minor*, but *well-defined*, personality features. Currently present are a mix of manifest, but *clinically insignificant* traits that fall clearly in the range of *normality*.

Style: A distinctive and characteristic *configuration* of personality traits that is essentially *subclinical* in nature; that is, although there are *occasional adaptive difficulties*, *treatment* on these grounds alone is *not indicated*.

Disorder: The personality pattern is sufficiently problematic to justify a *clinical diagnosis*. Characteristics *definitely impair life functioning*, resulting in periodic but *significant adaptive difficulties*. (Note: schizotypal, paranoid, and borderline personality ratings should be judged at least at the level of "disorders" rather than "styles" or "traits"). Outpatient *treatment* is *indicated*.

Marked disorder: Personality characteristics are of a *severe* and *persistent* nature. They *markedly and repeatedly impair* psychosocial functioning. *Treatment* is *definitely called for*, mostly on an outpatient basis, but frequently in an inpatient setting.

Extreme disorder: Personality features are *intense*, *chronic*, and *pervasive*, often of an idiosyncratic and graphic character, and invariably *debilitating*. Inpatient/residential *treatment* is *required*.

Step 4: Record Your Confidence in the Preceding Ratings

The degree to which you feel sure about your rating depends in large measure on the complexity of the case, and the extent to which you have had an opportunity to study its symptoms and characteristics. Using the guide that follows, indicate in the appropriate grids the degree of your confidence regarding each of your rated syndromes and disorders.

High: Judgment based on considerable information and a secure understanding of the symptoms/features rated above; these judgments may be assumed to be accurate.

Medium: Judgment based on reasonably good information and an adequate clinical understanding of the symptoms/features rated above. More precise appraisals, however, may result with additional information.

Low: Judgment is modestly informed; an understanding of the symptoms/features rated above is only of a surface nature at this time. Additional information is likely to increase the validity of these judgments.

Step 5: Record the Actual MCMI-III BR Scores of This Patient

Recall: Do not review the MCMI-III BR scores of your patients before you rate them in the sections below the dark line. Write in their BR score numbers in both columns *after* completing your ratings.

Illustrative Clinical Rating Form

[In Figure 17.1] we have printed a sample of a completed Clinician's Rating Form. As you can see, the patient's gender and age were completed by the clinician. Also completed were three judgments in the Clinical Syndromes Axis I grid. "Dysthymia" was placed in the first column to signify that it was judged the most prominent or clinically significant syndrome. Alcohol Abuse was placed in the second column, and Somatoform was rated in the third column. As you can note, Dysthymia was also judged to be a "marked syndrome," whereas the other two syndromes were rated "mild." In the Personality grid, schizotypal was judged the best fit and hence was placed in the first column. Avoidant, judged to be second "best fit," was recorded in the second column, and Negativistic was assigned to the third column; all other personalities were left blank. Both Schizotypal and Avoidant personalities were rated as "Disorders," whereas Negativistic was judged a "Style."

All of the clinician's confidence ratings were marked as "medium," except for Schizotypal, which was judged to have been "high." At the bottom of the form are the MCMI-III BR scores for this patient as completed by the clinician.

Axis I Criteria

Anxiety Disorder

The parallel MCMI-III scale is intended to assess the general symptoms of anxiety and to operate as a screener for the more specific Anxiety Disorders. No one DSM-IV criteria set exactly parallels the item content of this scale. High scoring subjects report such cognitive symptoms as excessive worry (generalized anxiety disorder) and obsessional thoughts (obsessive–compulsive disorder), such cognitive–somatic symptoms as feeling tense and panicky when away from home (agoraphobia and panic disorder), somatic symptoms such as sweating, and behavioral symptoms such as compulsive checking to reduce anxiety (obsessive–compulsive disorder)

Somatoform Disorder

The MCMI-III Somatoform Disorder scale represents a constellation of physical symptoms, including difficulty keeping balance, feeling weak and tired much of the time, loss of sensation of various parts of the body, difficulty sleeping, and loss of appetite.

Abbreviated DSM-IV criteria for undifferentiated somatoform disorder are as follows:

A. One or more physical complaints.
B. Either (1) or (2):
   (1) after appropriate investigation, the symptoms cannot be fully explained by a known general medical condition or the direct effects of a substance.
   (2) when there is a general medical condition, the physical complaints or resulting social or occupational impairment is in excess of what would be expected from the history, physical examination, or laboratory findings.
C. The symptoms have endured at least 6 months and have caused clinically significant distress or impairment in social, occupational, or other important areas of functioning.

Instructions: Use the *Clinician Rating Reference Booklet* to guide your thinking about the clinical syndrome and personality ratings, to be made on the two upper columns. Below the dark line, fill in the MCMI-III BR scores obtained by the patient you have just rated. Also, fill in the patient's age and gender. We will record a letter to represent your setting and patient's number.

Age: <u>32</u>   Gender: M (F)   Setting: <u>XYZ</u>   Patient #: <u>19</u>

Axis II Clinical Syndromes	Prominence		
	1st	2nd	3rd
Anxiety	1	2	3
Somatoform	1	2	●
Bipolar	1	2	3
Dysthymia	●	2	3
Alcohol Abuse	1	●	3
Drug Abuse	1	2	3
PTSD	1	2	3
Thought Disorder	1	2	3
Major Depression	1	2	3
Paranoid Delusions	1	2	3
Axis I Severity Rating			
SLIGHT	O	O	O
MILD (SUBSYNDROME)	O	●	●
SYNDROME	O	O	O
MARKED SYNDROME	●	O	O
EXTREME SYNDROME	O	O	O
Confidence in Ratings			
HIGH	O	O	O
MEDIUM	●	●	●
LOW	O	O	O

Axis II Personality Features	Pattern		
	1st	2nd	3rd
Schizoid	1	2	3
Avoidant	1	●	3
Depressive	1	2	3
Dependent	1	2	3
Histrionic	1	2	3
Narcissistic	1	2	3
Antisocial	1	2	3
Sadistic	1	2	3
Compulsive	1	2	3
Negativistic (P-Agg)	1	2	●
Masochistic (S-Def)	1	2	3
Schizotypal	●	2	3
Borderline	1	2	3
Paranoid	1	2	3
Axis II Severity Rating			
TRAIT	O	O	O
STYLE (SUB-DISORDER)	O	O	●
DISORDER	●	●	O
MARKED DISORDER	O	O	O
EXTREME DISORDER	O	O	O
Confidence in Ratings			
HIGH	●	O	O
MEDIUM	O	●	●
LOW	O	O	O

Instructions: Please be mindful *not* to review or transcribe these actual BR scores before making your ratings above.

MCMI SCALE	Actual BR
Schizoid	72
Avoidant	80
Depressive	78
Dependent	62
Histrionic	22
Narcissistic	31
Antisocial	14
Sadistic	20
Compulsive	41
Negativistic (P-Agg)	64
Masochistic (S-Def)	84
Schizotypal	91
Borderline	85
Paranoid	58

MCMI SCALE	Actual BR
Anxiety	78
Somatoform	84
Bipolar	23
Dysthymia	88
Alcohol Abuse	95
Drug Abuse	67
PTSD	70
Thought Disorder	80
Major Depression	70
Paranoid Delusions	47

FIGURE 17.1. Clinician Rating Form: MCMI Validation Study.

Bipolar: Manic Disorder

The MCMI-III Bipolar: Manic Disorder scale includes such features as wanting to do so many things the patient finds it difficult to decide exactly what to do, that he or she may feel cheerful and excited for no apparent reason, that in the past the patient has been told by others that they have become too excited, and that they have annoyed others due to their manic behaviors.

Abbreviated DSM-IV criteria for manic episode are as follows:

A. A distinct period of abnormally and persistently elevated, expansive, irritable mood, lasting at least I week.

B. During the period of mood disturbance, three (or more) of the following symptoms have persisted and been present to a significant degree:

    (1) inflated self-esteem or grandiosity
    (2) decreased need for sleep
    (3) more talkative than usual or pressure to keep talking
    (4) flight of ideas or subjective experience that thoughts are racing
    (5) distractibility
    (6) increase in goal-directed activity
    (7) excessive involvement in pleasurable activities that have potential for painful consequences

C. The mood disturbance is sufficiently severe to cause marked impairment in occupational functioning or in usual social activities or relations with others, or to necessitate hospitalization to prevent harm to self or others, or there are psychotic features.

D. The symptoms are not due to the direct physiological effects or general medical condition (e.g., hyperthyroidism).

Dysthymic Disorder

Patients scoring high on the parallel MCMI-III scale report feeling like a failure, feeling guilty for not being able to do things right, long-standing feelings of discouragement and sadness, and lack of energy.

Abbreviated DSM-IV criteria include:

A. Depressed mood for most of the day, for more days than not, as indicated either by subjective account or observation by others, for at least 2 years.

B. Presence, while depressed, of two (or more) of the following:

    (1) poor appetite or overeating
    (2) insomnia or hypersomnia
    (3) low energy or fatigue
    (4) low self-esteem
    (5) poor concentration or difficulty making decisions
    (6) feelings of hopelessness

C. During the 2-year period of the disturbance, the person has never been without the symptoms for more than 2 months at a time.

D. No major depressive episode has been present during the first 2 years of the disturbance.

Alcohol Dependence

High scorers on the parallel MCMI-III scale report problems with alcohol dependence in many areas of life, specifically, that they have a drinking problem that they have tried unsuccessfully to end, that they have had difficulty controlling impulses to drink, that their problem has created difficulties for themselves and their families, that they sometimes abuse alcohol as a means of coping with depression, and that their parents have had problems with alcohol, as well.

　　Partial DSM-IV descriptions of alcohol abuse include: School and job performance may suffer from the aftereffects of drinking or from actual intoxication on the job or at school; child care or household responsibilities may be neglected; and alcohol-related absences may occur from school or job. The person may use alcohol in physically hazardous ways. Legal difficulties may arise because of alcohol use. Finally, individuals with alcohol abuse may continue to consume alcohol despite the knowledge that continued consumption poses significant social or interpersonal problems for them.

Drug Abuse

High scorers on this MCMI-III scale report that drugs have gotten them into trouble in the past, that they have missed work because of drug use, that there have been times when they couldn't get through the day without drugs, that their drug use has led to family difficulties, and that they have spent more money than they should buying drugs.

　　Categories relevant to drug dependence in the DSM-IV are broken down by type of drug, for example, amphetamine, cannabis, cocaine, hallucinogen, and so on. As with alcohol, the severity of abuse of these substances is perhaps judged in terms of the effects of abuse across many domains of life, creating problems in school, at work, within the family in terms of spousal relations or child care, and involving the person in various legal entanglements. Abuse often continues despite knowledge that further consumption only perpetuates these problems.

Posttraumatic Stress Disorder

On the MCMI-III, high scorers on the Post-traumatic Stress Disorder scale report memories of upsetting experiences that keep coming back to haunt them, nightmares about a life-threatening event, flashbacks, terrifying recurring thoughts about a life-threatening event, and that these experiences cause them difficulties in their current life. DSM-IV include the following:

A. The person has been exposed to a traumatic event.

B. The traumatic event is persistently reexperienced.

C. Persistent avoidance of stimuli associated with the trauma and numbing of general responsiveness.

D. Persistent symptoms of increased arousal (not present before trauma).

E. Duration of the disturbance is more than 1 month.

F. The disturbance causes clinically significant distress or impairment in social, occupational, or other important areas of functioning.

　　Depending on the length and course of the problem, these patients are usually classified as "schizophrenic," "schizophreniform," or "brief reactive psychosis." They may periodically exhibit incongruous, disorganized, or regressive behavior, often appearing confused and disoriented and occasionally displaying inappropriate affect, scattered hallucinations, and unsystematic delusions. Thinking may be fragmented or bizarre. Feelings may be blunted, and there may be a pervasive sense of being isolated and misunderstood by others. Withdrawn and seclusive or secretive behavior may be notable.

The criteria for these disorders are complex. Clinicians are invited to consult the DSM-IV if assistance is required.

The criteria for these disorders are complex. Clinicians are invited to consult the DSM-IV if assistance is required.

Major Depression

These patients are usually incapable of functioning in a normal environment, are severely depressed, and express a dread of the future, suicidal ideation, and a sense of hopeless resignation. Some exhibit a marked motor retardation, whereas others display an agitated quality, incessantly pacing about and bemoaning their sorry state. Several somatic processes are often disturbed during these periods, notably, a decreased appetite, fatigue, weight loss or gain, insomnia, or early rising. Problems of concentration are common, as are feelings of worthlessness or guilt. Repetitive fearfulness and brooding are frequently in evidence.

Abbreviated DSM-IV criteria for major depressive episode include the following:

A. Five (or more) of the following symptoms have been present during the same 2-week period and represent a change from previous functioning; at least one of the symptoms is either (1) depressed mood or (2) loss of interest or pleasure.

   (1) depressed mood most of the day, nearly every day, as indicated by either subjective report (e.g., feels sad or empty) or observation made by others
   (2) markedly diminished interest or pleasure in all, or almost all, activities most of the day, nearly every day
   (3) significant weight loss when not dieting or decrease or increase in appetite nearly every day
   (4) insomnia or hypersomnia nearly every day
   (5) psychomotor agitation or retardation nearly every day
   (6) fatigue or loss of energy nearly every day
   (7) feelings of worthlessness or excessive or inappropriate guilt (which may be delusional) nearly every day
   (8) diminished ability to think or concentrate, or indecisiveness, nearly every day
   (9) recurrent thoughts of death, recurrent suicidal ideation without a specific plan, or a suicide attempt or a specific plan for committing suicide

Delusional Disorder

This patient, frequently considered acutely paranoid, may become periodically belligerent, voicing irrational but interconnected sets of delusions of a jealous, persecutory, or grandiose nature. Depending on the constellation of other concurrent syndromes, there may be clearcut signs of disturbed thinking and ideas of reference. Moods usually are hostile, and feelings of being picked on and mistreated are expressed. A tense undercurrent of suspiciousness, vigilance, and alertness to possible betrayal are typical concomitants.

Axis II Criteria[1]

Schizoid Personality Disorder: Millon Clinical Domains

Behavioral level

(F) *Expressively impassive* (e.g., appears to be in an inert emotional state, lifeless, undemonstrative, lacking in energy and vitality; is unmoved, boring, unanimated, robotic, phlegmatic, and displaying deficits in activation, motoric expressiveness, and spontaneity)

(F) *Interpersonally unengaged* (e.g., seems indifferent and remote, rarely responsive to the actions or feelings of others, chooses solitary activities, possesses minimal "human" interests; fades into the background, is aloof or unobtrusive, neither desires nor enjoys close relationships, prefers a peripheral role in social, work, and family settings)

Phenomenological level

(F) *Cognitively impoverished* (e.g., seems deficient across broad spheres of human knowledge and evidences vague and obscure thought processes, particularly about social matters; communication with others is often unfocused, loses its purpose or intention, or is conveyed via a loose or circuitous logic)

(S) *Complacent self-image* (e.g., reveals minimal introspection and awareness of self; seems impervious to the emotional and personal implications of everyday social life, appearing indifferent to the praise or criticism of others)

(S) *Meager objects* (e.g., internalized representations are few in number and minimally articulated, largely devoid of the manifold percepts and memories of relationships with others, possessing little of the dynamic interplay among drives and conflicts that typify well-adjusted persons)

Intrapsychic level

(F) *Intellectualization mechanism* (e.g., describes interpersonal and affective experiences in a matter-of-fact, abstract, impersonal, or mechanical manner; pays primary attention to formal and objective aspects of social and emotional events)

(S) *Undifferentiated organization* (e.g., given an inner barrenness, a feeble drive to fulfill needs, and minimal pressures either to defend against or resolve internal conflicts or cope with external demands, internal morphologic structures may best be characterized by their limited framework and sterile pattern)

Biophysical level

(S) *Apathetic mood* (e.g., is emotionally unexcitable, exhibiting an intrinsic unfeeling, cold, and stark quality; reports weak affectionate or erotic needs, rarely displaying warm or intense feelings, and apparently unable to experience most affects—pleasure, sadness, or anger—in any depth)

Avoidant Personality Disorder: Millon Clinical Domains

Behavioral level

(F) *Expressively fretful* (e.g., conveys personal unease and disquiet, a constant timorous, hesitant, and restive state; overreacts to innocuous events and anxiously judges them to signify ridicule, criticism, and disapproval)

---

[1]DSM criteria were listed in the booklet following the Millon clinical domains.

(F) *Interpersonally aversive* (e.g., distances from activities that involve intimate personal relationships and reports extensive history of social pananxiety and distrust; seeks acceptance, but is unwilling to get involved unless certain to be liked, maintaining distance and privacy to avoid being shamed and humiliated)

Phenomenological level

(F) *Cognitively distracted* (e.g., warily scans environment for potential threats and is preoccupied by intrusive and disruptive random thoughts and observations; an upwelling from within of irrelevant ideation upsets thought continuity and interferes with social communications and accurate appraisals)

(S) *Alienated self-image* (e.g., sees self as socially inept, inadequate, and inferior, justifying thereby his or her isolation and rejection by others; feels personally unappealing, devalues self-achievements, and reports persistent sense of aloneness and emptiness)

(S) *Vexatious objects* (e.g., internalized representations are composed of readily reactivated, intense, and conflict-ridden memories of problematic early relations; limited avenues for experiencing or recalling gratification, and few mechanisms to channel needs, bind impulses, resolve conflicts, or deflect external stressors)

Intrapsychic level

(F) *Fantasy mechanism* (e.g., depends excessively on imagination to achieve need gratification, confidence building, and conflict resolution; withdraws into reveries as a means of safely discharging frustrated affectionate, as well as angry impulses)

(S) *Fragile organization* (e.g., a precarious complex of tortuous emotions depends almost exclusively on a single modality for its resolution and discharge, that of avoidance, escape, and fantasy and, hence, when faced with personal risks, new opportunities, or unanticipated stress, few morphologic structures are available to deploy and few back-up positions can be reverted to, short of regressive decompensation)

Biophysical level

(S) *Anguished mood* (e.g., describes constant and confusing undercurrent of tension, sadness, and anger; vacillates between desire for affection, fear of rebuff, embarrassment, and numbness of feeling)

Depressive Personality Disorder: Millon Clinical Domains

Behavioral level

(F) *Expressively disconsolate* (e.g., appearance and posture conveys an irrelievably forlorn, somber, heavy-hearted, woebegone, if not grief-stricken quality; irremediably dispirited and discouraged, portraying a sense of permanent hopelessness and wretchedness)

(F) *Interpersonally defenseless* (e.g., owing to feeling vulnerable, assailable, and unshielded, will beseech others to be nurturant and protective; fearing abandonment and desertion, will not only act in an endangered manner, but will seek, if not demand, assurances of affection, steadfastness, and devotion)

Phenomenological level

(F) *Cognitively pessimistic* (e.g., possesses defeatist and fatalistic attitudes about almost all matters, sees things in their blackest form and invariably expects the worst;

feeling weighed down, discouraged, and bleak, gives the gloomiest interpretation of current events, despairing as well that things will never improve in the future)

(S) *Worthless self-image* (e.g., judges oneself of no account, valueless to self or others, inadequate and unsuccessful in all aspirations; barren, sterile, impotent, sees self as inconsequential and reproachable, if not contemptible, a person who should be criticized and derogated, as well as feel guilty for possessing no praiseworthy traits or achievements)

(S) *Forsaken objects* (e.g., internalized representations of the past appear jettisoned, as if life's early experiences have been depleted or devitalized, either drained of their richness and joyful elements or withdrawn from memory, leaving one to feel abandoned, bereft, and discarded, cast off, and deserted)

Intrapsychic level

(F) *Asceticism mechanism* (e.g., engages in acts of self-denial, self-punishment, and self-tormenting, believing that one should exhibit penance and be deprived of life's bounties; not only is there a repudiation of pleasures, but there are harsh self-judgments, as well as self-destructive acts)

(S) *Depleted organization* (e.g., the scaffold for morphologic structures is markedly weakened, with coping methods enervated and defensive strategies impoverished, emptied, and devoid of their vigor and focus, resulting in a diminished, if not exhausted capacity to initiate action and regulate affect, impulse, and conflict)

Biophysical level

(S) *Melancholic mood* (e.g., is typically woeful, gloomy, tearful, joyless, and morose; characteristically worrisome and brooding, the low spirits and dysphoric state rarely remits)

Dependent Personality Disorder: Millon Clinical Domains

Behavioral level

(F) *Expressively incompetent* (e.g., withdraws from adult responsibilities by acting helpless and seeking nurturance from others; is docile and passive, lacks functional competencies, and avoids self-assertion)

(F) *Interpersonally submissive* (e.g., needs excessive advice and reassurance, as well as subordinates self to stronger, nurturing figure, without whom may feel anxiously alone and helpless; is compliant, conciliatory, and placating, fearing being left to care for oneself)

Phenomenological level

(F) *Cognitively naive* (e.g., rarely disagrees with others and is easily persuaded, unsuspicious, and gullible; reveals a Pollyanna attitude toward interpersonal difficulties, watering down objective problems and smoothing over troubling events)

(S) *Inept self-image* (e.g., views self as weak, fragile, and inadequate; exhibits lack of self-confidence by belittling own attitudes and competencies, and hence not capable of doing things on one's own)

(S) *Immature objects* (e.g., internalized representations are composed of infantile impressions of others, unsophisticated ideas, incomplete recollections, rudimentary drives, and childlike impulses, as well as minimal competencies to manage and resolve stressors)

Intrapsychic level

(F) *Introjection mechanism* (e.g., is firmly devoted to another to strengthen the belief that an inseparable bond exists between them; jettisons independent views in favor of those of others to preclude conflicts and threats to relationship)

(S) *Inchoate organization* (e.g., owing to entrusting others with the responsibility to fulfill needs and to cope with adult tasks, there is both a deficient morphologic structure and a lack of diversity in internal regulatory controls, leaving a miscellany of relatively undeveloped and undifferentiated adaptive abilities, as well as an elementary system for functioning independently)

Biophysical level

(S) *Pacific mood* (e.g., is characteristically warm, tender, and noncompetitive; timidly avoids social interaction)

Histrionic Personality Disorder: Millon Clinical Domains

Behavioral level

(F) *Expressively dramatic* (e.g., is overreactive, volatile, provocative, and engaging, as well as intolerant of inactivity, resulting in impulsive, highly emotional, and theatrical responsiveness; describes penchant for momentary excitements, fleeting adventures, and short-sighted hedonism)

(F) *Interpersonally attention-seeking* (e.g., actively elicits praise and manipulates others to gain needed reassurance, attention, and approval; is demanding, flirtatious, vain, and seductively exhibitionistic, especially when wishing to be the center of attention)

Phenomenological level

(F) *Cognitively flighty* (e.g., avoids introspective thought, is overly suggestible, attentive to fleeting external events, and speaks in impressionistic generalities; integrates experiences poorly, resulting in scattered learning and thoughtless judgments)

(S) *Gregarious self-image* (e.g., views self as sociable, stimulating, and charming; enjoys the image of attracting acquaintances by physical appearance and by pursuing a busy and pleasure-oriented life)

(S) *Shallow objects* (e.g., internalized representations are composed largely of superficial memories of past relations, random collections of transient and segregated affects and conflicts, and insubstantial drives and mechanisms)

Intrapsychic level

(F) *Dissociation mechanism* (e.g., regularly alters and recomposes self-presentations to create a succession of socially attractive but changing facades; engages in self-distracting activities to avoid reflecting on and integrating unpleasant thoughts and emotions)

(S) *Disjointed organization* (e.g., there exists a loosely knit and carelessly united morphologic structure in which processes of internal regulation and control are scattered and unintegrated, with ad hoc methods for restraining impulses, coordinating defenses, and resolving conflicts, leading to mechanisms that must, of necessity, be broad and sweeping to maintain psychic cohesion and stability, and, when successful, only further isolate and disconnect thoughts, feelings and actions)

Biophysical level

(S) *Fickle mood* (e.g., displays rapidly shifting and shallow emotions; is vivacious, animated, impetuous, and exhibits tendencies to be easily enthused and as easily angered or bored)

Narcissistic Personality Disorder: Millon Clinical Domains

Behavioral level

(F) *Expressively haughty* (e.g., acts in an arrogant, supercilious, pompous, and disdainful manner, flouting conventional rules of shared social living, viewing them as naive or inapplicable to self; reveals a careless disregard for personal integrity and a self-important indifference to the rights of others)

(F) *Interpersonally exploitive* (e.g., feels entitled, is unempathic and expects special favors without assuming reciprocal responsibilities; shamelessly takes others for granted and uses them to enhance self and indulge desires)

Phenomenological level

(F) *Cognitively expansive* (e.g., has an undisciplined imagination and exhibits a preoccupation with immature and self-glorifying fantasies of success, beauty, or love; is minimally constrained by objective reality, takes liberties with facts, and often lies to redeem self-illusions)

(S) *Admirable self-image* (e.g., believes self to be meritorious, special, if not unique, deserving of great admiration, and acting in a grandiose or self-assured manner, often without commensurate achievements; has a sense of high self-worth, despite being seen by others as egotistic, inconsiderate, and arrogant)

(S) *Contrived objects* (e.g., internalized representations are composed far more than usual of illusory and changing memories of past relationships; unacceptable drives and conflicts are readily refashioned as the need arises, as are others often simulated and pretentious)

Intrapsychic level

(F) *Rationalization mechanism* (e.g., is self-deceptive and facile in devising plausible reasons to justify self-centered and socially inconsiderate behaviors; offers alibis to place oneself in the best possible light, despite evident shortcomings or failures)

(S) *Spurious organization* (e.g., morphologic structures underlying coping and defensive strategies tend to be flimsy and transparent and appear more substantial and dynamically orchestrated than they are in fact, regulating impulses only marginally, channeling needs with minimal restraint, and creating an inner world in which conflicts are dismissed, failures are quickly redeemed, and self-pride is effortlessly reasserted)

Biophysical level

(S) *Insouciant mood* (e.g., manifests a general air of nonchalance, imperturbability, and feigned tranquillity; appears coolly unimpressionable or buoyantly optimistic, except when narcissistic confidence is shaken, at which time either rage, shame, or emptiness is briefly displayed)

Antisocial Personality Disorder: Millon Clinical Domains

Behavioral level

(F) *Expressively impulsive* (e.g., is impetuous and irrepressible, acting hastily and spontaneously in a restless, spur-of-the-moment manner; is short-sighted, incautious, and imprudent, failing to plan ahead or to consider alternatives, no less to heed consequences)

(F) *Interpersonally irresponsible* (e.g., is untrustworthy and unreliable, failing to meet or intentionally negating personal obligations of a marital, parental, employment, or financial nature; actively intrudes upon and violates the rights of others and transgresses established social codes through deceitful or illegal behaviors)

Phenomenological level

(F) *Cognitively deviant* (e.g., construes events and relationships in accord with socially unorthodox beliefs and morals; is disdainful of traditional ideals, fails to conform to social norms, and is contemptuous of conventional values)

(S) *Autonomous self-image* (e.g., sees self as unfettered by the restrictions of social customs and the constraints of personal loyalties; values the image and enjoys the sense of being free, unencumbered, and unconfined by persons, places, obligations, or routines)

(S) *Debased objects* (e.g., internalized representations comprise degraded and corrupt relationships that spur revengeful attitudes and restive impulses which are driven to subvert established cultural ideals and mores, as well as to devalue personal sentiments and to sully, but intensely covet, the material attainments of society denied them)

Intrapsychic level

(F) *Acting-out mechanism* (e.g., inner tensions that might accrue by postponing the expression of offensive thoughts and malevolent actions are rarely constrained; socially repugnant impulses are not refashioned in sublimated forms, but are discharged directly in precipitous ways, usually without guilt or remorse)

(S) *Unruly organization* (e.g., inner morphologic structures to contain drive and impulse are noted by their paucity, as are efforts to curb refractory energies and attitudes, leading to easily transgressed controls, low thresholds for hostile or erotic discharge, few subliminatory channels, unfettered self-expression, and a marked intolerance of delay or frustration)

Biophysical level

(S) *Callous mood* (e.g., is insensitive, irritable, and aggressive, as expressed in a wide-ranging deficit in social charitableness, human compassion, or personal remorse; exhibits a coarse incivility, as well as an offensive, if not reckless, disregard for the safety of self or others)

Sadistic (Aggressive) Personality Disorder: Millon Clinical Domains

Behavioral level

(F) *Expressively precipitate* (e.g., is disposed to react in sudden, abrupt outbursts of an unexpected and unwarranted nature; recklessly reactive and daring, attracted to challenge, risk, and harm, as well as unflinching, undeterred by pain, and undaunted by danger and punishment)

(*F*) *Interpersonally abrasive* (e.g., reveals satisfaction in intimidating, coercing, and humiliating others; regularly expresses verbally abusive and derisive social commentary as well as exhibiting vicious, if not physically brutal, behavior)

Phenomenological level

(*F*) *Cognitively dogmatic* (e.g., is strongly opinionated and closed-minded, as well as unbending and obstinate in holding to one's preconceptions; exhibits a broad-ranging authoritarianism, social intolerance, and prejudice)

(*S*) *Combative self-image* (e.g., is proud to characterize self as assertively competitive, as well as vigorously energetic and militantly hardheaded; values aspects of self that present pugnacious, domineering, and power-oriented image)

(*S*) *Pernicious objects* (e.g., internalized representations of the past are distinguished by early relationships that have generated strongly driven aggressive energies and malicious attitudes, as well as by a contrasting paucity of sentimental memories, tender affects, internal conflicts, and shame or guilt feelings)

Intrapsychic level

(*F*) *Isolation mechanism* (e.g., can be cold-blooded and remarkably detached from an awareness of the impact of own destructive acts; views objects of violation impersonally, as symbols of devalued groups devoid of human sensibilities)

(*S*) *Eruptive organization* (e.g., despite a generally cohesive morphologic structure composed of routinely adequate modulating controls, defenses, and expressive channels, surging powerful and explosive energies of an aggressive and sexual nature threaten to produce precipitous outbursts which periodically overwhelm and overrun otherwise competent restraints)

Biophysical level

(*S*) *Hostile mood* (e.g., has an excitable and irritable temper which flares readily into contentious argument and physical belligerence; is cruel, mean-spirited, and fractious, willing to do harm, even to persecute others to gets one's way)

Compulsive Personality Disorder: Millon Clinical Domains

Behavioral level

(*F*) *Expressively disciplined* (e.g., maintains a regulated, highly structured, and strictly-organized life; perfectionism interferes with decision making and task completion)

(*F*) *Interpersonally respectful* (e.g., exhibits unusual adherence to social conventions and proprieties, as well as being scrupulous and overconscientious about matters of morality and ethics; prefers polite, formal, and correct personal relationships, usually insisting that subordinates adhere to personally established rules and methods)

Phenomenological level

(*F*) *Cognitively constricted* (e.g., constructs world in terms of rules, regulations, schedules, and hierarchies; is rigid, stubborn, and indecisive and notably upset by unfamiliar or novel ideas and customs)

(*S*) *Conscientious self-image* (e.g., sees self as devoted to work, industrious, reliable, meticulous, and efficient, largely to the exclusion of leisure activities; fearful of error or misjudgment and hence overvalues aspects of self that exhibit discipline, perfection, prudence, and loyalty)

(S) *Concealed objects* (e.g., only those internalized representations, with their associated inner affects and attitudes that can be socially approved, are allowed conscious awareness or behavioral expression; as a result, actions and memories are highly regulated, forbidden impulses sequestered and tightly bound, and personal and social conflicts are defensively denied, kept from awareness, and maintained under stringent control)

Intrapsychic level

(F) *Reaction formation mechanism* (e.g., repeatedly presents positive thoughts and socially commendable behaviors that are diametrically opposite one's deeper contrary and forbidden feelings; displays reasonableness and maturity when faced with circumstances that evoke anger or dismay in others)

(S) *Compartmentalized organization* (e.g., morphologic structures are rigidly organized in a tightly consolidated system that is clearly partitioned into numerous, distinct, and segregated constellations of drive, memory, and cognition, with few open channels to permit interplay among these components)

Biophysical level

(S) *Solemn mood* (e.g., is unrelaxed, tense, joyless, and grim; restrains warm feelings and keeps most emotions under tight control)

Negativistic (Passive–Aggressive) Personality Disorder: Millon Clinical Domains

Behavioral level

(F) *Expressively resentful* (e.g., resists fulfilling expectancies of others, frequently exhibiting procrastination, inefficiency, and obstinance, as well as contrary and irksome behaviors; reveals gratification in demoralizing and undermining the pleasures and aspirations of others)

(F) *Interpersonally contrary* (e.g., assumes conflicting and changing roles in social relationships, particularly dependent and contrite acquiescence and assertive and hostile independence; conveys envy and pique toward those more fortunate, as well as actively concurrently or sequentially obstructive and intolerant of others, expressing either negative or incompatible attitudes)

Phenomenological level

(F) *Cognitively skeptical* (e.g., is cynical, doubting, and untrusting, approaching positive events with disbelief and future possibilities with pessimism, anger, and trepidation; has a misanthropic view of life, is whining and grumbling, voicing disdain and caustic comments toward those experiencing good fortune)

(S) *Discontented self-image* (e.g., sees self as misunderstood, luckless, unappreciated, jinxed, and demeaned by others; recognizes being characteristically embittered, disgruntled, and disillusioned with life)

(S) *Vacillating objects* (e.g., internalized representations of the past comprise a complex of countervailing relationships, setting in motion contradictory feelings, conflicting inclinations, and incompatible memories that are driven by the desire to degrade the achievements and pleasures of others without necessarily appearing to do so)

Intrapsychic level

(F) *Displacement mechanism* (e.g., discharges anger and other troublesome emotions either precipitously or by employing unconscious maneuvers to shift them from their instigator to settings or persons of lesser significance; vents disapproval by substitute or passive means, such as acting inept or perplexed, or behaving in a forgetful or indolent manner)

(S) *Divergent organization* (e.g., there is a clear division in the pattern of morphologic structures such that coping and defensive maneuvers are often directed toward incompatible goals, leaving major conflicts unresolved and full psychic cohesion often impossible by virtue of the fact that fulfillment of one drive or need inevitably nullifies or reverses another)

Biophysical level

(S) *Irritable mood* (e.g., frequently touchy, temperamental, and peevish, followed in turn by sullen and moody withdrawal; is often petulant and impatient, unreasonably scorns those in authority, and reports being annoyed easily or frustrated)

Masochistic (Self-Defeating) Personality Disorder: Millon Clinical Domains

Behavioral level

(F) *Expressively abstinent* (e.g., presents self as nonindulgent, frugal, and chaste; is reluctant to seek pleasurable experiences, refraining from exhibiting signs of enjoying life; acts in an unpresuming and self-effacing manner, preferring to place self in an inferior light or abject position)

(F) *Interpersonally deferential* (e.g., distances from those who are consistently supportive, relating to others where one can be sacrificing, servile, and obsequious, allowing, if not encouraging them to exploit, mistreat, or take advantage; renders ineffectual the attempts of others to be helpful and solicits condemnation by accepting undeserved blame and courting unjust criticism)

Phenomenological level

(F) *Cognitively diffident* (e.g., hesitant to interpret observations positively for fear that, in doing so, they may not take problematic forms or achieve troublesome and self-denigrating outcomes; as a result, there is a habit of repeatedly expressing attitudes and anticipations contrary to favorable beliefs and feelings)

(S) *Undeserving self-image* (e.g., is self-abasing, focusing on the very worst personal features, asserting thereby that one is worthy of being shamed, humbled and debased; feels that one has failed to live up to the expectations of others and hence, deserves to suffer painful consequences)

(S) *Discredited objects* (e.g., object representations are composed of failed past relationships and disparaged personal achievements, of positive feelings and erotic drives transposed into their least attractive opposites, of internal conflicts intentionally aggravated, and of mechanisms for reducing dysphoria being subverted by processes which intensify discomfort)

Intrapsychic level

(F) *Exaggeration mechanism* (e.g., repetitively recalls past injustices and anticipates future disappointments as a means of raising distress to homeostatic levels; undermines personal objectives and sabotages good fortunes so as to enhance or maintain accustomed level of suffering and pain)

(S) *Inverted organization* (e.g., owing to a significant reversal of the pain–pleasure polarity, morphologic structures have contrasting and dual qualities—one more or less conventional, the other its obverse—resulting in a repetitive undoing of affect and intention, of a transposing of channels of need gratification with those leading to frustration and of engaging in actions which produce antithetical, if not self-sabotaging consequences)

Biophysical level

(S) *Dysphoric mood* (e.g., experiences a complex mix of emotions, at times anxiously apprehensive, at others forlorn and mournful, to feeling anguished and tormented; intentionally displays a plaintive and wistful appearance, frequently to induce guilt and discomfort in others)

Schizotypal Personality Disorder: Millon Clinical Domains

Behavioral level

(F) *Expressively eccentric* (e.g., exhibits socially gauche and peculiar mannerisms; is perceived by others as aberrant, disposed to behave in an unobtrusively odd, aloof, curious, or bizarre manner)

(F) *Interpersonally secretive* (e.g., prefers privacy and isolation, with few highly tentative attachments and personal obligations; has drifted over time into increasingly peripheral vocational roles and clandestine social activities)

Phenomenological level

(F) *Cognitively autistic* (e.g., capacity to "read" thoughts and feelings of others is markedly dysfunctional, mixes social communications with personal irrelevancies, circumstantial speech, ideas of reference, and metaphorical asides; often ruminative, appearing self-absorbed and lost in daydreams with occasional magical thinking, bodily illusions, obscure suspicion, odd beliefs, and a blurring of reality and fantasy)

(S) *Estranged self-image* (e.g., exhibits recurrent social perplexities and illusions as well as experiences of depersonalization, derealization, and dissociation; sees self as forlorn, with repetitive thoughts of life's emptiness and meaninglessness)

(S) *Chaotic objects* (e.g., internalized representations consist of a piecemeal jumble of early relationships and affects, random drives and impulses, and uncoordinated channels of regulation that are only fitfully competent for binding tensions, accommodating needs, and mediating conflicts)

Intrapsychic level

(F) *Undoing mechanism* (e.g., bizarre mannerisms and idiosyncratic thoughts appear to reflect a retraction or reversal of previous acts or ideas that have stirred feelings of anxiety, conflict, or guilt; ritualistic or magical behaviors serve to repent for or nullify assumed misdeeds or "evil" thoughts)

(S) *Fragmented organization* (e.g., possesses permeable ego boundaries; coping and defensive operations are haphazardly ordered in a loose assemblage of morphologic structures, leading to desultory actions in which primitive thoughts and affects are discharged directly, with few reality-based sublimations, and significant further disintegrations into a psychotic structural level, likely under even modest stress)

Biophysical level

(S) *Distraught* or *insentient mood* (e.g., excessively apprehensive and ill at ease, particularly in social encounters; agitated and anxiously watchful, evincing distrust of others and suspicion of their motives that persists despite growing familiarity *or* manifests drab, apathetic, sluggish, joyless, and spiritless appearance; reveals marked deficiencies in face-to-face rapport and emotional expression)

Borderline Personality Disorder: Millon Clinical Domains

Behavioral level

(F) *Expressively spasmodic* (e.g., displays a desultory energy level with sudden, unexpected, and impulsive outbursts; abrupt, endogenous shifts in drive state and inhibitory controls; not only places activation and emotional equilibrium in constant jeopardy, but engages in recurrent suicidal or self-mutilating behaviors)

(F) *Interpersonally paradoxical* (e.g., although needing attention and affection, is unpredictably contrary, manipulative, and volatile, frequently eliciting rejection rather than support; frantically reacts to fears of abandonment and isolation, but often in angry, mercurial, and self-damaging ways)

Phenomenological level

(F) *Cognitively capricious* (e.g., experiences rapidly changing, fluctuating, and antithetical perceptions or thoughts concerning passing events, as well as contrasting emotions and conflicting thoughts toward self and others, notably love, rage, and guilt; vacillating and contradictory reactions are evoked in others by virtue of one's behaviors, creating, in turn, conflicting and confusing social feedback)

(S) *Uncertain self-image* (e.g., experiences the confusions of an immature, nebulous, or wavering sense of identity, often with underlying feelings of emptiness; seeks to redeem precipitate actions and changing self-presentations with expressions of contrition and self-punitive behaviors)

(S) *Incompatible objects* (e.g., internalized representations comprise rudimentary and extemporaneously devised, but repetitively aborted learnings, resulting in conflicting memories, discordant attitudes, contradictory needs, antithetical emotions, erratic impulses, and clashing strategies for conflict reduction)

Intrapsychic level

(F) *Regression mechanism* (e.g., retreats under stress to developmentally earlier levels of anxiety tolerance, impulse control, and social adaptation; among adolescents, is unable to cope with adult demands and conflicts, as evident in immature, if not increasingly infantile behaviors)

(S) *Split organization* (e.g., inner structures exist in a sharply segmented and conflictful configuration in which a marked lack of consistency and congruency is seen among elements, levels of consciousness often shift and result in rapid movements across boundaries that usually separate contrasting percepts, memories, and affects, all of which lead to periodic schisms in what limited psychic order and cohesion may otherwise be present, often resulting in transient, stress-related psychotic episodes)

Biophysical level

(S) *Labile mood* (e.g., fails to accord unstable mood level with external reality; has either marked shifts from normality to depression to excitement, or has periods of dejection and apathy, interspersed with episodes of inappropriate and intense anger, as well as brief spells of anxiety or euphoria)

Paranoid Personality Disorder: Millon Clinical Domains

Behavioral level

(F) *Expressively defensive* (e.g., is vigilantly guarded, alert to anticipate and ward off expected derogation, malice, and deception; is tenacious and firmly resistant to sources of external influence and control)

(F) *Interpersonally provocative* (e.g., not only bears grudges and is unforgiving of those of the past, but displays a quarrelsome, fractious, and abrasive attitude with recent acquaintances; precipitates exasperation and anger by a testing of loyalties and an intrusive and searching preoccupation with hidden motives)

Phenomenological level

(F) *Cognitively suspicious* (e.g., is unwarrantedly skeptical, cynical, and mistrustful of the motives of others, including relatives, friends, and associates, construing innocuous events as signifying hidden or conspiratorial intent; reveals tendency to read hidden meanings into benign matters and to magnify tangential or minor difficulties into proofs of duplicity and treachery, especially regarding the fidelity and trustworthiness of a spouse or intimate friend)

(S) *Inviolable self-image* (e.g., has persistent ideas of self-importance and self-reference, perceiving attacks on one's character not apparent to others, asserting as personally derogatory and scurrilous, if not libelous, entirely innocuous actions and events; is pridefully independent, reluctant to confide in others, highly insular, experiencing intense fears, however, of losing identity, status and powers of self-determination)

(S) *Unalterable objects* (e.g., internalized representations of significant early relationships are a fixed and implacable configuration of deeply held beliefs and attitudes, as well as driven by unyielding convictions which, in turn, are aligned in an idiosyncratic manner with a fixed hierarchy of tenaciously-held but unwarranted assumptions, fears, and conjectures)

Intrapsychic level

(F) *Projection mechanism* (e.g., actively disowns undesirable personal traits and motives and attributes them to others; remains blind to one's own unattractive behaviors and characteristics, yet is overalert to, and hypercritical of, similar features in others)

(S) *Inelastic organization* (e.g., systemic constriction and inflexibility of undergirding morphologic structures, as well as rigidly fixed channels of defensive coping, conflict mediation, and need gratification, create an overstrung and taut frame that is so uncompromising in its accommodation to changing circumstances that unanticipated stressors are likely to precipitate either explosive outbursts or inner shatterings)

Biophysical level

(S) *Irascible mood* (e.g., displays a cold, sullen, churlish, and humorless demeanor; attempts to appear unemotional and objective, but is edgy, envious, jealous, and quick to take personal offense and react angrily)

RESULTS

As noted earlier in the chapter, the data of this MCMI-III validation study were based on knowledgeable clinicians as judges of their own patients. The results are presented in a series of tables which focus on a number of different issues. First, a basic set of MCMI-III results are summarized primarily in Tables 17.2 and 17.3. They are differentiated to highlight different aspects of DSM-IV Axis II performance. The second set of analyses encompasses both Axes I and II, and are essentially comparative. They compare diagnostic efficiency statistics across the three generations of the MCMI: the first, second, and third versions; these data are summarized primarily in Tables 17.4 through 17.8.

Although the method of data gathering for each generation of the MCMI reported has differed somewhat in each succeeding form (e.g., precise instructions given to clinical raters, diagnostic criteria, sampling procedures), the *essential* requirement of utilizing "informed" clinical raters was standard and uniform (e.g., all three generations of ratings were based on judgments by clinicians with substantially more knowledge of those they rated than was the case in other studies, for example, clinicians whose "uninformed" results were reported in the first edition of the MCMI-III manual).

Diagnostic Efficiency Statistics for the MCMI-III Study

Table 17.1 should aid the reader in following the discussions in this and later sections, as well as in analyzing the diagnostic efficiency data summarized in Tables 17.3 through 17.8. This table outlines the various procedures for evaluating the accuracy with which the MCMI-III classifies patients in accord with judgments made by the study's experienced clinicians, who served as the study's standard of comparison.

Table 17.2 reports the raw frequencies and prevalence rates for the 321 patients included at this midpoint of the validation study. To illustrate, in the first column of this table, we can see that 18 patients were rated *first* as schizoids by their clinicians; 34 were rated first as avoidants, and so on. The most frequently rated first personality disorder was the dependent ($N = 41$); next was the borderline ($N = 40$); third was the DSM-IV's new depressive personality disorder ($N = 37$). The second column of Table 17.2 translates

TABLE 17.1. Classification Efficiency Terminology

Above MCMI-III scale cutting lines	Clinician DSM-IV diagnosis	
	Positive	Negative
Positive	True positives (a)	False positives (b)
Negative	False negatives (c)	True negatives (d)
Total	Total positives ($a + c$)	Total negatives ($b + d$) = N

Note. Prevalence or base rate (BR) = $(a + c)/N$; Sensitivity or true positive rate = $a/(a + c)$; Specificity or true negative rate = $d/(b + d)$; Positive predictive power = $a/(a + b)$; Negative predictive power = $d/(c + d)$; Positive prevalence ratio = Positive predictive power/prevalence.

TABLE 17.2. Clinician-Judged and MCMI-III First and Second Highest Personality Diagnoses (N = 321)

MCMI-III scale	Clinician-judged 1st (of N = 321)	Prevalence 1st (N = 100%)	Clinician-judged 2nd (of N = 321)	Prevalence 2nd (N = 100%)	Clinician-judged 1st & 2nd (of N = 642)	Prevalence 1st & 2nd (N = 100%)	MCMI-BR 1st (of N = 321)	MCMI-BR 2nd (of N = 321)	MCMI-BR 1st & 2nd (of N = 642)
Schizoid	18	.06	20	.06	38	.06	15	21	36
Avoidant	34	.11	37	.12	71	.11	30	40	70
Depressive	37	.12	32	.10	69	.11	43	42	85
Dependent	41	.13	28	.09	69	.11	27	23	50
Histrionic	23	.07	19	.06	42	.07	27	13	40
Narcissistic	22	.07	25	.08	47	.07	18	27	45
Antisocial	18	.06	25	.08	43	.07	22	24	46
Sadistic	7	.02	16	.05	23	.04	7	14	21
Compulsive	30	.09	9	.03	39	.06	28	12	40
Negativistic	16	.05	28	.09	44	.07	18	21	39
Masochistic	12	.04	42	.13	54	.08	23	41	64
Schizotypal	11	.03	11	.03	22	.03	15	9	24
Borderline	40	.12	18	.06	58	.09	34	23	57
Paranoid	12	.04	7	.02	19	.03	15	12	27

TABLE 17.3. Axis II Diagnostic Efficiency Statistics
of Clinically Judged First Highest

MCMI-III scale	PPP	SENS	PPR
Schizoid	67	56	11.89
Avoidant	73	65	6.92
Depressive	49	57	4.24
Dependent	81	54	6.38
Histrionic	63	74	8.79
Narcissistic	72	59	10.54
Antisocial	50	61	8.92
Sadistic	71	71	32.76
Compulsive	79	73	8.41
Negativistic	39	44	7.80
Masochistic	30	58	8.14
Schizotypal	60	82	17.41
Borderline	71	60	5.66
Paranoid	79	92	21.02

Note. PPP, positive predictive power; SENS, sensitivity; PPR,
positive predictive ratio.

those who were judged first into their prevalences or BRs (e.g., dependent = 13%; border-line and depressive personalities = 12% each). The third and fourth columns of this table report the number and prevalence percent for personalities judged by their clinicians as *second* most prominent. Interestingly, the DSM-IV's newest (depressive) and its recently jettisoned (masochistic/self-defeating) personalities were two of the top three disorders judged second highest. The fifth and sixth columns of this table summarize the combined first and second raw frequencies and prevalences, as judged by participating clinicians. As can be seen, the avoidant, depressive, dependent, and borderline personalities rank highest; those judged least prevalent were the paranoid, schizotypal, and sadistic.

The final three columns of Table 17.2 report first and second highest results obtained on each scale of the MCMI-III; these results may be compared with the first and second highest disorders as judged by clinicians, as recorded on the first six columns of this table. The Depressive ($N = 43$) and Borderline ($N = 34$) were the two scales that achieved the most frequent high MCMI-III scores. The combined highest first and second scales were the Depressive ($N = 85$) and the Avoidant ($N = 70$). The least frequent to achieve the combined first and second highest MCMI-III scores were the Sadistic ($N = 21$), Schizotypal ($N = 24$), and Paranoid ($N = 27$). In summary, if we compare the fifth and ninth columns of Table 17.2 we see that the overall clinically judged most and least prevalent personality disorders correspond quite closely to those disorders that score highest and lowest on the MCMI-III.

MCMI-III diagnostic efficiency results may be seen in Table 17.3. The three columns report analyses pertaining to clinician-judged *first* highest personalities and their correspondence to the MCMI-III results. The positive predictive power (PPP) statistic represents the percentage of those diagnosed for which true positives constitute the total number of positives identified by the test, while sensitivity (SENS) represents the percentage of those diagnosed for which true positives constitute the total number of patients identified as positive by their clinicians, whether or not they are also identified as positive by the test. Thus, of all the patients identified by the MCMI as Schizoid, 67% are in fact true positives. Similarly, of all patients identified by the MCMI as Compulsive, 79% are true positives. Highest predictive power results for highest-rated personalities were obtained for the dependent (.81), the paranoid (.78), and the compulsive (.79) disorders. The least impressive PPP scores were obtained with the masochistic (.30), negativistic (.39), and the depressive (.49); whether the poorer PPP statistics for these three personalities can be attributed, at least in part, to the fact that the masochistic/self-defeating was fully deleted from the DSM-IV, and the negativistic and depressive comprise the only personality disorders relegated to the manual's Appendix, should certainly be considered.

Moving forward, the SENS statistics reported in Table 17.3 identify the percentage of those judged clinically to exhibit a primary personality disorder who, in fact, obtain their highest score on the parallel MCMI-III scale, for example, 57% of those rated primarily as depressives by clinicians obtained their highest MCMI-III scores on the Depressive Personality scale.

The PPR score compares the predictive success rate (PPP) actually achieved in contrast to what would have been achieved by chance alone (e.g., if the prevalence rate of a disorder was 5%, then 5 such cases in a group of 100 patients would have been identified by chance). What the PPR statistics tells us is how much *better than chance* the test results are. For example, if 5% was what chance should result in, then obtaining a 30% PPR on the MCMI-III would be appreciably greater than chance; in fact, it would be six times better; that is, it would result in a PPR of 6.0. To illustrate from Table 17.3, we can note that the MCMI-III's PPR for the avoidant personality is 6.92, that is, close to 7 times greater than chance alone would have produced. The PPR incremental accuracy is most impressive among disorders with low prevalence rates: sadistic (32+), paranoid (21+), schizotypal (17+), and schizoid (11+). Lesser, yet quite impressive PPRs are obtained with disorders possessing high prevalence rates, for example, depressive (4+), borderline (5+), dependent (6+), and avoidant (6+). In our judgment, PPR is the single most useful and important diagnostic efficiency statistic in that it tells the reader how much "better" the MCMI-III (or any other psychometric) instrument may be than an uninformed and nondiscriminating (i.e., chance) diagnostic assignment (Millon, Bockian, Tringone, Antoni, & Green, 1989).

Looking ahead to Tables 17.7 and 17.8, we will find the *Axis I* diagnostic efficiency statistics for MCMI-III scales as appraised by the clinician's judgments. The final column of Table 17.7 compares the clinician's *highest* rated Axis I judgment and the parallel MCMI-III scale at the cutting score of BR 85; MCMI-III scores at this BR level provide the most stringent comparison—highest to highest. As can be seen in this last column of Table 17.7, the range of the PPP statistics is .33 delusional disorder to .93 (drug dependence). The two most Prevalent Axis I disorders, anxiety and dysthymia, achieve PPPs of .75 and .81, respectively. SENS gauges were likewise good, achieving modal values in the mid-60s. Calculations derived from Table 17.7 show PPR statistics that are similarly impressive, ranging from four MCMI-III–Axis I scales that are 10 or more times greater than chance, to three MCMI-III scales that are two to three times that of chance.

A less discriminating set of efficiency statistics are reported in 17.8. Here the clinician's highest rated Axis I disorder is gauged using the more modest MCMI-III cutting score of BR 75. As anticipated, the SENS gauge was increased relative to that achieved utilizing the BR 85 cutting score. By contrast, both PPP and PPR statistics were somewhat reduced.

Overall, the study's diagnostic efficiency statistics for the Axis I and Axis II scales match the convincing results achieved by the MCMI-III's predecessor, the MCMI-II, perhaps even superseding them at several comparison points, as can be appraised by analyses presented in the following section.

Comparing MCMI, MCMI-II and MCMI-III Diagnostic Efficiency Statistics

Comparative results may be seen in Tables 17.4 through 17.8; these present three generations of SENS and PPP statistics (specificities and negative predictive power statistics are not presented, as these statistics tend to be grossly inflated, averaging about .95, as a byproduct of the number of scales included in the configural calculations). Evaluation of an instrument in terms of these statistics requires that both SENS and PPP be considered conjointly. As noted in a previous paragraph, they tend to be inversely related—one goes up as the other goes down. Either can be almost perfect, while the other is atrocious. For example, assume that 100 patients of a sample of 1,000 are labeled by clinical judges as thought disordered. If all 100 are identified on a Thought Disorder scale, then the SENS of the instrument is perfect. So far, so good. If, however, the other 900 are also identified as thought disordered, then our appraisal is dramatically changed. Here, perfect SENS is gained at the expense of a large number of false positives. Conversely, if all the patients identified as thought disordered by a Thought Disorder scale are also labeled as such by the clinical judges, the PPP of the instrument is perfect. So far, so good. If, however, the scale succeeds in identifying only one of a total of 100 thought disorder patients, our appraisal is dramatically changed. These two examples, of course, are merely illustrative; actual trade-offs between SENS and PPP tend to be far more modest.

The results of Tables 17.4 through 17.8 are presented in a manner which allows corresponding statistics to be directly compared, as their continued calculation assumes, de facto, that such comparisons will automatically be made. In spite of the fact that these statistics must be viewed as generally favorable within any given version of the MCMI, it must be said that their comparability across the various generations of MCMIs may be problematic. Perhaps the foremost feature of science is experimental control—that is, that manipulations across sample conditions be known in advance and built explicitly into the research design.

TABLE 17.4. Axis II Diagnostic Efficiency Statistics of Clinically Judged First Highest over Three MCMI Generations

MCMI scale	Sensitivity			Positive predictive power		
	MCMI	MCMI-II	MCMI-III	MCMI	MCMI-II	MCMI-III
Schizoid	38	33	56	50	38	67
Avoidant	67	67	65	70	72	73
Depressive	*	*	57	*	*	49
Dependent	63	77	54	69	70	81
Histrionic	58	53	74	65	48	63
Narcissistic	50	59	59	65	55	72
Antisocial	42	60	61	55	68	50
Sadistic	*	68	71	*	*	71
Compulsive	53	66	73	53	61	79
Negativistic	47	59	44	62	50	39
Masochistic	*	48	58	*	*	30
Schizotypal	58	38	82	74	47	60
Borderline	60	67	60	64	60	71
Paranoid	54	31	92	79	40	79

TABLE 17.5. Axis II Diagnostic Efficiency Statistics of Clinically Judged First and Second Highest over Three MCMI Generations

	Sensitivity			Positive predictive power		
	MCMI	MCMI-II	MCMI-III	MCMI	MCMI-II	MCMI-III
Schizoid	88	62	68	68	71	72
Avoidant	88	76	62	80	79	63
Depressive	*	*	75	*	*	61
Dependent	80	79	56	80	76	78
Histrionic	79	68	75	79	65	79
Narcissistic	74	74	72	59	69	77
Antisocial	62	71	81	61	80	76
Sadistic	*	78	74	*	71	81
Compulsive	58	73	74	57	67	76
Negativistic	78	72	59	73	64	67
Masochistic	*	72	85	*	58	73
Schizotypal	74	57	73	68	69	67
Borderline	77	72	79	71	66	81
Paranoid	71	50	89	68	65	65

The structure and content of the MCMI, however, has often been informed as much by the desultory course of historical change as by self-conscious evolution. This would include changes (1) in the number of personality disorders—the addition of the aggressive/sadistic and self-defeating personalities from MCMI to MCMI-II, and the addition of the depressive personality in MCMI-III; each of these increases tends to lower the upper boundaries of SENS and PPP that can be practically obtained for any one disorder; (2) two kinds of changes in the nature of the constructs assessed—the repositioning of the antisocial and passive–aggressive personalities from MCMI to make room for the aggressive/sadistic and self-defeating in MCMI-II, and the weighting of item content more toward conformity with DSM-IV criteria in MCMI-III, from relatively greater conformity with Millon's theory in MCMI-II—and (3) changes in clinical habits of diagnosis that have evolved over time, tending both to reflect and inform the two influences just noted. Accordingly, the comparability of these statistics across time is not something that can be directly quantified, but instead

TABLE 17.6. Axis II Frequency of Sensitivity and Positive Predictive Power Levels Comparing MCMI-II and MCMI-III

	Combined 1st and 2nd highest personalities				1st highest personality			
	SENS-II	SENS-III	PPP-II	PPP-III	SENS-II	SENS-III	PPP-II	PPP-III
.30 to .39					3		1	2
.40 to .49					1	1	3	
.50 to .59	2	2	1		3	4	2	1
.60 to .69	2	2	7	4	5	3	3	3
.70 to .79	9	6	4	7	1	3	2	6
.80 to .89		3	1	2		1		1
≥.90								

Note. The depressive personality is not included in these results because it was not part of the MCMI-II.

TABLE 17.7. Prevalence, Sensitivity, and Positive Predictive Power of MCMI Axis I Scales at BR ≥ 85

MCMI–Axis I scale	Prevalence rates				Sensitivity				Positive predictive power			
	M-I	M-II	M-III[a]	M-III[b]	M-I	M-II	M-III[a]	M-III[b]	M-I	M-II	M-III[a]	M-III[b]
Anxiety Disorder	24	23	46	28	67	69	57	64	73	74	80	75
Somatoform Disorder	13	5	24	12	37	43	25	24	44	33	53	39
Bipolar Disorder	4	3	6	4	49	40	44	64	50	53	57	58
Dysthymia	26	29	38	23	73	76	55	65	76	72	88	81
Alcohol Dependence	12	8	30	17	56	79	65	80	66	88	91	88
Drug Dependence	6	9	19	11	52	62	78	82	63	78	92	93
PTSD	*	*	18	6	*	*	53	88	*	*	73	67
Thought Disorder	3	2	10	4	15	20	52	100	19	30	59	52
Major Depression	3	6	20	11	24	47	65	84	27	50	72	66
Delusional Disorder	2	1	9	2	15	25	40	50	23	40	63	33

[a]Statistic calculated using all disorders judged by clinicians as present.
[b]Statistic calculated using disorders judged by clinicians as most prominent.

becomes a matter of judgment. Obviously, comparisons of MCMI with MCMI-II, and of MCMI-II with MCMI-III, are likely to be less problematic than is comparison between MCMI and MCMI-III.

Fortunately, as comparisons across the columns of Table 17.4 and 17.5 show, with some exceptions, there is generally good conformity between the MCMI and the expert judges across all three generations. In terms of individual scales in Table 17.4, the lowest MCMI-III PPP statistics were obtained for the DSM-IV-jettisoned masochistic disorder (.30) and the two that comprise the DSM-IV Appendix, the negativistic (.39) and depressive (.49) disorders. The lowest MCMI-III SENS statistics were obtained for the negativistic (.44) and the dependent (.54) personalities. Each of these are acceptable, but not quite in the running with the rest of the statistics. While the PPP of the Masochistic and Negativistic scales indicate that these constructs are not as often identified as highest in the Axis II MCMI-II and -III configuration of scales as they are by clinicians, their SENS and PPPs, at first and second highest (Table 17.5), are quite respectable, indicating in our view that these

TABLE 17.8. Prevalence, Sensitivity, and Positive Predictive Power of MCMI Axis I Scales at BR ≥ 75

MCMI–Axis I scale	Prevalence rates			Sensitivity			Positive predictive power		
	M-I	M-II	M-III	M-I	M-II	M-III	M-I	M-II	M-III
Anxiety Disorder	34	39	46	88	80	88	79	84	70
Somatoform Disorder	18	13	24	42	57	59	51	53	49
Bipolar Disorder	8	4	6	56	42	67	55	55	55
Dysthymia	41	46	38	91	81	85	84	80	61
Alcohol Abuse	17	15	30	74	87	86	63	92	83
Drug Abuse	11	13	19	78	72	92	71	82	89
PTSD	*	*	18	*	*	82	*	*	52
Thought Disorder	6	4	10	39	37	74	45	50	51
Major Depression	6	14	20	41	68	85	46	73	51
Delusional Disorder	5	5	9	32	34	77	36	61	61

Note. Statistic calculated using all disorders judged by clinicians as present. PTSD, posttraumatic stress disorder.

relatively more complex and inferential personality disorders may not be adequately judged by knowledgeable clinicians.

While it is difficult to get a sense of the MCMI-II as compared with the MCMI-III by attempting to digest Tables 17.4 and 17.5 in total, examining the frequency of personality scales found at various levels of SENS and PPP is more revealing. Table 17.6 presents these frequency data across first and second highest and first highest alone. These results show that the SENS and PPP statistics are somewhat higher for the MCMI-III than for the MCMI-II. In effect, these data show that the MCMI-III is a somewhat better diagnostic instrument, at least as far as expert judges are concerned.

Insofar as Axis II is concerned, a direct comparison of diagnostic efficiency analyses of MCMI, MCMI-II, and MCMI-III shows that each form of the instrument achieved a satisfactory to high level of predictive and clinical accuracy. Where clinicians are well-informed about the theoretical and clinical grounding of personality constructs and, most importantly, know the personality of the patients they judge quite well, the results of the MCMI-III are very impressive. The shift in diagnostic efficiency Axis II statistics from MCMI to MCMI-II to MCMI-III shows a modest but general upward trend in the instrument's SENS and PPP.

Tables 17.7 and 17.8 relate to efficiency statistics calculated to appraise the correspondence between clinical judgments and MCMI-III scale scores for DSM-IV Axis I. These tables compare the PPRs, SENSs, and PPPs for the MCMI Axis I scales at the BR 75 and BR 85 cutting scores.

Two columns for the MCMI-III are presented in Table 17.7. The first, labeled M-III[a], calculates prevalence, SENS, and PPP for all disorders judged present, not merely those judged to be both present and prominent (ranked of greatest clinical importance) by clinicians. By this gauge, the prevalence rates in this study are much higher than those obtained with MCMI and MCMI-II. Given this increase in prevalence, the SENS and PPP statistics are not fully comparable. Nevertheless, compared with the MCMI-II, the statistics seem to obey the general principle outlined above, that when SENS decreases, PPP tends to increase, and vice versa. The SENS of the Basic Axis I disorders are lower— and significantly lower for the Somatoform scale—while those of the severe Axis I disorders are uniformly higher. When the data are presented this way, the PPPs for the Basic and Severe Axis I scales are shown to be higher in every case. In particular, the three Severe Axis I scales—Thought Disorder, Major Depression, and Delusional Disorder— appear somewhat improved. While these statistics are, as noted, not really comparable to the operating characteristics presented for MCMI and MCMI-II, the M-III[a] column would seem to possess greater ecological validity at the BR 85 cutting score—clinicians should be interested in the SENS and PPP of any disorder at a given cutting score, not merely to the most prominent disorder.

Column M-III[b] of Table 17.7 presents the SENS and PPP statistics for MCMI-III at BR≥85, that is, those Axis I disorders judged as most in need of clinical attention. While MCMI-III[b] prevalence rates of every Axis I disorder, except dysthymia, are higher than those reported for the MCMI-II, these figures are more comparable to the MCMI-II than those presented in column M-III[a]. The MCMI-III SENS statistics are essentially mixed; some are higher and some are lower. The MCMI-III PPPs, however, are generally higher, and in some cases, much higher, than those obtained for MCMI-II.

In summary, it would appear justified to conclude that the MCMI-III has proven for most scales to be equal to or marginally superior to their comparable scales on the MCMI-II.

REFERENCES

American Psychiatric Association. (1994). *Diagnostic and statistical manual of mental disorders* (4th ed.). Washington, DC: Author.

Cronbach, L. J., & Meehl, P. E. (1955). Construct validity in psychological tests. *Psychological Bulletin, 52,* 281–302.

Millon, T. (1987). *Millon Clinical Multiaxial Inventory—II manual.* Minneapolis: National Computer Systems.

Millon, T. (1990). *Toward a new personology: An evolutionary model.* New York: Wiley-Interscience.

Millon, T., Bockian, N., Tringone, R., Antoni, M., & Green, C. (1989). New diagnostic efficiency statistics: Comparative sensitivity and predictive/prevalence ratio. *Journal of Personality Disorders, 3,* 163–171.

Millon, T., Millon, C., & Davis, R. (1994). *Millon Clinical Multiaxial Inventory—III manual.* Minneapolis: National Computer Systems.

Retzlaff, P. (1996). MCMI-III diagnostic validity: Bad test or bad validity study. *Journal of Personality Assessment, 66,* 431–437.

III

THE MACI, MBHI, MBMC, AND MPDC

18

The MACI: Composition and Clinical Applications

JOSEPH T. McCANN

Over the course of human development there are distinct phases of change and growth that create unique challenges for the person. The period of adolescence marks a time of many developmental changes and conflicts (Coleman, 1992; Petersen, 1988). Biological forces bring about such changes as the increase in hormonal activity, development of secondary sex characteristics, and physical maturation that leads to a more adultlike physique. Social pressures also define adolescence as a time of conflict. There is the desire in U.S. culture to break away from family influences and to adopt the norms of one's peer group, but adolescents also recognize the frequent need for a certain degree of emotional and economic dependence on family. In the teenager's continuing individual growth, there is a developing sense of autonomy that leads to questions about one's identity and direction in life, as well as a greater inconsistency in managing interpersonal relationships. In short, adolescence marks a transitional phase that finds change in all aspects of development, including biological, psychological, and social growth.

Because of the distinct nature of adolescence, it should be obvious that psychological assessment procedures need to be designed specifically for the measurement of adolescent personality and adjustment. Strangely, however, the early phases of adolescent psychodiagnosis were characterized by the adaptation of instruments originally designed for adults to the assessment of adolescents (Archer & Ball, 1988). This was usually done under the assumption that adolescents were "mini-adults," and assessment required merely renorming and slight alterations in the test, perhaps through changing instructions and items or modifying scoring procedures.

Only in recent years has there been an attempt to design objective personality instruments specifically for adolescents. One such instrument, the newly developed Minnesota Multiphasic Personality Inventory—A (MMPI-A) (Butcher et al., 1992), reflects the trend in clinical assessment toward acknowledging the need for specialized measures for adolescents. The major difficulty with many psychological instruments, including the MMPI-A, is that they lack any grounding in a coherent and meaningful theoretical diagnostic model. Theory, as a guiding framework in psychological test development, has several advantages, including the ability to test hypotheses more readily, the ability to organize interpretation around different scales, and the facilitation of clinical diagnosis and test interpretation.

363

The Millon Adolescent Clinical Inventory (MACI; Millon, 1993) represents a psycho-diagnostic instrument that has been constructed with these issues in mind. As a test designed especially for adolescents, the MACI measures clinical symptomatology, personality characteristics, and expressed concerns that are common among and unique to teenagers. Moreover, the MACI is grounded in a comprehensive theory of personality and psychopathology (Millon, 1969, 1981, 1990). In addition to these attributes, the MACI has also been developed for clinical assessment in settings where the adolescent is being evaluated for mental health treatment and where the identification of clinical symptomatology and psychopathology is of primary concern. As such, the MACI scales have been designed to correspond to the diagnostic criteria and syndromes which are outlined by current diagnostic nomenclature in the fourth edition of the *Diagnostic and Statistical Manual of Mental Disorders* (DSM-IV; American Psychiatric Association, 1994).

No diagnostic instrument represents a perfect measure of DSM-IV criteria. However, the MACI does incorporate several innovations and attributes which reflect the diagnostic conceptual model that is represented in DSM-IV. Among the ways in which the MACI conforms with current nosology is the existence of two sets of scales to separately measure transient clinical syndromes associated with Axis I of DSM-IV and the more stable personality characteristics of Axis II. The MACI also has individual scales which correspond to each personality disorder in the DSM-IV classification system.

Another major feature of the MACI which makes it particularly useful for clinical diagnosis and evaluation is the focus on clinical symptomatology. The MACI is a major revision of the original Millon Adolescent Personality Inventory (MAPI; Millon, Green, & Meagher, 1982). Among the reasons for revising the MAPI was the need to create a version of the test that corresponds to changes in diagnostic nomenclature, make the test concurrent with changes in the underlying theory, obtain a normative sample that was more clinically based, and develop scales to measure symptomatology and syndromes that are commonly found in clinical settings and thus of interest to practitioners.

This chapter is meant to serve as a brief overview of the procedures that were followed in developing the MACI and to outline various strategies for interpretation and clinical application. Individual scales are described, along with the meaning of high scores, and strategies are reviewed for integrating various sections of the MACI profile. Finally, case examples are presented which demonstrate some approaches to making effective use of the MACI for clinical diagnosis.

APPLICATIONS AND LIMITATIONS

The MACI is a 160-item objective personality inventory which has been designed for use in settings where adolescents come to the attention of mental health professionals. Therefore, unlike its predecessor, the MAPI, the MACI maintains a more clinical focus which emphasizes evaluation of the various psychological disturbances which are likely to be encountered in clinical settings, including depression, anxiety, eating disorders, substance abuse potential, and other similar forms of pathology. Given the fact that the normative sample upon which the MACI was developed comes from inpatient and outpatient treatment settings as well as correctional and residential treatment programs, the test is appropriate for use in any setting where the individual being evaluated resembles an individual from one of these settings. Because of the need to create scales that measure clinical syndromes on the MACI, several scales originally found on the MAPI which measured a teenager's academic confidence, scholastic achievement concerns, and academic attendance consistency were necessarily dropped from consideration for the MACI. Thus, the MAPI may still be the preferred instrument where academic concerns are being evaluated (Dyer, 1985), and psychopathology is not present or is only a minor consideration. Where psychological disturbances are believed to be the major reason for scholastic difficulties, then the MACI would be the preferred instrument.

Given the nature of adolescent behavior and development, there are several practical considerations to recognize when evaluating this age group with an objective, self-administered test such as the MACI. One of the most important considerations is readability of the items. The MACI assumes a sixth-grade reading level (Millon, 1993), thus limiting the ways in which the test can be administered to those teenagers with reading difficulties. In such instances, the test can be read to the subject either by a nonintrusive, neutral evaluator, or by standardized tape recording (available from the test publisher, NCS Assessments). Another major limitation of the MACI is its normative age range. Originally developed and normed on adolescents ages 13 to 19, the MACI is not suitable for individuals outside this range, as such use may lead to inaccurate diagnostic information.

An additional consideration that is important in adolescent psychodiagnostic testing is the issue of test length (Dyer, 1985). The MACI is brief relative to other similarly styled instruments and clinical experience reveals that adolescents have noticeably less concern about the length of the MACI, compared with other, lengthier instruments.

While the MACI has several advantages with its clinical focus, brevity, and suitability for adolescent concerns, the clinician may encounter some limitations as well in its use. The more severe forms of pathology, such as thought disturbances, bipolar mood disorders, paranoid ideation, and other more serious conditions are not directly measured by MACI scales. While other assessment techniques such as clinical interviews, patient history, collateral reports, and projective measures can be of assistance in answering such diagnostic questions, the MACI can still be useful, particularly in revealing the major problem areas as the adolescent sees them via the Expressed Concerns scales. Thus, the clinician using the MACI must be mindful of not only the advantages in utilizing the test, but also the limitations which may dictate conservative interpretation strategies or prudent applications in specific settings.

SCALE DEVELOPMENT AND COMPOSITION

Those scales and indices which make up the entire MACI profile were selected according to a number of criteria (Millon, 1993). Scales needed to reflect the basic personality patterns that are represented in the underlying theory of personality and psychopathology (Millon, 1981, 1990). Additionally, scales needed to assess the clinical syndromes that are of greatest importance to a broad band of clinicians working with adolescents, including eating disturbances, delinquency problems, impulsivity, substance abuse, anxiety, depression, and suicide potential. Given the recent interest in borderline personality disorders in adolescence, a scale was added to measure this form of pathology as well. Also of importance was the selection of scales which reflect primary adolescent concerns and difficulties which define this stage of development. Finally, response style indices were necessary to evaluate the impact of various response styles and levels of openness on overall validity of the test profile.

The result of this strategy was the formation of the 31 scales and indices which appear in Table 18.1. This table outlines the names of each MACI scale along with the number of items on each scale and a sample item to represent scale composition.

A major distinguishing feature of the MACI, as with all Millon inventories, is the use of a base rate (BR) score as the standardized measure for converting, plotting, and inter-

TABLE 18.1. MACI Scales and Sample Items

Scale		No. of items	Sample item
Modifying indices			
VV	Reliability	2	I flew across the Atlantic thirty times last year.
X	Disclosure	N/A[a]	N/A
Y	Desirability	17	I always try to do what is proper.
Z	Debasement	16	So little of what I have done has been appreciated by others.
Personality patterns			
1	Introversive	44	I don't need to have close friendships like other kids do.
2A	Inhibited	37	I often feel that others do not want to be friendly to me.
2B	Doleful	24	It's not unusual to feel lonely and unwanted.
3	Submissive	48	I worry a great deal about being left alone.
4	Dramatizing	41	I seem to fit in right away with any group of new kids I meet.
5	Egotistic	39	Some people think of me as a bit conceited.
6A	Unruly	39	Punishment never stopped me from doing whatever I wanted.
6B	Forceful	22	I sometimes scare other kids to get them to do what I want.
7	Conforming	39	I always try to do what is proper.
8A	Oppositional	43	I often resent doing things others expect of me.
8B	Self-Demeaning	44	I guess I'm a complainer who expects the worst to happen.
9	Borderline Tendency	21	I seem to make a mess of the good things that come my way.
Expressed concerns			
A	Identity Diffusion	32	I often feel as if I'm floating around, sort of lost in life.
B	Self-Devaluation	38	I see myself as falling far short of what I'd like to be.
C	Body Disapproval	17	Most people are better looking than I am.
D	Sexual Discomfort	37	Thinking about sex confuses me much of the time.
E	Peer Insecurity	19	Most other teenagers don't seem to like me.
F	Social Insensitivity	39	Becoming involved in other people's problems is a waste of time.
G	Family Discord	28	I would rather be anyplace but home.
H	Childhood Abuse	24	I hate to think about some of the ways I was abused as a child.
Clinical syndromes			
AA	Eating Dysfunctions	20	Although people tell me I'm thin, I still feel overweight.
BB	Substance Abuse Proneness	35	I used to get so stoned that I did not know what I was doing.
CC	Delinquent Predisposition	34	I'm no different from lots of kids who steal things now and then.
DD	Impulsive Propensity	24	As soon as I get the impulse to do something, I act on it.
EE	Anxious Feelings	42	I often fear I'm going to panic or faint when I'm in a crowd.
FF	Depressive Affect	33	Things in my life just go from bad to worse.
GG	Suicidal Tendency	25	More and more often I have thought of ending my life.

Note. Sample items are from Millon (1993). Copyright 1993 by Theodore Millon. Reproduced by permission.
[a]Disclosure is calculated based on the raw score sum of Scales 1 through 8B.

preting raw scores. These scores are derived in a manner which reflects the prevalence rates of various disorders and syndromes in a clinical setting to enhance the instrument's use as a diagnostic test. The MACI BR scores were derived by first arriving at a set of items that survived repetitive cycling through a three-stage validation process in which the items met strict theoretical–substantive, internal–structural, and external–criterion forms of validity (Millon, 1993). Once items were written to correspond with the underlying theoretical prototypic personality descriptions and DSM-IV diagnostic criteria, they were tested to make sure they had adequate endorsement frequencies and internal consistency. Thus, the items would be expected to adequately discriminate between various diagnostic groups while also achieving high levels of internal consistency. Items and scales were also selected based on their correspondence to external diagnostic criteria.

Once the MACI was established in its standard form, the prevalence rates for each diagnostic category measured by Scales 9 (Borderline Tendency) through GG (Suicidal Tendency) on the profile were established in the normative sample. Raw score frequency distributions were also constructed for each scale and five anchor points were selected at arbitrary levels on the BR scale to convert the raw score frequencies. Base rate (BR) scores of 0, 60, 75, 85, and 115 were selected to correspond to various points along the distribution. Base rate scores of 0 and 115 were selected to represent the minimum and maximum raw score on each scale respectively, while a BR score of 60 corresponds to the median raw score across all scales. A BR score of 75 corresponds to the percentile on the raw score distribution which reflects the percentage of adolescents in the normative sample rated as having a personality trait, expressed concern, or clinical syndrome as being *present*. The BR score of 85 corresponds to the raw score percentile which reflects the percentage of adolescents in the sample rated as having a trait, concern, or syndrome as being *prominent*. Through the process of algebraic interpolation, the BR score conversion tables were developed for each MACI scale with separate norms for 13- to 15-year-old males, 13- to 15-year-old females, 16- to 19-year-old males, and 16- to 19-year-old females.

The BR conversions for Scales 1 (Introversive) through 8B (Self-Demeaning) followed a slightly different procedure. According to Millon (1993), these scales were developed in such a manner that a restriction on BR transformations was maintained. The restriction was such that a specific scale would be the highest among the personality style scales at a rate which matched the prevalence for the same characteristic when rated most *prominent* among patients in the normative sample. The BR score conversions were also designed to have a scale be the second-highest elevation among the personality style scales at a rate that matched the prevalence of the characteristic when rated as *present*. Thus, linear interpolation was not always uniformly calculated for each of the BR scores for the basic personality scales.

The modifier indices had BR cutoffs based on percentiles. Thus, on Disclosure (Scale X), Desirability (Scale Y), and Debasement (Scale Z), BR scores above 85 represent the top 10% of patients, whereas a BR between 75 and 84 includes the next 15%. The lowest 15% of the population falls below a BR of 35, with the rest of the patients falling between a BR score of 35 and 74.

ADMINISTRATION AND SCORING

Because the number of items on the MACI is quite small compared with most other adolescent personality inventories, the instrument is ideally suited for most instances where the teenager meets appropriate criteria in terms of age and reading level. Various methods are available for scoring the MACI, including both handscoring and computerized scoring. The complexity of scoring procedures and profile adjustment algorithms on the MACI generally render the test better suited for computerized scoring; however, handscoring can be useful as a learning tool for understanding the various nuances of MACI scoring.

Among the major features and considerations in MACI scoring are the use of selective item weighting and various profile adjustments to correct for the influences of various state and trait characteristics that can result in under- or overreporting of problem areas. Each item on the MACI was selected based on its substantive connection to a particular construct and its psychometric properties. However, each item may be connected to one or more various constructs. Thus, keying of items is such that items contribute various raw score points to different scales based on how close an item represents the particular trait or characteristic being measured.

In addition, once MACI raw scores are converted to BR scores, various adjustments to the profile are implemented to correct for such influences as the overall level of disclosure, the impact of acute anxiety and depression on self-reports of personality, social desirability, or overly negative self-report styles, and characterological tendencies to be overly complaining or denying of problem areas. While each of these adjustments are carefully described in the MACI manual (Millon, 1993), users of the test are often unclear as to the validity or utility of such adjustments. Essentially, the MACI profile adjustments serve to maintain scale elevation frequencies which reflect the prevalence rates of the personality styles, expressed concerns, and clinical syndromes in the normative sample upon which the test was developed. The adjustments make intuitive sense, but they also serve the psychometric goal of maintaining correspondence between the frequency of MACI scale elevations and diagnostic prevalence rates in clinical settings.

INTERPRETATION OF THE MACI

There are several procedural steps which outline interpretation of the MACI. At a more basic and preliminary level, the effects of response styles on the meaning of scale elevations and overall profile validity give way to an analysis of individual scale elevations. More complex interpretation leads to different meanings being given to particular scales, depending on other elevations in the profile; moreover, various sections of the MACI profile are integrated with other sections. Thus, for example, an elevation on Peer Insecurity (Scale E) and Anxious Feelings (Scale EE) will take on different meaning if the adolescent's basic personality pattern can be characterized as egotistic–dramatizing (Scales 5 and 4), as opposed to inhibited–introversive (Scales 2A and 1). Other complex interpretive strategies thus include the analysis of various two-, three-, and four-point codetypes within and across various sections of the profile. Also, demographic characteristics of the adolescent and the context or setting in which the MACI is administered will have an impact on test interpretation.

Useful clinical information can be derived not only from the resultant profile, but also from the responses to individual items on the MACI. There has traditionally been recognized in objective test interpretation the need to examine individual items. This process reveals useful information to the clinician. While individual item responses have less psychometric reliability, they can still be interpretively useful. The brief length of the MACI and the printing of individual responses to noteworthy items makes individual item analysis a relatively easy procedure during MACI interpretation.

In this section, various strategies for interpreting the MACI will be discussed. Space limitations prevent a full discussion of the most frequently occurring scale combinations and their particular meaning. Instead, individual scales are reviewed in terms of their clinical significance. Various strategies will be reviewed for integrating sections of the MACI profile and where particularly relevant, common scale combinations will be highlighted to assist in more complex interpretation. Finally, strategies for dealing with MACI profiles which appear to be a "poor fit" with what is known about a particular adolescent will be discussed, revealing ways in which such profiles can still be of clinical use.

Modifying Indices and Response Styles

The four scales or indices on the MACI which measure response style and test-taking attitude are Reliability (Scale VV), Disclosure (Scale X), Desirability (Scale Y), and Debasement (Scale Z). Together they can be used to discern among adolescents who respond to the test questions honestly, those who distort their results with a tendency toward denial and underreporting, teenagers who magnify problems, and those who are careless or in other ways inaccurate in their self-reports.

Scale VV

The Reliability scale is not contained as an actual measure on the MACI profile, but rather it consists of two items (114 and 126) which are bizarre in content and are rarely, if ever, endorsed by even the most disturbed of adolescents. If either item is answered in the affirmative, it suggests various possibilities, including random responding, extreme oppositionality, concentration difficulties, poor reading skills, and extreme confusion that impairs the adolescent's ability to accurately report his or her difficulties. The exact same items on this scale are also contained on a similar index on the adult version of the test, the MCMI-III. Research has effectively shown that this index will accurately identify over 95% of all random response sets when a cutoff of one item is utilized (Bagby, Gillis, & Rogers, 1991). Therefore, only one Reliability scale item endorsed in the true direction is sufficient to invalidate the entire MACI profile.

Scale X

The Disclosure scale is designed as a general measure of an adolescent's willingness or ability to be open about personal attributes and concerns. In general, the intent is to be neutral as to the response style in either high or low scorers. However, this scale correlates highly in the positive direction with Debasement (Z) and moderately in the negative direction with Desirability (Y; Millon, 1993). Low scores are thus reflective of a teenager who is defensive and unwilling to be forthcoming about personal attributes and concerns. This lack of openness may be due to several factors, including a general concern about how self-reports will be utilized by the evaluator, a need to appear adjusted and emotionally healthy, or a general suspicion of adults. High scores on this scale reveal a teenager who is quite open, forthright, and direct in revealing personal concerns. In those cases where Scale X is highly elevated, the adolescent may be searching for attention, support, or some other source of secondary gain.

Scale Y

All items from this (Desirability) scale are found on other MACI scales, particularly Scales 4 (Dramatic), 5 (Egotistic), and 7 (Conforming). As a measure of socially desirable response sets, it is not uncommon to see elevations on one or more of these other scales when Scale Y is elevated. High scores on Desirability reflect attempts at having others see the teenager as a well-adjusted individual with few, if any, personal faults. There may be a need to be seen in an unrealistically favorable light and personal concerns are denied or markedly downplayed. Although Scale Y elevations are not sufficient by themselves to invalidate a MACI computer profile printout, as the BR score approaches 90, a socially desirable response set must be considered as potentially blurring much of the diagnostic information in the profile.

Scale Z

Some teenagers may be motivated to present their problems or concerns in a manner which conveys extreme emphasis on negative self-attributes and a magnification of minor or moderate symptoms or concerns. The Debasement scale is designed to measure such response styles. High scores reflect an adolescent who has some motivation to exaggerate, overreport, or in some other way distort problem areas in the negative direction. As with the Desirability (Y) scale, the Debasement scale will not, by itself, invalidate the computerized report and profile for the MACI. However, as scores begin to approach a BR of 90, the MACI profile's overall validity should be seriously questioned as being disrupted by a self-report style that is characterized by feeling helpless over extremely distressing feelings, malingering, or overreporting of problems as a psychological "cry for help."

Modifying Indices Configurations

Generally, a valid MACI profile is characterized by scales X, Y, and Z all falling below a BR of 75 and the Disclosure level (Scale X) falling above a raw score value of 200. As the response style approaches one of social desirability, Scale Y will be elevated above a BR score of 75 and Scales X and Z will fall below this level. Conversely, a response style characterized by the overreporting of psychopathology will be characterized by an elevation on Scale Z above a BR of 75 and Scale Y falling below this level; Scale X usually begins to elevate over a BR of 75 as well, given its strong correlation with Scale Z. In rare instances, both Scales Y and Z will be elevated above a BR of 75, reflecting conflicting and antithetical self-reports. Clinical experiences have generally revealed that this response style configuration represents inconsistent responding, or it is found in gregarious, self-centered, and egocentric adolescents who are experiencing an acute period of agitated depression.

Personality Patterns Scales

There are some distinguishing features of the MACI personality scales which differentiate them from other scales on the adult version of the Millon inventories, the MCMI. Like the MCMI personality scales, the MACI scales are designed to measure the more stable and enduring characteristics associated with personality, rather than more transient, state-related symptomatology. Also, the scale names on the MACI Personality Patterns scales denote distinct personality styles that correspond to a DSM-IV or theory-based character disorder. However, the scales have less pathological names; thus there is no mention of distinct DSM-IV personality disorders as there is on the MCMI. The purpose for this language change is to emphasize the clinical nature of adolescent personality disturbances, while also recognizing that personality styles may still be developing in adolescence and that further modification in the teenager's personality may occur as he or she enters into adulthood.

To assist with interpretation of the personality patterns scales, Millon (1995) has developed a set of factor analytically derived content subscales for each scale. The purpose of these subscales is to provide a theoretically and clinically useful set of scales that can assist in refining the particular components and attributes that contribute to elevations on individual personality pattern scales. Table 18.2 outlines these psychometrically derived dimensions of each scale and the alpha level for each content subscale. As the interpretive significance of each personality patterns scale is discussed below, the content subscales and the items which comprise each of them will be delineated.

Scale 1

The Introversive scale reflects those features which are associated with the schizoid personality described in DSM-IV criteria. High scores on this scale reflect a diminished capacity for experiencing either pleasure or pain in one's life. There is much restriction in the adolescent's expression of emotion and the teenager may appear apathetic, remote, and detached. Interpersonal relationships are scarce and high scorers prefer to engage in solitary activities that are not likely to bring them into contact with other people. When faced with challenge or demands, these teenagers respond with indifference or very little overt discomfort or concern. The ability to focus on more complex aspects of one's environment is limited; thus, high scorers may experience difficulty in articulating their concerns. Moderate elevations are also common in chronically depressed and dysphoric adolescents, though other scales in the profile suggestive of such pathology are usually elevated as well.

There are four content scales depicted in Table 18.2 which define prominent dimensions assessed by Scale 1. Existential Aimlessness is comprised of four items endorsed in the True direction (items 34, 115, 147, and 154) and two items in the False direction (items 2 and 145). This scale taps generalized feelings of hopelessness and a lack of direction in life. A second dimension of Scale 1 is Anhedonic Affect, comprised of five items in the True direction (items 12, 47, 61, 85, and 91), and assesses bland emotional experiences and weakened feelings of pleasure. The third dimension in Scale 1 is Social Isolation and it is defined by six items in the True direction (items 13, 35, 38, 69, 119, and 142) and two items in the False direction (items 24 and 70). A fourth content scale for Scale 1 is Sexual Indifference; it is comprised of two items in the True direction (items 51 and 116) and two in the False direction (items 59 and 143).

Scale 2A

The Inhibited scale is designed to assess those features associated with the avoidant personality described in DSM-IV criteria. Elevations on this scale reflect an extreme sensitivity to unpleasant and painful experiences that interfere with the teenager's ability to enjoy life. Initiative and planning of activities are avoided because of the fear that things will turn out badly, and interpersonal relationships are actively avoided because of extreme fears that others will be critical and rejecting. Thus, high scores are found for teenagers who appear shy, ill-at-ease, and socially awkward. Their lives are generally lonely and they lack the self-confidence and self-assurance that will permit them to excel in various aspects of their life. Any relationships that the inhibited teenager does have are usually characterized by both anxious clinging due to a fear of rejection and the constant seeking of reassurance that others are accepting and tolerant.

There are six content scales for Scale 2A and these are outlined in Table 18.2. The first of these taps a dimension of Existential Sadness, marked by feelings of despondency

TABLE 18.2. MACI Personality Pattern Content Subscales

Scale	Subscale	α
1. Introversive (Schizoid)	Existential Aimlessness	.80
	Anhedonic Affect	.60
	Social Isolation	.80
	Sexual Indifference	.50
2A. Inhibited (Avoidant)	Existential Sadness	.77
	Preferred Detachment	.52
	Self-Conscious Restraint	.55
	Sexual Aversion	.60
	Rejection Feelings	.82
	Unattractive Self-Image	.80
2B. Doleful (Depressive)	Brooding Melancholia	.80
	Social Joylessness	.55
	Self-Destructive Ideation	.69
	Abandonment Fears	.67
3. Submissive (Dependent)	Deficient Assertiveness	.70
	Authority Respect	.61
	Pacific Disposition	.75
	Attachment Anxiety	.59
	Social Correctness	.55
	Guidance Seeking	.41
4. Dramatizing (Histrionic)	Convivial Sociability	.82
	Attention-Seeking	.50
	Attractive Self-Image	.80
	Optimistic Outlook	.67
	Behavioral Disinhibition	.54
5. Egotistic (Narcissistic)	Admirable Self-Image	.84
	Social Conceit	.53
	Confident Purposefulness	.72
	Self-Assured Independence	.58
	Empathic Indifference	.44
	Superiority Feelings	.55
6A. Unruly (Antisocial)	Impulsive Disobedience	.76
	Socialized Substance Abuse	.75
	Authority Rejection	.64
	Unlawful Activity	.60
	Callous Manipulation	.60
	Sexual Absorption	.50
6B. Forceful (Sadistic)	Intimidating Abrasiveness	.78
	Precipitous Anger	.79
	Empathic Deficiency	.45
7. Conforming (Compulsive)	Interpersonal Restraint	.78
	Emotional Rigidity	.80
	Rule Adherence	.58
	Social Conformity	.64
	Responsible Conscientiousness	.51
8A. Oppositional (Negativistic)	Self-Punitiveness	.74
	Angry Dominance	.74
	Resentful Discontent	.77
	Social Inconsiderateness	.52
	Contrary Conduct	.50

(continued)

TABLE 18.2. (*continued*)

Scale	Subscale	α
8B. Self-Demeaning (Self-Defeating)	Self-Ruination	.73
	Low Self-Valuation	.84
	Undeserving Self-Image	.57
	Hopeless Outlook	.72
9. Borderline Tendency	Empty Loneliness	.72
	Capricious Reactivity	.70
	Uncertain Self-Image	.78
	Suicidal Impulsivity	.63

Note. Term in parentheses indicates MCMI-III scale equivalent.

and unhappiness, and is comprised of five items in the True direction (items 64, 80, 84, 140, and 153). A second content dimension defined as Preferred Detachment, assessing the teenager's preference for being isolated from others, is made up of three items in the True direction (items 36, 85, and 100) and one item in the False direction (item 24). Self-Conscious Restraint is the third content dimension for Scale 2 and is made up of four items in the False direction (items 18, 77, 117, and 149). The fourth content scale is Sexual Aversion, reflecting the avoidant person's discomfort in intimate and/or sexual relationships, and is comprised of two items in the True direction (items 51 and 116) and three items in the False direction (items 59, 62, and 143). A fifth content scale for Scale 2 is Rejection Feelings and is comprised of eight items in the True direction (items 13, 35, 38, 69, 87, 106, 119, and 142) and one item in the False direction (item 70). The last content scale listed in Table 18.2 for the Inhibited scale is one that assesses Unattractive Self-Image and is made up of five items in the True direction (items 26, 31, 71, 99, and 127) and two items in the False direction (items 10 and 68). Perusal of the items from each of these content scales can assist in determining the major personality dimensions being assessed by elevations on Scale 2A.

Scale 2B

Characteristics associated with the depressive personality disorder in DSM-IV are measured by the Doleful scale. Elevations on this scale are associated with long-standing feelings of dysphoria and depression. Doleful adolescents have great difficulty in experiencing joy or pleasure because of their lack of hope about the future. They expect that nothing can be done to change the sad state in which they see their life. This pessimism also carries over into other areas of their life, including low self-esteem, feelings of worthlessness, and inadequacy over their ability to perform specific activities. Socially, high scorers are lonely and withdrawn because they do not feel interested or hopeful enough that a friendship will lead to any positive consequences. Thus, these teenagers are prone to excessive worry and rumination and they may often be preoccupied by feelings of guilt over past transgressions that are either real or exaggerated.

The four content scales for the Doleful scale are listed in Table 18.2. The first of these taps a dimension of chronic, intense depressed mood and is referred to as Brooding Melancholia; 12 items in the True direction make up this scale (items 19, 25, 42, 43, 79, 84, 110, 118, 121, 140, 147, and 154). A second content scale is defined by unhappiness within the context of interpersonal relationships and is named Social Joylessness; four items in the True direction make up this scale (items 47, 85, 91, and 98). Self-Destructive Ideation is the third content scale and is made up of three items in the True direction (items 54, 95, 107). Finally, Abandonment Fears constitutes the last of the content scales and is comprised of five items in the True direction (items 20, 63, 64, 153, and 158). Again, examination of the items in each of these scales can assist in refining interpretations of Scale 2B elevations.

Scale 3

The Submissive scale is designed to measure those personality attributes which are associated with the DSM-IV dependent personality. When scores are elevated on this scale, they reflect an adolescent who is passive and submissive in interpersonal relationships. Submissive teenagers avoid taking any active leadership role in peer groups and they are concerned that others may not always be there for them; thus, there may be clinging behaviors. Because there may be excessive fears that others will leave or abandon them, teenagers who score highly on this scale will frequently downplay their own achievements and abilities and they favor connecting with those who can take a more assertive and confident role. Elevations also reveal strong needs for attention and affection and they also reflect strong needs for encouragement and support. There is a lack of self-confidence in many areas and reassurance is often needed from others. When in relationships, submissive teenagers will be sentimental and their behavior will be directed toward maintaining connection to others, even when relationships are problematic or filled with turmoil.

There are six content scales for MACI Scale 3 listed in Table 18.2; as noted before, review of the items on these scales can help identify the specific personality dimensions being measured. Deficient Assertiveness is the first of these scales and consists of six items keyed in the False direction (items 18, 21, 44, 92, 117, and 148). The second Submissive content scale is Authority Respect, measuring the teenager's willingness to follow those in positions of authority, and is comprised of three items in the True direction (items 6, 93, and 96) and one item in the False direction (item 158). Pacific Disposition is a third content scale comprised of seven items, all keyed in the False direction (items 28, 41, 52, 78, 97, 128, and 157). The fourth content scale listed for the Submissive scale in Table 18.2 has been labeled Attachment Anxiety and is made up of four items in the True direction (items 63, 71, 109, and 132). Social Correctness is a dimension tapping socially proper and conforming behavior and is comprised of four items in the True direction (items 5, 9, 23, and 130). Finally, Guidance Seeking is the sixth content scale, tapping the teenager's proclivity to seek out assistance and guidance from others, and is made up of four items keyed in the True direction (items 1, 87, 122, and 151).

Scale 4

The DSM-IV histrionic personality represents the underlying construct that is measured by the MACI Dramatizing scale. Elevations on this scale reflect a teenager who is quite sociable and who thrives on having numerous friendships and people in their life. Emotions are displayed in a dramatic and changeable pattern and they can often lead to poorly planned and impulsive decisions. The social behavior of these teenagers is characterized by excessive talkativeness, sensation-seeking, and drawing of attention to oneself. Long-term and lasting relationships are not tolerated well because the dramatizing adolescent becomes easily bored and requires constant stimulation. Others may find them interesting and fun at first, but the excessive focus on only the superficial aspects of life situations and the dramatizing adolescent's concern over physical appearances quickly causes their friends and acquaintances to become disillusioned and lose interest.

There are five content scales which define the major personality dimensions being measured by Scale 4. The first of these scales is Convivial Sociability, tapping the adolescent's ease in making friends and socializing; there are two items in the True direction (items 24 and 70) and 10 items in the False direction (items 13, 35, 36, 38, 69, 85, 100, 106, 119, and 142). Attention Seeking is the second of the content scales and is made up of four items in the True direction (items 56, 59, 103, and 135). The third content scale for the Dramatizing scale is Attractive Self-Image, reflecting comfort with one's appearance and self; it is comprised of one item in the True direction (item 10) and five items in the False direction (items 26, 31, 84, 99, and 127). Four items keyed in the False direction (items 19, 34, 43, 47, and 110) make up the Optimistic Outlook scale, while a fifth content dimension is Behavioral Disinhibition, which is made up of six items in the True direction (items 28, 77, 92, 111, 143, and 148). As stated earlier, examination of the items from these content scales can help to refine interpretations made on the Dramatizing scale.

Scale 5

As its name implies, the Egotistic scale is designed to measure features which define the narcissistic personality in DSM-IV criteria. High scorers exude self-confidence and self-assurance that leads to others seeing these teenagers as self-centered, arrogant, and conceited. In relationships, these adolescents require constant admiration, respect, and reinforcement. In fact, egotistic teenagers expect that others will recognize their talents and abilities and they will become easily upset and angered if others fail to give them proper recognition. Also, these teenagers are quite entitled and will easily exploit others to achieve the gratification that they expect. High scores reveal an inability to experience empathy or concern for others, thus other people are frequently given little respect. There are often periods of being caught up in fantasies of unlimited success and power, thus the egotistic teenager may at times appear on the surface to be quiet and aloof. In their relationships with friends and family, others are likely to feel unappreciated or taken for granted.

There are six content-based scales which have been derived for the Egotistic scale and these are listed in Table 18.2. The first of these is Admirable Self-Image and it is made up of three items keyed in the True direction (items 10, 68, and 131) and four items in the False direction (items 26, 31, 99, and 127). Social Conceit, measuring the need to have attention drawn to one's self, is the second content scale and it contains five items in the True direction (items 7, 56, 59, 103, and 135) and one item in the False direction (item 1). The third content scale is Confident Purposefulness and measures feelings of having a direction in life; four items make up the scale, with two keyed in the True direction (items 2 and 145) and two keyed in the False direction (items 34 and 115). Self-Assured Independence is the fourth content-based dimension for Scale 5 and is made up of six items in the False direction (items 19, 20, 25, 63, 71, and 151). The fifth content-based dimension is Empathic Indifference, measuring a lack of sensitivity and empathy for others; five items in the True direction make up this scale (items 39, 41, 52, 104, and 139). Superiority Feelings makes up the last of the Scale 5 subscales and has three items keyed in the True direction (items 86, 101, and 146) and two items in the False direction (items 84 and 140).

Scale 6A

The personality characteristics which are measured by the Unruly scale are those which define the DSM-IV antisocial personality. High scorers exhibit conduct problems due to their rejection of socially acceptable standards of behavior. They are rebellious in their attitudes and they reject any efforts to have limits placed on their actions. While cooperative activity with others is generally rejected, the unruly teenager may frequently exhibit cooperative types of behavior with others who share similar antisocial attitudes; the goals of such group cooperation are generally directed toward illegal or other rebellious ends. High scorers also value autonomy and they do not like having limits placed on their behavior. Thus, they engage in impulsive and irresponsible actions such as stealing, truancy, fighting, and other forms of acting-out. In relationships, unruly adolescents have little or no compassion for others and they are prone to seeking revenge for perceived injustices or advantages that others have taken. These adolescents do not learn from mistakes or problems they have encountered; thus, they are often caught in a cycle of acting out, having their behavior limited or corrected, and responding with rebellion and revenge at their punishers, followed by more acting-out.

Six content scales have been derived for the Unruly scale and they are listed in Table 18.2. The first of these subscales has been labeled Impulsive Disobedience and is comprised of eight items in the True direction (items 18, 21, 44, 77, 104, 117, 148, and 149). The second content dimension is Socialized Substance Abuse and is made up of four items keyed in the True direction (items 57, 120, 150, and 152) and one item in the False direction (item 8). Authority Rejection is the third content scale for the Unruly scale and is made up of one item in the True direction (item 155) and five items in the False direction (items 5, 9, 23, 93, and 96). Unlawful Activity represents the fourth content dimension and contains two items keyed in the True direction (items 73 and 111) and two items in the False direction (items 15 and 45). The last two content scales are Callous Manipulation, made up of seven True-keyed items (items 28, 41, 52, 58, 76, 92, and 135), and Sexual Absorption, made up of two items in the True direction (items 59 and 143) and two items in the False direction (items 51 and 116).

Scale 6B

The Forceful scale is very useful for assessing features associated with very aggressive and sadistic adolescents, along with the characteristics which define the sadistic personality disorder originally described in DSM-III-R. High scorers are those teenagers who are extremely strong-willed and tough-minded. Their constant conflict with authority is related to their intolerance for being controlled or in other ways having their self-determination limited or restricted. Socially, they are blunt, hostile, and often cruel toward others because these adolescents have no empathy or sensitivity for others. In fact, they often derive much satisfaction and pleasure from humiliating, verbally attacking, or in other ways violating the rights of others. When attempts are made to confront these teenagers with the consequences of their actions, they go on the offensive, becoming hostile and combative. In relationships, they are controlling and intimidating. While behaviorally they may appear antisocial or conduct disordered, the high score on the Forceful scale usually denotes that the adolescent derives pleasure from the harm or turmoil that their acting-out behavior can inflict on others. They tend to see themselves as dominant and authoritarian.

There have been three content subscales derived for the Forceful scale. The first of these is Intimidating Abrasiveness, reflecting the tendency to exert power and harsh behaviors in relationships; seven items in the True direction make up this content scale (items 28, 52, 78, 97, 128, 139, and 157). Precipitous Anger, assessing abrupt displays of hostility and extreme oppositionality, is the second scale and is made up of seven items keyed in the True direction (items 18, 21, 74, 104, 117, 148, and 149). The third of the content subscales for Scale 6B is Empathic Deficiency, reflecting extreme deficits in the ability to experience sensitivity to the feelings of others. It is made up of two items in the True direction (items 41 and 60) and two items in the False direction (items 5 and 81).

Scale 7

The Conforming scale corresponds to the compulsive personality in DSM-IV. High scorers are generally emotionally constricted and very serious-minded. They hold rigid ideas about what is morally right and wrong and they are compliant with rules. In relationships, they keep a tight hold on their feelings and have difficulty accepting others who go against their fixed beliefs and ideas. They are intolerant of those who enjoy being spontaneous or unpredictable and the conforming adolescent has a self-image that is characterized as industrious and hard-working. Given the fact that many of these characteristics are also somewhat desirable (e.g., follows rules, hard-working, etc.), it is not uncommon to see this scale elevated in those teenagers who are not necessarily compulsive in their personality style, but who are exhibiting a socially desirable response set on the MACI. Thus, elevations may be found in impulsive, emotional, acting-out adolescents who only wish to be seen as hard-working, compliant, serious-minded, and conforming.

Table 18.2 lists the five content-based subscales which can be used to help refine interpretations of elevations on Scale 7. The first content scale is Interpersonal Restraint and is comprised of six items keyed in the False direction (items 18, 21, 74, 104, 117, and 149). Emotional Rigidity is the second of the subscales and is comprised of one item in the True direction (item 145) and nine items in the False direction (items 19, 34, 42, 43, 107, 110, 118, 133, and 154). The third content scale reflects attitudes that contribute to the following of rules and guidelines and is appropriately named Rule Adherence; it is made up of four items in the True direction (items 50, 93, 96, and 159) and one item in the False direction (item 4). The last two content subscales are Social Conformity, comprised of one item in the True direction (item 15) and four in the False direction (items 73, 90, 148, and 150), and Responsible Conscientiousness, made up of three True-keyed items (items 9, 23, and 130) and one False item (item 58).

Scale 8A

The Oppositional scale, while measuring some of the attributes associated with oppositional–defiant disorder, is more accurately viewed as a measure of the DSM-IV negativistic personality disorder. Elevations on this scale are found in teenagers who are very resentful over having demands made upon them. They are resistant and oppositional toward others when something is asked of them and their moods are easily prone to irritability and moodiness. There tends to be much confusion about their feelings because these adolescents are not used to controlling their feelings for very long. They feel misunderstood and unappreciated, thus leading to sullen and discontented feelings. In relationships, the oppositional adolescent is often quick to spoil the pleasures or enjoyment that others may experience by either passive–aggressive and indirect hostile comments or the expression of irritable and sour moods. Their stubborn and resistant behavior often gets them into trouble with teachers, parents, and other authority figures and they are very difficult to engage in productive discussion in treatment.

Again, to assist with the interpretation of primary scale elevations, there are five content-based subscales for the Oppositional scale listed in Table 18.2. Self-Punitiveness is the first of these subscales and it is made up of six items in the True direction (items 16, 54, 66, 88, 95, and 107). The second content dimension is Angry Dominance, which is comprised of six items (items 28, 78, 97, 128, 149, and 157), all keyed in the True direction. Resentful Discontent is the third of the content subscales and is made up of 12 items in the True direction (items 4, 19, 25, 34, 67, 91, 105, 110, 118, 127, 136, and 158) and one item in the False direction (item 23). Social Inconsiderateness, the fourth content subscale, has five items in the True direction (items 37, 39, 41, 49, and 117) and one item in the False direction (item 5). The last of the subscales listed in Table 18.2 is Contrary Conduct, assessing oppositional behavioral tendencies, and has three True items (items 18, 73, and 148) and one False item (item 45).

Scale 8B

Although the self-defeating personality disorder was dropped from DSM-IV criteria, the Self-Demeaning scale was retained on the MACI as a measure of that particular personality style. As such, high scores reflect strong self-effacing and self-punitive beliefs and attitudes. These teenagers often undermine the opportunities for personal growth and fulfillment and they feel undeserving of any successes or rewards they may experience. They have extremely poor self-esteem and put the needs of others ahead of their own. Adolescents scoring high on this scale also internalize the tension and conflict that can arise under stress. Thus, they will blame themselves when problems arise, expect the worst things to happen, and frequently complain that they are incapable of doing anything to change their lives. When others offer support or help, self-demeaning adolescents thwart any assistance by claiming they are unworthy of help or by undermining the helpful efforts of others. This scale is also frequently elevated in chronically depressed or dysphoric adolescents, as well as those who have been abused or victimized and have long-standing unresolved issues over the abuse.

Four content scales have been derived for the Self-Demeaning scale and are listed in Table 18.2. The first of these measures is labeled Self-Ruination and assesses the self-perception that most of the teenager's misfortunes are self-inflicted; six items in the True direction (items 19, 34, 46, 121, 140, and 141) and one in the False direction (item 2) make up this scale. Low Self-Valuation, reflecting self-loathing and low self-esteem, is the second content scale and is made up of five items in the True direction (items 26, 84, 99, 112, and 127) and two in the False direction (items 10 and 68). The last two content scales for the Self-Demeaning scale are Undeserving Self-Image, made up of five items in the True direction (items 66, 80, 89, 108, and 160) and Hopeless Outlook, which is comprised of seven items keyed in the True direction (items 20, 25, 64, 110, 118, 136, and 153).

Scale 9

The Borderline Tendency scale is designed to measure the characteristics which define the borderline personality disorder in the DSM-IV. High scorers are adolescents who experience a great deal of emotional turmoil and instability. Their moods change from periods of anxiety, to depression, anger, joy, or sadness. Instability is also found in many areas of the teenager's life. Relationships are characterized by changing feelings and attitudes toward others, from positive idealization to devaluation and rejection. These adolescents will also experience instability in their feelings about long-term career goals, personal interests and preferences, and other aspects reflecting a sense of identity. Behaviorally, the borderline adolescent is also unstable and engages in self-destructive, impulsive, and risky behavior in such areas as substance abuse, suicidal acting-out, promiscuous sexual behavior, or other forms of reckless actions. There are often long-standing needs for attention and support that are never fully satisfied; thus the borderline teenager fears rejection or abandonment and may go to extreme lengths to keep others close and involved in his or her life. Based on the nature of borderline disturbances, elevations on this scale are generally reflective of a moderate to severe level of psychopathology.

There are four content scales listed in Table 18.2 for the Borderline Tendency scale. The first of these is the Empty Loneliness subscale, which is made up of six items in the True direction (items 63, 64, 84, 121, 141, and 153). Capricious Reactivity, reflecting angry and hostile feelings, is assessed with six items (items 4, 18, 44, 78, 104, and 117), all endorsed in the True direction. A third content scale is labeled Uncertain Self-Image and is comprised of three items in the True direction (items 34, 115, and 154) and two items in the False direction (items 2 and 145). The last content subscale for Scale 9 is Suicidal Impulsivity and it is assessed with four items (items 54, 88, 107, and 149), all keyed in the True direction.

Expressed Concerns Scales

The expressed concerns scales of the MACI assess issues that the adolescent, from his or her perspective, finds troublesome or problematic. Generally, these scales can be very useful in beginning a course of treatment because elevations generally reveal particular concerns that the teenager is willing to acknowledge. As the elevations on these scales increase, the intensity of the problems or concerns in those particular areas will be greater. Thus, the clinician can use the Expressed Concerns scales to prioritize particular treatment issues.

Scale A

The Identity Diffusion scale measures concerns an adolescent may have about who they are and the direction life is heading. Future goals and aspirations are vague and not clearly formulated. Such issues as future career plans, education, life interests, and values are a source of confusion. High scorers often report themselves to be lost, directionless, and unclear about what they want out of life. They have no consistent framework within which to understand or think about their needs and interests.

Scale B

The Self-Devaluation scale measures a general discontent or distress that an adolescent experiences over personal adequacy, achievements, and competence. High scorers exhibit low self-esteem and they are very unhappy with their self-image. They fear taking on demands because they expect to fall short in their striving for personal goals. Thus, weakness, inadequacy, and lack of self-worth are frequently expressed.

Scale C

High scores on the Body Disapproval scale reflect prominent concerns and unhappiness with the way that the adolescent's physical maturation is occurring. Although such concerns are typical in adolescence, elevations on this scale are suggestive of those concerns about one's physical attractiveness and social appeal that are of great concern to the teenager. These adolescents may focus on the worst features of their physical appearance and when comparing themselves to other peers, they perceive themselves as deviant, unusual, or physically inadequate.

Scale D

The Sexual Discomfort scale is designed to reveal excessive confusion or discomfort that a teenager has over the sexual impulses that develop during adolescence. High scores reveal conflict over the various social roles sexuality may require and there may also be anxieties or concerns over the physical changes that occur with the onset of stronger sexual interests and secondary sex characteristics. Thoughts and feelings about sexuality are generally unwanted and a cause of constant turmoil.

Scale E

Elevations on the Peer Insecurity scale are indicative of sadness, discouragement, or anxiety over feeling rejected by peers. Although close personal relationships are desired, high scorers are likely to withdraw due to an expectation of ridicule or the failure to obtain needed acceptance. Thus, these adolescents tend to withdraw into an isolated and socially unassuming lifestyle.

Scale F

The Social Insensitivity scale is elevated in those adolescents who have a cold and indifferent attitude toward others. Thus, these teens have little regard for the welfare of others. They will take advantage of others to gain personal advantage and they have little empathy toward others. In some instances, this scale can be a useful prognostic indicator in treatment. Remembering that the Expressed Concerns scales reflect difficulties as the adolescent sees them, elevations on the Social Insensitivity scale can reveal an adolescent who has at least some insight into the fact that he or she has little sensitivity toward others. Thus, this insight, minimal as it may appear, can be capitalized upon in therapy.

Scale G

High scores on the Family Discord scale reflect conflicted and strained family relationships. These adolescents generally report their family as being tense and full of conflict. They feel unsupported by their family and cut off from their parents. The specific nature of the adolescent's role in the family disruption can be determined by looking at the personality scales, which will reveal if the teenager is overly sensitive to parental rejection, oppositional, rebellious, indifferent, or has adopted some other posture toward the family as part of a basic personality style.

Scale H

The Childhood Abuse scale is generally designed to assess shame, disgust, ruminative ideation, or some other adverse consequence to physical, emotional, or sexual abuse as a child. The scale is generally robust and is sensitive to both long-standing issues related to abuse which occurred remotely in the past, or to more acute exacerbations related to recent trauma.

Clinical Syndromes Scales

There are some problems and concerns frequently seen among adolescents in mental health settings that represent diagnostically significant symptoms. The Clinical Syndromes scales are designed to assess those difficulties which may warrant a diagnosis.

Scale AA

The Eating Dysfunctions scale measures problems related to an array of eating difficulties including bulimia, anorexia, and overeating. High scores are indicative of body image disturbances as well as intense fears or concerns over gaining weight and getting fat. Behavior problems characterized by laxative abuse and self-induced vomiting after eating are also commonly seen.

Scale BB

As its name implies, the Substance Abuse Proneness scale is designed to measure problems an adolescent has with excessive alcohol and drug use. High scorers spend large amounts of time trying to seek out situations where they can gain access to illicit substances or alcohol, and they have little or no insight into the negative effects such substances have on their functioning in relationships, at school, or at work. In some instances where there is no documented history of substance abuse, this scale may still be elevated in adolescents who have been raised in a family where substance abuse was common and who hold attitudes and beliefs which create a risk of future substance abuse.

Scale CC

The Delinquency Predisposition scale is designed to assess features that are common in conduct-disordered and delinquent youths. High scores reflect a general disregard for societal norms and the rights of others. These adolescents have little empathy for others and are quite threatening and hostile. Also, these teenagers can be quite deceptive and will lie frequently to get out of trouble. Stealing, fighting, use of weapons, and other such antisocial behavior is common.

Scale DD

High scores on the Impulsive Propensity scale reflect an adolescent who is prone to act out in an erratic and unstable manner in response to feelings. There is often a small provocation that results in quick and impulsive actions without consideration of the adverse consequences. The impulsivity is seen in many different areas, including sexual activity, risk-taking behaviors, angry outbursts, fighting, or other similar types of actions.

Scale EE

The Anxious Feelings scale is designed to measure general feelings of tension, apprehension, and nervousness. The adolescents scoring highly on this scale often describe feelings of uneasiness about the future and they have a sense of foreboding that something bad is about to happen. Others may feel tense and agitated because of feelings that they are limited or confined in their ability to freely live their life. Also evident in high scorers may be social anxiety, specific fears, or physical signs of tension and worry.

Scale FF

The characteristics of high scorers on the Depressive Affect scale are sad and despondent mood, a lack of energy, feelings of guilt, and social withdrawal. Also in keeping with the symptoms of clinical depression, adolescents with elevations describe a loss of confidence, feelings of inadequacy, disinterest in pleasurable activities, and diminished levels of vitality. Restlessness, rumination, and passive suicidal ideation may also be present.

Scale GG

The Suicidal Tendency scale is a measure of suicidal ideation and planning. Many of the items reflect passive thoughts such as feeling that others would be better off without the teenager around, general feelings of hopelessness, and a lack of purpose in one's life. However, more active planning may also be evident and the clinician should consider direct intervention, such as the involvement of family members or other collateral supports, when the scale is elevated.

Integrating the Profile

The process of MACI interpretation involves not only an analysis of single scale elevations, but also integrating various sections of the profile. For instance, each of the Expressed Concerns and Clinical Syndromes scales takes on different significance and meaning depending on the personality style of the individual adolescent. For example, an elevation on the Anxious Feelings (EE) scale generally denotes tension, worry, or anxiety over confinement or getting into legal troubles for an unruly–oppositional teenager (Scales 6A and 8A), while the same elevation on Scale EE may signify excessive social anxiety and uneasiness in an inhibited–self-demeaning (Scales 2A and 8B) adolescent.

Another factor to consider when integrating sectional components of the MACI profile is the influence of item overlap. While differential item weights and profile adjustments control to some extent the impact of item overlap, there are still common patterns that are likely to occur with some frequency. In particular, Scales A (Identity Diffusion) and 9 (Borderline Tendency) understandably share items, as do Scales 6A (Unruly), F (Social Insensitivity), and CC (Delinquent Predisposition). Common items are also found on Scales 2A (Inhibited) and E (Peer Insecurity), as they are on Scales 2B (Doleful) and FF (Depressive Affect). Thus, some Expressed Concerns and Clinical Syndromes scales may reflect extensions of underlying personality characteristics and difficulties, and various combinations across the various profile sections are to be expected.

There are no simple rules or guidelines to follow in a mechanistic fashion that will facilitate MACI profile integration. The best tools that the clinician has to approach integrative interpretation are sound clinical experience, an understanding of the underlying theory and diagnostic criteria upon which the MACI is based, a clear understanding of the psychometric properties of the test, and a good working knowledge of the adolescent being evaluated. While skill is gained by utilizing the MACI frequently in a given setting, experience in other varied types of applications and settings can also be invaluable.

Interpretation Challenges: The "Poor-Fit" Profile

In a majority of the cases, clinicians will find that the MACI provides an accurate and useful assessment of the adolescent's personality and psychopathology. However, given that the test is a self-report instrument, it is prone to some of the problems that such instruments have. The impact of response sets, lack of insight on the part of the adolescent, defensiveness, biased self-reports, and other such factors undoubtedly have an adverse influence on psychological test results. While adjustments are made in the MACI profile to control for such influences, in some cases the clinician will find a MACI profile that appears valid based on a review of the Modifier Indices, but which does not seem to fit with what is known about the teenager's history and clinical presentation.

In these instances, it is tempting to discard the MACI results as inaccurate and useless. However, with careful consideration of the results within the context of the assessment setting, much useful information can usually be obtained from these seemingly inaccurate profiles and reports. A good place to begin an analysis of these profiles is by characterizing the nature of the error that is believed to have occurred. Perhaps a scale is not elevated when the history suggests a problem in that particular area. For example, Scales D (Sexual Discomfort) and H (Childhood Abuse) are not elevated when the history reveals that the teenager was sexually abused. Whenever any of the Expressed Concerns scales are expected to be elevated, but they are not, this generally reflects the adolescent's unwillingness or inability to recognize the particular area of difficulty as a concern. Such information can be useful in planning treatment. This same guideline can be utilized for other unexpected results on individual MACI scales.

Another step in analyzing inaccurate profiles is to recognize that personality style scale patterns that do not describe the adolescent may, in fact, reflect how the adolescent wants to be seen by others. For example, in severely conduct-disordered adolescents who are in correctional settings or undergoing evaluations for legal proceedings, it is common to find elevations on Scales 3 (Submissive) and 7 (Conforming) because such adolescents want to be perceived as cooperative and conforming to those individuals who are in a position to evaluate their performance and who can influence how they are treated within the legal system.

In other instances, some adolescents may report themselves as manifesting certain personality characteristics, clinical symptoms, and other concerns in response to long-term difficulties. Thus, chronic schizophrenic and severely disabled adolescents may report excessive submissive or self-demeaning traits because of the perception these teenagers have of themselves as excessively reliant on others or the system and as generally inadequate in being able to function more independently.

A basic guideline to follow is to rationally analyze the problematic MACI profile when it happens to arise. It is helpful to ask the question: "Why did *this* adolescent produce *this* profile under *these* circumstances?" Though the MACI will not be accurate 100% of the time, some useful information can generally be obtained from those profiles which appear to be either slightly or totally inaccurate.

CASE EXAMPLES

The following two cases were selected for presentation based on their ability to illustrate clinically useful interpretive strategies. Case illustrations which demonstrated differing levels of severity in various problem areas were needed. Likewise, cases were selected based on similarities in the profiles (e.g., similar high-point elevations) which would allow for different interpretations given to the same scale patterns, based on other secondary elevations in the profile. The purpose of these case selection procedures was to be able not only to present the cases individually, but also to make a comparative analysis, thus highlighting some of the interpretive strategies discussed earlier. Table 18.3 contains data on the MACI profiles for the two adolescents who will be discussed.

Case 1: Janet

History and Background

Janet was a 17-year-old, white female who was evaluated in an inpatient setting following an admission for suicidal ideation she had expressed to her parents. She had always been a very lonely and socially isolated child who had never fit in well with friends and she had func-

TABLE 18.3. MACI Profiles for Case Example Adolescents

		BR Scores	
Scale		Janet	Martin
Modifier indices			
VV.	Reliability	0	0
X.	Disclosure	97^b	70
Y.	Desirability	03	20
Z.	Debasement	75^a	77^a
Personality patterns			
1.	Introversive	94^b	103^c
2A.	Inhibited	73	101^c
2B.	Doleful	65	77^a
3.	Submissive	18	61
4.	Dramatizing	01	16
5.	Egotistic	08	12
6A.	Unruly	58	41
6B.	Forceful	85^b	28
7.	Conforming	01	45
8A.	Oppositional	86^b	71
8B.	Self-Demeaning	72	102^c
9.	Borderline Tendency	79^a	63
Expressed concerns			
A.	Identity Diffusion	88^b	91^b
B.	Self-Devaluation	87^b	98^b
C.	Body Disapproval	108^c	69
D.	Sexual Discomfort	54	49
E.	Peer Insecurity	88^b	95^b
F.	Social Insensitivity	73	13
G.	Family Discord	85^b	30
H.	Childhood Abuse	98^b	10
Clinical syndromes			
AA.	Eating Dysfunctions	84^a	33
BB.	Substance Abuse Proneness	63	21
CC.	Delinquent Predisposition	44	34
DD.	Impulsive Propensity	85^b	51
EE.	Anxious Feelings	47	49
FF.	Depressive Affect	104^c	89^b
GG.	Suicidal Tendency	97^b	53

^{a} = BR≥75; ^{b} = BR≥85; ^{c} = BR≥100.

tioned marginally in an academic setting. She had always "hated" school and was occasionally truant because she was frequently teased by peers due to her unusual appearance. She was very tall and uncoordinated, had poor personal hygiene, and made poor eye contact.

Janet complained that her home life was very unhappy due to a number of factors. Her mother was extremely overprotective and her father, though usually mild-mannered, sometimes exploded into angry outbursts that Janet perceived as emotionally abusive. On her mental status examination, Janet was very negative and hostile. She had recently stopped eating to "punish" herself, which she often did to retaliate against her parents' overinvolvement in her life. Janet ruminated excessively about a lengthy history of being sexually molested by a family friend, something she had not told her parents until recently, and she experienced impaired sleep and depressed mood, along with vague passive suicidal ideation. There was no history of prior hospitalizations, suicide attempts, substance abuse, or psychotic symptomatology.

Profile Results

Overall, the MACI results in Table 18.3 revealed a moderate to high level of psychopathology across a number of areas. The profile was valid, with a high level of openness and frankness about her problems and a slight tendency toward focusing upon the more negative aspects of herself. Janet's basic personality style was marked by an introverted, socially withdrawn, and isolated exterior with intense hostility, conflict, and negative emotions harboring underneath. She was conflicted in her relationships and intense rage and anger characterized her feelings toward important people. The elevated borderline tendency score (Scale 9) revealed a prominent level of disturbance and disruption in her life.

Consistent with her clinical picture was the presence of numerous expressed concerns in a variety of areas, including significant body image disturbances, rumination over her sexual abuse, family conflict, identity diffusion, feelings of inadequacy, and fear of peer rejection. These all were consistent with her history and, together with her high disclosure level, suggest a willingness on Janet's part to address these concerns in treatment. In fact, she became quite invested in the treatment program, to the point that she did not want to return home during a major portion of her inpatient stay.

Also, the clinical syndrome scales revealed a pattern that was consistent with extreme depression, suicidal preoccupation, and eating problems. Clinically, her diagnosis was Dysthymia on Axis I and Schizotypal Personality Disorder on Axis II. Surprisingly, there was an elevation on the Impulsive Propensity scale (DD) which was not consistent with her history. When explored further, Janet revealed that she viewed her anger and hostility as so overwhelming that at times she was unable to adequately cope with the negativistic and passive–aggressive defenses she had frequently utilized. Thus, she saw herself as being guided by her emotions and unable to think through problems and stresses.

Treatment and Outcome

Given the large degree of psychopathology, the major goals for Janet were stabilization, a return to her previous functional level, and engagement in an outpatient treatment program. Despite the family's objection at first, she was started on a course of antidepressant medication, after they ultimately gave consent, which met with some success. Family therapy was directed at enabling the parents to be less intrusive and to permit Janet more flexibility and autonomy in her personal decisions, which defused some of her hostility and oppositionality. She was eager to enter a day treatment program, partially to keep from returning to her school. However, her family entered into a lengthy outpatient program of therapy. At 2-month follow-up, there were some slight improvements in Janet's school performance and with the family's overall level of satisfaction with their interactions together.

Case 2: Martin

History and Background

Martin was a 15-year-old, white male who was admitted to an inpatient adolescent unit for intense and debilitating depression. He had refused to go to school, was sleeping very poorly, and had a passive wish to be dead, though he denied any suicidal plans or intent.

He was extremely unmotivated to do any work and his family relationships were very strained. His mother was supportive and caring, but she could not protect Martin or the family from the hostile, belittling, and rejecting emotional abuse of his alcoholic father.

Martin had no history of legal problems, prior psychiatric history, or substance abuse. His school performance was poor, as his grades were very low due to the large amount of school he had missed. Peer relationships were also impaired in that Martin would stay at home and socialize very little with others.

Profile Results

The MACI profile was valid, though characterized by a somewhat self-debasing response style. The personality scales revealed a very introverted and inhibited youth who was socially isolated, uncertain of himself, and harbored long-standing feelings of insecurity, inadequacy, and self-loathing. The elevations on Scales A (Identity Diffusion), B (Self-Devaluation), and E (Peer Insecurity) were all consistent with his presentation. Likewise, the clinical scale elevation on Scale FF (Depressive Affect) was consistent with the diagnosis of Major Depression that Martin had on Axis I. Interestingly, it is important to note some scale elevations that were expected, but not present. For instance, Scale G (Family Discord), and to a lesser extent Scale H (Childhood Abuse), were not elevated, despite the history of marked family disruption and emotional abuse. During the initial evaluation and subsequent treatment, Martin was unwilling to talk about his family problems, and his father in particular. In fact, he had attempted emotionally to cut his father out of his life. Thus, Martin's unwillingness to consider family relationships and his refusal to view the abuse he experienced as problematic were evidence of his extreme denial in those particular areas.

Treatment and Outcome

Martin responded well to a course of antidepressant medication and individual supportive therapy. However, it took him several weeks of hospitalization before he began to participate socially in group and milieu therapy. Once he was more socially involved, Martin found it difficult to leave the hospital and the prospect of returning home intensified his depression. Upon discharge he was less depressed, but required intensive structured therapy in a day treatment setting. The family problems could not be adequately addressed at that time due to Martin's resistance, and his father's refusal, to deal with family conflict.

Comparative Case Analysis

The similarities between the cases of Janet and Martin were quite significant. Both suffered intense depression, severe family discord, and poor adjustment in both peer relationships and academic performance. The MACI profiles were also similar in that both Janet and Martin exhibited schizoid/introversive personality features as their prominent style and each of them harbored deep concerns as to their identity, personal adequacy, and security in peer relationships. Also, both MACI profiles were consistent with a depressive disorder diagnosis.

However, the variations among the two MACI profiles also revealed meaningful differences between these two adolescents and how they experienced their depression within the context of their basic personality style. Despite both profiles having Scale 1 (Introversive) as the highest personality scale, the other secondary elevations reveal differences in the meaning of those elevations. With Janet, her social isolation and indifference masked deep hostility and resentment toward her parents (see elevations on Scales 6B and 8A) which she would abruptly display in angry tirades. With Martin, his introverted and socially isolated style served to protect him from expected rejection and criticism (see elevations on Scales 2A and 8B).

Another meaningful difference was in the way each of these teenagers managed family discord and the abusive experiences they had encountered. With Janet, she was able to acknowledge her concerns (Scales G and H were elevated), while Martin could not overtly deal with his family disruption and the emotional abuse to which he was subjected (Scales G and H were low). In treatment, therefore, Janet was more successful in beginning a useful course of family therapy, while Martin was not able to adequately address family concerns in treatment.

Finally, the clinical scales revealed meaningful differences in the nature of the depression experienced by these two adolescents. Janet's anorexic tendencies, suicidal preoccupation, and angry agitation were reflected in the elevations on Scales AA (Eating Dysfunctions), DD (Impulsive Propensity), and GG (Suicidal Tendency). On the other hand, Martin experienced none of these difficulties, but rather was suffering only intense depressed mood, low energy, and withdrawal, which were characterized by the sole elevation on Scale FF (Depressed Affect).

CONCLUSION

The purpose of this chapter was to provide an overview of the composition and clinical uses of the MACI. Also, strategies for interpretation were discussed and case examples were utilized to illustrate some of these issues. One of the main points that I made involves the interpretation of MACI scales and profiles that do not appear at first glance to fit the adolescent's history or clinical presentation. I suggest that by being familiar with the MACI's composition and psychometric properties, gaining sufficient experience in the use of the test, having a good working knowledge of personality theory and clinical diagnosis, and understanding the patient's background and history, the MACI will prove to be useful not only in the apparently "well fitting" cases, but also in those instances where the test results are at odds with the clinical picture.

REFERENCES

American Psychiatric Association. (1994). *Diagnostic and statistical manual of mental disorders* (4th ed.). Washington, DC: Author.

Archer, R. P., & Ball, J. D. (1988). Issues in the assessment of adolescent psychopathology. In R. L. Greene (Ed.), *The MMPI: Use with specific populations* (pp. 259–277). Philadelphia: Grune & Stratton.

Bagby, R. M., Gillis, J. R., & Rogers, R. (1991). Effectiveness of the Millon Clinical Multiaxial Inventory validity index in the detection of random responding. *Psychological Assessment, 3,* 285–287.

Butcher, J. N., Williams, C. L., Graham, J. R., Archer, R. P., Tellegen, A., Ben-Porath, Y. S., & Kaemmer, B. (1992). *MMPI: A manual for administration, scoring, and interpretation.* Minneapolis: University of Minnesota Press.

Coleman, J. C. (1992). The nature of adolescence. In J. C. Coleman & C. Warren-Adamson (Eds.), *Youth policy in the 1990s: The way forward* (pp. 8–27). London: Routledge.

Dyer, F. J. (1985). Millon Adolescent Personality Inventory. In D. J. Keyser & R. C. Sweetland (Eds.), *Test critiques* (Vol. IV, pp. 425–433). Kansas City, MO: Test Corporation of America.

Millon, T. (1969). *Modern psychopathology: A biosocial approach*. Philadelphia: Saunders.

Millon, T. (1981). *Disorders of personality: DSM-III: Axis II*. New York: Wiley.

Millon, T. (1990). *Toward a new personology: An evolutionary model*. New York: Wiley.

Millon, T. (1993). *Millon Adolescent Clinical Inventory manual*. Minneapolis: National Computer Systems.

Millon, T. (1995). *Factor analytically derived content scales for the MACI*. Unpublished raw data.

Millon, T., Green, C. J., & Meagher, R. B. (1982). *Millon Adolescent Personality Inventory manual*. Minneapolis: National Computer Systems.

Petersen, A. C. (1988). Adolescent development. *Annual Review of Psychology, 39*, 583–607.

19

The MBHI: Composition and Clinical Applications

GEORGE S. EVERLY, JR.
EILEEN C. NEWMAN

Recent trends in the delivery of health care services have rekindled interest in the psychological assessment of medical patients. The Millon Behavioral Health Inventory (MBHI; Millon, Green, & Meagher, 1982a) is a standardized, objective psychological assessment tool that offers significant utility in the assessment of medical patients and as such may be a significant addition to the assessment technologies of the primary care physician as well as the consultation/liaison psychiatrist and psychologist.

BACKGROUND

Now more than ever, the health care system is being challenged to provide efficient, cost-effective patient care. This challenge has caused organized health care to focus introspectively as never before. Questions pertaining to who uses the health care system, how frequently, and why, are all questions being posed not only by managed care entities, but by health care providers, as well. The answers to these and related queries are expected to facilitate the quest for efficient and cost-effective patient care. While the arduous task of scrutinizing the health care delivery system has just begun, one phenomenon in particular shows promise as a point of intervention in the quest to increase the efficiency and cost effectiveness of health care delivery: patterns of frequent medical care utilization. Frequent utilizers of medical services may be categorized into four somewhat overlapping categories:

1. Patients who experience recurrent or chronic objectively diagnosed physical illnesses.
2. Patients who amplify or exaggerate the severity or disabling aspects of their physical illness.
3. Patients who report the symptoms of a physical disease in the absence of objective medical evidence.
4. Patients who are medically noncompliant.

While there is reason to be concerned with all four categories of frequent users of medical services, the latter three have proven somewhat more enigmatic to the medical profession.

Consider the following. Medical patients who are psychologically disordered or dysfunctional (e.g., those with a somatization disorder or personality disorder) are likely to utilize primary medical care twice as frequently and are likely to incur 6 to 14 times the medical costs (Smith, Monson, & Ray, 1986; Borus, Olendzki, Kessler, Burns, Brandt, Broverman, & Henderson, 1985) as those who are not. Yet it is not only primary care patients with diagnosable mental disorders who are high utilizers of medical services. Cummings and colleagues have found that up to 60% of all visits to physicians' offices failed to result in a confirmed biological diagnosis (Cummings, 1985; Follette & Cummings, 1967; Cummings & Follette, 1968). Similarly, Barsky and colleagues (Barsky & Klerman, 1983; Barsky, Wyshak, & Klerman, 1986) estimated that 50% of the cost of ambulatory health care was accounted for by the so-called "worried well." According to Costa and McCrae (1980, 1985), the tendencies to overreport physical complaints and to then overutilize medical care for those complaints are highly correlated with a neurotic personality style. Studies conducted at both primary care and specialty medical clinics in the United States and England found that frequent utilizers of medical services, who were also considered difficult or frustrating to help, tended to exhibit unexplained somatic complaints and tended to suffer from some form of psychosocial discord (Sharpe et al., 1994; Lin et al., 1991). The prevalence of difficult patients among high utilizers ranged from 20% to 37%. Based upon a lengthy review of studies, Saravay and Lavin (1994) concluded that the provision of medical care becomes more complex and more costly when provided to patients for whom physical disorders are accompanied by psychological discord or dysfunction.

After reviewing key studies involving medical patients who were both high utilizers of services and frustrating to physicians, Mayou and Sharpe (1995) concluded that one key element for improving frequent overutilization problems, a condition that leaves patients feeling uncared for and physicians feeling frustrated and ineffective, dissatisfied, is gaining a better understanding of each patient and their physical disease within the broader psychosocial context, thus rapidly identifying both the patient's psychological and physical needs. Achievement of this goal involves the effective assessment of the "person," that is, the entire psychosocial–personologic–medical complex as it relates to each individual and unique patient. This form of assessment goes beyond mere assessment of psychopathology, as is often the practice of many consultation/liaison specialists. Hahn, Thompson, Wills, Stern, and Budner (1994) argue in support of a similar conclusion. They noted that there is a need to understand the complete patient, especially the personality, if one expects to understand difficult doctor–patient relationships and people with somatization disorders.

Psychological testing can be a rapid and effective aid in the formulation of the psychological aspects of the medical patient. However, such psychological testing must go beyond the screening of psychopathology to provide an elucidation of the aforementioned psychosocial–personologic–medical complex. As noted by Pallak, Cummings, Dorken, and Henke (1985), "Medical and emotional problems do not exist in clinical isolation but rather [they] interact to complicate treatment and drive medical utilization upward" (p. 7).

Unfortunately, in this age of "managed" health care, psychological testing appears to have fallen from favor. Such testing is often viewed as redundant, time consuming, and expensive. In a managed care setting, any of those three characteristics might be reason for exclusion from the standard diagnostic and treatment protocol, but the presence of all three, if correct, could be damning indeed. On the other hand, if any technology, including psychological testing, could facilitate the diagnostic and treatment process in a significant yet logistically reasonable manner, it would have great value, *especially* in a managed health care setting. Any technology that could do the following reliably would be an extremely valuable addition to any "managed" clinical protocol: (1) identify the manner in which a given medical patient is likely to react to, or cope with, a physical disease or symptoms, including the propensity to utilize or overutilize medical services; (2) predict patterns of or barriers to medical compliance; (3) objectively document the patient's status, or change, regarding important psychosocial factors believed to moderate physical illness; (4) offer general prognostic insight from a psychosocial perspective; and finally, (5) assist in the demonstration or comparison of the clinical efficacy of selected therapeutic interventions. Interestingly enough, appropriate psychological testing can yield valuable data so as to potentially achieve not one, but all of these five desired outcomes. Certainly, for a psychiatric population, similar outcome would be desirable, but for a medical population such outcome could lead to improved clinical efficiency, especially if instituted at the primary care level. As O'Conner and Eggert (1994) note, therefore:

> There are compelling reasons for the clinical use of standardized psychosocial assessments. Such assessment documents a client's status . . . providing a basis for systematic treatment selection and making possible the reliable documentation of change. . . . Indeed, the use of such measures is requisite for responding to the demands . . . for controlled studies that demonstrate exactly what works . . . (p. 31)

The Millon Behavioral Health Inventory (MBHI) is one standardized psychological assessment tool that may be used to shed valuable light upon the complex psychosocial–personologic–medical interface, thus going far toward achieving the recommendation of Mayou and Sharpe (1995) that each patient and their physical disease be understood within the broader psychosocial and personologic context (Hahn et al., 1994).

OVERVIEW OF THE MBHI
Introduction

The MBHI is a brief (150 items), self-report inventory designed to assess the personologic and psychological coping factors related to the physical health care of adult medical patients and behavioral medicine patients. The MBHI serves to facilitate the formulation of a comprehensive treatment plan for each patient.

The MBHI evolved from a comprehensive clinical theory of personality developed by Theodore Millon (Millon, 1969, 1981). There are eight basic personality-based coping styles according to Millon. Each of these eight styles is represented on the MBHI and is described in detail in a later section of this chapter. In addition, the MBHI contains six Psychogenic Attitude scales which reflect psychosocial stressors found in the research literature to be significant precipitators or exacerbators of physical illness. The three Psychosomatic Correlates scales gauge the extent to which the patient's responses are similar to comparably diagnosed patients whose illnesses have been judged primarily psychosomatic or complicated by emotional or social factors. The three Prognostic Indices scales seek to identify future treatment problems or difficulties that may arise in the course of the patient's illness.

The MBHI items were selected on the basis of data comparing groups of general medical populations, rather than normal or psychiatric comparison groups, to optimize the discrimination efficiency of the scales. Because it is normed on medical patients, the MBHI can be used in managed care settings, providing useful information for treatment planning. It can be useful in the evaluation and screening of individuals in specialty clinics or specialty programs (e.g., pain, stress, headache) and in workers' compensation evaluations to help assess stress-related claims and to develop rehabilitation programs for claims related to physical injuries. Finally, in medical settings, physically ill, injured, and surgical patients can be evaluated and screened to identify possible psychosomatic complications or to help predict a person's response to illness or treatment (i.e., Psychogenic Attitude and Psychosomatic Correlates scales).

Administration

The MBHI consists of 150 true/false self-report items. It requires an eighth grade reading level and should be administered to adults 18 years of age and older. Administration time is about 20 minutes. Formats for administration include paper and pencil, audiocassette, or online computer administration.

Norms

The norms for the MBHI are based upon medical and nonmedical samples of adults aged 18 years and older. The norm group consisted of 343 males and 410 females drawn from diverse medical and nonmedical settings. The ethnic distribution for the MBHI consisted of 82% white, 13% black, 3% Hispanic, 1% Asian, and 1% Other. Norming the MBHI on medical patients, as opposed to psychiatric patients, creates a unique advantage in the use of the MBHI.

Base Rate Scores

The MBHI utilizes base rate (BR) scores rather than traditional standard scores. Standard scores assume a "normal" distribution which may not be truly reflective of the population at hand. The characterological coping styles of medical patients are clearly not normally distributed. Therefore, the MBHI transforms raw scores into BR scores. BR scores are scale score transformations based upon estimated coping style prevalence data integrated with the concept of utilizing ordinal cutting lines which maximize correct classifications. Such transformations maximize the valid positive to false positive ratios obtained by the MBHI. Psychometrically, this concept is far superior, and far more practical for the clinical utility of the MBHI, than is using traditional standardized scores.

Reliability

The reliability estimates for the MBHI scales are provided in Table 19.1 below. Table 19.1 summarizes test–retest reliability estimates as well as the Kuder–Richardson Formula 20 (K-R 20) estimates for internal consistency. Test–retest reliability is a measure of the temporal stability of the scales. K-R 20 estimates are reflective of the internal consistency of the scales.

The test–retest coefficients for the Coping scales ranged from .77 to .88. The coefficients for the Psychogenic Attitude scales ranged from .78 to .90, while the coefficients for the Psychosomatic correlates ranged from .79 to .83. Finally, the Prognostic Index scales ranged from .59 to .82.

The median K-R 20 coefficients for all scales was .83, ranging from .66 to .90.

Validation

Following the recommendations of Loevinger (1957) and Jackson (1970), the MBHI went through three stages of validation. The theoretical–substantive stage involved creating a

TABLE 19.1. Estimates of Reliability for MBHI Scales

MBHI domain	Scale	Test–retest	KR 20
Coping Style	1. Introversive	.79	.72
	2. Inhibited	.84	.84
	3. Cooperative	.81	.68
	4. Sociable	.83	.82
	5. Confident	.86	.66
	6. Forceful	.77	.72
	7. Respectful	.78	.74
	8. Sensitive	.88	.86
Psychogenic Attitude	A. Chronic Tension	.90	.77
	B. Recent Stress	.87	.74
	C. Premorbid Pessimism	.85	.90
	D. Future Despair	.78	.86
	E. Social Alienation	.85	.84
	F. Somatic Anxiety	.79	.86
Psychosomatic Correlate	MM. Allergic Inclination	.83	.81
	NN. Gastrointestinal Susceptibility	.81	.83
	OO. Cardiovascular Tendency	.79	.85
Prognostic Index	PP. Pain Treatment Responsivity	.82	.86
	QQ. Life Threat Reactivity	.76	.83
	RR. Emotional Vulnerability	.59	.82

Note. Mean time elapsed between test and retest was 4.5 months. Used with permission of National Computer Systems, Inc.

theory-derived (Millon, 1969) pool of test items. Over 1,000 test items were originally generated. The items were initially reduced largely on the basis of theoretical homogeneity as determined by the convergence of the opinions of 10 health professionals.

The internal–structural validation stage was the next stage to follow in the overall validation process. This stage consisted of administering the item pool to over 2,500 individuals in a variety of settings. Item–scale homogeneities were then calculated, further reducing the item pool. The final stage in the validation process was the external–criterion stage. In this stage, items were given to specific clinical groups and were then compared with other comparison groups. The retained items were those which demonstrated the greatest discriminating validity. Finally, the psychological scales were correlated against other existing psychological scales so as to yield convergent and divergent validity indices (see Chapter IV of the MBHI manual). See Tables 19.2 and 19.3 below.

THE SCALES OF THE MBHI

Previous sections of the chapter have provided a brief overview of the nature and development of the MBHI; let us now take a closer look at the scales which constitute the MBHI.

The value of the MBHI resides not only in the statistical psychometric properties of its scales, but also in the qualitative *content* of the scales. This is the essence of the MBHI, and that which determines clinical suitability.

TABLE 19.2. Selected External Validation Criteria for the MBHI Coping Scales

MBHI scale	Scale name	Criterion instrument and scale	α
Scale 1	Introversive Style	MMPI Social Introversion	.55
		CPI Good Impression	−.59
Scale 2	Inhibited Style	MMPI Social Introversion	.54
		CPI Sociability	−.56
Scale 3	Cooperative Style	CPI Tolerance	.32
		JAS Type A Standard Style	−.55
Scale 4	Sociable Style	CPI Sociability	.64
		MMPI Social Introversion	−.49
Scale 5	Confident Style	CPI Sociability	.50
		MMPI Depression	−.52
Scale 6	Forceful Style	JAS Type A Standard Style	.53
		CPI Tolerance	−.42
Scale 7	Respectful Style	CPI Responsibility	.48
		CPI Flexibility	−.50
Scale 8	Sensitive Style	MMPI Hypochondriasis	.49
		CPI Tolerance	−.61

Note. MMPI, Minnesota Multiphasic Personality Inventory; CPI, California Personality Inventory; JAS, Jenkins Activity Survey.

Basic Coping Styles (Scales 1–8)

The source of the following descriptions of each of these scales is the MBHI manual (Millon et al., 1982). Rooted in Millon's biosocial learning theory of personality and empirically honed, Scales 1 through 8 are referred to as the Basic Coping scales. These scales provide the physician or consulting psychologist with important clinical information through an examination of the patient's characteristic style of coping with physical illness. More specifically, these scales provide personologic insight into (1) the manner in which the patient is likely to react or cope with a physical disorder; (2) the existence of significant barriers to medical compliance; and (3) personologic propensities to be a frequent utilizer of medical services.

TABLE 19.3. Selected External Validation Criteria for the MBHI Psychogenic Attitude Scales

MBHI scale	Scale name	Criterion instrument and scale	α
Scale A	Chronic Tension	JAS Type A Standard Score	.59
		CPI Tolerance	−.46
Scale B	Recent Stress	LES Subjective Change	.58
		CPI Well-being	−.47
Scale C	Premorbid Pessimism	MMPI Depression	.57
		CPI Well-being	−.60
Scale D	Future Despair	MMPI Depression	.53
		CPI Well-being	−.52
Scale E	Social Alienation	MMPI Social Introversion	.51
		CPI Sociability	−.51
Scale F	Somatic Anxiety	MMPI Hypochondriasis	.60
		CPI Well-being	−.51

Note. JAS, Jenkins Activity Survey; CPI, California Personality Inventory; LES, Life Experiences Survey; MMPI, Minnesota Multiphasic Personality Inventory.

Scale 1: The Introversive Style

Patients who score high on this scale tend to appear emotionally flat and colorless. They typically lack energy, are vague concerning their physical symptoms, and may take a rather passive approach to their health care. Treating professionals will need to provide such patients clear directions. One must pin them down when obtaining clinical information and not expect such patients to take the initiative in following a treatment plan. Simple concrete steps in a structured treatment plan will be most helpful.

Scale 2: The Inhibited Style

Patients scoring high on this scale tend to be hesitant, shy, and ill at ease with others. They tend to be highly anxious patients. As they tend to have a history of being criticized or ridiculed they are easily hurt and are often somewhat hypervigilant, fearing others may take advantage of them. Clinicians should take extra care to establish rapport with inhibited individuals. Concerned about what doctors may do to them, they may withhold information about their problems but such patients are also eager to gain the understanding and attention of the health caregiver. If the clinician adopts a sympathetic attitude, chances are good that inhibited patients will cooperate with the treatment plan.

Scale 3: The Cooperative Style

Patients scoring high on this scale tend to attach themselves to caregivers in a dependent manner. Consequently, they may resist when referred to new and different doctors or clinics. Cooperative individuals may deny the existence of real problems and fail to take the initiative in seeking treatment. Thus, health care personnel may have to probe and ask explicit questions. Finally, when clinicians give advice, they should keep in mind such patients will expect to be told exactly what to do, deriving a sense of security from such directions. Providing cooperative patients with too many therapeutic options may actually prove anxiogenic. Cooperative patients tend to look to their doctors for directive care and recommendations.

Scale 4: The Sociable Style

Patients scoring high on this scale tend to be outgoing, sociable, and charming. Appearance and attractiveness take precedence over solving problems. Although seemingly cooperative initially, their changeable nature may result in short-lived cooperation with the treatment plan. Also, they may not be reliable in keeping appointments and taking required medications. Such patients often challenge the provider's ability to keep a "professional distance." Some of these patients may actually appear seductive. Physical complaints tend to be more numerous than average among general medical patients. Symptoms are often vague and dramatically presented with an undue urgency.

Scale 5: The Confident Style

Patients scoring high on this scale tend to act in a confident, calm manner. Nonetheless, they are concerned about bodily ailments and are generally motivated to follow recommendations to increase well-being. Confident individuals may expect special treatment and be demanding of doctors, but if treated professionally and given thorough expectations of the treatment, they will usually follow recommendations. Some confident patients may present with a sense of entitlement. Some may even "talk down" to their health care providers. Such patients can be quite demanding, but respond well to a little "extra" attention and respect.

Scale 6: The Forceful Style

Patients scoring high on this scale will be somewhat domineering and tough-minded. They tend to be mistrustful, so the clinician must work hard to gain patient cooperation. By employing a direct, straightforward approach and by refusing to be intimidated or provoked by these patients, clinicians will increase the likelihood of compliance. Fear and doubt are seldom expressed by these patients. Rather, they react to threatening situations with frustration or anger. Forceful patients commonly challenge and "test" their doctors. They will commonly discharge a health care provider for indecisiveness as well as being too authoritarian.

Scale 7: The Respectful Style

Patients who score highly on this scale appear to be well-controlled, responsible, serious-minded, cooperative, and conforming individuals. Being sick signifies weakness and laziness, so that respectful individuals may deny symptoms and delay seeking treatment. However, they tend to be very responsible about taking medications and following professional advice. Such patients will tend to ask many questions of their providers. They expect detailed and informed responses to their queries. These patients want to feel part of the treatment team. Denial and the need for control are critical elements of their persona. Maintenance of perceived self-efficacy is an important factor in compliance. These patients do not typically cope well with change. Outpatient procedures are tolerated better than are inpatient procedures, typically.

Scale 8: The Sensitive Style

Patients who score high on this scale appear moody. They are unpredictable and often erratic in following advice. Rapport with such patients will be easier some days, harder on others. Sensitive individuals often seem displeased and complain about their physical and psychological states and treatment. They vacillate between expressing their dissatisfaction and having feelings of guilt for complaining. They may be perceived as passive–aggressive and demanding. They tend not to be forgiving of mistakes, tending to be adept at second-guessing the opinions of providers. They also tend to complain frequently. They require inordinate amounts of attention.

Psychogenic Attitude Scales

Scales A through F, collectively entitled *psychogenic attitudes*, provide the physician or consulting psychologist with information regarding important psychosocial factors believed to play a role in the course of physical illness.

Scale A: Chronic Tension

Patients who score high on this scale are prone to suffer various psychosomatic and physical illnesses as a result of a self-imposed, pressured lifestyle. Cardiovascular and digestive system problems are more commonly seen. Recommendations would include a reduction in the rapid pace such patients maintain as well as education in the management of stress and tension.

Scale B: Recent Stress

Patients who score high on this scale have experienced recent life changes resulting in increased susceptibility to illness and poor physical and psychological health. During this critical time, contact with the physician should be more frequent to prevent more serious illness.

Scale C: Premorbid Pessimism

Patients who score high on this scale tend to view the world in a negative manner. This "negativity" filters their perceptions, resulting in interpretations of their situation as more serious and intense so that they report more discomfort, having a tendency to exaggerate their difficulties. Health care providers will need to make careful, objective assessments of patient complaints.

Scale D: Future Despair

Unlike Scale C, this scale addressees the patient's response to current difficulties rather than a lifelong tendency to be pessimistic. Patients who score high on this scale view medical procedures as very distressing and even life-threatening. Such a bleak outlook makes for a poor prognosis. Such patients require a considerably high level of support and encouragement to improve treatment response.

Scale E: Social Alienation

Patients who score high on this scale lack the familiar support and friendship necessary for coping with stressful experiences. They will be prone to physical and psychological ailments and may not seek treatment until their illnesses are very serious. A poor adjustment to hospitalization is common. The health care team will want to provide ample opportunities for such patients to develop rapport and confidence in their health care providers.

Scale F: Somatic Anxiety

Somatic anxiety means having fear concerning or being preoccupied with one's physical state. Patients who score high on this scale tend to be hypochondriacal. Their fear concerning bodily functions is abnormal and may result in increased susceptibility to illness. These patients tend to overreact to surgery and hospitalization. Professionals should be sensitive to such patients' irrational fears and help reduce their anxiety by providing support, reassurance, and informative decisions.

Psychosomatic Correlates Scales

Scales MM through OO, collectively titled the Psychosomatic Correlates, provide the physician or consulting psychologist with information regarding the degree to which the patient's illness is similar to illnesses judged to be primarily psychosomatic or complicated by emotional or social factors.

Scale MM: Allergic Inclination

Patients who have been previously diagnosed with allergic disorders and score high on this scale experience emotional factors as significant precipitants of their disease.

Scale NN: Gastrointestinal Susceptibility

Patients previously diagnosed with gastrointestinal (GI) disorders who score high on this scale typically react to stress with an increase in the number of GI symptoms and in the severity of the symptoms.

Scale OO: Cardiovascular Tendency

Patients previously diagnosed with cardiovascular disorders who score high on this scale are prone to experience an increase in cardiovascular symptoms under conditions of stress and tension.

Prognostic Indicators Scales

Scales PP through RR, collectively titled the Prognostic Indicators, provide the physician or consulting psychologist with information regarding any further treatment problems or potential difficulties in treating the patient.

Scale PP: Pain Treatment Responsivity

Patients who score high on this scale will likely experience less than satisfactory results after treatment in a traditional medical treatment program. Pain-related behaviors such as complaining about symptoms, depression, and social withdrawal, may be maintained by psychological factors in these patients.

Scale QQ: Life Threat Reactivity

Patients who score high on this scale and who are suffering chronic or potentially life-threatening illness tend to do more poorly than other patients with the same condition. Psychological support is highly encouraged for these patients.

Scale RR: Emotional Vulnerability

Patients about to undergo major surgery or similar life-saving treatment who score high on this scale are more vulnerable to severe emotional reactions such as disorientation, psychotic episodes, or clinical depression than are other patients. Both preoperative and postoperative psychological support may mitigate symptoms.

THE MBHI AS AN ASSESSMENT TOOL
IN MEDICAL SETTINGS

In support of the notion that it is important to understand the psychosocial–persono-logic–medical complex in the formulation of the medical patient (Mayou & Sharpe, 1995; Hahn et al., 1994), the MBHI, as an index of this complex, has been useful in the assessment and prediction of important variables related to medical treatment.

The MBHI was used in a modified prospective design to assess risk of developing postconcussion syndrome (PCS) subsequent to a mild head injury (Middelboe, Birket-Smith, Anderson, & Friis, 1992). The authors concluded that "patients demonstrating high scores on the MBHI scales Forceful Personality Style and Sensitive Personality Style, due to their coping strategies, seem at risk of developing PCS. Correspondingly, a risk group is consti-tuted by patients with high scores on the scales Chronic Tension and Recent Stress, these being also possible predictors of poor outcome" (p. 254).

Somatization is a major contributor to the frequent utilization syndrome as well as to poor treatment outcome (Hahn et al., 1994; Sharpe et al., 1994; Smith et al., 1986). The MBHI has been utilized to successfully identify a profile of somatizing patients. The so-called anxious/moody, Sensitive/Inhibited MBHI profile (elevated Scales 8 and 2) was found in 49% of the somatizing population, but was found in only 18% of the control group (Dickson et al., 1992). Somatizing patients also scored high on the Premorbid Pessimism, Somatic Anxiety, and Pain Treatment Response scales.

Clearly, chronic pain is one of the most significant problems challenging the mod-ern health care system and is a major contributor to the frequent utilization syndrome. Psychological factors are such an important aspect of the chronic pain patient's presen-tation that Sternbach (1974) discouraged attempts to differentiate "functional" from "organic" pain. The MBHI has been found to be capable of predicting recovery of physical function in patients with low back pain such that decreases in the Introversive Style and Emotional Vulnerability scales predicted functional restoration; further, the Sensi-tive Style, Recent Stress, Emotional Vulnerability, and Gastrointestinal Susceptibility scales discriminated patients who dropped out of the functional restoration program from those who completed the program (Gatchel, Mayer, Capra, Barnett, & Diamond, 1986).

Finally, the MBHI was used in an attempt to directly assess frequent utilizers of ambu-latory health care services in direct contrast to the low utilizers of care. Frequent utilizers tended to be more sensitive and inhibited (elevated Scales 8 and 2) compared with low utilizers of care (Marron, Fromm, Snyder, & Greenberg, 1984). This finding is in concert with the somatization profile discussed earlier.

Thus, while illness behavior is a complex phenomenon, the MBHI shows great prom-ise as one assessment technology which can contribute significantly to an understanding of the patient.

THE MBHI OUTPUT

Previous sections of this chapter have introduced the MBHI as a potentially useful stan-dardized psychosomatic instrument which may have great utility in health care settings. Its psychometric development and properties have been described as well as the content of its scales. Yet these descriptions do little in having the MBHI "come to life" for the reader. Therefore we have included in this chapter a sample computer-generated MBHI interpretive report.

The MBHI is a computer-scored instrument which yields a complete interpretive report or merely a computer-scored profile summary sheet. The complete interpretive report is provided in Figure 19.1.

THE MBHI IN CLINICAL PRACTICE

Having reviewed the nature and composition of the MBHI, let us examine an actual clinical profile.

Roberta was a 21-year-old female referred for psychological assessment subsequent to a repetitive motion hand injury.

A high school graduate, Roberta was born and raised in a suburban community on the East Coast. An only child, Roberta described both her mother and father as highly critical. "Nothing I ever did was good enough . . . my parents second guessed every decision I ever made." She noted, "My father was disappointed that I wasn't a boy, he really wanted a son." At age 18, Roberta moved out of her parent's household to avoid the familial tension that was so problematic for her. She described both her parents as "argumentative."

After graduating from high school, Roberta went to work in a remanufacturing plant performing repetitive tasks on an assembly line. After 1.5 years, Roberta developed carpal tunnel syndrome in her dominant hand. Surgery was performed to correct the compression. The surgeon considered surgery a success. Nerve conduction studies proved normal postoperatively, yet Roberta continued to complain of pain, more vague than before. When her surgeon indicated that he didn't know what was wrong, she became extremely angry, threatening to sue him. Roberta received consultations from several surgeons and had been in a pain treatment program for 3 months until she was referred for psychological assessment.

Upon clinical interview, Roberta's most florid presentation was that of an angry young woman. She noted, "They hurt me and I want them to pay. . . . they will have to pay me for my pain, my scars, my lost wages, and for lying to me." She further added, "I want an apology from the company, they knew I could have been injured." Roberta had actually refused another surgery stating, "I don't want to get better until after I win my lawsuit." Roberta was suing both her employer and her surgeon. She had previously sued two other individuals for situations not related to this injury.

Roberta was given the MBHI. Roberta's MBHI profile (Figure 19.2) represents a rather classic sensitive/inhibited profile suggesting a negative, moody, vindictive, pessimistic personologic presentation. Her familial background is consistent with the factors known to engender that personologic style (Millon, 1981). Chronic pain certainly contributes to and exacerbates such a clinical picture. Roberta also scored high on the Pain Treatment Responsivity and Emotional Vulnerability scales. Previous research noted that individuals with such a profile had poor recovery prognoses. Indeed, a 3-month enrollment in a pain treatment program revealed no clinical improvement in either reported pain or in expressed depressive symptoms; in fact, some worsening was noted. While secondary gain is certainly an issue for this patient, one is impressed with the convergence between this profile and the somatization profile described earlier. The Noteworthy Responses (Figure 19.3) help the profile come to life for the reader.

MBHI
Interpretive Report
Theodore Millon, PhD
ID Number 110110110
SAMPLE MBHI
Male
Age 51

9/15/94

This report assumes that the MBHI answer form was completed by a person undergoing professional medical evaluation or treatment. It should be noted that MBHI data and analyses do not provide physical diagnoses. Rather, the instrument supplements such diagnoses by identifying and appraising the potential role of psychogenic and psychosomatic factors in medical disease. The statements printed below are derived from cumulative research data and theory. As such, they must be considered as suggestive or probabilistic references, rather than definitive judgments, and should be evaluated in that light by clinicians. The specific statements contained in the report are of a personal nature and are for confidential professional use only. They should be handled with great discretion and not be shown to patients or their relatives.

COPING STYLE

The following paragraphs pertain to those longstanding traits of the patient that have characterized most personal, social, and work relationships. In addition to summarizing these more general features of psychological functioning, this section will briefly review the manner in which the patient is likely to relate to health personnel, services, and regimens.

In most settings the patient is seen by others as being socially domineering, if not overbearing. This public posture of assertiveness, competitiveness, and self-assurance is important as an image that the patient tries to maintain. The patient seeks to avoid displaying weaknesses before others, or expressing feelings of warmth, closeness, and intimacy. Keeping a cool distance and exhibiting a tough and uncompromising veneer is, in large measure, a protection against significant insecurities within the patient. Exposing personal inadequacies and failures is intolerable, as there are fears that such imperfections and deficiencies will lead others to be derogatory and humiliating. To prevent such reactions, the patient presents a bluff exterior and often acts defensively vigilant, that is, on guard and distrustful of others, even when their intentions are benign.

Being seen by others as sick or ailing is experienced as extremely discomforting to the patient. Used to feeling strong and unassailable, the patient is likely to react to the news of a significant illness by denial, indifference, or anger. Not only do things like this not happen to the patient, but the individual will resist accepting what is seen as the vulnerable and weak role of patient. Always thinking of oneself as strong and capable, the patient will experience this role not only as humiliating, but as being exposed to the power and malice of others. If seriously ill and actively debilitated, the patient will feel especially threatened and be apt to attack or blame others for any and every problem or discomfort experienced. Sarcasm and temper tantrums are likely to typify such periods, although their frequency and intensity will diminish if the patient learns to believe that others are genuinely supportive and helpful.

Trust is a significant issue in dealing with this patient. Persons in power are viewed either as demigods or, more likely, they are viewed suspiciously as potentially malignant. To evoke the former attitude, that of eliciting respect and a willingness to be compliant with prescribed regimens, great care must be taken on the part of health care personnel to act in a straightforward, honest, and businesslike manner with the patient. Inclined to engage in power games with those in control, such as doctors and other personnel, it may be a sound strategy to bring the patient in as a collaborator in planning and carrying out the treatment program.

It is quite important to avoid being drawn into unnecessary wrangles with this patient. Furthermore, being intimidated by confrontations or, in contrast, reacting to arrogant behaviors by irritation or threat is also extremely unwise. Consistent, firm, and authoritative dealings are the only way to prevent the patient from undoing or otherwise resisting medical advice.

(continued)

FIGURE 19.1. Sample MBHI interpretive report. Copyright 1992 by Theodore Millon, PhD. All rights reserved. Published and distributed exclusively by National Computer Systems, Inc., Minneapolis, MN.

PSYCHOGENIC ATTITUDES

The scales comprising this section compare the feelings and perceptions expressed by the patient to those of a cross-section of both healthy and ill adults of the same sex. The results of these scales are summarized here, as they may be associated with an increase in the probability of psychosomatic pathogenesis, or with tendencies to aggravate the course of an established disease, or with attitudes that may impede the effectiveness of medical or surgical treatment.

The patient portrays life as moderately demanding insofar as responsibilities and the expectations of others. Although pressures may exist, they are not seen as persistent or beyond what is reasonably managed. This moderate level of stress does not preclude tension-related ailments, but it generally signifies a less than average probability of such difficulties.

Recent life events are depicted by the patient as having been unusually distressing, with a marked increase in both the number and severity of significant personal difficulties. This is seen by the patient as a major departure from a past pattern of normal life experiences. Perceptions such as these often signify an increased risk in both the onset of illness and the exacerbation of preexisting conditions. Frequent contact with the patient would appear advisable to both identify and prevent the possibility of these sequelae.

The patient perceives the events of both the past and the present in a balanced fashion. Life is depicted as one in which both good and bad things happen, that is, a mixture of happy experiences and difficulties that are largely overcome. This balanced inclination suggests that the patient is likely to respond to illness in an average or unexceptional way.

Disposed to view life positively, the patient shows typical levels of concern regarding life and the ability to manage whatever problems may arise. Reasonably confident, the patient is likely to cope with physical difficulties in a relatively benign and unexceptional manner.

The patient finds the attentions and concerns of family and friends sufficient, but not overwhelming. There is confidence that this support network will be available in times of need. This expectation of interest and encouragement is a good prognostic sign in the event that illness occurs.

An average level of concern is conveyed by the patient regarding matters of personal health and bodily functioning. Neither excessively fearful nor particularly indifferent, the patient is likely to bear the pains and handle the anxieties and discomforts of illness with a reasonable measure of equanimity.

PSYCHOSOMATIC CORRELATES

The scales comprising this section are designed for use only with patients who have previously been diagnosed by physicians as suffering one of a number of specific disease entities or syndromes, for example, hypertension, colitis, or allergy. Note that these scales do not provide data confirming such medical diagnoses, nor do they include statements which may be construed as supporting them. Rather, the primary intent of this section is to gauge the extent to which the patient is similar to comparably diagnosed patients whose illness has been judged to be substantially psychosomatic, or whose course has been judged to be complicated by emotional or social factors.

If the patient has a diagnosed allergic disorder, for example, pruritus, urticaria, dermatitis, or asthma, the probabilities are that psychosocial elements contribute minimally, if at all, as precipitants of the disease process.

If the patient has a history of chronic gastrointestinal disorder, for example, peptic ulcer, colitis, dyspepsia, or irritable colon, there appears to be no indication that psychosocial stress plays a part in its etiology or its likeliness to complicate treatment.

If the patient has been medically diagnosed as manifesting the symptoms of certain cardiovascular disorders, notably hypertension or angina pectoris, there is an indication that emotional tensions may contribute to a modest degree to the periodic exacerbation of symptoms.

PROGNOSTIC INDICES

The scales comprising this section have been empirically constructed to assist clinicians in appraising the impact of psychosocial factors which can complicate the usual prognostic course of patients who have a history of either a chronic or life-threatening illness, or who are under review for a life-sustaining surgical or medical procedure.

FIGURE 19.1. *cont.*

If there has been a medical history of a periodic or persistent pain disorder, for example, low back pain, headache, or TMJ, it is likely that the patient will have an uncomplicated and favorable response to traditional outpatient treatment of the disorder.

If the patient is suffering from a chronic and progressive life-threatening illness, for example, metastatic carcinoma, renal failure, or congestive heart disease, it is probable that it will follow an especially benign course attributable in part to the optimistic belief of being cared for and supported by others.

If faced with major surgery or a candidate for ongoing, life-dependent treatment programs, for example, open heart procedures, hemodialysis, or cancer chemotherapy, there is little likelihood that the patient will react with either serious depressive episodes or disorientation.

NOTEWORTHY RESPONSES

The following statements were answered by the patient in the direction noted in the parentheses. These items suggest specific problem areas that may deserve further inquiry on the part of the clinician.

Potential Noncompliance
Suggests a disinclination to follow medical advice.

   8. I always take the medicine a doctor tells me to even if I don't think it is working. (False)
   21. I have a lot of faith that doctors can cure any sickness. (False)
   32. No matter what, seeing a doctor can make me feel better. (False)
   73. Doctors have always been helpful to me. (False)
   87. I dislike going to doctors, and do so only after trying everything myself. (True)

Health Preoccupations
Denotes an excessive attention to physical ailments.

   16. I am in better health than most of my friends. (False)

Illness Overreaction
Signifies tendencies to magnify illness consequences.

None endorsed.

Depressive Feelings
Indicates dejection and/or dysphoric mood.

   38. I have had more than my share of troubles in the past year. (True)
   92. Even when things seem to be going well, I expect that they'll soon get worse. (True)

Psychiatric Possibility
Provides indices of a potential mental disturbance.

   143. I become very excited or upset once a week or more. (True)

CAPSULE SUMMARY

This patient seeks to dominate by presenting an aggressive and combative exterior. Such a self-concept means that the patient role is experienced as personally humiliating. Unwilling to trust others, the patient is likely to engage in power games with health care personnel. Bringing the patient in as contributor and collaborator in planning the treatment programs may be necessary to gain a measure of compliance to the therapeutic regimen.

FIGURE 19.1. *cont.*

ITEM RESPONSES

1: 2	2: 2	3: 1	4: 2	5: 1	6: 1	7: 1	8: 2	9: 2	10: 2
11: 1	12: 2	13: 2	14: 2	15: 1	16: 2	17: 2	18: 2	19: 2	20: 2
21: 2	22: 2	23: 2	24: 1	25: 1	26: 1	27: 2	28: 2	29: 2	30: 2
31: 2	32: 2	33: 2	34: 2	35: 1	36: 2	37: 1	38: 1	39: 1	40: 2
41: 1	42: 1	43: 2	44: 1	45: 1	46: 2	47: 1	48: 2	49: 1	50: 2
51: 2	52: 2	53: 1	54: 1	55: 1	56: 1	57: 1	58: 2	59: 2	60: 2
61: 2	62: 1	63: 2	64: 2	65: 2	66: 2	67: 2	68: 2	69: 1	70: 2
71: 2	72: 2	73: 2	74: 2	75: 2	76: 2	77: 2	78: 2	79: 1	80: 1
81: 1	82: 1	83: 1	84: 1	85: 1	86: 2	87: 1	88: 1	89: 2	90: 2
91: 2	92: 1	93: 2	94: 1	95: 2	96: 2	97: 2	98: 2	99: 2	100: 1
101: 2	102: 2	103: 2	104: 2	105: 2	106: 2	107: 1	108: 2	109: 1	110: 2
111: 1	112: 2	113: 2	114: 1	115: 1	116: 2	117: 2	118: 1	119: 1	120: 1
121: 1	122: 1	123: 2	124: 1	125: 2	126: 1	127: 2	128: 1	129: 2	130: 2
131: 2	132: 2	133: 2	134: 2	135: 2	136: 2	137: 1	138: 1	139: 2	140: 2
141: 1	142: 2	143: 1	144: 1	145: 2	146: 1	147: 2	148: 1	149: 1	150: 2

End of Report

MILLON BEHAVIORAL HEALTH INVENTORY
CONFIDENTIAL INFORMATION FOR PROFESSIONAL USE ONLY

CODE: - ** - *654281 +37 '//B ** - *// - ** - *// - ** - *//

Valid Report   DATE: 12/01/92

SCALES		SCORE RAW	SCORE BR	PROFILE OF BR SCORES	DIMENSIONS
	1	17	40		INTROVERSIVE
	2	10	53		INHIBITED
	3	16	23		COOPERATIVE
BASIC PERSONALITY STYLE	4	26	60		SOCIABLE
	5	24	65		CONFIDENT
	6	17	70		FORCEFUL
	7	21	22		RESPECTFUL
	8	12	51		SENSITIVE
	A	16	69		CHRONIC TENSION
	B	13	85		RECENT STRESS
PSYCHOGENIC ATTITUDES	C	11	62		PREMORBID PESSIMISM
	D	8	51		FUTURE DESPAIR
	E	7	53		SOCIAL ALIENATION
	F	11	58		SOMATIC ANXIETY
PSYCHO-SOMATIC	MM	7	35		ALLERGIC INCLINATION
	NN	6	47		GASTRO SUSCEPTIBILITY
	OO	14	65		CARDIOVAS TENDENCY
	PP	11	59		PAIN TREATMENT RESPONSE
PROGNOSTIC	QQ	9	50		LIFE-THREATENING REACT
	RR	2	45		EMOTIONAL VULNERABILITY

Profile of BR scores columns: 35, 60, 75, 85, 100

FIGURE 19.1. *cont.*

Any therapy process, to be effective for Roberta, must focus as much on her personologic style as on her chronic pain. The MBHI suggests that the chronic pain syndrome is but the most florid clinical aspect of a far more salient personologic dysfunction. Failure to focus on the personality will likely lead to frustration and treatment failure. As the MBHI correctly prognosticated "it is likely the patient will not respond favorably to traditional outpatient treatment." At the 3-month mark in treatment, such was certainly the case.

Finally, assessment for assessment's sake alone serves little purpose. Assessment should serve as a foundation for improved treatment. Pallak et al. (1995) found that Medicaid enrollees who used mental health services experienced a reduction in their annual medical costs of 9.5% to 21%, while Medicaid enrollees who did not utilize mental health services actually experienced a 15% increase in medical costs.

THE MILLON BEHAVIORAL HEALTH INVENTORY

I.D. Number: 000000795   Date: 07/18/95

Code:
82 ** - *61 +7534 ´´//CDE **F *//MMOONN ** - *//PPQQRR ** - *//

VALID REPORT

Scale	Raw	BR	Profile of BR Scores	DIMENSIONS
			35 60 75 85 100	
BASIC PERSONALITY STYLE				
1	18	50	**************	Introversive
2	28	115	**	Inhibited
3	14	5	*	Cooperative
4	9	0	*	Sociable
5	14	12	**	Confident
6	14	58	*****************	Forceful
7	21	21	****	Respectful
8	31	115	**	Sensitive
PSYCHOGENIC ATTITUDES				
A	16	56	****************	Chronic Tension
B	12	63	*********************	Recent Stress
C	27	90	**	Premorb Pessimism
D	25	88	***	Future Despair
E	20	86	**	Social Alienation
F	23	82	**	Somatic Anxiety
PSYCHOSOMATIC CORRELATES				
MM	23	97	**	Allergic Inclin
NN	17	89	***	Gastro Susceptbl
OO	25	94	*** **********	Cardio Tendency
PROGNOSTIC INDICES				
PP	23	106	**	Pain Treat Respon
QQ	26	102	**	Life-Threat React
RR	8	85	**	Emotional Vulner

FIGURE 19.2. MBHI profile for Roberta, a 21-year-old woman.

NOTEWORTHY RESPONSES

Potential Noncompliance
Suggests a disinclination to follow medical advice.

21. I have a lot of faith that doctors can cure any sickness. (False)
32. No matter what, seeing a doctor can make me feel better. (False)
59. I feel that the doctors I have seen are not interested in my problems. (True)
73. Doctors have always been helpful to me. (False)

Health Preoccupations
Denotes an excessive attention to physical ailments.

16. I am in better health than most of my friends. (False)
41. I almost never worry about my health. (False)
68. I worry a lot about my health. (True)

Illness Overreaction
Signifies tendencies to magnify illness consequences.

  7. If I were very sick, I'm sure that everything would work out well. (False)
71. If I had a very serious sickness, I think I would fall apart mentally. (True)
101. I'd rather be dead than have a very serious sickness. (True)

Depressive Feelings
Indicates dejection and/or dysphoric mood.

13. I have a feeling that things in my life just go from bad to worse. (True)
38. I have had more than my share of troubles in the past year. (True)
44. I look forward to the future with lots of hope. (False)
50. I feel pretty upset about most things in my life. (True)
63. I often think about unhappy things that have happened to me. (True)

FIGURE 19.3. Noteworthy Responses section of Roberta's MBHI profile.

While the MBHI is not the sole answer to medical overutilization, it can be a useful beginning.

SUMMARY

The new health care environments are challenging medical and psychiatric delivery systems as never before. They demand rapid, efficient, and economical service provision without any sacrifice in the quality of care. In this chapter, we have proposed that the MBHI can facilitate the provision of high quality medical services through (1) the identification of psychological coping patterns in response to physical illness, including utilization propensities; (2) the prediction of patterns of medical compliance; (3) the documentation of the patient's status on selected psychosocial variables; (4) the provision of prognostic indices provided from a psychosocial perspective; and (5) the documentation of clinical efficacy as measured in psychosocial terms.

If, indeed, medical care is best when the patient's physical illness is considered within the broader psychosocial context, the MBHI may be reconsidered from being a "luxury" to being an indispensable aspect of quality health care, for if we are truly to understand the patient, we must understand the patient's personality. The MBHI achieves that goal in a far richer manner than does a mere psychiatric screening tool.

REFERENCES

Barsky, A., & Klerman, G. (1983). Overview: Hypochondriasis, bodily complaints and somatic styles. *American Journal of Psychiatry, 140,* 273–283.

Barsky, A., Wyshak, G., & Klerman, G. (1986). Medical and psychiatric determinants of outpatient medical utilization. *Medical Care, 24,* 548–560.

Borus, J. F., Olendzki, M., Kessler, L., Burns, B., Brandt, U., Broverman, C., & Henderson, P. (1985). The "offset effect" of mental health treatment on ambulatory medical care utilization and charges. *Archives of General Psychiatry, 42,* 573–580.

Costa, P., & McCrae, R. (1980). Somatic complaints in males as a function of age and neuroticism. *Journal of Behavioral Medicine, 3,* 245–257.

Costa, P., & McCrae, R. (1985). Hypochondriasis, neuroticism and aging: When are somatic complaints unfounded? *American Psychologist, 40,* 19–28.

Cummings, N. A. (1985, May). *Saving health care dollars through psychological service.* Paper presented at a meeting cosponsored by Hon. D. Inouye, Hon. M. Baucus, and the American Psychological Association, Washington, DC.

Cummings, N., & Follette, W. (1968). Psychiatric services and medical utilization in a prepaid health setting. Part II. *Medical Care, 6,* 31–41.

Dickson, L., Hays, L., Kaplan, C., Scherl, E., Abbott, S., & Schmitt, F. (1992). Psychological profile of somatizing patients attending the integrative clinic. *International Journal of Psychiatry in Medicine, 22,* 141–153.

Follette, W. T., & Cummings, N. (1967). Psychiatric services and medical utilization in a prepaid health plan setting. *Medical Care, 5,* 25–35.

Gatchel, R., Mayer, T., Capra, P. , Barnett, J., & Diamond, P. (1986). MBHI: Its utility in predicting physical function in patients with low back pain. *Archives of Physical Medicine and Rehabilitation, 67,* 878–882.

Gough, H. G. (1970). *California Psychological Inventory.* Palo Alto: Consulting Psychologists Press.

Hahn, S., Thompson, K., Wills, T., Stern, V., & Budner, N. (1994). The difficult doctor–patient relationship: Somatization personality and psychopathology. *Journal of Clinical Epidemiology, 47,* 647–657.

Hathaway, S., & McKinley, J. (1967). *The Minnesota Multiphasic Personality Inventory Manual.* New York: Psychological Corporation.

Jackson, D. (1970). A sequential system for personality scale development. In C. Spielberger (Ed.), *Current topics in clinical and community psychology* (Vol. 2, pp. 61–92). New York: Academic Press.

Jenkins, D. C., Zyzanski, S., & Rosenman, R. (1979). *Jenkins Activity Survey Manual.* New York: Psychological Corporation.

Lin, E., Kanton, W., Von Korff, M., Bush, T. , Lipscomb, P., Russo, J., & Wagner, E. (1991). Frustrating patients. *Journal of General Internal Medicine, 6,* 241–246.

Loevinger, J. (1957). Objective tests as instruments of psychological theory. *Psychological Reports, 3,* 635–694.

Marron, J., Fromm, B., Snyder, V., & Greenberg, D. (1984). Use of psychologic testing in characterizing the frequent use of ambulatory health care services. *Journal of Family Practice, 19,* 802–806.

Mayou, R., & Sharpe, M. (1995). Patients whom doctors find difficult to help. *Psychosomatics, 36,* 323–325.

Middelboe, T., Birket-Smith, M., Anderson, H., & Friis, M. (1992). Personality traits in patients with postconcussional sequelae. *Journal of Personality Disorders, 6,* 246–255.

Millon, T. (1969). *Modern psychopathology.* Philadelphia: Saunders.

Millon, T. (1981). *Disorders of personality.* New York: Wiley.

Millon, T., Green, C., & Meagher, R. (1982a). *Millon Behavioral Health Inventory manual* (3rd ed.). Minneapolis: National Computer Systems.

Millon, T., Green, C., & Meagher, R. (Eds.). (1982b). *Handbook of clinical health psychology.* New York: Plenum.

O'Connor, F. W., & Eggert, L. L. (1994). Psychosocial assessment for treatment planning and evaluation. *Journal of Psychosocial Nursing, 32,* 31–42.

Pallak, M., Cummings, N., Dorken, H., & Henke, C. (1995). Effect of mental health treatment on medical costs. *Mind/Body Medicine, 1,* 7–12.

Sarason, I. G., Johnson, J., & Siegel, J. (1978). Assessing the impact of life change: Development of the Life Events Survey. *Journal of Consulting and Clinical Psychology, 46,* 932–941.

Saravay, S., & Lavin, M. (1994). Psychiatric comorbidity and length of stay in the general hospital. *Psychosomatics, 35,* 233–252.

Sharpe, M., Mayou, R., Seagroatt, V., Surawy, C., Warwick, H., Bulstrode, C., Dawber, R., & Lane, D. (1994). Why do doctors find some patients difficult to help? *Quarterly Journal of Medicine, 87,* 187–193.

Smith, G., Monson, R., & Ray, D. (1986). Patients with multiple unexplained symptoms. *Archives of Internal Medicine, 146,* 69–72.

Sternbach, R. (1974). *Pain patients: Traits and treatment.* New York: Academic Press.

20

The Role of Psychological Assessment in Health Care: The MBHI, MBMC, and Beyond

MICHAEL H. ANTONI
CARRIE M. MILLON
THEODORE MILLON

THE ROLE OF PSYCHOSOCIAL FACTORS IN HEALTH PRESERVATION AND HEALTH CARE DELIVERY

Maintaining our nation's health has been one of the most poignant, perplexing, and costly agendas weighing on the minds of scientists, academicians, administrators, practitioners, and policy makers during the past decade and will most assuredly occupy a center stage throughout the remainder of this millenium. Because medical diseases influence millions of American lives and consume billions of American dollars each year, the health care revolution may be one of the largest wars that we as a nation have ever fought. At the close of the last decade, it was apparent that chronic medical diseases-those maladies that are the most expensive to treat—were the major health challenge in the United States (Taylor & Aspinwall, 1990). The most prevalent among these diseases included arthritis (Lawrence et al., 1989), cancers (American Cancer Society, 1989), diabetes (American Diabetes Association, 1986; Centers for Disease Control, 1993), cerebrovascular disease (stroke; American Heart Association, 1988), and coronary heart disease (American Heart Association, 1988). Other conditions, though lower in prevalence, may be equally devastating and costly. These include but are not limited to asthma, acquired immune deficiency syndrome (AIDS), kidney disease, liver disease, spinal cord injury, and neurological disease as well as disturbances in physiological regulation related to circulation (e.g, hypertension), digestion (e.g., gastrointestinal disorders), respiration (e.g., chronic obstructive pulmonary disease), arousal (e.g., chronic fatigue syndrome), sensation (e.g., chronic pain), reproduction (e.g., gynecologic disorders), metabolism (e.g., thyroid disorders), and immune function (e.g., allergies and autoimmune diseases).

Because people often live for many years with several of these conditions, health care costs for chronic disease management are astronomical. At the end of the last decade cost figures were surpassing half a trillion dollars annually (Taylor & Aspinwall, 1990). By 1992 the total cost of health care in the United States was $838 billion, accounting for 1/7 of the money spent on all domestic goods and services (United States Department of Health and Human Services, 1992) and the increase was running at three times the general inflation rate. *Were more people getting sicker, were the services getting costlier, or were the providers getting greedier?* One alarming trend identified in the same report showed that up to 20% of the 1992 health care costs were incurred on unnecessary procedures. The trend toward accelerating increases in overall health care costs as well as the significant evidence of abuse in the use of medical interventions led in part to what is often termed the health care or managed care revolution (Regier, 1994). This revolution has as a central mission the long-term reform of our nation's health care system addressing in particular methods to increase the accessibility, efficacy, and cost efficiency of procedures and services designed to preserve health and manage disease.

One exciting potential interface between clinical health psychology and this revolution is revealed in a report by Regier (1994) stating that clinical behavioral medicine (e.g., educational, behavioral, and psychosocial) interventions may reduce the frequency of medical utilization by 17% to 56% for services such as total ambulatory care visits, pediatric acute illness visits, acute asthma services, cesarean section and epidural anesthesia during labor and delivery, and major surgery. For instance, these interventions have also been associated with an average reduction of 1.5 hospital days for surgical patients. This report goes on to note that:

- A substantial proportion of health care costs are for treatments for conditions with *psychosocial sources.*
- Increasing a person's *sense of control and optimism* can improve health outcomes and decrease health care costs.
- *Social support building groups* are cost-effective ways to deliver interventions to medical patients.

Finally, the report notes that there already exists convincing data for the health and cost benefits of psychosocial interventions in conditions such as minor and acute illnesses, stress-related disorders, chronic pain, diabetes, asthma, arthritis, surgery, and childbirth. Much ongoing research is addressing similar questions in the context of other major medical conditions such as coronary heart disease, different forms of cancer, and AIDS, among others. Most of the gains made in these areas of clinical research and practice were initiated following the observation that patients with similar medical diagnoses and treatments showed a wide variability in the physical course and psychological sequelae of the disease being treated and much of this variance could be predicted on the basis of the psychosocial characteristics that the patients presented at the time of screening or intake. Because the focus of this volume is on psychological assessment in a wide variety of populations, it seems timely to include this chapter on the use of psychological assessment with medical patients.

The first section of this chapter identifies many points of intersection between psychosocial processes and the optimization of health maintenance and health care delivery. We have separated these intersection points into those concerned with health maintenance and those dealing with health care delivery. As regards the *health maintenance* arena we will focus on psychosocial factors related to (1) health preservation and the primary prevention of disease and (2) patient responses to disease and secondary prevention efforts. Within the context of *health care delivery* we focus on the role of psychosocial factors in (1) medical utilization and health care cost containment, as well as (2) treatment success and reha-bilitation/recovery from disease. After summarizing these potential roles for psychosocial factors in these various contexts we describe some of the methods available for assessing psychosocial characteristics of patients in specific medical environments. Here we sum-marize the empirical support for the use of the Millon Behavioral Health Inventory (MBHI; Millon, Green, & Meagher, 1982) to address both primary and secondary prevention questions in different medical populations. We then review the limitations of the MBHI for addressing other issues in the health care environment and present the rationale for the domains targeted by the newest Millon instrument, the Millon Behavioral Medicine Con-sult (MBMC). We are currently engaged in a series of pilot studies with this new instru-ment, including special populations of cardiac, transplant, pain, oncologic, and diabetic patients. The remainder of this chapter relates to factors that have influenced the selection of items and scales of the MBMC.

Importance of Psychosocial Factors in Health Maintenance

Health Preservation and Primary Prevention

One aspect of health maintenance can be conceptualized as encompassing efforts to pre-serve a healthy, nondiseased state including activities that reduce the likelihood of devel-oping disease among healthy individuals who are at risk for the development of a specific disease (i.e., primary prevention). Psychosocial factors have been associated with several aspects of health maintenance including *frequency of risk behaviors* (e.g., substance use, smoking); *decisions to utilize diagnostic screening tests* (e.g., cholesterol testing, skin can-cer screening, mammography, Pap smears); *the practice of adequate self-care behaviors* (e.g., adherence to dietary guidelines), *susceptibility* to stress-related or trauma-induced symptoms; and *resistance to the promotion* of preclinical physical and physiologic abnor-malities *and the onset of clinical disease.*

Psychosocial Factors and Risk Behaviors

Psychosocial factors associated with engaging in risk behaviors include but are not limited to an individual's

- *Appraisals* of self-worth, current health status and perceived susceptibility to disease, general outlook toward their future, the health protective effects of ceasing the risk behaviors, and their personal efficacy for making behavior changes (Becker, Maiman, Kirscht, Haefner, & Drachman, 1977; Rosenstock, 1974; Turk & Meichenbaum, 1989; McCann et al., 1995).
- *Repertoire of coping strategies* for dealing with internal and external forces that perpetuate the practice of the behaviors.
- Social, economic, familial, and spiritual *resources available* to them for gaining the *tangible and emotional support* necessary to make substantial lifestyle changes (Wallston, Alagna, De Vellis, & De Vellis, 1983).
- *Context* (e.g., external stressors) in which they are attempting to make these changes.

Accordingly, individuals who have a low sense of self-worth, are unconcerned with their health, have a low sense of self-efficacy, maintain a pessimistic outlook, practice maladap-tive coping strategies, have few resources for gaining tangible or emotional support, and who live in a very stressful environment might be seen as those persons who are most likely to continue to engage in health-compromising risk behaviors. These factors may also act as obstacles to practicing positive self-care behaviors (McCann et al., 1995; Wilson et al., 1986). They might also work to deter healthy individuals from pursuing diagnostic screenings such as annual physical exams, Pap smears, mammography, and other widely available medical tests that have been shown to dramatically reduce morbidity and mortality as well as health care costs.

Psychosocial Factors and Help Seeking

Similarly, these factors may also contribute to a symptomatic patient's delay in seeking prompt medical attention after the initial onset of physical symptoms (Cameron, Leventhal, & Leventhal, 1995; Neal, Tilley, & Vernon, 1986). On the other hand, a person's appraisals, coping strategies, resources, and life context may also cause them to "overutilize" the health care system when their condition does not warrant such use (Pallak, Cummings, Dorken, & Henke, 1994). Obviously these aspects of health preservation can have a potentially huge impact on the quality and quantity of patients' lives as well as the costs of providing them with health care.

Psychosocial Factors and Vulnerability to Developing Stress-Related Symptoms

Psychosocial factors may also contribute to an individual's susceptibility to stress-related symptoms. The experience of stressful life events ranging from daily hassles and marital discord to more traumatic events such as sexual and physical abuse, a devastating diagnosis, war, and natural disasters has been related to the onset or exacerbation of mental and physical symptoms, and underlying physiological changes have been demonstrated in both healthy people (Kiecolt-Glaser & Glaser, 1992; Ironson, Antoni, & Lutgendorf, 1995; Ironson, Wynnings, Schneiderman, et al., in press; Cohen, Tyrell, & Smith, 1991) and those with a preexisting medical condition (Grady et al., 1991; Lutgendorf, Antoni, et al., 1995).

Moreover, several psychosocial factors have been shown to be capable of moderating the influence of stressors on physical health changes and physiological regulatory processes, some of these including the individual's appraisals of *self-efficacy* (Bandura, Taylor, Williams, Mefford, & Barchas, 1985; O'Leary, 1992; Wiedenfield et al., 1990), an *optimistic outlook* toward the future (Lutgendorf, Antoni, et al., 1995), *adaptive coping strategies* such as acceptance, positive reframing, and active coping (Folkman & Lazarus, 1980; Carver et al., 1993; Taylor, Lichtman, & Wood, 1984; Taylor & Brown, 1988; Antoni, Goldstein, et al., 1995) as well as *emotional expressivity* (Esterling, Antoni, Kumar, & Schneiderman, 1990; Esterling, Antoni, Fletcher, Marguilles, & Schneiderman, 1994; Pennebaker, Kiecolt-Glaser, & Glaser, 1988) and *adequate social support* resources (Zuckerman & Antoni, 1995; Cohen & Wills, 1985).

Psychosocial Factors and the Promotion of Subclinical and Overt Disease Processes

Finally, psychosocial factors may also contribute to an individual's resistance or vulnerability to the promotion of a subclinical pathogenic or pathophysiologic process, or the onset of clinically manifest disease. Some subclinical processes that have been associated with psychosocial factors include

- Coronary artery disease (Contrada, Wright, & Glass, 1985; Hecker, Chesney, Black, & Frautschi, 1988).
- Hypertension (Dimsdale et al., 1986; Krantz et al., 1987; James, Hartnett, & Kalsbeek, 1984).
- Glucose control (Frenzel, McCaul, Glasgow, & Schafer, 1988; Brand, Johnson, & Johnson, 1986).
- Neoplastic changes in tissue (Goodkin, Antoni, & Blaney, 1986; Antoni & Goodkin, 1988, 1989).
- Immune system functioning (Kiecolt-Glaser, 1992; Antoni, Esterling, et al., 1995) including the surveillance of acute (Cohen et al., 1993) and chronic viral infections (Esterling et al., 1994; Lutgendorf, Antoni, Kumar, et al., 1994; McKinnon, Weisse, Reynolds, Bowles, & Baum, 1989).

Some of the psychosocial factors implicated as contributing to these processes include affective disorders (Fox, 1978, 1981) *and* distress states (depressed mood; Herbert & Cohen, 1993) as well as anger and hostility (Dembroski & Costa, 1987); appraisals of self-efficacy or personal control (Cohen & Edwards, 1989; O'Leary, 1992) and optimism (Peterson, Seligman, & Vaillant, 1988; Antoni & Goodkin, 1988; Scheier & Carver, 1985); various coping strategies ranging from active coping and engagement to denial, avoidance, and emotional suppression (Holohan & Moos, 1986; Pettingale, Greer, & Tee, 1977; Goodkin et al., 1986; Antoni & Goodkin, 1988); resources such as social support (House, Landis, & Umberson, 1988; Cohen & Wills, 1985; Cohen, 1988; Zuckerman & Antoni, 1995), religiosity, and spirituality (Levin, 1994; Pressman et al., 1992); and contextual factors such as stressful events (Antoni & Goodkin, 1989; Schwartz, Springer, Flaherty, & Kiani, 1986).

Many of these same psychosocial factors may also contribute directly or indirectly to the development of clinical endpoints such as myocardial infarction (Booth-Kewley & Friedman, 1987; Friedman & Booth-Kewley, 1987; Kamarck & Jennings, 1991), different cancers (Fox, 1981; Holland, 1990; Kaplan & Reynolds, 1988; Mulder, Van der Pompe, Spiegel, Antoni, & de Vries, 1992; Goodkin, Antoni, Fox, & Sevin, 1993; Goodkin, Antoni, Sevin, & Fox, 1993; Sklar & Anisman, 1981), Type II diabetes mellitus (Glasgow, Toobert, Hampson, & Wilson, 1995; Surwit & Feinglos, 1988), gastrointestinal symptoms (Friedman & Booth-Kewley, 1987), rheumatoid arthritis (Anderson, Bradley, Young, McDaniel, & Wise, 1985), and AIDS (Zuckerman & Antoni, 1995; Ironson, Solomon, Cruess, Barroso, & Stivers, 1995).

In summary, many psychosocial factors have been associated with health-compromising risk behaviors, including: decisions to seek diagnostic screening and help-seeking following the onset of symptoms; susceptibility to stress-induced emotional, physiologic, and physical health status changes; and the promotion of pathophysiologic processes and development of clinical disease. These psychosocial factors, while not unilaterally associated with all of these aspects of health preservation, do appear to cluster around a finite number of domains including *affective and other psychiatric disorders* (depression and anxiety conditions), *cognitive appraisals* (self-efficacy, optimism/pessimism, perceived control), *coping strategies* (active behaviors, acceptance and cognitive reframing, avoidance, and denial), *resources* (social, economic, familial, spiritual), and the *individual's life context* (stressful events, perceived stress level and functional capacity).

Patient Responses to Diagnosis of Disease and Secondary Prevention

A second major domain encompassing health maintenance concerns the patient's coping responses and resources that determine the sequelae of the initial diagnosis of disease (i.e., secondary prevention). Secondary prevention can refer to the prevention of extreme or maladaptive behavioral or emotional responses to a new diagnosis, treatment regime, or any of the life-changing aspects of a chronic medical condition with which an individual must deal. Secondary prevention also reflects processes that contribute to recovery from, relapse of, or progression of physical disease. Psychosocial factors that have been associated with secondary prevention phenomena include characteristics predictive of a patient's *initial reaction to a new diagnosis* (e.g., based on positive mammography, Pap smear, or HIV-1 antibody testing), patients' *responses to a stressful or invasive "curative" medical procedure* (e.g, surgical mastectomy, hysterectomy, cytotoxic chemotherapy, radiotherapy, cardiac catheterization, or tissue transplantation), patients' *adjustment to the burdens of a chronic disease* (e.g., limitations in physical, mental, vocational, and social activities) *and those regimens concerned with its management* (e.g., renal dialysis, insulin injections, antiviral medications, or lifestyle behavior changes), and the *actual physical course of the disease* (e.g., recovery, relapse, recurrence, symptom flares, and progressive decline).

Psychosocial Factors and Emotional Response to Diagnosis

There is wide variability in patients' initial psychological reaction to a serious medical diagnosis, with responses often involving either anxiety or depression-related conditions (Taylor & Aspinwall, 1990; Antoni, 1991). Some of the factors that may act to buffer an individual from extreme reactions to serious or life-threatening diagnoses are actually quite similar to those noted in the previous section on health preservation and primary prevention. These include but are not limited to

- *Appraisals* (interpretation of the meaning of the diagnosis and its ramifications; outlook toward the future, self-efficacy, and treatment efficacy).
- *Repertoire of coping strategies* (active coping, denial, giving up, cognitive reframing, acceptance).
- *Available resources* (support of friends and family, spiritual sources of support, economic means).
- *Contextual factors* (ongoing life stressors, prior experience with serious disease, functional ability).

There is growing evidence that maintaining an optimistic attitude (Carver et al., 1993) and accepting the reality of and having social or spiritual resources available for dealing with a serious medical diagnosis can be predictive of less distress in the weeks or months after receiving the diagnosis (Lutgendorf et al., 1996; Taylor & Aspinwall, 1990; Zuckerman & Antoni, 1995; Woods, Antoni, Ironson, & Kling, 1996). Conversely, maintaining a pessimistic or hopeless attitude (Carver et al., 1993), using coping strategies such as denial and giving up and inadequate social support (Zuckerman & Antoni, 1995) may be predictive of greater depression and anxiety reactions after diagnosis of conditions ranging from breast cancer to HIV infection. These initial psychological reactions may abate over the ensuing weeks or months (Jacobson, Perry, & Hirsch, 1990) or may persist and act as obstacles to the patient's future adjustment . For example, patients who used denial to deal with an HIV seropositive diagnosis showed greater depressive and anxiety symptoms 3 weeks as well as 1 year later (Antoni et al., 1991).

Psychosocial Factors and Adjustment to Chronic Disease

Psychiatric Disturbances. The most widely studied psychological problems that come in the period after initial reactions to diagnosis and which are common across the course of chronic diseases are those involving anxiety and depression (Taylor & Aspinwall, 1990). Beyond the obvious emotional pain and burden associated with these emotional reactions it is important to note that anxiety and depression can act as obstacles to the patient's ability to make and adapt to lifestyle changes, to recover from demanding medical procedures, to engage successfully in a rehabilitation program, and in some cases, to return to the work force or to premorbid levels of physical, mental, and interpersonal functioning (Bremer, 1995; Taylor & Aspinwall, 1990). Taylor and Aspinwall (1990) note that sources of excessive anxiety in medical patients may include invasive procedures, aversive medication side effects, and fears of disease recurrence, among others. Of course, the likelihood of anxiety reactions may vary considerably across patients as a function of their premorbid personality characteristics and psychiatric histories. In addition, these reactions can vary as a function of the specific disease, its stage at the time of diagnosis, and the nature of the medical regimen. For instance, mastectomy patients' greatest concerns and sources of anxiety include fears of disease recurrence, loss of femininity, and their partner's reaction to their surgery (Carver et al., 1993; Taylor & Aspinwall, 1990). On the other hand, uncertainties about the risk that behaviors (e.g., sexual relations) carry for future heart attacks are one key source of anxiety among myocardial infarction patients (Christman et al., 1988). It is plausible that other psychosocial characteristics (e.g., dependence, self-esteem, pessimism) may delineate which of these potential anxiety sources is most salient for different patient populations.

Another very prevalent set of emotional sequelae experienced by medical patients are symptoms associated with depression. It has been estimated that up to 25% of medical inpatients suffer from severe depression (Taylor & Aspinwall, 1990). The prevalence of Axis I affective disorders is known to be substantial among men diagnosed with HIV infection. In fact, the suicide rate in this population has been documented as 36 times higher than that observed in men in the same age group in the general population. Depressive symptoms may last for years after surgery for conditions such as breast cancer (Meyerowitz, 1980). Depressed affect and related symptoms may interfere with adjustment to the lifestyle changes and treatment regimens that accompany a variety of medical diseases. Lustman, Griffith, and Clouse (1988) found that depressed diabetics had significantly greater difficulties with glucose control than did their nondepressed counterparts.

Personality and Coping Style. In general, coping strategies characterized by avoidance are associated with increased distress in people dealing with stressors (Holohan & Moos, 1986; Taylor & Aspinwall, 1990). There is also evidence that these associations hold in patients from varying chronic disease groups who are dealing with the stress of the disease (Taylor & Aspinwall, 1990; Young, 1992). One study found that across patients diagnosed with cancer, hypertension, diabetes, and rheumatoid arthritis—four major chronic disease categories—cognitive restructuring predicted better emotional adjustment while self-blame and fantasizing, among others, were associated with poorer adjustment (Felton & Revenson, 1984). There is some evidence that those psychosocial characteristics associated with patients' immediate emotional reactions to diagnosis are also predictive of their psychological responses (depressive and anxiety symptoms) to the medical treatment regimens that are administered in the initial postdiagnosis period. Breast cancer patients who showed an optimistic attitude, accepted their diagnosis, and used positive reframing displayed better emotional adjustment over the months after surgical mastectomy (Carver et al., 1993). Other work noted that positive active responses to stress, a high locus of control, and greater perceived control over an illness are predictive of better psychological adjustment in patients with different chronic diseases such as cancer (Burgess, Morris, & Pettingale, 1988). One study found that lower levels of helplessness were associated with better psychological functioning and less symptom severity in rheumatoid arthritis patients (Stein, Wallston, Nicassio, & Castner, 1986). Another study provided evidence for a vicious cycle operating among rheumatoid arthritis patients involving helplessness appraisals and the use of passive coping strategies with resulting psychosocial impairments that obviate the patient's ability to adapt to this chronic disease (Smith & Wallston, 1992).

The relative merits of using denial coping strategies to deal with an illness and surrounding stressors remains a hotly debated topic. Some have suggested that the effectiveness of denial as a coping strategy in patients with chronic disease may vary as a function of the type as well as the stage of disease (Meyerowitz , 1980). One study found that denial among myocardial infarction (MI) patients actually predicted fewer days in intensive care and less cardiac dysfunction during hospitalization but was associated with poorer adaptation to disease in the long term, including poorer adherence to aftercare recommendations and a greater number of days of rehospitalization (Levine et al., 1988). However, another study showed that greater use of denial and behavioral disengagement among breast cancer patients predicted higher levels of distress in the months after surgical mastectomy (Carver et al., 1993). HIV-infected men who used denial to cope with their initial seropositivity diagnosis showed more depressive symptoms 1 year later (Antoni et al., 1991). Other work suggests that the ability of cancer patients to use multiple coping strategies (e.g., flexibility) was predictive of greater effectiveness in managing stressful events (Taylor & Aspinwall, 1990). These studies suggest that the coping strategies that medical patients employ in dealing with the challenges surrounding the initial diagnosis and initial treatment for their disease can have lasting effects on their ability to emotionally adjust.

Social Support and Other Resources. Another psychosocial factor that has been widely related to patients' ability to adjust to the stressors of their disease is social support. Social support provisions are often grouped into one of several categories such as tangible aid, information, and emotional assistance (House, 1981; Schaefer, Coyne, & Lazarus, 1981), though others have broken down these categories further into areas such as nurturance, social integration, and sense of belongingness (Cutrona & Russell, 1987). The existence of rewarding personal relationships that provide one or more of these assets in the lives of medical patients has been associated with better psychological adjustment to conditions such as cancer (Siegal, Calsyn, & Cuddihee, 1987; Taylor et al., 1984; Helgeson & Cohen, 1996), end-stage renal disease (Siegel et al., 1987), and arthritis (Fitzpatrick, Newman, Lamb, & Shipley, 1988). The literature relating different aspects of social support to emotional adjustment in cancer patients is substantial and has generated evidence that perceptions of greater emotional support from family and health care professionals is associated with better emotional adjustment in breast cancer patients dealing with the stress of mastectomy (Jamison, Wellisch, & Pasnau, 1978; Funch & Mettlin, 1982; Northouse, 1988; Helgeson & Cohen, 1996).

Social support may affect patients' adjustment to a chronic illness by way of multiple pathways, including ways in which it acts as a stress buffer (Cohen & Wills, 1985; Zich &

Temoshok, 1987), facilitates the use of adaptive coping strategies (Dunkel-Schetter, Folkman, & Lazarus, 1987; Leserman et al., 1992; Thoits, 1987), and enhances adherence to medication regimens (Wallston et al., 1983). The effects of social support on well-being may be mediated specifically by: (1) the availability of resources that make stressful events appear less overwhelming: (2) the opportunity that support provides for an open expression of ongoing fears and frustrations; (3) the information that guidance can offer to help patients refute their irrational appraisals about their illness and related stressors; (4) the feelings of connectedness derived from social ties that enhance one's perceived self-worth, belongingness, and sense of purpose and meaning; and (5) the ability of supportive others to facilitate the patient's use of and persistence in using active coping strategies for dealing with demanding medical regimens and the lifestyle changes accompanying a chronic disease (Cohen & Wills, 1985; Zuckerman & Antoni, 1995). It is also possible that patients' adverse emotional reactions to the stressors of their disease may act to drive away potential sources of social support (Zuckerman & Antoni, 1995; Wortman & Conway, 1985). Social isolation (Turner, Hays, & Coates, 1993) and social conflict (Lesserman et al., 1995) may in turn forestall a person's ability to manage the demands of a chronic disease resulting in greater distress, depression, and withdrawal, thereby creating a vicious circle.

Contextual Factors. The influence of a patient's coping strategies and resources on their psychological adjustment does not act in a vacuum, but rather it must operate in the context of contextual factors such as ongoing major life events and minor hassles, prior skills obtained for dealing with illness, and actual functional ability to carry out role-associated responsibilities, vocations, and social activities. The experience of elevated numbers of stressful life events has been associated with depressive symptoms and increased risk of emotional difficulties (Uhlenhuth & Paykel, 1973; Murphy & Brown, 1980; Brown & Siegel, 1988). The increased emotional burden associated with ongoing life events may overwhelm the patient's coping strategies, making it all the more difficult to deal with the challenges of the disease and the associated treatment regime (Antoni & Emmelkamp, 1995; Antoni et al., 1991). Stressful life events may also interact with health-compromising behaviors (e.g., alcohol consumption; Morrisey & Schuckitt, 1978; Newcomb & Harlow, 1986) that can in turn further hamper their attempts to cope with new challenges. A patient's perception of their overall quality of life and their ability to carry on premorbid activities can also contribute to their ability to adjust to a demanding medical regimen. Previously, measures such as the Sickness Impact Profile (Bergner, Bobbitt, Carter, & Gilson, 1981) and the Index of Daily Activities (Katz, Ford, Moskowitz, Jackson, & Jaffe, 1983) have been used to assess functional status (across psychosocial and physical dimensions) in medical patients, though these measures often do not measure how much the illness has compromised personal or role functioning (Taylor & Aspinwall, 1990). The acute side effects of certain treatments such as chemotherapy and radiation can often have a substantial impact on a patient's perceived quality of life (Lichtman, Taylor, & Wood, 1987), while more subtle chronic side effects of longer-term medication regimens can also greatly compromse patient's coping resources (Anderson et al., 1985; Zachariah, 1987).

Psychosocial Interventions. There is also evidence that focused psychosocial interventions (e.g., cognitive–behavioral stress management, CBSM) which attempt to modify several of the psychosocial factors just noted (e.g., cognitive appraisals, coping strategies, social support) may offset the initial impact of a serious diagnosis (e.g., HIV-1 seropositivity) on distress levels (depressive and anxiety symptoms) and related physiological measures (immune system components; Antoni et al., 1991). There is support for the notion that these sorts of interventions can modify depressed affect and anxiety in medical patients by altering their cognitive appraisals, coping strategies, and social resources for managing the disease-specific stressors and challenges emanating from other contextual factors (Antoni et al., in press). While some have argued that the risk of depressive reaction may be greatest at the time of the initial medical disease diagnosis (Cassileth et al., 1984), others have suggested that depressive symptoms may actually worsen after a patient has had more time to process the extent of limitations that the disease places on his or her life (Baum, 1982; Hughes & Lee, 1987). Although the severity of depression likely increases in parallel with disease severity and number of years of disability, other characteristics such as premorbid personality characteristics (and related coping strategies), social support loss, and external life events and role change stress are also likely to play a major role in a patient's emotional adjustment to a chronic disease (Taylor & Aspinwall, 1990). One stressor associated with affective disturbance is bereavement, a common phenomenon that is superimposed over the stress of having HIV infection. Chesney and Folkman (1994) have demonstrated that a time-limited coping effectiveness training intervention is successful in reducing distress and improving adaptive coping in HIV-infected gay men who are dealing with multiple losses (Chesney, Folkman, & Chambers, 1996). Another study found that a 10-week expressive supportive group therapy intervention was effective in lowering depression in HIV-infected gay men dealing with partner loss (Goodkin et al., 1996).

There are many other research studies demonstrating that psychosocial intervention can be used successfully to help cancer patients deal with the emotional challenges of their disease (Andersen, 1992; Trijsburg, van Knippenberg, & Rijma, 1992). Many of these interventions feature a social support component and offer patients the opportunity to challenge and change maladaptive cognitive appraisals and coping strategies. Psychosocial interventions have also been shown to facilitate adjustment to other chronic diseases such as congestive heart disease (CHD) (Oldenberg, Perkins, & Andrews, 1985; Razin, 1982; Gruen, 1975; Williams & Chesney, 1993), arthritis (McCracken, 1991), diabetes mellitus (Glasgow et al., 1995), and melanoma (Fawzy Cousins et al., 1990), as well as other syndromes such as chronic pain (Keefe, Dunsmore, & Burnett, 1992). The point here is that knowledge of the presence of a psychiatric disturbance or significant emotional distress in a medical patient, information regarding the patient's relative strengths and weaknesses in the domains of cognitive appraisals and coping strategies, support derived from social, familial, or spiritual sources, and an understanding of the ongoing life context can be very useful in determining the ways in which patients will adjust to a new diagnosis and the demands that a chronic disease places on them. This information can in turn be used to choose appropriate psychosocial services that should be made available to facilitate the adjustment process.

Psychosocial Factors and the Physical Course of Disease

The psychosocial factors associated with the actual physical course of many different chronic diseases are similar in many ways to those factors predictive of psychological adjustment that were previously mentioned. In fact, it is plausible that factors such as appraisals, coping styles, and different support resources may relate to a better disease course by way of their ability to moderate the influence of disease-related (and contextual) stressors on emotional adjustment. Better emotional adjustment might in turn relate to a better disease course through its association with physiological mechanisms that have a protective effect against the pathogen (e.g., the immune system) or homeostatic dysregulation (e.g., the endocrine system) causing the primary disease.

Personality and Coping Styles. There is a growing, albeit slow-growing, collection of studies suggesting that patients who use certain coping strategies for dealing with the demands of their disease, as well as with life stressors in general, may show the ability to outlive their physician's prognosis for the course of their disease. While this literature was primarily focused on patients with different types of cancer during the 1960s and '70s, changes in prevalence patterns of other chronic diseases have broadened this literature to studies of psychosocial characteristics associated with the course of other progressive and usually terminal diseases such as AIDS as well as with chronic but non-life-threatening diseases such as arthritis (Grady et al., 1991; Blalock, DeVellis, & Giordino, 1995) and more recently, chronic fatigue syndrome (Lutgendorf, Antoni, et al., 1995), all of which are usually tracked in terms of flare-ups. Greater denial coping at the time of a diagnosis of HIV infection was also predictive of greater impairments in immune function 1 year later (Antoni, Goldstein, et al., 1995) and a greater likelihood of progression to full-blown AIDS 2 years later (Ironson et al., 1994). At least three studies have related coping strategies such as active confrontation (Mulder, Antoni, Duivenvoorden, et al., 1995), and realistic acceptance (Reed, Kemeny, Taylor, Wang, & Visseher, 1994) to differences in disease progression for HIV-infected individuals.

Appraisals and Attitudes toward Health and Illness. There is a large literature suggesting that the cognitive appraisals that patients use to process life stressors as well as those that are specific to the burdens of a chronic disease may be associated with the course of their disease. For instance, having a fighting spirit was associated with a slower development of HIV-related symptoms and slower decline in the immune system among HIV-infected men (Solano et al., 1993). Others have found that HIV-infected individuals who show the longest survival time after a diagnosis of AIDS are more likely to maintain an attitude of hope, greater life involvement, and a greater sense of meaningfulness than do those who have shorter survival times (Ironson, Soloman, et al., 1995; Solomon, Benton, Harker, Bonavida, & Fletcher, 1993). Patients maintaining a "fighting spirit" in the face of a breast cancer diagnosis have been shown to have longer survival times than those with a more passive attitude toward the disease (Greer, Morris, Pettingale, & Haybittle, 1990). Women with the combination of a pessimistic attitude and elevated negative life events showed greater promotion of cervical carcinoma (Antoni & Goodkin, 1988, 1989; Goodkin et al., 1993). Other studies have identified associations between attitudinal factors and physiological regulatory indicators that may mediate a faster disease progression. For instance, an external locus of control was associated with poorer diabetes control in both children and adults (Burns, Green, & Chase, 1986).

Social Support. Resources such as social support have been associated with a faster recovery from certain illnesses and may reduce the risk of mortality in some cases (House et al., 1988; Neal et al., 1986). More specifically, adequate levels of social support have related to faster recovery or rehabilitation from a wide range of diseases, including stroke (Robertson & Suinn, 1968), leukemia (Magni, Silvestro, Tamiello, Zanesco, & Carl, 1988), congestive heart failure (Chambers & Reiser, 1953), and kidney disease (Dimond, 1979). There is also evidence that social support may influence the course of other chronic diseases by improving diabetes control (Marteau, Bloch, & Baum, 1987; Schwartz et al., 1986), by reducing the risk of mortality from MI (Wiklund et al., 1988), by reducing the risk of recurrence for breast cancer patients (Levy, Herberman, Lippman, D'Angelo, & Lee, 1991), and by slowing down the progressive decline in the immune system (Theorell et al., 1995; Zuckerman & Antoni, 1995) and progression to the clinical manifestations of AIDS in those with HIV infection (Ironson, Soloman, et al., 1995). Another study found that greater perceived emotional support predicted longer survival time among breast cancer patients, though this relationship was limited to women who had localized disease at the time of testing (Ell, Nishimoto, Mediansky, Mantell, & Hamovitch, 1992).

Other Resources. There is also a growing appreciation for the importance of other resources. For instance, the ability of patients to use spiritual/religious resources has been related to physiological functions such as blood pressure (Levin & Vanderpool, 1989) and immune function (Woods et al., 1996). One review of over 100 epidemiological studies noted that religiosity was consistently associated with better physical health (Levin, 1994). Religious involvement or spirituality may influence health in medical patients by multiple pathways, including enhanced social support through the fellowship of organized religious activities (attending services and praying together), less fear of death, a greater acceptance of the efficacy of self-regulation techniques, and a decreased likelihood of engaging in health-compromising lifestyle behaviors. One study found that elderly coronary patients who lacked a sense of strength and comfort from religion were more likely to die in the 6 months after open heart surgery as compared with their more religiously comforted counterparts (Oxman, Freeman, & Manheimer, 1995). A review of people who regularly practice a religious activity suggested that religion may reduce morbidity and mortality by prescribing health-enhancing behaviors (e.g., adequate sleep and moderation in consummatory activities) while discouraging health-compromising risk behaviors (e.g., substance use; Jarvis & Northcott, 1987).

Lifestyle Behaviors. In addition to these psychosocial factors, there are other behavioral factors—many associated with the patient's daily "lifestyle"—that may play a role in health preservation or adjustment to disease. Those factors that have been most convincingly associated with primary and secondary prevention of disease include *alcohol use* (Vaillant, Schnurr, Baron, & Gerber, 1991) , *illicit drug use* (National Institute on Drug Abuse, 1990), *overeating patterns* (Brownell & Wadden, 1992), *caffeine use* (Lovallo et al., 1996), *tobacco smoking* (Epstein & Perkins, 1988), and *physical exercise* (Dubbert, 1992). Several of these behaviors have also been associated with many of the psychosocial factors mentioned previously including *coping strategies* (Marlatt, 1985; Myers, Brown, & Mott, 1993) and *social support* (Richter, Brown, & Mott, 1991). In addition there is evidence that *contextual factors* such as life stressors may increase the likelihood of health-compromising behaviors such as smoking and drug use (King, Beals, Manson, & Trimble, 1992; Duberstein, Conwell, & Yeates, 1993) and may decrease the frequency of health-promoting behaviors such as a balanced diet and adequate physical exercise (Epstein & Perkins, 1988; Baum, 1994; Grunberg & Baum, 1985). Moreover, poor emotional adjustment to a chronic disease or to related treatment demands may also increase the risk of relapse of smoking, drug, or alcohol use or decrease a patient's ability to maintain a restricted nutritional regimen, and several of these could in turn affect physiological changes in the circulatory system (Krantz, Grunberg, & Baum, 1985) and immune system that are associated with the progression of certain diseases (Levy et al., 1991; Baum, 1994).

Psychosocial Interventions. There is mounting evidence that psychosocial interventions that attempt to modify several of these factors may be associated with a decreased rate of clinical progression in conditions such as coronary heart disease (Frasure-Smith & Prince, 1989; Oldenberg et al., 1985; Razin, 1982; Gruen, 1975; Williams & Chesney, 1993), HIV infection (Ironson et al., 1994; Auerbach, Olson, & Solomon, 1992; Mulder & Antoni,

1994), breast cancer (van der Pompe et al., 1994; Mulder et al., 1992; Spiegel, Kraemer, Bloom, & Gottheil, 1989; Andersen, Kiecolt-Glaser, & Glaser, 1994), and malignant melanoma (Fawzy et al., 1993).

In sum, a set of psychosocial factors associated with health preservation (primary prevention) and adjustment to disease (secondary prevention) appear to cluster around a finite number of domains including *cognitive appraisals* (self-efficacy, optimism/pessimism, and perceived control), *coping strategies* (active coping, acceptance and cognitive reframing, avoidance and denial, and emotional suppression), *resources* (social, economic, familial, and spiritual), and the *individual's life context* (stressful events, perceived stress level, and functional ability). The influence of these psychosocial factors on health preservation may be mediated by changes in patients' decisions to engage in risk behaviors, decisions to seek diagnostic screening services, and help-seeking responses after the onset of overt symptoms. The impact of these factors on adjustment to disease and disease course may be mediated by changes in patients' susceptibility to stress-induced emotional (e.g., depressive and anxiety symptoms), physiological (e.g., endocrine, immunological, cardiovascular dysregulation), and physical (e.g., muscle tension, sleep disorders, pain perception) sequelae.

Importance of Psychosocial Factors in Health Care Delivery

In addition to the psychosocial factors that may be associated with health maintenance, there are those psychosocial processes that may also contribute to optimal health care delivery. The identification of these factors through clinical research and their routine application to medical practice, made possible by comprehensive screening and assessment, may play a pivotal role in containing our nation's accelerating health care cost basis, a liability that has become quite salient in the face of the ongoing managed care revolution. In this section we summarize the effects of this revolution on the delivery of health care in this country, noting the potentially beneficial effects of efforts directed at cost containment. We then highlight the research providing empirical support for links between specific psychosocial factors and patient medical utilization patterns and how these associations, in turn, can drive up health care costs in the short term. We also point to research relating psychosocial factors to the success rates of certain treatments and patient recovery and rehabilitation rates from specific illnesses, outcomes that are both instrumental in longer-term cost containment.

The Influence of the Managed Care Revolution on Health Care Delivery

The most prominent trends being dealt with in our government's current attempts to manage the escalating costs in medical care delivery include: providing increases in services to underserved populations, determining the basic criteria for medical need, setting fair prices for services, emphasizing the role of primary care, and monitoring public health through nationally funded research programs (Regier, 1994). Arguably, the success of all of these missions could be greatly enhanced with systematic and valid methods for assessment of physical as well as psychological status of the patients making use of health care services. Improved screening and assessment is obviously relevant for identifying underserved populations who could benefit from enhanced services, determining whether a patient meets criteria for one medical procedure or another, and surveying the usual and customary costs for services and their relative cost effectiveness. In addition, one of the most critical ingredients of cost-effective primary care is understanding the factors that predict patients' decisions to utilize early screening and detection services. Another important aspect of primary care involves developing the most valid and reliable techniques for detecting physical and mental disorders in children and adults at the earliest possible stage. Finally, direct and comprehensive assessment of medical patients is a key source of data for predicting and monitoring the effects of medical decisions on recovery and rehabilitation rates, as well as the quality of life of the patients receiving care. In many cases, however, the amount and level of psychosocial/mental health assessment may be grossly disproportionate to the amount of effort and resources spent on high-technology biomedical assessments—in many cases psychosocial assessment may be totally absent from the screening, intake, and follow-up procedures, despite the remarkably low cost/high payoff potential of these tests.

Evidence justifying the potential cost savings and quality assurance that is made possible by integrating adequate mental health benefits into the overall physical health delivery package is only now being disseminated. This evidence comes from many sources, including epidemiologic investigations, health services research, health costs analyses, and treatment efficacy studies. Epidemiological studies have indicated that 29% of people diagnosed with mental disorders also have substance abuse disorders (Regier, 1994). This research suggests that people may utilize services for those forms of pathology that have a comorbid condition that can motivate them to seek out health care. Patients with equally serious medical conditions who are lacking such comorbidities may delay or fail to seek treatment as soon or as often as they should. Conversely, many patients with mental disorders utilize medical services (emergency services, private practice physicians) that are inappropriate for their presenting pathology (e.g., affective disorder, substance dependence). The integration of epidemiological and health services research can identify disease comorbidities that account for the highest utilization patterns. Health costs analyses consider the costs of illness and treatment and are important in defining the amounts that should be allocated to benefits packages. Finally, treatment efficacy studies are helpful for developing empirically validated guidelines for primary prevention strategies, as well as recommendations for treatment choices (i.e., triaging) for people already diagnosed with a medical condition. In some cases these triaging decisions may result in a recommendation for a synergistic combination of pharmacological (e.g., antidepressant) and psychosocial interventions (e.g., supportive group therapy or individual counseling) that can complement the treatment of the primary medical condition (e.g., cancer) by enhancing adherence to a self-care routine/lifestyle change or adjustment to the side effects of the medication. The upshot of these different lines of investigation is that *knowledge of patients' psychosocial characteristics and health-relevant behavior patterns could aid in the reduction of the costs of health care delivery* across a wide range of medical conditions in affected or at-risk populations.

There are several ways in which researchers have operationalized outcomes for the purpose of studying the influence of psychosocial factors in health maintenance and health care costs. These include indicators of health status, behavior changes, and cost effectiveness. Health status indicators may range from broad categorizations of morbidity and mortality to more disease-specific measures of progression, relapse, or remission, to more functional indices concerning physical and mental capacity or general quality of life. Many of these were used in the studies presented in the previous section. Behavior changes are usually indexed in terms of risk-increasing (e.g., cigarette smoking, fat intake, sun exposure) and risk-decreasing (e.g., exercise, relaxation) activities. Some of these were also included in the studies mentioned previously. Finally, cost effectiveness can be tracked through actual cash outlay or through hospital admissions, lengths of stay, number of outpatient visits for follow-up, and the use of expensive (e.g., surgery) and less expensive (e.g., medications) procedures. Some of the psychosocial factors associated with health care costs involve those directly related to medical utilization (short-term cost effects) while others relate more directly to treatment success and recovery and rehabilitation rates (longer-term cost effects).

The Influence of Psychosocial Factors on Medical Utilization and Health Care Costs

Anxiety and Depression

There is good evidence that medical patients who display psychiatric disorders or who are in some way evidencing a poor emotional adjustment to their illness may generate greater health care costs than do their better adjusted counterparts (Jacobs, Kopans, & Reizes, 1995). For instance, greater state anxiety in gall bladder patients was associated with longer postoperative hospital stays (Boeke, Stronks, Vehage, & Zwaveling, 1991). Medical patients with depressive disorders may also generate greater costs in the process of obtaining their health care (Greenberg, Stiglin, Finkelstein, & Berndt, 1993; Klerman & Weissman, 1992). Some work has indicated that depressed patients tend to show greater medical utilization (Barsky, Wyshak, & Klerman, 1986), have longer hospital stays (Jacobs et al., 1995; Narrow, Regier, & Rae, 1993; Cushman, 1986), require more custodial care (e.g., nursing homes; Cushman, 1986), are less able to maintain improvements made during rehabilitation (Thompson, Sobolew-Shubin, Graham, & Janigian, 1989), and may be less able to recapture their premorbid quality of life (Niemi, Laaksonen, Kotila, & Waltimo, 1988), thus increasing the need for further psychological intervention. There is also growing evidence that depressed cardiac patients may be at heightened risk for rehospitalization (Stern, Pascale, & Ackerman, 1977) and reinfarct (Carney, Freedland, Rich, & Jaffe, 1995; Frasure-Smith, Lesperance, & Talajic, 1993) in the years following their initial MI.

Other work has found that chronically ill patients (drawn from oncology, rheumatology, and gastroenterology services) who showed poor psychosocial adjustment to their illness showed the greatest utilization of medical services (including use of specialist services and number of hospital episodes in the prior 6 months) and generated the highest costs associated with these services (Browne, Arpin, Corey, Fitch, & Gafni, 1990). Other work has indicated that patients displaying significant levels of psychopathology showed 40% longer hospital stays, 35% greater hospital charges, and also used more procedures, independent of gender, race, age, and medical diagnosis (Levenson, Hamer, & Rossiter, 1990). A large study of over 50,000 medical/surgical patients discharged from two major hospitals during 1984 found that patients with psychiatric comorbidity had nearly double the length of hospital stays of patients without comorbidity (Fulop, Strain, Vita, Lyons, & Hammer, 1987). Here, affective disorders and substance abuse disorders were the most prevalent and of these affective disorders were associated with the greatest length of stay.

Personality and Coping Style

Stone and Porter (1995) presented a theoretical model for the multiple pathways through which *coping* can affect outcomes in medical patients. They suggested that a patient's coping efforts, guided in part by their appraisals of some medical event (e.g., perceiving a physical symptom) can affect their emotional response, their health behaviors, communications with their health care provider, and their adherence to primary and secondary prevention efforts. These intermediary outcomes may in turn predict the patient's further help-seeking, sense of well-being, and possibly their disease course (Stone & Porter, 1995). To the degree that maladaptive coping strategies lead to poor emotional adjustment, resumption of health risk behaviors, disturbed patient–physician communications, and reduced adherence to the recommended treatment regime, they may require additional medical care with associated escalation in costs.

Psychological Issues

Other work has found that many of the psychological factors previously associated with emotional adjustment to illness (e.g., social support, life stress) are also associated with medical utilization patterns. One set of psychological characteristics of medical patients that may be related to utilization and health care costs involves *resources such as social support*. For instance, in a study of *social support* factors among medical patients attending 43 family practices, those with lower confidante support and lower emotional support showed a significantly greater number of office visits and a greater number of total charges over a 1-year period (Broadhead, Hehlbach, DeGruy, & Kaplan, 1989). *Contextual factors* such as elevated life stress predicted a greater frequency of medical visits, and this association was strongest among patients with personality traits characterizing a tendency toward somaticizing (Miranda, Perez-Stable, Munoz, Hargreaves, & Henke, 1991). This study suggested that stress reduction interventions might be particularly cost effective in reducing overutilization of outpatient medical services, especially among patients who (1) possess this personality characteristic and (2) are undergoing significant life stressors. Thus, assessment of *key psychological characteristics of medical outpatients within their life context* may facilitate triaging to time-limited, focused psychological intervention to substantially contain health care expenditures.

Lifestyle Behaviors

The health-compromising behaviors that people engage in may be one of the most important factors influencing the cost of their health care. When 2,238 medical records were randomly sampled from over 42,000 discharges from six different hospital populations, *lifestyle behaviors* such as alcohol use and cigarette smoking were found to be consistently higher among the 13% of patients classified as high-cost utilizers as compared with the other 87%, the low-cost utilizers (Zook & Moore, 1980). Repeat hospitalizations and unexpected complications during treatment were among the primary causes for the expenditures in the high cost group. Importantly, these are behaviors that may be modifiable by psychosocial interventions.

Psychosocial Interventions

Is there any evidence that psychosocial interventions can significantly reduce health care costs in medical patients? Several reviews addressing the utility of mental health interventions in reducing costs for medical patients have been published in the last 5 years (e.g., Levenson, 1992). Using the example of behavioral medicine interventions (e.g., educational, behavioral, and psychosocial interventions) it is possible to experimentally demonstrate the importance of psychosocial factors in cost containment. For instance, one study found that educating patients on self-care reduced doctor's visits for minor illness and related symptoms by 33%, and did so without compromising their health (Vickery, 1983). This program in particular appeared to save $2.50 for every $1 that it cost to implement. Psychological distress-related physical discomfort (e.g., headaches, gastrointestinal problems, sleep difficulties) is believed to be the most common cause of health care utilization, with up to 60% of all medical visits made by the "worried well" (Cummings & Van den Bos, 1981). Interventions that are directed at the psychosocial sources of these complaints (i.e., stress-reducing techniques) have been estimated to provide a savings of up to $4 for every dollar invested (Schneider, 1987). In one randomized trial, behavioral medicine techniques were found to reduce physical discomfort and to trim off two office visits, on average, in a cohort of patients presenting with stress-related problems (Hellman, 1990). After controlling for the costs of the psychosocial intervention, the health maintenance organization (HMO) saved thousands of dollars in the first 6 months alone. Pallak and colleagues (1994) found that a managed mental health treatment intervention reduced medical costs by up to 21% among Medicaid patients and that these reductions held at 6, 12, and 18 months posttreatment (Pallak et al., 1994). Another study found that an 11-day psychosocial intervention conducted with inpatints referred for stress-related conditions reduced average numbers of days hospitalized by 68% with an average cost savings of $3 for each dollar invested (Gonik, 1981).

A large meta-analytic review of this literature revealed that medical utilization was reduced by 10% to 33% and hospital stays were cut by 1.5 days after brief psychotherapy (Mumford, Schlesinger, Glass, Patrick, & Cuerdon, 1984). Schlesinger and colleagues observed that patients diagnosed with one of four major medical conditions (chronic lung disease, diabetes, ischemic heart disease, and hypertension) showed significantly lower costs for medical services after receiving mental health treatment (Schlesinger, Mumford, Glass, Patrick, & Sharfstein, 1983). Behavioral interventions were also shown to provide relief to *chronic pain patients* at a fraction of the cost of medical interventions (Caudill, 1991). This group noted that medical office visits plummeted by 36% in the first year after the program and persisted at this low level over the second year of follow-up, with an average savings achieved by the program of $3.50 for every dollar invested. Jacobs (1987) reviewed the medical cost offsets of different forms of psychosocial intervention in patients presenting with various pain-related disorders. This analysis indicated that biofeedback treatment reduced hospital and clinic utilization by 72% and 63%, respectively; vocational rehabilitation reduced hospital and clinical visits by 89% and 41%, respectively; and a chronic pain program reduced hospital and clinical utilization by 72% and 50%, respectively. On average these programs were associated with a sustained 47% reduction in hospital utilization and a total of over $7 million in cost savings over a 4-year follow-up period (Jacobs, 1987).

The Influence of Psychosocial Factors in Treatment Success and Recovery from Disease

It is difficult, if not impossible, to separate out the contribution of psychosocial interventions to health care utilization versus treatment success. However, some studies have provided some additional information that may support the role of psychosocial intervention in actually improving the efficacy of a medical intervention regime. Here we present some examples of the application of behavioral medicine interventions (designed to modify many of the psychosocial factors previously reviewed) to patients with specific diseases.

Diabetes Mellitus

One area that is relevant in this regard is the care of patients who are diagnosed with diabetes. One study found that among nearly 1,000 diabetic patient records reviewed, inadequate self-care contributed to one in every six hospitalizations. At least three major studies involving over 20,000 total patients showed that psychosocial interventions substantially reduced costs incurred by *diabetics*. Some of these studies found a reduction in hospitalization rates of 73% and lengths of stay of 78%, resulting in an estimated savings of over $2,000 per patient participating in the program (Miller & Goldstein, 1972; Miller, 1981). Another found that an outpatient education program reduced the incidence of severe ketoacidosis by 65% and the frequency of lower extremity amputations by nearly 50% for a cost savings of over $400,000 per year (Davidson, 1983). Finally, a brief outpatient education program reduced the number of hospital days by over 50% in a group of diabetics (Assal et al., 1985; Mulhauser et al., 1983). Similar forms of interventions conducted with *pregnant women with diabetes* have also been shown to lower medical costs for both the mother's and the baby's care with savings up to 30.3%, resulting in over $5 saved for each dollar invested. Beyond these impressive cost savings, the results of this last study suggest that the child's health might be affected to some degree by the diabetic mother's access to psychosocial intervention.

Asthma

Among *patients with asthma*, psychosocial interventions delivered in small groups resulted in more symptom-free days, greater physical activity improvements, and 49% fewer office visits for acute attacks compared with patients receiving usual care over a 2-year follow-up period (Wilson et al., 1993).

Arthritis

Among *chronic rheumatoid arthritis* sufferers, one health education program was found to reduce pain reports by 20% and physician visits by 43%. Importantly, this program also significantly increased patients' perceived self-efficacy, a key characteristic in consistent self-management, adherence to medical regimens, and reducing vulnerability to stressors and mood disturbances. For rheumatoid arthritis patients the program saved an estimated $12 over a 4-year period (or $3 annually) for each dollar invested (Lorig et al., 1993).

Surgery Patients

There is some evidence that *surgery patients* may recover faster with *preoperative* psychosocial intervention. Studies conducted over the past two decades have indicated that psychological interventions may speed actual physical recovery rates from surgery. Interventions ranging from muscle relaxation to intensive psychotherapy have been associated with improvements in several surgery-related outcome variables, including fewer days in intensive care, fewer total days in the hospital, and fewer incidents of congestive heart failure (e.g., Aiken & Henricks, 1971). Among the nearly 200 studies addressing this topic between 1963 and 1989 beneficial effects for various forms of psychosocial intervention have been reported 79% to 84% of the time (Devine, 1992). Similar to other work with hospital inpatients, length of hospital stay was reduced by 1.5 days on average. Using a conservative estimate of projected cost savings of such changes in length of stay, these programs may save up to $10 for each dollar invested. Across 13 other studies, psychosocial intervention reduced hospital days post-MI or postsurgery by 2 full days (Mumford, Schlesinger, & Glass, 1982). One study also revealed that conducting an adequate psychological screen and triaging surgery patients to receive psychiatric intervention reduced the average hospital stay by 2.2 days, for a savings of over $8 for each dollar invested (Strain et al., 1991). Thus, greater attention to the role of psychosocial factors is warranted to contain health care costs and to improve success rates of medical regimens over a wide range of disease conditions.

Disease Complications

Psychosocial interventions may play a significant role in reducing long-term health care costs by reducing the likelihood of phenomena such as diabetic complications, recurrence of heart attacks in MI patients, and extended rehabilitation costs for spinal injury or stroke due to reinjury. Other long-term effects of psychosocial interventions are currently being explored in terms of reducing the progression rate of conditions such as HIV infection, the recurrence rate of certain cancers (e.g., breast cancer), and life-threatening and costly complications, such as kidney failure, which result from other disease processes.

Psychosocial Assessment-Directed Intervention Choices

Despite the impressive cost savings that may be achieved with psychosocial interventions it is important to note that these are average costs savings and do not reflect individual cases. It is entirely likely that there are subsets of patients who possess certain psychosocial characteristics that make them more or less likely to benefit from psychosocial interventions. The ability to identify these characteristics at the point of screening and intake would further increase cost savings because all patients in need of such services would be caught while those not in need of such services would not incur the costs or burden of psychosocial services unnecessarily.

To summarize the first two sections of this chapter, there are several psychosocial characteristics that are capable of influencing health maintenance on the one hand and health care costs on the other. Together these factors can be grouped into four major categories as follows:

1. Psychiatric indicators (anxiety, depression, and other Axis I-related disturbances)
2. Personality coping style (behavioral, cognitive, and interpersonal coping style and strategies)
3. Psychosocial issues (appraisals, resources, and contextual factors)
4. Lifestyle behaviors (health-compromising and health-promoting behaviors)

In addition, knowledge the patient's *communication style* may be critical for the health care provider to understand the needs and symptoms that they present. At least four components of a patient's communication style may be relevant here: (1) the tendency to be open about sharing personal information; (2) inclinations to present themselves in a very positive light even at the expense of concealing symptoms; (3) inclinations to present many minor as well as major symptoms, sensations, and experiences; and (4) receptivity to specific details about diagnostic, prognostic, and treatment procedures and outcomes. The ability to identify systematic distortions, biases, and preferences in patients' self-reports to their health care provider can improve the precision of history taking and symptom monitoring and facilitate patient–provider rapport, potentially resulting in improved help seeking upon emergence of new symptoms and better adherence to prescribed and self-care regimens.

Figure 20.1 lists these five sets of psychosocial factors and their relations to various domains of health maintenance (including primary and secondary prevention) and health care delivery. Ideally, all of this information can be synthesized to predict a wide range of medical outcomes that are relevant to the management of the patient's health care. Some of these *treatment prognostics* might include:

- Patients' compliance with medical regimens.
- Potential difficulties with or misuses of medications.
- Adverse emotional reactions to demanding protocols.
- Managing risks of treatment complications due to the resumption of risk behaviors.
- The patient's potential for positive responses to psychosocial interventions.

The Role of Psychological Assessment in Health Preservation and Health Care Delivery

What psychological characteristics identify patients who are most likely to need and benefit from psychosocial interventions in terms of health outcomes and cost savings? While we are a long way from being able to identify all the factors that predict who does and who does not benefit from psychosocial interventions, there is a plethora of evidence to suggest that certain sets of psychosocial characteristics (as reviewed here) may contribute to health maintenance and health care utilization. If psychosocial interventions are effective at modulating these factors in ways that promote health and contain costs, then developing ways to identify their presence and configuration in patients at the earliest phases of the medical utilization process could make a major contribution to the health care revolution. The remainder of this chapter will focus on the instruments that are available for assessing these patient characteristics.

The Use of the Minnesota Multiphasic Personality Inventory (MMPI) with Medical Patients

For years investigators have attempted to gather support for the use of psychological instruments such as the MMPI (Dahlstrom, Welsh, & Dahlstrom, 1972) to examine the associations between psychosocial characteristics of medical patients and the etiology and physical course of their illness as well as the effectiveness of their medical treatment (Stoddard, Tsushima, & Heiby, 1988). Fewer investigations have explored the use of psychological assessments to predict medical utilization and related costs or the cost offset potential of psychosocial interventions; none of these employed accepted instruments such as the MMPI (Cummings & Follete, 1968; Marron, Fromm, Snyder, & Greenberg, 1984; Westhead, 1985).

One study empirically derived a utilization prediction scale (UPS) made up of MMPI items that discriminated between medical outpatients who did versus those who did not significantly decrease their medical utilization after psychosocial intervention (Stoddard et al., 1988). They found that patients with UPS profiles characterized by the presence of self-confidence, patience, good social skills, and a low endorsement of items reflecting anxiety and depression symptoms, showed the greatest reductions in utilization after the

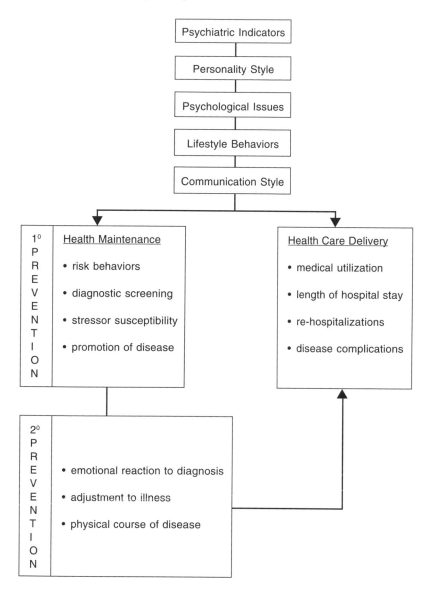

FIGURE 20.1. Five sets of psychosocial characteristics (psychiatric indicators, personality style, psychological issues, lifestyle behaviors, and patient communication style) and their relationship to multiple aspects of health maintenance (primary and secondary prevention) and health care delivery.

intervention. These findings are intriguing in light of the fact that these psychosocial interventions were a heterogeneous collection of techniques such as psychodynamic psychotherapy, behavioral techniques, and combined psychopharmacologic and psychosocial approaches. Importantly, none of the MMPI clinical scales was able to make such discriminations. This latter point illuminates the fact that very few instruments have been developed for the purpose of specifically and simultaneously assessing all of the psychosocial characteristics—*psychiatric indicators, personality style, psychological issues* (appraisals, coping strategies, resources, and contextual factors), *lifestyle behaviors, and patient com-*

munication style—that may play a role in health preservation and health care delivery in medical patients.

The Use of the MBHI with Medical Patients

One other objective instrument that has attempted to provide some of this information in a more systematic and explicitly synthesized format than the MMPI is the Millon Behavioral Health Inventory (MBHI; Millon et al., 1982). This instrument was described in detail in Chapter 19 by Everly and Newman. Here we describe some of the MBHI-based research evaluating ways in which psychosocial factors relate to various aspects of health maintenance, including questions relevant to primary as well as to secondary prevention.

The Use of the MBHI in Health Preservation and Primary Prevention

MBHI and Help Seeking in Response to Life-Threatening Symptoms. The MBHI has been used to examine how personality style relates to behavioral and cognitive responses immediately after the onset of acute coronary symptoms in patients experiencing their first MI (Kolitz, Antoni, & Green, 1988). Advances in cardiotechnology have facilitated the development of life-saving interventions such as angioplasty and chemical agents capable of removing arterial blockage accompanying MI in as many as 75% of treated cases (Topol et al., 1987). However, these forms of intervention are generally most effective during the first few hours after the onset of acute MI symptoms, after which time the cardiac muscle may be damaged irreparably. Understanding the psychosocial factors (e.g., personality/coping style) that are associated with a patient's decisions to pursue help versus delaying help seeking after the onset of such symptoms may have significant implications for reducing the severity of the MI and its associated costs.

In the first study, 30 patients diagnosed with an MI (23 men and 7 women) completed the MBHI, the Beck Depression Inventory (BDI; Beck, 1978), and a lifestyle behavior interview after they had been transferred from the coronary care unit (CCU) to the cardiac ward. Using a base rate (BR) cutoff score of 70 on the MBHI, three personality code groups were formed and designated as follows: Angry–Moody (elevations on Scales 2, 6, and 8), Dependent–Conforming (elevations on Scales 1, 3, and 7), and Confident–Outgoing (elevations on Scales 4, 5, and 6). Kolitz and colleagues (1988) found that members of the Angry–Moody group tended to attribute the cause of their MI to external stress, while memmbers of the Dependent–Conforming and Confident–Outgoing groups attributed their heart attacks to their poor lifestyle habits. The Angry–Moody group also reported the longest delay time in seeking medical attention after the onset of their MI symptoms—81% took longer than 4 hours and fully 65% took longer than 14 hours to seek help. On the other hand, 91% of the patients in the Confident–Outgoing group and 75% of Dependent–Conforming group members sought medical attention in the first 1 to 4 hours after the onset of MI symptoms. Interestingly, the Angry–Moody group also showed significantly higher BDI scores, higher recent stress, and greater pessimism, hopelessness, and somatic anxiety than did patients in the other two groups, suggesting that these subjects were having the most difficulty adjusting emotionally to their MI during their hospital convalescence.

A second study by this same group largely replicated these findings in 40 first-time MI patients drawn from two different hospitals (Kolitz et al., 1988). Again patients were recruited 3 to 5 days after their MI and after transfer from the CCU. As in the previous study, an identical 81% of patients classified in the Angry–Moody group delayed seeking treatment for more than 4 hours after the onset of acute symptoms. All of the patients in the other two personality groups sought treatment within 4 hours of symptom onset. The average delay time in the Angry–Moody group (*M* = 8.2 hrs) was approximately 10 times the delay time among members of the other two groups (*M* = 0.8 hrs). In addition to replicating the findings of the first study, this investigation also revealed that patients in the Angry–Moody group did indeed show New York Heart Association (NYHA)-based evidence of greater average tissue destruction than did patients in the other two groups, despite the fact that all groups were equivalent on the size and type of MI and the nature of the acute symptoms they experienced (Kolitz et al., 1988). The Angry–Moody group also showed higher pessimism, hopelessness, and social alienation than did the other two groups. These findings, taken together with results of the first study, suggest that *personality/coping style, cognitive appraisals* (pessimism and hopelessness, as well as attributions for the cause of MI symptoms), and *social support resources* may act together to play a role in determining patients' decisions to seek help after the onset of life-threatening symptoms.

MBHI and the Promotion of Subclinical Neoplastic Changes. There is a growing interest in relating psychosocial factors such as personality coping style, optimism, self-efficacy, social support, and contextual factors such as stressful life events to increased risk for the manifestation of clinical disease in at-risk patients. However, little empirical work has been conducted to support these associations in a reliable fashion. This line of investigation focuses on identifying samples of people who possess a genetic, pathophysiological, behavioral, or environmental risk factor for the development of a disease and then evaluating the incremental proportion of the variance in disease manifestation that can be predicted by knowledge of psychosocial and contextual factors. One application of this paradigm might involve identifying persons who are at risk for the development of coronary heart disease due to their possessing genetic (family history), pathophysiological (e.g., hypertension, hypercholesterolemia), behavioral (e.g., tobacco smoking and other lifestyle behaviors), and contextual (e.g., high stress job) risk factors, and examining the incremental predictive power that knowledge of the patient's *psychiatric status* (e.g., depressive disorder), *personality coping style* (e.g., hard-driving, time-urgent, hostile), and *psychosocial factors* (e.g., low self-esteem, pessimism, social alienation, and lack of resources) provides for predicting the development of overt coronary disease.

One medical disease that has received some research attention in this regard involves predicting the development of specific forms of cancer. At least four studies have related MBHI-indexed personality coping styles and other psychosocial factors to the subclinical promotion of cervical neoplasia, the cellular changes that precede the development of invasive cervical carcinoma. In one study, 73 women presenting to an Obstetric/Gynecology (OB/GYN) clinic with evidence of repeated abnormal Pap smears completed the MBHI, the Life Experiences Survey (LES; Sarason, Johnson, & Spiegel, 1978), and a lifestyle behavior interview before being colposcopically examined for evidence of neoplastic changes on the surface of the cervix (Goodkin et al., 1986). This examination required insertion of a colposcope to magnify the surface of the cervix to locate any lesions suspicious for cervical neoplasia. A sample of the cervical tissue was biopsied and sent to a pathology lab for histological determination of neoplastic promotion. This study found that after controlling for risk factors for cervical cancer, women with the greatest number of negative life events experienced in the recent past showed the greatest level of cervical neoplastic growth. The women with the highest MBHI Premorbid Pessimism, Future Despair, Social Alienation, and Somatic Anxiety scores showed the strongest association between negative life event stress and level of cervical neoplasia (Goodkin et al., 1986). A second study used a similar paradigm with 75 women undergoing colposcopic examinations for abnormal Pap smears. Women were subsequently diagnosed with either varying levels of cervical neoplasia or the absence of cervical neoplasia infection despite being infected with the human papilloma virus (HPV), a viral risk factor for cervical carcinoma (Antoni & Goodkin, 1988). They found that after controlling for other risk factors such as Pap smear frequency and cigarette smoking, women with higher scores on MBHI Respectful style and MBHI Preorbid Pessimism, Future Despair, and Somatic Anxiety scales displayed the greatest level of biopsy-determined cervical neoplasia (Antoni & Goodkin, 1988). They also found that women who showed evidence of invasive cervical carcinoma had the highest Respectful style scores as well as the highest Premorbid Pessimism, Future Despair, Social Alienation, and Somatic Anxiety scores, and the mean scores for these women were all above the clinical cutoff of 74 BR points. Conversely, women showing evidence of HPV infection but who remained free of cervical neoplasia showed the lowest scores on these MBHI scales, none of which showed a mean value above the clinical cutoff criterion. A follow-up to this study indicated that MBHI Respectful style and psychogenic attitude scales interacted with recent life event stress in predicting greater levels of cervical neoplasia (Antoni & Goodkin, 1989).

These latter two studies showed that the MBHI was useful in identifying those HPV-infected women who were at heightened risk for developing cervical carcinoma by examining the systematic associations between the subclinical cervical neoplastic process and psychosocial factors (personality/coping style, appraisals, social support) while controlling for pathophysiologic (HPV infection), and behavioral lifestyle (smoking, Pap smear frequency) risk factors. These authors proposed that the association between these psychosocial factors and the promotion of cervical neoplasia might be mediated by immune system changes that are associated with stressors and psychosocial factors on the one hand and the surveillance of HPV-induced cervical neoplastic changes on the other (Goodkin, Antoni, Sevin, et al., 1993). A fourth study used the MBHI to pursue this line of reasoning by examining the association between psychosocial factors (personality/coping style, pessimism, contextual factors) and immune system functioning (natural killer cell cytotoxicity, NKCC) in 38 women at risk for the development of cervical carcinoma due to the presence of multiple risk factors (HPV infection, HIV infection; Byrnes et al., 1996). This study found that after controlling for the presence or absence of two specific types of HPV infection (based on *in-situ* hybridization of tissue removed by cervical swabs) and amount of cigarette smoking, that higher MBHI Respectful scores in combination with a greater number of recently experienced negative life events were associated with poorer NKCC. This finding held even after controlling for other factors such as Pap smear frequency, dietary factors, physical exercise, and the frequency of unprotected sexual intercourse (Byrnes et al., 1996). These findings collectively suggest that the MBHI may be useful in identifying psychosocial (personality/coping style, appraisals, resources, and contextual factors) characteristics that combine with lifestyle behavioral risk factors and pathophysiological risk actors to be incrementally predictive of the development of neoplastic disease as well as changes in underlying surveillance mechanisms that control the growth of the primary pathogenic process.

Another study used the MBHI to examine the association between personality coping styles and immune system functioning in men ultimately diagnosed with HIV infection (Lutgendorf et al., 1996). Healthy, symptom-free and sexually active gay men enrolled in a study designed to examine the psychological and physiological effects of HIV antibody testing and notification. They completed a battery of psychological tests, including the MBHI, and underwent a blood draw to evaluate the status of their immune systems, approximately 5 weeks before they were tested for and notified of their HIV antibody status.

MBHI personality coping style scores were then correlated with different indices of immune system status within the men who ultimately turned out to be HIV seropositive (Lutgendorf et al., 1996). This is an important analysis because, as in the case of the cervical neoplasia studies just summarized, the men were unaware of their disease status at the time of psychological testing, thus diminishing the likelihood that test responses were mere reactions to the news of diagnosis, and increasing the likelihood that MBHI responses pertained to long-standing personality/coping styles. Interestingly, HIV+ men scoring above the group median on the MBHI Sensitive style showed significantly higher NKCC than men with scores above the median on the Introversive style scale and the Sensitive group also had better T-cell responsivity to mitogen challenge than did the men with MBHI profiles reflecting a Respectful style. Moreover, higher Respectful style scores at baseline were associated with poorer immunological control (reflected in rising IgG antibody titers) of Epstein-Barr virus (EBV), a virus that may act as a cofactor in HIV-related disease progression (see Antoni, Esterling, Lutgendorf, et al., 1995, for review). Interestingly, these associations only held in the HIV-infected group and not in the men who later turned out to be HIV seronegative (Lutgendorf et al., 1996). As in the case of the cervical neoplasia study, an emotionall nonexpressive coping style (as measured on the MBHI Respectful and Introversive style scales) was associated with greater impairments in indices of immune system functioning relevant to viral infection surveillance (NKCC and EBV IgG antibody titers) in this cohort of HIV-infected men. Men with greater impairments in immune system surveillance functions at this early, asymptomatic stage of the infection may be at greater risk for a faster progression to full-blown AIDS.

The Use of the MBHI in Assessing Adjustment to Disease and Secondary Prevention

MBHI and Reactions to Diagnosis. The MBHI has also been used to predict how individuals react to a new medical diagnosis. As noted previously, one study enrolled gay men who were unaware of their HIV antibody status and tested them with a battery of psychosocial tests including the MBHI before randomizing them to either a stress management intervention or control condition, and then followed them over the 5 weeks before and after notification of their HIV antibody status. Among the men enrolled in the study, approximately one-third turned out to be HIV seropositive (Ironson et al., 1990). Over the ensuing 5-week period the men participated in one of two stress management interventions, or in an assessment-only control condition. The men who tested positive based on the week 6 antibody test showed significantly greater pre–post notification changes in distress, as compared with the men who tested negative (Ironson et al., 1990). However, the HIV+ men who were randomized to a stress management intervention showed significantly lower pre–post notification increases in distress (Antoni et al., 1991; LaPerriere et al., 1990) than did those randomized to the assessment-only control. When the MBHIs of the HIV+ men assigned to the stress management intervention were examined, the investigators observed that higher MBHI Respectful scores predicted decreased positive outlook and increased denial coping over the course of the study. Importantly, subsequent analyses revealed that greater increases in denial coping over the postnotification period predicted greater decrements in immune system functioning 1 year later (Antoni et al., 1995) and a greater likelihood of progression to full-blown AIDS over a 2-year follow-up period (Ironson et al., 1994). These findings suggest that the MBHI may be useful in predicting patients' initial psychological response to a life-threatening diagnosis, and these initial reactions may have health implications in the long term.

MBHI and Adjustment to Chronic Disease. There has also been work testing the utility of the MBHI for identifying associations between personality/coping style and the ways in which HIV-infected people, already manifesting clinical symptoms, adapt to this chronic disease. A number of MBHI coping style scales were found to be associated with several indices of psychosocial and behavioral adjustment in a cohort of symptomatic HIV-infected gay men (Starr et al., 1996). Specifically, elevations of the Inhibited, Forceful, and Sensitive scales (2, 6, and 8, respectively), as well as higher (Scales) 2–6–8 composite scores, were associated with higher BDI scores, a lower sense of self-efficacy, less perceived social support, and more frequent use of COPE-indexed (Carver, Scheier, & Weintraub, 1989) denial as a coping strategy for dealing with their infection. On the other hand, higher scores on the MBHI Sociable (Scale 4) and Confident (Scale 5) scales were associated with lower BDI depression scores, greater self-efficacy, and less frequent use of denial. Subjects in the highest tercile for the (Scales) 2–6–8 composite score showed an average BDI score in the clinical range of moderate depression, while the mean of subjects in the remaining 2/3 of the sample had mean BDI scores below the cutoff for mild depression. These results suggested that certain MBHI coping styles may identify HIV-infected persons who are less able to adjust emotionally to their disease.

These psychosocial characteristics may also relate to difficulties in maintaining lifestyle behavior changes that are critical for health maintenance and for controlling transmission in HIV-infected people. Further, this study found that higher scores on MBHI Scales 6 and 8 were associated with a greater number of sex partners in the past month and higher (Scales) 2–6–8 composite scores were associated with a greater number of different partners and a higher frequency of unprotected sexual episodes (Starr et al., 1996). Transcripts of interviews with these men were rated by independent judges and revealed that men with higher (Scales) 2–6–8 composites displayed lower self-esteem, poorer problem-solving skills, and less insight as they discussed the ways that they have been dealing with their infection (Starr et al., 1996). This study suggests that HIV-infected individuals (in this study, gay men) with MBHI coping styles characterized according to Millon's theory by active avoidance, active independence, and/or active ambivalence, may be less able to adjust emotionally to this life-threatening disease and may be less able or willing to make the lifestyle changes that are required to maintain their health. Moreover, these individuals appear to maintain a low sense of self-esteem, utilize maladaptive coping styles such as denial, display poor problem-solving skills, have inadequate social support resources, and lack insight into the ways their infection has affected their lives. This work suggests that the MBHI may be useful in identifying HIV-infected persons who could benefit from psychosocial interventions designed to change some of these psychosocial factors.

MBHI and the Efficacy of Secondary Prevention Efforts. At least two studies have used the MBHI to predict patient's success with interventions designed to help them manage chronic disease. Wilcoxin and colleagues found that a composite score based on several MBHI scales (Chronic Tension, Recent Stress, Allergic Inclination, Inhibited style, Respectful style, Pain Treatment Responsivity, Life-Threat Reactivity, and Premorbid Pessimism) successfully predicted gains in time sitting, time standing, number of stairs climbed, time on a treadmill, treadmill speed, and hand-grip strength among male and female pain patients completing a 20–day outpatient pain rehabilitation program (Wilcoxin, Zook, & Zarski, 1988). Using a composite score reflecting success across all of these areas of treatment improvement, a discriminant function analysis revealed that these eight MBHI scales, in combination with demographic information on age, gender, marital status, and educational level, correctly classified 96% (29/30) of patient outcomes.

Another study used the MBHI to relate 42 dialysis patients' psychosocial characteristics to their preferences for types of dialysis and their adjustment to treatment (Weisberg & Page, 1988). All patients completed the MBHI and a patient questionnaire assessing general emotional factors and current adjustment to dialysis at the time of their visit to the Kidney Unit at a large hospital. Patients choosing to receive hospital-based dialysis showed higher scores on the MBHI Chronic Tension, Recent Stress, Premorbid Pessimism, Future Despair, Social Alienation, Somatic Anxiety, Life-Threat Reactivity, and Emotional Vulnerability scales as compared with patients choosing home-based dialysis. Analysis of personality coping styles indicated that the patients choosing the hospital-based program had significantly higher MBHI Respectful style scores than did those choosing home-based dialysis. In terms of adjustment to dialysis, higher Recent Stress and Premorbid Pessimism scores were associated with patients' reports of greater difficulty in accepting help from their partners and lower satisfaction with their chosen dialysis modality. Higher scores on Premorbid Pessimism, Future Despair, Social Alienation, Life-Threatening Reactivity, and Emotional Vulnerability were associated with a greater likelihood of the patients viewing themselves as "sick." Several different MBHI psychogenic attitude scales were associated with poorer sexual adjustment and feelings of loss of femininity/masculinity (Weisberg & Page, 1988). Patients scoring higher on the MBHI Respectful style were less satisfied with the treatment modality chosen, showed poorer sexual adjustment, and felt less in control of treatment procedures. Higher scores on the Forceful scale were associated with greater difficulty in asking partners for help, while patients scoring higher on the Sociable style were less likely to view themselves as sick and reported greater satisfaction with their treatment. This study demonstrates the usefulness of the MBHI in predcting patient treatment choices and their ensuing adjustment to the demands of chronic disease. The latter study may have implications for health care delivery, as home-based dialysis is associated with substantial cost savings over hospital-based programs. Identifying psychosocial characteristics of kidney disease patients might help to predict those who are the best candidates for both home- and hospital-based dialysis and might also direct practitioners to issues that may act as obstacles to successfully implementing either choice.

MBHI and the Course of Disease. The MBHI has also been used to examine associations between personality/coping styles and the progression of breast cancer (Goldstein & Antoni, 1989). Forty-four women diagnosed with breast cancer completed the MBHI within the first month after diagnosis. All patients received a mastectomy as well as some form of adjuvant therapy. When the MBHI profiles of these women were compared with those of 34 women attending a GYN clinic (and who were subsequently shown to be free of neoplastic disease), they found that the cancer patients were significantly more likely to display an emotionally nonexpressive coping style (higher MBHI Respectful, Introversive, or Cooperative scores). Among the 44 breast cancer patients, those with the most severe prognosis (metastatic disease) were the only cases to show clinically elevated MBHI Respectful scores (Goldstein & Antoni, 1989). Follow-up analyses revealed that higher nonexpressive coping style scores were correlated with a greater tumor size in these women. As noted previously, MBHI Respectful scores were found to be predictive of increases in the use of denial coping among men adjusting to a diagnosis of HIV infection, and increases in denial were in turn predictive of poorer immune functioning 1 year later (Antoni et al., 1995) and progression to AIDS 2 years later (Ironson et al., 1994). Therefore, although it would be premature to claim a casual relationship, it appears that certain MBHI personality coping styles are associated with a greater likelihood of disease progression in some patient populations. These findings point to the potential utility of the MBHI as a research tool for investigating psychosocial factors as they relate to disease course and to underlying pathophysiological processes that may determine the course of different medical diseases.

Psychosocial Characteristics Not Assessed by the MBHI

Despite the impressive results generated by studies using the MBHI to assess psychosocial characteristics relevant to a variety of primary and secondary prevention domains in different patient populations, there remain several important psychosocial characteristics that this instrument does not provide explicit information on. Some areas not tapped by the MBHI include (1) information on the presence of psychiatric indicators that may influence the patient's adjustment to their medical condition; (2) information on coping styles reflecting recently derived personality disorders such as depressive personality disorder, sadistic personality disorder, and masochistic personality disorder (Millon & Davis, 1995); (3) information on other psychological factors related to cognitive appraisals (e.g., self-esteem, general efficacy), resources (e.g., spiritual and religious), and contextual factors (e.g., functional abilities); (4) information on specific lifestyle behaviors (e.g., alcohol and substance abuse, smoking, eating patterns, and exercise routine); (5) information on the patient's communication style (tendencies toward disclosure, social desirability, devaluation when communicating, and preference for more or less details when receiving medical information); and (6) information useful for predicting patient adherence to recommended regimen, medication abuses, and emotional responses to stressful medical procedures which in turn can be useful in informing health care management decision making and mental health treatment triaging. Awareness of the potential usefulness of this information for maximizing health maintenance and minimizing health care costs has provided the impetus for our work toward the forthcoming expanded health-oriented instrument we have entitled the Millon Behavioral Medicine Consult (MBMC).

SUMMARY

In this chapter we have presented the rationale for the use of psychological assessment in various health care settings. In the first section we presented a review of the literature providing empirical and theoretical support for the role of a finite set of psychosocial patient characteristics in two major aspects of health maintenance—health preservation/primary prevention, and adjustment to disease/secondary prevention. This review revealed that psychosocial characteristics such as patient communication styles, psychiatric status, personality/coping style, psychosocial issues (appraisals, resources, and contextual factors), and lifestyle behaviors may all contribute additively or interactively to the probability of optimal health preservation as manifest in engagement in risk behaviors, decisions to pursue diagnostic testing or medical help after the onset of symptoms, vulnerability to stress-related symptoms, and the promotion of subclinical pathophysiological changes that may in turn increase the risk of developing clinically manifest physical disease. The behavioral medicine and health psychology literature also provide evidence that many of these same psychosocial characteristics can potentially affect the patient's adjustment to disease in the form of their initial emotional reaction to diagnosis and their adjustment to the stressful demands, limitations, and lifestyle changes brought about by a chronic illness. These factors may also have direct or indirect effects on the physical course of the disease, possibly facilitating or thwarting secondary prevention efforts. In the next section we reviewed the health services literature and noted a plethora of studies showing that many of these psychological patient characteristics are associated with optimal health care delivery at the level of both medical utlization and treatment success and recovery, these improvements corresponding to potential reductions in short-term and longer-term health care costs, respectively. This extensive body of literature(s), in combination with Millon's personality theory, forms the rationale for the use of psychological assessment instruments such as the MBHI and the forthcoming MBMC in a wide variety of health care environments. It is our hope that these instruments and others will address several critical but often overlooked psychosocial characteristics that medical patients bring to the health care arena and in so doing facilitate the health care provider's efforts to maintain their patient's health through the delivery of a theoretically guided and empirically supported plan of action.

REFERENCES

Aiken, L., & Henricks, T. (1971). Sytematic relaxation as a nursing intervention technique with open heart surgery patients. *Nursing Research, 20,* 212–217.

American Cancer Society. (1989). *Cancer facts and figures: 1989.* Atlanta, GA: Author.

American Diabetes Association. (1986). *Diabetes: Facts you need to know.* Alexandria, VA: Author.

American Heart Association. (1988). *1989 Heart Facts.* Dallas, TX: Author.

American Psychiatric Association. (1994). *Diagnostic and statistical manual of mental disorders* (4th ed.). Washington, DC: Author.

Anderson, B. L. (1992). Psychological interventions for cancer patients to enhance the quality of life. *Journal of Consulting and Clinical Psychology, 60,* 552–568.

Andersen, B., Kiecolt-Glaser, J., & Glaser, R. (1994). A biobehavioral model of cancer stress and disease outcome. *American Psychologist, 49,* 389–404.

Anderson, K. O., Bradley, L.A., Young, L.D., McDaniel, L. K., & Wise, C.M. (1985). Rheumatoid arthritis: Review of psychological factors related to etiology, effects and treatment. *Psychological Bulletin, 98,* 358–387.

Antoni, M. H. (1991). Psychosocial stressors and behavioral interventions in gay men with HIV infection. *International Reviews in Psychiatry, 3,* 383–389.

Antoni, M. H., Baggett, L., Ironson, G., August, S., LaPerriere, A., Klimas, N., Schneiderman, N., & Fletcher, M. A. (1991). Cognitive–behavioral stress management intervention buffers distress responses and immunologic changes following notification of HIV-1 seropositivity. *Journal of Consulting and Clinical Psychology, 59*(6), 906–915.

Antoni, M. H., & Emmelkamp, P. (1995). Editorial on special issue on HIV/AIDS. *Clinical Psychology and Psychotherapy, 2*(4), 199–202.

Antoni, M. H., Esterling, B., Lutgendorf, S., Fletcher, M. A., & Schneiderman, N. (1995). Psychosocial stressors, herpes virus reactivation and HIV-1 infection. In M. Stein & A. Baum (Eds.), *AIDS and oncology: Perspectives in behavioral medicine.* Hillsdale, NJ: Erlbaum.

Antoni, M. H., Goldstein, D., Ironson, G., LaPerriere, A., Fletcher, M. A., & Schneiderman, N. (1995). Coping responses to HIV-1 serostatus notification predict concurrent and prospective immunologic status. *Clinical Psychology and Psychotherapy, 2*(4), 234–248.

Antoni, M. H., & Goodkin, K. (1988). Life stress and moderator variables in the promotion of cervical neoplasia. I: Personality facets. *Journal of Psychosomatic Research, 32*(3), 327–338.

Antoni, M. H., & Goodkin, K. (1989). Life stress and moderator variables in the promotion of cervical neoplasia. II: Life event dimensions. *Journal of Psychosomatic Research, 33*(4), 457–467.

Antoni, M. H., Schneiderman, N., & Ironson, G. (in press). Stress management for HIV-infection. In *Society of Behavioral Medicine clinical research guidebook series: From behavioral medicine research to behavioral medicine practice.* Hillsdale, NJ: Erlbaum.

Assal, J. P., et al. (1985). Patient education as the basis for diabetes care in clinical practice and research. *Diabetologia, 28,* 602–613.

Auerbach, J. E., Olsson, T. D., & Solomon, G. F. (1992). A behavioral medicine intervention as an adjunctive treatment for HIV-related illness. *Psychology and Health, 6,* 325–334.

Bandura, A., Taylor, C. B., Williams, S., Mefford, I., & Barchas, J. (1985). Catecholamine secretion as a function of perceived coping self-efficacy. *Journal of Consulting and Clinical Psychology, 53,* 406–414.

Barsky, A., Wyshak, G., & Klerman, G. (1986). Medical and psychiatric determinants of outpatient medical utilization. *Medical Care, 24,* 548–560.

Baum, A. (1994). Behavioral, biological, and environmental interactions in disease processes. In S. Blumenthal, K. Matthews, & S.Weiss (Eds.), *New research frontiers in behavioral medicine: Proceedings of the National Conference* (NIH Publication No. 94-3772, pp. 61–69). Washington, DC: U.S. Government Printing Office.

Baum, J. (1982). A review of the psychological aspects of neumatic diseases. *Seminars in Arthritis and Rheumatism, 11,* 352–361.

Beck, A. T. (1978). *The Beck Depression Inventory.* Philadelphia, PA: Center for Cognitive Therapy.

Becker, M. H., Maiman, L., Kirscht, J., Haefner, D., & Drachman, R. (1977). The health belief model and dietary compliance: A field experiment. *Journal of Health and Social Behavior, 18,* 348–366.

Bergner, M., Bobbitt, R. A., Carter, W. B., & Gilson, B. S. (1981). The sickness impact profile: Development and final revision of a health status measure. *Medical Care, 19,* 787–805.

Blalock, S., DeVellis, B., & Giordino, K. (1995). The relationship between coping and psychological well-being among people with osteoarthritis: A problem-solving approach. *Annals of Behavioral Medicine, 17,* 107–115.

Boeke, S., Stronks, D., Vehage, F., & Zwaveling, A. (1991). Psychological variables as predictors of the length of post-operative hospitalization. *Journal of Psychosomatic Research, 35,* 281–288.

Booth-Kewley, S., & Friedman, H. S. (1987). Psychological predictors of heart disease: A quantitative review. *Psychological Bulletin, 101,* 343–362.

Brand, A. H., Johnson, J. H., & Johnson, S. B. (1986). Life stress and diabetic control in children and adolescents with insulin-dependent diabetes. *Journal of Pediatric Psychology, 11,* 481–495.

Bremer, B. (1995). Absence of control over health and the psychological adjustment to end-stage renal disease. *Annals of Behavioral Medicine, 17,* 227–233.

Broadhead, W., Hehlbach, S., DeGruy, F., & Kaplan, B. (1989). Functional versus structural social support and health care utilization in a family medicine outpatient practice. *Medical Care, 27,* 221–233.

Brown, J., & Siegel, J. (1988). Attributions for negative life events and depression: The role of perceived control. *Journal of Personality and Social Psychology, 54,* 316–322.

Browne, G., Arpin, K., Corey, P., Fitch, M., & Gafni, A. (1990). Individual correlates of health service utilization and the cost of poor adjustment to chronic illness. *Medical Care, 28,* 43–58.

Brownell, K. D., & Wadden, T. A. (1992). Etiology and treatment of obesity: Understanding a serious, prevalent, and refractory disorder. *Journal of Consulting and Clinical Psychology, 60,* 505–517.

Burgess, C., Morris, T., & Pettingale, K. W. (1988). Psychological response to cancer diagnosis: II. Evidence for coping styles (coping styles and cancer diagnosis). *Journal of Psychosomatic Research, 32,* 263–272.

Burns, K., Green, P., & Chase, H. (1986). Psychosocial correlates of glycemic control as a function of age in youth with insulin-dependent diabetes. *Journal of Adolescent Health Care, 7,* 311–319.

Byrnes, D., Antoni, M. H., Goodkin, K., Efantis-Potter, J., Simon, T., & Munaij, J. (1996, March) *Life stress, HPV infection, immunity, and cervical intraepithelial neoplasia in HIV-1 seropositive minority women.* Paper presented at the annual meeting of the Society of Behavioral Medicine, Washington, DC.

Cameron, L., Leventhal, E., & Leventhal, H. (1995). Seeking medical care in response to symptoms and life stress. *Psychosomatic Medicine, 57,* 37–47.

Carney, R., Freedland, K., Rich, M., & Jaffe, A. (1995). Depression as a risk factor for cardiac events in established coronary heart disease: A review of possible mechanisms. *Annals of Behavioral Medicine, 17,* 142–149.

Carver, C. S., Pozo, C., Harris, S. D., Noriega, V., Scheier, M. F., Robinson, D. S., Ketcham, A. S., Moffat, F. L., Jr., & Clark, K. C. (1993). How coping mediates the effect of optimism on distress: A study of women with early stage breast cancer. *Journal of Personality and Social Psychology, 65,* 375–390.

Carver, C., Scheier, M., & Weintraub, J. (1989). Assessing coping strategies: A theoretically-based approach. *Journal of Personality and Social Psychology, 56,* 267–283.

Cassileth, B. R., Lusk, E. J., Strouse, T. B., Miller, D. S., Brown, L. L., Cross, P. A., & Tenaglia, A. N. (1984). Psychosocial status in chronic illness: A comparative analysis of six diagnostic groups. *New England Journal of Medicine, 331,* 506–511.

Caudill, M. (1991). Decreased clinic use by chronic pain patients: Response to behavioral medicine interventions. *Journal of Clinical Pain, 7*(4), 305–310.

Centers for Disease Control. (1993). *Diabetes surveillance, 1993.* Atlanta, GA: Centers for Disease Control, Division of Diabetes Translation.

Chambers, W. N., & Reiser, M. F. (1953). Emotional stress in the precipitation of congestive heart failure. *Medicine, 15,* 38–60.

Chesney, M. A., & Folkman, S. (1994). Psychological impact of HIV disease and implications for intervention. *Psychiatric Clinics of North America, 17,* 163–181.

Chesney, M., Folkman, S., & Chambers, D. (1996). The impact of a cognitive–behavioral intervention on coping with HIV disease. *Psychosomatic Medicine, 58,* 86.

Christman, N. J., McConnell, E. A., Pfeiffer, C., Webster, K. K., Schmitt, M., & Ries, J. (1988). Uncertainty, coping, and distress following myocardial infarction: Transition from hospital to home. *Research in Nursing and Health, 11,* 71–82.

Clarkin, J. F., & Lenzenweger, M. F. (Eds.). (1996). *Major theories of personality disorder.* New York: Guilford Press.

Cohen, S. (1988). Psychosocial models of the role of social support in the etiology of physical disease. *Health Psychology, 7,* 269–297.

Cohen, S., & Edwards, J. R. (1989). Personality characteristics as moderators of the relationship between stress and disorder. In R. W. J. Neufeld (Ed.), *Advances in the investigation of psychological stress* (pp. 235–283). Hillsdale, NJ: Erlbaum.

Cohen, S., Tyrrell, D. A., & Smith, A. P. (1991). Psychological stress in humans and susceptibility to the common cold. *New England Journal of Medicine, 325,* 606 612.

Cohen, S., & Wills, T. A. (1985). Stress social support, and the buffering hypothesis. *Psychological Bulletin, 98,* 310–357.

Contrada, R. J., Wright, R. A., & Glass, D. C. (1985). Psychophysiological correlates of Type A behavior: Comments on Houston (1983) and Holmes (1983). *Journal of Research in Personality, 19,* 12–30.

Cummings, N. A., & Follette, W. T. (1968). Psychiatric services and medical utilization in a prepaid health plan setting: Part II. *Medical Care, 6,* 31–41.

Cummings, N. A., & Van den Bos, G. R. (1981). The twenty year Kaiser Permanente experience with psychotherapy and medical utilization: Implications for national health policy and national health insurance. *Health Policy Quarterly: Evaluation and Utilization, 1*(2), 159–175.

Cushman, L. A. (1986). Secondary neuropsychiatric complications in stroke: Implications for acute care. *Archives of Physical Medicine Rehabilitation, 69,* 877–879.

Cutrona, C., & Russell, D. (1987). The provision of social relationships and adaptation to stress. In W. H. Jones & D. Perlman (Eds.), *Advances in personal relationships* (Vol. 1, pp. 37–67). Greenwich, CT: JAI Press.

Dahlstrom, W., Welsh, G., & Dahlstrom, L. (1972). *An MMPI handbook* (Vols. I & II). Minneapolis: University of Minnesota Press.

Davidson, J. K. (1983). The Grady Memorial Hospital Diabetes Programme. In J. I. Mann, K. Pyorala, & A. Teuscher (Eds.), *Diabetes in epidemiological perspective.* Edinburgh: Churchill Livingstone.

Dembroski, T. M., & Costa, P. R., Jr. (1987). Coronary prone behavior: Components of the Type A pattern and hostility. *Journal of Personality, 55,* 211–235.

Devine, E. C. (1992). Effects of psychoeducational care for adult surgical patients: A meta-analysis of 191 studies. *Patient Education and Counseling, 19,* 129–142.

Dimond, M. (1979). Social support and adaptation to chronic illness: The case of maintenance hemodialysis. *Research in Nursing and Health, 2,* 101–108.

Dimsdale, J. E., Pierce, C., Schoenfeld, D., Brown, A., Zusman, R., & Graham, R. (1986). Suppressed anger and blood pressure: The effects of race, sex, social class, obesity, and age. *Psychosomatic Medicine, 48,* 430–436.

Dubbert, P. (1992). Exercise in behavioral medicine. *Journal of Consulting and Clinical Psychology, 60,* 613–618.

Duberstein, P. R., Conwell, Y., & Yeates, E. (1993). Interpersonal stressors, substance abuse, and suicide. *Journal of Nervous and Mental Disease, 181*(2), 80–85.

Dunkel-Schetter, C., Folkman, S., & Lazarus, R. S. (1987). Correlates of social support receipt. *Journal of Personality and Social Psychology, 53,* 71–80.

Ell, K., Nishimoto, R., Mediansky, L., Mantell, J., & Hamovitch, M. (1992). Social relations, social support and survival among patients with cancer. *Journal of Psychosomatic Research, 36,* 531–541.

Epstein, L. H., & Perkins, K. A. (1988). Smoking, stress, and coronary heart disease. *Journal of Consulting and Clinical Psychology, 56,* 342–349.

Esterling, B. A., Antoni, M. H., Kumar, M., & Schneiderman, N. (1990). Emotional repression, stress disclosure responses, and Epstein-Barr viral capsid antigen titers. *Psychosomatic Medicine, 52,* 397–410.

Esterling, B., Antoni, M. H., Fletcher, M. A., Marguilles, S., & Schneiderman, N. (1994). Emotional disclosure through writing or speaking modulates latent Epstein–Barr virus reactivation. *Journal of Consulting and Clinical Psychology, 62*(1), 130–140.

Fawzy, F. I., Cousins, N., Fawzy, N. W., Kemeny, M., Elashoff, R., & Morton, D. (1990). A structured psychiatric intervention for cancer patients: I. Changes over time in methods of coping and affective disturbance. *Archives of General Psychiatry, 47,* 720–725.

Fawzy, F. I., Fawzy, N., Hyun, C., Elashoff, R., Guthrie, D., Fahey, J. L., & Morton, D. L. (1993). Malignant melanoma: Effects of an early structured psychiatric intervention, coping, and affective state on recurrence and survival 6 years later. *Archives of General Psychiatry, 50,* 681–689.

Fawzy, F. I., Kemeny, M. E., Fawzy, N. W., Elashoff, R., Morton, D., Cousins, N., & Fahey, J. L. (1990). A structured psychiatric intervention for cancer patients. II. Changes over time in immunological measures. *Archives of General Psychiatry, 47,* 729–735.

Felton, B. J., Revenson, T. A., & Hinrichsen, G. (1984). Coping and adjustment in chronically ill adults. *Social Science and Medicine, 18,* 889–898.

Fitzpatrick, R., Newman, S., Lamb, R., & Shipley, M. (1988). Social relationships and psychological well-being in rheumatoid arthritis. *Social Science and Medicine, 27,* 399–403.

Folkman, S., & Lazarus, R. S. (1980). An analysis of coping in a middle-aged community sample. *Journal of Health and Social Behavior, 21,* 219–239.

Fox, B. H. (1978). Premorbid psychological factors as related to cancer incidence. *Journal of Behavioral Medicine, 1,* 45–134.

Fox, B. H. (1981). Psychosocial factors and the immune system in human cancer. In R. Ader (Ed.), *Psychoneuroimmunology.* New York: Academic Press.

Frasure-Smith, N., Lesperance, F., & Talajic, M. (1993). Depression following myocardial infarction. *Journal of the American Medical Association, 270*(15), 1819–1825.

Frasure-Smith, N., & Prince, R. (1989). Long-term follow-up of the ischemic heart disease life stress monitoring program. *Psychosomatic Medicine, 51,* 485–513.

Frenzel, M. P., McCaul, K. D., Glasgow, R. E., & Schafer, L. C. (1988). The relationship of stress and coping to regimen adherence and glycemic control of diabetes. *Journal of Social and Clinical Psychology, 6,* 77–87.

Friedman, H. S., & Booth-Kewley, S. (1987). The "disease prone" personality: A meta-analytic view of the construct. *American Psychologist, 42,* 539–555.

Fulop, G., Strain, J., Vita, J., Lyons, J., & Hammer, J. (1987). Impact of psychiatric comorbidity on length of hospital stay for medical/surgical patients: A preliminary report. *American Journal of Psychiatry, 144*, 878–882.

Funch, D. P., & Mettlin, C. (1982). The role of support in relation to recovery from breast cancer. *Social Science and Medicine, 16*(1), 91–98.

Glasgow, R., Toobert, D., Hampson, S., & Wilson, W. (1995). Behavioral research on diabetes at the Oregon Research Institute. *Annals of Behavioral Medicine, 17*, 32–40.

Goldstein, D., & Antoni, M. H. (1989). The distribution of repressive coping styles among nonmetastatic and metastatic breast cancer patients as compared to non-cancer patients. *Psychology and Health: An International Journal, 3*, 245–258.

Gonik U.L. (1981). Cost-effectiveness of behavioral medicine procedures in the treatment of stress-related disorders. *American Journal of Clinical Biofeedback, 4*(1), 16–24.

Goodkin, K., Antoni, M., & Blaney, P. (1986). Stress and hopelessness in the promotion of cervical intraepithelial neoplasia to invasive squamous cell carcinoma of the cervix. *Journal of Psychosomatic Research, 30*, 67–76.

Goodkin, K., Antoni, M. H., Fox, B. H., & Sevin, B. (1993). A partially testable model of psychosocial factors in the etiology of cervical cancer: II. Psychoneuroimmunological aspects, critique and prospective integration. *Psychooncology, 2*(2), 99–121.

Goodkin, K., Antoni, M. H., Sevin, B., & Fox, B. H. (1993). A partially testable model of psychosocial factors in the etiology of cervical cancer: I. A review of biological, psychological, and social aspects. *Psychooncology, 2*(2), 79–98.

Goodkin, K., Tuttle, R., Blaney, N., Feaster, D., Shapshak, P., Burhalter, J., Leeds, B., Baldewicz, T., Kumar, M., & Fletcher, M. A. (1996). A bereavement support group intervention is associated with immunological changes in HIV-1+ and HIV-1– homosexual men. *Psychosomatic Medicine, 58*, 83.

Grady, K., Reisine, S., Fifield, J., Lee, N., McVay, J., & Kelsey, M. (1991). The impact of Hurricane Hugo and the San Francisco Earthquake on a sample of people with rheumatoid arthritis. *Arthritis Care and Research, 2*, 106–110.

Greenberg, P. E., Stiglin, L. E., Finkelstein, S. N., & Berndt, E. R. (1993). The economic burden of depression in 1990. *Journal of Clinical Psychiatry, 54*, 405–417.

Greer, S., Morris, T., Pettingale, K., & Haybittle, J. (1990). Psychological response to breast cancer and 15-year outcome. *Lancet, i*, 49–50.

Gruen, W. (1975). Effects of brief psychotherapy during hospitalization period on the recovery process in heart attacks. *Journal of Consulting and Clinical Psychology, 43*, 232–233.

Grunberg, N., & Baum, A. (1985). Biological commonalities of stress and substance abuse. In S. Schiffman & T. Willis (Eds.), *Coping and substance abuse*. Orlando, FL: Academic Press.

Hecker, M. L., Chesney, M. A., Black, G. W., & Frautschi, N. (1988). Coronary-prone behaviors in the Western collaborative group study. *Psychosomatic Medicine, 50*, 153–164.

Helgeson, V., & Cohen, S. (1996). Social support and adjustment to cancer: Reconciling descriptive, correlational, and intervention research. *Health Psychology, 15*, 135–148.

Hellman, C. J. C. (1990). A study of the effectiveness of two group behavioral medicine interventions for patients with psychosomatic complaints. *Behavioral Medicine, 16*, 165–173.

Herbert, T., & Cohen, S. (1993). Depression and immunity: A meta-analytic review. *Psychological Bulletin, 113*, 472–486.

Holahan, C. J., & Moos, R. H. (1986). Personality, coping, and family resources in stress resistance: A longitudinal analysis. *Journal of Personality and Social Psychology, 51*, 389–395.

Holland, J. (1990). Behavioral and psychosocial risk factors in cancer: Human studies. In J. Holland & J. Rowland (Eds.), *Handbook of psychooncology*. New York: Oxford University Press.

House, J. A. (1981). *Work stress and social support*. Reading, MA: Addison-Wesley.

House, J. S., Landis, K. R., & Umberson, D. (1988). *Social Relationships and Health Science, 241*, 540–545.

Hughes, J. E., & Lee, D. (1987). Depression symptoms in patients with terminal cancer. In M. Watson & S. Greer (Eds.), *Psychosocial issues in malignant disease*. Oxford, England: Pergamon Press.

Ironson, G., Antoni, M., & Lutgendorf, S. (1995). Can psychological interventions affect immunity and survival? Present findings and suggested targets with a focus on cancer and human immunodeficiency virus. *Mind/Body Medicine, 1*(2), 85–110.

Ironson, G., Friedman, A., Klimas, N., Antoni, M. H., Fletcher, M. A., LaPerriere, A., Simoneau, J., & Schneiderman, N. (1994). Distress, denial and low adherence to behavioral intervention predict faster disease progression in gay men infected with human immunodeficiency virus. *International Journal of Behavioral Medicine, 1*, 90–105.

Ironson, G., LaPerriere, A., Antoni, M. H., O'Hearn, P., Schneiderman, N., Klimas, N., & Fletcher, M. A. (1990). Changes in immune and psychological measures as a function of anticipation and reaction to news of HIV-1 antibody status. *Psychosomatic Medicine, 52*, 247–270.

Ironson, G., Solomon, G., Cruess, D., Barroso, J., & Stivers, M. (1995). Psychosocial factors related to long-term survival with HIV/AIDS. *Clinical Psychology and Psychotherapy, 2*, 249–266.

Ironson, G., Wynings, C., Schneiderman, N., Baum, A., Rodriguez, M., Greenwood, D., Benight, C., Antoni, M., LaPerriere, A., Huang, H., Klimas, N., & Fletcher, M. A. (in press). Post traumatic stress symptoms, intrusive thoughts, and loss of immune function after Hurricane Andrew. *Psychosomatic Medicine.*

Jacobs, D. (1987). Cost-effectiveness of specialized psychological programs for reducing hospital stays and outpatient visits. *Journal of Clinical Psychology, 43*, 729–735.

Jacobs, D., Kopans, B., & Reizes, J.M. (1995). Reevaluation of depression: What the general practitioner needs to know. *Mind/Body Medicine, 1*, 17–22.

Jacobson, P., Perry, S., & Hirsch, D. (1990). Behavioral and psychological responses to HIV antibody testing. *Journal of Consulting and Clinical Psychology, 58*, 31–37.

James, S. A., Hartnett, S., & Kalsbeek, W. D. (1984). John Henryism and blood pressure differences among Black men. *Journal of Behavioral Medicine, 7*, 259–276.

Jamison, K., Wellisch, D., & Pasnau, R. (1978). Psychosocial aspects of mastectomy: I. The woman's perspective. *American Journal of Psychiatry, 135*, 432–436.

Jarvis, G., & Northcott, H. (1987). Religion and differences in morbidity and mortality. *Social Science and Medicine, 25*, 813–824.

Kamarck, T., & Jennings, J. (1991). Biobehavioral factors in sudden cardiac death. *Psychological Bulletin, 109*, 42–75.

Kaplan, G. A., & Reynolds, P. (1988). Depression and cancer mortality and morbidity: Prospective evidence from the Alameda County study. *Journal of Behavioral Medicine, 11*, 1–13.

Katz, S., Ford, A., Moskowitz, R., Jackson, B., & Jaffe, M. (1983). Studies of illness in the aged: The index of ADL. *Journal of the American Medical Association, 185*, 914–919.

Keefe, F., Dunsmore, J., & Burnett, R. (1992). Behavioral and cognitive–behavioral approaches to chronic pain: Recent advances and furture directions. *Journal of Consulting and Clinical Psychology, 60*, 528–536.

Kiecolt-Glaser, J. K., & Glaser, R. (1992). Psychoneuroimmunology: Can psychological interventions modulate immunity? *Journal of Consulting and Clinical Psychology, 60*(4), 569–575.

King, J., Beals, J., Manson, S., & Trimble, J. (1992). A structural equation model of factors related to substance use among American Indian adolescents. *Drugs and Society, 6*(3–4), 253–268.

Klerman, G., & Weissman, M. (1992). The course, morbidity, and costs of depression. *Archives of General Psychiatry, 49*, 831–834.

Kolitz, S., Antoni, M. H., & Green, C. (1988). Personality style and immediate help-seeking responses following the onset of myocardial infarction. *Psychology and Health, 2*, 259–289.

Krantz, D. S., Grunberg, N. E., & Baum, A. (1985). Health psychology. *Annual Review of Psychology, 36*, 349–383.

Krantz, D. S., DeQuattro, V., Blackburn, H. W., Eaker, E., Haynes, S., James, S. A., Manuck, S. B., Myers, H., Shekelle, R. B., Syme, S. L., Tyroler, H. A., & Wolf, S. (1987). Task Force 1: Psychosocial factors in hypertension. *Circulation, 76* (Suppl. 1), 184–188.

LaPerriere, A., Antoni, M. H., Ironson, G., Klimas, N., Ingram, F., Fletcher, M. A., & Schneiderman, N. (1990). Exercise Training buffers emotional distress and immune decrements in gay males learning of their HIV-1 antibody status. *Biofeedback and Self-Regulation, 15*(3), 229–242.

Lawrence, R. C., Hochberg, M. C., Kelsey, J. L., McDuffie, F. C., Medsger, T-A., Felts, W. R., & Shulman, L. E. (1989). Estimates of the prevalence of selected arthritis and musculo-skeletal diseases in the U.S. *Journal of Rheumatology, 16,* 427–441.

Leserman, J., DiSantostefano, R., Perkins, D., Murphy, C., Golden, R., & Evans, D. (1995). Longitudinal study of social support and social conflict as predictors of depression and dysphoria among HIV-positive and HIV-negative gay men. *Depression, 2,* 189–199.

Leserman, J., Perkins, D., & Evans, D. (1992). Coping with the threat of AIDS: The role of social support. *American Journal of Psychiatry, 149,* 1514–1520.

Levenson, J. L. (1992). Psychosocial interventions in chronic medical illness: An overview of outcome research. *General Hospitals in Psychiatry, 14* (Suppl.), 43–49..

Levenson, J., Hamer, R., & Rossiter, L. (1990). Relation of psychopathology in general medical inpatients to use and cost of services. *American Journal of Psychiatry, 147,* 1498–1503.

Levin, J. (1994). Religion and health: Is there an association, is it valid, and is it causal? *Social Science and Medicine, 38*(11), 9–36.

Levin, J., & Vanderpool, H. (1989). Is religion therapeutically significant for hypertension? *Social Science and Medicine, 29,* 69–78.

Levine, M. N., Guyatt, G. H., Gent, M., DePauw, S., Goodyear, M.D., Hryniuk, W. M., Arnold, A., Findlay, B., Skillings, J. R., Bramwell, V. H., Levin, L., Bush, H., Abu-Zahra, H., & Kotalik, J. (1988). Quality of life in Stage II breast cancer: An instrument for clinical trials. *Journal of Clinical Oncology, 6,* 1798–1810.

Levy, S., Herberman, R., Lippman, M., D'Angelo, T., & Lee, J. (1991). Immunological and psychosocial predictors of disease recurrence in patients with early-stage breast cancer. *Behavioral Medicine, 17,* 67–75.

Lichtman, R., Taylor, S., & Wood, J. (1987). Responses to treatment and quality of life after radiation therapy for breast cancer. In H. P. Withers & L. Peters (Eds.), *Innovations in radiation oncology research.* New York: Springer-Verlag.

Lorig, K. et al. (1993). Evidence suggesting that health education for self-management in patients with chronic arthritis has sustained health benefits while reducing health care costs. *Arthritis and Rheumatism, 36,* 439–446.

Lovallo, W., d'Absi, M., Pincomb, G., Everson, S., Sung, B., Passey, R., & Wilson, M. (1996). Caffeine and behavioral stress effects on blood pressure in borderline hypertensive caucasian men. *Health Psychology, 15,* 11–17.

Lustman, P. J., Griffith, L. S., & Clouse, R. E. (1988). Depression in adults with diabetes: Results of a 5-year follow-up study. *Diabetes Care, 11,* 605–612.

Lutgendorf, S., Antoni, M. H., Ironson, G., Fletcher, M., Penedo, F., Baum, A., Schneiderman, N., & Klimas, N. (1995). Physical symptoms of chronic fatigue syndrome are exacerbated by the stress of Hurricane Andrew. *Psychosomatic Medicine, 57,* 310–323.

Lutgendorf, S., Antoni, M. H., Ironson, G., Klimas, N., Starr, K., Schneiderman, N., & Fletcher, M.A. (1996, March) *Coping and social support predict distress changes in symptomatic HIV-seropositive gay men following a cognitive behavioral stress management intervention.* Paper presented at the annual conference of Society of Behavioral Medicine, Washington, DC.

Lutgendorf, S., Antoni, M., Kumar, M., & Schneiderman, N. (1994). Changes in cognitive coping strategies predict EBV-antibody titre change following a stressor disclosure induction. *Journal of Psychosomatic Research, 38*(1), 63–78.

Magni, G., Silvestro, A., Tamiello, M., Zanesco, L., & Carl, M. (1988). An integrated approach to the assessment of family adjustment to acute lymphocytic leukemia in children. *Acta Psychiatrica Scandinavia, 78,* 639–642.

Marlatt, G. (1985). Coping and substance abuse: Implications for research, prevention, and treatment. In T. Wills & S. Shiffman (Eds.), *Coping and substance abuse.* Orlando, FL: Academic Press.

Marron, J., Fromm, B., Snyder, V., & Greenberg, D. (1984). Use of psychologic testing in characterizing the frequent user of ambulatory health services. *Journal of Family Practice, 19,* 802–806.

Marteau, T. M., Bloch, S., & Baum, J. D. (1987). Family life and diabetic control. *Journal of Child Psychology and Psychiatry*, 28, 823–833.

Marzuk, P., Tierney, H., Tardiff, K., Gross, E., Morgan, E., Hsu, M., & Mann, J. (1988). Increased risk of suicide in persons with AIDS. *Journal of the American Medical Association*, 259, 1333–1337.

McCann, B., Bovbjerg, V., Brief, D., Turner, C., Follete, W., Fitzpatrick, V., Dowdy, A., Retzlaff, B., Walden, C., & Knopp, R. (1995). Relationship of self-efficacy to cholesterol lowering and dietary change in hyperlipidemia. *Annals of Behavioral Medicine*, 17, 221–226.

McCracken, L. (1991). Cognitive–behavioral treatment of rheumatoid arthritis: A preliminary review of efficacy and methodology. *Annals of Behavioral Medicine*, 13, 57–65.

McKinnon, W., Weisse, C., Reynolds, C., Bowles, C., & Baum, A. (1989). Chronic stress, leukocyte subpopulations, and humoral response to latent viruses. *Health Psychology*, 8, 399–402.

Meyerowitz, B. E. (1980). Psychosocial correlates of breast cancer and its treatments. *Psychological Bulletin*, 87, 108–131.

Miller, L. V. (1981). Assessment of program effectiveness at the Los Angeles County–University of Southern California Medical Center. In G. Stein & P. A. Lawrence (Eds.), *Educating diabetic patients* (pp. 349–359). New York: Springer.

Miller, L. V., & Goldstein, J. (1972). More efficient care of diabetes in a county hospital setting. *New England Journal of Medicine*, 286, 1388–1391.

Millon, T., & Davis, R. (1996). *Disorders of personality: DSM-IV and beyond* (2nd ed.). New York: Wiley-Interscience.

Millon, T., Green, C., & Meagher, R. (1982). *The Millon Behavioral Health Inventory manual*. Minneapolis: National Computer Services.

Miranda, J., Perez-Stable, E., Munoz, R., Hargreaves, W., & Henke, C. (1991). Somatization, psychiatric disorder, and stress in utilization of ambulatory medical services. *Health Psychology*, 10, 46–51.

Morrissey, E., & Schuckitt, M. (1978). Stressful life events and alcohol problems among women seen at a detoxification center. *Journal of Studies on Alcohol*, 39, 1559.

Muhlhauser, I. (1983). Bicentric evaluation of a teaching and treatment program for Type I (insulin-dependent) diabetic patients: Improvement of metabolic control and other measures of diabetes care for up to 22 months. *Diabetologia*, 25, 470–476.

Mulder, N., & Antoni, M. H. (1994). Acquired immunodeficiency syndrome (AIDS) in homosexual men: Psychological distress and psychotherapy. *Clinical Psychology and Psychotherapy*, 2, 69–81.

Mulder, C. L., Antoni, M. H., Duivenvoorden, H. J., Kauffman, R. H., & Goodkin, K. (1995). Active confrontational coping predicts decreased clinical progression over a one year period in HIV-infected homosexual men. *Journal of Psychosomatic Research*, 39, 957–965.

Mulder, C. L., Van der Pompe, G., Spiegel, D., Antoni, M. H., & deVries, M. (1992). Do psychosocial factors influence the course of breast cancer? A review of recent literature, methodological problems and future directions. *Psychooncology*, 1, 155–167.

Mumford, E., Schlesinger, H. J., & Glass, G. V. (1982). The effects of psychological intervention on recovery from surgery and heart attacks: An analysis of the literature. *American Journal of Public Health*, 72(2), 141–151.

Mumford, E., Schlesinger, H. J., Glass, G. V., Patrick, C., & Cuerdon, T. (1984). A new look at evidence about reduced cost of medical utilization following mental health treatment. *American Journal of Psychiatry*, 141(10), 1145–1158.

Murphy, E., & Brown, G. (1980). Life events, psychiatric disturbances, and physical illness. *British Journal of Psychiatry*, 136, 326–338.

Myers, M. G., Brown, S. A., & Mott, M. (1993). Coping as a predictor of substance abuse treatment outcome. *Journal of Substance Abuse*, 5(1), 15–29.

Narrow, W. E., Regier, D. A., & Rae, D. S.(1993). Use of services by persons with mental and addictive disorders: Findings from the National Institute of Mental Health Epidemiologic Catchment Area Program. *Archives of General Psychiatry*, 50, 95–107.

National Institute on Drug Abuse. (1990). *Alcohol and health* (DHHS Publication No. ADM 87-1519). Rockville, MD: Department of Health and Human Services.

Neal, A. V., Tilley, B. C., & Vernon, S. W. (1986). Marital status, delay in seeking treatment and survival from breast cancer. *Social Science and Medicine, 23,* 305–312.

Newcomb, M., & Harlow, L. (1986). Life events and substance use among adolescents: Mediating effects of preceived loss of control and meaninglessness in life. *Journal of Personality and Social Psychology, 51,* 564.

Niemi, M. L., Laaksonen, R., Kotila, M., & Waltimo, O. (1988). Quality of life 4 years after stroke. *Stroke, 19,* 1101–1107.

Northouse, A. (1988). Social support in patients' and husbands' adjustment to breast cancer. *Nursing Research, 37,* 91–95.

Oldenberg, B., Perkins, R., & Andrews, G. (1985). Controlled trial of psychological intervention in myocardial infarction. *Journal of Consulting and Clinical Psychology, 53,* 852–859.

O'Leary, A. (1992). Self-efficacy and health: Behavioral and stress–physiological mediation. *Cognitive Therapy and Research, 16,* 229–245.

Oxman, T., Freeman, D., & Manheimer, E. (1995). Lack of social participation or religious strength and comfort as risk factors for death after cardiac surgery in the elderly. *Psychosomatic Medicine, 57,* 5–15.

Pallak, M. S., Cummings, N. A., Dorken, H., & Henke, C. J. (1994). Medical costs, Medicaid, and managed mental health treatment: The Hawaii study. *Management Care Questionnaire, 2,* 64–70.

Pennebaker, J. W., Kiecolt-Glaser, J. K., & Glaser, R. (1988). Disclosure of traumas and immune function: Health implications for psychotherapy. *Journal of Consulting and Clinical Psychology, 56,* 239–245.

Peterson, C., Seligman, M. E. P., & Vaillant, G. E. (1988). Pessimistic explanatory style is a risk factor for physical illness: A thirty-five year longitudinal study. *Journal of Personality and Social Psychology, 55,* 23–27.

Pettingale, K., Greer, S., & Tee, D. (1977). Serum IgA and emotional expression in breast cancer patients. *Journal of Psychosomatic Research, 21,* 395–399.

Razin, A. (1982). Psychosocial intervention in coronary artery disease: A review. *Psychosomatic Medicine, 44,* 363–387.

Reed, G. M., Kemeny, M. E., Taylor, S. E., Wang, H. J., & Visscher, B. R. (1994). Realistic acceptance as a predictor of decreased survival time in gay men with AIDS. *Health Psychology, 13*(4), 299–307.

Regier, D. (1994). Health care reform: Opportunities and challenge. In S. Blumenthal, K. Matthews, & S. Weiss (Eds.), *New research frontiers in behavioral medicine: Proceedings of the National Conference* (NIH Publication No. 94–3772, pp. 19 -24). Washington, DC: U.S. Government Printing Office.

Richter, S., Brown, S., & Mott, M. (1991). The impact of social support and self-esteem on adolescent substance abuse treatment outcome. *Journal of Substance Abuse, 3*(4), 371–385.

Robertson, E. K., & Suinn, R. M. (1968). The determination of rate of progress of stroke patients through empathy measures of patient and family. *Journal of Psychosomatic Research, 12,* 189–191.

Rosenstock, I. M. (1974). The health belief model and preventive health behavior. *Health Education Monographs, 2,* 354–386.

Sarason, I., Johnson, J., & Spiegel, J. (1978). Assessing the impact of life changes: Development of the Life Experiences Survey. *Journal of Consulting and Clinical Psychology, 46,* 932–946.

Schaefer, C., Coyne, J. C., & Lazarus, R. S. (1981). The health-related functions of social support. *Journal of Behavioral Medicine, 4,* 381–406.

Scheier, M. F., & Carver, C. S. (1985). Optimism, coping, and health: Assessment and implication of generalized outcome expectancies. *Health Psychology, 4,* 219–247.

Schlesinger, H. J., Mumford, E., Glass, G. V., Patrick, C., & Sharfstein, S. (1983). Mental health treatment and medical care utilization in a fee-for-service system: Outpatient mental health treatment following the onset of a chronic disease. *American Journal of Public Health, 73*(4), 422–429.

Schneider, C. J. (1987). Cost-effectiveness of biofeedback and behavioral medicine treatments: A review of the literature. *Biofeedback and Self-Regulation, 12*(2), 71–92.

Schwartz, L. S., Springer, J., Flaherty, J. A., & Kiani, R. (1986). The role of recent life events and social support in the control of diabetes mellitus. *General Hospital Psychiatry, 8,* 212–216.

Siegal, B. R., Calsyn, R. J., & Cuddihee, R. M. (1987). The relationship of social support to psychological adjustment in end-stage renal disease patients. *Journal of Chronic Disease, 40,* 337–344.

Sklar, L. W., & Anisman, H. (1981). Stress and cancer. *Psychological Bulletin, 89,* 369–406.

Smith, C., & Wallston, K. (1992). Adaptation in patients with chronic rheumatoid arthritis: Application of a general model. *Health Psychology, 11,* 151–162.

Sobel, D. (1994). Mind matters, money matters: The cost-effectiveness of clinical behavioral medicine. In S. Blumenthal, K. Matthews, & S. Weiss (Eds.), *New research frontiers in behavioral medicine: Proceedings of the National Conference* (NIH Publication No. 94-3772, pp. 25–36). Washington, DC: U.S. Government Printing Office.

Solano, L., Costa, M., Salvati, S., Coda, R., Aiuta, F., Mezzaroma, I., & Bertini, M. (1993). Psychosocial factors and clinical evolution in HIV-1 infection: A longitudinal study. *Journal of Psychosomatic Research, 37*(1), 39–51.

Solomon, G. F., Benton, D., Harker, J., Bonavida, B., & Fletcher, M. A. (1993). Prolonged asymptomatic states in HIV-seropositive persons with 50 CD4+ T-cells/mm^3. Preliminary psychoimmunologic findings. *Journal of Acquired Immunodeficiency Syndromes, 6*(10), 1173.

Spiegel, D., Kraemer, H. C., Bloom, J. R., & Gottheil, E. (1989). Effect of psychosocial treatment on survival of patients with metastatic breast cancer. *Lancet, 2,* 888–891.

Starr, K., Antoni, M.H., Penedo, F., Costello, N., Lutgendorf, S., Ironson, G., & Scheiderman, N. (1996, March). *Cognitive and affective correlates of emotional expression in symptomatic HIV-infected gay men.* Paper presented at the annual meeting of the Society of Behavioral Medicine, Washington, DC.

Stein, M. J., Wallston, K. A., Nicassio, P. M., & Castner, N. M. (1988). Correlates of a clinical classification schema for the arthritis helplessness subscale. *Arthritis and Rheumatism, 31,* 876–881.

Stern, M. J., Pascale, L., & Ackerman, A. (1977). Life adjustment postmyocardial infarction: Determining predictive variables. *Archives of Internal Medicine, 137,* 1680–1685.

Stoddard, V., Tsushima, W., & Heiby, E. (1988) MMPI predictors of outpatient medical utilization rates following psychotherapy. *Psychotherapy, 25,* 370–376.

Stone, A., & Porter, L. (1995). Psychological coping: Its importance for treating medical problems. *Mind/Body Medicine, 1,* 46–54.

Strain, J., Lyons, J., Hammer, J., Fahs, M., Lebovitz, A., Paddison, P., Snyder, S., Strauss, E., Burton, R., Nuber, G., Abernathy, T., Sacks, H., Nordlie, J., & Sacks, C. (1991). Cost offset from a psychiatric consultation-liaison intervention with elderly hip fracture patients. *American Journal of Psychiatry, 148*(8), 1044–1049.

Surwit, R. S., & Feinglos, M. N. (1988). Stress and autonomic nervous system in Type II diabetes: A hypothesis. *Diabetes Care, 11,* 83–85.

Taylor, S. E., Lichtman, R. R., & Wood, J. V. (1984). Attributions, beliefs about control, and adjustment to breast cancer. *Journal of Personality and Social Psychology, 46,* 489–502.

Taylor, S. E., & Aspinwall, L. G. (1990). Psychosocial aspects of chronic illness. In P. Costa & G. van den Bos (Eds.), *Psychological aspects of serious illness: Chronic conditions, fatal diseases, and clinical care* (pp. 7–60). Washington, DC: American Psychiatric Association Press.

Taylor, S. E., & Brown, J. (1988). Illusion and well-being: A social psychological perspective on mental health. *Psychological Bulletin, 103,* 193–210.

Theorell, T., Blomkvist, V., Jonsson, H., Schulman, S., Berntorp, E., & Stigendal, L. (1995). Social support and the development of immune function in human immunodeficiency virus infection. *Psychosomatic Medicine, 57,* 32–36.

Thoits, P. A. (1987). Gender and marital status differences in control and distress: Common stress versus unique stress explanations. *Journal of Health and Social Behavior, 28,* 7–22.

Thompson, S. C., Sobolew-Shubin, A., Graham, M. A., & Janigian, A. S. (1989). Psychosocial adjustment following a stroke. *Social Science and Medicine, 28,* 239–247.

Topol, E., Califf, R., George, B., Kereiakes, D., Abbotsmith, C., Candela, R., Lee, K., Pitt, B., Strack, R., O'Neill, W., & the Thrombolysis and Angioplasty in Myocardial Infarction Study Group (1987). A randomized trial of immediate versus delayed elective angioplasty after intravenous tissue plasminogen activator in acute myocardial infarction. *New England Journal of Medicine, 317*(10), 581–588.

Trijsburg, R. W., van Knippenberg, F. C. E., & Rijma, S. E. (1992). Effects of psychological treatment on cancer patients: A critical review. *Psychosomatic Medicine, 54,* 489–517.

Turk, D., & Meichenbaum, D. (1989). Adherence to self-care regimens: The patient's perspective. In R. H. Rozensky, J. Sweet, & S.Tovian (Eds.), *Handbook of clinical psychology in medical settings.* New York: Plenum Press.

Turner, H. A., Hays, R. B., & Coates, T. J. (1993). Determinants of social support among gay men: The context of AIDS. *Journal of Health and Social Behavior, 34,* 37–53.

Uhlenhuth, E., & Paykel, E. (1973). Symptom intensity and life events. *Archives of General Psychiatry, 28,* 473–477.

U.S. Department of Health and Human Services. (1992). *1992 HCFA Statistics: U.S. Department of Health and Human Services, Health Care Financing Administration, Bureau of Data Management and Strategy* (HCFA Publication No. 03333, pp. 212–216). Baltimore, MD: U.S. Government Printing Office.

Vaillant, G. E., Schnurr, P. P., Baron, J. R., & Gerber, P. D. (1991). A prospective study of the effect of smoking and alcohol abuse on mortality. *Journal of General Internal Medicine, 6,* 299–304.

van der Pompe, G., Antoni, M. H., Mulder, N., Heijnen, C., Goodkin, K., de Graeff, A., Garssen, B., & de Vries, M. (1994). Psychoneuroimmunology and the course of breast cancer, an overview: The impact of psychosocial factors on progression of breast cancer through immune and endocrine mechanisms. *Psychooncology, 3,* 271–288.

Vickery, D. M. (1983). Effect of a self-care education program on medical visits. *Journal of the American Medical Association, 250*(21), 2952–2956.

Wallston, B. S., Alagna, S. W., De Vellis, B., & DeVellis, R. F. (1983). Social support and physical health. *Health Psychology, 2,* 367–391.

Westhead, J. (1985). Frequent attenders of general practice: Medical, psychological, and social characteristics. *Journal of the Royal College of General Practitioners, 35,* 337–340.

Weisberg, M., & Page, S. (1988). Millon Behavioral Health Inventory and perceived efficacy of home and hospital dialysis. *Journal of Social and Clinical Psychology, 6,* 408–422.

Wiedenfield, S., O'Leary, A., Bandura, A., Brown, S., Levine, S., & Raska, K. (1990). Impact of perceived self-efficacy in coping with stressors on components of the immune system. *Journal of Personality and Social Psychology, 59,* 1082–1094.

Wiklund, I., Oden, A., Sanne, H., Ulvenstam, G., Wilhelmsson, C., & Wilhemsen, L. (1988). Prognostic importance of somatic and psychosocial variables after a first myocardial infarction. *American Journal of Epidemiology, 128,* 786–795.

Wilcoxin, M., Zook, A., & Zarski, J. (1988). Predicting behavioral outcomes with two psychological assessment methods in an outpatient pain management program. *Psychology and Health, 2,* 319–333.

Williams, R. B., & Chesney, M. (1993). Psychosocial factors and prognosis in established coronary artery disease: The need for research on interventions. *Journal of the American Medical Association, 279,* 1860–1861.

Wilson, S., Scamagas, P., German, D., Hughes, G., Lulla, S., Coss, S., Chardon, L., Thomas, R., Starr-Scheiderkraut, N., Stancavage, F., & Arsham, G. (1993). A controlled trial of two forms of self-management education for adults with asthma. *American Journal of Medicine, 94,* 564–576.

Wilson, W., Ary, D. V., Biglan, A., Glasgow, R. E., Toobert, D. J., & Campbell, D. R. (1986). Psychosocial predictors of self-care behaviors (compliance) and glycemic control in non-insulin-dependent diabetes mellitus. *Diabetes Care*, *9*, 614–622.

Woods, T., Antoni, M.H., Ironson, G., & Kling, D. (1996, March). *Religiosity is associated with affective and immune status in HIV-infected gay men.* Paper presented at the annual meeting of the Society of Behavioral Medicine, Washington, DC.

Wortman, C., & Conway, T. (1985). The role of social support in adaptation and recovery from physical illness. In S. Cohen & S. Syme (Eds.), *Social support and health* (pp. 281–302). New York: Academic Press.

Young, L. (1992). Psychological factors in rheumatoid arthritis. *Journal of Consulting and Clinical Psychology*, *60*, 619–627.

Zachariah, P. (1987). Quality of life with antihypertensive medication. *Journal of Hypertension*, *5* (Suppl.), 105–110.

Zich, J., & Temoshok, L. (1987). Perceptions of social support in men with AIDS and ARC: Relationships with distress and hardiness. *Journal of Applied Social Psychology*, *17*, 193–215.

Zook, C. J., & Moore, F. D. (1980). High cost users of medical care. *New England Journal of Medicine*, *302*, 996–1002.

Zuckerman, M., & Antoni, M. H. (1995). Social support and its relationship to psychological physical and immune variables in HIV infection. *Clinical Psychology and Psychotherapy*, *2*(4), 210–219.

21

The MPDC: Composition and Clinical Applications

ROBERT F. TRINGONE

In the construction and validation phases of the Millon inventories, there has been a tradition of gathering clinicians' impressions through rating scales. The research instruments have been included to compare the new self-report instruments to an external criterion and to maximize their diagnostic accuracy. The Millon Personality Diagnostic Checklist (MPDC) represents the most developed of these research instruments.

The MPDC was initially developed to assist in the construction and validation of the MCMI-II (Millon, 1987a). Without a "gold standard" to serve as a comparison point for any of the personality disorders (PDs), clinicians were asked to complete the MPDC and provide up to three PD diagnoses, in their order of salience, while their patients completed the MCMI-II research form. The clinician diagnoses helped set the prevalence rates and, in turn, the presence and prominence levels of the MCMI-II personality pattern scales. Concordance rates were then generated between the clinicians' diagnostic impressions and the self-report inventory. The diagnostic efficiency of each MPDC item across all the PDs was then calculated to investigate its strength and utility in the diagnostic process.

The MPDC was developed during a period of transition in the approach to classification and psychodiagnosis. This context will be discussed because it had a direct impact on the conceptualization and early use of the instrument. Steps taken in the construction and validation of the MPDC will be presented, as well as some of the available data on the instrument's internal and external validity. Clinical and research applications will then be demonstrated and future directions proposed.

CLASSIFICATION MODELS

Over the past two decades, there has been renewed interest in the area of personology. The most significant catalyst was the development and introduction of the DSM-III (American Psychiatric Association, 1980) with its multiaxial format, the placement of the PDs on a separate axis, and the delineation of specific diagnostic criteria. These changes marked a "paradigmatic shift" in the approach to classification and psychodiagnosis (Klerman, 1986;

449

Millon, 1986a). While DSM-I and DSM-II employed a "classic" perspective to psycho-diagnosis, DSM-III utilized a prototypic typology which recognized the diagnostic syndromes' intrinsic heterogeneity due to the probabilistic nature of their diagnostic features.

Wittgenstein (1953) received much credit with regard to recognizing the inherent ambiguity and multidimensionality involved in categorization. Researchers extrapolated from his notions of the multiplicity of "language games" and applied them to the PDs. The DSM-III (American Psychiatric Association, 1980) represented progress toward a prototypic typology (Frances, 1980; Millon, 1986a, 1987b), however, the advances were not complete (Frances, 1982; Frances & Widiger, 1986). For example, some of the DSM-III Axis II PDs were conceptualized within the prototypic typology (borderline, compulsive, and schizotypal PDs) while others (histrionic, narcissistic, antisocial, passive–aggressive, and paranoid PDs) required the presence of all their diagnostic criteria within a multiple choice format. DSM-III holdouts still under the "classic" monothetic format which required all diagnostic criteria to be present to meet a diagnosis were the schizoid, avoidant, and dependent PDs. In the DSM-III-R (American Psychiatric Association, 1987) and, now, the DSM-IV (American Psychiatric Association, 1994), all Axis II PDs are conceptualized according to the polythetic, prototypic typology.

Much debate has taken place and continues to take place in the shift from a "classic" model to a prototypal model and to the current consideration of dimensional models. Historically, psychology and psychiatry have tended to align their views of diagnosis with those of medicine and biology (Garfield, 1986) and the "classic" approach views categories as possessing clear demarcations indicative of distinct entities. Membership is determined by the presence of distinctive, "necessary and sufficient" characteristics which differentiate persons into homogeneous categories. Advantages of the "classic" perspective include the ease and convenience through which pertinent information can be communicated. Well-established categories are highlighted by a set of the most salient characteristics and they provide a standard reference for clinicians (Millon, 1987b). The failure to meet the assumptions of monothetic criteria and homogeneous group membership, however, argues against this position (Cantor, Smith, French, & Mezzich, 1980). There are also no studies available that have empirically determined the thresholds or cutoff points that make a clear distinction between the presence or absence of a PD (Widiger, 1992). Additionally, Frances and Widiger (1986) noted that attempts to delineate restrictive diagnostic criteria in an effort to increase the sameness of members in a category have led to an increase in the number of "wastebasket" categories. Ironically, the DSM-III-R Axis II revisions led to dramatic increases in the prevalence rates of the PDs as well as their comorbidity (Morey, 1988).

The prototypal model allows that instances within categories may display quantitative as well as qualitative differences. The critical contribution of the prototypal model is the assumption of probabilistic features, which demands greater flexibility in determining diagnostic categorization. There is a deemphasis on the presence of "necessary and sufficient" characteristics and instances are viewed along a continuum of prototypicality or "goodness of fit." Attributes serve as correlated indicators of disorders and carry varying degrees of diagnostic efficiency and validity (Clarkin, Widiger, Frances, Hurt, & Gilmore, 1983; Widiger, Hurt, Frances, Clarkin, & Gilmore, 1984). Within the prototypal model, category members are not likely to meet all inclusive and exclusive criteria of a category. Therefore, one anticipates heterogeneity within a disorder, numerous borderline, "atypical" cases, and varying degrees of similarity to the standard of comparison (e.g., DSM-IV PD). Other than the issue of within-group heterogeneity, the prototypal model allows for the overlap of categories. While it has been argued that categories may then no longer be very distinctive, the very nature of personality is one of overlap and covariation between personalities. Research with the MPDC has provided considerable support for the prototypal model (Millon & Tringone, 1989; Tringone, 1990).

Two variants have been proposed within a prototypic typology: summary prototypes and exemplar prototypes (Cantor & Genero, 1986). The most relevant examples of summary prototypes are the DSM-IV diagnostic criteria sets, whereas exemplar prototypes emphasize the use of multiple examples for any category. The difference lies in the latter's reliance on known instances or "exemplars" of a category rather than on the abstract image of a cognitive structure (Cantor & Genero, 1986). Millon's writings on PD subtypes (Millon & Davis, 1996) provide theoretically derived exemplars within each PD category. For example, while a person may have a primary narcissistic PD, they may also possess salient features of the histrionic PD (amorous narcissist), the antisocial PD (unprincipled narcissist), or the paranoid PD (elitist narcissist).

A common counterargument to the "classic" position states that persons cannot be divided into homogeneous, discrete units (Frances, 1980). In an effort to alleviate the qualitative problems of the "classic" model, a dimensional perspective has been proposed and has generated considerable interest. Viewing characteristics and disorders along a continuum of severity which ranges from normal to pathological, this model emphasizes quantitative gradations rather than qualitative, all-or-none distinctions (Skinner, 1986; Millon, 1987b). Such latitude allows an individual to possess certain features indicative of various disorders in matters of degree. Though perceived in opposition, "classic" and dimensional approaches complement one another (Frances, 1982; Millon, 1987b). While such dimensions account for quantitative differences for criteria, personality constructs can be perceived as qualitative sets of attributes. Dimensional scores can also be translated into categorical diagnoses through the use of cutoff points.

Classification systems which employ dimensions are viewed as more flexible and informative than the "classic" perspective (Widiger, 1982). Also, they are better able to classify borderline cases than is a "forced choice" paradigm. Their utility may be lessened, however, when descriptions become too complex and unwieldy (Frances, 1982). Other noted problems involve defining the core dimensions, agreeing on the number of core dimensions needed to represent the personality disorders, and identifying the meaningfulness of increments within the chosen dimensions (Millon, 1987b). At the present time, the five-factor model has generated the most interest and activity (Costa & McCrae, 1992, 1995; Shopshire & Craik, 1994).

With the shift from the "classic" perspective to the prototypic view, there has been a dramatic increase in the number of studies investigating the PDs. While we are progressing in our empirical understanding of these disorders, advancements must still be made in our theoretical understanding of their origins, their self-perpetuating tendencies, and how clinicians must intervene and treat them (Millon, 1969, 1981, 1990; Millon & Davis, 1996).

DEVELOPMENT OF THE MPDC

As with the other Millon inventories, the development of the MPDC has followed the validation sequence proposed by Loevinger (1957) and Jackson (1970). In her classic monograph, Loevinger delineated three components of construct validity: substantive, structural, and external. She suggested that these components were construction and validation stages that could be followed sequentially. Her schema incorporates the conceptualizations of Cronbach and Meehl (1955) on construct validity and of Campbell and Fiske (1959) on convergent and discriminant validity. The intent of following this model was to enhance the MPDC's reliability and validity and to maximize its efficiency in assessing personality characteristics. Millon's biosocial learning theory (1969, 1981, 1990) serves as the underlying theoretical model for the MPDC's conceptualization of the DSM-III-R and DSM-IV PDs, as the recognized constructs can each be theoretically deduced from Millon's three polarities model. This model also proposes the relationships of the different constructs to one another. Furthermore, it proposes prototypical features of each PD within common domains.

Stage I: Substantive Validation

The first validation stage, relabeled "theoretical–substantive," is the initial "guiding light" in the development of an assessment instrument. According to Loevinger (1957), the "substantive component of validity is the extent to which the content of the items included in . . . the test can be accounted for in terms of the trait believed to be measured and the context of measurement" (p. 661). Therefore, one of the primary objectives of the theoretical–substantive stage is to establish adequate content validity, which requires that a test's items sample the "universe" of "signs" of the construct(s) under investigation. Two steps were involved in compiling and developing items to meet this requirement with the MPDC: (1) creating an initial item pool based on theoretical and empirical grounds and (2) reducing the initial item pool on empirical and rational grounds.

Item Generation

In its original form, the MPDC (then named the Millon Personality Disorder Ratings Scale) was comprised of 240 items or descriptors of the 13 proposed DSM-III-R PDs, including the sadistic and masochistic PDs which were eventually placed in the Appendix. Each PD was initially represented by 18 or 19 descriptors distributed across five clinical domains. The MPDC items were chosen from personality characteristics according to Millon's biosocial learning theory of personality (1969, 1981, 1986b) and from the DSM-III-R Axis II diagnostic criteria. These sources were viewed as having theoretical and empirical support for defining the PDs.

A classification system becomes content valid when all of its categories are defined across the full range of clinically relevant domains. The criteria sets of the DSM-III-R and DSM-IV personality disorders are both "noncomprehensive" and "noncomparable" (Millon & Davis, 1996). They are distorted in various ways. Some of the constructs' criteria are narrow and restricted to behavior-oriented features, while other constructs' criteria are redundant and reiterate a single theme across multiple criteria. Shea (1992) also noted that the criteria sets vary in the number of underlying dimensions they address and the level of inference required to assess the criteria, with the latter issue amplified in regard to whether or not the underlying motivations of the manifest behaviors have been made explicit. This point is especially important because similar behaviors can have different determinants and different behaviors can share similar determinants (Stricker & Gold, 1988).

Millon (1986b, 1990) has outlined defining features for each PD across eight domain areas. Those features which are manifest between the person and his or her environment have been labeled "functional domains." These domains represent the "behaviors, social conduct, cognitive processes, and unconscious mechanisms which manage, adjust, transform, coordinate, balance, discharge, and control the give and take of inner and outer life" (1990, p. 136). Three functional domains have been incorporated into the MPDC: Expressive Acts, Interpersonal Conduct, and Cognitive Style. A second group of clinically relevant characteristics has been labeled "structural domains" which represent "a deeply embedded and relatively enduring template of imprinted memories, attitudes, needs, fears, conflicts, and so on, which guide experience and transform the nature of ongoing life events" (1990, p 147). The "structural domains" assessed with the MPDC are Self-Image and Mood/Temperament. These five domains were selected because they are generally more objective and require less inference on the part of clinicians than do the three remaining domains: Regulatory Mechanisms, Object Representations, and Morphologic Organization. While each domain is informative in its own respect, an assessment which involves multiple domains is much more thorough and clinically relevant.

Item Selection

Data were collected on the 240-item version of the MPDC as part of an MCMI–MCMI-II cross-validation study. A nationwide sample of clinicians who administered the MCMI as a regular component of a clinical assessment were asked to complete an MPDC and to provide up to three Axis II diagnoses for clients they believed had a PD. Instructions encouraged them to endorse between 35 and 50 items and then to reread the items and choose the 8 to 12 items that represented the client's most prominent characteristics. Data were initially collected on 238 subjects. The diagnostic efficiency of each item was then analyzed for each PD. From these analyses, 66 descriptors were eliminated, reducing the MPDC to 174 items. Items were dropped for the following reasons:

1. The endorsement frequency was so low as not to be a good discriminator between the PDs;
2. The endorsement frequency was so high as to be characteristic of the clinical population in general; and/or
3. The descriptor was redundant with other items, expressing similar ideas with only slight changes in its phrasing.

Item Weights

After this initial reduction, item weights were assigned in accordance with the prototypal model wherein the defining features of a PD may not be exhibited by all members of that PD diagnosed group and members of one PD diagnosed group often exhibit some of the defining features of other PD prototypes. Both trends create diagnostic mixtures and overlaps of varying degrees. For example, a person who meets the cutoff number of criteria for a Histrionic PD will receive this diagnosis without possessing all of the Histrionic PD diagnostic criteria and may also possess some of the Narcissistic PD criteria.

According to Loevinger (1957), the "empirical relations among the items, and perhaps between items and criteria, serve as basis for selection of items from the pool to form a scoring key" (1957, p. 661). The "empirical relations" between the MPDC items and the diagnostic categories were investigated with the diagnostic efficiency statistics. The four primary statistics are sensitivity, specificity, positive predictive power, and negative predictive power (Baldessarini, Finklestein, & Arana, 1983, 1988), and the two secondary statistics are comparative sensitivity and predictive prevalence ratio (Millon, Bockian, Tringone, Antoni, & Green, 1989). The sensitivity of a "sign" represents the true-positive rate of a particular criterion (e.g., affective instability) given the presence of a diagnosis (e.g., borderline PD [BPD]), otherwise expressed as the percentage of the criterion group which possesses the feature. In contrast, specificity is a measure of the true-negative rate and is expressed as the percentage of persons who do not have a particular disorder (e.g., BPD) and who do not possess the feature in question (e.g., affective instability). Measures of sensitivity and specificity are valuable in the determination of prototypes because they help assign inclusion and exclusion criteria. Given the presence or absence of a disorder, one is interested in the rate of the presence or absence of a "sign" in the criterion and noncriterion groups. High sensitivity and specificity values minimize false-negative and false-positive rates, respectively, and enable one to discriminate between groups with greater confidence. Positive predictive power represents the ratio of true-positive "signs" to all positive "signs" (e.g., conditional probability of BPD given affective instability) and negative predictive power is a measure of true-negative results to all negative results.

Millon and colleagues (1989) introduced two new diagnostic efficiency statistics which address some of the limitations inherent in the sensitivity and positive predictive power measures. A limitation in the sensitivity statistic resides in determining the significance and relative meaningfulness between different values across the PDs. Therefore, comparative sensitivity was derived to help compare sensitivity values and is calculated as follows:

$$\frac{\text{Sensitivity of target disorder}}{\text{Sensitivity of target disorder} + \text{Sensitivity of other disorder}} \times 2$$

The comparative sensitivity measure provides a midpoint of 1.0 which is met when the sensitivity of two groups is equal to one another on a particular criterion. It has a fixed range of 0 to 2.0. Fluctuations in either direction have relevance depending on one's reference point. At this time, intuitive judgments determine what values constitute a significant and meaningful deviation from 1.0. Comparative sensitivity compares multiple disorders and demonstrates overlap between disorders on particular criteria while maintaining a common midpoint for each comparison.

The problem inherent in positive predictive power is the unequal prevalence rate of various disorders in the population, and moreso, the lack of a systematic manner in which to take this information into account when analyzing the diagnostic efficiency of PD criteria. The predictive prevalence ratio is a simple measure which was developed to compare positive predictive power values between groups while adjusting for their unequal base rates (BRs) in the population. The measure is calculated as follows:

$$\frac{\text{Positive predictive power of target disorder}}{\text{Prevalence of target disorder}}$$

By chance, a target disorder could have a positive predictive power equal to its prevalence in the population. If this were the case, the predictive prevalence ratio would equal 1.0. Depending on one's criterion measure, one would anticipate higher or lower positive predictive power values relative to their prevalence values for the various disorders. Similar to the comparative sensitivity measure, the predictive prevalence ratio relies on intuitive judgments to determine the values which indicate significant and meaningful deviations from chance occurrence, although the general rule is a value of 1.5 or higher, as this means that the positive predictive power value is at least 50% higher than the PD's prevalence rate. The predictive prevalence ratio provides its most valuable information when analyzing criteria with adequate sensitivity values.

MPDC item weights of 0, 1, 2, and 3 points were assigned according to the patterns of the diagnostic efficiency statistics, in particular, the distribution of the predictive prevalence ratio. Translated to assigning weights on the MPDC, the PD with the highest predictive prevalence ratio for an item is assigned an item weight of 3. These are considered prototype items for the "home" scale and only one scale can receive 3 points on an item. An item weight of 2 can be assigned to one or more PD scales, depending on the distribution and relative strengths of the predictive prevalence ratio. An item weight of 1 can also be assigned to more than one PD scale but will always have a lower predictive prevalence ratio value than those PD scales assigned 2 units. Negative weights have not been assigned.

Raw Score to Base Rate (BR) Transformations

The MPDC cumulative unit weight values or "raw scores" are transformed into BR scores. The distribution of these cumulative raw scores is transformed to correspond with the underlying distribution or prevalence of the PD constructs in the clinical population. For this purpose, the appropriate transformation is into BR scores rather than standard or *T*-scores, which assume a normal, bell-shaped distribution. Whereas the latter scores provide a person's relative position in a normal frequency distribution, the BR scores optimize the diagnostic efficiency toward reaching a decision as to whether a person is or is not a member of a particular category. While the "base rate issue" was expounded upon decades ago (Meehl & Rosen, 1955), Gibertini, Brandenburg, and Retzlaff (1986) recognized that the lack of an explicit and reliable classification system hampers our ability to develop reliable tests which can determine, with a reasonable amount of confidence, whether a person does or does not possess a particular disorder. The DSM-III and DSM-III-R provided the first, albeit imperfect standards.

The MPDC BR scores range from 0 to 120. For each PD scale, the median raw score corresponds to a BR score of 60. The other BR scores are more complicated and are based on the prevalence rates of the PDs as calculated according to the primary diagnoses given by the clinicians. A BR score of 85 indicates the *prominence* of a personality pattern or PD and a BR score of 75 indicates the *presence* of a personality pattern or PD. The raw score in a frequency distribution for each PD scale which corresponds to the prevalence rate of each PD in the clinical population is assigned a BR score of 85. For example, the prevalence rate for the BPD is 20%. The raw score which is equal to the 80th percentile in a frequency distribution of all subjects' raw scores on the Borderline scale is equal to a BR score of 85. In other words, 20% of the Borderline scale scores from the initial sample will have a BR score of 85 and above. The clinicians' secondary PD diagnoses provide the percentages which correspond to BR scores of 75 to 84. For example, if 10% of the subjects were given a secondary diagnosis of BPD, then the raw scores which were between the highest 20% to 30% in the frequency distribution would correspond to these scores. The MPDC has separate transformations for males and females. For example, the same raw score will result in higher BR scores for females versus males on the Schizotypal and Paranoid scales and a lower BR score on the Borderline scale.

Correction Factor

One other component in the scoring system of the MPDC has been named the "correction factor." The majority of clinicians endorsed between 32 and 50 descriptors; however, a substantial number endorsed more or fewer items. The profiles obtained in the latter instances either "overpathologize" the person in the first situation or fail to have any personality scale BR score exceed 75 in the second. As a result, a correction factor was developed for adjusting the extreme profiles. For example, when a clinician endorses more than 50 items, the raw score values for each personality scale are multiplied by a value less than 1.0. In a similar manner, when fewer than 32 items are endorsed, the raw score values for each personality scale are multiplied by a value greater than 1.0. The adjustment factor seeks to maintain a clinician's approach to the test. It will raise or lower the profile but not overcompensate for the clinician's response style. An MPDC with fewer items endorsed, when corrected, will not exceed the median number of items endorsed, and an MPDC with more endorsements will not be adjusted below the mean.

After these revisions, data were collected on 222 subjects, bringing the sample size to 460. All 174 items were reanalyzed and 24 more were removed. Subsequent to these revisions the DSM-IV introduced the depressive PD and 10 prototypal items were added. Although the DSM-IV dropped the sadistic and masochistic PDs, these personality patterns are still included in the MPDC due to their theoretical underpinnings within the Millon model as well as the empirical support found for them in the MPDC and MCMI-II and MCMI-III analyses.

Stage II: Structural Validation

The second validation stage, relabeled "internal–structural," pertains to the test's congruence with its underlying theory, where the relationship between the scales and their items should be consistent with the theory's predictions. For those instruments developed within a factor analytic model, the scales are expected to be homogeneous and independent of one another. With regard to Millon's personality theory and the prototypal model, each MPDC scale is designed to possess a high degree of internal consistency and to display overlap with other theoretically related scales. According to Loevinger (1957):

> The structural component of validity refers to the extent to which structural relations between test items parallel the structural relations of other manifestations of the trait being measured. . . . The concept of structural validity includes both the fidelity of the structural model to the structural characteristics of non-test manifestations of the trait and the degree of inter-item structure. (p. 661)

The following statistics were computed to assess the MPDC's internal–structural validity:

- Internal consistency–reliability
- Correlations between scale scores
- Correlations between each item and its total scale score
- Correlations between each item and all total scale scores

Reliability

Alpha coefficients were calculated for each personality scale. These range from .78 to .91, with a mean of .84, well within usual acceptable levels and comparable with other gauges of personality traits and clinical patterns.

Interscale Correlations

Correlations between the MPDC scales represent the most basic analyses of the test's internal structure and its correspondence to the underlying personality theory. Table 21.1 provides supportive data in this regard. The three detached scales (Schizoid, Avoidant, and Schizotypal) all have significant positive correlations with one another. The Dependent and Self-Defeating (Masochistic) scales have a significant correlation with one another as well as with the Avoidant scale. All three of these scales have negative correlations with the scales marked by independent and hostile orientations (Narcissistic, Antisocial, Aggressive/Sadistic, and Passive–Aggressive/Negativistic). The Paranoid scale has significant positive correlations with the Narcissistic, Antisocial, Aggressive/Sadistic, and Passive–Aggressive/Negativistic scales. The Histrionic scale has significant correlations with the Narcissistic and Antisocial scales and lower but still significant correlations with the Dependent and Aggressive/Sadistic scales. The Borderline scale was found to have significant positive correlations with many other scales. The highest correlations were found with the Antisocial and Aggressive/Sadistic scales, due to their common impulsive behaviors and impetuous moods. Second-tier correlations with the Borderline scale were found with the Self-Defeating/Masochistic, Passive–Aggressive/Negativistic, and Schizotypal scales, while significant negative correlations were found between the Borderline scale and the Obsessive–Compulsive and Schizoid scales.

Item–Scale Correlations

More specific analyses of the internal structure of the MPDC involved the correlations between each item and the personality scales. These analyses were conducted to reflect the "convergence" (positive correlations) and "discriminability" (negative correlations) of each item with each personality scale. The vast majority of the MPDC items had their strongest correlations with their original, "home" personality scale. Overall, only three items had stronger correlations with a personality scale other than the original, "home" scale when they were correlated to total raw score values. Also, fewer than 10% of the items had stronger correlations with another personality scale when they were correlated with the

TABLE 21.1. Intercorrelation Matrix for MPDC Personality Scales

	SZD	AVD	DPD	HST	NAR	ATS	AGG	OCP	PAG	SDF	SZT	BDL
SZD												
AVD	.60**											
DPD	.14	.48**										
HST	−.59**	−.66**	.22*									
NAR	−.45**	−.66**	−.56**	.74**								
ATS	−.39**	−.51**	−.66**	.46**	.72**							
AGG	−.35**	−.36**	−.57**	.22*	.46**	.81**						
OCP	.16	−.02	.25**	−.09	−.17**	−.46**	−.48**					
PAG	−.13	−.18	−.47**	−.03	.26**	.55**	.70**	−.40**				
SDF	.14	.44**	.76**	−.22*	−.51**	−.47**	−.25**	.04	−.28**			
SZT	.68**	.61**	.06	−.47**	−.43**	−.17	−.05	−.25**	.02	.18*		
BDL	−.24**	−.00	−.02	.15	.05	.35**	.48**	−.57**	.22*	.30**	.21*	
PRN	−.13	−.08	−.57**	.05	.39**	.62**	.70**	−.33**	.62**	−.43**	.17	.18

Note. SZD, Schizoid; AVD, Avoidant; DPD, Dependent; HST, Histrionic; NAR, Narcissistic; ATS, Antisocial; AGG, Aggressive/Sadistic; OCP, Obsessive–Compulsive; PAG, Passive–Aggressive/Negativistic; SDF, Self-Defeating; SZT, Schizotypal; BDL, Borderline; PRN, Paranoid.
*p < .01; **p < .001.

BR scores. A consistent pattern for the vast majority of the MPDC items was that the correlations with the raw scores were higher than those with the BR scores for the "home" scale. Additionally, these "home" scale correlations tended to increase in magnitude from the BR scores to raw scores while decreasing in magnitude for the other personality scales (Tringone, 1990). A similar pattern had been noted with the MCMI-II (Millon, 1987a).

Stage III: External Validation

The third phase of validation, relabeled "external–criterion," requires the comparison of test scores to some external, "nontest" measure. To this point, the MPDC has been subjected to three tests of external–criterion validation:

- Concordance analyses between clinicians' diagnoses and the MPDC "high-point" scale
- Interscale correlations with the MCMI-II
- MPDC mean profiles with subjects grouped according to their primary Axis II diagnosis

Concordance Analyses

A concordance analysis tests the correspondence between the MPDC profiles derived from the clinician's endorsements (which were then converted to BR scores) and the primary diagnosis they provided. Three factors that potentially affected the concordance rates were in operation. One factor was that the diagnoses and endorsements were provided by the same person. A second factor was that the clinicians' endorsement patterns served to set the item weights as well as the raw score-to-BR transformations. A third factor that had to be considered was the unreliability of clinicians' diagnoses. Table 21.2 presents the concordance analysis between the clinicians' diagnoses and the MPDC. Two separate analyses are contained within this table. One is the distribution of high-point scales given the diagnosis which, in essence, is a measure of sensitivity: the percentage of cases given a particular diagnosis that have that corresponding scale as the high-point scale. The second is the correspondence between the high point scale and the clinicians' diagnoses, in essence, a measure of positive predictive power: the percentage of cases with a particular high-point scale that were assigned that diagnosis.

The concordance values range from 50% to 82% with a median agreement rate of just over 60%. Clinicians seemed to have their greatest difficulty identifying the dependent, narcissistic, and borderline PDs based on the "range" of high point scales for these cases. The positive predictive power values range from a low of 36% to a high of 72%, with a median concordance rate of just under 60%. The Aggressive/Sadistic and Self-Defeating/Masochistic scales had the lowest positive predictive power values. Such a finding was not unexpected, given their relative "newness" and the clinicians' lack of familiarity with them at that time.

MPDC–MCMI-II Correlations

Only one analysis has been performed testing the convergent and discriminant validity (Campbell & Fiske, 1959) of the MPDC with an uncontaminated external criterion. Correlations were computed between the MPDC and MCMI-II BR scores from more than 200 subjects from the original sample. Table 21.3 presents the data from this analysis. The

TABLE 21.2. Concordance between Clinician's Primary Diagnosis and MPDC High-Point Scale

Clinician's diagnosis		SZD	AVD	DPD	HST	NAR	ATS	AGG	OCP	PAG	SDF	SZT	BDL	PRN
							MPDC high-point scale							
Schizoid (N = 22)	N	13	2	1	0	0	0	1	0	1	1	2	1	0
	%	59	9	5	0	0	0	5	0	5	5	9	5	0
Avoidant (N = 57)	N	4	35	6	1	0	0	0	3	3	1	0	4	0
	%	7	61	11	2	0	0	0	5	5	2	0	7	0
Dependent (N = 74)	N	4	5	37	4	0	1	0	7	3	7	0	6	0
	%	5	7	50	5	0	1	0	10	4	10	0	8	0
Histrionic (N = 38)	N	0	0	4	24	2	1	0	4	1	0	0	1	1
	%	0	0	11	63	5	3	0	11	3	0	0	3	3
Narcissistic (N = 36)	N	1	1	1	7	18	2	2	1	0	0	1	1	1
	%	3	3	3	19	50	6	6	3	0	0	3	3	3
Antisocial (N = 11)	N	0	0	0	0	0	9	0	0	0	0	0	1	1
	%	0	0	0	0	0	82	0	0	0	0	0	9	9
Aggressive (N = 6)	N	0	0	0	0	0	2	3	0	0	0	0	0	1
	%	0	0	0	0	0	33	50	0	0	0	0	0	17
Compulsive (N = 49)	N	1	2	3	1	0	0	0	37	3	1	1	0	0
	%	2	4	6	2	0	0	0	76	6	3	3	0	0
Passive–Aggressive (N = 35)	N	1	1	1	1	0	0	0	2	22	0	0	4	3
	%	3	3	3	3	0	0	0	6	63	0	0	11	9
Self-Defeating (N = 16)	N	1	0	4	0	0	1	0	0	1	9	0	0	0
	%	6	0	25	0	0	6	0	0	6	56	0	0	0
Schizotypal (N = 17)	N	1	1	0	0	0	1	0	0	1	0	12	1	0
	%	6	6	0	0	0	6	0	0	6	0	71	6	0
Borderline (N = 86)	N	0	3	6	3	4	1	2	2	1	6	3	52	3
	%	0	4	7	4	5	1	2	2	1	7	4	61	4
Paranoid (N = 13)	N	0	0	0	0	1	0	0	0	0	0	0	2	10
	%	0	0	0	0	8	0	0	0	0	0	0	15	77
PPP		50	70	59	59	72	50	38	66	61	36	63	71	50

Note. PPP (positive predictive power) = True positive results/All positive results. All other abbreviations as in Table 21.1.

459

TABLE 21.3. Interscale Correlations between MPDC and MCMI-II BR Scores

MCMI-II	MPDC personality scales												
	SZD	AVD	DPD	HST	NAR	ATS	AGG	OCP	PAG	SDF	SZT	BDL	PRN
SZD	36**	47**	22*	-42**	-43**	-27**	-11	00	09	18*	41**	-01	-01
AVD	28**	48**	26**	-34**	-36**	-19*	00	-26**	05	31**	43**	24**	-06
DPD	04	12	33**	01	-19*	-20*	-16	-08	-15	25**	05	10	-30**
HST	-42**	-45**	-16	39**	35**	23**	17	-11	-00	-10	-31**	11	01
NAR	-30**	-36**	-25**	22**	32**	21*	14	-04	09	-22*	-29**	-03	15
ATS	-09	-09	-18*	00	13	21*	20*	-29**	16	-08	04	11	15
AGG	-16	-17	-25**	01	18*	23**	25**	-13	21*	-21*	-07	02	26**
OCP	11	03	-03	-13	-06	-17*	-19*	29**	-03	-18*	-11	-30**	03
PAG	-02	14	06	-12	-09	10	25**	-38**	21*	13	21*	29**	13
SDF	04	26**	28**	-12	-22*	-06	11	-36**	03	38**	30**	41**	-10
SZT	28**	41**	14	-38**	-34**	-16	-03	-23**	05	18*	43**	14	-02
BDL	-05	13	09	-08	-11	10	24**	-43**	11	23**	25**	47**	04
PRN	-04	-06	-11	-03	03	04	04	-12	11	-15	-02	-05	13

Note. Abbreviations as in Table 21.1.
*p < .01; **p < .001. N = 217.

correlations for the same personality scales ranged from a low of .13 (Paranoid scales) to a high of .48 (Avoidant scales) with a median correlation of .33. The majority of the scales had their highest correlations with their corresponding scales and all of these, except for the Paranoid scale, were significant. While some of these scale correlations between the two sources are not as strong as I would like, the correlations between similar scales on self-report inventories and similar constructs on self-report inventories and structured interviews have often been weaker than those reported here.

MPDC Mean Profiles of Clinician-Diagnosed Groups

Mean profiles provide a graphic representation of the concordance between the clinicians' primary diagnoses and the MPDC. However, they provide a "condensed image" of the diagnostic group, as the averaged BR scores lose their ability to represent individual differences or subtype diversity. While these profiles demonstrate the prototypal model quite well, they collapse valuable information across individuals and subtypes. The results of these analyses have been presented elsewhere (Tringone, 1990).

CLINICAL APPLICATIONS

While the MPDC-IV was initially developed as a research instrument, its link to Millon's personality theory and its capacity to assess 14 personality disorders across five domains enables it to provide information that is clinically quite valuable. The next section will demonstrate its utility in checking a clinician's diagnostic impressions through comparing MPDC profiles with client-generated MCMI-III profiles. Although the MPDC was developed in conjunction with the MCMI-II, the strong correlations between the MCMI-II and MCMI-III scales (Millon, 1994) suggest that the MPDC should have similar correspondences with the MCMI-III. A number of factors are potentially in operation at any time that can affect the concordance between measures. These same factors have been noted with regard to structured interviews and self-report inventories. For example, a person can deny or conceal certain issues or features on a very conscious level or they may not be aware of these issues or features. In the other direction, people can exaggerate their symptoms or misuse clinically loaded descriptions of their lives. In the examples provided, MPDC and MCMI-III profiles are compared.

Case A

Anne was a 22-year-old woman who was referred for individual psychotherapy due to severe depression with persistent suicidal ideation. She had suffered two significant losses within the past year and was struggling academically in her new graduate school program. She expressed a passive wish to die and end her pain and suffering. She came from an intact but conflict-ridden family. Her parents argued often and her father was verbally and emotionally abusive toward her and her mother. In spite of very legitimate academic achievements in high school and college, she attached her self-worth to her most recent grades and, at the time she started treatment, she felt like a failure. She also experienced severe panic attacks which caused her to miss many scheduled exams. Her fear of failure immobilized her and further set her up to feel ashamed.

Anne's MCMI-III profile (Figure 21.1) captured the acute and chronic components of her depressive condition. Her inner pain and torment were unmistakable. She possessed a

MILLON CLINICAL MULTIAXIAL INVENTORY - III
CONFIDENTIAL INFORMATION FOR PROFESSIONAL USE ONLY

ID NUMBER: 8755   Valid Profile
PERSONALITY CODE: 2B ** 8B * 7 2A + 5 3 4 1 " 8A 6A 6B ' ' // - ** - * //
SYNDROME CODE: D ** A * // CC ** - * //
DEMOGRAPHIC: 8755/ON/F/22/W/N/17/MA/SC/-----/02/-----/

CATEGORY		SCORE		PROFILE OF BR SCORES					DIAGNOSTIC SCALES
		RAW	BR	0	60	75	85	115	
MODIFYING INDICES	X	89	57						DISCLOSURE
	Y	9	43						DESIRABILITY
	Z	21	78						DEBASEMENT
CLINICAL PERSONALITY PATTERNS	1	5	50						SCHIZOID
	2A	9	65						AVOIDANT
	2B	17	89						DEPRESSIVE
	3	8	53						DEPENDENT
	4	11	51						HISTRIONIC
	5	10	55						NARCISSISTIC
	6A	1	12						ANTISOCIAL
	6B	1	12						AGGRESSIVE (SADISTIC)
	7	20	74						COMPULSIVE
	8A	3	20						PASSIVE-AGGRESSIVE
	8B	7	75						SELF-DEFEATING
SEVERE PERSONALITY PATHOLOGY	S	9	65						SCHIZOTYPAL
	C	7	49						BORDERLINE
	P	3	45						PARANOID
CLINICAL SYNDROMES	A	9	80						ANXIETY DISORDER
	H	10	69						SOMATOFORM DISORDER
	N	2	24						BIPOLAR: MANIC DISORDER
	D	17	85						DYSTHYMIC DISORDER
	B	1	25						ALCOHOL DEPENDENCE
	T	0	0						DRUG DEPENDENCE
	R	8	64						POST-TRAUMATIC STRESS
SEVERE SYNDROMES	SS	12	68						THOUGHT DISORDER
	CC	16	92						MAJOR DEPRESSION
	PP	0	0						DELUSIONAL DISORDER

FIGURE 21.1. MCMI-III profile for a 22-year-old woman. Copyright 1994 by Dicandrien, Inc. All rights reserved. Reproduced by permission. Published and distributed exclusively by National Computer Systems, Inc., Minneapolis, MN 55440. "Million Clinical Multiaxial Inventory-III" and "MCMI-III" are trademarks of Dicandrien, Inc.

pervasive sadness, a pessimistic outlook, and an inadequate self-image. While she was often self-sacrificing in her efforts to secure acceptance, she tended to focus on past injustices and anticipate future disappointments. She experienced extended periods of dejection and harbored a sense of worthlessness. Family relationships were generally dissatisfying and she often felt mistreated and unappreciated. Guilt-ridden over her perceived deficiencies and failures, she believed that she deserved to suffer. Her life became a vicious circle of pain and unhappiness where she could not turn to others and she turned away from herself. Her presentation was consistent with the self-derogating, depressive subtype (Millon & Davis, 1996). Obsessive–compulsive features helped her to function well in more structured environments. Her MCMI-III profile further suggested that anger and resentment were often suppressed or turned inward.

Her MPDC profile (Figure 21.2) was quite similar to her MCMI-III profile, with the two highest elevations on the Depressive and Self-Defeating/Masochistic scales. While the Obsessive–Compulsive scale was the third highest MCMI-III scale, the Dependent scale was in this position on the MPDC. This tertiary elevation suggests that the clinician has sensed significant dependence needs which Anne may not have acknowledged or recognized to the same extent or may not manifest at this level when she is under less acute stress. The following were her prototypal depressive features clustered within the Mood/Temperament domain:

Is characteristically gloomy and dejected
Is almost always sad and downcast
Is preoccupied with guilt feelings

and the Cognitive Style domain:

Broods about past and worries about future
Exhibits ingrained pessimistic outlook

At the same time, her prototypal self-defeating/masochistic features within the Interpersonal Conduct domain were as follows:

	Raw	BR	Millon Personality Diagnostic Checklist					
			0	30	60	75	85	115
Schizoid	15	52	*********************					
Avoidant	25	65	*****************************					
Depressive	55	115	**					
Dependent	42	89	**					
Histrionic	3	21	********					
Narcissistic	0	0						
Antisocial	0	0						
Sadistic	7	21	********					
Obsessive–Compulsive	34	86	**					
Negativistic	3	21	********					
Masochistic	69	115	**					
Schizotypal	10	32	*************					
Borderline	19	39	****************					
Paranoid	1	8	***					

FIGURE 21.2. MPDC profile for a 22-year-old woman.

Engages in self-sacrifice and martyrdom
Courts undeserved blame and criticism
Permits others to be exploitative and mistreating

and in the Self-Image domain were as follows:

Claims to deserve being shamed and debased
Belittles own aptitudes and competencies

A closer inspection of the MPDC descriptors revealed that her prototypal dependent features were also within the Interpersonal Conduct domain:

Is compliant, submissive, and placating
Subordinates desires to please nurturing person
Prefers others to make major decisions

as well as in the Self-Image domain:

Sees self as inept and/or fragile
Is notably lacking in self-confidence

There is good concordance in this case between the self-report and clinician-rated instruments, as the profile configurations are quite similar with a common two-point high code (2B–8B). Her treatment plan should include psychotherapeutic and pharmacologic interventions. Working through her grieving and mourning within the context of both the etiology (history) and self-perpetuation processes (present and future) of her personality style will be the primary focus of her treatment. I would also anticipate that the Self-Image, Interpersonal Conduct, and Mood/Temperament domains would be targeted through cognitive and assertiveness training interventions.

Cases B and C

Vincent, a 37-year-old man, and Marie, a 32-year-old woman, had been married for 4 years. They were seen for marital therapy due to frequent conflicts, poor communication, and mutual dissatisfaction with their marriage. He is a money market broker and she is a former teacher who stays home to raise their 3-year-old daughter. Each expressed that their needs were not met and that they were frustrated with one another. She described her husband as a "self-centered king" who expected to be catered to while he described his wife as an "indecisive child." The issues of differing parenting styles and whether to have another child were the areas they initially wanted to address. Marie did not want a second child if the marriage did not improve and Vincent did not help more, while he saw her stance as a way of gaining "power and control" over him and forcing him to change. Their arguments were intense and often led to one or the other threatening to leave or telling the other to leave.

Vincent's MCMI-III profile (Figure 21.3) suggested that he was quite self-centered, with an inflated sense of self-importance which was combined with an underlying sense of mistrust. His inner anger and resentment was quick to be projected outward and he can be abrasive and provocative. A sense of self-determination and self-reliance were important to him. A primary theme for him was to remain in a dominant position of power over others

MILLON CLINICAL MULTIAXIAL INVENTORY - III
CONFIDENTIAL INFORMATION FOR PROFESSIONAL USE ONLY

ID NUMBER: 4020   Valid Profile
PERSONALITY CODE: 5 ** 8A 6B * 3 + 4 7 6A 2B 1 " 2A 8B ' ' // - ** P * //
SYNDROME CODE: - ** A * // - ** - * //
DEMOGRAPHIC: 4020/ON/M/37/W/F/16/MA/SX/----/10/----/

CATEGORY		SCORE RAW	BR	PROFILE OF BR SCORES	DIAGNOSTIC SCALES
MODIFYING INDICES	X	96	61		DISCLOSURE
	Y	18	84		DESIRABILITY
	Z	5	49		DEBASEMENT
CLINICAL PERSONALITY PATTERNS	1	3	36		SCHIZOID
	2A	2	23		AVOIDANT
	2B	2	39		DEPRESSIVE
	3	8	70		DEPENDENT
	4	19	56		HISTRIONIC
	5	23	100		NARCISSISTIC
	6A	6	45		ANTISOCIAL
	6B	15	75		AGGRESSIVE (SADISTIC)
	7	15	49		COMPULSIVE
	8A	11	77		PASSIVE-AGGRESSIVE
	8B	0	0		SELF-DEFEATING
SEVERE PERSONALITY PATHOLOGY	S	3	59		SCHIZOTYPAL
	C	7	61		BORDERLINE
	P	15	75		PARANOID
CLINICAL SYNDROMES	A	7	82		ANXIETY DISORDER
	H	0	0		SOMATOFORM DISORDER
	N	7	64		BIPOLAR: MANIC DISORDER
	D	2	40		DYSTHYMIC DISORDER
	B	3	45		ALCOHOL DEPENDENCE
	T	2	30		DRUG DEPENDENCE
	R	4	60		POST-TRAUMATIC STRESS
SEVERE SYNDROMES	SS	7	64		THOUGHT DISORDER
	CC	0	0		MAJOR DEPRESSION
	PP	9	74		DELUSIONAL DISORDER

(BR scale markers: 0, 60, 75, 85, 115)

FIGURE 21.3. MCMI-III profile for a 37-year-old man. Copyright 1994 by Dicandrien, Inc. All rights reserved. Reproduced by permission. Published and distributed exclusively by National Computer Systems, Inc., Minneapolis, MN 55440. "Million Clinical Multiaxial Inventory-III" and "MCMI-III" are trademarks of Dicandrien, Inc.

before they had an opportunity to exploit him. His desire to intimidate and control others stemmed from a need to overcome his sense of inner weakness and to vindicate real or imagined injustices. Risk-taking and decisiveness are admired attributes while sensitivity, tenderness, and warmth are considered weaknesses.

Vincent's narcissistic orientation was quite pervasive and obvious. His MPDC profile (Figure 21.4) captured this with the very prominent elevation on the Narcissistic scale. On a secondary basis, features of the paranoid, antisocial, histrionic, and aggressive/sadistic PDs are manifest in his assertive and reactive demeanor. The Antisocial scale is presumed to be elevated due to its high correlation with the Narcissistic scale (.72) and the Aggressive/Sadistic scale (.81).

Marie's MCMI-III profile (Figure 21.5), on the other hand, portrayed a woman who was almost the opposite of her husband. Her "spike" high-point code on the Histrionic scale indicated that she required affection and recognition from significant others and often acted in a gregarious and outgoing manner. She tended to be compliant, accommodating, and giving and she emphasized maintaining harmony in her relationships. It was crucial for her to be attentive and responsive to others, as her self-esteem was attached to others' approval.

Marie's MPDC profile (Figure 21.6) added supplementary information to her MCMI-III profile with regard to the possible underlying determinants of her basically histrionic presentation. Her histrionic, dependent, and obsessive–compulsive configuration on the MPDC was consistent with the appeasing histrionic subtype (Millon & Davis, 1996) which possesses many of the primary histrionic features. It was probable that as a child she was taught to be other-directed and that she learned to satisfy others', in particular, her parents' desires and expectations to receive attention and affection. Her efforts, however, may not have been "good enough"; therefore, she could not please them or elicit praise and recognition from them on a consistent basis. As a result, she may have developed an underlying fear that she was inferior to others and she may have harbored an inadequate or unworthy self-image.

The insight gained from the MCMI-III and MPDC suggest that marital therapy with this couple will need to focus on the interplay of their personality styles and how their core differences (polarity levels) are played out in their relationship. Their basic needs are, in

	Raw	BR	Millon Personality Diagnostic Checklist					
			0	30	60	75	85	115
Schizoid	9	41	****************					
Avoidant	2	8	***					
Depressive	0	0						
Dependent	0	0						
Histrionic	20	71	**********************************					
Narcissistic	59	112	**					
Antisocial	53	73	***************************************					
Sadistic	43	68	**********************************					
Obsessive–Compulsive	6	42	*****************					
Negativistic	13	54	*********************					
Masochistic	1	4	**					
Schizotypal	8	24	*******					
Borderline	5	15	*****					
Paranoid	50	77	**					

FIGURE 21.4. MPDC profile for a 37-year-old man.

MILLON CLINICAL MULTIAXIAL INVENTORY - III
CONFIDENTIAL INFORMATION FOR PROFESSIONAL USE ONLY

ID NUMBER: 4010   Valid Profile
PERSONALITY CODE: - ** 4 * 3 5 7 + - " 2B 6B 8A 8B 1 2A 6A ' ' // - ** - * //
SYNDROME CODE: - ** - * // - ** - * //
DEMOGRAPHIC: 4010/ON/F/32/W/F/18/MA/SX/-----/10/-----/

CATEGORY		SCORE		PROFILE OF BR SCORES					DIAGNOSTIC SCALES
		RAW	BR	0	60	75	85	115	
MODIFYING INDICES	X	59	33						DISCLOSURE
	Y	15	70						DESIRABILITY
	Z	6	52						DEBASEMENT
CLINICAL PERSONALITY PATTERNS	1	1	11						SCHIZOID
	2A	1	10						AVOIDANT
	2B	5	34						DEPRESSIVE
	3	9	61						DEPENDENT
	4	16	79						HISTRIONIC
	5	11	61						NARCISSISTIC
	6A	0	1						ANTISOCIAL
	6B	2	25						AGGRESSIVE (SADISTIC)
	7	15	61						COMPULSIVE
	8A	2	14						PASSIVE-AGGRESSIVE
	8B	1	13						SELF-DEFEATING
SEVERE PERSONALITY PATHOLOGY	S	0	1						SCHIZOTYPAL
	C	3	23						BORDERLINE
	P	2	31						PARANOID
CLINICAL SYNDROMES	A	4	49						ANXIETY DISORDER
	H	6	52						SOMATOFORM DISORDER
	N	5	61						BIPOLAR: MANIC DISORDER
	D	5	34						DYSTHYMIC DISORDER
	B	2	61						ALCOHOL DEPENDENCE
	T	0	1						DRUG DEPENDENCE
	R	1	11						POST-TRAUMATIC STRESS
SEVERE SYNDROMES	SS	1	10						THOUGHT DISORDER
	CC	5	39						MAJOR DEPRESSION
	PP	0	1						DELUSIONAL DISORDER

FIGURE 21.5. MCMI-III profile for a 32-year-old woman. Copyright 1994 by Dicandrien, Inc. All rights reserved. Reproduced by permission. Published and distributed exclusively by National Computer Systems, Inc., Minneapolis, MN 55440. "Million Clinical Multiaxial Inventory-III" and "MCMI-III" are trademarks of Dicandrien, Inc.

Millon Personality Diagnostic Checklist

	Raw	BR	0	30	60	75	85	115
Schizoid	6	37	****************					
Avoidant	15	41	******************					
Depressive	11	31	**************					
Dependent	38	85	***					
Histrionic	33	87	**					
Narcissistic	13	57	**************************					
Antisocial	6	28	**************					
Sadistic	5	14	******					
Obsessive–Compulsive	30	79	***					
Negativistic	3	21	********					
Masochistic	31	58	***************************					
Schizotypal	10	32	*****************					
Borderline	22	44	**********************					
Paranoid	7	30	*****************					

FIGURE 21.6. MPDC profile for a 32-year-old woman.

many respects, counter to one another. As a result, the self-perpetuating processes inherent in their respective styles set up vicious circles which, at their most intense levels, threaten their marriage. For example, Marie was preoccupied with soliciting Vincent's approval. As he continually failed to recognize her needs and did not respond to her in a positive and supportive way, her efforts became more desperate. Vincent, in turn, began to feel smothered and eventually verbally castigated and demeaned her. His uncensored barrage caused her self-esteem to plummet. Under these circumstances, Vincent failed to recognize the pain he had inflicted and often attempted to justify his actions. Marie, on the other hand, was left to struggle with brief but recurring depressive episodes.

RESEARCH APPLICATIONS

When the MPDC was initially developed, its primary roles were to serve as an external criterion to the MCMI-II and to investigate the diagnostic efficiency of the DSM-III-R diagnostic criteria and other criteria which were theoretically consistent with the recognized and proposed PDs. What follow are examples of how the diagnostic efficiency statistics and the prototypic perspective were applied on an item basis with the MPDC. Schizotypal and borderline PD items were chosen because numerous articles have addressed their diagnostic overlap and covariation since Spitzer, Endicott, and Gibbon (1979/86) "split" them and established their respective DSM-III diagnostic criteria. Widiger, Frances, Warner, and Bluhm (1986) compared the diagnostic efficiency of the schizotypal and borderline PD DSM-III criteria using 84 inpatients. Substantial overlap was found, as they co-occurred in almost half the cases given either diagnosis. While each of their respective criteria had higher sensitivity and positive predictive power values for the "home" PD, these values were high for each PD. Nevertheless, given these limitations, the cognitive–perceptual criteria were the most effective discriminators for the schizotypal PD, while the most efficient borderline PD criteria were impulsivity and self-damaging acts. In a follow-up paper, Widiger, Frances, and Trull (1987) elaborated that, in particular, these cognitive–perceptual criteria were paranoid ideation, odd speech, ideas of reference, and peculiar illusions. Jacobsberg, Hymowitz, Barasch, and Frances (1986) reported similar results; the most effective discriminators between these PDs were inadequate rapport, odd speech, ideas of reference, magical thinking, and paranoid ideation. McGlashan (1987) also found that the most effective discriminators among the schizotypal PD criteria were magical thinking, odd speech, and paranoid ideation and the most efficient discriminators among the borderline PD criteria were impulsivity, self-damaging acts, and unstable relationships.

Table 21.4 presents the diagnostic efficiency statistics for two schizotypal PD items which are included within the MPDC's Cognitive Style domain section. The first criterion, "evidences impoverished or digressive speech," is an excellent inclusion criterion for this PD. The sensitivity value of 50% indicates that half of the subjects with a schizotypal PD diagnosis were rated to possess this feature. Its positive predictive power value of 31%

TABLE 21.4. Diagnostic Efficiency Statistics for Two Schizotypal PD Items

Prevalence:	SZD	= 4.45	[N = 26]		OCP	= 10.27	[N = 60]
	AVD	= 11.99	[N = 70]		PAG	= 7.19	[N = 42]
	DPD	= 14.55	[N = 85]		SDF	= 4.62	[N = 27]
	HST	= 7.53	[N = 44]		SZT	= 3.42	[N = 20]
	NAR	= 8.39	[N = 49]		BDL	= 20.21	[N = 118]
	ATS	= 2.40	[N = 14]		PRN	= 2.74	[N = 16]
	AGG	= 2.23	[N = 13]				

Scale	Phi	SEN	SPE	PPP	NPP	CS	PPR
Item: Evidences impoverished or digressive speech							
SZT	368	50	96	31	98		9.14
SZD		15	95	13	96	1.53	2.81
AVD		6	95	13	88	1.80	1.04
DPD		4	94	9	85	1.87	.64
HST		2	94	3	92	1.91	.42
NAR		4	94	6	91	1.85	.74
ATS		14	95	6	98	1.56	2.60
AGG		8	95	3	98	1.73	1.40
OCP		0	94	0	89	2.00	.00
PAG		2	94	3	93	1.91	.44
SDF		4	94	3	95	1.86	.68
BDL		3	94	9	79	1.90	.46
PRN		0	94	0	97	2.00	.00
Item: Exhibits magical thinking or superstitious beliefs							
SZT	384	80	90	22	99		6.41
SZD		31	88	11	96	1.44	2.46
AVD		9	87	8	87	1.81	.69
DPD		6	86	7	84	1.86	.47
HST		5	87	3	92	1.89	.36
NAR		6	87	4	91	1.86	.49
ATS		0	87	0	97	2.00	.00
AGG		0	87	0	97	2.00	.00
OCP		12	87	10	90	1.75	.93
PAG		2	87	1	92	1.94	.19
SDF		11	87	4	95	1.76	.89
BDL		17	89	27	81	1.65	1.36
PRN		13	88	3	97	1.73	1.00

Note. SEN, sensitivity; SPE, specificity; PPP, positive predictive power; NPP, negative predictive power; CS, comparative sensitivity; PPR, predictive prevalence ratio. All other abbreviations as in Table 21.1.

indicates that about one out of three subjects who possessed this feature were from the schizotypal PD group. The true diagnostic strength of this criterion, however, is captured in the predictive prevalence ratio, which exceeds 9.0. This value indicates that, for this sample, it is nine times more probable than chance that if a subject evidenced impoverished or digressive speech on the MPDC that they were in the schizotypal PD group. Secondary elevations were noted for the schizoid and antisocial PDs. On the other hand, very few subjects with a borderline PD diagnosis were rated to possess this feature.

The second criterion, "exhibits magical thinking or superstitious beliefs," is also a strong inclusion criterion for the schizotypal PD. Eighty percent of the schizotypal PD group possessed this feature, which resulted in a positive predictive power value of 22%. Seventeen percent of the BPD group possessed this feature, which resulted in a higher positive predictive power value of 27%. This discrepancy is due to the different prevalence rates for these groups. The predictive prevalence ratio statistic again clarifies that this criterion is a strong inclusion criterion for the schizotypal PD and does not contribute much beyond chance in reaching a BPD diagnosis.

The diagnostic efficiency statistics for two BPD items are presented in Table 21.5. The first item, "has made suicidal threats or attempts," is included within the Expressive Acts domain and has often been found to be the most discriminating criterion for BPD (Grueneich, 1992). These previous findings are supported with the current data. Almost three-fourths of the BPD subjects met this criterion, and almost half of the subjects in the total sample who met this criterion were within the BPD group. The second item, "has persistent identity disturbances," is included in the Self-Image domain and has not found overwhelming support in previous studies. Nevertheless, the current data suggest again that this can be a strong BPD discriminator, although clinicians would need to be wary that a significant proportion of the schizotypal PD subjects also exhibit this feature. Hurt and colleagues (1990) presented intriguing data in regard to "joint conditional probabilities" of diagnostic criteria wherein combining different criteria, even those with lower sensitivity values, can improve diagnostic accuracy. Their analysis grouped the BPD criteria into identity, affective, and impulse clusters and found the presence of criteria from at least two out of three clusters maximized diagnostic accuracy.

FUTURE DIRECTIONS

In the past two decades, numerous structured interviews and self-report inventories have been developed to assess the personality disorders. Most studies investigating the concordance between self-report instruments have found disappointing results, to say the least (Dubro, Wetzler, & Kahn, 1988; Streiner & Miller, 1988) and studies which have compared structured interviews and self-report inventories also have not fared well (Hyler, Skodol, Kellman, Oldham, & Rosnick, 1990; Zimmerman & Coryell, 1989). Much work needs to be done with the MPDC to determine its utility in various clinical settings. Its interrater reliability and relationship to other inventories and interviews must be explored.

The MPDC can also be employed to test out the diagnostic efficiency of new or proposed diagnostic criteria by adding them to the test. In this manner, convergent and discriminant validity estimates can be obtained according to the new items' relationships with the present MPDC items. Some current items may need to be refined and scale overlap reduced.

A large-scale study needs to be completed with the MPDC. While the sample chosen (e.g., inpatient versus outpatient) will have an effect on the PDs' prevalence and comorbidity

TABLE 21.5. Diagnostic Efficiency Statistics for Two Borderline PD Items

Prevalence:							
SZD = 4.45 [N = 26]				OCP = 10.27 [N = 60]			
AVD = 11.99 [N = 70]				PAG = 7.19 [N = 42]			
DPD = 14.55 [N = 85]				SDF = 4.62 [N = 27]			
HST = 7.53 [N = 44]				SZT = 3.42 [N = 20]			
NAR = 8.39 [N = 49]				BDL = 20.21 [N = 118]			
ATS = 2.40 [N = 14]				PRN = 2.74 [N = 16]			
AGG = 2.23 [N = 13]							

Scale	Phi	SEN	SPE	PPP	NPP	CS	PPR
Item: Has made suicidal threats or attempts							
BDL	459	72	80	48	92		2.39
SZD		12	69	2	94	1.72	.38
AVD		26	69	10	87	1.47	.85
DPD		21	68	10	84	1.55	.70
HST		30	70	7	92	1.42	.98
NAR		12	68	3	89	1.71	.41
ATS		29	70	2	98	1.43	.95
AGG		38	70	3	98	1.30	1.27
OCP		3	67	1	86	1.91	.11
PAG		24	69	6	92	1.50	.79
SDF		30	70	5	95	1.42	.98
SZT		15	69	2	96	1.66	.50
PRN		6	69	1	96	1.84	.21
Item: Has persistent identity disturbances							
BDL	295	39	89	46	85		2.30
SZD		12	83	3	95	1.54	.68
AVD		14	83	10	88	1.46	.84
DPD		13	82	11	85	1.50	.76
HST		9	82	4	92	1.62	.54
NAR		4	82	2	90	1.81	.24
ATS		14	83	2	98	1.46	.84
AGG		15	83	2	98	1.43	.91
OCP		8	82	5	89	1.65	.49
PAG		10	82	4	92	1.61	.56
SDF		19	83	5	95	1.36	1.09
SZT		25	83	5	97	1.22	1.48
PRN		0	83	0	97	2.00	.00

Note. Abbreviations as in Table 21.4.

rates (Grueneich, 1992), day treatment programs may serve as the most appropriate setting for this purpose. On an inpatient basis, active Axis I syndromes often distort (exaggerate or overshadow) patients' underlying personality styles, and outpatient settings often do not offer opportunities for more than one clinician to know the patient well. Day treatment programs, on the other hand, often work with patients who have had their acute Axis I disorders at least stabilized, which allows their Axis II disturbances to become more apparent. The multiple treatments and activities offered in these programs provide the opportunity for multiple clinicians to observe the patient in a variety of settings. Because the MPDC requires just a short amount of time to administer and score, it can be completed multiple times and lends itself quite well to addressing the issue of aggregation (Overholser, 1992).

CONCLUSION

The MPDC is a unique instrument which allows clinicians to rate Axis II diagnostic criteria across the 14 DSM-III-R and DSM-IV PDs and 5 clinical domains. Developed according to the three stages of construction and validation common to all of the Millon inventories, preliminary studies on the MPDC have shown reasonable internal and external validity consistent with Millon's theoretical formulations. The MPDC has proven to be quite valuable in determining the diagnostic efficiency of the DSM-III-R and DSM-IV Axis II diagnostic criteria and in serving as a significant data source to support the prototypal model of classification. The MPDC's potential utility was demonstrated in clinical and research applications; however, much work remains to be done to refine and improve the instrument.

REFERENCES

American Psychiatric Association. (1980). *Diagnostic and statistical manual of mental disorders* (3rd ed.). Washington, DC: Author.

American Psychiatric Association. (1987). *Diagnostic and statistical manual of mental disorders* (3rd ed., rev.). Washington, DC: Author.

American Psychiatric Association. (1994). *Diagnostic and statistical manual of mental disorders* (4th ed.). Washington, DC: Author.

Baldessarini, R. J., Finklestein, S., & Arana, G. W. (1983). The predictive power of diagnostic tests and the effect of prevalence of illness. *Archives of General Psychiatry, 40,* 569–573.

Baldessarini, R. J., Finklestein, S., & Arana, G. W. (1988). Predictive power of diagnostic tests. In F. Flach (Ed.), *Psychobiology and psychopharmacology* (pp. 175–189). New York: Norton.

Campbell, D. T., & Fiske, D. W. (1959). Convergent and discriminant validation by the multitrait–multimethod matrix. *Psychological Bulletin, 56,* 81–105.

Cantor, N., & Genero, N. (1986). Psychiatric diagnosis and natural categorization: A close analogy. In T. Millon & G. L. Klerman (Eds.), *Contemporary directions in psychopathology: Toward the DSM-IV* (pp. 233–256). New York: Guilford.

Cantor, N., Smith, E. E., French, R., & Mezzich, J. (1980). Psychiatric diagnosis as prototype categorization. *Journal of Abnormal Psychiatry, 89,* 181–193.

Clarkin, J. F., Widiger, T. A., Frances, A., Hurt, S. W., & Gilmore, M. (1983). Prototypic typology and the borderline personality disorder. *Journal of Abnormal Psychology, 92,* 263–275.

Costa, P. T., Jr., & McCrae, R. R. (1992). The five-factor model of personality and its relevance to personality disorders. *Journal of Personality Disorders, 6,* 343–359.

Costa, P. T., Jr., & McCrae, R. R. (1995). Domains and facets: Hierarchical personality assessment using the Revised NEO Personality Inventory. *Journal of Personality Assessment, 64,* 21–50.

Cronbach, L. J., & Meehl, P. E. (1955). Construct validity in psychological tests. *Psychological Bulletin, 52,* 281–302.

Dubro, A. F., Wetzler, S., & Kahn, M. W. (1988). A comparison of three self-report questionnaires for the diagnosis of DSM-III personality disorders. *Journal of Personality Disorders, 2,* 256–266.

Frances, A. (1980). The DSM-III personality disorders section: A commentary. *American Journal of Psychiatry, 137,* 1050–1054.

Frances, A. (1982). Categorical and dimensional systems of personality diagnosis: A comparison. *Comprehensive Psychiatry, 23,* 516–527.

Frances, A., & Widiger, T. A. (1986). Methodological issues in personality disorder diagnosis. In T. Millon & G. L. Klerman (Eds.), *Contemporary directions in psychopathology: Toward the DSM-IV* (pp. 381–400). New York: Guilford Press.

Garfield, S. (1986). Problems in diagnostic classification. In T. Millon & G. L. Klerman (Eds.),

Contemporary directions in psychopathology: Toward the DSM-IV (pp. 99–114). New York: Guilford Press.

Gibertini, M., Brandenburg, N. A., & Retzlaff, P. D. (1986). The operating characteristics of the Millon Clinical Multiaxial Inventory. *Journal of Personality Assessment, 50,* 554–567.

Grueneich, R. (1992). The borderline personality disorder diagnosis: Reliability, diagnostic efficiency, and covariation with other personality disorder diagnoses. *Journal of Personality Disorders, 6,* 197–212.

Hurt, S. W., Clarkin, J. F., Widiger, T. A., Fyer, M. R., Sullivan, T., Stone, M. H., & Frances, A. (1990). Evaluation of DSM-III decision rules for case detection using joint conditional probability structures. *Journal of Personality Disorders, 4,* 121–130.

Hyler, S. E., Skodol, A. E., Kellman, H. D., Oldham, J. M., & Rosnick, L. (1990). Validity of the Personality Diagnostic Questionnaire—Revised: Comparison with two structured interviews. *American Journal of Psychiatry, 147,* 1043–1048.

Jackson, D. N. (1970). A sequential system for personality scale development. In C. D. Spielberger (Ed.), *Current topics in clinical and community psychology* (Vol. 2, pp. 61–92). New York: Academic Press.

Jacobsberg, L. B., Hymowitz, P., Barasch, A., & Frances, A. J. (1986). Symptoms of schizotypal personality disorder. *American Journal of Psychiatry, 143,* 1222–1227.

Klerman, G. L. (1986). Historical perspective on contemporary schools of psychopathology. In T. Millon & G. L. Klerman (Eds.), *Contemporary directions in psychopathology: Toward the DSM-IV* (pp. 3–28). New York: Guilford Press.

Loevinger, J. (1957). Objective tests as instruments of psychological theory. *Psychological Reports, 3,* 635–694.

McGlashan, T. H. (1987). Testing DSM-III symptom criteria for schizotypal and borderline personality disorders. *Archives of General Psychiatry, 44,* 143–148.

Meehl, P. E., & Rosen, A. (1955). Antecedent probability and the efficiency of psychometric signs, patterns, or cutting scores. *Psychological Bulletin, 52,* 194–216.

Millon, T. (1969). *Modern psychopathology: A biosocial approach to maladaptive learning and functioning.* Philadelphia: W. B. Saunders.

Millon, T. (1981). *Disorders of personality: DSM-III Axis II.* New York: Wiley.

Millon, T. (1986a). On the past and future of the DSM-III: Personal recollections and projections. In T. Millon & G. L. Klerman (Eds.), *Contemporary directions in psychopathology: Toward the DSM-IV* (pp. 29–70). New York: Guilford Press.

Millon, T. (1986b). Personality prototypes and their diagnostic criteria. In T. Millon & G. L. Klerman (Eds.), *Contemporary directions in psychopathology: Toward the DSM-IV* (pp. 671–712). New York: Guilford Press.

Millon, T. (1987a). *Millon Clinical Multiaxial Inventory—II manual.* Minneapolis: National Computer Systems.

Millon, T. (1987b). On the nature of taxonomy in psychopathology. In M. Hersen & C. Last (Eds.), *Issues in diagnostic research* (pp. 3–85). New York: Plenum Press.

Millon, T. (1990). *Toward an integrated personology: Providing an evolutionary and ecological foundation for Murray's scaffolding.* New York: Wiley.

Millon, T., Bockian, N., Tringone, R., Antoni, M., & Green, C. J. (1989). New diagnostic efficiency statistics: Comparative sensitivity and predictive/prevalence ratio. *Journal of Personality Disorders, 3,* 163–173.

Millon, T., & Davis, R. D. (1996). *Disorders of personality: DSM-IV and beyond* (2nd ed.). New York: Wiley.

Millon, T., Millon, C., & Davis, R. (1994). *Millon clinical multiaxial inventory—III manual.* Minneapolis: National Computer Systems.

Millon, T., & Tringone, R. (1989). *Co-occurrence and diagnostic efficiency statistics.* Unpublished raw data.

Morey, L. C. (1988). Personality disorders in DSM-III and DSM-III-R: Convergence, coverage, and internal consistency. *American Journal of Psychiatry, 145,* 573–577.

Overholser, J. C. (1992). Aggregation of personality measures: Implications for personality disorder research. *Journal of Personality Disorders, 6,* 267–277.

Shea, M. T. (1992). Some characteristics of the Axis II criteria sets and their implications for assessment of personality disorders. *Journal of Personality Disorders, 6,* 377–381.

Shopshire, M. S., & Craik, K. H. (1994). The five-factor model of personality and the DSM-III-R personality disorders: Correspondence and differentiation. *Journal of Personality Disorders, 8,* 41–52.

Skinner, H. A. (1986). Construct validation approach to psychiatric classification. In T. Millon & G. L. Klerman (Eds.), *Contemporary directions in psychopathology: Toward the DSM-IV* (pp. 307–330). New York: Guilford.

Spitzer, R. L., Endicott, J., & Gibbon, M. (1986). Crossing the border into borderline personality and borderline schizophrenia: The development of criteria. In M. Stone (Ed.), *Essential papers on borderline disorders: One hundred years at the border.* New York: New York University Press. (Original work published 1979)

Streiner, D. L., & Miller, H. R. (1988). Validity of MMPI scales for DSM-III personality disorders: What are they measuring? *Journal of Personality Disorders, 2,* 238–242.

Stricker, G., & Gold, J. R. (1988). A psychodynamic approach to the personality disorders. *Journal of Personality Disorders, 2,* 350–359.

Tringone, R. (1990). *Construction of the Millon Personality Diagnostic Checklist—III—R and personality prototypes.* Unpublished doctoral dissertation, University of Miami, Coral Gables, FL.

Widiger, T. A. (1982). Prototypic typology and borderline diagnoses. *Clinical Psychology Review, 2,* 115–135.

Widiger, T. (1992). Categorical versus dimensional classification. *Journal of Personality Disorders, 6,* 287–300.

Widiger, T. A., Frances, A., & Trull, T. J. (1987). A psychometric analysis of the social–interpersonal and cognitive–perceptual items for the schizotypal personality disorder. *Archives of General Psychiatry, 44,* 741–745.

Widiger, T. A., Frances, A., Warner, L., & Bluhm, C. (1986). Diagnostic criteria for the borderline and schizotypal personality disorders. *Journal of Abnormal Psychology, 95,* 43–51.

Widiger, T. A., Hurt, S. W., Frances, A., Clarkin, J. F., & Gilmore, M. (1984). Diagnostic efficiency and DSM-III. *Archives of General Psychiatry, 41,* 1005–1012.

Wittgenstein, L. (1953). *Philosophical investigations.* Oxford: Blackwell.

Zimmerman, M., & Coryell, W. (1989). The reliability of personality disorder diagnoses in a nonpatient sample. *Journal of Personality Disorders, 3,* 53–57.

IV

THE PACL AND MIPS

22

The PACL: Gauging Normal Personality Styles

STEPHEN STRACK

gauge (gāj)—To appraise, estimate, or judge;
to determine the exact dimensions, capacity, quantity,
or force of; measure.[1]

The Personality Adjective Check List (PACL) is a 153-item, self-report and rating measure of Theodore Millon's (1969/1983a) eight basic personality patterns for use with normal adults and nonpsychiatric patients. It features a problem indicator (PI) scale that taps aspects of Millon's three severe schizoid, cycloid, and paranoid styles, and may be used as a measure of personality disorder. PACL personality scales assess theoretically derived, *normal* versions of the character types most frequently seen in clinical settings. Test results yield rich descriptions of respondents in a language that closely resembles that found in the DSM-IV (American Psychiatric Association, 1994). The measure is frequently used by therapists and personnel psychologists who work with relatively high-functioning individuals and who want to understand the *strengths* of their clients as well as their weaknesses. The PACL has been used in numerous research studies which tested various propositions of Millon's theory and addressed the interface between normal and abnormal personality (e.g., Strack, 1991a, 1993; Millon & Davis, 1994).

In this chapter I present the PACL from the ground up. I begin with its conception and theoretical foundation in Millon's (1969/1983a) biopsychosocial model of personality pathology and describe its development according to Loevinger's (1957) three-stage model of test construction. Next I present clinical and research findings from a variety of studies and descriptions of persons who obtain high scale scores. Clinical and research uses of the test are then outlined, and I finish with examples of personality ratings of some nontraditional subjects: Mozart and Beethoven.

---

[1]From *The Random House College Dictionary* (Rev., 1975).

477

CONCEPTION OF THE PACL
AND THEORETICAL FOUNDATION

The PACL originated at the University of Miami in the early 1980s in a research group led by Theodore Millon, Catherine Green, and the late Robert Meagher, Jr.[2] This was an exciting time. The DSM-III (American Psychiatric Association, 1980) had just been published and the new multiaxial diagnostic system incorporated much of Millon's (1969/1983a, 1981) personality theory into its taxonomy of character disorders. The MCMI (Millon, 1977, 1983a) had recently been published and the Millon Adolescent Personality Inventory (MAPI) (Millon, Green, & Meagher, 1982a) and Millon Behavioral Health Inventory (MBHI; Millon, Green, & Meagher, 1982b) were just being launched. At that time very little empirical work had been accomplished using Millon's model of personality and we sought ways of changing this. Many theses and dissertations were spawned in the research group, including my second year (master's level) project, *Development and Preliminary Validation of the Personality Adjective Check List* (Strack, 1981). The purpose of creating the PACL was to open the door for research on normal subjects. Although Millon's model posits a direct link between normal and abnormal personalities, the MCMI, MAPI, and MBHI were designed for clinical populations. By developing a measure of Millon's personalities for normal individuals we hoped to capitalize on the large pool of nonclinical research subjects available to investigators in college and business settings. Our long-term goals included building an analogue model of personality disorders among normal people and demonstrating the inherent continuity between the normal and abnormal domains of personality functioning.

LINKING NORMALITY AND PATHOLOGY

An attractive feature of Millon's (1969/1983a, 1981, 1986a, 1986b, 1990, 1994a) model, and one that makes the PACL possible, is its assumption that normal and abnormal personalities lie along a continuum, with disordered character representing an exaggeration or distortion of normal traits. Normal and abnormal persons are viewed as sharing the same basic styles. Disordered individuals are depicted as a small subset of the pool of all persons who, for various biological, psychological, environmental, and social reasons, have developed traits that are rigid and maladaptive.

In deriving his personality taxonomy, Millon (1981, 1986a, 1986b, 1990, 1994a) distinguished four points along the normal–abnormal continuum, that is, normal character, and styles exhibiting mild, moderate, and severe pathology. Eight[3] personality types are considered to exist in normal form and/or in mild or moderate pathological form, namely, asocial, avoidant, submissive (dependent), gregarious (histrionic), narcissistic, aggressive, conforming (compulsive), and negativistic. Three severe styles—schizoid (schizotypal), cycloid (borderline), and paranoid—are thought to be variants of the mildly and

---

[2]Other members of the research group were Leonard Bard, Nancy Firestone, Richard Garvine, and Steven Hentoff.

[3]The three personalities added later by Millon (1986a, 1986b, 1994a)—aggressive (sadistic), depressive, and self-defeating (masochistic)—were placed among the basic styles. Aggressive (sadistic) was formulated as a variant of his original aggressive personality, depressive as a variant of the avoidant style, and self-defeating (masochistic) as an aspect of the negativistic pattern. Whether these new styles exist in normal form has not been empirically established. On the surface, they do not appear to have normal counterparts.

moderately pathological personalities which do not have direct counterparts in the normal domain.

Two sets of concepts were outlined by Millon to distinguish his personalities at the various continuum points. One set of concepts defines the relative position of normal and pathological individuals on his three evolutionary polarities, that is, active–passive, pleasure–pain, and self–other (Millon, 1990). Normal individuals are thought to be balanced in each of these areas, for example, possessing both moderate self-esteem and empathic regard for others. Mild or moderate pathology is apparent among persons showing excesses or deficits in self- or other-regard, active or passive coping, and/or pleasure–pain orientation. Severe pathology is marked by extremes or distortions on these polarities.

A second set of ideas used by Millon to distinguish normal and abnormal personalities focuses on interpersonal functioning, namely, an individual's level of flexibility, stability, and tendency to foster vicious cycles (1969/1983a, 1986a). Healthy persons are viewed as interpersonally flexible, adaptive in coping, ego resilient, and able to avoid, escape from, or move beyond pathogenic attitudes, behaviors, or situations. In contrast, mildly and moderately pathological persons exhibit rigidity in interpersonal relations, nonadaptive coping, low ego strength, and a tendency to become mired in dysfunctional schemas or transactions with others and the environment. More severely disturbed individuals are viewed as strongly rigid and inflexible, lacking in adaptive coping skills, possessing extreme ego deficits, and unable to avoid, escape, or move through pathological thought processes and relationships.

In a recent expansion of his theory, Millon (1994b; Millon & Davis, 1994) explicated a number of new dimensions that he believes underlie the manifest forms of normal personalities. His pathological personality styles, and their normal variants measured by the PACL, were conceived on the basis of three *motivating* aims: active–passive, pleasure–pain, and self–other. To encompass a wider array of normal personality forms, Millon introduced four new axes differentiating various *cognitive* styles and five axes delineating *interpersonal* styles. Interested readers may consult the MIPS chapter (Chapter 23) in this volume for a complete description of these new theoretical principles.

DEVELOPMENT OF THE PACL

In deciding on a format for creating this measure, two factors were primary. First, Millon's empirical work had taught him that fast and simple tests were the ones most often selected for use by investigators and completed successfully by subjects. Second, I wanted the measure to build on the interpersonal roots of Millon's theory, a strong attraction for me given my previous training and work at Berkeley. Therefore, in the tradition of LaForge and Suczek's (1955) Interpersonal Check List, and Gough and Heilbrun's (1983) Adjective Check List, we decided to develop a quick and easy-to-complete adjective measure that would allow for both self-reports and observer ratings.

The check list was developed using a method outlined by Loevinger (1957) and used by Millon and his colleagues for creating his clinical measures. In this method test construction is theory driven and follows a step-by-step process with development and validation occurring together.

In the first stage of development and validation, dubbed the substantive phase, 405 theory-derived adjectives were selected to measure normal versions of Millon's (1969/1983a) eight basic and three severe personality styles. Items were drawn from numerous sources, including *Modern Psychopathology* (Millon, 1969/1983a), and were selected based on rater judgments that each item had a clear best fit for one style (see Strack, 1987, 1991a, for details).

The second phase of test construction, structural validity, involves creating scales that match the underlying theory. Toward this end, the 405-item experimental check list was given to 207 men and 252 women from colleges in Ohio and Florida. Preliminary scales were created from items that were endorsed by at least 5% and by no more than 80% of subjects and had minimum item–scale correlations of .25 and maximum within-scale item–item correlations of .49 (to prevent redundancy; Strack, 1987). Using these criteria, measures were created for each of Millon's eight basic styles that had satisfactory internal consistency and temporal reliability. Alpha coefficients ranged from .76 to .89 (new sample median = .83; Strack, 1987), while test–retest correlations over a three-month period ranged from .60 to .85 (Median = .72 across sexes; Strack, 1987). Additional data showed the scales to be relatively free from social desirability bias (Strack, 1987).

Unfortunately, measures could not be developed for the three severe (schizoid, cycloid, and paranoid) personalities because of extremely low endorsement rates (< 5%) for most keyed items. Rather than throw away the handful of good items that remained for these measures, they were combined into an experimental problem indicator scale, PI, which we thought might be useful in identifying persons with personality disorders.

In addition to the personality and experimental scales, I developed three response bias indices to aid in the detection of faked protocols (Strack, 1991a), namely, Random (R), Favorable (F), and Unfavorable (UF). Separate groups of college students were asked to complete the PACL randomly, or with intent to give an overly favorable or overly unfavorable self-report. Discriminant function analyses were used to distinguish the faked tests from PACLs completed under the normal instructional set. Equations were derived from these analyses (separately for men and women) and were cross-validated with independent samples. The equations were able to correctly identify a large majority of faked (75%–91%) and normal tests (60%–94%).

In accord with the third stage of test development, the criterion stage, extensive external validity data have been reported for the PACL by myself and a number of independent researchers in the form of correlations with tests of personality, mood, and dispositional variables and reports from subjects about current and past behavior (Chung, 1993; Durff, 1994; Horton & Retzlaff, 1991; Pincus & Wiggins, 1990; Strack, 1987, 1991a, 1991b, 1994; Strack & Lorr, 1990a; Strack, Lorr, & Campbell, 1989; Wiggins & Pincus, 1989, 1994). My own research demonstrated that each PACL scale is in line with theoretical expectations and measures milder versions of Millon's (1969/1983a) pathological styles. For example, the scale measuring the avoidant personality (Inhibited) was positively associated with measures of shyness, submissiveness, and social anxiety, and negatively associated with measures of sociability, dominance, and emotional well-being (Strack, 1991a). The scale measuring aggressive traits (Forceful) was positively linked to measures of arrogance, dominance, assertiveness, and autonomy, and negatively linked to measures of deference, submissiveness, and conscientiousness (Strack, 1991a). In a study comparing the PI scores of psychiatric patients (n = 124) and normal adults (n = 140) who completed the PACL using standard instructions, I found that 84% of the PI scores of T = 60 and above were obtained by patients (only 16% of the normals had scores over 59; Strack, 1991c).

Other investigators have reported expected relationships between PACL scales and a variety of measures. For example, Horton and Retzlaff (1991) correlated the PACL with Moos' (1974) *Family Environment Scale* in a sample of 65 undergraduates. They found that family cohesion and expressiveness were strongly associated with cooperative and sociable personality styles, while conflict was most prevalent in the families of sensitive and forceful persons. High scores on the Respectful scale were linked to family environments in which cohesion, organization, and religiosity were salient features.

Wiggins and Pincus (1989; Pincus & Wiggins, 1990) examined the PACL in relation to Minnesota Multiphasic Personality Inventory (MMPI) personality disorder scales (Morey, Waugh, & Blashfield, 1985), the Big Five Interpersonal Adjective Scales (IAS-B5; Trapnell & Wiggins, 1988), the NEO Personality Inventory (NEO-PI; Costa & McCrae, 1985), and a circumplex version of the Inventory of Interpersonal Problems (Alden, Wiggins, & Pincus, 1990). PACL scales exhibited anticipated relationships with each of the tests in correlational, canonical, and factor analyses. For example, PACL Introversive and Sociable scales were loaded (in opposite directions) on a factor that included the MMPI Schizoid and Histrionic scales, NEO-PI Extraversion, and IAS-B5 Dominance. The PACL Forceful scale was correlated .59 with interpersonal problems associated with dominance behavior, while the PACL Cooperative scale was correlated .48 with problems involving exploitation by others.

In keeping with the emphasis on normality, PACL scales were normed as *T*-scores rather than as base rate (BR) scores. Normative data (Strack, 1991a) were obtained from 2,507 normal adults between the ages of 16 and 72. Subjects were sampled between 1980 and 1986 with 90% coming from colleges and 10% from businesses. Men comprised 47.4% of the sample and women, 52.6%. Ethnic makeup was 65.2% non-Hispanic European American, 17.3% Hispanic, 9.1% African American, 7.6% Asian, and 0.8% Native American Indian or Eskimo.

The PACL is currently available as a paper-and-pencil measure that can be hand scored or entered into a computer file via an optical scanner. Full-color, computerized versions of the check list for DOS (AUTOPACL; Robbins, 1991) and Windows (WinPACL; Robbins, 1994) that permit computer administration of the test, scoring, and printing of profile plots of scores as well as narrative interpretations are available. These programs allow for unlimited uses on a single computer and, as an aid to researchers, can produce exportable files containing test data for multiple subjects. The narrative interpretations were written by me for use in counseling and personnel settings and were based on Millon's writings, empirical information obtained during test construction and validation, and clinical experience with the test. A sample printout from WinPACL, including a narrative interpretation of results, is presented in Figure 22.1. PACL items are given on the last page of the printout. Adjectives endorsed for this sample subject are identified in capital letters.

COMPARISON WITH THE MCMIs

The PACL was designed exclusively on the basis of Millon's (1969/1983a) original model of personality and measures normal trait characteristics. This is in contrast to the three editions of the MCMI, which were designed to match DSM Axis II criteria for personality disorders. Additionally, Millon's original model differs somewhat from that found in his more recent writings (1986a, 1986b, 1990, 1994a, 1994b; Millon & Davis, 1994).

In accordance with Millon's (1969/1983a, 1987, 1994b) model and akin to the MCMI, PACL personality scales contain varying numbers of overlapping items, ranging from one for the Respectful scale to nine for the Sensitive scale. The percentage of overlapping items on PACL scales is substantially lower than that for MCMI scales and ranges from 5% to 35%. As a result, scale intercorrelations for the PACL are somewhat lower than are those for the MCMI (median *r* = |.35| across sexes; Strack, 1987). Also as a result, PACL scales

PERSONALITY ADJECTIVE CHECK LIST

REPORT

produced by WinPACL

Jane Clinician, Ph.D.
123 Main Street
Anytown, USA 98765

Name: Susan Sample

ID:002123111

Age: 38

Sex: Female

Education:12

Ethnicity: Non-Hispanic White

Marital: First Marriage

Religion: Protestant

Research code: 00000

Test date: 12/11/94

Report date: 03/06/95

(*continued*)

FIGURE 22.1. A sample print-out from the WinPACL (Robbins, 1994) computer program.

Personality Adjective Check List Profile

IDENTIFYING INFORMATION

Name: Susan Sample
Age: 38
Education: 12
Marital: First Marriage

Sex: Female
Research code: 00000
Ethnicity: Non-Hispanic White
Religion: Protestant

VALIDITY INDICES

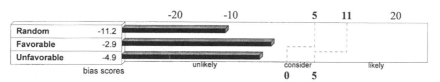

Number of adjectives checked = 36: Number checked is OK
Random response set is UNLIKELY
Favorable response set is UNLIKELY
Unfavorable response set is UNLIKELY

SCALE *T* SCORES

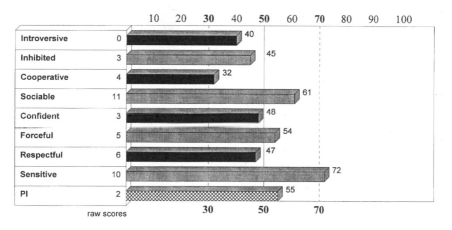

FIGURE 22.1. *cont.*

ID: 002123111   Test date: 12/11/94   Report date: 03/06/95

Introduction

The Personality Adjective Check List (PACL) is a comprehensive, objective measure of eight basic personality styles outlined by Theodore Millon. A ninth PI scale measures aspects of three more severe personality styles and may be used as an indicator of personality disturbance. This test was designed for use with normal adults who read at minimally the eighth grade level. The PACL was developed, validated, and normed using the responses of over 2500 men and women from across the United States. All of the people measured in the course of test development were presumed to have normal personalities. Therefore, even extreme elevations on PACL scales should not be interpreted as indicating disordered personality.

Computer-generated PACL test reports are intended for use by qualified professionals only. Interpretive statements made in the test reports are based on empirical data and theoretical inference. They are probabilistic in nature and cannot be considered definitive. The report should be evaluated along with other information available about the respondent, for example, background characteristics and other test and interview data, before conclusions are made. Users of the test reports should be familiar with the PACL's assets and limitations as described in the test manual.

Respondent Characteristics and Test Validity

This 38-year-old, non-Hispanic white, Protestant, married, female respondent, with 12 years of education, completed the PACL on 12/11/94. She marked 36 adjectives as self-descriptive, which is within the valid range of 20–110 items checked. Response style indices indicate no unusual test-taking biases.

Narrative Description

This active, extroverted person is unconventional and individualistic in her approach to life. She views herself as being different from others and as having unique interests and talents. Seeking high levels of stimulation and attention, she is dramatic, colorful, excitable, and impulsive. She uses her interpersonal sensitivity to get what she wants, and she can be exploitive in this regard. Impatient with the status quo, this person does not like adhering to accepted standards. Whether appropriate or not, she will often take a routine task and shape it to meet her own needs. If others do not go along with her or if she is forced to work within boundaries that do not match her own, she can be angry and disruptive. In spite of the considerable efforts she makes to gratify her needs, this person frequently seems disgruntled. She is often unhappy with the way things are but can't seem to find satisfying alternatives. Her dissatisfaction is often noted in temporary displays of indignation and hostile pessimism. When experiencing unhappiness, this person's normally effusive, buoyant style gives way to a self-absorbed, critical, and brooding demeanor.

FIGURE 22.1. *cont.*

ID: 002123111   Test date: 12/11/94   Report date: 03/06/95

With her best side forward, this person is charming, clever, and appropriately assertive and individualistic. These qualities make her well-suited for work environments in which she can be somewhat independent in interpreting task requirements. Jobs that involve unusual duties and impose few rules and restrictions are most likely to bring out her good qualities. This person's angry, pessimistic side may provoke problems with supervisors, co-workers, and colleagues. In general, she cannot tolerate group or team work environments. However, if this person does work with a group, she will perform best in one that is fairly stable and that can tolerate her emotional, individualistic nature.

Generalized anger, dysphoria, pessimism, and feelings of inadequacy are frequently experienced by persons with this personality style who seek professional assistance. They may feel scattered, disconnected, or bitter. Dependency conflicts and feelings of being unable to cope are common. Therapists can expect these persons to fluctuate in their level of cooperation and be somewhat pessimistic in carrying out therapeutic suggestions. Because these persons often have trouble separating their evaluation of a situation from its objective characteristics, problem clarification is essential to therapeutic success. A supportive approach can be helpful in restoring a sense of emotional stability and self-worth. Problem-solving techniques aimed at correcting self-defeating behaviors may be useful. With highly motivated persons, insight-oriented therapy can be effective in working through unconscious anxieties and building adaptive defenses. Group treatment may also be utilized to help these persons develop self-control and more consistent social behavior.

WinPACL V1.1 copyright © 1994 Brian Robbins, Ph.D.
PACL and interpretations copyright © 1986, 1990, 1994 Stephen Strack, Ph.D.
Published by 21st Century Assessment, South Pasadena, California

FIGURE 22.1. *cont.*

ID: 002123111	Test Date: 12/11/94	Report date: 03/06/95

Item Endorsements [36]

1. playful	52. annoyed	103. self-admiring
2. self-satisfied	53. LIVELY	104. gentle
3. reserved	54. rigid	105. theatrical
4. consenting	55. naive	106. sweet
5. ignored	56. irritable	107. formal
6. insecure	57. shy	108. grouchy
7. BOASTFUL	58. disciplined	109. overlooked
8. strict	59. uninspired	110. self-contented
9. EXTRAVAGANT	60. excluded	111. bossy
10. oversensitive	61. fearless	112. suspicious
11. apprehensive	62. BAFFLING	113. EFFICIENT
12. careful	63. NEAT	114. self-conscious
13. intimidating	64. solitary	115. egoistic
14. bubbly	65. touchy	116. CONFUSING
15. EDGY	66. secretive	117. mean
16. remote	67. OUTGOING	118. moralistic
17. COURAGEOUS	68. traditional	119. conceited
18. timid	69. subdued	120. disagreeable
19. erratic	70. FICKLE	121. powerful
20. innocent	71. ANIMATED	122. HELPFUL
21. COMPETITIVE	72. MOODY	123. dependent
22. industrious	73. TALKATIVE	124. organized
23. uneasy	74. NAGGING	125. self-important
24. chaotic	75. decent	126. domineering
25. GREGARIOUS	76. expressionless	127. revengeful
26. arrogant	77. conforming	128. righteous
27. fragmented	78. coy	129. ill-at-ease
28. afraid	79. DRAMATIC	130. rejected
29. yielding	80. militant	131. unafraid
30. virtuous	81. BLUNT	132. serious
31. sluggish	82. ADVENTUROUS	133. COOPERATIVE
32. UPRIGHT	83. hesitant	134. immodest
33. selfish	84. indifferent	135. FORCEFUL
34. WORRIED	85. PROPER	136. trustful
35. straight-laced	86. commanding	137. tough
36. aggravated	87. nervous	138. respectful
37. PRECISE	88. care-free	139. FLIRTATIOUS
38. cool	89. unnoticed	140. disinterested
39. vivacious	90. orderly	141. impersonal
40. daring	91. docile	142. inexpressive
41. apathetic	92. lonely	143. sweet-tempered
42. FLUCTUATING	93. SOCIABLE	144. VAIN
43. agreeable	94. obedient	145. hard-headed
44. peppy	95. ANXIOUS	146. pessimistic
45. TEMPERAMENTAL	96. combative	147. warm-hearted
46. self-centered	97. COMPLAINING	148. HARD-WORKING
47. testy	98. despondent	149. merry
48. depressed	99. detached	150. distant
49. unemotional	100. apologetic	151. UNDERSTANDING
50. fearful	101. seductive	152. aggressive
51. overconfident	102. uncomfortable	153. hostile

FIGURE 22.1. *cont.*

containing only nonoverlapping items have been found to be quite reliable on their own, and to yield essentially the same factors as the overlapping scales (Pincus & Wiggins, 1990; Wiggins & Pincus, 1989; Strack, 1991a).

Table 22.1 lists corresponding personality measures for the PACL, the MCMI, the MCMI-II, and the MCMI-III. Two MCMI scales are listed for PACL Inhibited, Forceful, and Sensitive scales. This is because Millon (1986a, 1986b, 1994a) divided his original avoidant (inhibited) personality into avoidant and depressive aspects; his original aggressive (forceful) style into antisocial and aggressive, and his original negativistic (sensitive)

TABLE 22.1. Corresponding Scales for the PACL, MCMI, MCMI-II, and MCMI-III

PACL	MCMI	MCMI-II	MCMI-III
Introversive	Schizoid	Schizoid	Schizoid
Inhibited	Avoidant	Avoidant	Avoidant
			Depressive
Cooperative	Dependent	Dependent	Dependent
Sociable	Histrionic	Histrionic	Histrionic
Confident	Narcissistic	Narcissistic	Narcissistic
Forceful	Antisocial	Antisocial	Antisocial
		Aggressive	Aggressive
Respectful	Compulsive	Compulsive	Compulsive
Sensitive	Passive–Aggressive	Passive–Aggressive	Passive–Aggressive
		Self-Defeating	Self-Defeating

Note. The PACL Problem indicator (PI) scale measures aspects of the schizotypal, borderline, and paranoid styles but does not directly assess these personalities.

style into passive–aggressive and self-defeating. An examination of items for these scales suggests that the MCMI, MCMI-II, and MCMI-III Avoidant, Aggressive, and Passive–Aggressive scales may be closer to the PACL Inhibited, Forceful, and Sensitive scales, respectively, than to the MCMI, MCMI-II, and MCMI-III Depressive, Antisocial, and Self-Defeating scales, although research is needed to verify this impression.

In practice, correspondence between the PACL and various versions of the MCMI is reduced by the dissimilar test formats (adjectives versus statements), models used, and focus on normality versus pathology. In spite of these differences, I found 8 PACL and 10 MCMI-II basic personality scales which correlated between .39 and .67 (median = .52, using MCMI-II weighted raw scores; Strack, 1991b) in a sample of 65 male and 75 female college students. The lowest values were found for PACL Sensitive–MCMI-II Self-Defeating (.39) and for PACL Forceful–MCMI-II Antisocial (.41), suggesting that these MCMI-II scales are not strongly aligned with Millon's original (1969/1983a) model. By comparison, the MCMI-II Aggressive scale was correlated .53 with the PACL Forceful scale, and the MCMI-II Passive–Aggressive scale was correlated .51 with the PACL Sensitive scale.

Factor analyses of PACL, MCMI, and MCMI-II personality scales have revealed very similar results. The three dimensions found to underlie the PACL (Strack, 1987), that is, neuroticism, assertiveness–aggressiveness, and social extraversion–introversion, correspond to the three factors found among the MCMI's basic eight personality scales (Retzlaff & Gibertini, 1987), and for the MCMI-II's 13 personality measures (Strack, Lorr, Campbell, & Lamnin, 1992). A joint factor analysis of PACL and MCMI-II basic personality scales among college students also yielded three factors (using residual scores), with corresponding PACL and MCMI-II scales loading on the same dimensions (Strack, 1991b).

Strack, Lorr, and Campbell (1990) examined the circular ordering of MCMI-II personality disorder scales in a mixed group of psychiatric patients and compared results with those from the PACL among normal adults. Plotted against the orthogonally rotated first two principal components, they found a reasonably good circle for MCMI-II scales (using residual scores) that, for the most part, followed Millon's (1987) predictions. Ordering for the PACL scales was similar, although a less complete circle was noted: the Sociable, Confident, and Forceful scales were loaded opposite the Introversive, Inhibited, and Sensitive scales on one dimension, while the Cooperative and Respectful scales defined one end of a second dimension but had no opposing scales.

MILLON'S PERSONALITIES AS MEASURED BY THE PACL

Correlational evidence demonstrates that normal versions of Millon's basic styles are milder variants of the personalities as disorders. Unfortunately, behavioral studies and side-by-side comparisons of matched groups of normals and patients on the PACL and MCMI-II and -III have not yet been carried out. As a result, important data are still needed to address the precise nature of similarities and differences between normal and disordered forms of Millon's personalities.

With regard to the appearance of Millon's personalities in normal form, what can be offered at this point is a portrait of each style based on Millon's theory, empirical findings from studies associating PACL scales with other measures, and clinical experience with the test. Summaries of empirical findings can be found in Strack (1991a, 1993). The following descriptions represent normal prototypes of persons who obtain high scores on the individual scales. In practice, of course, people are seldom prototypical, instead exhibiting a mixture of traits from multiple styles. Nevertheless, these descriptions flesh out various aspects of normal personality not readily grasped by extrapolations from Millon's writings on pathological character. Especially noteworthy among the normal styles are their positive dispositional features and interpersonal attitudes. Even less desirable traits are placed within a normal frame of reference.

Scale 1: Introversive

Aloof, introverted, and solitary, these persons usually prefer distant or limited involvement with others and have little interest in social activities, which they find unrewarding. Appearing to others as nonchalant and untroubled, they are often judged to be easy going, mild mannered, quiet, and retiring. They frequently remain in the background of social life and work quietly and unobtrusively at a job. At school or in the workplace these people do well on their own, are typically dependable and reliable, are nondemanding, and are seldom bothered by noise or commotion around them. They are often viewed as level headed and calm. However, these individuals may appear unaware of, or insensitive to, the feelings and thoughts of others. These characteristics are sometimes interpreted by others as signs of indifference or rejection, but reveal a sincere difficulty in being able to sense others' moods and needs. Introversive persons can be slow and methodical in demeanor, lack spontaneity and resonance, and be awkward or timid in social or group situations. They frequently view themselves as being simple and unsophisticated, and are usually modest in appraising their own skills and abilities. At the same time, their placid demeanor and ability to weather ups and downs without being ruffled are traits frequently prized by friends, family members, and coworkers.

Scale 2: Inhibited

As with the introversive style, the inhibited personality is marked by a tendency toward social withdrawal. However, for inhibited individuals this pattern is motivated not by disinterest, but by a fear of negative consequences. Inhibited persons tend to be sensitive to their own feelings and to those of others. They often anticipate that others will be critical or rejecting of them, and because of this they frequently seem shy or skittish in unfamiliar surroundings. In this regard, family members and acquaintances may see them as being unnecessarily nervous, wary, and fearful. Although inhibited persons tend to get along reasonably well with others, they are often difficult to get to know on a personal level.

These individuals usually wish that they could be at ease with others and tend to desire closeness, but they often are just too uncertain of the consequences of closeness and intimacy to let their guard down. As a result, they may experience feelings of loneliness, but be unable or unwilling to do anything about them. Because of their sensitivity to others, inhibited persons are often described as kind, considerate, and empathic by close acquaintances. Inhibited persons often prefer to work alone or in a small group with people they can come to know well. They do best in a stable work environment where stimulation and commotion are kept at low to moderate levels. Persons working with inhibited types need to appreciate their sensitivity to both positive and negative feedback, as well as their need to build trust over a long period of time.

Scale 3: Cooperative

Cooperative persons can be identified by a need for approval and affection, and by a willingness to live in accord with the desires of others. They usually adapt their behavior to the standards of others but in the process may deny their own needs. Interpersonally, these individuals are often cooperative, reliable, considerate of others, and deferential. They may appear even tempered, docile, obliging, self-effacing, ingratiating, or naive. Cooperative individuals often see themselves as being modestly endowed in terms of skills and abilities. They are often pleased when they can rely on others and may feel insecure when left on their own. Especially when faced with difficult or stressful situations, cooperative persons seek others to provide authority, leadership, and direction. They often prefer group work environments and will typically excel in them if given support and guidance. They are usually willing to follow directions and cooperate with coworkers in team efforts.

Scale 4: Sociable

Like those with cooperative personalities, sociable individuals have a need for attention and approval. However, unlike cooperative persons, sociable types take the initiative in assuring their reinforcements by being "center stage." They are characterized by an outgoing, talkative, and extroverted style of behavior and tend to be lively, dramatic, and colorful. These people are typically viewed by others as spontaneous, clever, enthusiastic, and vigorous. They can be quite sensitive to the needs and wants of others, at least to those aspects which will help them get the attention they seek. Sociable individuals may also be seen as fickle in their attachments. They may have quickly shifting moods and emotions, and may come across as shallow and ungenuine. These persons tend to prefer novelty and excitement, and are bored by ordinary or mundane activities. Like cooperative personalities, sociable individuals seem uncomfortable or deflated when left on their own. Not surprisingly, sociable types often excel in group work environments where they can exercise their showy style. They often do well interacting with the public, may be skilled and adept at rallying or motivating others, and will usually put their best side forward even in difficult circumstances.

Scale 5: Confident

Aloof, calm, and confident, these persons tend to be egocentric and self-reliant. They may have a keen sense of their own importance, uniqueness, or entitlement. Confident individuals enjoy others' attention and may be quite bold socially, although they are seldom garish. They can be self-centered to a fault and may become so preoccupied with themselves that they lack concern and empathy for others. These persons have a tendency to believe that others share, or should share, their sense of worth. As a result, they may expect others to submit to their wishes and desires, and to cater to them. Ironically, the confident individual's secure appearance may cover feelings of personal inadequacy and a sensitivity to criticism and rejection. Unfortunately, they usually do not permit others to see their vulnerable side. When feeling exposed or undermined these individuals are frequently disdainful, obstructive, or vindictive. In the workplace, confident persons like to take charge in an emphatic manner, often doing so in a way that instills confidence in others. Their self-assurance, wit, and charm often win them supervisory and leadership positions.

Scale 6: Forceful

Like confident persons, forceful individuals can be identified by an inclination to turn toward the self as the primary source of gratification. However, instead of the confident personality's internalized sense of self-importance, forceful people seem driven to prove their worthiness. They are characterized by an assertive, dominant, and tough-minded personal style. They tend to be strong-willed, ambitious, competitive, and self-determined. Feeling that the world is a harsh place where exploitiveness is needed to assure success, forceful individuals are frequently gruff and insensitive in dealing with others. In contrast to their preferred, outwardly powerful appearance, these individuals may feel inwardly insecure and be afraid of letting down their guard. In work settings, these persons are often driven to excel. They work hard to achieve their goals, are competitive, and do well where they can take control or work independently. In supervisory or leadership positions these persons usually take charge and see to it that a job gets done. However, they often need to temper an inclination to demand as much of others as they do of themselves.

Scale 7: Respectful

Responsible, industrious, and respectful of authority, these individuals tend to be conforming and work hard to uphold rules and regulations. They have a need for order and are typically conventional in their interests. These individuals can be rule-abiding to a fault, however, and may be perfectionistic, inflexible, and judgmental. A formal interpersonal style and notable constriction of affect can make some respectful persons seem cold, aloof, and withholding. Underneath their social propriety there is often a fear of disapproval and rejection, or a sense of guilt over perceived shortcomings. Indecisiveness and an inability to take charge may be evident in some of these persons due to a fear of being wrong. However, among coworkers and friends, respectful personalities are best known for being well-organized, reliable, and diligent. They have a strong sense of duty and loyalty, are cooperative in group efforts, show persistence even in difficult circumstances, and work well under supervision.

Scale 8: Sensitive

Sensitive persons tend to be unconventional and individualistic in their response to the world. They march to the beat of a different drummer and are frequently unhappy with the status quo. They may be quick to challenge rules or authority deemed arbitrary and unjust. They may also harbor resentment without expressing it directly and may revert to passive–aggressive behavior to make their feelings known. Many sensitive people feel as if they don't fit in and view themselves as lacking in interpersonal skills. In fact, to others they often appear awkward, nervous, or distracted, and seem angry or dissatisfied with themselves and others. They can be indecisive and have fluctuating moods and interests. An air of uncertainty and general dissatisfaction may reflect an underlying dependence and sense of personal inadequacy. With their best side forward, sensitive persons can be spontaneous, creative, and willing to speak out for what they believe in. These qualities make them especially suited to jobs that are not rule-bound, that give them a certain independence from supervision, and that require unusual duties or creative expression.

Scale 9: Problem Indicator

Items for this scale were compiled from adjectives measuring the schizoid, cycloid, and paranoid personalities, for example, "chaotic," "fragmented," "depressed," and "suspicious." While the scale does not define a personality style, high scores are indicative of personality problems and the potential for disorder. High scorers possess personality disorder traits and symptoms such as low ego strength and affective instability. They are likely to appear anxious, dysphoric, and fearful, exhibit strong self-doubt, and express dissatisfaction with themselves and others. They may have long-standing adjustment problems in major areas of life such as work, school, and relationships. Those who score high on this scale are not likely to fit the same picture of normality as are low scorers (e.g., by exhibiting interpersonal rigidity and maladaptiveness), but further assessment is advised before drawing conclusions regarding the presence of a disorder.

CLINICAL AND RESEARCH USES

Clinical Applications

The PACL is appropriate for use with persons 16 years of age and older who read at minimally the eighth-grade level. The measure has been successfully employed by therapists working in high school and college counseling centers and employee assistance programs; by vocational counselors, personnel psychologists, and marriage and family counselors; by therapists doing custody and worker's compensation evaluations; and by general practitioners who work with relatively high-functioning clients. Because the PACL is quick (it takes approximately 10 minutes to complete) and easy to administer, it is often given during initial screening visits to assess personality style and identify persons who may have more serious character problems. Clinicians have found it useful with people who can't or won't complete questionnaire measures, for example, some medical patients, teenagers, and the elderly.

A number of clinicians use the PACL as a rating instrument to assess their clients' personality styles and to have couples and family members assess each other. I have experimented with the PACL in these areas, utilizing the norms in the PACL Manual (Strack, 1991a) for scoring. Although the norms are based on self-reports, they worked remarkably well with a variety of ratings.

An important factor to keep in mind when using the PACL in clinical settings is that the test measures normal trait characteristics, not personality disorder features. High scores on the PACL indicate that an individual possesses more of the traits of a particular normal personality style than do other adults in the general population. For example, the higher an individual's T-score is above 50 on any particular scale, the more likely it is that he or she will fit the prototype descriptions given earlier. The test does not assess disordered personality features beyond those measured by the PI scale.

Research Applications

Because the PACL is fast and easy to administer, researchers have found that it can be easily added to a test battery without taxing subjects' time and attentional resources. Concerning important research uses, I encourage studies that further explicate Millon's personalities in normal form and examine major premises of his model thought to differentiate normal from abnormal persons (Millon, 1969/1983a; Millon & Davis, 1994; Strack, 1991a). In this regard, there may be some value in using the PACL with psychiatric samples and/or in combining the PACL with the MCMI-III. PACL item responses may provide information about the normal characteristics of psychiatric patients not tapped by the MCMI, and the scale scores can show how subjects deviate from a normal mean, something MCMI BR scores cannot do.

There is still much to be learned about the appearance and function of Millon's basic personalities in normal form, for example, their vocational interests (Strack, 1994), work behavior, and coping styles. Correlational research employing measures pertinent to Millon's constructs will be helpful, as will experimental and rating studies that focus on real-life behavior. In addition to the regular PACL scale scores, investigators may use scores from nonoverlapping scales (Strack, 1991a), factor scores derived from the scales (Strack, 1987) or items (Strack & Lorr, 1990b), and profile clusters (Strack, 1992).

Millon's ideas about the differences between normal and abnormal personalities are important targets for research. At this point we simply do not have empirical evidence addressing whether disordered styles are less interpersonally flexible and stable and more pathogenic than are normal styles. Likewise, there is no research information available concerning the relative position of normal and abnormal types on Millon's active–passive, pleasure–pain, and self–other polarities.

In describing personality development, Millon (e.g., 1969/1983a, 1981, 1990) emphasized a number of individual difference and process elements thought to be influential in creating either normal or dysfunctional character, for example, biological predisposition (including temperament), early learning experiences, and parent–child relations. Many of these elements are central to his model and deserve careful scrutiny in both retrospective and longitudinal investigations.

Cross-cultural research is needed to assess the similarities and differences in trait structure of Millon's personalities based on cultural influences. As an interpersonal model, one would expect cultural differences to be evident among Millon's personalities at the nomothetic (normative) level of measurement. From an idiographic perspective, one would also expect test interpretation to differ somewhat by culture. For example, in mainstream America independence is valued more than dependence. This may be reflected in our assessment of an individual's strengths and weaknesses when, for example, we suggest that a confident and forceful style will help a person get ahead in business while a cooperative style may be a liability in the same environment. In some other cultures dependence and cooperativeness are more highly valued than are traits of independence, and changes in test interpretation would follow. The PACL is now available for research use in the Chinese, Dutch, Italian, Portuguese, and Spanish languages, and I strongly support cross-cultural investigations of any kind.

Novel Approaches

Creative research studies beyond those traditionally associated with personality assessment are encouraged. For example, self report does not have to be limited to self-report of *cur-*

rent personality. Subjects can be asked to describe their ideal self, how they were as a child or before a major life event, and how they imagine themselves in a variety of roles and personas, such as company president, homeless person, someone of the opposite sex, and their shadow or "dark side."

I noted earlier that some PACL users have had couples and family members rate each other. In this context, self-report data can be readily contrasted with ratings to reveal similarities and differences between self and other viewpoints. If more than one person rates an individual, scores can be combined or weighted to produce composite profiles. Of course, ratings do not have to be limited to individuals, or even to people. Raters can be asked to assess the characteristics of a group of people (e.g., coworkers, a sports team, the United States Congress), a business, an environment, a piece of art, the ideal automobile, etc. Data from such ratings are not just for academic consumption. They can illuminate the salient features of an elusive or abstract subject in a language that facilitates communication and understanding.

Rating Mozart and Beethoven

To exemplify the utility of nontraditional approaches to personality assessment, I had groups of psychology graduate students rate a musical piece by Wolfgang Mozart and the personality of Ludwig Beethoven (N = 13 and 15, respectively). My supposition was that raters would have little trouble providing word portraits of the subjects, and would produce very similar PACL profiles for each subject that could be readily understood in terms of Millon's theoretical formulations.

For the Mozart piece, students were asked to describe the "personality" of the second (andante) movement of his 21st piano concerto (Casadesus & Szell, 1983/1965) (K. 467; sometimes referred to as the Elvira Madigan concerto). Readers may know this movement as one of Mozart's most lyrical compositions. It is intimate, slow, rhythmic, sweet, and melodic, but also very emotional, often evoking feelings of tender love, longing, and resigned sadness. Students were asked to imagine the music in personality form as they listened to the 7¾-minute composition in its entirety. When giving their ratings they were asked to limit themselves to the music (i.e., to exclude information that they had about Mozart from other sources).

For Beethoven, students were given a short description (approximately 300 words) of his personal background and character traits as compiled from a number of biographies and letters from contemporaries. For example, they were told that Beethoven suffered emotional abuse at the hands of his father, was erudite, never married, worked hard, was perfectionistic, and was experienced by various persons as intense, passionate, opinionated, self-absorbed, moody, and petulant. They also listened to short passages from his 3rd (Szell, 1990), 5th (Bernstein, 1985), 7th (Von Karajan, 1985), and 9th (Winter, 1991) symphonies that demonstrated a variety of his musical interests and compositional styles. When completing the PACL, raters were asked to give their impression of Beethoven's personality based on any and all information available to them (i.e., they did not have to limit themselves to the stimulus materials).

As noted by their relatively quick completion time (5–15 minutes), raters did not seem to have trouble recording their impressions. A few persons commented that they would have used additional words in their portraits if they had been included on the check list (e.g., passionate). Each student's rating was entered into the WinPACL (Robbins, 1994) computer program and scored using standard norms. The profiles for each set of ratings were remarkably similar. All of the students gave Mozart's music a high point on Scale 2,

Inhibited, with the second high point on Scale 3, Cooperative (favored by the men), or Scale 8, Sensitive (favored by the women). The PI scale was elevated above 60 on most of the profiles. Beethoven was given a high point on Scale 8, Sensitive, by 12 of 15 raters, with a second high point on Scale 6, Forceful, or Scale 2, Inhibited, by 14 of 15 persons.

Composite profiles are given in Figure 22.2. These were obtained by entering, on a single test protocol, all of the adjectives checked by the raters for each subject. Adjectives were not weighted, so items endorsed by more than one person were entered only once. Both profiles show good definition and represent code types commonly found for men in the normative sample (Strack, 1991a). The 2–3 (elevations on Scales 2 and 3) profile for Mozart describes his musical piece as timid, self-effacing, sensitive, agreeable, deferential, and modest. The elevated PI scale suggests intense, even disturbing affect. Beethoven was viewed as individualistic, unconventional, tough, competitive, and emotional. His 8–6 profile describes him as someone who fluctuates between feelings of confidence and power

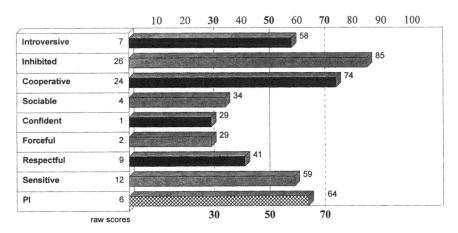

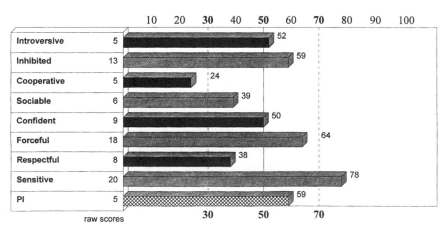

FIGURE 22.2. Composite PACL profiles for the second movement of Mozart's 21st piano concerto (top), and Beethoven's personality (bottom) based on student ratings.

on the one hand, and feelings of self-doubt and inadequacy and on the other. To close acquaintances he might come across as hard-boiled, irritable, self-absorbed, and moody.

The student raters found these profiles to be quite accurate in terms of reflecting their feelings about the subjects. Many of the raters had no training or interest in classical music and were surprised that their impressions aligned so closely with those of raters who knew the composers well. The results gave way to lively discussions about the meaning of personality, how music, emotion, and language fit together, and the broad utility of Millon's ideas.

There are a number of noteworthy features about this rating exercise, but I think the main point to be taken links it with the rest of the chapter: Millon's model of personality pathology extends itself well to normal character—however the subject matter is defined—and the PACL readily lends itself to explorations of this model in ways that are limited only to the investigator's imagination.

ACKNOWLEDGMENTS

I am grateful to Peter Graves, Maurice Lorr, and Brian Robbins for their helpful comments on earlier drafts of this chapter.

REFERENCES

Alden, L. E., Wiggins, J. S., & Pincus, A. L. (1990). Construction of circumplex scales for the Inventory of Interpersonal Problems. *Journal of Personality Assessment, 55*, 521–536.

American Psychiatric Association. (1980). *Diagnostic and statistical manual of mental disorders* (3rd ed.). Washington, DC: Author.

American Psychiatric Association. (1994). *Diagnostic and statistical manual of mental disorders* (4th ed.). Washington, DC: Author.

Bernstein, L. (1985). *Beethoven's 5th and Schubert's 8th "unfinished" symphonies* [CD]. New York: CBS Inc.

Casadesus, R., & Szell, G. (1983/1965). *Mozart piano concertos nos. 21 "Elvira Madigan" & 24* [CD]. New York: CBS Inc. (Original recording published 1965)

Chung, Y. (1993). *Relationship between types and degree of acculturation and Millon's personality types of Koreans in the United States*. Unpublished doctoral dissertation, California School of Professional Psychology, Los Angeles.

Costa, P. T., & McCrae, R. R. (1985). *The NEO Personality Inventory manual*. Odessa, FL: Psychological Assessment Resources.

Durff, T. (1994). *The relationship between Millon's basic personality styles and the cognitive style of field dependence–independence*. Unpublished doctoral dissertation, California School of Professional Psychology, Los Angeles.

Gough, H. G., & Heilbrun, A. B. (1983). *The Adjective Check List manual*. Palo Alto, CA: Consulting Psychologists Press.

Horton, A. D., & Retzlaff, P. D. (1991). Family assessment: Toward DSM-III-R relevancy. *Journal of Clinical Psychology, 47*, 94–100.

LaForge, R., & Suczek, R. F. (1955). The interpersonal dimensions of personality: III. An interpersonal check list. *Journal of Personality, 24*, 94–112.

Loevinger, J. (1957). Objective tests as instruments of psychological theory. *Psychological Reports, 3*, 635–694.

Millon, T. (1977). *Millon Clinical Multiaxial Inventory manual*. Minneapolis: National Computer Systems.

Millon, T. (1981). *Disorders of personality*. New York: Wiley.

Millon, T. (1983a). *Millon Clinical Multiaxial Inventory manual* (3rd ed.). Minneapolis: National Computer Systems.

Millon, T. (1983b). *Modern psychopathology.* Prospect Heights, IL: Waveland Press. (Original work published 1969)

Millon, T. (1986a). A theoretical derivation of pathological personalities. In T. Millon & G. L. Klerman (Eds.), *Contemporary directions in psychopathology: Toward the DSM-IV* (pp. 639–670). New York: Guilford Press.

Millon, T. (1986b). Personality prototypes and their diagnostic criteria. In T. Millon & G. L. Klerman (Eds.), *Contemporary directions in psychopathology: Toward the DSM-IV* (pp. 639–670). New York: Guilford Press.

Millon, T. (1987). *Manual for the Millon Clinical Multiaxial Inventory—II* (2nd ed.). Minneapolis: National Computer Systems.

Millon, T. (1990). *Toward a new personology.* New York: Wiley.

Millon, T. (1994a). *Millon Clinical Multiaxial Inventory—III manual.* Minneapolis: National Computer Systems.

Millon, T. (1994b). *Millon Index of Personality Styles manual.* San Antonio, TX: Psychological Corporation.

Millon, T., & Davis, R. D. (1994). Millon's evolutionary model of normal and abnormal personality: Theory and measures. In S. Strack & M. Lorr (Eds.), *Differentiating normal and abnormal personality* (pp. 79–113). New York: Springer.

Millon, T., Green, C., & Meagher, R. B. (1982a). *Millon Adolescent Personality Inventory manual.* Minneapolis: National Computer Systems.

Millon, T., Green, C., & Meagher, R. B. (1982b). *Millon Behavioral Health Inventory manual.* Minneapolis: National Computer Systems.

Moos, R. H. (1974). *The Family Environment Scale.* Palo Alto, CA: Consulting Psychologists Press.

Morey, L. C., Waugh, M. H., & Blashfield, R. K. (1985). MMPI scales for DSM-III personality disorders: Their derivation and correlates. *Journal of Personality Assessment, 49,* 245–251.

Pincus, A. L., & Wiggins, J. S. (1990). Interpersonal problems and conceptions of personality disorders. *Journal of Personality Disorders, 4,* 342–352.

Retzlaff, P. D., & Gibertini, M. (1987). Factor structure of the MCMI basic personality scales and common-item artifact. *Journal of Personality Assessment, 51,* 588–594.

Robbins, B. (1991). *AUTOPACL user's guide.* South Pasadena, CA: 21st Century Assessment.

Robbins, B. (1994). WinPACL user's guide. South Pasadena, CA: 21st Century Assessment.

Strack, S. (1981). *Development of the Personality Adjective Check List and preliminary validation in a normal college population.* Unpublished manuscript.

Strack, S. (1987). Development and validation of an adjective check list to assess the Millon personality types in a normal population. *Journal of Personality Assessment, 51,* 572–587.

Strack, S. (1991a). *Manual for the Personality Adjective Check List (PACL)* (rev.). South Pasadena, CA: 21st Century Assessment.

Strack, S. (1991b). Factor analysis of MCMI-II and PACL basic personality scales in a college sample. *Journal of Personality Assessment, 57,* 345–355.

Strack, S. (1991c). *Comparison of PACL PI scale elevations in samples of psychiatric patients and normal adults.* Unpublished manuscript.

Strack, S. (1992). Profile clusters for men and women on the Personality Adjective Check List. *Journal of Personality Assessment, 59,* 204–217.

Strack, S. (1993). Measuring Millon's personality styles in normal adults. In R. J. Craig (Ed.), *The Millon Clinical Multiaxial Inventory: A clinical research information synthesis* (pp. 253–278). Hillsdale, NJ: Erlbaum.

Strack, S. (1994). Relating Millon's basic personality styles and Holland's occupational types. *Journal of Vocational Behavior, 45,* 41–54.

Strack, S., & Lorr, M. (1990a). Three approaches to interpersonal behavior and their common factors. *Journal of Personality Assessment, 54,* 782–790.

Strack, S., & Lorr, M. (1990b). Item factor structure of the Personality Adjective Check List (PACL). *Journal of Personality Assessment, 55,* 86–94.

Strack, S., Lorr, M., & Campbell, L. (1989, August). *Similarities in Millon personality styles among normals and psychiatric patients.* Paper presented at the annual convention of the American Psychological Association, New Orleans, LA.

Strack, S., Lorr, M., & Campbell, L. (1990). An evaluation of Millon's circular model of personality disorders. *Journal of Personality Disorders, 4,* 353–361.

Strack, S., Lorr, M., Campbell, L., & Lamnin, A. (1992). Personality and clinical syndrome factors of MCMI-II scales. *Journal of Personality Disorders, 6,* 40–52.

Szell, G. (1990). *Beethoven symphony no. 3 "Eroica–Heroique" and symphony no. 8* [CD]. New York: Sony Classical.

Trapnell, P., & Wiggins, J. S. (1988). *Extension of the Interpersonal Adjective Scales to include the Big Five dimensions of personality (IASR-B5).* Unpublished manuscript, University of British Columbia, Vancouver, Canada.

Von Karajan, H. (1985). *Ludwig Van Beethoven symphonien nos. 4 & 7.* Hamburg, Germany: Polydor International.

Wiggins, J. S., & Pincus, A. L. (1989). Conceptions of personality disorders and dimensions of personality. *Psychological Assessment, 1,* 305–316.

Wiggins, J. S., & Pincus, A. L. (1994). Personality structure and the structure of personality disorders. In P. T. Costa & T. A. Widiger (Eds.), *Personality disorders and the five-factor model of personality* (pp. 73–93). Washington, DC: American Psychological Association.

Winter, R. (1991). *Multimedia Beethoven: The ninth symphony.* Redmond, WA: Microsoft Corporation.

23

The MIPS: Gauging the Dimensions of Normality

LAWRENCE G. WEISS

The newest of the Millon family of instruments, the Millon Index of Personality Styles (MIPS; Millon, Weiss, Millon, & Davis, 1994), is designed to measure the personal styles of normally functioning adults.

As the senior project director responsible for directing the prepublication research program on the MIPS while the test was under development at The Psychological Corporation, I had the professional fortune to work very closely with Dr. Millon on the development of this test over a period of several years. My favorable review of the MIPS may be partially due to my personal connection with it, but it is largely based on an intimate knowledge of the research data we have collected.

AN OVERVIEW OF THE MIPS

The MIPS is a carefully developed, 180-item, true–false questionnaire available through The Psychological Corporation. It is appropriate for ages 18 to 65+. Most MIPS items require an eighth–grade education to complete, and most individuals finish it in 30 minutes or less.

The MIPS can be administered, scored, and interpreted on a personal computer, administered in paper-and-pencil format and hand-scored, or scanned on a desktop scanner. A mail-in scoring service is also available. Computer-generated reports provide either a single page profile (i.e., graph) of the scores, or a complete narrative interpretation of the profile pattern. The user's guide to the software includes a complete explanation of the logic that the computer program uses to analyze MIPS profiles and to generate the interpretive reports (The Psychological Corporation, 1994).

THE MIPS SCALES

The MIPS consists of 24 scales grouped into 12 pairs. Each pair contains two juxtaposed scales. For example, the Retiring and Outgoing scales are considered a pair. As shown in

Table 23.1 the 12 pairs of MIPS scales are organized into three major areas: Motivating Aims, Cognitive Modes, and Interpersonal Behaviors. A brief definition of each of the 24 MIPS scales is given in Table 23.2. The MIPS also contains a composite of overall adjustment called the Adjustment Index, and three validity indicators: Positive Impression, Negative Impression, and Consistency.

The Motivating Aims Scales

Three pairs of Motivating Aims scales assess the person's orientation toward obtaining reinforcement from the environment. Millonian theorists will recognize these three pairs of scales as normal range variations of Millon's pleasure–pain, active–passive, and self–other dimensions. The first pair of scales (Enhancing and Preserving) examines the extent to which the respondent's behavior is motivated by obtaining positive reinforcement (e.g., pleasure) or avoiding negative stimulation (e.g., pain) from the world. The second pair assesses the extent to which the individual's activities reflect an active (Modifying) or passive (Accommodating) approach toward the world. The third pair of scales focuses on the source of reinforcement, assessing the extent to which the person is primarily motivated by Individuating (referring to self) or Nurturing (referring to others) aims.

These three motivating aims are broad and powerful constructs that have an important history in the field of psychology. In brief, the pleasure–pain dimension is related to drive theory, the active–passive dimension to ego psychology, and the self–other dimension to self psychology and object relations theory.

The Cognitive Modes Scales

Four pairs of Cognitive Modes scales examine styles of information processing. The first two pairs of scales in this area, Extraversing–Introversing, and Sensing–Intuiting, assess information-gathering strategies. The second two pairs, Thinking–Feeling, and Systematizing–Innovating, assess different styles of processing information once it has been gathered.

The astute reader will observe that the Cognitive Modes scales are highly consonant with the model formulated by Jung in 1921 (1921/1971) and subsequently popularized in the Myers–Briggs Type Indicator (MBTI; Myers & McCaulley, 1985). The MBTI Judging and Perceiving scales have been renamed Systematizing and Innovating in the MIPS to more

TABLE 23.1. MIPS Scales by Domain

Motivating Aims	Cognitive Modes	Interpersonal Behaviors
Enhancing Preserving	Extroversing Introversing	Retiring Outgoing
Modifying Accommodating	Sensing Intuiting	Hesitating Asserting
Individuating Nurturing	Thinking Feeling	Dissenting Conforming
	Systematizing Innovating	Yielding Controlling
		Complaining Agreeing

Note. Data and table copyright 1994 by Dicandrien, Inc. All rights reserved.

TABLE 23.2. Brief Definitions of MIPS Scales

Motivating Aims

Enhancing. Persons scoring high on this scale tend to look for the bright side of life, are optimistic about future possibilities, find it easy to enjoy themselves, and face the ups and downs of their lives with equanimity.

Preserving. Persons scoring high on this scale focus on and intensify the problems of life. Perceiving the past as having been personally troubling, they always seem to be waiting for something else to go wrong, and feel that things are likely to go from bad to worse. They are easily upset by minor concerns and disappointments.

Modifying. Persons scoring high on this scale take charge of their lives and make things happen rather than wait for them to occur. They are busily involved in modifying their environments and arranging events to suit their needs and desires.

Accommodating. Persons scoring high on this scale undertake little to shape or alter their lives. They react to the passing scene, accommodating to circumstances created by others; they seem acquiescent, are unable to rouse themselves, lack initiative, and do little to generate the outcomes they desire.

Individuating. Persons scoring high on this scale are oriented to actualize their own needs and wishes—that is, they seek to fulfill themselves first, worry little about the impact of their behavior on others, and tend to be both independent and egocentric.

Nurturing. Persons scoring high on this scale are motivated to meet the needs of others first—to attend to other people's welfare and desires at the expense of themselves. They are seen as nurturant and protective, taking care of others before taking care of themselves.

Cognitive Modes

Extraversing. Persons scoring high on this scale turn to others to find stimulation and encouragement. They draw upon friends and colleagues for ideas, guidance, inspiration, and energy, as well as garnering assurances of self-worth from them and taking comfort in their presence.

Introversing. Persons scoring high on this scale prefer to use their own thoughts and feelings as resources, gaining inspiration and stimulation primarily from themselves rather than from others. By contrast with extraversers, introversers experience greater serenity and comfort by distancing themselves from external sources, preferring to heed the prompting that comes from within.

Sensing. Persons scoring high on this scale gather their knowledge from the tangible and concrete, trusting direct experience and observable phenomena over the use of inference and abstraction. The practical and "real," the literal and factual are what give these individuals comfort and confidence.

Intuiting. Persons scoring high on this scale prefer the symbolic and unknown to the concrete and observable. They are open to the intangibles of life and are inclined to seek out and enjoy the more mysterious experiences and speculative sources of knowledge.

Thinking. Persons scoring high on this scale prefer to process the knowledge they have by means of logic and analytic reasoning. Decisions are based on cool, impersonal, and "objective" judgments, rather than on subjective emotions.

Feeling. Persons scoring high on this scale form their judgments by heeding their own affective responses to circumstances, by evaluating subjectively the impact of their actions upon those involved, and by following their personal values and goals.

Systematizing. Persons scoring high on this scale are highly organized and predictable in their approach to life's experiences. They transform new knowledge in line with what is known and are careful, if not perfectionistic, in arranging even minor details. As a result, they are seen by others as orderly, conscientious, and efficient.

(continued)

TABLE 23.2. *cont.*

Innovating. Persons scoring high on this scale are inclined to be creative and to take risks, ready to alter and recast whatever they come upon. They seem discontented with the routine and the predictable, spontaneously modifying what is given by following their hunches and seeking to effect novel, unanticipated consequences.

Interpersonal Behaviors

Retiring. Persons scoring high on this scale are characterized by their lack of affect and their social indifference. They tend to be quiet, passive, and uninvolved; they may be viewed by others as quiet, colorless, and unable to make friends, as well as apathetically disengaged.

Outgoing. Persons scoring high on this scale seek social stimulation, excitement, and attention. They often react dramatically to situations around them, but they typically lose interest quickly. Colorful and charming socialites, they also can be demanding and manipulative.

Hesitating. Persons scoring high on this scale are usually shy, timid, and nervous in social situations, strongly wanting to be liked and accepted, yet often fearing that they will be rejected. At the same time that they are sensitive and emotionally responsive, they are mistrusting, lonely, and isolated.

Asserting. Persons scoring high on this scale tend to feel that they are more competent and gifted than the people around them. They are often ambitious and egocentric, self-assured and outspoken. Others may see them as arrogant and inconsiderate.

Dissenting. Persons scoring high on this scale tend to act out in an independent and nonconforming manner. They often resist following traditional standards, displaying an audaciousness that may be seen either as reckless or as spirited and enterprising.

Conforming. Persons scoring high on this scale are likely to be upstanding and self-controlled. They relate to authority in a respectful and cooperative manner, tend to behave in a formal and proper manner in social situations, and are unlikely to be self-expressive or to act spontaneously.

Yielding. Persons scoring high on this scale are their own worst enemies: They are accustomed to suffering rather than pleasure, are submissive, and tend to act in self-demeaning ways. Their behavior renders ineffective the efforts of others to assist them and causes the yielders to bypass opportunities for rewards and to fail repeatedly to achieve, despite possessing abilities to do so.

Controlling. Persons scoring high on this scale are forceful and often domineering and socially aggressive. They tend to see themselves as fearless and competitive. To them, warmth and gentleness are signs of weakness, which they avoid by being strong-willed and ambitious.

Complaining. Persons scoring high on this scale are characterized by their tendency to be passive–aggressive, sullen, and generally dissatisfied. Their moods and behavior are highly changeable. At times, they relate to others in a sociable and friendly manner; on other occasions, they are irritable and hostile, expressing the belief that they are misunderstood and unappreciated.

Agreeing. Persons scoring high on this scale tend to be highly likable socially, often relating to others in an amenable manner. They form strong loyalties and attachments to others. They cover any negative feelings, however, especially when these feelings may be viewed as objectionable by the people they wish to please.

Note. Data and table copyright 1994 by Dicandrien, Inc. All rights reserved.

accurately capture the original Jungian meaning. More important, however, Millon has recast these constructs in terms of their influence on one's cognitive style of dealing with the voluminous influx of information required for daily living in the information age. This is an important contribution because cognitive differences in how individuals respond to information and the manner in which these differences are expressed in daily life have been much overlooked in generating and appraising personality traits.

The Interpersonal Behaviors Scales

Five pairs of Interpersonal Behaviors scales assess the person's style of relating to others. Millonian theorists will recognize these five pairs of scales as normal range variations of Millon's ten personality disorders (Millon, 1990). The MIPS retiring and outgoing interpersonal styles are the normal variants of the schizoid and histrionic personality disorders respectively. The hesitating and asserting styles are related to the avoidant and narcissistic disorders. The dissenting and conforming personality styles are consonant with the antisocial and obsessive–compulsive disorders in the pathological range. The yielding and controlling styles are the normal range variants of the self-defeating/masochistic and the sadistic personalities—although these are not formally recognized as disorders in DSM-IV. Finally, the interpersonal styles characterized by the Complaining and Agreeing scales on the MIPS are on the same continuum as the negativistic/passive–aggressive and the dependent personality disorders, respectively.

As a group, the MIPS scales have a rich theoretical foundation in a model of personality that is deeply rooted in biosocial and evolutionary theory (Millon, 1969, 1990, 1991).

APPLICATIONS OF THE MIPS

The MIPS is appropriate for use with normally functioning adults. It is especially useful in organizational settings. One important application is to screen employees for general adjustment. This is particularly relevant for employees in high-risk fire and safety occupations. The MIPS is also frequently used to assist in identifying managerial potential, or as developmental feedback to improve existing managerial talent. The MIPS also can be used to help form work or project teams and to improve the effectiveness with which teams make decisions and work together. Feedback of MIPS results can be integrated into many team-building exercises and other organizational training and development programs. Practitioners using the MIPS in organizational settings should be aware of relevant legal and ethical issues regarding testing of job applicants.

Appropriate applications of the MIPS also include settings in which counselors seek to identify, understand, and assist normally functioning adults. Such settings include employee assistance programs, vocational guidance and career development programs, university counseling centers, and marriage and family counseling centers. Also appropriate are independent and group practice settings in which reasonably functional individuals seek assistance with real-life problems such as divorce, child management, drinking, work stress, etc.

THE MIPS INTERPRETIVE REPORTS

Interpretive reports are available with the computer version of the MIPS. The interpretive reports carry the flare, depth, and insightful wit for which Theodore Millon's writings have become widely known. Upon reviewing these works one has the feeling of reading carefully crafted prose rather than an automated psychological report.

More than 400 reports are built into the software. The reports differ from many computerized interpretations because the narratives do not follow a simplistic, scale-by-scale procession of scores. The reports print a description of the individual as an integrated and wholistic person. Practitioners often find the reports rich with discourse on the person's style that goes beyond a simple description of behavior and fosters a new understanding of and sensitivity toward the client.

The reading level is high and practitioners should exercise appropriate clinical judgment in deciding to give a report directly to the client. College-educated individuals easily understand the reports. Those with a high school education grasp most of the report, although parts of it will be beyond their comprehension.

It has been my experience that most normally functioning adults easily recognize themselves in these narratives and favorably receive the message. Individuals whose interpersonal styles occasionally cause some real life problems, however, may need to have the reports placed in an appropriate context for them. Practitioners should review each report carefully before deciding whether it is appropriate for the client to read.

TECHNICAL CHARACTERISTICS OF THE MIPS

Item Development

The writing of items for the MIPS scales was guided by an explicit theory of normal personology elucidated elsewhere (Millon, 1990). Items were reviewed by content experts for correspondence with the constructs that were intended to be measured by each of the MIPS scales.

MIPS items are scored on more than one scale. This multiple keying of items on conceptually related scales forces higher intercorrelations among some scales, but this is believed to mirror the phenomenological relatedness of these constructs in the naturally occurring world. This scale design follows a theory of prototypes in which all construct domains are assumed to be composed of a set of core or prototypical characteristics and a set of related behaviors that commonly occur but are not essential characteristics of the core trait. Core characteristics of one trait may be nonessential but related characteristics for another trait. For example, outgoing behavior is one component of an asserting style of relating to others. For each trait, the core items receive more weight in the scoring of that scale than do the supporting items. Because of this item overlap, which is common in Millon's inventories, certain statistical procedures based on scale intercorrelations may not be appropriate. For example, factor analyses should be conducted at the item level rather than on the scale intercorrelation matrix.

Representativeness of Norm Samples

After multiple pilot tests, the items were refined and the test was then standardized on 1,000 adults in community settings in eight cities. This sample was carefully selected to closely represent the United States population of adults in terms of racial/ethnic group, educational level, age, gender, and region of the country. A separate set of college norms were also developed based on a standardization sample of 1,600 students at 14 colleges and universities around the country. The student sample was carefully selected to be representative of the population of college students in terms of racial/ethnic group, age, year in school, major area of study, region of the country, and type of institution attended. We considered the representativeness of the standardization samples to be critical because we planned to use a new norming procedure that would take into account the prevalence rates of the constructs measured in the population.

THE MIPS PREVALENCE SCORE SYSTEM
Concept and Use

The MIPS Prevalence Score (PS) system is a unique and powerful synergy of dimensional and categorical approaches to personality measurement. Categorical models sort individuals into one or another classification group. Dimensional models estimate the amount of a trait an individual possesses or describe his or her position relative to others on some dimension of interest. To view these two approaches as inconsistent would be an unfortunate misinterpretation of the naturally occurring world, and would result in a loss of meaningful information for both the researcher and the practitioner. To accurately reflect the percentage of each of the MIPS traits occurring in the real world, the measurement approach begins with a simple classification into trait groups based on population prevalence data and then proceeds to a more sophisticated rating of the individual's position on the underlying dimension relative to others in that particular trait group.

MIPS PSs range from PS 0 to PS 100. The system was designed in such a way that the proportion of individuals who score at or above PS 50 on each scale matches the prevalence of individuals in the general population who possess that trait. We accomplished this by the following procedure: For each MIPS scale, PS 49 was set in such a manner that the percentage of the standardization sample scoring at or above PS 50 would correspond as closely as possible to the actuarial estimate of the prevalence rate for that trait in the general population. The population prevalence rates were estimated based on an extensive literature review of studies measuring related constructs across a wide variety of nonclinical samples, as described in the MIPS manual (Millon et al., 1994).

The reference point for interpretation of individual score profiles is always PS 50. An individual who obtains scores at or above PS 50 on any particular scale is classified as a member of the trait group defined by that scale. For example, a person scoring above PS 50 on the Extroversing scale is considered extroverted. Once individuals have been classified as members of particular trait groups, individual score profiles are interpreted in terms of their distance from PS 50 on each scale. Scores higher than PS 50 indicate higher positions within that trait group on the underlying dimension measured by the scale. Higher-scoring individuals are likely to possess the trait to a greater degree and to demonstrate the trait with greater frequency and intensity than are lower-scoring individuals within the same trait group. Simply put, two persons scoring PS 50 and PS 69, respectively, on the Extroversing scale are both categorized as members of the extrovert group, but the person scoring PS 69 is more extroverted than is the person scoring PS 50. In fact, a score of PS 69 on the Extroversing scale is at the median of all extroverts. A score of PS 89 on the Extroversing scale is at the 84th percentile of all members of that trait group. PSs have the same meaning across all the MIPS scales.

Although the use of gender-based norms is required to represent empirically demonstrated gender differences in the prevalence of various personality styles in the population, for some situations, referencing a person to a combined sample of men and women also may be of interest. For this reason, total group norms are provided for the general adult sample and for the general college sample.

Comment

The PS scaling procedure used for the MIPS is preferred to both linear and normalized standard score conversions (e.g., *T*-scores) because PSs more accurately reflect differences in the prevalence of various personality traits in the population. The use of either linear or normalized *T*-score transformations with a standard psychometric cutoff score, such as one or two standard deviations above the mean, would impose an arbitrary statistical rule of thumb that bears little resemblance to the reality of population prevalence rates.

Unlike intelligence, personality variables are not necessarily distributed normally in the population. Normalized *T*-scores would, by definition, require half the population to score above 50 on all scales, which is clearly an inaccurate representation of the distribution of many personality traits in the normal population. It is simply not true that half the population is introverted and the other half extroverted, so that developing tests that result in these simplistic dichotomies is unjustified by the available actuarial data.

Linear *T*-scores would center the scale at the sample mean—that is, the average score. To describe an individual as "average" on Introversing, however, is meaningless, because most people are not introverted. The use of PS conversions is empirically justified by population prevalence rate data and is consistent with the test authors' biosocial/evolutionary model of personology.

Reliability

The internal consistency of the MIPS scales is quite adequate for a personality test. The median coefficient alphas are $r = .78$ for adults ($n = 1,000$) and $r = .77$ for students ($n = 1,600$). Median split-half reliabilities are $r = .82$ and $r = .80$ for the adult ($n = 1,000$) and college ($n = 1,600$) samples, respectively. The median retest reliability is $r = .85$ for adults after 2 months ($n = 50$), and $r = .84$ for students after 3 weeks ($n = 110$). Reliabilities are very comparable for females and males.

Construct Validity

The test manual presents correlations with a wide variety of other personality tests, including the Sixteen Personality Factor Questionnaire (16 PF; Cattell, Eber, & Tatsuoka, 1970), Myers–Briggs Type Indicator (MBTI; Myers & McCaulley, 1985), California Psychological Inventory (CPI; Gough, 1987), NEO Personality Inventory (NEO; Costa & McCrae, 1985), Gordon Personal Profile—Inventory (GPP-I; Gordon, 1978), Beck Depression Inventory (BDI; Beck & Steer, 1987), College Adjustment Scales (CAS; Anton & Reed, 1991), Minnesota Multiphasic Personality Inventory (MMPI; Hathaway & McKinley, 1967), Minnesota Multiphasic Personality Inventory—2 (MMPI-2; Butcher, Dahlstrom, Graham, Tellegen, & Kaemmer, 1989), Strong Interest Inventory (SII; Hansen & Campbell, 1985), and the Jackson Personality Research Form (PRF; Jackson, 1985). These studies are strengthened by the fact that most of the subject samples were selected to be representative of working adults in the United States population, and were not based on samples of convenience such as college freshman. The pattern of convergent and divergent correlations between the MIPS and these tests, obtained to demonstrate external validity, were largely consonant with expectations, based on the test authors' theory of normal personology and on the item content of the respective scales. The MIPS constructs can be said to be well positioned within a larger nomological network of personality domains. Correlations with the MMPI, MBTI, and the NEO-PI were selected for discussion in this chapter.

The MIPS was correlated with the MMPI-2 in a sample of 62 Air Force recruits referred for psychological evaluation, and with the MMPI-1 in a sample of 58 police officer applicants. Interestingly, the MIPS and MMPI showed a pattern of convergent validity in the clinically referred sample and a pattern of divergent validity in the job applicant sample. In the sample of clinically referred Air Force recruits, the MIPS Preserving, Accommodating, Hesitating, and Introversing scales correlated very highly ($r > .65$) with several indicators of psychopathology on the MMPI-2, most notably Scale Pt (Psychasthenia), Scale Sc (Schizophrenia), and Scale Si (Social Introversion). By comparison, the magnitude of the correlations between the MIPS and the MMPI-1 in the police applicant sample were generally quite low (Millon et al., 1994). This finding may suggest that when used with normal populations, such as job applicants, the MIPS and MMPI measure essentially different domains. While the ability of the MMPI to screen out obvious psychopathology has been well demonstrated, the use of the MMPI to predict job performance among normally functioning employees is less accepted (Butcher, 1979) and can be legally problematic in many employment settings.

THE MIPS COGNITIVE MODES
Relationship with the MBTI

The MIPS and the MBTI were administered to 100 adults with a median age of 40 years. Strong correlations were observed between MBTI scales and the MIPS Cognitive Modes developed to measure similar Jungian constructs. When these data were arranged in a multitrait–multimethod matrix using continuous bipolar scores, the correlations between the complementary scales on the MIPS and MBTI ranged from $r = .71$ to $r = .75$.

In a separate sample of displaced executives and upper-level managers ($n = 47$), these multitrait–multimethod correlations were also strong, ranging from $r = .67$ to $r = .86$. The magnitude of these correlations clearly supports the hypothesis that the MIPS Cognitive Modes scales measure essentially the same constructs as do the MBTI.

Relation with the MIPS Interpersonal Styles

Many other meaningful relationships were observed between certain of the MIPS Motivating Aims and Interpersonal Behaviors bipolarities and the MBTI scales. The MBTI Thinking (T) and Feeling (F) scales were moderately correlated with the MIPS Individuating–Nurturing bipolarity. The direction of these correlations suggests that individuals oriented toward obtaining reinforcement from others in their environment (Nurturing on the MIPS) are likely to be classified as "feelers" on the MBTI, while those oriented toward obtaining reinforcement from self (Individuating on the MIPS) are more likely to be classified as "thinkers" on the MBTI. The MBTI Thinking scale was also correlated with the MIPS Controlling scale, while the MBTI Feeling scale was correlated with the MIPS Agreeing scale.

Further, the MIPS Dissenting–Conforming bipolarity was moderately correlated with the MBTI Judging (J) and Perceiving (P) scales. The direction of these correlations suggests an important relationship between judgmental thinking and conforming interpersonal behavior. Finally, the MBTI Intuiting (N) scale is moderately correlated with the Innovating scale on the MIPS, suggesting that innovative thinking may be related to an intuiting style of processing information.

The MIPS 16 Types

There are 16 possible combinations of the four MBTI bipolar scales that are typically presented in MBTI research (Myers & McCaulley, 1985). An analogous set of 16 types can be produced using the four MIPS Cognitive Modes bipolarities. The MIPS manual shows the percentages in each of these 16 MIPS types for the adult (n = 1,000) and college (n = 1,600) standardization samples, by gender and overall. The largest percentage of adult males (24%) is found in the ESTZ (Extroversing–Sensing–Thinking–Systematizing) type. The largest percentages of adult females are found in the ENFV (Extroversing–Intuiting–Feeling–Innovating) type (15.8%) and in the ESFZ (Extroversing–Sensing–Feeling–Systematizing) type (14.4%). The percentages obtained can be considered representative of the general population because of the closeness of proportions of age, education level, and race/ethnicity in the samples to those in the United States Census data.

Shown in Table 23.3 are the percentages of the 16 typologies in specific occupational groups, including sales personnel, clerical and technical workers, upper-level managers, Air Force recruits, police applicants, and general laborers. These data are interesting because they show differences in characteristic modes of gathering and processing information across occupational groups. For example, approximately 18% of those in technical occupations were classified as ISTZ (Introversing–Sensing–Thinking–Systematizing), compared with about 7% of salespersons. More than half of the police officer applicants (58%) were classified as ESTZ (Extroversing–Sensing–Thinking–Systematizing), compared with only 24% of males in the adult standardization sample. The MIPS typologies by occupational group shown in this section should be used with caution because these data do not imply a connection to effective job performance. Studies concerning job performance are discussed below in the section on Organizational Research.

Summary

The MIPS Cognitive Modes scales operate in very similar ways to the MBTI scales, and the integration of these typologies with the MIPS Motivating Aims and Interpersonal Behaviors may provide an enriched understanding of the person taking the test.

APPLIED ORGANIZATIONAL RESEARCH WITH THE MIPS

I conducted six large applied research studies in various organizations and corporations around the country as part of the MIPS prepublication research program. Several of these studies are summarized in this section. Interested researchers can read about the technical details of each study in the MIPS manual.

Managerial Performance

The MIPS was administered to a sample of mid-level managers in a large telecommunications firm in the southeastern United States (n = 51). These were mostly white and well-educated men in the third tier of the corporation's management structure. The subjects participated in a three-day management assessment center that included two simulated board meetings with different agendas: one meeting involved a competitive resource allocation decision, and the other involved a cooperative organizational problem-solving discussion. Other activities included an in-basket exercise; a formal presentation of a business plan to a

TABLE 23.3. MIPS Percentages for Each of the 16 Cognitive Modes Types by Occupational Group

	ISTZ	ISFZ	INFZ	INTZ
Upper management	10.1	2.3	1.5	3.2
Clerical/secretarial	8.7	9.7	1.0	1.0
Sales	7.2	4.5	1.8	0.9
Technical	18.2	1.8	1.8	3.6
General labor	10.7	10.7	0.0	0.0
Air Force recruits	9.4	3.1	3.6	1.6
Police applicants	9.2	0.3	0.3	1.4
	ISTV	**ISFV**	**INFV**	**INTV**
Upper management	3.9	3.1	1.5	0.7
Clerical/secretarial	2.9	1.9	7.8	1.0
Sales	0.9	1.8	9.0	6.3
Technical	9.1	0.0	1.8	7.3
General labor	1.8	8.9	10.7	7.1
Air Force recruits	1.0	4.2	8.3	3.6
Police applicants	1.7	0.3	1.4	0.0
	ESTV	**ESFV**	**ENFV**	**ENTV**
Upper management	12.5	0.8	7.8	13.2
Clerical/secretarial	1.0	3.9	11.7	2.9
Sales	1.8	7.2	15.3	7.2
Technical	9.1	0.0	7.3	5.5
General labor	10.7	5.4	8.9	3.6
Air Force recruits	5.2	4.2	6.8	3.1
Police applicants	5.6	2.0	1.4	3.4
	ESTZ	**ESFZ**	**ENFZ**	**ENTZ**
Upper management	22.0	10.2	0.8	6.2
Clerical/secretarial	16.5	18.4	10.7	1.0
Sales	20.7	7.2	2.7	5.4
Technical	20.0	7.3	0.0	7.3
General labor	10.7	7.1	3.6	0.0
Air Force recruits	21.9	7.8	8.3	7.8
Police applicants	58.0	3.6	3.4	8.1

Note. The sizes of the samples are as follows: Upper management (*n* = 130), Clerical (*n* = 103), Sales (*n* = 111), Technical (*n* = 55), General labor (*n* = 56), Air Force recruits (*n* = 206), and Police applicants (*n* = 349). I, Intraversing; S, Sensing; T, Thinking; Z, Systematizing; F, Feeling; N, Intuiting; V, Innovating; E, Extroversing. Data and table copyright 1994 by Dicandrien, Inc. All rights reserved.

superior, based on review of a standardized packet of information; a personnel counseling session with a disgruntled subordinate; and the preparation of a written business plan, based on the review of another standardized packet of information. Each manager's performance was rated by three trained assessors on 10 dimensions of managerial performance.

The mean MIPS profile for the managers was quite interesting. The profile suggested that these men actively sought positive reinforcement from their world by modifying surrounding circumstances and asserting themselves interpersonally in a socially confident and poised manner. The highest mean MIPS scores were on the MIPS Enhancing (PS = 80.6), Asserting (PS = 72.9), Outgoing (PS = 70), Modifying (PS = 68.5), and Extroversing (PS = 68.5) scales. A moderate elevation was observed on the MIPS Controlling scale (PS = 55.1).

Several a priori hypotheses about the relationship of the MIPS scales to the 10 dimensions of managerial performance were supported. As predicted, oral communication was related to the MIPS Modifying, Extroversing, Outgoing, and Asserting scales. Oral defense, or the ability to offer persuasive verbal responses in the face of challenges and criticism, was positively related to the MIPS Outgoing, Asserting, and Controlling scales, and inversely related to the Yielding scale. Strategic analysis was related to the MIPS Modifying and Controlling scales. Interactive problem solving was positively correlated with the MIPS Extroversing, Outgoing, and Asserting scales and negatively correlated with the Hesitating scale. Team management was related to the MIPS Controlling scale.

Although not anticipated, the MIPS Intuiting and Innovating scales were correlated significantly with several dimensions of managerial performance, including strategic analysis, interactive problem solving, oral defense, and oral communication. Because the business decisions and situations encountered at higher levels of management are both more complex and less structured, this finding may suggest that an ability to deal with novelty and ambiguity, which sensing and systematizing individuals often lack, may be helpful to effective managerial performance at the higher levels on management. Further research is needed on this topic.

Also not anticipated was a significant correlation between team management and the MIPS Preserving, Complaining, and Feeling scales. While a feeling style of cognitive processing may relate to team management because of the tendency to attend to the views of others, the positive relationship of high ability in this dimension with the Preserving and Complaining scales is more difficult to interpret. According to MIPS theory, the Complaining scale represents a tendency to be discontented with situations in general, and the Preserving scale reflects a basic motivation to avoid negative reinforcement from the environment. If the current findings can be replicated, they may suggest that this increased alertness to negative feedback, if appropriately channeled, can be adaptive when managing a team.

The present findings are consistent with definitions of leadership as a process of interpersonal influence involving persuasion rather than dominance (Hogan, Curphy, & Hogan, 1993).

Law Enforcement Performance

The relationship between the MIPS and police officer performance was studied in a predominantly Hispanic metropolitan city in the southwestern United States. The mean MIPS profile for those applicants offered admission to the training academy ($n = 47$) was noteworthy for the relatively moderate elevation on the Controlling (PS = 47) scale, as well as the balance of scores on the Individuating (PS = 41) and Nurturing (PS = 41) bipolarity. The highest MIPS scores were observed on the Thinking (PS = 71), Asserting (PS = 74), and Enhancing (PS = 81) scales. Also noteworthy was the mean score on the Adjustment Index ($T = 59$), which was almost one full standard deviation above average.

A structured job analysis was conducted to determine the personality traits that are considered essential to effective performance as an entry level patrol officer, with consensus ratings provided by five field training officers. The results suggested that four personality dimensions were essential to effective performance: (1) adherence to work ethic, (2) thoroughness and attentiveness to details, (3) sensitivity to the interests of others, and (4) emotional stability. The job analysis was conducted using a research version of An Inventory of General Position Requirements (Bowling Green State University, 1992), which was developed to provide an empirical basis for matching position requirements and personality traits in specific occupations (Guion, 1991).

MIPS composites were developed to measure each of the four dimensions identified in the job analysis. After 6 months of academy training, these composites were correlated with ratings on simulated tactical police exercises. The MIPS Emotional Stability composite was correlated with the use of secure police tactics during a barroom disturbance and with appropriately removing a suspect from the disturbance. Appropriate removal of the suspect was also correlated with the MIPS composite for Sensitivity to the Interests of Others and the MIPS composite for Adherence to Work Ethic. In another exercise, the MIPS composite for Thoroughness and Attentiveness to Detail and the MIPS composite for Adherence to Work Ethic were both correlated with properly issuing a traffic citation.

After graduation from the academy, the cadets were followed through 4 months of field training. They were rated multiple times on tasks, attitude, knowledge, and appearance. The MIPS Controlling scale showed a pattern of medium to large inverse correlations with all areas of field performance measured in this study. According to MIPS theory, individuals with moderately high scores on the MIPS Controlling scale demonstrate a pervasively forceful and domineering style of relating to others. Individuals with very high Controlling scores may be chronically combative, tending toward a contentious, even hostile, tone in their relationships. In the author's theory of personality disorders, these individuals are on the same continuum (although not as extreme) as those diagnosed with aggressive personality disorders. As written previously about these individuals, "Although many may cloak their more malicious and power-oriented tendencies in publicly approved roles and vocations, they give themselves away in their dominating, antagonistic, and frequent persecutory actions" (Millon, Millon, Davis, Choca, & Van Denburg, 1994, pp. 12–13).

On the other hand, the polar opposite MIPS scale, Yielding, was uncorrelated with field performance. This suggests a nonlinear relationship between dominance and police performance in which either too little or too much of this trait is associated with problematic performance as a law enforcement officer. This finding is also consistent with the results of the job analysis in which the police department's field training officers indicated that sensitivity to the interests of others is essential to effective performance of police duties. Overall, these results mirror the changing conceptualization of the police officer's role from "carrying a big stick" to a highly technical position requiring considerable interpersonal skill and judgment.

Screening for Psychological Adjustment

The MIPS was administered to 297 U.S. Air Force recruits during the first week of basic training as part of a routine screening program designed to identify individuals who are psychologically incapable of adjusting to military service. MIPS results were not available to the psychologists making these decisions. One hundred and sixty-nine recruits passed the initial mass screening based on their responses to a structured life history questionnaire. Ninety-five recruits were referred for further testing, but were then cleared for duty based on the test results. Thirty-three recruits were recommended for discharge from the military after a complete psychological evaluation.

The mean MIPS profiles for these groups were dramatically different. Whereas the group that passed the initial screening was reasonably balanced on the pleasure–pain bipolarity, for example, the group found unfit for duty scored extremely high on pain (Preserving PS = 98) and extremely low on pleasure (Enhancing PS = 1).

An Adjustment Index was developed based on a composite of MIPS scales. The following six MIPS PS values were placed on the positive side of the Adjustment Index: Enhancing, Outgoing, Asserting, Conforming, Controlling, and Agreeing. The Enhancing scale was weighted twice as heavily as the other five scales. The following six MIPS PS values entered the negative side of the equation for the Adjustment Index: Preserving, Retiring, Hesitating, Dissenting, Yielding, and Complaining. The Preserving scale was weighted twice as heavily as the other five scales. This Adjustment Index was then converted to a *T*-score using the mean and *SD* of the standardization sample.

The unfit for duty group scored more than two and a half standard deviations below average on the Adjustment Index (*T* = 23). A *T*-score less than or equal to 35 points on the Adjustment Index was identified as a cutoff score because it correctly classified 100% of recruits in the unfit for duty group while misclassifying fewer than 20% of recruits who were actually fit for duty. The correlation of the Adjustment Index with fit versus unfit designations was at the upper limit of the statistic. This study suggested that use of the Adjustment Index in the screening program could have significantly reduced the caseload of the examining psychologists.

While the cutoff score should be cross-validated in an independent sample, the MIPS Adjustment Index holds considerable promise in a wide variety of organizational settings in which screening for overall adjustment is considered job relevant, such as safety-sensitive positions or positions working with children or the elderly. Individuals who score below *T*-35 on this index should be administered a clinical range instrument such as the MCMI-III (Millon et al., 1994) to assess for psychopathology.

Absenteeism and Disciplinary Personnel Actions

The MIPS was administered to a sample of hourly workers employed by a medium-sized municipal government in the southeastern United States (*n* = 41) and absenteeism and disciplinary records were obtained. These employees were predominantly laborers working in the city maintenance, landscape, and sanitation departments. The sample was largely male (76%) and African American (56%), with a high school education or less (70%). The median age was 35 years.

The mean MIPS Interpersonal Behaviors scales for this sample were characterized by high scores on the Conforming (PS = 60) and Agreeing (PS = 61) scales. These employees tended to use more Sensing (PS = 63) modes of gathering information and Systematizing (PS = 55) strategies for processing information. In general, this sample of laborers was considerably more introversing, retiring, and yielding, as well as less enhancing and modifying, than were samples of managers and executives.

MIPS scores were correlated with personnel records for the preceding 12 months. The MIPS Controlling scale was inversely correlated with both disciplinary personnel action taken against an employee (*r* = −.35, *p* < .01) and absenteeism (*r* = −.33, *p* < .01). In addition, the MIPS Hesitating scale was positively related to absenteeism (*r* = .32, *p* < .01). Thus, we can speculate that employees with high scores on the Controlling scale and low scores on the Hesitating scale will have better attendance records than other employees. According to MIPS theory, individuals who score high on the Controlling scale seek to arrange and control the events in their lives to meet their schedules, needs, and priorities. In addition, individuals scoring low on the Hesitating scale tend to feel more secure about their personal worth and to be more decisive about taking action than those who score higher. Perhaps these employees take better command of potential conflict between their personal and work schedules than those who are absent more often.

Career Decision Making

Two studies examined the use of the MIPS in career decision making. In the first study, the MIPS was administered to 70 clients participating in career management counseling at a large, nationally based firm which specializes in executive outplacement and management consulting to Fortune 500 companies. The sample consisted of all upper-level managers who had been displaced during corporate downsizing. The mean MIPS profile for this sample suggested that, on average, these managers werre people who actively sought positive reinforcement from the environment and who were assertive and outgoing in interpersonal relations. Their preferred information-gathering styles were extraversing and sensing, while their preferred information-processing styles were thinking and systematizing.

Correlations with the Strong Interest Inventory (Hansen & Campbell, 1985) show that a systematizing style of processing information is significantly correlated with conventional occupations involving methodical, organized, or clerical tasks. The polar opposite MIPS scale, Innovating, is correlated with interest in enterprising activities, which require entrepreneurial, persuasive, and political behaviors. The Strong Enterprising scale is also significantly correlated with the MIPS Modifying, Extroversing, Outgoing, Asserting, and Controlling scales.

An interest in business management on the Strong was positively correlated with the MIPS Controlling and Asserting scales and negatively correlated with the MIPS Accommodating scale. By contrast, an interest in office practices on the Strong was correlated with systematizing style of processing information and a conforming and agreeing style of interpersonal behavior. Further, an outgoing style of relating, as measured on the MIPS, was correlated with an interest in both sales and merchandising as expressed on the Strong.

In the second study, the MIPS and the Strong were administered to a sample of 100 community college students identified as expressing uncertainty about their career goals and describing their uncertainty as troublesome and an unresolved issue for them. A canonical analysis yielded three distinct patterns of relationships between the MIPS and Strong scales labeled the retreator, the feeler, and the conscientious conformer. Retreators were characterized by the Hesitating and Agreeing scales on the MIPS. They do not trust others or take risks easily. They prefer disconnection from the world of work and may develop interpersonally defensive career intentions. For the retreator, career indecision may reflect a lack of receptivity to the social relations that are part of most work settings. There was a hint at some compatibility with highly structured subordinate/follower roles in work.

The feeler was characterized by the Nurturing, Feeling, and Agreeing scales on the MIPS. Although retreators and feelers both tended to have agreeing personalities, they differed in their approach toward others. Retreators may have used agreeing behavior as a way of avoiding more meaningful and, perhaps, threatening interpersonal communication; feelers, on the other hand, were socially open and their agreeing behavior lacked the defensive quality shown by retreators. Feelers showed a pattern of being people-oriented and avoiding activities that were highly regulated and that involved calculation or the use of standardized procedures to find solutions.

The conscientious conformer was characterized by the MIPS Conforming, Sensing, and Systematizing scales. This variant was very similar to the pattern of MIPS scales found to correlate with the Conscientiousness factor of the NEO (see below). These students tended to express interest in office practice, domestic activities, social service, and religious activities.

General negative affectivity—that is, the propensity to focus on and experience painful emotional states—may provide a framework for understanding chronic career indecision. Perhaps the strong need for systems that was characteristic of the conscientious conformer, and the willingness to defer to the wishes of others, characteristic of both the retreator and feeler, represent two methods of avoiding possible negative stimulation from the work environment. Students who exhibit pervasive career indecision present unique challenges for counselors in traditional vocational guidance programs. The often-used career counseling techniques of exploration, job shadowing, and placement assistance may be inadequate for these clients. To remediate chronic career indecision, counselors may need to address the underlying personality issues (Super, 1983; Tango & Dziuban, 1984).

Summary

The studies reviewed in this section provide empirical support for many of the applications of the MIPS suggested earlier in this chapter.

FACTOR STRUCTURE OF THE MIPS

Results of Factor Analysis

We studied the factor structure of the MIPS using a principal components analysis at the item level in a sample of 2,600 subjects (Weiss & Lowther, 1995). This study suggested five factors that were consistent with the five-factor model of personality and which accounted for 24.8% of the total variance. Subjects with high scores on the first factor were likely to endorse items such as "I often feel on edge, waiting for something to happen." The first factor was interpreted as measuring maladaptation. The second dimension was interpreted as representing extroversion or surgency. It was marked by items such as "I have great confidence in my social abilities." The third factor, termed conscientiousness, was defined by items such as "I plan ahead and then act decisively to make my plans happen." The fourth dimension, interpreted as disagreeableness, contained items such as "I look out for myself first, and then think of others." The fifth factor was marked by items such as "I am a realistic person who does not like to speculate about things." This factor was interpreted as representing the opposite pole of openness to experience, namely closed-mindedness. These findings were consonant with the five-factor model of personality (Goldberg, 1993) except that we obtained the reverse poles of the agreeableness and openness to experience factors, namely, disagreeableness and closed-mindedness.

Relation to the Five-Factor Model of Personality

We (Weiss & Lowther, 1995) correlated the MIPS factors with several measures of the five-factor model of personality, including the NEO Personality Inventory (Costa & McCrae, 1985), the Goldberg Adjective Checklist (Goldberg, 1992), and the second-order factors of the 16 PF (Cattell et al., 1970). The pattern of correlations was consistent with expectations. For example, the MIPS Maladaptation, Surgency, Conscientiousness, Disagreeableness, and Closed-mindedness factors correlated $r = .81$, $r = .70$, $r = .72$, $r = -.43$, and $r = -.33$ with the NEO Neuroticism, Extroversion, Conscientiousness, Agreeableness, and Openness scales in a sample of 61 adults.

Factor Patterns by Occupational Group

Mean MIPS *T*-scores for the five factors were examined in several occupational samples (Weiss & Lowther, 1995) and some very interesting patterns emerged. Among the five occupational groups studied, the police officers ($n = 354$) had the highest Conscientiousness score ($\bar{X} = 56$) and the lowest Maladaptation score ($\bar{X} = 39$). Mid-level managers ($n = 83$) had the highest mean scores on the Surgency factor ($\bar{X} = 54$) and the lowest mean scores on the Closed-Mindedness factor ($\bar{X} = 45$). Conversely, a sample of hourly municipal employees (n = 41) had the lowest scores on the Surgency factor ($\bar{X}$ = 46) and the highest score on Closed-mindedness factor ($\bar{X}$ = 57). Air Force recruits (n = 288) also had high Closed-mindedness scores ($\bar{X}$ = 54). Perhaps most interestingly, the sample of displaced executives (n = 72) had the highest Disagreeableness score ($\bar{X}$ = 55).

Factor Scores by Gender and Age

T-score means for the factor scores were also examined by gender for the adult sample (n = 500 males and n = 500 females) and the college sample (n = 800 females and n = 800 males). The mean scores for Closed-mindedness and Conscientiousness factors were higher in the adult than in the college samples, while the college samples presented higher mean scores on Maladaptation. Most intuitive of all, however, was the finding that the highest mean score for males was Disagreeableness, while the lowest mean score for females was Disagreeableness. This was true for both adults and college students.

Using the MIPS Factor-Based Scales

Researchers and practitioners can calculate the appropriate T-score for each factor by using the information contained in Table 23.4 and applying the following formula:

$$\frac{RS - M}{SD} \times 10 + 50$$

where RS is the sum of the items in the factor, M is the raw score mean, and SD is the raw score standard deviation. For each of the five factors, this procedure will yield a linear T-score. Note that T-scores have a mean of 50 and a standard deviation of 10. Thus, a person scoring T-60 on Maladaptation, for example, would be one standard deviation above the mean on this trait. Note that using the M and SD of the combined sample (n = 2,600) allows natural age and gender differences to emerge in the transformed scores.

Theoretical Implications of the Five-Factor Model

The five-factor model has emerged as an important force in the investigation of personality structure (Digman, 1990). The MIPS appears to factor into five dimensions that are consistent with the five-factor model of personality. This finding is important because of the parallels between the theoretically derived MIPS scales and the empirically derived five-factor model. The MIPS scales have a rich theoretical foundation in a model of personality that is deeply rooted in biosocial and evolutionary theory (Millon, 1969; Millon, 1981; Millon, 1990). The five-factor model, on the other hand, is largely devoid of theory, having its roots in the statistical analysis of lists of adjectives used by ordinary people to describe others (Goldberg, 1993). The parallels between the Millonian taxonomy and the five-factor model observed in this study could launch an effort to theoretically bootstrap the five-factor model into two well-established and accepted theoretical frameworks of personology, the beginnings of which are outlined below.

The first factor, termed Maladaptation or Neuroticism, is marked by several items from the MIPS Enhancing–Preserving bipolarity (e.g., pleasure versus pain). According to the theory, persons scoring high on this factor are likely to show a significant tendency to focus attention on potential threats to one's emotional and physical security, an expecta-

TABLE 23.4. MIPS Items That Define the Five Factors, and the Raw Score Mean (M) and Standard Deviation (SD) for each Factor

Maladaptation (*M* = 13.61, *SD* = 8.82)
  True: 11, 13, 17, 18, 25, 27, 34, 38, 39, 40, 45, 49, 52, 54, 56, 57, 60, 62, 63, 68, 69, 72, 82, 85, 86, 87, 95, 100, 105, 111, 122, 126, 139, 148, 155
  False: 58, 81, 94, 106

Surgency (*M* = 13.07, *SD* = 4.63)
  True: 3, 28, 41, 47, 65, 73, 123, 132, 149, 158, 162, 166, 167, 170, 172, 174, 180
  False: 20, 91, 142, 143

Conscientiousness (*M* = 13.95, *SD* = 5.28)
  True: 4, 33, 48, 59, 67, 79, 84, 112, 119, 135, 137, 153, 157, 159, 163, 168, 171, 173, 177, 179
  False: 42, 107

Disagreeableness (*M* = 6.76, *SD* = 4.02)
  True: 43, 75, 83, 89, 96, 108, 113, 116, 118, 133, 147, 150
  False: 71, 80, 92, 99, 121, 127, 144

Closed mindedness (*M* = 6.87, *SD* = 3.06)
  True: 16, 21, 29, 37, 46, 64, 78, 88, 90, 102, 114, 117, 125, 130

Note. To obtain the raw score for each factor, count 1 point for each item endorsed in the keyed direction. Data and table copyright 1995 by Dicandrien, Inc. All rights reserved.

tion of and heightened alertness to the signs of potential negative feedback that can lead them to disengage from everyday relationships and pleasurable experiences. Those scoring low on Maladaptation are likely to be motivated more by pleasure than pain, possess attitudes and behaviors designed to foster and enrich life, and to generate joy, pleasure, contentment, and fulfillment, and thereby strengthen their capacity to remain competent physically and mentally. The Maladaptation factor also contains several items from the MIPS Complaining and Hesitating scales, which are the normal range variants of the avoidant and negativistic disorders.

The second factor, termed Extraversion or Surgency, contains items from the MIPS Extraversing–Introversing scales. These scales are derived from the work of Jung (1921/1971) and reflect the direction of the individual's attentions and interests. They are part of a cognitive mode in which high scorers on this factor look to the external environment for sources of information and inspiration (Millon et al., 1994). In terms of interpersonal behaviors, the Surgency factor also contains items from the MIPS Outgoing and Controlling scales, which are the normal range variants of the histrionic and sadistic personalities.

The Conscientiousness factor is marked by items from the Modifying–Accommodating scales and from the Systematizing scale. The Modifying–Accommodating bipolarity corresponds to the active–passive dimension of Millon's theory. Those who score high on Conscientiousness are instrumental in actively seeking to modify their lives and to intrude on passing events by energetically and busily shaping their circumstances. In the cognitive sphere, they exhibit a systematizing style of processing information akin to the judgment preference abstracted from Jung's notions (Myers, 1962). Disposed to operate within established perspectives, systematizers assimilate new information to previous points of view, exhibiting thereby a high degree of dependability and consistency, if not rigidity, in their functioning. It is noteworthy that only two of the items from the MIPS Conforming–Dissenting bipolarity load on this factor. This is important in light of Loevinger's (1994) criticism of the operationalization of the conscientiousness construct in the five-factor model as merely measuring interpersonal conformity. The current formulation of conscientiousness appears to be more cognitive than interpersonal.

The Disagreeableness factor is marked by the Individuating–Nurturing (e.g., self versus other) bipolarity in Millon's taxonomy and the Thinking–Feeling bipolarity derived from Jungian theory. Self-focused, those scoring high on the Individuating scale tend to make up their own minds and reach their own decisions without perceiving the need to seek input or gain approval from others. At best, they are self-starting and self-actualizing. At times, however, they may become self-absorbed, caring little about the needs and priorities of others and focusing largely on their own interests. Persons scoring high on Disagreeableness also present a thinking style of processing information in which experiences are interpreted in light of reason and logic and decisions are made based on tangible and impersonal facts with less consideration for the feelings or interests of others.

The Closed-mindedness factor is marked by a sensing cognitive style in the Jungian typology, and a conforming and agreeing interpersonal style in the Millonian taxonomy. Sensing individuals are inclined toward information-gathering strategies based on tangible facts and decision-making strategies based on realistic options. They are less inclined to consider the possibilities of intangible, unstructured, or ambiguous situations. The conforming and agreeing interpersonal behaviors are the normal range variants of the obsessive–compulsive and dependent personality disorders, respectively. Conformers are notably respectful of tradition and authority and do their best to uphold conventional rules and standards. Agreeing individuals are noted for their dependence on safe and supportive relationships and lack of openness to new and unusual experiences that may threaten their emotional security.

Summary

This section expanded the five-factor model by showing the empirical relationships of those five dimensions with the theoretical works of Millon and Jung. Future research on the five-factor model should seek to place that model into the larger nomological network of established personality theories to further our understanding of the structure of normal personality.

EXPANDING THE DIMENSIONS OF NORMALITY

Millon's model is perhaps one of the most thorough and coherent theories of personality offered by the field's great thinkers. Nonetheless, the model may still have room for expansion. Recall that the Millon taxonomy as originally proposed was based on a 2 × 4 matrix in which the Active and Passive domains were crossed with Self, Other, Self–Other Ambivalence, and Pain to produce his original eight personality types. The model was subsequently extended by Millon into a 2 × 5 matrix in which Active and Passive were also crossed with Pain–Pleasure Discordance for a total of ten personality types. Millon further extended his thinking about normal range personality by incorporating the Jungian-like cognitive styles of information gathering and processing into the MIPS.

Over the past 2 years I have begun to consider an extension of Millon's matrix in which the Active and Passive dimensions are crossed with Pleasure. These crossings were excluded in Millon's earlier taxonomies because they were judged to have little relevance for the elucidation of psychopathological personality types (personal communication, Theodore Millon, 1993).

Many forms of psychopathology have been related to forces that either impede or confuse one's strivings for pleasure. Paul Meehl (1975) challenged the classic analytic view that anhedonia (e.g., the inability to experience pleasure) is always a function of some impedance in one's pleasure strivings often due to guilt or anxiety. He asserted that some individuals simply have low capacity to experience pleasure. This opens the door to viewing hedonic capacity on a continuum from high to low ability to experience pleasure, or strong to weak responsivity to rewards. Observing that some individuals seem to experience pleasure in almost any situation, Meehl (1987, p. 37) wrote, "I conjecture that these people are the lucky ones at the high end of the hedonic capacity continuum, i.e., they were 'born three drinks' ahead." Individuals with a normal capacity to experience pleasure are also subject to many of the same life stresses as are those with anhedonia. Their experience of stress is buffered, however, by an ability to feel a sense of enjoyment in life's occasional rewards. This ability to experience pleasure may provide them with a prophylactic against depressogenic cognitions and reduce susceptibility to various forms of psychopathology.

Responsiveness to pleasure is a spectrum phenomenon. The ability to experience pleasure reaches broadly into every aspect of personality. The experience of pleasure provides motivation for a host of appropriate social, occupational, and recreational behaviors that are essential for the maintenance of self esteem, if not for personal growth and self-actualization. Any formulation of normality should therefore include a discussion of pleasure and the various means by which individuals seek to obtain pleasure in their daily lives. Perhaps the two most basic variants of the pleasure-seeking orientation are the active pleasure and passive pleasure styles.

The Active Pleasure Style

This style is characterized by a normal predisposition to experience reinforcement from positive events (as opposed to the absence of pain), combined with a tendency to arrange and modify actively the circumstances of one's life to obtain the desired reinforcement. Individuals with this style differ to the extent that they find positive reinforcement in diverse stimuli. Some find pleasure in the usual rewards of successful careers and energetically pursue this course in an outgoing and confident, but sometimes controlling manner.

Others are more inclined toward recreational pleasures. They frequently seek to combine work with play and look for opportunities to have fun while conducting business. They are likable colleagues, workmates, and bosses who set a tone of enjoying work. In the extreme, they are somewhat ill-disposed to attend to the mundane details of responsible adult life, choosing to focus their attentions in that regard only when the demands of the situation are forced upon them, and then only with sufficient effort to remove the immediate threat of negative environmental stimuli and return their attentions to the active pursuit of pleasure. They are adventurous, fun-loving, enjoyable companions, who are often viewed by significant others as less responsible and mature than most people of their age and station in life. At times, their behavior may result in some minor inefficiencies in daily living and perhaps real life problems as well. The data show that this personality style is common. Approximately 37% of adults 34% of college students could reasonably be classified as presenting an active pleasure style.[1]

---

[1]For this analysis, individuals in the MIPS adult (n = 1,000) and college (n = 1,600) standardization samples were classified as active pleasure types if their MIPS PS values met both of the following conditions: (1) Modifying PS > Accommodating PS, and Modifying PS > 59, and (2) Enhancing PS > Preserving PS, and Enhancing PS > 59.

Following Millon's (1981) format for elaborating personality types, I have characterized the active pleasure type in terms of five functional processes and three structural attributes. In terms of functional processes, the behavioral presentation of these individuals is characterized as energetic and their interpersonal style is best described as catalytic. That is, they are often the catalysts in interpersonal relations who make things happen. Their cognitive style is characterized as enriched, active, and lively; they are always thinking of how best to modify their environments to suit their needs and desires. Expressed mood is best characterized as happy; they usually enjoy what they are doing. When events go wrong, they respond with appropriate affect and then quickly return to their usual mood. The dominant unconscious mechanism for dealing with intrapsychic conflict is rationalization. This is a second line defense, however, as these individuals are usually confrontive; they attempt to deal forcefully yet appropriately with the progenitor of any inner turmoil. Only when this is not possible or successful are they likely to resort to rationalization, often devaluing that reinforcement which they could not achieve.

In terms of structural attributes, the self-image of the active pleasure type is characterized by a sense of competence; they see themselves as tough and able to influence, if not dominate, others, but always in a socially skilled manner. Because of their high energy and drive, they often see themselves as competitive as well as competent. Internalized content is best described as ambitiousness; inner representations are characterized by a strong drive to achieve that which they find reinforcing or pleasurable. Impulses to take advantage of others in the service of these drives are modulated by choosing socially acceptable goals and methods of influence. Intrapsychic organization is integrated, consisting of wholistic, well-formed, stable mechanisms of internal regulation adequately modulating controls, defenses, and expressive channels.

The Passive Pleasure Style

This style is also noted for a normal orientation toward enjoying positive reinforcement, but is combined with a general tendency to wait passively for such reinforcement. These individuals expect good things to happen to them without any real effort on their part. They are likable because of their easygoing style and positive outlook, but are often hesitating and yielding in their interpersonal relations. They are self-indulgent and optimistic about future events, although they lack the exaggerated self-worth and sense of entitlement of those who lean toward being narcissistic. Their optimism often seems unwarranted in the view of significant others who know their circumstances and history. They are unlikely to be proactive in dealing with life, often waiting for situations to force them to move off a dead center position. They may see no need, for example, to look for another apartment or a better job even when circumstances might suggest otherwise, assuming that things will work out in their own time and in their own way. Things do work themselves out often enough to maintain the behavior and avoid serious troubles.

When pervasive, however, this style can begin to cause significant inefficiencies in daily living. Those with this style seem to ignore the real life difficulties their behavior may create and are not appropriately distressed by these circumstances. In some cases, they may be brought to counseling by significant others who view them as lacking motivation to better themselves. Their behavior may have a dependent quality in the view of those who care for them, but the behavior is not motivated by dependence strivings or attachment needs. In today's vernacular, the passive pleasure type might well be referred to as a "couch potato" (e.g., someone whose idea of pleasure is to lay on a comfortable couch eating snacks and watching television).

The data show that although the passive pleasure style is not extremely rare, it is much less common than the active pleasure style. About 1 in every 12 people may show this pattern. In terms of percentages, approximately 8% of adults and 8% of college students present a passive pleasure style.[2]

In terms of functional processes, the behavioral presentation of these individuals is best characterized as hedonic, and their interpersonal style can be summarized as easy going or "laid back". They readily experience pleasures that are laid on their plate, but are not motivated to pursue such rewards. Their cognitive style is marked by optimism, and expressed mood is untroubled. These individuals seem unphased by most daily stresses. The primary unconsciousness mechanism is suppression. Conflicts that cannot be reframed with a positive outlook are simply put out of mind. In terms of structural attributes, the passive pleasure type maintains a self-image characterized as lucky, or perhaps blessed. Internalized content may be best characterized as relaxed; they have few strong drives or impulses and their inner representations revolve around finding ways to remove themselves from normal daily stresses. Finally, intrapsychic organization is naive; few things bother them so there is little need for strong mechanisms of internal regulation and control, nor are there strong impulses and drives toward change or self-actualization. Internal structures are not well formed but are adequate to modulate the diluted affect which does occur, and there is a high threshold for impulse discharge.

Summary

The ability to experience pleasure is important in understanding normality. Both the active pleasure and passive pleasure types have adequate hedonic capacity. The passive pleasure type can enjoy the rewards that come his or her way but does not anticipate pleasure and is not motivated to pursue it. The active pleasure type plans to obtain rewards and works to bring them to fruition.

Clearly, these ideas are inchoate and I invite elaboration by others. For example, do the active pleasure and passive pleasure types take on a different forms if the individual is also high on the Self or Other dimension of Millon's theory? Only time will tell if these two personality styles will stand the test of clinical experience.

FUTURE RESEARCH WITH THE MIPS

There are many areas of fruitful research for the MIPS, especially differentiating normal from abnormal personality styles, expanding our understanding of normality, and further validating organizational applications. Perhaps the most obvious research study that has not yet been conducted is examining the relationship between the MIPS the other Millon inventories, most importantly the MCMI-III. How do the personality disorder scales on the MCMI-III relate to the personality styles measured by the MIPS? Where is the line between normality and abnormality? A joint item-level factor analysis of responses from both personality disordered and nonclinical samples would allow one to establish a cutoff point to determine if treatment has moved the client into the functional distribution (see

---

[2]For this analysis, individuals in the MIPS adult (n = 1,000) and college (n = 1,600) standardization samples were classified as passive pleasure types if their MIPS PS values met both of the following conditions: (1) Accommodating PS > Modifying PS, and Accommodating PS > 59, and (2) Enhancing PS > Preserving PS, and Enhancing PS > 59.

Jacobson & Truax, 1991, for appropriate formulas). In this way, we may more clearly draw the elusive line between clinical and nonclinical populations which is so important in gauging the dimensions of normality.

The early applications of the MIPS have largely been in organizational settings. Thus, numerous industrial–personnel and organizational training and development research projects are appropriate. The MIPS Adjustment Index cutoff score of T-35, described above, needs to be cross-validated in an independent sample. The importance of the MIPS intuiting and innovating styles of information processing for effective functioning among higher-level managers, suggested above, needs to be explored further. Also suggested above, the possible effect of the MIPS preserving and complaining styles in managing teams needs further research. The role of the MIPS in the initial formation of work teams should also be explored. Further exploration of the use of the MIPS in vocational counseling and career development is appropriate.

When studying job performance it is critical to begin with a job analysis. The Inventory of General Position Requirements (IGPR; Bowling Green State University, 1992) is the only job analysis instrument that was developed to provide an empirical basis for matching job requirements and personality traits in specific occupations (Guion, 1991). The relationship between the MIPS personality styles and the IGPR dimensions is an important area for future researchers. This would allow practitioners to make empirically supported hypotheses about connections between job requirements and personality styles, thus selecting job candidates based on defensible scientific principals rather than on professional opinion alone. Such research would represent an important scientific advance in an era when the use of personality tests for personnel selection is under intense legal and professional scrutiny.

Areas of research that have not yet been touched are applications in the marriage and family arena, as well as the use of the MIPS to assist in making classification and placement decisions with prison inmates.

On the theoretical front, the active pleasure and passive pleasure styles I described above need serious research attention. How can these styles be operationalized, what are the correlates of these types with other personality styles, and how are individuals with these styles perceived by significant others?

On the treatment front, Beck and Freeman (1990) and their associates have proposed an elaborate schema of typical core cognitive beliefs held by individuals with each of the personality types. They suggest that these beliefs are at the core of individuals' uncomfortable emotions and inefficient behaviors, and they offer well-articulated cognitive treatment strategies targeting these beliefs. The relationship between these core cognitive belief structures and particular personalities needs to be explored empirically. Do each of the personalities endorse these belief sets differentially? Do individuals with nonpathological personality styles endorse the relevant belief sets with less intensity than do those with personality disorders, or do they have a different set or beliefs? Do these sets of beliefs have implications for helping normal individuals understand and improve themselves?

CONCLUSIONS

Just past its third birthday at this writing, the MIPS already has an impressive collection of validation studies to support its application in a variety of settings with normally functioning adults. The MIPS is an important and useful addition to the Millon family of inventories.

REFERENCES

Anton, W. D., & Reed, J. R. (1991). *College Adjustment Scales: Professional manual.* Odessa, FL: Psychological Assessment Resources, Inc.

Beck, A. T., Freeman, A., & Associates. (1990). *Cognitive therapy of personality disorders.* New York: Guilford Press.

Beck, A. T., & Steer, R. A. (1987). *Manual for the revised Beck Depression Inventory.* San Antonio, TX: The Psychological Corporation.

Butcher, J. N. (Ed). (1979). *New developments in the use of the MMPI.* Minneapolis: University of Minnesota Press.

Butcher, J. N., Dahlstrom, W. G., Graham, J. R., Tellegen, A., & Kaemmer, B. (1989). *Minnesota Multiphasic Personality Inventory—2: Manual for administration and scoring.* Minneapolis: University of Minnesota Press.

Bowling Green State University. (1992). *An inventory of general position requirements.* Bowling Green, OH: Author.

Cattell, R. B., Eber, H. W., & Tatsuoka, M. M. (1970). *Handbook for the Sixteen Personality Factor Questionnaire (16 PF).* Champaign, IL: Institute for Personality and Ability Testing.

Costa, P. T., & McCrae, R. R. (1985). *The NEO Personality Inventory manual.* Odessa, FL: Psychological Assessment Resources.

Digman, J. M. (1990). Personality structure: Emergence of the five-factor model. *Annual Review of Psychology, 41,* 417–440

Goldberg, L. R. (1992). The development of markers for the Big-Five factor structure. *Psychological Assessment, 4*(1), 26–42.

Goldberg, L. R. (1993). The structure of phenotypic personality traits. *American Psychologist, 48,* 26–34.

Gordon, L. V. (1978). *Gordon Personal Profile—Inventory manual* (rev.). New York: Psychological Corporation.

Gough, H. G. (1987). *California Psychological Inventory: Administrator's guide.* Palo Alto, CA: Consulting Psychologists Press.

Guion, R. M. (1991, May). *Matching position requirements and personality traits.* Paper presented at the annual convention of the Society of Industrial and Organizational Psychology, Montreal, Quebec.

Hansen, J. C., & Campbell, D. P. (1985). *Manual for the Strong Interest Inventory* (4th ed.). Palo Alto, CA: Consulting Psychologist Press, Inc.

Hathaway, S. R., & McKinley, J. C. (1967). *Minnesota Multiphasic Personality Inventory manual.* New York: The Psychological Corporation.

Hogan, R., Curphy, G. J., & Hogan, J. (1993, April). *What we know about leadership: Effectiveness and personality.* Paper presented at the annual convention of the Society for Industrial and Organizational Psychology, San Francisco.

Jacobson, N. S., & Truax, P. (1991). Clinical significance: A statistical approach to defining meaningful change in psychotherapy research. *Journal of Consulting and Clinical Psychology, 59*(1), 12–19.

Jackson, D. N. (1985). *Personality Research Form manual* (3rd ed.). Port Huron, MI: Research Psychologists Press.

Jung, C. G. (1971). *Psychological types* (H. G. Baynes, Trans., rev. by R. F. C. Hull). *The collected works of C. G. Jung* (Vol. 6). Princeton, NJ: Princeton University Press. (Original work published 1921)

Loevinger, J. (1994). Has psychology lost its conscience? *Journal of Personality Assessment, 62*(1), 2–8.

Meehl, P. E. (1987). Hedonic capacity: some conjectures. In D. C. Clark & J. Fawcett (Eds.), *Anhedonia and affect deficit states* (pp. 33–50). New York: PMA Publishing Corporation.

Millon, T. (1969). *Modern psychopathology: A biosocial approach to maladaptive learning and functioning.* Philadelphia: Saunders.

Millon, T. (1981). *Disorders of personality: DSM-III, Axis II*. New York: Wiley.

Millon, T. (1990). *Toward a new personology: An evolutionary model*. New York: Wiley.

Millon, T. (1991). Normality: What may we learn from evolutionary theory? In D. Offer & M. Sabshin (Eds.), *The diversity of normal behavior* (pp. 100–150). New York: Basic Books.

Millon, T., Millon, C., & Davis, R. (1994). *Millon Clinical Multiaxial Inventory—III manual*. Minneapolis: National Computer Systems.

Millon, T., Weiss, L. G., Millon, C., & Davis, R. (1994). *The Millon Index of Personality Styles manual*. San Antonio, TX: Psychological Corporation.

Myers, I. B. (1962). *The Myers–Briggs Type Indicator*. Palo Alto, CA: Consulting Psychologist Press.

Myers, I. B., & McCaulley, M. H. (1985). *Manual: A guide to the development and use of the Myers–Briggs Type Indicator*. Palo Alto, CA: Consulting Psychologist Press.

The Psychological Corporation. (1994). *User's guide for the Millon Index of Personality Styles computer program*. San Antonio, TX: Author.

Super, D. E. (1983). Assessment in career guidance: Toward truly developmental counseling. *Personnel and Guidance*, 61(9), 555–562.

Tango, R. A., & Dziuban, C. D. (1984). The use of personality components in the interpretation of career indecision. *Journal of College Student Personnel*, 25(6), 509–512.

Weiss, L. G., & Lowther, J. (March, 1995). *The factor structure of the Millon Index of Personality Styles*. Paper presented at the annual convention of the Society for Personality Assessment, Atlanta.

V

EPILOGUE

24

The Millon Inventories: Present and Future Directions

ROGER D. DAVIS
THEODORE MILLON

All of the Millon Inventories have been refined and strengthened on a regular basis by both theoretical logic and research data. This aspiration will continue. The new MCMI-III, for example, has been coordinated with the most recent official diagnostic schema, the DSM-IV (American Psychiatric Association, 1994) in an even more explicit way than before. Although the publication of the first version of the MCMI (MCMI; Millon, 1977) preceded the publication of the DSM-III (American Psychiatric Association, 1980), its author played a major role in formulating the official manual's personality disorders, contributing thereby to their conceptual correspondence. The DSM-III-R (American Psychiatric Association, 1987) was subsequently published in the same year as the MCMI-II; the inventory was modified in its final stages to make it as consonant as possible with the conceptual changes introduced in the forthcoming classification. The MCMI-III (Millon, 1994a), strengthens these correspondences further by drawing on many of the criteria of the DSM-IV as the basis for drafting the inventory's items. This chapter reports on a select set of theoretical and empirical developments that are being carefully weighed for inclusion in future Millon inventories, or as a guide in the refinement process of future inventories in the Millon family of instruments. Although we will refer mainly to the MCMI, the developments are broad enough to apply to all the Millon instruments.

Before proceeding, however, a brief historical review may be in order. Like the evolving MCMIs, future Millon inventories will not be cast in stone, but instead will remain subject to modification, significantly upgraded and refined to reflect substantive advances in knowledge, be they from theory, research, or clinical experience. For example, what prompted the introduction of MCMI-III changes? First, the taxonomic theory of which the first two MCMI versions were deductive and operational measures had undergone further developments (Millon, 1986a, 1986b, 1990). Consequently, two new MCMI personality disorder scales were introduced in the second version, and an additional personality scale was added in this most recent, or third version. Similarly, owing to its increas-

525

526 V. EPILOGUE

ing importance in diagnostic work, a new clinical syndrome scale (Post-Traumatic Stress Disorder) was added to the MCMI-III. Second, there had been a continuous growth of interest in personality and its disorders. The *Journal of Personality Disorders* and the recently established International Society for the Study of Personality Disorders illustrate the emergence of these syndromes as a major focus for mental disorders. This surge of clinical, theoretical, and research literature reflect the late 1970s, '80s, and '90s as a time of renaissance in personality theory and assessment (Millon, 1984, 1990). Enriched by this knowledge (much of which has been incorporated into the DSM), an increasingly solid base for making refined diagnostic decisions has been found well beyond the literature of the late 1970s and early '80s. In addition, Millon's work has led him to articulate an expanding base of diagnostic criteria and personality concepts (e.g., Millon, 1990, 1994b), much more extensive than those of earlier DSMs. This growing body of clinical literature provides much of the knowledge base for the MCMI-III. To the extent that DSM-IV also reflects these advances, its correspondence to MCMI-III has been further strengthened. Third, numerous cross-validation and cross-generalization studies have been and continue to be executed with the goal of evaluating and improving each of the several elements that embody both MCMI instruments, their items, scales, scoring procedures, algorithms, and interpretive text (see Choca, Shanley, & Van Denburg, 1992; Craig, 1993; Hsu & Maruish, 1992; Maruish, 1994). These ongoing investigations will continue to provide an empirical grounding for further upgrading each of these components.

With the preceding information as a base, a number of changes were introduced to create the MCMI-III:

1. One additional personality scale—the Depressive Personality—has been added to the 13 that constituted the personality segment of MCMI-II. Also, a Post-Traumatic Stress Disorder scale was added to the clinical syndromes group, as well as a small set of items to strengthen the utility of the Noteworthy Responses section in the areas of Child Abuse, Anorexia, and Bulimia. Modifications have been made also in procedures for correcting distortion effects (e.g., random responding, faking, denial, complaining), that simplify the scoring procedures developed in the MCMI-II.
2. To provide for additional scales and to optimize MCMI item–DSM-IV criteria correspondence, as well to reflect generalization studies, 95 new MCMI-III items were introduced to replace 95 MCMI-II items.
3. An item weighting system ranging from 1 to 3 points was introduced in MCMI-II scoring to reflect item differences in the variety and strength of their supporting validation data. In the MCMI-III, prototypal items are given a weight of 2 points; all others receive 1 point in the scoring system. Because the prototypal items demonstrate substantive, structural, and external validation on their "home" scale (Loevinger, 1957) they are given a higher weight than subsidiary items selected on the basis of external validation alone.
4. Interpretive texts were expanded and refined to reflect general advances in knowledge, changes introduced in the MCMI-III's underlying theory and the DSM-IV, and progress in treatment planning utilizing short-term and circumscribed methods.

A principal goal in constructing the MCMIs was to keep the total number of items small enough to encourage use in diverse diagnostic and treatment settings, yet large enough to permit the assessment of a wide range of clinically relevant behaviors. At 175 items, the final form is shorter than comparable instruments, with terminology geared to an eighth-grade reading level. The majority of clients can complete the MCMI-III in 20 to 30 minutes, facilitating relatively simple and rapid administration and minimizing client resistance and fatigue. This chapter reports on some of the theoretical and empirical developments that are in the pipeline for future MCMIs, as well as for other forthcoming Millon inventories.

THEORETICAL DEVELOPMENTS: ASSESSMENT OF PERSONALITY SUBTYPES

Personality disorders are best thought of as prototypes. Within each prototype, however, lie numerous variations. There is no one single schizoid or avoidant or depressive or histrionic type, but instead, there are several variations, different forms in which the core or prototypal personality expresses itself. With the publication of *Disorders of Personality: DSM-IV and Beyond*, Millon and Davis (1995) elaborated a series of personality subtypes for each of the major prototypes deduced from Millon's evolutionary theory (1990). These subtypes essentially represent a reading of the modern and historical literature in convergence with clinical wisdom, cultural myth, and empirical fact. Often, they are simply mixtures of major types. The deficient conscience, fraudulent dealings, and arrogant attitude of the "unprincipled" narcissist, for example, is reminiscent of the conman or charlatan, a cultural stereotype incarnated as a kind of antisocial narcissist. Likewise, the "nomadic" antisocial, represented as a gypsylike roamer, vagrant, or itinerant railroad bum existing as a scavenger at the margins of society, essentially reflects a mixture of the schizoid and antisocial.

In other cases, the subtypes exist at the confluence of Millon's evolutionary theory and other organizing principles. Psychodynamic thinkers, for example, have described the "compensating" narcissist, an individual who counteracts deep feelings of inferiority and lack of self-esteem by creating for oneself the illusion of being superior and exceptional. Similarly, the "hypersensitive" avoidant represents a more manifestly cognitive variant of a major type, being intensely wary and suspicious, alternately panicky, terrified, edgy, and timorous, and then thin-skinned, high-strung, petulant, and prickly. Table 24.1 lists the subtypes described by Millon and Davis (1995) for the narcissistic personality, along with their hypothesized MCMI-III profiles. Descriptions for the 14 personality disorders of DSM-IV and DSM-III-R are available in comprehensive form in *Disorders of Personality: DSM-IV and Beyond* (Millon & Davis, 1996).

TABLE 24.1. Narcissistic Subtypes and Their MCMI Profiles

Elitist: Feels privileged and empowered by virtue of special childhood status and pseudo-achievements; entitled facade bears little relation to reality; seeks favored and good life; is upwardly mobile; cultivates special status and advantages by association. MCMI: 5

Amorous: Sexually seductive, enticing, beguiling, tantalizing; glib and clever; disinclines real intimacy; indulges hedonistic desires; bewitches and inveigles the needy and naive; pathological lying and swindling. MCMI: 5–4

Unprincipled: Deficient conscience; unscrupulous, amoral, disloyal, fraudulent, deceptive, arrogant, exploitive, a conman and charlatan, dominating, contemptuous, vindictive. MCMI: 5–6A

Compensatory: Seeks to counteract or cancel out deep feelings of inferiority and lack of self-esteem; offsets deficits by creating illusions of being superior, exceptional, admirable, noteworthy; self-worth results from self-enhancement. MCMI: 5–8A/2A

Beside the obvious relationship of each subtype to its cousins, all the subtypes share an important feature: Each is a statement of particular truth about the nature of the personologic landscape, a claim that the world contains such-and-such personalities in it, more by historical accident than by ontological necessity. Each is a specific manifestation of a major type in the context of our particular times and culture, and if history or culture were different, then the subtypes would likely be different, also. The major prototypes, on the other hand, are, in a sense, required by the theory, just as existence, adaptation, and replication are required by the laws of evolution. While the subtypes lack the deductive inevitability of major prototypes, they nevertheless bring the major types down to a level of unparalleled descriptive specificity, and, it is hoped, proportionately increased clinical utility.

However, it is precisely because the subtypes are not inevitable products of the evolutionary theory that they bear a greater burden of validational evidence than do the major types, and also they present a greater challenge for reliable and valid assessment. In particular, the issue of base rates (BRs), the prevalence of the various subtypes, is of particular importance. Because the BRs for some of the major types are quite low (the schizoid and the sadistic, for example), many of the subtypes are likely to be quite rare. A particular clinician, in fact, might go years between seeing a particular subtype, making such validational research almost impossible in any one clinical setting. Moreover, some subtypes may be seen quite frequently, while others will hardly ever be observed. All of the problems associated the prediction of low BR phenomena, like the prediction of suicide or murder, are also problems here.

Nevertheless, several directions could be pursued in order to advance the assessment utility of the Millon inventories in relation to the subtypes. Millon (1995), for example, presented MCMI-III codetypes for each personality disorder subtype. Thus, on theoretical grounds, it is expected that the unprincipled narcissist will appear as a 5–6A, while the "compensating" narcissist is more likely to appear is a 5–8A or a 5–2A. Such a codetype approach would seem to be the most straightforward, especially where these subtypes exist predominately as a mixture of two or more major types. In the coming years, as clinicians already skilled in Millon's theory become well enough acquainted with these subtypes to provide useful external validity ratings, studies which examine the diagnostic efficiency of these MCMI-III profile patterns will become possible. Not all 5–8A codetypes, for example, are likely to be classified as "compensating" narcissists. Conversely, some "compensating" narcissists may produce profiles other than the 5–8A. Eventually, the items most directly responsible for each subtype profile will be identified and examined against the content of the subtypes, and a feedback process will begin through which the item content of the inventories and the content of the subtypes themselves are mutually refined. Items for future Millon inventories will be written with accurate classification of these subtypes in mind.

How an emphasis on personality subtypes will affect the length of future instruments and their exact item compositions, are, of course, open questions at the current time. The answers in part are dependent upon the nature of the empirical problems encountered. Certainly, it would seem difficult to provide an accurate assessment of over 60 subtypes with tests of less than 200 items. Even if all of the MCMI items were oriented toward Axis II, for example, that would still leave fewer than 3 unique items per subtype, far too few to protect discriminant validity. Fortunately, the BRs of some the major personality patterns, namely the antisocial and borderline, make their subtypes more important than those of the schizoid, for example. Where compromises in inventory length must be made, then, they will favor the assessment of those subtypes that are most clinically relevant, at least for pencil and paper forms. Future computer-administered versions of the Millon tests, programmed to optimize the selection of items based on the client's pattern of prior responses, need not administer an entire item bank, and are much more likely to yield highly specific, subtype-relevant information.

EMPIRICAL DEVELOPMENTS: TRAIT SUBSCALES

Psychological instruments may be interpreted at several levels. At the lowest level lie individual test items. Because any single item is too unreliable and narrow as a predictor of broader individual differences, many items are usually aggregated together to form scales. Each scale, in turn, represents only a single dimension of the total personality, and consequently scales are usually examined conjointly as set, or profile configuration. Assuming test validity and assuming that the inventory has some claim, either deductive–theoretical or inductive–statistical, as a representation of all of personality, the profile configuration essentially becomes an intervening variable for individuality.

A level of interpretation that is becoming more important in modern inventories is the personality trait (see Weiss, this volume). Traits are assessed at a level between what are variously called types, styles, syndromes, or higher-order dimensions, and the level of individual items. Each personality disorder may be thought of as consisting of a set of such trait characteristics. Conversely, the covariation of a particular set of personality traits may be thought of as a personality style. There are, then, four levels of clinical interpretation within an inventory—item level, trait level, scale level, and profile configuration.

Trait subscales are clinically useful. Recall that each personality syndrome is viewed in the prototypal model as a covariant attribute structure whose features, taken one by one, are neither necessary nor sufficient for the diagnosis of the syndrome. While theoretically the most prototypal member of a syndrome possesses all its features, most individuals will not. As astute clinicians know, no two narcissistic personalities are exactly alike, no two antisocial personalities are exactly alike, and so on. In the DSM-IV, nine criteria are listed for the borderline personality disorder, of which five are required for diagnosis. Conceivably, then, two individuals might both be diagnosed with the disorder while having only one feature or criterion in common, allowing for considerable trait or criterion heterogeneity within any personality type. The specific personality traits that an individual possesses are of interest when we want to know what kind of schizoid the person is, what kind of dependent, and so on, a fact that is obviously relevant to the identification of adult subtypes described above. However, an individual may also receive specific disorder subscales elevations in the absence of a diagnosis. These correspond to problematic trait characteristics which deserve attention but are not so pervasively expressed as to constitute full-fledged personality disorders (Millon, 1994b). The DSM-IV allows problematic traits to be noted on Axis II, but apparently this possibility is rarely used clinically, perhaps because the DSM is criterion- rather than trait-oriented.

The existence of personality traits as a legitimate level of organization in human personality, and their utility in clinical interpretation, argues that they should be represented in any personality disorders inventory. Because of its relative brevity, traits have not yet been explicitly represented in the MCMIs. Instead, the structure of the inventory at levels before that of syndrome or disorder has drawn upon an item-weighting system informed by the strength of each item's validational data, the intrinsic interrelatedness of the personality disorders, and the prototypal structure of mental disorders generally. An item weighting system ranging from 1 to 3 points was introduced in the MCMI-II; in the

MCMI-III, prototypal items are given a weight of 2 points; all others are weighted at 1 point only. Because the prototypal items demonstrate substantive, structural, and external validation (Loevinger, 1957) on their "home" scale, they are given a heavier weight than are subsidiary items selected on the basis of external validation alone. Prototypal items represent features of their respective disorders and are doubly weighted. Nonprototypal items represent features which, while not central, are nevertheless relevant to their respective disorders. Thus, an item such as "I like to be the center of attention when I'm in a group," might be weighted 2 points on the Histrionic scale, and 1 point on the Narcissistic scale.

Such multiple assignments have caused some (Wiggins, 1982) to express concern regarding the discriminant validity of the MCMI scales. Exploratory studies (Davis, 1994) with the Millon Adolescent Clinical Inventory (MACI; designed according to the 3-2-1 weighting system, show that factoring the items assigned to each personality scale separately results in brief subscales that often share over half their items. Similar results would likely emerge for the MCMI-II. In contrast, the MCMI-III personality scales were designed to be shorter, using a 2-1 weighting system. Factor studies currently underway reveal, not unexpectedly, that the item overlap of the resulting MCMI-III factor traits is substantially more favorable to clinical use. The results of these inductive, or "bottom-up" studies must, of course, be examined in conjunction with theoretical, or "top-down" considerations to appraise their value. Trait subscales need not be designed for every Axis II disorder, but might instead be constructed only for those disorders of greater clinical relevance frequently seen in clinical settings—certainly the antisocial, borderline, and paranoid, and perhaps the narcissistic and dependent, but not, for example, the schizoid or sadistic.

CONJOINT DEVELOPMENT AND REFINEMENT OF INSTRUMENTS ACROSS DIVERSE DATA SOURCES

One of the fundamental principles in instrument construction is that validity should be built into an instrument from the beginning. Loevinger (1957), Jackson (1970), and Skinner (1986) have discussed test construction as an iterative three-stage process. In the first, rational stage, the content of each construct to be measured is defined as precisely as possible. Items may be written and refined by multiple so-called experts in the theory of the construct, sorted according to their discriminative characteristics, ranked in terms of difficulty level, and so on, all before being put to actual subjects. In the second, internal stage, the items are given to real individuals. Various statistics are then calculated to ensure that the items tap a single dimension. Items with strong relationships to scales for which they were not intended may be deleted or reassigned. In addition, a correlation matrix of the instrument's scales may be examined for anomalies and items may be reassigned or dropped to bring this pattern in line with theoretical expectations. In the third, external stage, the newly developed scales are assessed against other instruments of established reputation. Items which pass through all three stages are said to have been validated theoretically, statistically, and empirically. The Millon inventories have essentially been constructed according to this tripartite logic.

While inventories should be constructed to mirror our expectations regarding relationships between constructs both internal and external to the instrument as precisely as possible, they should also possess a generative value. That is, an inventory should assist in the accumulation of new knowledge. If our test is intended to assess personality disorders, we might expect, for example, that individuals classified as dependent personalities will also be classified as experiencing depressive episodes more often than, say, antisocials, simply because dependents are likely to feel helpless and hopeless more often than are antisocials, who take the initiative in changing their external world, albeit usually in a destructive fashion. As noted in Chapter 17, these internal–internal and internal–external expectations form a set of constraints that our inventory must be constructed to satisfy. Each such constraint is an additional point through which the instrument's predictions are triangulated with reality as it is assumed to exist. The larger this set of constraints, the better, for if the inventory can satisfy many such constraints at the beginning, then we can have greater confidence that it will meet future challenges.

Sometimes, for example, after an instrument has been constructed, certain variables about which we had no preformed ideas show a significant relationship. Perhaps in the beginning we believed that those with antisocial personalities should also report high family distress and a high incidence of alcoholism. Perhaps we also believed that those with dependent personalities should report overprotective parents and an inability to end relationships, and these expectations were built into the instrument. About the relationship between dependent personality and the incidence of alcoholism, however, we may have no expectations at all, so that the magnitude of this second relationship is "free to vary," simply because we do not know much about it, how it should be evaluated, or whether it should even exist at all. How do we evaluate this observed, but unexpected, relationship? Having constructed our instrument to satisfy multiple constraints in the form of theoretically driven expectations, we are no longer working with just any item pool. The more our test satisfies many different constraints, the greater our expectations of the generalizability of the entire system of instrumentation. Demonstrated validity in diverse areas of the nomological network becomes a promissory note that observed relationships between intervening variables elsewhere is not peculiar to their particular mode of operationalization, but is instead representative of nature's structure and, so, worthy of genuine scientific interest. In general, the more constraints an instrument satisfies at the outset, the more confidence we can have in the validity of relationships that are unanticipated.

At the current time, most psychological instruments are developed within a single data source, be it self-report, clinical ratings, observer ratings, or projective testing observations, and then validated against instruments of already-established utility within that same data source. Validation against instruments from other data sources, while important, is usually secondary. Thus, a new self-report scale to measure dependence finds evidence for its validity first against other self-report dependence scales, and then, against observer ratings and projectives, and so on. Lower correlations between self-report and rated forms are attributed to method considerations, and often rightfully so. Unfortunately, this rather haphazard style of instrument development often leads to confusing results where such instruments are paired against each other in a multitrait–multimethod matrix. The Narcissistic scale of a self-report instrument may correlate more highly with the Histrionic rating scale, and so on. Many such mismatches are likely to be found for any given set of personality instruments, a fact which has undermined confidence in the valid assessment of personality disorders.

A much better method blurs the distinction between internal and external by viewing test construction as a system of relations or constraints to be satisfied across multiple data sources. Here, the goal is to build an entire suite of instruments informed one by the others across the entire construction process. The more data sources that can be involved, the better. For example, a self-report inventory for the personality disorders, an observer-rated version of the same inventory, and a clinical checklist would be constructed simultaneously, not one at a time. Correlation matrices between all instruments would be inspected at every stage. Thus, if during development it was found that the observer-rated Narcissistic scale correlated more highly with the self-report Histrionic scale than with its parallel self-report Narcissistic scale, indicating a lack of convergent validity, the items from both pools would be examined, not only with regard to their content characteristics and correlation to their assigned scale, but also in terms of their cross-method correlations. Violations of multitrait–multimethod considerations would be tracked to particular items, and these would be reassigned, dropped, or rewritten. Thus, rather than being examined post hoc, multitrait–multimethod considerations become a fundamental part of the item selection process, considered from the beginning, allowing each instrument to strengthen the others. Validity is built into an entire system of instrumentation, and not simply into a single instrument. Future versions of some Millon inventories are likely to be constructed in this fashion.

What are the requirements for the construction of such a test suite? The first is essentially practical, reflecting a much larger investment on the part of participants and the need for more iterations in the development process. Both patients and their clinicians must be subjected to the agonies of providing data for a large item pool. The second is theoretical, and is the more difficult of the two, requiring expert clinical judgment concerning the constructs the test seeks to embrace. The construction process is begun knowing that correlations between like scales across diverse data sources will be less than unity, and that this reflects measurement error as it does the informational biases of the respective sources. Persons can be expected to differ in terms of their levels of self-knowledge and the extent to which they distort objective information. The egocentricity of the narcissist and his or her tendency to construe reality in ways favorable to self makes him or her less likely than the pessimistic and self-focused depressive to provide valid self-report information. We might conjecture, then, that the correlation between self-reported and clinician-rated narcissistic personality is likely to be less than that between self-reported and clinician-rated depressive personality. This is the problem the theorist faces. Knowing that the multitrait–multimethod matrix reflects informational biases as well as measurement error, the theorist must provide a substantive framework within which to evaluate the direction and magnitude of its correlations and to determine the path in which the results are best refined. In turn, this involves knowing (1) those traits or characteristics for which each personality can typically be expected to provide valid self-report information, (2) those traits or characteristics for which each personality cannot be expected to provide such information, (3) those traits or characteristics for which clinicians can typically be expected to provide valid ratings, and (4) those traits or characteristics which, for whatever reason, clinicians will not easily be able to rate.

Unfortunately, the DSM's Axis II, deliberately formulated to be atheoretical and so existing at a descriptive rather than explanatory level, cannot provide the substantive framework necessary to guide such research. Rather than providing a coherent deductive foundation within which to ask questions about the various personalities, Axis II is best viewed as a body of descriptive material collated across several perspectives but not really coordinated with any of them. While the periodic table is the unique province of chemistry, the problematic behaviors which are to be carved up into diagnostic categories are often given to psychopathologists by parties whose standards are extrinsic to psychopathology as a science. Perhaps we live in a more enlightened age, but was it not so long ago that Sullivan, a founder of the interpersonal school, proposed the "homosexual personality"? Or that the "masochistic personality" came under fire as reflecting biases against women? Philosophers of science agree that the system of kinds undergirding any domain of inquiry must itself be answerable to the question which forms the very point of departure for the scientific enterprise: Why does nature take this particular form rather than some other? Why these particular diagnostic groups rather than others? One cannot merely accept any list of kinds or dimensions as given. Committee consensus is not science. Instead, a taxonomic scheme must be justified, and to be justified scientifically, it must be justified theoretically. Taxonomy and theory are intimately linked.

Item writers involved in attempts to construct a coordinated suite of multimethod instruments, future versions of the MCMI, the Millon Index of Personality Styles (MIPS; Millon, 1994b) and the Millon Personality Diagnostic Checklist (MPDC; Tringone, Chapter 21, this volume) require a strong theoretical basis on which the various personality disorders can be compared and contrasted for their manifestations across different data sources. Relevant example questions are "What traits does the narcissist possess about which he or she is likely to have self-knowledge and will admit to?", and "What traits does the narcissist possess about which he or she is unlikely to have self-knowledge?" For the authors, this basis is Millon's Evolutionary theory (Millon, 1990). While a detailed exposition is beyond the scope of this paper, the theory essentially seeks to explicate the structure and styles of personality with reference to deficient, imbalanced, or conflicted modes of ecological adaptation and reproductive strategy. As noted in earlier chapters, four phases in which evolutionary principles are demonstrated are labeled as existence, adaptation, replication, and abstraction. The first relates the serendipitous transformation of random or less organized states into those possessing distinct structures of greater organization; the second refers to homeostatic processes employed to sustain survival in open ecosystems; the third pertains to reproductive styles that maximize the diversification and selection of ecologically effective attributes; and the fourth concerns the emergence of competencies that foster anticipatory planning and reasoned decision making. Polarities derived from the first three phases—pleasure–pain, passive–active, and other–self, respectively—are used to form "traits" as in the MIPS (Millon, 1994b) as well as to construct a theoretically embedded classification system of personality disorders, as in the MCMI-III. Personalities we have termed *deficient* lack the capacity to experience or to enact certain aspects of the three polarities (e.g., the schizoid has a faulty substrate for both "pleasure" and "pain"); those spoken of as *imbalanced* lean strongly toward one or another extreme of a polarity (e.g., the dependent is oriented almost exclusively to receiving the support and nurturance of "others"); and those we judge *conflicted* struggle with ambivalence toward opposing ends of a bipolarity (e.g., the passive–aggressive vacillates between adhering to the expectations of "others" versus enacting what is wished for one's "self"). Figure 24.1 illustrates the place of the DSM personality disorders within the polarity model. These polarities lend the model a holistic, cohesive structure which facilitates the comparison and contrast of groups along fundamental axes, sharpening the meanings of the derived constructs, preventing their definitions from being coopted by one perspective or school to the exclusion of others, and "fixing" them against construct drift.

In addition to providing a polarity model by which to derive the entire constellation of personality disorders, Millon and associates have also stressed that personality is an intrinsically multioperational construct. That is, personality disorders are not simply about behavior, or about cognition, or about unconscious conflicts, but rather, as disorders of the entire matrix of the person, they embrace all of these data domains. In past (Millon, 1986a, 1986b) and current writings (Millon & Davis, 1996), Millon and associates have set forth comprehensive (exhaustive of the major domains of personality) and comparable (existing at approximately equal levels of abstraction) attributes for eight functional and structural domains of the personality. Each cell of the resulting 8 × 14, domain-by-disorder circumplex contains the diagnostic attribute which in our judgment best captures the expression of each personality style within that particular domain (see Figure 24.2).

	Existential Aim		Replication Strategy		
	Life Enhancement	Life Preservation	Reproductive Propagation	Reproductive Nurturance	
Polarity	Pleasure–Pain		Self–Other		
Deficiency, Imbalance, Conflict	Pleasure – Pain – +	Pleasure Pain (Reversal)	Self – Other +	Self + Other –	Self – Other (Reversal)
Adaptation Mode	DSM Personality Disorders				
Passive: Accommodation	Schizoid / Depressive	Masochistic	Dependent	Narcissistic	Compulsive
Active: Modification	Avoidant	Sadistic	Histrionic	Antisocial	Negativistic
Structural Pathology	Schizotypal	Borderline, Paranoid	Borderline	Paranoid	Paranoid

FIGURE 24.1. Polarity model and its personality disorder derivatives.

In contrast, the criteria of the DSM-IV are both noncomprehensive (no real scheme through which to meaningfully distribute personality attributes has been developed) and noncomparable (the criteria run the gamut from very broad to very narrow). Noncomprehensive criteria lead to redundancies and omissions. Noncomparable criteria lead to a mixture of levels. Consider, for example, the dependent personality disorder. Criterion 1 states "Has difficulty making everyday decisions without an excessive amount of advice and reassurance from others." Criterion 2, however, says almost the same: "Needs others to assume responsibility for most major areas of his or her life." In fact, five of the eight dependent personality criteria seem oriented toward the interpersonal conduct domain, two seem oriented toward the Self-Image domain, and only one is concerned with Cognitive Style, leaving the domains of Regulatory Mechanisms, Object Representations, Morphologic Organization, Mood/Temperament, and Expressive Acts completely unaddressed. Consider the obsessive–compulsive personality disorder. Criterion 5 is relatively narrow and behavioral: "Is unable to discard worn-out or worthless objects even when they have no sentimental value." In contrast, criterion 8 requires more inference: "Shows rigidity and stubbornness." In fact, the inability to discard worthless objects could well be considered simply a behavioral manifestation of the trait of rigidity.

Failure to multioperationalize the personality disorders via comprehensive and comparable attributes almost certainly contributes to diagnostic inefficiency and invalidity, and provides a critique of the content validity of the DSM-IV criteria sets. Even more problematic, because the DSM-IV is usually taken as the "gold standard" by which other measures of personality disorder are judged, and because most modern measures seek to conform to the DSM in some way, the degree to which these criteria sets distort the practice of modern clinical science is an open question—there is no gold standard for the gold standard. Because most test authors consider it necessary to construct their instruments in accordance with the diagnoses and criteria of the DSM-IV, we can conclude that almost every extant instrument that emphasizes the DSM is to an unknown extent contaminated by this problem, a

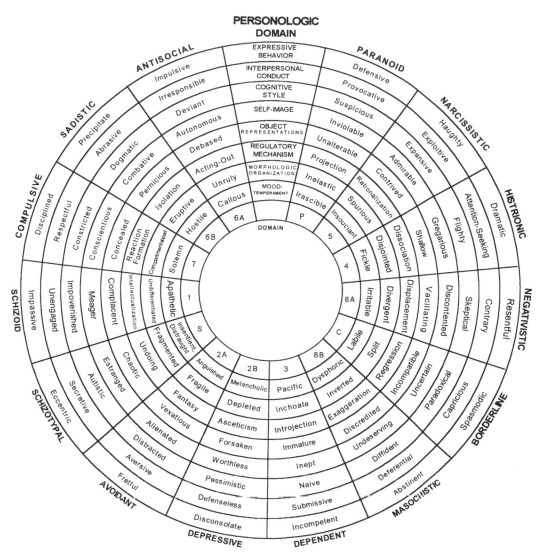

FIGURE 24.2. Expression of personality disorders within personologic domains.

consideration which argues strongly for the role of theory as a guide when selecting attributes, criteria, or items by which to operationalize personality disorders.

Obviously, its atheoretical shortcomings, together with its noncomprehensive and noncomparable format, makes the DSM difficult to regard even now as a gold standard for the MCMI-II, MCMI-III (which actually features many items as rephrases of the official criteria), and MPDC. Because of its theoretical anchoring, the MCMI-III and MPDC are perhaps best regarded as measures of the DSM-IV constructs, but more, the "more" being the surplus meaning provided by the theory. However, as the theory continues to evolve along the lines necessary to construct a coordinated suite of instruments (of which the MCMI will be only one essential leg), the relationship between future MCMIs and the DSM-IV will require close consideration and perhaps even a reevaluation. That an

atheoretical, but official, classification should act as the criterion against which a theoretically grounded system is judged can only be described as a paradox, one faced not only by
integrative theorists, but by interpersonal and psychodynamic thinkers as well.

CONCLUSIONS

While we have chosen to review only a select set of present theoretical and empirical fronts,
additional developments in the "Millonian tradition," unfortunately beyond the scope of
this paper, will undoubtedly influence the direction and content of future inventories,
indirectly at first, but more directly as time proceeds. One of these is the formation of a
Research Network to coordinate researchers interested in Millon's theory and inventories,
using the rapidly developing resources of the internet (for information, email
IASPP@aol.com). The advances in communications technology, such as the ability, for
example, to pilot large numbers of items with readily obtained, sizable samples gathered
from sites as small as the individual private practice clinician and as large as the largest
hospital or university setting, will undoubtedly speed the development, validation, and
coordination of inventories of all types.

REFERENCES

American Psychiatric Association. (1980). *Diagnostic and statistical manual of mental disorders*
(3rd ed.). Washington, DC: Author.
American Psychiatric Association. (1987). *Diagnostic and statistical manual of mental disorders*
(3rd ed., rev.). Washington, DC: Author.
American Psychiatric Association. (1994). *Diagnostic and statistical manual of mental disorders*
(4th ed.) Washington, DC: Author.
Choca, J. P., Shanley, L. A., & Van Denburg, E. (1992). *Interpretive guide to the Millon Clinical
Multiaxial Inventory (MCMI)*. Washington, DC: American Psychological Association.
Craig, R. J. (Ed.). (1993). *The Millon Clinical Multiaxial Inventory: A clinical research informa-
tion synthesis*. Hillsdale, NJ: Erlbaum.
Davis, R. D. (1994). *The development of content scales for the Millon Adolescent Clinical Inven-
tory*. Unpublished master's thesis.
Hsu, L. M., & Maruish, M. E. (1992). *Conducting publishable research with the MCMI-II: Psy-
chometric and statistical issues*. Minneapolis: National Computer Systems.
Jackson (1970). A sequential system for personality scale development. In C. D. Spielberger (Ed.),
Current topics in clinical and community psychology (Vol. 2, pp. 61–92). New York: Aca-
demic Press.
Loevinger, J. (1957). Objective tests as instruments of psychological theory. *Psychological Reports*,
3, 635–694.
Maruish, M. (Ed.). (1994). *The use of psychological testing for treatment planning and outcome
assessment*. Hillsdale, NJ: Erlbaum.
Millon, T. (1977). *Manual for the Millon Clinical Multiaxial Inventory (MCMI)*. Minneapolis:
National Computer Systems.
Millon, T. (1984). On the renaissance of personality assessment and personality theory. *Journal of
Personality Assessment*, *48*, 450–466.
Millon, T. (1986a). Personality prototypes and their diagnostic criteria. In T. Millon & G. L. Klerman
(Eds.), *Contemporary directions in psychopathology: Toward the DSM-IV* (pp. 671–712). New
York: Guilford Press.
Millon, T. (1986b). A theoretical derivation of pathological personalities. In T. Millon & G. L.

Klerman (Eds.), *Contemporary directions in psychopathology: Toward the DSM-IV* (pp. 639–670). New York: Guilford Press.

Millon, T. (1990). *Toward a new personology.* New York: Wiley.

Millon, T. (1994a). *Millon Clinical Multiaxial Inventory—III manual.* Minneapolis: National Computer Systems.

Millon, T. (1994b). *Millon Index of Personality Styles (MIPS) manual.* San Antonio, TX: Psychological Corporation.

Millon, T. (1995, August). *Subtypes of the personality disorders.* Paper presented at the second annual Conference on the Millon Inventories, Minneapolis.

Millon, T., & Davis, R. D. (1996). *Disorders of personality: DSM-IV and beyond.* New York: Wiley-Interscience.

Skinner, H. A. (1986). Construct validation approach to psychiatric classification. In T. Millon & G. L. Klerman (Eds.), *Contemporary directions in psychopathology: Toward the DSM-IV* (pp. 307–330). New York: Guilford Press.

Wiggins, J. S. (1982). Circumplex models of interpersonal behavior in clinical psychology. In P. Kendall & J. Butcher (Eds.), *Handbook of research methods in clinical psychology.* New York: Wiley-Interscience.

Index